Employment Discrimination

Selected Cases and Statutes – 2016

Employment Discrimination

Selected Cases and Statutes – 2016

Michael J. Zimmer

Late Professor of Law
Loyola University Chicago
&
Late Professor of Law Emeritus
Seton Hall University

Charles A. Sullivan

Associate Dean for Finance and Faculty
&
Professor of Law
Seton Hall University

Rebecca Hanner White

Dean and J. Alton Hosch Professor of Law Emeritus
University of Georgia

SUSTAINABLE FORESTRY INITIATIVE   Certified Sourcing
www.sfiprogram.org
SFI-00756

About Wolters Kluwer Legal & Regulatory US

Wolters Kluwer Legal & Regulatory US delivers expert content and solutions in the areas of law, corporate compliance, health compliance, reimbursement, and legal education. Its practical solutions help customers successfully navigate the demands of a changing environment to drive their daily activities, enhance decision quality and inspire confident outcomes.

Serving customers worldwide, its legal and regulatory portfolio includes products under the Aspen Publishers, CCH Incorporated, Kluwer Law International, ftwilliam.com and MediRegs names. They are regarded as exceptional and trusted resources for general legal and practice-specific knowledge, compliance and risk management, dynamic workflow solutions, and expert commentary.

Contents

Case Supplement

Statutes

Regulations

Preface

Since the publication of the Eighth Edition in early 2013, the Supreme Court and the circuit courts of appeals have been busy not merely in addressing second-order questions but also in reframing bedrock principles of the field. Perhaps most significant were opinions that recast the law both of pregnancy discrimination (*Young v. UPS*) and religious accommodation (*EEOC v. Abercrombie & Fitch Stores, Inc.*) as well as decisions narrowing the definition of "supervisor" for purposes of sexual harassment liability (*Vance v. Ball State University*), and holding that "motivating factor" liability did not reach to Title VII retaliation cases (*University of Texas Southwestern Medical Center v. Nassar*). All four of these decisions are included as principal cases in this 2016 Supplement together with Notes exploring their implications.

Somewhat less important for employment discrimination law, but still significant are three additional cases. *Texas Department of Housing & Community Affairs v. Inclusive Communities Project, Inc.* approved the disparate impact theory under the Fair Housing Act and in the process providing some insights into that theory under Title VII. The second is *Burwell v. Hobby Lobby Stores, Inc.*, which may (or may not) have significant implications for the applicability of the antidiscrimination laws to employers who can plausibly claim a religious objection to statutory demands. Third, and most recently, the Supreme Court issued a somewhat surprising opinion in its second encounter with *Fisher v. University of Texas*, upholding racial preferences in admissions against an equal protection challenge. To facilitate efficient treatment, all three of these cases are discussed in text.

Finally, three opinions have more direct implications for Title VII enforcement but are of limited effect. One decision allowed very limited judicial review of EEOC pre-suit efforts to conciliate (*Mach Mining, LLC v. EEOC*), a second held that the administrative exhaustion timing requirements run from notice of resignation in a constructive discharge claim (*Green v. Brennan*), and a third considered a defendant's entitlement to attorneys' fees when it "prevails" against a discrimination claim (*CRST Van Expedited, Inc. v. EEOC*). *Green* is reproduced as a principal case for those who wish to teach time limitations in more detail while the others are explained in text.

In the lower courts, much was also percolating. Particularly interesting are the Americans with Disability Act cases, where appellate opinions interpreting the changes wrought by the ADAAA continue to multiply. As usual, Notes are updated throughout to reflect these and other changes.

CAS
RHW

August 2016

Acknowledgments

The authors offer their heartfelt thanks to their research assistants, who, operating under often unreasonable deadlines, did a great job in ensuring that our supplements are both accurate and up to date:

Samira Paydar, Seton Hall class of 2017.
John G. Dumnich, Seton Hall class of 2016.
Angela R. Raleigh, Seton Hall class of 2016.

Professor Sullivan would also like to thank Teresa Rizzo, his assistant, who incorporated many new developments into the manuscript as well as making his workplace both efficient and cheerful.

Employment Discrimination

Selected Cases and Statutes – 2016

Case Supplement

1   *Individual Disparate Treatment Discrimination*

Page 11, add at end of carryover paragraph:

Samuel R. Bagenstos, *Disparate Impact and the Role of Classification and Motivation in Equal Protection Law after* Inclusive Communities, 101 Cornell L. Rev. 1115 (2016), notes that, for the first time, the Supreme Court equated "unconscious prejudices" with intentional discrimination), citing *Tex. Dep't of Hous. & Cmty. Affairs v. Inclusive Cmtys. Project, Inc.*, 135 S. Ct. 2507, 2511-12 (2014) ("Recognition of disparate-impact liability under the FHA plays an important role in uncovering discriminatory intent: it permits plaintiffs to counteract unconscious prejudices and disguised animus that escape easy classification as disparate treatment.").

Page 14, add at end of second paragraph of carryover Note 1, *Mixed Motives & Causation*:

See also Burrage v. United States, 134 S. Ct. 881, 888 (2014) ("The same conclusion follows if the predicate act combines with other factors to produce the result, so long as the other factors alone would not have done so — if, so to speak, it was the straw that broke the camel's back. Thus, if poison is administered to a man debilitated by multiple diseases, it is a but-for cause of his death even if those diseases played a part in his demise, so long as, without the incremental effect of the poison, he would have lived."). *See generally* Leora F. Eisenstadt & Jeffrey R. Boles, *Intent and Liability in Employment Discrimination*, Am Bus. L. J. (forthcoming), available at http://ssrn.com/abstract=2756109 (arguing for incorporation of a version of criminal law's approaches to intent into Title VII such that the extent of liability would turn on the degree of intent); Leora F. Eisenstadt, *Causation in Context*, 36 Berkeley J. Emp. & Lab. L. 1 (2015).

Page 15, delete Note 2; replace with the following:

2. *Getting Inside the Employer's Mind to Prove Age Discrimination.* The Hazen cousins made several "stray comments" about Biggins's age, i.e., comments showing that his age was on their minds, but these were not made at the moment of his discharge. Does that support finding that age may have played a role in his discharge but not sufficiently to show that, but for his age, he would not have been fired? Suppose an employer asks an older worker about her plans for retirement. Some courts have been very reluctant to see bias in comments related to potential retirement. *See Fleishman v. Cont'l Cas. Co.*, 698 F.3d 598, 605-06 (7th Cir. 2012) (inquiry about plaintiff's retirement plans and promise that he would receive severance pay if he decided to retire was not connected with his age as opposed to his fall-off in performance). In contrast, in *Sharp v. Aker Plant Servs. Group, Inc.*, 726 F.3d 789, 799 (6th Cir. 2013), an employee tape-recorded a conversation regarding his layoff, which provided "a window into the mind of an employment decision maker." The comments recorded were that the employer's "succession plan was to hire or retain younger workers at the expense of older workers because it was more likely that the former would stay with the company longer than the latter." The statements "disclose[d] no analytical step between computing an employee's potential longevity with the company and his age." *Id.* at 801. *See also Hilde v. City of Eveleth*, 777 F.3d 998, 1006 (8th Cir. 2015) (to assume that a candidate "was uncommitted to a position because his age made him retirement-eligible is age-stereotyping that the ADEA prohibits"); *Tramp v. Associated Underwriters, Inc.*, 768 F.3d 793, 802-03 (8th Cir. 2014) (unlike age and pension benefits, "[a]ge and health care costs are not so analytically distinct if Associated Underwriters presumed the rise in one necessitated a rise in the other").

Page 15, add in second paragraph of Note 3, *Age Discrimination as Acting on Stereotypes*, after "Or does the implicit bias literature explain this?":

See Michael Winerip, *Three Men, Three Ages. Which Do You Like?*, N.Y. TIMES, July 27, 2013, B-1 (reporting a study in which versions of the same person at three different ages were treated differently by a test group of Princeton undergraduates; the "assertive" version of the character was viewed more negatively than the younger versions even when saying the same thing).

Page 21, add at end of carryover paragraph in carryover Note 3, *The First Step: The Prima Facie Case*:

Another such reason would be the failure of plaintiff to apply for a vacancy. *See EEOC v. Audrain Health Care, Inc.*, 756 F.3d 1083, 1087-88 (8th Cir. 2014) (male plaintiff neither applied for a vacant position nor made "every reasonable attempt" to communicate his interest in the position; his failure to do so was not excused by employer statements indicating a preference for female nurses). But even in this setting, lack of an existing opening is not fatal to a discrimination claim. *See Chambers v. Burwell*, 2016 U.S. App. LEXIS 9769, at *7-8 (D.C. Cir. May 31, 2016) (lack of an existing vacancy for promotion does not necessarily foreclose a discrimination claim; "As a matter of law, at least where a manager regularly requests and receives upgraded vacancies that are earmarked for his subordinates, his decision not to engage in that process because of an employee's disability or race can be an adverse employment action").

Page 21, add after *Berquist* cite in Note 4, *Other Versions of the Prima Facie Case*:

Cf. Zayas v. Rockford Mem'l Hosp., 740 F.3d 1154, 1158 (7th Cir. 2014) (prior satisfactory performance evaluations did not establish that plaintiff was meeting the employer's legitimate job expectations at the time she was fired given more recent disciplinary actions; in any event analysis of satisfactory performance is not limited to actual job performance but includes "factors such as insubordination and workplace camaraderie").

Page 22, add at end of carryover paragraph before cross-reference:

One court has treated the "inference of discrimination" prong as essentially subsuming the entire *McDonnell Douglas* litigation structure. *Young v. Builders Steel Co.*, 754 F.3d 573 (8th Cir. 2014) (plaintiff failed to prove a prima facie case because he could not establish the inference-of-discrimination element by showing that the defendant's reason was pretextual, which obviated the need to engage in the *McDonnell Douglas* burden-shifting analysis).

Page 24, add before *Upshaw* cite in Note 8, *The Third Step: Proving Pretext*:

Evance v. Trumann Health Servs., LLC, 719 F.3d 673, 678 (8th Cir. 2013) (since the court is not a "super-personnel department" with "the power to second-guess employers' business decisions," it was not unlawful for a company to make employment decisions based upon erroneous information);

Page 27, add at end of carryover Note 10, *A Process of Elimination?*:

Cf. William R. Corbett, *Unmasking a Pretext for Res Ipsa Loquitur: A Proposal to Let Employment Discrimination Speak for Itself*, 62 Am. U. L. Rev. 447, 454-55 (2013) ("the *McDonnell Douglas* pretext proof structure is a thinly veiled version of res ipsa loquitur," but using this approach in employment discrimination law "has become not just unhelpful, but an impediment to proving discrimination in many disparate treatment claims").

Page 34, add at end of Note 3, *Rejecting the Lower Court's "Direct" Evidence Rule*:

Some courts have elaborated different approaches depending on whether direct evidence is present. Thus, the court in *Reed v. Neopost USA, Inc.*, 701 F.3d 434, 441 (5th Cir. 2012), wrote

> Where a plaintiff offers remarks as direct evidence, we apply a four-part test to determine whether they are sufficient to overcome summary judgment, [whether the remarks are] 1) age related; 2) proximate in time to the terminations; 3) made by an individual with authority over the employment decision at issue; and 4) related to the employment decision at issue. . . . Where a plaintiff offers remarks as circumstantial evidence alongside other alleged discriminatory conduct, however, we apply a more flexible two-part test. In that circumstance, a plaintiff need only show (1) discriminatory animus (2) on the part of a person that is either primarily responsible for the challenged employment action or by a person with influence or leverage over the relevant decisionmaker.")

(citations and internal quotations omitted).

Page 36, add at end of carryover Note 5, *Rejecting the "Pretext-Plus" Rule:*

But see Flowers v. Troup Cnty., 803 F.3d 1327 (11th Cir. 2015) ("it is insufficient for Flowers merely to make a prima facie case and—assuming that he could do so—call into question the School District's proffered legitimate, nondiscriminatory reason. The burden placed on Title VII plaintiffs to produce additional evidence suggesting discrimination after contradicting their employer's stated reasons is not great, but neither is it nothing.").

Page 36, add at end of first paragraph in Note 6, *The Plausibility of Alternative Explanations*:

See also Latowski v. Northwoods Nursing Ctr., 549 F. App'x 478, 484 (6th Cir. 2013) (while "a policy is not necessarily pretext for discrimination merely because we find it ill-advised," an unreasonable decision might suggest discriminatory motivation; thus, an employer's policy terminating otherwise qualified workers when their doctors imposed restrictions arising from non-workplace injuries, even if those restrictions had no effect on job performance, could be found to be "so lacking in merit as to be a pretext for discrimination.").

Page 36, add in Note 6, *The Plausibility of Alternative Explanations*, before Derum cite:

See also Johnson v. Koppers, Inc., 726 F.3d 910, 915 (7th Cir. 2013) (even assuming a co-worker made a false report regarding plaintiff, there was no evidence it was racially motivated, given a long-standing dislike between the two).

1. Individual Disparate Treatment Discrimination

Page 37, add before *Keys* cite in last full paragraph:

McCleary-Evans v. Md. DOT, 780 F.3d 582, 587-88 (4th Cir. 2015) (*Swierkiewicz*'s more lenient pleading standard has been superseded, and plaintiff's averments of discrimination were mere conclusions when she failed to allege a prima facie case or other basis for inferring more than the possibility of discrimination). *See also Connelly v. Lane Constr. Corp.*, 809 F.3d 780, 791 (3d Cir. 2016) (complaint sufficient when it alleged that plaintiff was the only female truck driver qualified to drive her employer's trucks but was not rehired while the employer recalled six males, including two with less seniority; there was no need to allege facts regarding pretext since, at the pleading stage, plaintiff "is not obliged to choose whether she is proceeding under a mixed-motive or pretext theory, nor is she required to establish a prima facie case, much less to engage in the sort of burden-shifting rebuttal that *McDonnell Douglas* requires at a later stage in the proceedings.").

Another potentially important decision is *Littlejohn v. City of New York*, 795 F.3d 297, 310 (2d Cir. 2015), which agreed that *Iqbal* applied to Title VII complaints but found it not to affect

> the benefit to plaintiffs pronounced in the *McDonnell Douglas* quartet. To the same extent that the *McDonnell Douglas* temporary presumption reduces the facts a plaintiff would need to *show* to defeat a motion for summary judgment prior to the defendant's furnishing of a non-discriminatory motivation, that presumption also reduces the facts needed to be *pleaded* under *Iqbal*. . . . The facts alleged must give plausible support to the reduced requirements that arise under *McDonnell Douglas* in the initial phase of a Title VII litigation. The facts required by *Iqbal* to be alleged in the complaint need not give plausible support to the ultimate question of whether the adverse employment action was attributable to discrimination. They need only give plausible support to a minimal inference of discriminatory motivation.

Of course, this analysis would permit a suit if a prima faciè case was plead, which is more than *Swierkiewicz* required.

Page 38, add at end of carryover paragraph:

Michael J. Zimmer, *Title VII's Last Hurrah: Can Discrimination Be Plausibly Pled?*, 2014 U. Chi. L. F. 19.

Page 43, delete Note 4; replace with:

4. *Comparator Cases.* Another way to view cases like *Santa Fe* is as literally "disparate treatment" cases: a plaintiff prevails by proving that she was treated differently than a "comparator" (a similarly situated person of the other sex or a different race). And that difference in treatment supports the inference that the different treatment was because of race. Most lower courts try to frame the analysis in *McDonnell Douglas* terms rather than as straightforward unequal treatment;

under this approach, the similarities establish the prima facie case and the asserted differences between plaintiff and the comparator are the nondiscriminatory reason that plaintiff must prove to be pretext. *See Baker v. Macon Res., Inc.*, 750 F.3d 674 (7th Cir. 2014) (selective enforcement of a policy for reporting abuse, combined with the inconsistencies in distinguishing the plaintiff from a younger person treated less harshly, was sufficient pretext evidence to allow a reasonable jury to find age discrimination when plaintiff was fired but a younger worker was not after both violated the same rule). But it can be argued that the difference in treatment of a sufficiently close comparator is enough to infer discrimination.

In any event, the problem is less the label than how close a comparator must be in order to count. Some lower courts seem to require the comparator to be "nearly identical" to the plaintiff, *e.g., Castillo v. Roche Labs., Inc.*, 467 F. App'x 859, 862 (11th Cir. 2012) ("To prevent courts from second-guessing employers' reasonable decisions and confusing apples with oranges, the quantity and quality of the comparator's misconduct must be nearly identical"); *Holmes v. Trinity Health*, 729 F.3d 817, 823 (8th Cir. 2013) (plaintiff, hospital COO, was unable to show sex discrimination when the comparator she chose, although at a comparable level, did not engage in the same conduct she did — criticizing the CEO's management style).

However, *Crawford v. Indiana Harbor Belt R.R. Co.*, 461 F.3d 844, 846 (7th Cir. 2006), disapproved of a trend "to require closer and closer comparability between the plaintiff and the members of the comparison group." It explained:

> The requirement is a natural response to cherry-picking by plaintiffs. . . . If a plaintiff can make a prima facie case by finding just one or two male or nonminority workers who were treated worse [better?] than she, she should have to show that they really are comparable to her in every respect. But if as we believe cherry-picking is improper, the plaintiff should have to show only that the members of the comparison group are sufficiently comparable to her to suggest that she was singled out for worse treatment. Otherwise plaintiffs will be in a box: if they pick just members of the comparison group who are comparable in every respect, they will be accused of cherry-picking; but if they look for a representative sample, they will unavoidably include some who were not comparable in every respect, but merely broadly comparable. The cases that say that the members of the comparison group must be comparable to the plaintiff in all material respects get this right.

See also White v. Baxter Healthcare Corp., 533 F.3d 381, 395 (6th Cir. 2008).

The cases that require the same supervisor may make more sense than others requiring near identity precisely because they focus on the intent of the individual decisionmaker. The argument is that supervisor A's intent can't be inferred from what Supervisor B did. So if A thinks tardiness is a firing offense for an African American, the fact that B allows her white workers to be tardy does not prove that A had any discriminatory intent. *But see Henry v. Abbott Labs.*, No. 15-4165, 2016 U.S. App. LEXIS 10604, at *17-18 (6th Cir. June 10, 2016) (plaintiff need not limit comparators to those with the same immediate supervisor where all workers had the same job duties and were governed by the same policies and procedures, and were reviewed by the same ultimate decisionmaker). This "me too" proof issue is treated in more detail in Note on Special Issues of Proof at p. 98. More detailed

1. Individual Disparate Treatment Discrimination

analysis of comparator proof is found in Charles A. Sullivan, *The Phoenix from the Ash: Proving Discrimination by Comparators*, 60 ALA. L. REV. 191 (2009). *See also* Suzanne Goldberg, *Discrimination by Comparison*, 120 YALE L.J. 728, 742 (2011) ("The judicial default to comparators crowds out not only other heuristics, but also other more textured conceptions of discrimination.").

Page 45, add before *Hafford* cite in Note 7, *Intersectionalism*:

Shazor v. Prof'l Transit Mgmt., 744 F.3d 948, 958 (6th Cir. 2014) (plaintiff can make a claim for intersectional discrimination: "African American women are subjected to unique stereotypes that neither African American men nor white women must endure.");

Page 46, add at end of carryover Note 7, *Intersectionalism*:

Jennifer Bennett Shinall, *The Substantially Impaired Sex: Uncovering the Gendered Nature of Disability Discrimination*, MINN. L. REV. (forthcoming) *available at* http://ssrn.com/abstract=2759457.

Page 46, replace *Greene* cite in Note 8, *Discrimination by Mistake* with:

D. Wendy Greene, *Categorically Black, White, or Wrong: "Misperception Discrimination" and the State of Title VII Protection*, 47 U. MICH. J.L. REFORM 87 (2013).

Page 46, add at the end of Note 8, *Discrimination by Mistake*:

Reconsider this question when you have read *EEOC v. Abercrombie & Fitch Stores*, reproduced at p. 84 of this Supplement.

Page 47, add before *Coulton* cite toward end of carryover paragraph:

Deets v. Massman Constr. Co., 811 F.3d 978 (7th Cir. 2016) (white construction worker who was told when laid off that the employer's "minority numbers" were too low produced direct evidence of discrimination sufficient to avoid summary judgment and which was supported by other evidence, including the fact that the employer had been out of compliance with its minority participation goals for three consecutive weeks and the hiring of a racial minority the day after plaintiff's termination);

Page 52, add before Risch cite in carryover paragraph of carryover Note 3, *Role of Qualifications in McDonnell Douglas Cases*:

Miller v. Polaris Labs., LLC, 797 F.3d 486 (7th Cir. 2015) (even though plaintiff failed to meet her production quotas over her eight-month employment, there was a triable question as to whether her failure was caused by sabotage by two co-workers who had racial animus);

Page 52, add in Note 4, *Methods of Proving Pretext* before *Lott* cite:

See also Goudeau v. Nat'l Oilwell Varco, L.P., 793 F.3d 470 (5th Cir. 2015) (doubts about the validity and timing of supposed written warnings would permit a jury to find age was the reason for termination, even though the employer had no duty to issue warnings before discharging an at-will employee); *Ridout v. JBS USA, LLC*, 716 F.3d 1079, 1084 (8th Cir. 2013) ("[A] strong showing that the plaintiff was meeting his employer's reasonable expectations at the time of termination may create a fact issue as to pretext when the employer claims that the employee was terminated for poor or declining performance.");

Page 53, add at end of first sentence in Note 4 (d) *"Unreasonable" Decision vs. "Business Judgment"*:

See Burton v. Freescale Semiconductor, Inc., 798 F.3d 222 (5th Cir. 2015) (triable issue of pretext existed when defendant relied on old, and not especially negative, performance evaluations, created an extensive post-discharge paper trail to justify its decision, and supervisors had inconsistent explanations for plaintiff's discharge).

Page 54, add before *Jones* cite in second paragraph of Note 5, *Several Nondiscriminatory Reasons*:

Pierson v. Quad/Graphics Printing Corp., 749 F.3d 530 (6th Cir. 2014) (shifting explanations by the decisionmaker created a fact issue as to whether the decision in question was due to a reduction in force or whether that reason was a pretext for age discrimination);

Page 59, delete Note 2; replace with:

2. *Whose Motive/Intent?* Given the Court's continued focus on intent for individual disparate treatment cases, it is not surprising for the majority to hold that, "to find an entity has discriminated," we must "look[ ] to the intent of particular individuals within that entity." Whether such a requirement is inevitable is another question — since the "intent" of a collective body is sometimes used without any connection to

any particular human actor, as in "legislative intent." *See* Richard W. Murphy, *NeuroCongress,* 37 Seton Hall L. Rev. 221 (2006). But, of course, individual human beings did have the requisite mental state in *Straub* and, according to the Court, a jury could find not only that they were motivated by antimilitary bias but also that they desired to have their reports result in an adverse employment action.

Straub seems likely to shift the focus from what the employing entity did to the particular manager whose decision (or influence) is claimed to be biased. *Sharp v. Aker Plant Servs. Group, Inc.,* 726 F.3d 789, 797 (6th Cir. 2013) (although a manager was not the ultimate decisionmaker, those who were relied solely on his forced rankings and recommendation of who could be fired and there was no process to scrub any bias); *Haire v. Bd. of Supervisors of La. State Univ. Agric. & Mech. Coll.,* 719 F.3d 356, 366-67 (5th Cir. 2013) (University Chancellor could be found to be cat's paw for biased campus police officer when he was new to the university and unfamiliar with its security policies and attributed plaintiff's supposed violation of those policies to misinformation regarding them provided to him by the biased individual).

However, employers have escaped liability when plaintiff could not establish the causal link between the actions of the biased subordinate and those of the actual decisionmaker. *E.g., Woods v. City of Berwyn,* 803 F.3d 865, 870 (7th Cir. 2015) (although an allegedly biased supervisor initiated disciplinary proceedings, the Board made its determination to discharge after a full hearing and without relying on any of his statements); *Thomas v. Berry Plastics Corp.,* 803 F.3d 510, 517 (10th Cir. 2015) ("We conclude that Berry's independent termination review process broke the causal chain between Morton's purported retaliatory animus and Thomas's termination."); *Jones v. SEPTA,* 796 F.3d 323 (3d Cir. 2015) (the fact that a supervisor reported and initiated an investigation is not sufficient to establish that the subsequent adverse action was tainted when there was a subsequent investigation independent of the supervisor); *Lawrence v. Sch. Dist. No. 1,* 560 F. App'x 791, 796 (10th Cir. 2014) (hearing before "an independent and mutually chosen arbitrator" broke the chain of causation).

Page 60, add at end of Note 4, *Proximate Cause*:

Sandra F. Sperino, *Statutory Proximate Cause,* 88 Notre Dame L. Rev. 1199 (2013). Other articles on this topic appear in a symposium sponsored by the Ohio State Law Journal and appearing in 75 Ohio St. L.J. (2014) by Deborah L. Brake; Martha Chamallas; William R. Corbett; Camille Hébert; Maria L. Ontiveros; Laura Rothstein; Sandra F. Sperino; Catherine E. Smith; and Charles A. Sullivan.

Page 60, add at end of Note 5, Co-Workers and Cats' Paws:

In *Velázquez-Pérez v. Developers Diversified Realty Corp.,* 763 F.3d 265, 274 (1st Cir. 2014), the court answered this question when a jilted co-worker's claims of poor job performance, motivated by jealousy, resulted in another employee's termination. Co-worker statements maligning the plaintiff, for discriminatory reasons and with the intent to cause the plaintiff's firing can be actionable when they "proximately cause the plaintiff to be fired, and the employer acts negligently by allowing the co-worker's acts to achieve their desired effect though it knows (or reasonably should know) of the discriminatory motivation."

Page 65, replace Note 2, *Materiality* with the following:

2. *Materiality.* As *Minor* suggests, the lower courts have generally required more than a mere showing that the employer discriminated in order for its conduct to be actionable. They have required an "adverse employment action," which they have usually defined to require some material effect on the terms and conditions of employment. Obviously, "ultimate employment actions" — hiring and firing — suffice, but meaningful changes in compensation have also been held actionable. *E.g., Davis v. N.Y.C. Dep't of Educ.*, 804 F.3d 231 (2d Cir. 2015) (denial of a discretionary bonus could be an adverse employment action based on a prohibited factor); *Alexander v. Casino Queen, Inc.*, 739 F.3d 972, 980 (7th Cir. 2014) (floor assignments could constitute an adverse employment action because of the importance of tips for cocktail waitresses); *Farrell v. Butler Univ.*, 421 F.3d 609, 614 (7th Cir. 2005) (while denial of bonuses is not an adverse employment action, denial of a raise can be).

When it comes to less direct economic effects on employees' lives, however, the lower courts decisions are divergent. A few examples of cases holding no adverse employment action illustrate the problem:

- mid-range evaluation, *Primes v. Reno*, 190 F.3d 765 (6th Cir. 1999), or even negative evaluation when future prospects were hindered, *Davis v. Town of Lake Park, Fla.*, 245 F.3d 1232, 1242-1243 (11th Cir. 2001).
- lateral transfer usually defined to mean no reduction in pay or title or any diminution in pay "indirect and minor," *Williams v. Bristol-Myers Squibb Co.*, 85 F.3d 270 (7th Cir. 1996), even though the transfer might be to a distant location, *Reynolds v. Ethicon Endo-Surgery*, Inc., 454 F.3d 868 (8th Cir. 2006); *see also Youssef v. F.B.I.*, 687 F.3d 397 (D.C. Cir. 2012 (transferring agent to less important work than counterterrorism not materially adverse). *But see Bonenberger v. St. Louis Metro. Police Dep't*, 810 F.3d 1103 (8th Cir. 2016) (supervisory duties, regular schedule and hours, greater prestige, and potential increased opportunity for promotion constituted a material change in working conditions" sufficient for denial of promotion to be an adverse employment action); *Thompson v. City of Waco*, 764 F.3d 500 (5th Cir. 2014) (restrictions of job duties that functioned to reduce an African-American detective to the status of assistant detective constituted an adverse employment action).
- investigation of plaintiff, *Kuhn v. Washtenaw Cnty.*, 709 F.3d 612 (6th Cir. 2013) (investigation of a complaint of employee wrongdoing was not an

adverse employment action when there was no disciplinary action, demotion, or change in job responsibilities), or a paid administrative leave, *Jones v. SEPTA*, 796 F.3d 323 (3d Cir. 2015).

On the other hand, some decisions with no present adverse economic or other tangible consequences have sometimes been held actionable. *E.g., Tolbert v. Smith*, 790 F.3d 427 (2d Cir. 2015) (even though plaintiff was offered another year of probationary employment, the denial of tenure was actionable since it denied him a material improvement in the conditions of employment). *See also Deleon v. Kalamazoo Cnty. Rd. Comm'n*, 739 F.3d 914, 919 (6th Cir. 2014) (a transfer may be a materially adverse employment action when it gives rise to "some level of objective intolerability," such as daily exposure to toxic fumes), *cert denied*, 135 S. Ct. 783 (2015) (Alito, J. dissenting)

Page 67, delete Note 6; replace with:

6. *Constructive Discharge and Contaminated Work Environment.* Some conduct by the employer may be so severe as to justify a reasonable employee in quitting. This is the equivalent of formal discharges and is therefore an adverse employment action. *See Pennsylvania State Police v. Suders*, 542 U.S. 129, 134 (2004) (to establish "constructive discharge," the plaintiff must not only make a case of an abusive working environment but that that environment "became so intolerable that her resignation qualified as a fitting response"). *See also Nassar v. University of Tex. Southwestern Med. Ctr.*, 674 F.3d 448, 453 (5th Cir. 2012), *rev'd on other grounds*, 133 S. Ct. 2517 (2013) (for constructive discharge plaintiff must prove not only a contaminated work environment but also an "aggravating factor" such as demotion, reduction in salary or job responsibility, reassignment to degrading work, or harassment calculated to encourage the employee's resignation); *Wright v. Ill. Dep't of Children & Family Servs.*, 798 F.3d 513 (7th Cir. 2015) (for a constructive discharge claim to be predicated on resignation in the face of imminent discharge, the employer must communicate to a reasonable employee in plaintiff's position that the termination of her employment was imminent; employer actions that may lead to termination are not sufficient).

Some courts required not only intolerable working conditions but also proof that such conditions were imposed in order to force plaintiff to leave. If this theory were ever tenable, it has likely been laid to rest by the Supreme Court's recent decision in *Green v. Brennan*, reproduced at p. 139 of this Supplement, which also held that resort to EEOC procedures is timely if filed within the relevant period following the employee's notice of resignation.

Page 68, add before last sentence of carryover paragraph in carryover Note 7, *Discrimination vs. Retaliation*:

See also Smith v. City of Greensboro, No. 15-11643, 2016 U.S. App. LEXIS 6586, at *9 (11th Cir. Apr. 12, 2016) (a change of shift, which precluded plaintiff from working a second job, is not sufficiently adverse to support a Title VII discrimination claim but can constitute an adverse employment action for purposes of retaliation claims).

Page 84, add at end of first paragraph:

See generally Jeffrey A. Van Detta, *The Strange Career of Title VII's §703(m): An Essay on the Unfulfilled Promise of the Civil Rights Act of 1991,* 89 St. John's L. Rev. 883 (2016) (exploring the tortured history of *Ash* both before and after the Supreme Court's decision); Leora F. Eisenstadt, *The N-Word at Work: Contextualizing Language in the Workplace,* 33 Berkeley J. Emp. & Lab. L. 299, 303 (2012) (arguing for "expert testimony to inform courts about the way in which linguistic meaning is created in our culture and the contextually-based meanings of specific terms").

Page 85, add at end of Note 9, *The "Jerk" Possibility*:

See also Hall v. City of Chicago, 713 F.3d 325 (7th Cir. 2013) (mistreatment of the only female plumber was not sufficient to establish a gender basis; however, the harasser's statements about wanting to "slap that woman" allowed a jury to find a sex basis).

Page 87, add at end of Note 13, *"A Motivating Factor" Causation*:

Cf. Brian S. Clarke, *A Better Route Through the Swamp: Causal Coherence in Disparate Treatment Doctrine,* 65 Rutgers L. Rev. 723, 772-73 (2013) (critiquing Katz's reading of "motivating factor" as "minimal causation" because (1) both the Court and Congress used the term in the sense of playing a substantial part in the adverse employment action and (2) it is "artificially narrow" since the intermediate stage between traditional but-for and "minimal causation" is found in the notion of "necessary element of a sufficient set" of factors causing a decision).

Page 87, replace Note 14 with the following:

14. *Has Desert Palace Trumped McDonnell Douglas?* Another way to ask the question is whether the addition of §§703(m) and 706(g)(2)(B) to Title VII by the 1991 Civil Rights Act changed all of Title VII or merely created an alternative to the "normal" analysis under §703(a), which, as we have seen, speaks in "because of" terms, a term the Court has read to mean but-for causation. Under the "alternatives" view, a plaintiff could use either avenue. *See Fogg v. Gonzales*, 492 F.3d 447 (D.C. Cir. 2007) ("On its face Title VII provides alternative ways of establishing liability for employment practices based upon the impermissible use of race or other proscribed criteria — one in §2000e-2(a), which has been the law since 1964, and another in §2000e-2(m), which the Congress added in 1991").

1. Individual Disparate Treatment Discrimination

Professor Sandra Sperino finds guidance in the Supreme Court's later decision in *University of Texas Southwestern Medical Center v. Nassar*, 133 S. Ct. 2517 (2013), reproduced at page 107 of this Supplement, where the Court wrote: "For one thing, §2000e–2(m) is not itself a substantive bar on discrimination. Rather, it is a rule that establishes the causation standard for proving a violation defined elsewhere in Title VII." *Id.* at 2530. Sperino argues that this makes clear that §703(m) does not create an alternative theory of liability but merely describes one way to prove a violation of §703: "[t]hese sentences mean that there is no such thing as a 'mixed-motive' claim or a 'single-motive' claim. Courts and litigants are entitled to use the 'motivating factor' definition of causation found in §2000e–2(m) for all intentional discrimination claims." *Nassar's Hidden Message*, http://law professors.typepad.com/laborprof_blog/2014/04/nassars-hidden-messag.html.

Are there reasons a plaintiff might want to forego the presumably less demanding motivating factor approach? *See Coe v. Northern Pipe Prods., Inc.*, 589 F. Supp. 2d 1055, 1097-98 (N. D. Iowa 2008) (while it is plaintiff's option to pursue a "mixed motives" claim under §703(m) . . . , plaintiffs might well choose to avoid §703(m) because of the strong possibility that a jury verdict will result in liability but no backpay or damages).

Page 87, add at end of Note 15(a):

Griffith, however, is increasingly an outlier. *Quigg v. Thomas Cnty. Sch. Dist.*, 814 F.3d 1227, 1232-33 (11th Cir. 2016), concluded that mixed-motive claims based on circumstantial evidence required only proof sufficient to convince a jury that a protected characteristic was a motivating factor for an adverse employment action against the plaintiff. It viewed the Eighth Circuit as "alone in holding that, post-*Desert Palace*, the *McDonnell Douglas* approach must be applied" in the summary judgment context. *Id.* at 1239. *Quigg* looked mainly to *White v. Baxter Healthcare Corp.*, 533 F.3d 381 (6th Cir. 2008), but also found a number of other circuits approving deviations from the *McDonnell Douglas* framework.

Page 89, delete Note 16; replace with:

16. *Is "Direct" Evidence Still the Gold Standard?* The kind of evidence that might have been characterized as "direct" before *Desert Palace* remains very important as a way of proving discrimination. *See Tolbert v. Smith*, 790 F.3d 427 (2d Cir. 2015) (principal's pejorative references to an African American's cooking "black food" during the year when plaintiff was informed he would not receive tenure suggested racial bias and were related to plaintiff's qualifications as a teacher); *Etienne v. Spanish Lake Truck & Casino Plaza, L.L.C.*, 778 F.3d 473 (5th Cir. 2015) (repeated statements by general manager that waitress was "too black" to be promoted in a casino was direct evidence of discrimination necessitating a trial); *Wilson v. Cox*, 753 F.3d 244, 247 (D.C. Cir. 2014) (statements by decisionmaker such as "you didn't come here to work, you came here to retire" were sufficient direct evidence

to require a trial on plaintiff's claim of discriminatory termination). *Cf. Roberts v. Int'l Bus. Machs. Corp.*, 733 F.3d 1306, 1308 (10th Cir. 2013) (reference to plaintiff's exceeding his "shelf life" not direct evidence of age discrimination in his eventual discharge; translating an instant message's "euphemisms and acronyms" into English "unmistakably suggests that 'shelf life' was nothing worse than an inartful reference to Mr. Roberts's queue of billable work").

One court tried to sketch the differing analyses when statements were at issue in direct and circumstantial evidence cases:

> when a direct evidence claim is made, the subject remarks must "be proximate in time to the terminations, made by an individual with authority over the employment decision, and related to the challenged decision"; however, when the remarks are offered in a circumstantial evidence case, they are "just one ingredient in the overall evidentiary mix" and so subject to more flexible standard, showing "(1) discriminatory animus (2) on the part of a person that is either primarily responsible for the challenged employment action or by a person with influence or leverage over the relevant decisionmaker."

Goudeau v. Nat'l Oilwell Varco, L.P., 793 F.3d 470, 475-76 (5th Cir. 2015) (internal quotations omitted)

Page 90, add after *Barner* cite in second paragraph of *Note on Evidence Issues About Admissions Testimony*:

Cf. Back v. Nestlé USA, Inc., 694 F.3d 571, 577-78 (6th Cir. 2012) (while evidence that a Human Resources Director said there was a plan to get rid of the three oldest employees would be admissible since it was made within the scope of his employment, the particular statement was actually hearsay within hearsay since the Director was saying that "higher management" had made the statement and there was no showing that the unidentified declarants were speaking on a matter within the scope of their employment).

Page 91, add at end of carryover subsection (a) *What did the agent actually say?*:

See also Johnson v. Perez, No. 15-5034, 2016 U.S. App. LEXIS 9229, at *20-22 (D.C. Cir. May 20, 2016) (rejecting any view that parties or coworker testimony is somehow insufficient proof; questions about the credibility of either, regardless of self-interest or other motives, are ordinarily for the jury, not the court on summary judgment).

Page 91, add before *McGinest* cite in (b), *Does the statement show illegitimate considerations?*:

Abrams v. Dep't of Pub. Safety, 764 F.3d 244 (2d Cir. 2014) (statements about plaintiff not "fitting in" could be found to refer to race when the elite unit consisted of white officers only, almost half the officers in the unit also lacked a college degree, and other criticism of him stemmed from supposed deficiencies years earlier);

Page 97, delete Note 1; replace with:

1. *The Holding.* The Court decided that in all ADEA individual disparate treatment cases the plaintiff must carry the burden of production and of persuasion that age was the but-for cause of the adverse employment action that is challenged. However, the circuit courts have so far read *Gross* not to affect the application of *McDonnell Douglas* analysis in ADEA cases in carrying that burden. *E.g., Jones v. Okla. City Pub. Schs,* 617 F.3d 1273 (10th Cir. 2010) ("Although we recognize that *Gross* created some uncertainty regarding burden-shifting in the ADEA context, we conclude that it does not preclude our continued application of *McDonnell Douglas* to ADEA claims."); *Smith v. City of Allentown,* 589 F.3d 684, 691 (3d Cir. 2009) (same). They have also continued to look to something like "direct evidence" — not as a burden shifting device but rather as a reason to find that age was a determinative factor. *E.g., Soto-Feliciano v. Villa Cofresí Hotels, Inc.,* 779 F.3d 19 (1st Cir. 2015) (negative age-related comments directed at plaintiff, including by the key decisionmaker regarding his termination in the context of a performance evaluation within two weeks of that decision created a fact question as to pretext); *Scheick v. Tecumseh Pub. Schs,* 766 F.3d 523 (6th Cir. 2014) (plaintiff's testimony as to the school board's expressed desire for a younger worker was sufficient to deny summary judgment to the employer despite real questions about both plaintiff's performance and the existence of a budget crisis).

But even where there is direct evidence, the causation requirement can be outcome determinative. *E.g., Arthur v. Pet Dairy,* 593 F. App'x 211, 221 (4th Cir. 2015) (while a supervisor's comments were direct evidence of age bias, summary judgment for the employer was still appropriate because no reasonable jury could find but-for causation in light of record evidence demonstrating that his employer terminated plaintiff for other lawful reasons); *Johnson v. Securitas Sec. Servs. USA, Inc.,* 769 F.3d 605, 614 (8th Cir. 2014) (age-related comments — he was "too old" and "needed to hang up his Superman cape and retire" — by one of the three decisionmakers in plaintiff's termination were not enough to create a jury question as to pretext regarding his unauthorized departure from the scene and delay in reporting an accident).

Page 98, delete Note 3; replace with:

3. *Gross's Effect on Other Discrimination Statutes. Desert Palace* and *Gross* create separate analytic regimes for Title VII and the ADEA respectively. But the world did not have long to wait before the reverberations of *Gross* were felt across the spectrum of antidiscrimination laws. The most dramatic manifestation was within Title VII itself, where a majority of the Court in *University of Texas Southwestern Medical Center v. Nassar,* 133 S. Ct. 2517 (2013), reproduced at page 107 of this

Supplement, held that, even the Title VII prohibition of retaliation, which is found in a separate section from its prohibitions of "status-based" discrimination, is subject to but-for causation analysis. The significance of these holdings for other antidiscrimination laws is considered in Note 7 on page 126.

Page 99, add at end of second full paragraph of Note 1, *"Same Actor" Rule v. Inference*:

See Blasdel v. Nw. Univ., 687 F.3d 813, 820 (7th Cir. 2012) (while not a "presumption," the same actor proof undermined any inference of prejudice against female scientists by the person who hired plaintiff).

Page 100, add at end of carryover Note 1, *"Same Actor" Rule v. Inference*:

At least one court has taken up this theme. *See Perez v. Thorntons, Inc.*, 731 F.3d 699, 710 (7th Cir. 2013) (noting the "interesting linkage, or perhaps a disconnect" between the same actor inference and the "stray remark" doctrine: the former assumes that "if a person was unbiased at Time A (when he decided to hire the plaintiff), he was also unbiased at Time B (when he fired the plaintiff)," but the latter posits that "if a person was racist or sexist at Time A (time of the remark), it is *not* reasonable to infer that the person was still racist or sexist at Time B (when he made or influenced the decision to fire the plaintiff)"). *See also* Victor D. Quintanilla & Cheryl R. Kaiser, *The Same-Actor Inference of Nondiscrimination: Moral Credentialing and the Psychological and Legal Licensing of Bias*, 104 CAL. L. REV. 1 (2016) (same-actor evidence should be viewed as merely one datum in the analysis partly due to empirical evidence suggesting that non-biased actions (such as hiring a minority or woman) can actually establish a kind of "moral licensing" that privileges subsequent manifestations of bias).

Page 100, add after Green citation in Note 2, *Same Supervisor*:

See generally Emma Pelkey, Comment, *The "Not Me Too" Evidence Doctrine in Employment Law: Courts' Disparate Treatment of "Me Too" Versus "Not Me Too" Evidence in Employment Discrimination Cases*, 92 OR. L. REV. 545 (2014).

Page 101, add at end of Note 3, *Age Difference in ADEA Cases*:

See also Liebman v. Metro. Life Ins. Co., 808 F.3d 1294, 1299 (11th Cir. 2015 (seven years is nor sufficiently "substantially younger" than plaintiff to establish this prong of the prima facie case);

1. Individual Disparate Treatment Discrimination

Page 102, add at end of first full paragraph of carryover Note 4, *Replacement by a Member of the Same Race or Sex*:

Blasdel v. Nw. Univ., 687 F.3d 813, 822 (7th Cir. 2012) ("In the seven years that the dean had been in office when he recommended against giving Blasdel tenure, the percentage of tenure track female faculty in the medical school had increased from 20.5 to 25.4 percent and their rate of obtaining tenure had exceeded that of the male faculty."). *But see Whitfield v. Int'l Truck & Engine Corp.*, 755 F.3d 438, 444 (7th Cir. 2014) (district court erred by "giving enormous weight" to the employer's hire of another African-American: the court should have recognized that hiring a member of the same protected class "does not magically negate the inference created by the evidence of Jackson's hiring and employment at the Plant, the evidence of intense racial hostility at the Plant or the cover page on Whitfield's personnel file identifying him as black.").

Page 102, add a new subsection:

5. Decisionmaker Within the Same Protected Class. It has sometimes been argued that the fact that the decisionmaker shares the same protected characteristic as the alleged victim precludes a finding of discrimination. The Supreme Court rejected this position as a matter of law in *Oncale v. Sundowner Offshore Servs.*, 523 U.S. 75, 79 (1998) ("nothing in Title VII necessarily bars a claim of discrimination 'because of . . . sex' merely because the plaintiff and the defendant (or the person charged with acting on behalf of the defendant) are of the same sex."), an opinion we will encounter at page 325. *See also Ross v. Douglas Cnty.*, 234 F.3d 391, 396 (8th Cir. 2000) ("we have no doubt that, as a matter of law, a black male could discriminate against another black male "because of such individual's race"). However, in a number of cases the fact that the plaintiff was of the same race or sex as the defendant's decisionmaker seems to have influenced a finding of no discrimination. *E.g., Walton v. Dalton*, No. 96-1408, 1997 U.S. App. LEXIS 5200, at *8 (4th Cir. Mar. 19, 1997). Any such tendency, however, can be overcome by other proof. *See Jackson v. VHS Detroit Receiving Hosp., Inc.*, 814 F.3d 769, 783-85 (6th Cir. 2016) (in a sex discrimination case largely predicated on comparator proof, summary judgment was denied although all of the decision-makers were female, as were most employees in the hospital's crisis center, when plaintiff was the only female out of fourteen individuals in her job category, which might imply that males were favored for that position).

2 Systemic Disparate Treatment Discrimination

Page 111, add after "See page 341" in Note 2. *No Sex Discrimination?*:

See also Bauer v. Lynch, 812 F.3d 340 (4th Cir. 2016) (upholding gender-normed physical fitness tests for FBI trainees by rejecting the simple *Manhart* test of whether "the evidence shows treatment of a person in a manner which but for that person's sex would be different" in favor of asking whether the test imposes a greater burden on one sex than the other).

Page 112, add before last sentence of Note 3, *A BFOQ*:

See also EEOC v. Exxon Mobil Corp., 560 F. App'x 282 (5th Cir. 2014) (Exxon's mandatory retirement policy of age 60 for its pilots, although not mandated by FAA regulations governing commercial pilots, is justified as a BFOQ by the same reasons as the FAA's policy, including the increased risk of in-flight incapacitation and the absence of adequate means of individually testing each pilot for risk for such incapacitation).

Page 131, add at end of first paragraph of Note 1, *What Happened to Systemic Disparate Treatment?*:

See generally Tristin K. Green, *Title VII and the Mirage of the* "Monell *Analogue*," 95 B.U.L. REV. 1077, 1097-98 (2015) (rejecting the argument that systemic disparate treatment discrimination should be actionable only if it results from a policy of a corporate employer rather than actions of individual employees).

2. Systemic Disparate Treatment Discrimination

Page 135, add after last full paragraph:

For an interesting take on using statistics in systemic cases, *see* Jason Bent, *Hidden Priors: Toward a Unifying Theory of Systemic Disparate Treatment Law*, 91 DENV. U. L. REV. 807 (2014), who views the current use of statistics as necessarily incorporating a view of discrimination as being relatively common. In other words, the theory supposes that the base rate is high, thus permitting the statistical proof to allow the factfinder to infer intentional discrimination by the particular defendant from a statistically significant underrepresentation. Looking to Bayesian analysis, Professor Bent argues that the base rate question should be analyzed as a Bayesian "prior" and that expert testimony should be allowed to inform jury decisions on the level of such priors before analyzing the claim of discrimination based on statistics in the case at hand. *See also* Jason R. Bart, *P-Values, Priors and Procedure in Administration Law*, 63 BUFFALO L. Rev. 85 (2015).

Page 141, add at end of carryover paragraph:

See also Chin v. Port Auth. of N.Y. & N.J., 685 F.3d 135, 153 (2d Cir. 2012) (a statistical analysis that concluded that underrepresentation of Asians in promotion decisions could have occurred by chance 13 percent of the time was not necessarily fatal to plaintiffs' case even though the generally accepted level of significance was 5% or less, there was "other evidence that reasonable jurors could have relied upon to find that an 87-percent likelihood that the disparity was not due to chance," including substantial evidence that the plaintiffs were more qualified than some white officers who were promoted).

Page 153, add at end of first paragraph of Note 2, *Defense or Rebuttal?*:

The Second Circuit agreed with the Seventh Circuit in *United States v. City of New York*, 717 F.3d 72 (2d Cir. 2013) (2-1), where a majority of the panel held summary judgment against the City inappropriate even where there was no effort by the employer to rebut the plaintiffs' statistical evidence of underrepresentation of minorities in the ranks of firefighters. While the results of civil service tests did justify disparate impact liability and an appropriate injunction, the underrepresentation was not a sufficient basis, even coupled with other evidence, to find disparate treatment when the City denied any intent to discriminate and put in evidence such as affidavits from the test designers that they did not intend to discriminate.

Page 155, add at end of Note 5, *Failure to Redress as Intentional Discrimination*:

But see Naomi Schoenbaum, *The Family and the Market at Wal-Mart*, 23 DEPAUL L. REV. 769 (2013) (arguing that some disparate impact suits, as presently framed, tend to reinforce stereotypes of women as less committed to the job market than men).

Page 157, add at end of first full paragraph:

See also Jessica Clarke, *Against Immutability*, 125 YALE L. J. 2, 4-7 (2015) (largely in response to the gay rights movement, some courts view "immutability" as not just characteristics that cannot be changed but as including traits so central to a person's identity that it would be abhorrent for government to penalize a person for refusing to change them; while useful in the equal protection arena, this approach "is a questionable strategy for reconceptualizing the broader project of equality law" because it "obscures critical questions about why some characteristics ought to be treated equally, offering only the empty assertion that they are fundamental to personhood."); Edward Stein, *Mutability and Innateness Arguments about Lesbian, Gay, and Bisexual Rights*, 89 CHI.-KENT L. REV. 597 (2014).

Page 167, add at end of Note 3, *Customer Preference as a BFOQ*:

A recent article considers how biased customer reactions can infiltrate the workplace even when the employer does not purport to be satisfying discriminatory preferences. Lu-in Wang, *When the Customer is King: Employment Discrimination as Customer Service*, http://papers.ssrn.com/sol3/papers.cfm?abstract_id=2657758.

Page 168, add before *Everson* cite in Note 5, *Privacy BFOQs*:

Teamsters Local Union No. 117 v. Wash. Dep't of Corr., 789 F.3d 979 (9th Cir. 2015) (a plan designating 110 female-only correctional positions to patrol housing units, prison grounds, and work sites was valid under the BFOQ exception since it reflected an individualized, well-researched response to problems in women's prisons of sexual abuse and misconduct by prison guards, breaches of inmate privacy, and security gaps);

Page 168, add before *Breiner* cite in Note 5, *Privacy BFOQs*:

Ambat v. City & Cnty. of S.F., 757 F.3d 1017 (9th Cir. 2014) (triable issue as to whether an employer's policy of prohibiting male deputies from supervising female jail inmates was a BFOQ);

Page 168, add before Buchanan cite towards end of Note 5, *Privacy BFOQs*:

Naomi Schoenbaum, *The Law of Intimate Work*, 90 WASH. L. REV. 1167, 1195 (2015) ("If consumers have their preferences accommodated, this reinforces their preexisting view that this is the only acceptable way these services may be delivered.

2. Systemic Disparate Treatment Discrimination

Employers' role in constructing discriminatory preferences then interferes with the free formation of meaningful intimate work relationships.");

Page 182, add at end of first paragraph of Note 1, *Litigation Structure*:

Cf. Shea v. Kerry, 796 F.3d 42 (D.C. Cir. 2015) (while the employer had the burden of production in establishing the validity of an affirmative action plan, it carried it by proof that the plan addressed manifest imbalances in senior-level positions in the Foreign Service Officer corps resulting from past discrimination and refrained from unnecessarily trammeling the rights of non-minority candidates).

Page 184, add before the last sentence of carryover Note 3, *Will* Weber *and* Johnson *Survive?*:

See generally Deborah C. Malamud, *The Strange Persistence of Affirmative Action under Title VII*, 118 W. VA. L. REV. 1, 23 (2015) ("it is by no means clear that even the remedial affirmative action permitted by *Weber* and *Johnson* will survive. It is even less likely, in my view, that this Court will see *Grutter* as creating a safe haven for corporate diversity practice."); Kingsley R. Browne, *Title VII and Diversity*, 14 NEV. L.J. 806, 829 (2014) ("If diversity preferences are to be made legal, at least in the private sector, it will take either a statutory amendment or a lawless decision by the Supreme Court that goes even farther than *Weber* and *Johnson*.");

Page 184, add at end of Note 5, *Is Avoiding Disparate Impact Permissible?*:

See also Shea v. Kerry, 796 F.3d 42, 54 (D.C. Cir. 2015) (finding *Weber/Johnson* to control a challenge to an affirmative action plan, despite *Ricci*, because those opinions "are directly applicable to this case" and the Supreme Court has cautioned against the lower courts finding its decisions overruled by implication)

Page 187, add after first full paragraph:

The Court revisited the question of diversity in college admissions in *Fisher v. University of Texas at Austin*, a case that many believed would overturn *Grutter*'s approval of this interest. Such predictions proved incorrect, but only after two trips to the Court. In its first encounter with the case, *Fisher I*, 133 S. Ct. 2411 (2013), the Court reversed the Fifth Circuit's decision upholding the University's admissions plan but did not disturb the core premise of *Grutter* that diversity could be a sufficiently compelling state interest to survive strict scrutiny. Rather, the *Fisher I* majority believed that the Fifth Circuit had been too deferential to the University's tailoring of its plan to the diversity interest claimed, looking only to its "good faith." For the Court,

> [o]nce the University has established that its goal of diversity is consistent with strict scrutiny, however, there must still be a further judicial determination that the admissions process meets strict scrutiny in its implementation. The University must prove that the means chosen by the University to attain diversity are narrowly tailored to that goal. On this point, the University receives no deference.

Id. at 2419-20. According to the Court, "[n]arrow tailoring also requires that the reviewing court verify that it is 'necessary' for a university to use race to achieve the educational benefits of diversity," *id.* at 2420, which requires "a careful judicial inquiry into whether a university could achieve sufficient diversity without using racial classifications." *Id.* That means "[t]he reviewing court must ultimately be satisfied that no workable race-neutral alternatives would produce the educational benefits of diversity." *Id.* The Court then remanded for an application of the correct standard to the litigation.

On remand, the Fifth Circuit, applying the new standard, again upheld the University's plan, and the Court again granted certiorari, this time affirming the Fifth Circuit. *Fisher II,* 195 L.Ed 2d 511 (2016), was a 4 to 3 decision (Justice Scalia having died and Justice Kagan having recused) written by Justice Kennedy, who had previously been almost uniformly hostile to affirmative action. He was joined by Justices Breyer, Sotomayor, and Kagan. An impassioned dissent by Justice Alito was joined by the Chief Justice and Justice Thomas, who also separately dissented to stress that *Grutter* itself was wrong when decided.

Given the procedural posture of the case, the majority opinion focused on whether the University's plan was narrowly tailored, but that inquiry necessarily entailed a focus on the diversity interest UT was pursuing. The Court began by sketching the outlines of the University's admissions process, which consisted of two components. Seventy-five percent of the entering class was admitted under the "Top Ten Percent Plan," a statutory scheme promising admissions to those in the top 10% of their high school classes. 195 L. Ed 2d at 518–19. The remaining 25% were admitted by a combination of academic index (a combination of SAT and high school grades) and "personal achievement index," a number computed on the basis of a "holistic review" of the application. *Id.* at 531–32. The PAI did consider race but only as "a factor of a factor of a factor." *Id.* at 520. In that process, "consideration of race is contextual and does not operate as a mechanical plus factor for underrepresented minorities." *Id.*

In analyzing the University's process, the Court stressed that *Fisher I* had (1) mandated strict scrutiny of any use of race, requiring the University to "demonstrate with clarity that its purpose or interest is both constitutionally permissible and substantial, and that its use of the classification is necessary . . . to the accomplishment of its purpose." *Id.* at 520–21 (internal quotation marks omitted); (2) accorded UT "some, but not complete, judicial deference" as to the educational benefits of diversity, *id.* at 521; but (3) provided no deference "when determining whether the use of race is narrowly tailored to achieve the university's permissible goals." *Id.*

Although this suggested a high hurdle for the University to surmount, the majority found it had done so. While *Fisher I* required a clear demonstration of the

2. Systemic Disparate Treatment Discrimination

University's goals, *Fisher II* rejected plaintiff's challenge to the concreteness of the compelling interest being pursued. First, UT need not, indeed, may not, set a goal of minority enrollment that is "reduced to pure numbers." *Id.* at 524. Second, while *Fisher II* stated that "asserting an interest in the educational benefits of diversity writ large is insufficient," because the goals "must be sufficiently measurable to permit judicial scrutiny of the policies adopted to reach them," *id.* at 524, the Court found the University had done so by identifying

> the educational values it seeks to realize through its admissions process: the destruction of stereotypes, the "'promot[ion of] cross-racial understanding,'" the preparation of a student body "'for an increasingly diverse workforce and society,'" and the "'cultivat [ion of] a set of leaders with legitimacy in the eyes of the citizenry.'" [The University] strives to provide an "academic environment" that offers a "robust exchange of ideas, exposure to differing cultures, preparation for the challenges of an increasingly diverse workforce, and acquisition of competencies required of future leaders." All of these objectives, as a general matter, mirror the "compelling interest" this Court has approved in its prior cases.

Id. (citations omitted).

The Court also rejected the plaintiff's argument that explicit consideration of race was unnecessary because the Ten Percent Plan already ensured a "critical mass" of minority enrollment. While race could be a factor in decisionmaking only if the benefits of diversity could not otherwise be achieved, the record revealed demographic data "show[ing] consistent stagnation in terms of the percentage of minority students enrolling at the University" during the relevant time period, *id.* at 525, as well as evidence that minority students admitted under the prior system "experienced feelings of loneliness and isolation." *Id.* That was bolstered by data showing how frequently classes had one or no minority students enrolled.

As for the plaintiff's argument that considering race in admissions was not necessary because it resulted in relatively few minority admissions, the majority found that increases in representation showed "a meaningful, if still limited, effect on the diversity of the University's freshman class"; in any event, "the fact that race consciousness played a role in only a small portion of admissions decisions should be a hallmark of narrow tailoring, not evidence of unconstitutionality." *Id.* at 526.

Rejecting the plaintiff's final argument that the University had other alternatives to explicit consideration of race, the Court found that UT made numerous efforts to improve diversity before turning to the current regime. As for the proposal that Texas uncap the Top Ten Percent Plan and admit more — or even all — students under that approach, the Court was dismissive on two grounds. First, the Top Ten Percent Plan, "though facially neutral, cannot be understood apart from its basic purpose, which is to boost minority enrollment." *Id.* Quoting Justice Ginsburg dissent's in *Fisher I*, the majority stressed that percentage plans are race conscious in their attempt to increase enrollment by utilizing the racial segregation of neighborhoods and schools. "Consequently, petitioner cannot assert simply that increasing the University's reliance on a percentage plan would make its admissions policy more race neutral." *Id.* at 527. Second, even if uncapping the plan would increase minority enrollment, college admissions would not be improved by becoming "a function of class rank alone," *id.*, since that would sacrifice all other admissions considerations.

Justice Alito authored an impassioned dissent, taking the majority of task for upholding the University's plan despite its failure to satisfy the demands of *Fisher I*. The dissent disagreed with the majority in almost every respect but it was especially critical of the failure of UT to

> [i]dentif[y] with any degree of specificity the interests that its use of race and ethnicity is supposed to serve. Its primary argument is that merely invoking "the educational benefits of diversity" is sufficient and that it need not identify any metric that would allow a court to determine whether its plan is needed to serve, or is actually serving, those interests. This is nothing less than the plea for deference that we emphatically rejected in our prior decision. Today, however, the Court inexplicably grants that request.

Id. at 529.

Although *Fisher II* is certainly historic in preserving *Grutter's* approval of diversity rationales for race consciousness, it is a very limited decision in two significant respects. First, the majority described the UT process at issue as "sui generis," *id.* at 521, thus suggesting that other colleges and universities will face different considerations. That was in part because most admissions decisions were dictated by the Ten Percent Plan, which plaintiff had not challenged and therefore "has been taken, somewhat artificially, as a given premise." *Id.* Because the record lacked data as to the diversity of students admitted to the University under that regime as compared to those 25% admitted where race was "a factor of a factor of a factor," *id.* at 520, the opinion's "value for prospective guidance" was undercut. *Id.* at 532. Second, and flowing from this reality, *Fisher II* did not necessarily validate even the current operation of the UT admissions system since the University had a "continuing obligation to satisfy the burden of strict scrutiny in light of changing circumstances." *Id* at 523.

And regardless of the status of race consciousness admissions in institutions of higher education, *Fisher II* provided no guidance on the limits of race consciousness in the employment context.

Page 188, add after carryover paragraph:

Assuming that *Grutter* does apply in the employment context in the sense of allowing diversity to be a compelling interest for at least some public employers, the *Fisher* saga suggests the current Court may be permissive. While *Fisher v. University of Texas at Austin*, 133 S. Ct. 2411 (2013), ("*Fisher I*,") suggested that a searching review is needed with respect to how "narrowly tailored" the plan is to the diversity goal, with no deference accorded to the employer's decision, *id.* at 2420, *Fisher II*, 195 L.Ed 2d 511 (2016), found that the plan at issue to satisfy that ostensibly higher standard. See discussion in this Supplement at p. 23.

3 *Systemic Disparate Impact Discrimination*

Page 204, add at end of carryover Note 2, *An Underlying Rationale for the Disparate Impact Theory?*:

Light may be shed on some of these issues by the posthumously published book of Professor Robert Belton, who was heavily involved in the *Griggs* litigation. Robert Belton, The Crusade for Equality in the Workplace: The *Griggs v. Duke Power* Story (Stephen L. Wasby ed., 2014)

Page 210, add new Note 0:

0. Although *Smith* approved disparate impact suits, it arguably did so only for those within §623(a)(2), which bars actions against "employees" that "would deprive or tend to deprive" them of job opportunities. In contrast, §623(1)(2), bars discrimination against any "individual," but it lacks the "tend to" language. Some cases prior to *Smith* accordingly recognized the disparate impact theory as available in suits by employees but not in those brought by applicants. *Villarreal v. R.J. Reynolds Tobacco Co.*, 806 F.3d 1288 (11th Cir. 2015) (2-1), however, held the theory also applied to claims of "disappointed job applicants." Although it found the statute ambiguous and the question not controlled by *Smith*, it held that the EEOC's reasonable interpretation to that effect was entitled to deference. The panel decision was vacated and rehearing en banc granted, No. 15-10602, 2016 U.S. App. LEXIS 2879 (11th Cir. Feb. 10, 2016).

Page 219, add at end of Note 1, *Employer Practices Subject to Disparate Impact*:

In addition, a plaintiff cannot challenge a policy that may have an adverse impact unless she was herself affected by that policy. *Tartt v. Wilson Cnty.*, 592 F. App'x 441, 448 (6th Cir. 2014) (plaintiff could not challenge policy of not advertising positions when he applied for only one); *Welch v. Eli Lilly & Co.*, 585 F. App'x 911, 913 (7th Cir. 2014) ("A plaintiff who was not injured by a challenged employment practice—even an objectionable practice—has no ground to complain, whether the theory be disparate impact or any other.").

Page 221, add at the end of first sentence in Note 5, *Pleading a Disparate Impact Case*:

See Adams v. City of Indianapolis, 742 F.3d 720, 733 (7th Cir. 2014) (the complaint was properly dismissed for failure to allege facts "tending to show that the City's testing process, or some particular part of it, caused a relevant and statistically significant disparity between black and white applicants for promotion" or "allegations about the racial makeup of the relevant workforce in the Indianapolis metropolitan area or the supervisory ranks in the police and fire departments").

Page 227, add at end of Note 1, *The Employment Practice Plaintiff Challenged*:

Such proof, however, can be much more complex. In *Tabor v. Hilti, Inc.*, 703 F.3d 1206 (10th Cir. 2013), for example, plaintiff made out a prima facie case of disparate impact of a particular promotion system by showing that the promotion rate for male sales representatives was substantially and significantly greater than that for female representatives. She alleged this was the result of managers exercising their discretion under the system in a discriminatory fashion by assigning subjective ratings differently for male and female employees. She was not required to show an impact on "otherwise qualified" employees when managers often used their discretion to waive the system's supposed minimum requirements to promote male employees with low or no ratings, while holding females to those requirements.

Page 229, add at end of carryover Note 7, *Incapable of Separation for Analysis*:

Chin v. Port Auth. of N.Y. & N.J., 685 F.3d 135, 154-55 (2d Cir. 2012) (while a promotion process formally involved three steps, the evidence established that the first two steps could not be separated from the rest for statistical analysis since both played an indeterminate role). *But see Tabor v. Hilti, Inc.*, 577 F. App'x 870, 873 (10th Cir. 2014), affirming holding that a Global Development and Coach program and interview process were separate, which meant that plaintiff had failed to isolate the impact of the former from that of the latter); *Davis v. Cintas Corp.*, 717 F.3d 476 (6th Cir. 2013) (plaintiff neither identified a "particular employment practice" by including several distinct subjective elements of a multi-interview hiring system nor showed that the "many steps were so intertwined that they were not capable of separation for analysis").

Page 230, add at end of Note 10, *Is Disparate Impact Constitutional?*

The constitutionality of disparate impact was reinforced by the Supreme Court's decision in *Texas Department of Housing & Community Affairs v. Inclusive Cmtys. Project, Inc.*, 135 S. Ct. 2507 (2014), which found the disparate impact theory applicable under the Fair Housing Act and in the process suggested interpretations that would ensure its constitutionality. *See* Richard Primus, *Of Visible Race-Consciousness and Institutional Role: Equal Protection and Disparate Impact after* Ricci *and* Inclusive Communities in TITLE VII OF THE CIVIL RIGHTS ACT AFTER 50 YEARS: PROCEEDINGS OF THE NEW YORK UNIVERSITY 67TH ANNUAL CONFERENCE ON LABOR (LexisNexis Publishing 2015) (arguing that *Inclusive Communities* suggests that the Supreme Court will not view disparate impact as definitionally inconsistent with equal protection but does not cast much light on likely future direction); Samuel R. Bagenstos, *Disparate Impact and the Role of Classification and Motivation in Equal Protection Law after* Inclusive Communities, 101 CORNELL L. REV. 1115 (2015) (Justice Kennedy's view that classifications are not constitutionally suspect because they are motivated to further racial integration has now been adopted by a majority of the Court).

The extent to which constitutional concerns will shape statutory disparate impact analysis, however, remains to be seen. *See Abril-Rivera v. Johnson*, 806 F.3d 599 (1st Cir. 2015) (looking to *Inclusive Communities* to hold that, when defendants present "legitimate business justifications for their actions," the disparate impact theory requires the plaintiff to prove a viable less discriminatory alternative; any other rule would too much constrain both business and government decisions and create the danger of racial quotas).

Page 231, add a new Note 11A:

11A. *"Voluntary" Quits.* In reductions in force, plaintiffs sometimes try to compare the proportions of protected class members retained with other groups. Employers respond that the correct focus should be on those involuntarily terminated and therefore exclude those who took a "voluntary" separation package, such as an early retirement incentive plan. *See Gambill v. Duke Energy Corp.*, 456 F. App'x 578, 587-88 (6th Cir. 2012) (a "simple percentage comparison of older and younger attorneys retained" was insufficient to make out disparate impact, in part because the plaintiffs included 13 attorneys who took a voluntary severance package and, therefore, were not subject to the RIF). Which is the appropriate comparison? Does it matter that many of those accepting severance offers did so because they anticipated discharge if they did not assent?

Page 237, add at end of carryover paragraph:

In *Jones v. City of Boston*, 752 F.3d 38 (1st Cir. 2014), plaintiffs challenged the police department's use of hair samples to test for illegal drug use, as causing a disparate impact. They claimed that black hair was more likely to yield false positives than white hair. Their proof of impact was that black officers tested positive for cocaine approximately 1.3% of the time, while white officers did so just under 0.3% of the time. The court held that was sufficient: the data was statistically significant, and there is no requirement that plaintiffs must also prove "practical significance," i.e., that the size of the disparity is large enough to matter. While the EEOC's 4/5's rule might be appropriate to guide an agency's enforcement priorities, it creates anomalies and should not be used to determine whether plaintiff establishes cognizable impact.

Page 249, add in Note 12, *Arrest Records and Discrimination* before "Ironically"

See generally Tammy R. Pettinato, *Employment Discrimination Against Ex-Offenders: the Promise and Limits of Title VII Disparate Impact Theory*, 98 MARQ. L. REV. 831(2014). *See also* Dallon Flake, *When Any Sentence Is a Life Sentence: Employment Discrimination Against Ex-Offenders*, 93 Wash. U. L. Rev. 45, 51 (2015) (recommending amendments to Title VII to prohibit discrimination against ex-offenders on the basis of a criminal record not directly related to the job at issue and to create a rebuttable presumption against admitting evidence of an offending employee's criminal record in negligent hiring cases).

Page 249, add new Notes:

12A. *Unemployment and Credit Scores.* There is also some concern as to discrimination on the basis of being unemployed or of having low credit scores (probably correlated phenomena). While there have been limited efforts on the state level to address "currently employed" requirements directly, *e.g.*, N.J. Stat. §34:8B-1, both grounds could be the basis of a disparate impact challenge. *See generally* Lea Shepard, *Seeking Solutions to Financial History Discrimination*, 46 CONN. L. REV. 993, 1000 (2014); Lea Shepard, *Toward a Stronger Financial History Antidiscrimination Norm*, 53 B.C. L. REV. 1695 (2012); Jennifer Jolly-Ryan, *Have a Job to Get a Job: Disparate Treatment and Disparate Impact of the "Currently Employed" Requirement*, 18 MICH. J. RACE & L. 189 (2012).

12B. *Who's Who?* Until recently, there was little problem with plaintiffs' proof of impact in terms of who counts as a member of a particular race. But *EEOC v. Kaplan Higher Educ. Corp.*, 748 F.3d 749 (6th Cir. 2014), raised precisely that question when the EEOC failed to prove the racial effects of a particular practice because of difficulties in identifying the race of affected individuals. The Sixth Circuit upheld dismissal of EEOC's disparate impact complaint when the agency could not prove that defendant's credit check policy had a disparate impact on blacks after the lower court appropriately excluded an expert report using "race raters" to ascertain the supposed race of rejected applicants on the basis of drivers' license photographs. *See generally* Charles A. Sullivan, *Who Counts as Black?*,

WORKPLACE PROF BLOG (Apr. 23, 2014), http://lawprofessors.typepad.com/laborprof_blog/2014/04/whats-race-once-again-.html.

12C. *The Universal Turn.* Some have argued that it is politically more feasible to challenge a variety of practices as objectionable without regard to race. *E.g.*, Katie R. Eyer, *That's Not Discrimination: American Beliefs and the Limits of Anti-Discrimination Law*, 96 MINN. L. REV. 1275, 1280 (2012) (arguing in favor of "litigation-based approaches that do not focus on group-based discrimination claims"). For example, prisoner re-entry has often been a subject of concern without focusing on the racial disparities of prison populations. Under this view, disparate impact challenges may be misguided if the real goal is systemic changes. Other scholars challenge this "universal turn." *E.g.*, Zev J. Eigen, Camille Gear Rich, & Charlotte Alexander, *Post-Racial Hydraulics: The Hidden Danger of the Universal Turn*, 91 N.Y.U.L. Rev. 1 (2016) (arguing against the "universal turn" — converting particular claims, like race discrimination claims, into broader universalist claims; the trend toward universalism" threatens to fundamentally reshape employment litigation and alter understandings of race discrimination); Jessica A. Clarke, *Beyond Equality? Against the Universal Turn in Workplace Protections*, 86 IND. L.J. 1219, 1240-51 (2011).

Page 256, add at end of Note 1, *Proposing an Alternative Employment Practice*:

See also Johnson v. City of Memphis, 770 F.3d 464, 467 (6th Cir. 2014) (trial court improperly shifted to the employer the plaintiff's burden of proof of alternative employment practices, and plaintiffs failed to present evidence establishing a genuine issue of fact regarding the availability of equally valid, less discriminatory alternative testing methods, even though there was proof that an earlier use had been successful).

Page 267, add at end of carryover paragraph in carryover Note 1, *Job Analysis*:

But see M.O.C.H.A. Soc'y, Inc. v. City of Buffalo, 689 F.3d 263, 286 (2d Cir. 2012) (2-1) ("[D]espite the lack of direct evidence [of the duties of lieutenant positions in] the Buffalo Fire Department, Buffalo carried its burden to demonstrate the examination's job relatedness by showing that the test derived from a valid statewide job analysis indicating that fire lieutenants across New York performed the same critical tasks and required the same critical skills.").

Page 267, add at end of first sentence of Note 2, *Developing the Test*:

The test need not try to assess performance on all aspects of the job but is supposed to test "critical" and "important" knowledge, skills, and abilities as identified in the job analysis. *Lopez v. City of Lawrence*, 823 F.3d 102 (1st Cir. 2016) (2-1).

Page 267, add to end of Note 3, *Choosing Validation Strategies*:

As the principal case suggests, a test can be valid enough to be of use but not valid enough to be used to select in rank order. However, recent cases have upheld such uses. *See Lopez v. City of Lawrence*, 823 F.3d 102 (1st Cir. 2016) ("Even accepting the district court's opinion that added scrutiny was called for because rank ordering was used, whatever added scrutiny one need apply here certainly falls short of the added scrutiny one would apply if rank ordering had been a material contributor to the disparate impact" since there had been no demonstration that "an increased number of Black and Hispanic applicants likely would have been selected" under an alternative approach); *Johnson v. City of Memphis*, 770 F.3d 464, 482 (6th Cir. 2014) (upholding rank-ordering on a content-validated police test because of "a substantial demonstration of job relatedness and representativeness," score variance, and an "adequate degree" of test reliability) (citation omitted).

4 The Interrelationship of the Three Theories of Discrimination

Page 279, after *Obrey* cite in add in Note 1, *The Role of Statistics in Individual Disparate Treatment Cases:*

Cf. Burgis v. New York City Dep't of Sanitation, 798 F.3d 63, 69 (2d Cir. 2015) (while statistics alone may be sufficient to plead a §1981claim, they "must not only be statistically significant in the mathematical sense, but they must also be of a level that makes other plausible non-discriminatory explanations very unlikely")

Page 279, add in Note 3, *Why Isn't* Baylie *a Systemic Case?* before first *Davis* cite:

Daniels v. UPS, 701 F.3d 620, 632-33 (10th Cir. 2012) (individual plaintiffs cannot bring pattern-or-practice claims — only the U.S. Attorney General or a certified class can do so)*; Chin v. Port Auth. of N.Y. & N.J.*, 685 F.3d 135, 147 (2d Cir. 2012) (rejecting the pattern-or-practice method of proof in private suits outside the class action context);

Page 283, add in first full paragraph before *McDowell* cite:

Fagerstrom v. City of Savannah, 627 F. App'x 803 (11th Cir. 2015) (plaintiff could not show racial discrimination against Asians, despite self-identifying as Asian based on his mother's ethnicity when he had originally listed his race as white, and at the point that the decisionmaker chose two white captains for the promotion, he believed plaintiff was white as well); *Hunter v. UPS*, 697 F.3d 697, 703-04 (8th Cir. 2012) (no sufficient evidence that employer's recruiter knew of plaintiff's transgender status at time of the interview despite plaintiff's use of a female first name while dressed and groomed more like a man);

Page 310, add at end of Note 6, *A Business Necessity as a Matter of Law?*

See also Ann C. McGinley, *Cognitive Illiberalism, Summary Judgment, and Title VII: An Examination of* Ricci v. DeStefano, 57 N.Y.L. Sch. L. Rev. 865, 889 (2012-13) (arguing that, even under the Court's standard, summary judgment should not have been granted to plaintiffs since Dr. Hornick's testimony created genuine issues of fact as to (1) the validity and accuracy of a test that had not been subjected to internal review; (2) the availability of different weighting of the written and oral tests, which would have allowed the City to consider additional black candidates; and (3) the alternative of using an assessment center).

Page 310, add at the end of Note 7, *Alternative Employment Practices*:

Lopez v. City of Lawrence, 823 F.3d 102 (1st Cir. 2016) (2-1), added a wrinkle to the analysis. Although it recognized that "as a general matter, incorporation of selection tools such as use of 'hurdles,' banding, oral interviews, so—called assessment centers, and open ended 'situational judgment' questions generally tend to result in less adverse impact than does a reliance on multiple choice exams," it found that plaintiffs had failed to rebut the city's expert who testified that "the low rates of job openings in the Boston sergeant ranks relative to the number of applicants made it unlikely that any alternative selection device would have materially reduced adverse impact."

Page 311, add before *Zisk* cite in Note 9, *Is* Ricci *Limited to End-Game Decisions?*:

See Maraschiello v. City of Buffalo Police Dep't, 709 F.3d 87, 95 (2d Cir. 2013) ("Even if it were determined that the City's choice to adopt a new test was motivated in part by its desire to achieve more racially balanced results . . . Maraschiello cannot demonstrate that the generalized overhaul of departmental promotional requirements amounted to the sort of race-based adverse action discussed in *Ricci*," which specifically permits employers to design a test to provide a fair opportunity for all individuals, regardless of race.").

5 *Special Problems in Applying Title VII, Section 1981, and the ADEA*

B. *Coverage of Title VII, Section 1981, and the ADEA*

Page 320, add before Carlson cite in Note 4, *Avoiding Liability by Using Independent Contractors*:

Charlotte Alexander, *Misclassification and Antidiscrimination: An Economic Analysis*, MINN. L. REV. (forthcoming), *available at* http://ssrn.com/abstract=2757822

Page 320, add after last full sentence on the page in Note 5, *Owners as Employees*:

See also Mariotti v. Mariotti Bldg. Prods., 714 F.3d 761 (3d Cir. 2013), (*Clackamas* applied to business, as well as professional, corporations, and its six factors address not only the extent of an individual's control but also the source of his authority, which includes whether the putative employee exercises authority by right or by delegation from those who ultimately possess the right to control the enterprise).

Page 321, add after *Sidley Austin* **cite in carryover Note 5,** *Owners as Employers*:

See also Bluestein v. Cent. Wis. Anesthesiology, S.C., 769 F.3d 944, 948 (7th Cir. 2014) (anesthesiologist properly found to have been an employer rather than an employee of a corporation as a shareholder and member of the board of directors and entitled to vote on all issues, including her own termination).

Page 321, add after first sentence in Note 6, *The Numbers Game*:

Sometimes, this determination requires an analysis of what entity constitutes the employer. *See Cink v. Grant Cnty.*, 635 Fed. App'x 470 (10th Cir. 2015) (the County

Sheriff was an agent of the County such that an employee of the Sheriff was employed by the County; thus, the fact that the Sheriff's office had too few employees, separately considered, to be a statutory employer was irrelevant).

Page 321, delete Note 7; replace with:

7. *Integrated Enterprises and Joint Employers*. Sometimes two or more formally distinct legal entities are viewed as being in reality a single employer, thus allowing the employees of all to be aggregated to reach the required minimum number, which has been called the "integrated enterprise" or "single employer" doctrine. *See Arculeo v. On-Site Sales & Mktg., L.L.C.*, 425 F.3d 193, 199 (2d Cir. 2005) ("although nominally and technically distinct, several entities [may be] properly seen as a single integrated entity"); *Davis v. Ricketts*, 765 F.3d 823 (8th Cir. 2014) (2-1) (despite evidence establishing common control and financial backing, two entities were not a single employer when there was little interrelation of operations and little shared control of labor relations).

Distinct from the single-employer doctrine is "joint employment," under which an employee of one entity may hold another entity liable; the premise is not that two entities are one but rather that they co-determine terms and conditions of employment. This is often a multifactor analysis, see, e.g., *Butler v. Drive Auto. Indus. of Am.*, 793 F.3d 404, 413 (4th Cir. 2015). Joint employment can arise in a number of settings.

One common one occurs when firms use staffing agencies to provide workers; in such cases, assuming the requirements are met, both the agency and its client can be found to be employers. *E.g., Faush v. Tuesday Morning, Inc.*, 808 F.3d 208 (3d Cir. 2015) (the store where a temporary staffing agency assigned plaintiff to work could be found to be his employer because it had control over his daily activities); *Burton v. Freescale Semiconductor, Inc.*, 798 F.3d 222 (5th Cir. 2015) (defendant held to be plaintiff's employer even though she was paid by a staffing agency when the defendant had the right to, and did, demand termination of her assignment, complaints were made by its personnel, her nominal agency supervisor worked elsewhere, and defendant's employees completed performance reviews of her work and made on-the-job corrections and admonishments).

Joint employment can also arise in other settings, such as contractor/subcontractor relationships. *E.g., EEOC v. Skanska USA Bldg., Inc.*, 550 F. App'x 253 (6th Cir. 2013) (finding contractor the joint employer of employees of a subcontractor when it did virtually all the supervision of the workers at the site), *but see Casey v. HHS*, 807 F.3d 395, 406 (1st Cir. 2015) (supervision of large government contracts by the purchasing agency does not convert the government into a joint employer when major employment decisions remain with the contractor); *Knitter v. Corvias Military Living, LLC*, 758 F.3d 1214, 1228 (10th Cir. 2014) (the defendant was not a joint employer with the plaintiff's primary employer when it did not lacked authority to supervise, discipline, or terminate plaintiff's employment. Another common setting is when affiliated but legally distinct corporate entities merge their employment practices. *Cf. Bridge v. New Holland Logansport, Inc.*, 815 F.3d 356 (7th

Cir. 2016) (three individuals who formally worked for a sister firm were not in reality employees of the defendant).

However, a determination of joint employment does not automatically render one employer liable for the violations of the other. *Whitaker v. Milwaukee Cnty.*, 772 F.3d 802, 811-12 (7th Cir. 2014) (a joint employer is liable for actions taken by the other employer only if it *participates* in the other employer's discrimination or if it knew or should have known about the other's discrimination and failed to take appropriate corrective measures); *Burton v. Freescale Semiconductor, Inc.*, 798 F.3d 222 (5th Cir. 2015) (same). *See generally* Richard R. Carlson, *The Small Firm Exemption and the Single Employer Doctrine in Employment Discrimination Law*, 80 St. John's L. Rev. 1197 (2006).

Page 321, delete Note 8; replace with:

8. *Interns and Volunteers.* In *Lerohl*, the court quotes approvingly an earlier case finding "silly" the claim that volunteer firefighters or volunteer rescue workers are employees "because the fire chief or the head of the rescue squad directs them." It may in fact be silly, but perhaps because "employment" entails both control and compensation. In other words, the firefighters are not employees because they are unpaid, even assuming their work is controlled by the putative employer. The courts have generally looked to remuneration either as an absolute requirement for employment or as an important factor in the determination. *See Marie v. Am. Red Cross*, 771 F.3d 344, 359 (6th Cir. 2014) (Catholic nuns claiming religious discrimination could not show they were employees under the common law agency test even in a circuit that did not find compensation a threshold requirement for Title VII coverage); *Juino v. Livingston Parish Fire Dist. No. 5*, 717 F.3d 431 (5th Cir. 2013) (looking to "remuneration" for volunteer firefighters as a threshold requirement to finding employment rather than merely one factor in the analysis). *But see Bryson v. Middlefield Volunteer Fire Dep't, Inc.*, 656 F.3d 348 (6th Cir. 2011) (given various benefits, volunteer firefighters might be employees even though not receiving compensation).

This means, for example, while graduate assistants in universities may be employees, *Cuddeback v. Florida Bd. of Educ.*, 381 F.3d 1230, 1234 (11th Cir. 2004), students interning at outside employers typically are held to lack statutory protection under the antidiscrimination laws even when the employers were for-profit entities. *See generally* David C. Yamada, *The Employment Law Rights of Student Interns*, 35 Conn. L. Rev. 215 (2002).

That may be changing, both as a result of recent decisions and because of state legislation providing interns with protection from discrimination and harassment, even if it does not address the minimum wage implications of unpaid work. *See generally* Stephanie A. Pisko, Comment, *Great Expectations, Grim Reality: Unpaid Interns and the Dubious Benefits of the DOL Pro Bono Exception*, 45 Seton Hall L. Rev. 613 (2015).

Then there's the question of prisoners, who are typically held not to be employees even when leased to private employers. *See Castle v. Eurofresh, Inc.*, 731

F.3d 901 (9th Cir. 2013) (prisoner not an "employee" of a state contractor under the ADA because his labor belonged to the State of Arizona, which put him to work at the contractor in order to comply with its statutory obligations). *See generally* Noah D. Zatz, *Working at the Boundaries of Markets: Prison Labor and the Economic Dimension of Employment Relationships*, 61 Vand. L. Rev. 857 (2008).

Page 322, add after *Garrett* cite in Note 9, *Governmental Employment*:

But see Brumfield v. City of Chicago, 735 F.3d 619, 622 (7th Cir. 2013) ("We join the Ninth and Tenth Circuits and hold that Title II of the ADA does not cover disability discrimination in public employment; this kind of claim must be brought under Title I.").

Page 322, add new Note 10A:

10A. *Successor Liability.* In some cases, a corporate employer goes out of business only to have its operations taken over by a second company. Some courts allow liability for discrimination to pass to the successor in appropriate circumstances. *See EEOC v. Northern Star Hospitality, Inc.*, 777 F.3d 898, 902 (7th Cir. 2015) (permissible to impose liability on the successor for discrimination by the predecessor when considering factors such as the successor's notice of the pending lawsuit; whether the predecessor could have provided the relief sought before or after the transition; and whether there is continuity between the operations and work force of the two entities).

Page 322, add at end of Note 11, *Exemptions*:

See also Toy v. Holder, 714 F.3d 881 (5th Cir. 2013), (refusing to allow review under Title VII of a denial of an FBI contract employee's access to a building based on national security considerations); *Foote v. Moniz*, 751 F.3d 656 (D.C. Cir. 2014) (Title VII claim foreclosed by doctrine barring judicial review of agency actions like the challenged refusal to certify an applicant under the Department of Energy's Human Reliability Program, despite absence of explicit statutory exception like that for security clearances).

Page 323, delete Note 12; replace with:

12. *Pushing the Coverage Envelope.* Some courts expand Title VII's reach in ways that are not obvious. Thus, entities that exercise control over another entity's employees are sometimes held to be "indirect employers." This can apply to state

agencies, *compare Ass'n of Mexican-Am. Educators v. California*, 231 F.3d 572 (9th Cir. 2000) (en banc) (Title VII applied to a California state credentialing agency in light of the power such agency exerted over employment as a teacher), *with Gulino v. N.Y. State Educ. Dep't*, 460 F.3d 361, 375 (2d Cir. 2006) (state defendants were not employers because the relationship between New York and its local school districts differed from that in California); *Lopez v. Massachusetts*, 588 F.3d 69 (1st Cir. 2009) (state agency that administered promotional exams for local police officers under state civil service system was not a Title VII "employer" when acting in that capacity). But it can also apply in the private sector. *See Love v. JP Cullen & Sons, Inc.*, 779 F.3d 697, 701-02 (7th Cir. 2015) (applying a five-factor test, the court held that a prime contractor was not an indirect employer of its subcontractor's employees even though it retained the right to exclude such persons from the job site when there was otherwise minimal control and the exclusion did not require the sub to discharge the employee).

In another context, physicians with clinical privileges were traditionally found not to be employees of the hospitals where they worked, *e.g.*, *Shah v. Deaconess Hosp.*, 355 F.3d 496, 500 (6th Cir. 2004), but the expanding control hospitals exercise over such physicians led one circuit to alter this. *See Salamon v. Our Lady of Victory Hosp.*, 514 F.3d 217 (2d Cir. 2008). More recent cases have not followed *Salamon's* lead. *Ashkenazi v. S. Broward Hosp. Dist.*, 607 F. App'x 968 (11th Cir. 2015) (physician not an employee under the ADEA even though hospital radically increased supervision of his work)); *Alexander v. Avera St. Luke's Hosp.*, 768 F.3d 756 (8th Cir. 2014) (pathologist not an employee of the hospital).

Page 323, add at end of Note on Coverage of §1981:

See Brown v. Sessoms, 774 F.3d 1016 (D.C. Cir. 2014) (finding that §1981 was enforced through §1983 but reversing dismissal for failure to state a claim under §1981 claim even though §1983 was not pled).

B. Sex Discrimination

Page 329, add in Note 3, *Proving the Harassment Was "Because of Sex"* before *Redd* cite:

Barrows v. Seneca Foods Corp., 512 F. App'x 115, 118 (2d Cir. 2013) (a reasonable jury could find that men were the primary targets of the conduct and could also consider that some "vulgar comments were sex-specific" and focused on male-specific body parts);

Page 329, add before *Cherry* cite in last paragraph of Note 3, *Proving the Harassment Was "Because of Sex."*:

Smith v. Rock-Tenn Servs., 813 F.3d 298 (6th Cir. 2016) (harassment could be found to be "because of sex" when supposed "horseplay" was aimed only at men in a mixed-sex workplace and included sexualized actions);

Page 336, add at end of carryover paragraph in carryover Note 1, *Sexual Orientation ± Sex Under Title VII*:

See also Leora F. Eisenstadt, *Fluid Identity Discrimination*, 52 Am. Bus. L. J. 789 (2015).

Page 336, add before *Prowel* cite in Note 2, *Distinguishing Sexual Orientation from Sex Stereotyping*:

EEOC v. Boh Bros. Constr. Co., L.L.C., 731 F.3d 444 (5th Cir. 2013) (en banc) ("nothing in *Oncale* overturns or otherwise upsets the Court's holding in *Price Waterhouse*: a plaintiff may establish a sexual harassment claim with evidence of sex-stereotyping. Thus, the EEOC may rely on evidence that Wolfe viewed Woods as insufficiently masculine to prove its Title VII claim.") *See generally* Luke A. Boso, *Real Men*, 37 Hawaii L. Rev. 107, 108 (2015) (arguing for a contextual approach to determining sex stereotyping in claims where male plaintiffs claim to have been discriminated against because they fail to look or behave like "real men": "If a plaintiff's gender presentation differs from the dominant gender norms in the relevant context, that difference, accompanied by harassment, should support an inference of discriminatory intent.")

Page 337, complete *Yuracko* cite near end of carryover paragraph in Note 2, *Distinguishing Sexual Orientation from Sex Stereotyping*:

161 U. Pa. L. Rev. 757 (2013).

Page 337, add at end of Note 2, *Distinguishing Sexual Orientation from Sex Stereotyping*:

See generally Brian Soucek, *Perceived Homosexuals: Looking Gay Enough for Title VII*, 63 Am. U. L. Rev. 715 (2014) (arguing that "employees who manifest traits coded as gay in observable ways at work often succeed under Title VII. But when an employee's sexuality is *cognitively* perceived—when co-workers *think* that a man is sleeping with another man or *know* that a woman lives with a female partner—courts refuse to extend Title VII's protections.").

Page 338, delete first full paragraph; replace with:

The Supreme Court is more recent decisions, although hard to classify doc-
trinally, nevertheless clearly view classifications based on sexual orientation with
hostility. *United States v. Windsor*, 133 S. Ct. 2675 (2013), struck down the federal
Defense of Marriage Act which barred same-sex partners from a wide array of federal
benefits offered to married couples. While it was widely believed to have portended a
more sweeping invalidation of state prohibitions on same-sex marriage, that did not
occur until *Obergefell v. Hodges*, 135 S. Ct. 2584 (2015), in which a majority of the
Court struck down such laws. *Obergefell* was grounded primarily in the Due Process
Clause but also looked to the Equal Protection Clause for its holding.

While there seems to be no direct application of these decisions to employment, certainly not employment in the private sector, they may portend a more
flexible approach to those issues under Title VII. A harbinger in this regard may
be the EEOC's recent decision in *Macy v. Holder*, No. 0120120821, 2012 EEOPUB
LEXIS 1181 (E.E.O.C. Apr. 20, 2012), holding that discrimination against transgender individuals based on their transgender status does constitute sex-based
discrimination in violation of Title VII. *See also Fowlkes v. Ironworkers Local 40*,
790 F.3d 378 (2d Cir. 2015) (recounting the change in the agency's views). Importantly, in July 2015, in a claim involving alleged discrimination in federal employment, the EEOC ruled (3-2) that discrimination on the basis of sexual orientation
is sex discrimination within the meaning of Title VII. See Complainant v. Foxx,
2015 WL 4397641 (E.E.O.C. July 15, 2015). The EEOC also has filed an amicus
brief in *Burrows v. The College of Central Florida*, No. 15-14554, a case pending
before the Eleventh Circuit, in which the agency asserts its position that discrimination on the basis of sexual orientation violates Title VII. *See generally* Keith
Cunningham-Parmeter, *Marriage Equality, Workplace Inequality: The Next Gay Rights
Battle*, 67 Fla. L. Rev. 1099 (2015); Stephen F. Befort & Michael J. Vargas, *Same-
Sex Marriage and Title VII*, 56 Santa Clara L. Rev. 207 (2016).

Page 341, add after first full paragraph:

In a class by itself is a state court case, *Nelson v. James H. Knight DDS, P.C.*, 834
N.W.2d 64 (Iowa 2013), which held that an employer did not engage in sex discrimination when he fired a female employee at the request of his wife due to her
concerns with the nature of his relationship with an employee. The basis was the
sexual attractiveness of the fired worker, not her involvement in any affair with the
boss.

Page 347, add before Render cite in first full paragraph:

Peter Brandon Bayer, *Debunking Unequal Burdens, Trivial Violations, Harmless
Stereotypes, and Similar Judicial Myths: The Convergence of Title VII Literalism,*

Congressional Intent, and Kantian Dignity Theory, 89 St. JOHN's L. REV. 401 (2016) (challenging the unequal burden test for dress and grooming codes on both textual and dignity theory grounds);

Page 353, add after second sentence in last paragraph of Note 1, *Is the PDA's Protection Only Status Protection?*:

See also Hubbard v. Meritage Homes of Fla., Inc., 520 F. App'x 859 (11th Cir. 2013) (plaintiff's comparator evidence of two other sales associates, who were not pregnant and were treated more favorably than she, failed because neither engaged in the same misconduct for which she was terminated).

Page 354, add at end of carryover Note 1, *Is the PDA's Protection Only Status Protection?*:

See also Hitchcock v. Angel Corps, Inc., 718 F.3d 733 (7th Cir. 2013) (at least four potentially different explanations for plaintiff's discharge were "sufficiently inconsistent or otherwise suspect to create a reasonable inference that they do not reflect the real reason for Hitchcock's firing" and were a pretext for pregnancy discrimination).

Page 356, delete Note 5, *The Question of Accommodation:*

Page 356, add at end of carryover Note 6, *Related Medical Conditions:*

See also EEOC v. Houston Funding II, Ltd., 717 F.3d 425 (5th Cir. 2013) (adverse employment action against a female employee because she was lactating or expressing milk constituted sex discrimination).

Page 358, add at end of carryover Note 9, *Using Title VII to Break Down the "Maternal Wall":*

Cf. Keith Cunningham-Parmeter, *Men at Work, Fathers at Home: Uncovering the Masculine Face of Caregiver Discrimination*, 24 COLUM. J. GENDER & L. 253 (2013) (evaluating the legal challenges that fathers and other male caregivers face in proving claims of workplace discrimination and explaining how masculine norms deter men from asserting their caregiving needs at work while undermining their ability to prosecute discrimination claims in court).

A counterintuitive article suggests that open discussion about family status in the hiring context is likely to assist women in returning to the job market; current law and practice, which discourage both employers and employees from raising the topic, plays into employer "ambiguity aversion." *See* Jodi Herch & Jennifer

Bennett Shinall, *Something to Talk About: Information Exchange under Employment Law*, U. PA. L. REV. (forthcoming), *available at* http://papers.ssrn.com/sol3/papers.cfm?abstract_id=2765455, (2016) (reporting the results of an empirical study on the question).

Page 358, add new principal case after carryover paragraph:

Young v. UPS
135 S. Ct. 1338 (2015)

JUSTICE BREYER delivered the opinion of the Court.

The Pregnancy Discrimination Act makes clear that Title VII's prohibition against sex discrimination applies to discrimination based on pregnancy. It also says that employers must treat "women affected by pregnancy . . . the same for all employment-related purposes . . . as other persons not so affected but similar in their ability or inability to work." 42 U.S.C. §2000e(k). We must decide how this latter provision applies in the context of an employer's policy that accommodates many, but not all, workers with nonpregnancy-related disabilities.

In our view, the Act requires courts to consider the extent to which an employer's policy treats pregnant workers less favorably than it treats nonpregnant workers similar in their ability or inability to work. And here — as in all cases in which an individual plaintiff seeks to show disparate treatment through indirect evidence — it requires courts to consider any legitimate, nondiscriminatory, nonpretextual justification for these differences in treatment. See *McDonnell Douglas Corp.* v. *Green*. Ultimately the court must determine whether the nature of the employer's policy and the way in which it burdens pregnant women shows that the employer has engaged in intentional discrimination. The Court of Appeals here affirmed a grant of summary judgment in favor of the employer. Given our view of the law, we must vacate that court's judgment.

I

A

We begin with a summary of the facts. The petitioner, Peggy Young, worked as a part-time driver for the respondent, United Parcel Service (UPS). Her responsibilities included pickup and delivery of packages that had arrived by air carrier the previous night. In 2006, after suffering several miscarriages, she became pregnant. Her doctor told her that she should not lift more than 20 pounds during the first 20 weeks of her pregnancy or more than 10 pounds thereafter.

UPS required drivers like Young to be able to lift parcels weighing up to 70 pounds (and up to 150 pounds with assistance). UPS told Young she could not work while under a lifting restriction. Young consequently stayed home without pay during most of the time she was pregnant and eventually lost her employee medical coverage.

Young subsequently brought this federal lawsuit. We focus here on her claim that UPS acted unlawfully in refusing to accommodate her pregnancy-related lifting restriction. Young said that her co-workers were willing to help her with heavy packages. She also said that UPS accommodated other drivers who were "similar in their . . . inability to work." She accordingly concluded that UPS must accommodate her as well.

UPS responded that the "other persons" whom it had accommodated were (1) drivers who had become disabled on the job, (2) those who had lost their Department of Transportation (DOT) certifications, and (3) those who suffered from a disability covered by the Americans with Disabilities Act of 1990. UPS said that, since Young did not fall within any of those categories, it had not discriminated against Young on the basis of pregnancy but had treated her just as it treated all "other" relevant "persons."

B

Title VII of the Civil Rights Act of 1964 forbids a covered employer to "discriminate against any individual with respect to . . . terms, conditions, or privileges of employment, because of such individual's . . . sex." In 1978, Congress enacted the Pregnancy Discrimination Act, which added new language to Title VII's definitions subsection. The first clause of the 1978 Act specifies that Title VII's 'ter[m] 'because of sex' . . . include[s] . . . because of or on the basis of pregnancy, childbirth, or related medical conditions." §2000e(k). The second clause says that

> women affected by pregnancy, childbirth, or related medical conditions shall be treated the same for all employment-related purposes . . . as other persons not so affected but similar in their ability or inability to work. . . .

This case requires us to consider the application of the second clause to a "disparate-treatment" claim — a claim that an employer intentionally treated a complainant less favorably than employees with the "complainant's qualifications" but outside the complainant's protected class. *McDonnell Douglas*. We have said that "[l]iability in a disparate-treatment case depends on whether the protected trait actually motivated the employer's decision." *Raytheon Co.* v. *Hernandez*, 540 U.S. 44, 52 (2003). We have also made clear that a plaintiff can prove disparate treatment either (1) by direct evidence that a workplace policy, practice, or decision relies expressly on a protected characteristic, or (2) by using the burden-shifting framework set forth in *McDonnell Douglas*. See *Trans World Airlines, Inc.* v. *Thurston*, 469 U.S. 111 (1985).

[The majority described the *McDonnell Douglas* litigation structure and then noted that employment discrimination law also recognized disparate-impact claims, but Young has not alleged such a claim. Nor did she assert a "pattern-or-practice" claim. In responding to UPS's motion for summary judgment on her claim of individual disparate treatment,] Young pointed to favorable facts that she believed were either undisputed or that, while disputed, she could prove. They include the following:

1. Young worked as a UPS driver, picking up and delivering packages carried by air.

2. Young was pregnant in the fall of 2006.

3. Young's doctor recommended that she "not be required to lift greater than 20 pounds for the first 20 weeks of pregnancy and no greater than 10 pounds thereafter."

4. UPS required drivers such as Young to be able to "[l]ift, lower, push, pull, leverage and manipulate . . . packages weighing up to 70 pounds" and to "[a]ssist in moving packages weighing up to 150 pounds."

5. UPS' occupational health manager, the official "responsible for most issues relating to employee health and ability to work" at Young's UPS facility, told Young that she could not return to work during her pregnancy because she could not satisfy UPS' lifting requirements.

6. The manager also determined that Young did not qualify for a temporary alternative work assignment.

7. UPS, in a collective-bargaining agreement, had promised to provide temporary alternative work assignments to employees "unable to perform their normal work assignments due to an *on-the-job* injury." (emphasis added).

8. The collective-bargaining agreement also provided that UPS would "make a good faith effort to comply . . . with requests for a reasonable accommodation because of a permanent disability" under the ADA.

9. The agreement further stated that UPS would give "inside" jobs to drivers who had lost their DOT certifications because of a failed medical exam, a lost driver's license, or involvement in a motor vehicle accident.

10. When Young later asked UPS' Capital Division Manager to accommodate her disability, he replied that, while she was pregnant, she was "too much of a liability" and could "not come back" until she "'was no longer pregnant.'"

11. Young remained on a leave of absence (without pay) for much of her pregnancy.

12. Young returned to work as a driver in June 2007, about two months after her baby was born.

As direct evidence of intentional discrimination, Young relied, in significant part, on the statement of the Capital Division Manager (10 above). As evidence that she had made out a prima facie case under *McDonnell Douglas*, Young relied, in significant part, on evidence showing that UPS would accommodate workers injured on the job (7), those suffering from ADA disabilities (8), and those who had lost their DOT certifications (9). That evidence, she said, showed that UPS had a light-duty-for-injury policy with respect to numerous "other persons," but not with respect to pregnant workers.

Young introduced further evidence indicating that UPS had accommodated several individuals when they suffered disabilities that created work restrictions similar to hers. UPS contests the correctness of some of these facts and the relevance of others. But because we are at the summary judgment stage, and because there is a genuine dispute as to these facts, we view this evidence in the light most favorable to Young, the nonmoving party:

13. Several employees received accommodations while suffering various similar or more serious disabilities incurred on the job [a 10-pound lifting limitation, foot injury, and an arm injury].

14. Several employees received accommodations following injury, where the record is unclear as to whether the injury was incurred on or off the job [recurring knee injury, ankle injury, knee injury, stroke, and leg injury].

15. Several employees received "inside" jobs after losing their DOT certifications [for a DUI conviction, high blood pressure, and sleep apnea diagnosis].

16. Some employees were accommodated despite the fact that their disabilities had been incurred off the job.

17. According to a deposition of a UPS shop steward who had worked for UPS for roughly a decade, "the only light duty requested [due to physical] restrictions that became an issue" at UPS "were with women who were pregnant."

[The District Court granted UPS' motion for summary judgment and the Fourth Circuit affirmed.]

D

We note that statutory changes made after the time of Young's pregnancy may limit the future significance of our interpretation of the Act. In 2008, Congress expanded the definition of "disability" under the ADA to make clear that "physical or mental impairment[s] that substantially limi[t]" an individual's ability to lift, stand, or bend are ADA-covered disabilities. ADA Amendments Act of 2008, 42 U.S.C. §§12102(1)-(2). As interpreted by the EEOC, the new statutory definition requires employers to accommodate employees whose temporary lifting restrictions originate off the job. See 29 CFR pt. 1630, App., §1630.2(j)(1)(ix). We express no view on these statutory and regulatory changes.

II

The parties disagree about the interpretation of the Pregnancy Discrimination Act's second clause. As we have said, the Act's first clause specifies that discrimination "'because of sex'" includes discrimination "because of . . . pregnancy." But the meaning of the second clause is less clear; it adds: "[W]omen affected by pregnancy, childbirth, or related medical conditions shall be treated the same for all employment-related purposes . . . as *other persons* not so affected but *similar in their ability or inability to work.*" 42 U.S.C. §2000e(k) (emphasis added). Does this clause mean that courts must compare workers *only* in respect to the work limitations that they suffer? Does it mean that courts must ignore all other similarities or differences between pregnant and nonpregnant workers? Or does it mean that courts, when deciding who the relevant "other persons" are, may consider other similarities and differences as well? If so, which ones?

The differences between these possible interpretations come to the fore when a court, as here, must consider a workplace policy that distinguishes between pregnant and nonpregnant workers in light of characteristics not related to pregnancy. Young poses the problem directly in her reply brief when she says that the Act requires giving "the same accommodations to an employee with a pregnancy-related work limitation as it would give *that employee* if her work limitation stemmed from a different cause but had a similar effect on her inability to work." Suppose the employer would not give "*that [pregnant] employee*" the "same accommodations" as another employee, but the employer's reason for the difference in treatment is that the pregnant worker falls within a facially neutral category (for example, individuals with off-the-job injuries). What is a court then to do?

The parties propose very different answers to this question. Young and the United States believe that the second clause of the Pregnancy Discrimination Act "requires an employer to provide the same accommodations to workplace disabilities caused by pregnancy that it provides to workplace disabilities that have other causes but have a similar effect on the ability to work." In other words, Young contends that the second clause means that whenever "an employer accommodates only a subset of workers with disabling conditions," a court should find a Title VII violation if "pregnant workers who are similar in the ability to work" do not "receive the same [accommodation] even if still other non-pregnant workers do not receive accommodations."

UPS takes an almost polar opposite view. It contends that the second clause does no more than define sex discrimination to include pregnancy discrimination. Under this view, courts would compare the accommodations an employer provides to pregnant women with the accommodations it provides to others *within* a facially neutral category (such as those with off-the-job injuries) to determine whether the employer has violated Title VII. Cf. (Scalia, J., dissenting) (hereinafter the dissent) (the clause "does not prohibit denying pregnant women accommodations . . . on the basis of an evenhanded policy").

A

We cannot accept either of these interpretations. Young asks us to interpret the second clause broadly and, in her view, literally. As just noted, she argues that, as long as "an employer accommodates only a subset of workers with disabling conditions," "pregnant workers who are similar in the ability to work [must] receive the same treatment even if still other nonpregnant workers do not receive accommodations." She adds that, because the record here contains "evidence that pregnant and nonpregnant workers were not treated the same," that is the end of the matter, she must win; there is no need to refer to *McDonnell Douglas*.

The problem with Young's approach is that it proves too much. It seems to say that the statute grants pregnant workers a "most-favored-nation" status. As long as an employer provides one or two workers with an accommodation — say, those with particularly hazardous jobs, or those whose workplace presence is particularly needed, or those who have worked at the company for many years, or those who are over the age of 55 — then it must provide similar accommodations to *all* pregnant workers (with comparable physical limitations), irrespective of the nature of their jobs, the employer's need to keep them working, their ages, or any other criteria.

Lower courts have concluded that this could not have been Congress' intent in passing the Pregnancy Discrimination Act. And Young partially agrees, for she writes that "the statute does not require employers to give" to "pregnant workers all of the benefits and privileges it extends to other" similarly disabled "employees when those benefits and privileges are . . . based on the employee's tenure or position within the company" [such as seniority, full-time work, and different job classifications.].

Young's last-mentioned concession works well with respect to seniority, for Title VII itself contains a seniority defense, see 42 U.S.C. §2000e-2(h). Hence, seniority is not part of the problem. But otherwise the most-favored-nation problem remains, and Young's concession does not solve it. How, for example, should a court treat special benefits attached to injuries arising out of, say, extra-hazardous duty? If Congress intended to allow differences in treatment arising out of special duties, special service, or special needs, why would it not also have wanted courts to take account of differences arising out of special "causes" — for example, benefits for those who drive (and are injured) in extrahazardous conditions?

We agree with UPS to this extent: We doubt that Congress intended to grant pregnant workers an unconditional most-favored-nation status. The language of the statute does not require that unqualified reading. The second clause, when referring to nonpregnant persons with similar disabilities, uses the open-ended term "other persons." It does not say that the employer must treat pregnant employees the "same" as "*any* other persons" (who are similar in their ability or inability to work), nor does it otherwise specify *which* other persons Congress had in mind.

Moreover, disparate-treatment law normally permits an employer to implement policies that are not intended to harm members of a protected class, even if their implementation sometimes harms those members, as long as the employer has a legitimate, nondiscriminatory, nonpretextual reason for doing so. See, *e.g., Raytheon; Burdine; McDonnell Douglas.* There is no reason to believe Congress intended its language in the Pregnancy Discrimination Act to embody a significant deviation from this approach. Indeed, the relevant House Report specifies that the Act "reflect[s] no new legislative mandate." H. R. Rep. No. 95-948, pp. 3-4 (1978) (hereinafter H. R. Rep.). And the Senate Report states that the Act was designed to "reestablis[h] the law as it was understood prior to" this Court's decision in *General Electric Co.* v. *Gilbert.* S. Rep. No. 95-331, p. 8 (1978) (hereinafter S. Rep.).

B

[The Court traced the somewhat inconsistent history of EEOC pronouncements. After certiorari had been granted in *Young,* the EEOC promulgated a guideline barring employers from looking to the source of an employee's limitations in any policy regarding accommodations. The majority refused to defer to this guidance in part because they seemed tailored to the present case, in part because its position was inconsistent with those the Government has long advocated, and in part because the positon was insufficiently rationalized.]

C

We find it similarly difficult to accept the opposite interpretation of the Act's second clause. UPS says that the second clause simply defines sex discrimination to include pregnancy discrimination. But that cannot be so.

The first clause accomplishes that objective when it expressly amends Title VII's definitional provision to make clear that Title VII's words "because of sex" and "on the basis of sex" "include, but are not limited to, because of or on the basis of pregnancy, childbirth, or related medical conditions." 42 U.S.C. §2000e(k). We have long held that "'a statute ought, upon the whole, to be so construed that, if it can be prevented, no clause'" is rendered "'superfluous, void, or insignificant.'" *TRW Inc.* v. *Andrews*, 534 U.S. 19, 31 (2001). But that is what UPS' interpretation of the second clause would do.

The dissent, basically accepting UPS' interpretation, says that the second clause is not "superfluous" because it adds "clarity." It makes "plain," the dissent adds, that unlawful discrimination "includes disfavoring pregnant women relative to other workers of similar inability to work." Perhaps we fail to understand. *McDonnell Douglas* itself makes clear that courts normally consider how a plaintiff was treated relative to other "persons of [the plaintiff's] qualifications" (which here include disabilities). If the second clause of the Act did not exist, we would still say that an employer who disfavored pregnant women relative to other workers of similar ability or inability to work had engaged in pregnancy discrimination. In a word, there is no need for the "clarification" that the dissent suggests the second sentence provides.

Moreover, the interpretation espoused by UPS and the dissent would fail to carry out an important congressional objective. [The PDA was designed to overturn both the holding and the reasoning of *Gilbert,* which had upheld a plan denying pregnancy-related health pregnancy was not comparable to the conditions covered by the plan because it was not a "disease" nor necessarily a result of accident.] In short, the *Gilbert* majority reasoned in part just as the dissent reasons here. The employer did "not distinguish between pregnant women and others of similar ability or inability *because of pregnancy.*" It distinguished between them on a neutral ground—*i.e.,* it accommodated only sicknesses and accidents, and pregnancy was neither of those.

Simply including pregnancy among Title VII's protected traits (*i.e.,* accepting UPS' interpretation) would not overturn *Gilbert* in full—in particular, it would not respond to *Gilbert*'s determination that an employer can treat pregnancy less favorably than diseases or disabilities resulting in a similar inability to work. . . .

III

The statute lends itself to an interpretation other than those that the parties advocate and that the dissent sets forth. Our interpretation minimizes the problems we have discussed, responds directly to *Gilbert,* and is consistent with long-standing interpretations of Title VII.

In our view, an individual pregnant worker who seeks to show disparate treatment through indirect evidence may do so through application of the *McDonnell Douglas* framework. That framework requires a plaintiff to make out a prima facie case of discrimination. But it is "not intended to be an inflexible rule." *Furnco Constr. Corp.* v. *Waters*, 438 U.S. 567, 575 (1978). Rather, an individual plaintiff may establish a prima facie case by "showing actions taken by the employer from which one can infer, if such actions remain unexplained, that it is more likely than not that such actions were based on a discriminatory criterion illegal under" Title VII. *Id.* The burden of making this showing is "not onerous." *Burdine*. In particular, making this showing is not as burdensome as succeeding on "an ultimate finding of fact as to" a discriminatory employment action. *Furnco*. Neither does it require the plaintiff to show that those whom the employer favored and those whom the employer disfavored were similar in all but the protected ways. See *McDonnell Douglas* (burden met where plaintiff showed that employer hired other "qualified" individuals outside the protected class); *Furnco* (same); *Burdine* (same). Cf. *Reeves* v. *Sanderson Plumbing Products, Inc.*, 530 U.S. 133, 142 (2000) (similar).

Thus, a plaintiff alleging that the denial of an accommodation constituted disparate treatment under the Pregnancy Discrimination Act's second clause may make out a prima facie case by showing, as in *McDonnell Douglas*, that she belongs to the protected class, that she sought accommodation, that the employer did not accommodate her, and that the employer did accommodate others "similar in their ability or inability to work."

The employer may then seek to justify its refusal to accommodate the plaintiff by relying on "legitimate, nondiscriminatory" reasons for denying her accommodation. But, consistent with the Act's basic objective, that reason normally cannot consist simply of a claim that it is more expensive or less convenient to add pregnant women to the category of those ("similar in their ability or inability to work") whom the employer accommodates. After all, the employer in *Gilbert* could in all likelihood have made just such a claim.

If the employer offers an apparently "legitimate, non-discriminatory" reason for its actions, the plaintiff may in turn show that the employer's proffered reasons are in fact pretextual. We believe that the plaintiff may reach a jury on this issue by providing sufficient evidence that the employer's policies impose a significant burden on pregnant workers, and that the employer's "legitimate, nondiscriminatory" reasons are not sufficiently strong to justify the burden, but rather — when considered along with the burden imposed — give rise to an inference of intentional discrimination.

The plaintiff can create a genuine issue of material fact as to whether a significant burden exists by providing evidence that the employer accommodates a large percentage of nonpregnant workers while failing to accommodate a large percentage of pregnant workers. Here, for example, if the facts are as Young says they are, she can show that UPS accommodates most nonpregnant employees with lifting limitations while categorically failing to accommodate pregnant employees with lifting limitations. Young might also add that the fact that UPS has multiple policies that accommodate nonpregnant employees with lifting restrictions suggests that its reasons for failing to accommodate pregnant employees with lifting restrictions are not sufficiently strong — to the point that a jury could find that its reasons for failing to accommodate pregnant employees give rise to an inference of intentional discrimination.

This approach, though limited to the Pregnancy Discrimination Act context, is consistent with our longstanding rule that a plaintiff can use circumstantial proof to rebut an employer's apparently legitimate, nondiscriminatory reasons for treating individuals within a protected class differently than those outside the protected class. See *Burdine*. In particular, it is hardly anomalous (as the dissent makes it out to be) that a plaintiff may rebut an employer's proffered justifications by showing how a policy operates in practice. In *McDonnell Douglas* itself, we noted that an employer's "general policy and practice with respect to minority employment" — including "statistics as to" that policy and practice — could be evidence of pretext. Moreover, the continued focus on whether the plaintiff has introduced sufficient evidence to give rise to an inference of *intentional* discrimination avoids confusing the disparate-treatment and disparate-impact doctrines.

Our interpretation of the Act is also, unlike the dissent's, consistent with Congress' intent to overrule *Gilbert*'s reasoning and result. The dissent says that "[i]f a pregnant woman is denied an accommodation under a policy that does not discriminate against pregnancy, she *has* been 'treated the same' as everyone else." This logic would have found no problem with the employer plan in *Gilbert*, which "denied an accommodation" to pregnant women on the same basis as it denied accommodations to other employees — *i.e.,* it accommodated only sicknesses and accidents, and pregnancy was neither of those. In arguing to the contrary, the dissent's discussion of *Gilbert* relies exclusively on the opinions of the dissenting Justices in that case. But Congress' intent in passing the Act was to overrule the *Gilbert majority* opinion, which viewed the employer's disability plan as denying coverage to pregnant employees on a neutral basis.

IV

[Under this interpretation, there was adequate evidence to deny the defendant summary judgment.] Viewing the record in the light most favorable to Young, there is a genuine dispute as to whether UPS provided more favorable treatment to at least some employees whose situation cannot reasonably be distinguished from Young's. In other words, Young created a genuine dispute of material fact as to the fourth prong of the *McDonnell Douglas* analysis.

Young also introduced evidence that UPS had three separate accommodation policies (on-the-job, ADA, DOT). Taken together, Young argued, these policies significantly burdened pregnant women. See (shop steward's testimony that "the only light duty requested [due to physical] restrictions that became an issue" at UPS "were with women who were pregnant"). The Fourth Circuit did not consider the combined effects of these policies, nor did it consider the strength of UPS' justifications for each when combined. That is, why, when the employer accommodated so many, could it not accommodate pregnant women as well?

We do not determine whether Young created a genuine issue of material fact as to whether UPS' reasons for having treated Young less favorably than it treated these other nonpregnant employees were pretextual. We leave a final determination of that question for the Fourth Circuit to make on remand, in light of the interpretation of the Pregnancy Discrimination Act that we have set out above. . . .

JUSTICE ALITO, concurring in the judgment.

[Violation of the first clause requires an employer's intent to discriminate because of or on the basis of pregnancy. Under this clause, it does not matter whether the employer's ground for the unfavorable treatment is reasonable; all that matters is the employer's actual intent. But the second clause raises more difficult questions of interpretation. Justice Alito started with the proposition that "this clause does not merely explain but instead adds to the language that precedes it," a reading consistent with the statutory text's use of the word "and." Further, the "second clause makes no reference to intent, which is the linchpin of liability under the first clause," and "the second clause is an affirmative command (an employer 'shall' provide equal treatment), while the first clause is negative (it prohibits discrimination). Finally, if the second clause does not set out an additional restriction on employer conduct, it would appear to be largely, if not entirely, superfluous.]

This leads to the second question: In determining whether pregnant employees have been given the equal treatment that this provision demands, with whom must the pregnant employees be compared? I interpret the second clause to mean that pregnant employees must be compared with employees performing the same or very similar jobs. Pregnant employees, the second provision states, must be given the same treatment as other employees who are "similar in their ability or inability to work." An employee's ability to work — despite illness, injury, or pregnancy — often depends on the tasks that the employee's job includes. Different jobs have different tasks, and different tasks require different abilities. Suppose that an employer provides a period of leave with pay for employees whose jobs require tasks, *e.g.*, lifting heavy objects, that they cannot perform because of illness or injury. Must the employer provide the same benefits for pregnant employees who are unable to lift heavy objects but have desk jobs that do not entail heavy lifting? The answer is no. The treatment of pregnant employees must be compared with the treatment of nonpregnant employees whose jobs involve the performance of the same or very similar tasks. . . .

This conclusion leads to a third, even more difficult question: When comparing pregnant employees to nonpregnant employees in similar jobs, which characteristics of the pregnant and nonpregnant employees must be taken into account? The answer, I believe, must be found in the reference to "other employees who are similar in their ability or inability to work." I see two possible interpretations of this language. The first is that the capacity to perform the tasks required by a job is the only relevant characteristic, but like the Court, I cannot accept this "most favored employee" interpretation. . . .

Recall that the second clause of §2000e(k) requires that pregnant women "be treated the same for all employment-related purposes . . . as *other persons* not so affected but similar in their ability or inability to work." (Emphasis added.) Therefore, UPS could say that its policy treated the pregnant employees the same as "other persons" who were similar in their ability or inability to work, namely, those nonpregnant employees [who were not accommodated]. But at the same time, the pregnant drivers like petitioner could say that UPS did not treat them the same as "other employees" who were similar in their ability or inability to work, namely, the nonpregnant employees [who were accommmdated]. An interpretation that leads to such a problem cannot be correct.

I therefore turn to the other possible interpretation of the phrase "similar in their ability or inability to work," namely, that "similar in the ability or inability to work" means "similar *in relation* to the ability or inability to work." Under this interpretation, pregnant and non-pregnant employees are not similar in relation to the ability or inability to work if they are unable to work for different reasons. And this means that these two groups of employees are not similar in the relevant sense if the employer has a neutral business reason for treating them differently. I agree with the Court that a sufficient reason "normally cannot consist simply of a claim that it is more expensive or less convenient to add pregnant women to the category of those . . . whom the employer accommodates."[5] Otherwise, however, I do not think that the second clause of the PDA authorizes courts to evaluate the justification for a truly neutral rule. The language used in the second clause of the PDA is quite different from that used in other antidiscrimination provisions that require such an evaluation. Cf. §12112(b)(5)(A) (discrimination against a person with a disability includes "not making *reasonable accommodations* to the known physical or mental limitations of an otherwise qualified . . . employee, unless [the employer] can demonstrate that the accommodation would impose *an undue hardship* on the operation of [its] business" (emphasis added)); §2000e(j) (employer must reasonably accommodate religious observance, practice, and belief unless that would impose an "undue hardship on the conduct of the employer's business"); §2000e-2(k)(1)(A)(i) (business necessity defense in Title VII disparate-impact cases).

III.

[Justice Alito agreed with the majority that the record was "sufficient (albeit barely)" to survive summary judgment under the first clause, but also agreed that

---

5. If cost alone could justify unequal treatment of pregnant employees, the plan at issue in *General Electric Co.* v. *Gilbert* would be lawful. But this Court has repeatedly said that the PDA rejected "'both the holding and the reasoning'" in *Gilbert*.

summary judgement should be denied under the second clause. Under the UPS policy, drivers physically unable to perform the usual tasks of the position fell into three groups.]

First, some drivers were reassigned to less physically demanding positions. Included in this group were (a) those who were unable to work as drivers due to an injury incurred on the job, (b) those drivers who were unable to work as drivers due to a disability as defined by the Americans With Disabilities Act of 1990 (ADA), and (c) those drivers who, as the result of a medical condition or injury, lost the Department of Transportation (DOT) certification needed to work in that capacity.

The second group of drivers consisted of those who were not pregnant and were denied transfer to a light-duty job. Drivers who were injured off the job fell into this category. The third group was made up of pregnant drivers like petitioner.

It is obvious that respondent had a neutral reason for providing an accommodation when that was required by the ADA. Respondent also had neutral grounds for providing special accommodations for employees who were injured on the job [since otherwise they would been eligible for workers' compensation benefits.]

The accommodations that are provided to drivers who lost their DOT certifications, however, are another matter. A driver may lose DOT certification for a variety of reasons, including medical conditions or injuries incurred off the job that impair the driver's ability to operate a motor vehicle. Such drivers may then be transferred to jobs that do not require physical tasks incompatible with their illness or injury. It does not appear that respondent has provided any plausible justification for treating these drivers more favorably than drivers who were pregnant.

The Court of Appeals provided two grounds for distinguishing petitioner's situation from that of the drivers who had lost their DOT certifications, but neither is adequate. First, the Court of Appeals noted that "no legal obstacle [stood] between [petitioner] and her work." But the legal obstacle faced by drivers who have lost DOT certification only explains why those drivers could not continue to perform all the tasks required by their ordinary jobs; it does not explain why respondent went further and *provided such drivers with a work accommodation*. Petitioner's pregnancy prevented her from continuing her normal work as a driver, just as is the case for a driver who loses DOT certification. But respondent had a policy of accommodating drivers who lost DOT certification but not accommodating pregnant women, like petitioner. The legal obstacle of lost certification cannot explain this difference in treatment.

Second, the Court of Appeals observed that "'those with DOT certification maintai[n] the ability to perform any number of demanding physical tasks,'" but it is doubtful that this is true in all instances. A driver can lose DOT certification due to a great variety of medical conditions, [but the record does not show that all such drivers were] nevertheless able to perform a great many physically demanding tasks. Nevertheless, respondent says that it was its policy to transfer such drivers to so-called inside jobs when such positions were available. Presumably, respondent did not assign these drivers to jobs that they were physically unable to perform. So in at least some instances, they must have been assigned to jobs that did not require them to perform tasks that they were incapable of performing due to the medical condition that caused the loss of DOT certification. Respondent has not explained why pregnant drivers could not have been given similar consideration. . . .

JUSTICE SCALIA, with whom JUSTICE KENNEDY and JUSTICE THOMAS join, dissenting.

Faced with two conceivable readings of the Pregnancy Discrimination Act, the Court chooses neither. It crafts instead a new law that is splendidly unconnected with the text and even the legislative history of the Act. To "treat" pregnant workers "the same . . . as other persons," we are told, means refraining from adopting policies that impose "significant burden[s]" upon pregnant women without "sufficiently strong" justifications. Where do the "significant burden" and "sufficiently strong justification" requirements come from? Inventiveness posing as scholarship—which gives us an interpretation that is as dubious in principle as it is senseless in practice.

I . . .

[Plaintiff did not establish liability under either the disparate treatment or disparate impact theories, which forced Young and the Court to turn to §2000e(k). But the] most natural way to understand the same-treatment clause is that an employer may not distinguish between pregnant women and others of similar ability or inability *because of pregnancy*. Here, that means pregnant women are entitled to accommodations *on the same terms* as other workers with disabling conditions. If a pregnant woman is denied an accommodation under a policy that does not discriminate against pregnancy, she *has* been "treated the same" as everyone else. UPS's accommodation for drivers who lose their certifications illustrates the point. A pregnant woman who loses her certification gets the benefit, just like any other worker who loses his. And a pregnant woman who keeps her certification does not get the benefit, again just like any other worker who keeps his. That certainly sounds like treating pregnant women and others the same.

There is, however, another way to understand "treated the same," at least looking at that phrase on its own. One could read it to mean that an employer may not distinguish *at all* between pregnant women and others of similar ability. Here, that would mean pregnant women are entitled, not to accommodations on the same terms as others, but to *the same accommodations* as others, no matter the differences (other than pregnancy) between them. UPS's accommodation for decertified drivers illustrates this usage too. There is a sense in which a pregnant woman denied an accommodation (because she kept her certification) has *not* been treated the same as an injured man granted an accommodation (because he lost his certification). He got the accommodation and she did not.

Of these two readings, only the first makes sense in the context of Title VII. The point of Title VII's bans on discrimination is to prohibit employers from treating one worker differently from another *because of a protected trait*. It is not to prohibit employers from treating workers differently for reasons that have nothing to do with protected traits. . . .

Prohibiting employers from making *any* distinctions between pregnant workers and others of similar ability would elevate pregnant workers to most favored employees. If Boeing offered chauffeurs to injured directors, it would have to offer chauffeurs to pregnant mechanics. And if Disney paid pensions to workers who can no longer work because of old age, it would have to pay pensions to workers who can no longer work because of childbirth. It is implausible that Title VII, which elsewhere creates guarantees of *equal* treatment, here alone creates a guarantee of *favored* treatment. . . .

II

The Court agrees that the same-treatment clause is not a most-favored-employee law, but at the same time refuses to adopt the reading I propose — which is the only other reading the clause could conceivably bear. The Court's reasons for resisting this reading fail to persuade.

The Court starts by arguing that the same-treatment clause must do more than ban distinctions on the basis of pregnancy, lest it add nothing to the part of the Act defining pregnancy discrimination as sex discrimination. Even so read, however, the same-treatment clause *does* add something: clarity. Just defining pregnancy discrimination as sex discrimination does not tell us what it means to discriminate because of pregnancy. Does pregnancy discrimination include, in addition to disfavoring pregnant women relative to the workplace in general, disfavoring them relative to disabled workers in particular? Concretely, does an employer engage in pregnancy discrimination by excluding pregnancy from an otherwise complete disability-benefits program? Without the same-treatment clause, the answers to these questions would not be obvious. . . .

This clarifying function easily overcomes any charge that the reading I propose makes the same-treatment clause "'superfluous, void, or insignificant.'" Perhaps, as the Court suggests, even without the same-treatment clause the best reading of the Act would prohibit disfavoring pregnant women relative to disabled workers. But laws often make explicit what might already have been implicit, "for greater caution" and in order "to leave nothing to construction." . . .

That brings me to the Court's remaining argument: the claim that the reading I have set forth would not suffice to overturn our decision in *Gilbert*. Wrong. *Gilbert* upheld an otherwise comprehensive disability-benefits plan that singled pregnancy out for disfavor. The most natural reading of the Act overturns that decision, because it prohibits singling pregnancy out for disfavor.

The Court goes astray here because it mistakenly assumes that the *Gilbert* plan excluded pregnancy on "a neutral ground" — covering sicknesses and accidents but nothing else. In reality, the plan in *Gilbert* was not neutral toward pregnancy [citing the dissenters in *Gilbert* to this effect.]

III

Dissatisfied with the only two readings that the words of the same-treatment clause could possibly bear, the Court decides that the clause means something in-between. It takes only a couple of waves of the Supreme Wand to produce the desired result. Poof!: The same-treatment clause means that a neutral reason for refusing to accommodate a pregnant woman is pretextual if "the employer's policies impose a significant burden on pregnant workers." Poof!: This is so only when the employer's reasons "are not sufficiently strong to justify the burden."

How we got here from the same-treatment clause is anyone's guess. There is no way to read "shall be treated the same"—or indeed anything else in the clause—to mean that courts must balance the significance of the burden on pregnant workers against the strength of the employer's justifications for the policy. That is presumably why the Court does not even *try* to connect the interpretation it adopts with the text it purports to interpret. The Court has forgotten that statutory purpose and the presumption against superfluity are tools for choosing among competing reasonable readings of a law, not authorizations for making up new readings that the law cannot reasonably bear.

The fun does not stop there. Having ignored the terms of the same-treatment clause, the Court proceeds to bungle the dichotomy between claims of disparate treatment and claims of disparate impact. Normally, liability for disparate treatment arises when an employment policy has a "discriminatory motive," while liability for disparate impact arises when the effects of an employment policy "fall more harshly on one group than another and cannot be justified by business necessity." *Teamsters.* In the topsy-turvy world created by today's decision, however, a pregnant woman can establish disparate *treatment* by showing that the *effects* of her employer's policy fall more harshly on pregnant women than on others (the policies "impose a significant burden on pregnant workers," and are inadequately justified (the "reasons are not sufficiently strong to justify the burden"). The change in labels may be small, but the change in results assuredly is not. Disparate-treatment and disparate-impact claims come with different standards of liability, different defenses, and different remedies. §§1981a, 2000e-2(k). For example, plaintiffs in disparate-treatment cases can get compensatory and punitive damages as well as equitable relief, but plaintiffs in disparate impact cases can get equitable relief only. See §§1981a, 2000e-5(g). A sound reading of the same-treatment clause would preserve the distinctions so carefully made elsewhere in the Act; the Court's reading makes a muddle of them.

But (believe it or not) it gets worse. In order to make sense of its conflation of disparate impact with disparate treatment, the Court claims that its new test is somehow "limited to the Pregnancy Discrimination Act context," yet at the same time "consistent with" the traditional use of circumstantial evidence to show intent to discriminate in Title VII cases. A court in a Title VII case, true enough, may consider a policy's effects and even its justifications—along with "'all of the [other] surrounding facts and circumstances'"—when trying to ferret out a policy's motive. *Hazelwood School Dist.* v. *United States.* The Court cannot possibly think, however, that its newfangled balancing test reflects this conventional inquiry. It has, after all, just marched up and down the hill telling us that the same-treatment clause is not (no-no!) "'superfluous, void, or insignificant.'" If the clause merely instructed courts to consider a policy's effects and justifications the way it considers other circumstantial evidence of motive, it *would* be superfluous. So the Court's balancing test must mean something else. Even if the effects and justifications of policies are not enough to show intent to discriminate under ordinary Title VII principles, they could (Poof!) still show intent to discriminate for purposes of the pregnancy same-treatment clause. Deliciously incoherent.

And all of this to what end? The difference between a routine circumstantial-evidence inquiry into motive and today's grotesque effects-and-justifications inquiry into motive, it would seem, is that today's approach requires judges to concentrate on effects and justifications to the exclusion of other considerations. But Title VII *already* has a framework that allows judges to home in on a policy's effects and justifications — disparate impact. Under that framework, it is *already* unlawful for an employer to use a practice that has a disparate impact on the basis of a protected trait, unless (among other things) the employer can show that the practice "is job related . . . and consistent with business necessity." §2000e-2(k)(1)(A)(i). The Court does not explain why we need (never mind how the Act could possibly be read to contain) today's ersatz disparate-impact test, under which the disparate-impact element gives way to the significant-burden criterion and the business-necessity defense gives way to the sufficiently-strong-justification standard. Today's decision can thus serve only one purpose: allowing claims that belong under Title VII's disparate-impact provisions to be brought under its disparate-treatment provisions instead.

IV

[The dissent also took issue with Justice Alito's concurrence for allowing an employer to] deny a pregnant woman a benefit granted to workers who perform similar tasks only on the basis of a "neutral business ground." This requirement of a "business ground" shadows the Court's requirement of a "sufficiently strong" justification, and, like it, has no footing in the terms of the same-treatment clause. . . . His] need to engage in this text-free broadening in order to make the concurrence's interpretation work is as good a sign as any that its interpretation is wrong from the start. . . .

JUSTICE KENNEDY, dissenting.

[Although joining Justice Scalia's dissent, this separate dissent noted "little doubt that women who are in the work force — by choice, by financial necessity, or both — confront a serious disadvantage after becoming pregnant." This reality is partially addressed by the PDA and the parental leave provisions of the FMLA, and perhaps by the ADA Amendments Act of 2008, as interpreted by implementing regulations that "may require accommodations for many pregnant employees, even though pregnancy itself is not expressly classified as a disability. Additionally, many States have enacted laws providing certain accommodations for pregnant employees. These Acts honor and safeguard the important contributions women make to both the workplace and the American family."]

NOTES

1. *How Big a Change?* The critical statutory language reads: "[W]omen affected by pregnancy, childbirth, or related medical condition shall be treated the same for all employment-related purposes as other persons not so affected but similar in their ability or inability to work." All the justices reject the "most-favored nation" reading of this second clause of the PDA, and the majority does so because this reading essentially writes intent to discriminate out of the statute for pregnancy accommodation disparate treatment cases. The majority then purports to apply *McDonnell Douglas*, which is all about intent, to the question of pregnancy accommodations, but it makes clear that its analysis applies only to the pregnancy question. In short, the Court seems to be reformulating what it means to intend to discriminate, but only for cases of pregnancy accommodation. For an analysis of the controversy leading up to *Young, see generally* Deborah A. Widiss, Gilbert *Redux: The Interaction of the Pregnancy Discrimination Act and the Amended Americans with Disabilities Act*, 46 U.C. DAVIS L. REV. 961 (2013). *See also* Nicole Buonocore Porter, *Mutual Marginalization: Individuals with Disabilities and Workers with Caregiving Responsibilities*, 66 FLA. L. REV. 1099, 1135-38 (2014).

2. *The Test.* The critical sentence seems to be: "We believe that the plaintiff may reach a jury on this issue by providing sufficient evidence that the employer's policies impose a significant burden on pregnant workers, and that the employer's 'legitimate, nondiscriminatory' reasons are not sufficiently strong to justify the burden, but rather—when considered along with the burden imposed—give rise to an inference of intentional discrimination." So the factfinder still has to find intent, but that issue gets to the jury when there's evidence of "a significant burden" and evidence that the employer's reasons are not "sufficiently strong."

Up to this point, you've learned that intent to discriminate requires, well, intent. *Cf. Personnel Administrator v. Feeney*, p. 146 The strength or weakness of the employer's reasons is irrelevant so long as the factfinder determines that a prohibited characteristic did not play a role in the decision. Of course, very weak reasons might allow a jury to infer intent since the jury might not credit that an employer in fact acted for what seemed a silly or irrational reason. Does *Young* change this? If it doesn't, why did the majority limit its rule to pregnancy? If it does, what does intent mean in the pregnancy setting? *See* William Corbett, Young v. United Parcel Service, Inc.: McDonnell Douglas *to the Rescue?*, 92 WASH. U. L. REV. 1683, 1686-87 (2015) (arguing that the Court's use of pretext analysis will probably rejuvenate the vexatious distinction between employment discrimination claims based on direct evidence and those based on circumstantial or indirect evidence, although the Court seemed to have laid that distinction to rest in 2003 in *Desert Palace, Inc. v. Costa*).

2. *Significant Burden and Sufficiently Strong.* The Court provided some guidance on the two key concepts for its new test. A plaintiff can get to the jury on a sig-

nificant burden "by providing evidence that the employer accommodates a large percentage of nonpregnant workers while failing to accommodate a large percentage of pregnant workers." As applied to the case before it, a showing would suffice that "UPS accommodates most nonpregnant employees with lifting limitations while categorically failing to accommodate pregnant employees with lifting limitations." The second half of the statement is certainly true, but did Young show that UPS accommodated "most nonpregnant employees with lifting limitations"? If so, is that because having a lifting limitation is an ADA-defined disability?

As for the strength of the employer's reasons, the majority noted, and Justice Alito agreed, that "consistent with the Act's basic objective, that reason normally cannot consist simply of a claim that it is more expensive or less convenient to add pregnant women to the category of those ('similar in their ability or inability to work') whom the employer accommodates." As for Young herself, she could argue that UPS's multiple policies accommodating nonpregnant employees with lifting restrictions suggest that its reasons for failing to accommodate pregnant employees "are not sufficiently strong — to the point that a jury could find that its reasons for failing to accommodate pregnant employees give rise to an inference of intentional discrimination."

But check out Justice Alito's concurrence. He would find compliance with the ADA and accommodations for those injured on the job to be sufficiently strong. Only the DOT disqualification apparently suffices. Do you think the majority would agree if forced to confront the issue? If so, is the decision really so sweeping?

In a post-*Young* decision, *Legg v. Ulster Cnty.*, 820 F.3d 67(2d Cir. 2016), the court overturned defendant's post trial judgment as a matter of law. Plaintiff had established a prima facie case by showing that she was denied light duty accommodation for her pregnancy when workers injured on the job were accommodated. While the employer's duty under state law to continue to pay workers injured on the job was a neutral reason, a reasonable jury could find it to be pretextual when no one testified that that was the reason for the denial and the evidence showed that a large number of other workers were accommodated when one woman was not. In addition, a "reasonable jury could also conclude that the defendants' reasons were not 'sufficiently strong,' when considered alongside the burden imposed, to justify the denial of accommodation to pregnant employees," when there was only one such worker and the cost of the accommodation could have been found to be a factor in the decision, contrary to *Young's* teaching. *Id.* at 74.

3. *Merging Disparate Treatment and Disparate Impact.* Looking to the strength of the employer's reasons (rather than merely their honesty) is a radical shift in approach to disparate treatment. Indeed, Justice Scalia's dissent accused the majority of importing disparate impact analysis into a disparate treatment framework. Is that a fair observation? Although we have seen that factfinders could always draw an inference of intent to discriminate from the use of a practice with a disparate impact, see Chapter 4, that was rare in the lower courts when sophisticated statistical evidence was not available. If Scalia is right, is that a bad thing? In any event, will this change in the pregnancy context leak out to other disparate treatment cases?

4. *Systemic Cases?* The majority views the case as a disparate treatment under the *McDonnell Douglas* framework, which we have described as individual disparate treatment. Although the Scalia dissent believes the analysis mimics disparate impact, the majority is explicit that no disparate impact claim is at issue. Suppose plaintiff had asserted disparate impact. How would the analysis differ? The majority also goes out of its way to state that no systemic disparate treatment claim is before it ("Nor has she asserted what we have called a "pattern-or-practice" claim."). But how can that be? The challenge isn't to an ad hoc decision but rather to the operation of an employer policy. And the proof is, at least in part, the effects of that policy. *See generally* L. Camille Hebert, *Disparate Impact and Pregnancy: Title VII's Other Accommodation Requirement*, 24 AM. U.J. GENDER SOC. POL'Y & L. 107 (2015).

5. *Stepping Back From the Doctrine.* Whatever the doctrinal implications of *Young* for either the pregnancy context or more broadly, the significance of the case for at least larger employers is clear: failing to accommodate pregnant workers when other workers are so accommodated is risky under Title VII. When the possible application of the Americans with Disabilities Act to pregnancy as a temporary disability is factored in, see Note 6, that risk becomes much greater. Finally, because of the growth of state laws requiring accommodation of pregnancy, see http://www.abetterbalance.org/web/ourissues/fairness-for-pregnant-workers/310, at least larger employers whose operations occur in such states will feel the need to revise their policies in a more pregnancy-friendly way.

6. *ADA to the Rescue?* Both the majority and the dissent refer to the ADA as requiring accommodation in a wide variety of cases, including those like *Young* itself. But neither opinion formally endorses the EEOC regulations that would require accommodation. Revisit this issue when you get to Chapter 7. *See also* Bradley A. Areheart, *Accommodating Pregnancy*, 67 ALA. L. REV. 1125 (2016) (arguing against accommodating through the ADA or statutes dealing with pregnancy per se because of the potential for increased discrimination against women; a better alternative is either universal accommodation or at least parental accommodation).

Page 364, add after second sentence of Note 1, *What Constitutes Harassment?*:

See McMiller v. Metro, 738 F.3d 185, 189 (8th Cir. 2013) (although sexual advances were not sufficiently severe or pervasive to contaminate plaintiff's work environment, a reasonable jury could find quid pro quo harassment in the supervisor causing her to be fired for refusing to cooperate with his attempts "to engage her sexually").

Page 365, add before *Hernandez* cite in last paragraph:

Ellis v. Houston, 742 F.3d 307 (8th Cir. 2014) (even if particular acts experienced by individual officers were insufficiently severe or pervasive, the pattern of harassment suffered by five African American prison guards sufficed, especially in light of evidence that supervisors made or condoned racist comments in group settings on nearly a daily basis); *Lambert v. Peri Formworks Sys., Inc.*, 723 F.3d 863, 868-69

(7th Cir. 2013) (racial harassment could be found even though the most offensive statements—reference to workers as "donkeys" and a "gorilla" and the use of "nigger"—occurred over a period of several years, were not physically threatening, and did not affect Lambert's work performance); *Ayissi-Etoh v. Fannie Mae*, 712 F.3d 572 (D.C. Cir. 2013) (a reasonable jury could find supervisors' behavior sufficiently severe or pervasive when one "used a deeply offensive racial epithet when yelling at [plaintiff] to get out of the office" and another explicitly linked his race to the denial of a raise).

Page 366, add after *Dediol* cite near end of carryover paragraph:

Griffin v. City of Portland, 2013 U.S. Dist. LEXIS 154204 (D. Or. Oct. 25, 2013) D. Or. Oct. 25, 2013) (cursing, including the use of "Jesus Christ" as an expletive, could be harassment on the basis of religion). See posting of Charles A. Sullivan, *Stop Cursing, Damn It!* to Workplace Prof, http://lawprofessors.typepad.com/labor-prof_blog/2013/11/damn-it-stop-cursing.html.

Page 366, add before *Colenberg* cite in first full paragraph:

Nichols v. Mich. City Plant Planning Dep't, 755 F.3d 594 (7th Cir. 2014) (one-time use of a racial epithet is not severe enough to trigger liability, and the collection of six incidents of harassment within a two-and-a-half-week period not sufficiently pervasive when none was physically threatening, they did not interfere with plaintiff's work performance, and a reasonable factfinder could not determine that all of the comments were directed at him);

Page 369, add before *Brown-Baumback* citation in first full paragraph in carryover Note 1, *How Bad Is Bad Enough?*:

Desardouin v. City of Rochester, 708 F.3d 102 (2d Cir. 2013) (comments made on a weekly basis over several months, though not threatening, were more than merely offensive and some could readily be found to be a solicitation for sexual relations coupled with a claim of sexual prowess); *Gerald v. Univ. of P.R.*, 707 F.3d 7 (1st Cir. 2013) (testimony that her supervisor grabbed plaintiff's breasts, sexually propositioned her, and crassly asked in front of others why she would not have sex with him could be found sufficiently egregious to be actionable);

Page 369, add before *Scruggs* cite at end of extract in carryover Note 1, *How Bad Is Bad Enough?*:

Watson v. Heartland Health Labs., Inc., 790 F.3d 856 (8th Cir. 2015) (a single racial slur, a sexual touching, four sexual slurs, and a threat from a patient with whom plaintiff had to deal at a facility over a 10-day period not sufficient to require a jury trial); *Butler v. Crittenden County*, 708 F.3d 1044, 1050 (8th Cir. 2013) ("Although there was evidence that Strong asked Butler on several dates, sought to touch her hair, and complimented her perfume, he never touched her inappropriately or engaged in 'physically threatening or humiliating' conduct.");

Page 370, add before *But see Paul* cite in Note 2, *Severe or Pervasive:*

See also Pryor v. United Air Lines, Inc., 791 F.3d 488 (4th Cir. 2015) (two anonymous death threats aimed at a black flight attendant could be found sufficiently severe to alter the conditions of her employment given the use of the word "nigger," the threat of violence, their being left in a secure mailroom at a major airport, and the context – including the same threats for other flight attendants and derogatory rumors).

Page 370, add at end of Note 2, *Severe or Pervasive*:

But some lower courts continue to require very dramatic conduct in order to find the harassment actionable. *See Walker v. Mod-U-Kraf Homes, LLC*, 775 F.3d 202 (4th Cir. 2014) (district court erred in requiring more than repeated comments for harassment to be severe or pervasive; it is sufficient if the pattern of such conduct is humiliating or demeaning).

Page 373, add after *Fuller* cite in carryover paragraph:

See generally Ann C. McGinley, *Reasonable Men?*, 45 Conn. L. Rev. 1, 1 (2012) (proposing a shift to a new universal standard for determining whether workplace behavior is sufficiently severe or pervasive that would inquire whether the victim's response is reasonable considering the identity factors of the victim and the workplace, and the social and individual context in which the behavior occurs.).

Page 373, add after *Cottrell* cite in second paragraph:

See also Adams v. Austal, U.S.A., L.L.C., 754 F.3d 1240, 1250 (11th Cir. 2014) (the district court correctly "limited its consideration to incidents of racial harassment of which the individual employees were aware since courts "conduct the objective assessment from the perspective of a reasonable person in the plaintiff's position, knowing what the plaintiff knew").

Page 373, add at end of second-to-last paragraph:

See also Gerald v. Univ. of P.R., 707 F.3d 7, 17 (1st Cir. 2013) (rejecting defendant's argument that plaintiff failed to prove the alleged harassment was unwelcome:

"We fail to see how an employee telling risqué jokes means that she is amenable to being groped at work."). *But see Souther v. Posen Constr., Inc.*, 523 F. App'x 352 (6th Cir. 2013) (plaintiff could not establish that a sexual relationship was unwelcome in view of her failure to complain to the supposed harasser, human resources, her union representative, or anyone else and when her conduct showed she was a willing participant and when there was no evidence that submitting to sexual advances was either an express or implied condition for gaining job benefits or avoiding job detriments).

Page 382, add to end of carryover Note 2, *The Use of Agency Principles*:

See generally Curtis J. Bankers, Note, *Identifying Employers' "Proxies" in Sexual-Harassment Litigation*, 99 Iowa L. Rev. 1785 (2014) (exploring how high in an employer's organization a harasser must be to trigger proxy liability).

Page 383, delete Note 3, *Who Is a Supervisor?*;

Page 383, add at end of carryover Note 4, *Tangible Employment Actions*:

But see Crockett v. Mission Hosp., Inc., 717 F.3d 348 (4th Cir. 2013) (seven-day suspension without pay not necessarily a tangible employment action when plaintiff presented no proof that she did not have paid time off available to cover the loss). Might such an approach lead to counterintuitive results? *See Kramer v. Wasatch County Sheriff's Office*, 743 F.3d 726, 743 (10th Cir. 2014) ("While rape is inarguably a severe form of sexual harassment, on the facts here it is not a 'tangible employment action'" since it did not involve "official act" of employer).

Page 384, add new principal case before asterisk breaker line:

Vance v. Ball State University
133 S. Ct. 2434 (2013)

Justice Alito delivered the opinion of the Court.

. . . We hold that [under the *Ellerth/Faragher* framework] an employee is a "supervisor" for purposes of vicarious liability under Title VII if he or she is empowered by the employer to take tangible employment actions against the victim. . . .

I

Maetta Vance, an African-American woman, began working for Ball State University (BSU) in 1989 as a substitute server in the University Banquet and

Catering division of Dining Services. In 1991, BSU promoted Vance to a part-time catering assistant position, and in 2007 she applied and was selected for a position as a full-time catering assistant.

Over the course of her employment with BSU, Vance lodged numerous complaints of racial discrimination and retaliation, but most of those incidents are not at issue here. For present purposes, the only relevant incidents concern Vance's interactions with a fellow BSU employee, Saundra Davis.

During the time in question, Davis, a white woman, was employed as a catering specialist in the Banquet and Catering division. The parties vigorously dispute the precise nature and scope of Davis' duties, but they agree that Davis did not have the power to hire, fire, demote, promote, transfer, or discipline Vance.

In late 2005 and early 2006, Vance filed internal complaints with BSU and charges with the Equal Employment Opportunity Commission (EEOC), alleging racial harassment and discrimination, and many of these complaints and charges pertained to Davis. Vance complained that Davis "gave her a hard time at work by glaring at her, slamming pots and pans around her, and intimidating her." She alleged that she was "left alone in the kitchen with Davis, who smiled at her"; that Davis "blocked" her on an elevator and "stood there with her cart smiling"; and that Davis often gave her "weird" looks.

Vance's workplace strife persisted despite BSU's attempts to address the problem. . . .

II . . .

B

[W]e have held that an employer is directly liable for an employee's unlawful harassment if the employer was negligent with respect to the offensive behavior. *Faragher.* Courts have generally applied this rule to evaluate employer liability when a co-worker harasses the plaintiff.

In *Ellerth* and *Faragher*, however, we held that different rules apply where the harassing employee is the plaintiff's "supervisor." In those instances, an employer may be vicariously liable for its employees' creation of a hostile work environment. And in identifying the situations in which such vicarious liability is appropriate, we looked to the Restatement of Agency for guidance. See, e.g., *Meritor*; *Ellerth*.

Under the Restatement, "masters" are generally not liable for the torts of their "servants" when the torts are committed outside the scope of the servants' employment. See 1 Restatement (Second) of Agency §219(2), p. 481 (1957) (Restatement). And because racial and sexual harassment are unlikely to fall within the scope of a servant's duties, application of this rule would generally preclude employer liability for employee harassment. See *Faragher*; *Ellerth*.

But in *Ellerth* and *Faragher*, we held that a provision of the Restatement provided the basis for an exception. Section 219(2)(d) of that Restatement recognizes an exception to the general rule just noted for situations in which the servant was "aided in accomplishing the tort by the existence of the agency relation." 2 Restatement 481.

[The opinion repeated the *Ellerth* and *Faragher* analytic structure which "identified two situations in which the aided-in-the-accomplishment rule warrants employer liability even in the absence of negligence." Both involved harassment by a "supervisor," as opposed to a co-worker. The first was the vicarious liability "when a supervisor takes a tangible employment action." Second, even absent a tangible employment action, "the employer can be vicariously liable for the supervisor's creation of a hostile work environment if the employer is unable to establish an affirmative defense.[3]]

C

Under *Ellerth* and *Faragher*, it is obviously important whether an alleged harasser is a "supervisor" or merely a co-worker, and the lower courts have disagreed about the meaning of the concept of a supervisor in this context. Some courts, including the Seventh Circuit below, have held that an employee is not a supervisor unless he or she has the power to hire, fire, demote, promote, transfer, or discipline the victim. Other courts have substantially followed the more open-ended approach advocated by the EEOC's Enforcement Guidance, which ties supervisor status to the ability to exercise significant direction over another's daily work. EEOC, Enforcement Guidance: Vicarious Employer Liability for Unlawful Harassment by Supervisors (1999), 1999 WL 33305874, *3 (hereinafter EEOC Guidance).

We granted certiorari to resolve this conflict.

III

We hold that an employer may be vicariously liable for an employee's unlawful harassment only when the employer has empowered that employee to take tangible employment actions against the victim, i.e., to effect a "significant change in employment status, such as hiring, firing, failing to promote, reassignment with significantly different responsibilities, or a decision causing a significant change in benefits." *Ellerth*. We reject the nebulous definition of a "supervisor" advocated in the EEOC Guidance[4] and substantially adopted by several courts of appeals. Petitioner's reliance on colloquial uses of the term "supervisor" is misplaced, and

---

3. . . . Neither party in this case challenges the application of *Faragher* and *Ellerth* [both of which involved sexual harassment] to race-based hostile environment claims, and we assume that the framework announced in *Faragher* and *Ellerth* applies to cases such as this one.

4. The United States urges us to defer to the EEOC Guidance, [citing *Skidmore* v. *Swift & Co.*, 323 U.S. 134, 140 (1944)]. But to do so would be proper only if the EEOC Guidance has the power to persuade, which "depend[s] upon the thoroughness evident in its consideration, the validity of its reasoning, [and] its consistency with earlier and later pronouncements." For the reasons explained below, we do not find the EEOC Guidance persuasive.

her contention that our cases require the EEOC's abstract definition is simply wrong.

As we will explain, the framework set out in *Ellerth* and *Faragher* presupposes a clear distinction between supervisors and co-workers. Those decisions contemplate a unitary category of supervisors, i.e., those employees with the authority to make tangible employment decisions. There is no hint in either decision that the Court had in mind two categories of supervisors: first, those who have such authority and, second, those who, although lacking this power, nevertheless have the ability to direct a co-worker's labor to some ill-defined degree. On the contrary, the *Ellerth/Faragher* framework is one under which supervisory status can usually be readily determined, generally by written documentation. The approach recommended by the EEOC Guidance, by contrast, would make the determination of supervisor status depend on a highly case-specific evaluation of numerous factors.

The *Ellerth/Faragher* framework represents what the Court saw as a workable compromise between the aided-in-the-accomplishment theory of vicarious liability and the legitimate interests of employers. The Seventh Circuit's understanding of the concept of a "supervisor," with which we agree, is easily workable; it can be applied without undue difficulty at both the summary judgment stage and at trial. The alternative, in many cases, would frustrate judges and confound jurors.

A

Petitioner contends that her expansive understanding of the concept of a "supervisor" is supported by the meaning of the word in general usage and in other legal contexts, but this argument is both incorrect on its own terms and, in any event, misguided.

[The majority looked to "general usage," as reflected in several dictionaries and to "colloquial business authorities" finding in both settings differing meanings; the term "is often used to refer to a person who has the authority to direct another's work," but is also used to mean someone with the authority to hire, fire, etc. The same is true of the use of the term in legal contexts. In a footnote, the Court described the admittedly broad use of the term in the National Labor Relations Act as an "outlier." The inclusive meaning in that context "reflect[s] the NLRA's unique purpose, which is to preserve the balance of power between labor and management. That purpose is inapposite in the context of Title VII, which focuses on eradicating discrimination. An employee may have a sufficient degree of authority over subordinates such that Congress has decided that the employee should not participate with lower level employees in the same collective-bargaining unit (because, for example, a higher level employee will pursue his own interests at the expense of lower level employees' interests), but that authority is not necessarily sufficient to merit heightened liability for the purposes of Title VII."]

More important, petitioner is misguided in suggesting that we should approach the question presented here as if "supervisor" were a statutory term.

"Supervisor" is not a term used by Congress in Title VII. Rather, the term was adopted by this Court in *Ellerth* and *Faragher* as a label for the class of employees whose misconduct may give rise to vicarious employer liability. Accordingly, the way to understand the meaning of the term "supervisor" for present purposes is to consider the interpretation that best fits within the highly structured framework that those cases adopted.

B

In considering *Ellerth* and *Faragher*, we are met at the outset with petitioner's contention that at least some of the alleged harassers in those cases, whom we treated as supervisors, lacked the authority that the Seventh Circuit's definition demands. This argument misreads our decisions.

[The majority revisited the facts of both cases and *Pennsylvania State Police v. Suders*, 542 U.S. 129 (2004), to conclude that the issue of the degree of authority that an employee must have in order to be classified as a supervisor was not before the Court.]

The dissent acknowledges that our prior cases do "not squarely resolve whether an employee without power to take tangible employment actions may nonetheless qualify as a supervisor," but accuses us of ignoring the "all-too-plain reality" that employees with authority to control their subordinates' daily work are aided by that authority in perpetuating a discriminatory work environment. As *Ellerth* recognized, however, "most workplace tortfeasors are aided in accomplishing their tortious objective by the existence of the agency relation," and consequently "something more" is required in order to warrant vicarious liability. The ability to direct another employee's tasks is simply not sufficient. Employees with such powers are certainly capable of creating intolerable work environments, but so are many other co-workers. Negligence provides the better framework for evaluating an employer's liability when a harassing employee lacks the power to take tangible employment actions.

C

Although our holdings in *Faragher* and *Ellerth* do not resolve the question now before us, we believe that the answer to that question is implicit in the characteristics of the framework that we adopted.

To begin, there is no hint in either *Ellerth* or *Faragher* that the Court contemplated anything other than a unitary category of supervisors, namely, those possessing the authority to effect a tangible change in a victim's terms or conditions of employment. The *Ellerth/Faragher* framework draws a sharp line between co-workers and supervisors. Co-workers, the Court noted, "can inflict psychological injuries" by creating a hostile work environment, but they "cannot dock another's pay, nor can one co-worker demote another." *Ellerth*. Only a supervisor has the power to cause "direct economic harm" by taking a tangible employment action. . . . The strong implication . . . is that the authority to take tangible employment actions is the defining characteristic of a supervisor, not simply a characteristic of a subset of an ill-defined class of employees who qualify as supervisors. . . .

Finally, the *Ellerth/Faragher* Court sought a framework that would be workable and would appropriately take into account the legitimate interests of employers and employees. The Court looked to principles of agency law for guidance, but the Court concluded that the "malleable terminology" of the aided-in-the-commission principle counseled against the wholesale incorporation of that principle into Title VII case law. *Ellerth*. Instead, the Court also considered the objectives of Title VII, including "the limitation of employer liability in certain circumstances." *Id.*

The interpretation of the concept of a supervisor that we adopt today is one that can be readily applied. In a great many cases, it will be known even before litigation is commenced whether an alleged harasser was a supervisor, and in others, the alleged harasser's status will become clear to both sides after discovery. And once this is known, the parties will be in a position to assess the strength of a case and to explore the possibility of resolving the dispute. Where this does not occur, supervisor status will generally be capable of resolution at summary judgment. By contrast, under the approach advocated by petitioner and the EEOC, supervisor status would very often be murky — as this case well illustrates.[12]

According to petitioner, the record shows that Davis, her alleged harasser, wielded enough authority to qualify as a supervisor. Petitioner points in particular to Davis' job description, which gave her leadership responsibilities, and to evidence that Davis at times led or directed Vance and other employees in the kitchen. The United States, on the other hand, while applying the same open-ended test for supervisory status, reaches the opposite conclusion. At least on the present record, the United States tells us, Davis fails to qualify as a supervisor. Her job description, in the Government's view, is not dispositive, and the Government adds that it would not be enough for petitioner to show that Davis "occasionally took the lead in the kitchen."

This disagreement is hardly surprising since the EEOC's definition of a supervisor, which both petitioner and the United States defend, is a study in ambiguity. . . . We read the EEOC Guidance as saying that the number (and perhaps the importance) of the tasks in question is a factor to be considered in determining whether an employee qualifies as a supervisor. And if this is a correct interpretation of the EEOC's position, what we are left with is a proposed standard of remarkable ambiguity.

The vagueness of this standard was highlighted at oral argument when the attorney representing the United States was asked to apply that standard to the situation in *Faragher*, where the alleged harasser supposedly threatened to assign the plaintiff to clean the toilets in the lifeguard station for a year if she did not date him. Since cleaning the toilets is just one task, albeit an unpleasant one, the authority to assign that job would not seem to meet the more-than-a-limited-number-of-tasks requirement in the EEOC Guidance. Nevertheless, the Government

---

12. The dissent attempts to find ambiguities in our holding, but it is indisputable that our holding is orders of magnitude clearer than the nebulous standard it would adopt. Employment discrimination cases present an almost unlimited number of factual variations, and marginal cases are inevitable under any standard.

attorney's first response was that the authority to make this assignment would be enough. He later qualified that answer by saying that it would be necessary to "know how much of the day's work [was] encompassed by cleaning the toilets." He did not explain what percentage of the day's work (50%, 25%, 10%?) would suffice.

The Government attorney's inability to provide a definitive answer to this question was the inevitable consequence of the vague standard that the Government asks us to adopt. . . .

Under the definition of "supervisor" that we adopt today, the question of supervisor status, when contested, can very often be resolved as a matter of law before trial. The elimination of this issue from the trial will focus the efforts of the parties, who will be able to present their cases in a way that conforms to the framework that the jury will apply. The plaintiff will know whether he or she must prove that the employer was negligent or whether the employer will have the burden of proving the elements of the *Ellerth/Faragher* affirmative defense. Perhaps even more important, the work of the jury, which is inevitably complicated in employment discrimination cases, will be simplified. The jurors can be given preliminary instructions that allow them to understand, as the evidence comes in, how each item of proof fits into the framework that they will ultimately be required to apply. And even where the issue of supervisor status cannot be eliminated from the trial (because there are genuine factual disputes about an alleged harasser's authority to take tangible employment actions), this preliminary question is relatively straightforward.

The alternative approach advocated by petitioner and the United States would make matters far more complicated and difficult. . . .

Courts and commentators alike have opined on the need for reasonably clear jury instructions in employment discrimination cases. And the danger of juror confusion is particularly high where the jury is faced with instructions on alternative theories of liability under which different parties bear the burden of proof. By simplifying the process of determining who is a supervisor (and by extension, which liability rules apply to a given set of facts), the approach that we take will help to ensure that juries return verdicts that reflect the application of the correct legal rules to the facts.

Contrary to the dissent's suggestions, this approach will not leave employees unprotected against harassment by co-workers who possess the authority to inflict psychological injury by assigning unpleasant tasks or by altering the work environment in objectionable ways. In such cases, the victims will be able to prevail simply by showing that the employer was negligent in permitting this harassment to occur, and the jury should be instructed that the nature and degree of authority wielded by the harasser is an important factor to be considered in determining whether the employer was negligent. The nature and degree of authority possessed by harassing employees varies greatly, and as we explained above, the test proposed by petitioner and the United States is ill equipped to deal with the variety of situations that will inevitably arise. This variety presents no problem for the negligence standard, which is thought to provide adequate protection for tort plaintiffs in many other situations. There is no reason why this standard, if accompanied by proper instructions, cannot provide the same service in the context at issue here.

D

The dissent argues that the definition of a supervisor that we now adopt is out of touch with the realities of the workplace, where individuals with the power to assign daily tasks are often regarded by other employees as supervisors. But in reality it is the alternative that is out of touch. Particularly in modern organizations that have abandoned a highly hierarchical management structure, it is common for employees to have overlapping authority with respect to the assignment of work tasks. Members of a team may each have the responsibility for taking the lead with respect to a particular aspect of the work and thus may have the responsibility to direct each other in that area of responsibility.

Finally, petitioner argues that tying supervisor status to the authority to take tangible employment actions will encourage employers to attempt to insulate themselves from liability for workplace harassment by empowering only a handful of individuals to take tangible employment actions. But a broad definition of "supervisor" is not necessary to guard against this concern.

As an initial matter, an employer will always be liable when its negligence leads to the creation or continuation of a hostile work environment. And even if an employer concentrates all decisionmaking authority in a few individuals, it likely will not isolate itself from heightened liability under *Faragher* and *Ellerth*. If an employer does attempt to confine decisionmaking power to a small number of individuals, those individuals will have a limited ability to exercise independent discretion when making decisions and will likely rely on other workers who actually interact with the affected employee. Under those circumstances, the employer may be held to have effectively delegated the power to take tangible employment actions to the employees on whose recommendations it relies. See *Ellerth*.

IV

[The dissent cites cases that it claims that our holding today would preclude employer liability, but, assuming that a harasser is not a supervisor, a plaintiff could still prevail by showing that his or her employer was negligent. Further, the standard we adopt "has been the law for quite some time in the First, Seventh, and Eighth Circuits." Finally, the majority was "skeptical that there are a great number of" cases in which negligence liability would not attach for the actions of an employee who cannot take tangible employment actions but who does direct the victim's daily work activities in a meaningful way, creates an unlawful hostile environment. "However, we are confident that, in every case, the approach we take today will be more easily administrable than the approach advocated by the dissent."

***

We hold that an employee is a "supervisor" for purposes of vicarious liability under Title VII if he or she is empowered by the employer to take tangible employment actions against the victim. Because there is no evidence that BSU empowered Davis to take any tangible employment actions against Vance, the judgment of the Seventh Circuit is affirmed. . . .

JUSTICE THOMAS, concurring.

I continue to believe that *Burlington Industries, Inc. v. Ellerth* and *Faragher v. Boca Raton* were wrongly decided. However, I join the opinion because it provides the narrowest and most workable rule for when an employer may be held vicariously liable for an employee's harassment.

JUSTICE GINSBURG, with whom JUSTICE BREYER, JUSTICE SOTOMAYOR, and JUSTICE KAGAN join, dissenting.

. . . The Court today strikes from the supervisory category employees who control the day-to-day schedules and assignments of others, confining the category to those formally empowered to take tangible employment actions. The limitation the Court decrees diminishes the force of *Faragher* and *Ellerth*, ignores the conditions under which members of the work force labor, and disserves the objective of Title VII to prevent discrimination from infecting the Nation's workplaces. I would follow the EEOC's Guidance and hold that the authority to direct an employee's daily activities establishes supervisory status under Title VII.

I

[The dissent summarized the employer liability structure of *Harris v. Forklift Systems, Inc.*, §219(2)(d) of the Restatement (Second) of Agency, *Faragher* and *Ellerth* and then wrote that the] distinction *Faragher* and *Ellerth* drew between supervisors and co-workers corresponds to the realities of the workplace. Exposed to a fellow employee's harassment, one can walk away or tell the offender to "buzz off." A supervisor's slings and arrows, however, are not so easily avoided. An employee who confronts her harassing supervisor risks, for example, receiving an undesirable or unsafe work assignment or an unwanted transfer. She may be saddled with an excessive workload or with placement on a shift spanning hours disruptive of her family life. And she may be demoted or fired. Facing such dangers, she may be reluctant to blow the whistle on her superior, whose "power and authority invests his or her harassing conduct with a particular threatening character." *Ellerth*. See also *Faragher*. In short, as *Faragher* and *Ellerth* recognized, harassment by supervisors is more likely to cause palpable harm and to persist unabated than similar conduct by fellow employees.

II

[The Court's view that supervisors are only those authorized to take tangible employment actions] is out of accord with the agency principles that, *Faragher* and *Ellerth* affirmed, govern Title VII. It is blind to the realities of the workplace, and it discounts the guidance of the EEOC, the agency Congress established to interpret, and superintend the enforcement of, Title VII. . . .

A

Until today, our decisions have assumed that employees who direct subordinates' daily work are supervisors. [The dissent reviewed the facts in *Faragher*, and noted that at least one of the harassers, David Silverman, would not be a supervisor under the Court's definition. Similarly, in *Pennsylvania State Police v. Suders*, the harassing employees "lacked authority to discharge or demote the complainant, but they were 'responsible for the day-to-day supervision' of the workplace and for overseeing employee shifts." While none of these cases "squarely resolve[d] whether an employee without power to take tangible employment actions may nonetheless qualify as a supervisor," the majority "misses the forest for the trees" in parsing the authority of the harassers: what mattered was the abuse of power vested in the harassers which facilitated their above.]

B

Workplace realities fortify my conclusion that harassment by an employee with power to direct subordinates' day-to-day work activities should trigger vicarious employer liability. The following illustrations, none of them hypothetical, involve in-charge employees of the kind the Court today excludes from supervisory status.[2]

Yasharay Mack: Yasharay Mack, an African-American woman, worked for the Otis Elevator Company as an elevator mechanic's helper at the Metropolitan Life Building in New York City. James Connolly, the "mechanic in charge" and the senior employee at the site, targeted Mack for abuse. He commented frequently on her "fantastic ass," "luscious lips," and "beautiful eyes," and, using deplorable racial epithets, opined that minorities and women did not "belong in the business." Once, he pulled her on his lap, touched her buttocks, and tried to kiss her while others looked on. Connolly lacked authority to take tangible employment actions against mechanic's helpers, but he did assign their work, control their schedules, and direct the particulars of their workdays. When he became angry with Mack, for example, he denied her overtime hours. And when she complained about the mistreatment, he scoffed, "I get away with everything." [*Mack v. Otis Elevator Co.*, 326 F.3d 116, 127 (CA2 2003).]

[The dissent then recounted the facts of *Rhodes v. Ill. Dept. of Transp.*, 359 F.3d 498, 501-503, 506-507 (CA7 2004), and *Whitten v. Fred's, Inc.*, 601 F.3d 231, 245-247 (CA4 2010).]

---

2. The illustrative cases reached the appellate level after grants of summary judgment in favor of the employer. Like the Courts of Appeals in each case, I recount the facts in the light most favorable to the employee, the nonmoving party.

Monika Starke: CRST Van Expedited, Inc., an interstate transit company, ran a training program for newly hired truckdrivers requiring a 28-day on-the-road trip. Monika Starke participated in the program. Trainees like Starke were paired in a truck cabin with a single "lead driver" who lacked authority to hire, fire, promote, or demote, but who exercised control over the work environment for the duration of the trip. Lead drivers were responsible for providing instruction on CRST's driving method, assigning specific tasks, and scheduling rest stops. At the end of the trip, lead drivers evaluated trainees' performance with a nonbinding pass or fail recommendation that could lead to full driver status. Over the course of Starke's training trip, her first lead driver, Bob Smith, filled the cabin with vulgar sexual remarks, commenting on her breast size and comparing the gear stick to genitalia. A second lead driver, David Goodman, later forced her into unwanted sex with him, an outrage to which she submitted, believing it necessary to gain a passing grade. See *EEOC v. CRST Van Expedited, Inc.*, 679 F.3d 657 (CA8 2012).

In each of these cases, a person vested with authority to control the conditions of a subordinate's daily work life used his position to aid his harassment. But in none of them would the Court's severely confined definition of supervisor yield vicarious liability for the employer. The senior elevator mechanic in charge, the Court today tells us, was Mack's co-worker, not her supervisor. . . . So were the lead drivers who controlled all aspects of Starke's working environment. . . .

As anyone with work experience would immediately grasp, [the harassers in the four cases] wielded employer-conferred supervisory authority over their victims. Each man's discriminatory harassment derived force from, and was facilitated by, the control reins he held. Cf. *Burlington N. & S.F. R. Co. v. White*, 548 U.S. 53 (2006) ("Common sense suggests that one good way to discourage an employee . . . from bringing discrimination charges would be to insist that she spend more time performing the more arduous duties and less time performing those that are easier or more agreeable."). Under any fair reading of Title VII, in each of the illustrative cases, the superior employee should have been classified a supervisor whose conduct would trigger vicarious liability.[3]

C

[The dissent argued in favor of "*Skidmore* deference" to the EEOC's definition of supervisor, deference that had been accorded other EEOC interpretations.]

---

3. The Court misses the point of the illustrations. Even under a vicarious liability rule, the Court points out, employers might escape liability for reasons other than the harasser's status as supervisor. . . . That, however, is no reason to restrict the definition of supervisor in a way that leaves out those genuinely in charge.

III . . .

A

The Court purports to rely on the *Ellerth* and *Faragher* framework to limit supervisor status to those capable of taking tangible employment actions. That framework, we are told, presupposes "a sharp line between co-workers and supervisors." The definition of supervisor decreed today, the Court insists, is "clear," "readily applied," and "easily workable," when compared to the EEOC's vague standard.

There is reason to doubt just how "clear" and "workable" the Court's definition is. A supervisor, the Court holds, is someone empowered to "take tangible employment actions against the victim, i.e., to effect a 'significant change in employment status, such as hiring, firing, failing to promote, reassignment with significantly different responsibilities, or a decision causing a significant change in benefits.'" Whether reassignment authority makes someone a supervisor might depend on whether the reassignment carries economic consequences. The power to discipline other employees, when the discipline has economic consequences, might count, too. So might the power to initiate or make recommendations about tangible employment actions. And when an employer "concentrates all decisionmaking authority in a few individuals" who rely on information from "other workers who actually interact with the affected employee," the other workers may rank as supervisors (or maybe not; the Court does not commit one way or the other).

Someone in search of a bright line might well ask, what counts as "significantly different responsibilities"? Can any economic consequence make a reassignment or disciplinary action "significant," or is there a minimum threshold? How concentrated must the decisionmaking authority be to deem those not formally endowed with that authority nevertheless "supervisors"? The Court leaves these questions unanswered, and its liberal use of "mights" and "mays," dims the light it casts.

That the Court has adopted a standard, rather than a clear rule, is not surprising, for no crisp definition of supervisor could supply the unwavering line the Court desires. Supervisors, like the workplaces they manage, come in all shapes and sizes. Whether a pitching coach supervises his pitchers (can he demote them?), or an artistic director supervises her opera star (can she impose significantly different responsibilities?), or a law firm associate supervises the firm's paralegals (can she fire them?) are matters not susceptible to mechanical rules and on-off switches. One cannot know whether an employer has vested supervisory authority in an employee, and whether harassment is aided by that authority, without looking to the particular working relationship between the harasser and the victim. That is why *Faragher* and *Ellerth* crafted an employer liability standard embracive of all whose authority significantly aids in the creation and perpetuation of harassment.

The Court's focus on finding a definition of supervisor capable of instant application is at odds with the Court's ordinary emphasis on the importance of particular circumstances in Title VII cases.[6] . . .

B . . .

The negligence standard allowed by the Court scarcely affords the protection the *Faragher* and *Ellerth* framework gave victims harassed by those in control of their lives at work. Recall that an employer is negligent with regard to harassment only if it knew or should have known of the conduct but failed to take appropriate corrective action. See 29 C.F.R. §1604.11(d); EEOC Guidance 405:7652 to 405:7653. It is not uncommon for employers to lack actual or constructive notice of a harassing employee's conduct. See Lindemann & Grossman [Employment Discrimination Law (4th ed. 2007)]. An employee may have a reputation as a harasser among those in his vicinity, but if no complaint makes its way up to management, the employer will escape liability under a negligence standard.

Faragher is illustrative. After enduring unrelenting harassment, Faragher reported Terry's and Silverman's conduct informally to Robert Gordon, another immediate supervisor. But the lifeguards were "completely isolated from the City's higher management," and it did not occur to Faragher to pursue the matter with higher ranking city officials distant from the beach. Applying a negligence standard, the Eleventh Circuit held that, despite the pervasiveness of the harassment, and despite Gordon's awareness of it, Boca Raton lacked constructive notice and therefore escaped liability. Under the vicarious liability standard, however, Boca Raton could not make out the affirmative defense, for it had failed to disseminate a policy against sexual harassment.

[In addition, dealing with cases such as these on the basis of negligence saddles plaintiffs with the burden of proving the employer's negligence whenever the harasser lacks the power to take tangible employment actions, whereas *Faragher* and *Ellerth* placed the burden squarely on the employer to make out the affirmative defense. This allocation of the burden was both sensible and deliberate: An employer has superior access to evidence bearing on whether it acted reasonably to prevent or correct harassing behavior, and superior resources to marshal that evidence.]

---

6. The Court worries that the EEOC's definition of supervisor will confound jurors who must first determine whether the harasser is a supervisor and second apply the correct employer liability standard. But the Court can point to no evidence that jury instructions on supervisor status in jurisdictions following the EEOC Guidance have in fact proved unworkable or confusing to jurors. Moreover, under the Court's definition of supervisor, jurors in many cases will be obliged to determine, as a threshold question, whether the alleged harasser possessed supervisory authority.

IV

... Because I would hold that the Seventh Circuit erred in restricting supervisor status to employees formally empowered to take tangible employment actions, I would remand for application of the proper standard to Vance's claim. On this record, however, there is cause to anticipate that Davis would not qualify as Vance's supervisor.

Supervisor status is based on "job function rather than job title," and depends on "specific facts" about the working relationship. EEOC Guidance 405:7654. Vance has adduced scant evidence that Davis controlled the conditions of her daily work. Vance stated in an affidavit that the general manager of the Catering Division, Bill Kimes, was charged with "overall supervision in the kitchen," including "reassign[ing] people to perform different tasks," and "control[ling] the schedule." The chef, Shannon Fultz, assigned tasks by preparing "prep lists" of daily duties. There is no allegation that Davis had a hand in creating these prep lists, nor is there any indication that, in fact, Davis otherwise controlled the particulars of Vance's workday. Vance herself testified that she did not know whether Davis was her supervisor. . . .

V . . .

Congress has, in the recent past, intervened to correct this Court's wayward interpretations of Title VII. The ball is once again in Congress' court to correct the error into which this Court has fallen, and to restore the robust protections against workplace harassment the Court weakens today. . . .

NOTES

1. *Fewer Supervisors = More Negligence Claims.* The majority's narrow definition of "supervisor" means that far fewer cases will trigger the strict or presumptive employer liability structure of *Faragher/Ellerth.* Instead, most harassment cases will proceed as negligence claims, which means that the employee has the burden of proving the employer knew (or should have known) of the harassment and failed to respond reasonably. *See Lambert v. Peri Formworks Sys., Inc.*, 723 F.3d 863, 867 (7th Cir. 2013) (while "yard leads" were not supervisors, they may have had sufficient authority to report claimed harassment to those who could take action and, therefore, failure of the employer to act after such reports may subject it to liability for negligence). Effectively, that eliminates strict liability and shifts the burden of proof from the employer to establish an affirmative defense to the employee to establish both elements of her claim.

Why does negligence provide "the better framework for evaluating an employer's liability when a harassing employee lacks the power to take tangible employment actions"? At one point, the majority seems to argue that its decision will have little effect in the real world because "victims will be able to prevail simply by showing that the employer was negligent in permitting this harassment to occur, and the jury should be instructed that the nature and degree of authority wielded by the harasser is an important factor to be considered in determining whether the employer was negligent." Further, while the EEOC's test is too vague to support the *Faragher/Ellerth* structure of strict or presumptive liability, these "present[] no problem for the negligence standard, which is thought to provide adequate protection for tort plaintiffs in many other situations. There is no reason why this standard, if accompanied by proper instructions, cannot provide the same service in the context at issue here."

If the court or jury is going to weigh all the same factors under either approach, what's the point of the restrictive definition of supervisor? Is shifting the burden of persuasion from employer to employee really so important? In *Velázquez-Pérez v. Developers Diversified Realty Corp.*, 753 F.3d 265 (1st Cir. 2014), the court, relying on both *Staub* and *Vance*, held that an employer could be liable in negligence when a co-worker's impermissibly motivated allegations against an employee resulted in his termination. It found employer liability could exist in a case that the court described as "quid pro quo" by a co-worker: when a jilted co-worker intended to cause the employee's firing, her allegations were the proximate cause of the firing, and the employer knew or should have known the co-worker's allegations were discriminatorily motivated.

2. *Delegating Decision-Making.* In response to the argument that an employer might try to "isolate itself from heightened liability under *Faragher* and *Ellerth*" by limiting decisionmaking power to a small number of individuals, Justice Alito noted that "those individuals will have a limited ability to exercise independent discretion when making decisions and will likely rely on other workers who actually interact with the affected employee. Under those circumstances, the employer may be held to have effectively delegated the power to take tangible employment actions to the employees on whose recommendations it relies." Note that the possibility of concentrating decisionmaking in a few individuals is not far-fetched: in most large firms, Human Resources has the formal power to hire and fire (and much in between) although in practice HR is likely to accord great deference to line managers.

In any event, this delegation argument echoes possibilities raised in *Staub v. Proctor Hospital*, reproduced at p. 54. Does it also suggest that the bright line the Court drew isn't so bright after all? Presumably, the point is that there are supervisors in practice who are not supervisors on paper.

Speaking of *Staub*, recall that the Court decided only that where "supervisors" influenced a decisionmaker, cat's paw liability can follow. But were the two individuals who influenced Buck, "Janice Mulally, Staub's immediate supervisor, and Michael Korenchuk, Mulally's supervisor," 131 S. Ct. at 1139, both "supervisors" under *Vance*? They certainly didn't have the power to fire Staub since they had to influence Buck in order to do so. Of course, they may have had other supervisory power (maybe they hired Staub), but, if not, *Vance* raises the question of whether *Staub*'s holding retains much significance. After all, the Court went out of its way to note that it wasn't deciding whether subordinate bias liability applied to acts of "co-workers." 131 S. Ct. at 194 n.3. Could the same statute have two different definitions of supervisor — a narrower one for harassment liability and a broader one for subordinate bias liability? *See generally* Charles A. Sullivan, WORKPLACE PROF BLOG, Vance *Negates* Staub?, http://lawprofessors.typepad.com/laborprof_blog/2014/03/vance-or-staub-or-both.html.

These issues came to the fore in *Kramer v. Wasatch County Sheriff's Office*, 743 F.3d 726, 741 (10th Cir. 2014), where the court recognized that, where the "harasser is empowered to effect significant changes in employment status indirectly through recommendations, performance evaluations, and the like, and where the person with final decision-making power does not work directly with the plaintiff, the harasser may be a 'supervisor' under Title VII." Applying that principle to the facts before it, the court recognized a genuine issue of fact whether the Sheriff's Department "effectively delegated to Sergeant Benson the power to cause tangible employment actions regarding Ms. Kramer by providing for reliance on recommendations from sergeants such as Benson when making decisions regarding firing, promotion, demotion, and reassignment." *Id.* Further, plaintiff "is not required to establish that the Sheriff would follow Sergeant Benson's recommendations blindly. Even if the Sheriff undertook *some* independent analysis when considering employment decisions recommended by Sergeant Benson, Sergeant Benson would qualify as a supervisor so long as his recommendations were among the proximate causes of the Sheriff's decision-making." *Id. See also Velázquez-Pérez v. Developers Diversified Realty Corp.*, 753 F.3d 265 (1st Cir. 2014) (relying on *Vance* to find biased individual was a co-worker, not a supervisor, but relying on *Staub* to find employer could be liable for co-worker's impermissibly motivated allegations that were the proximate cause of an employee's termination, where employer knew or should have known her allegations were impermissibly motivated).

3. *Workability.* If there is a single theme to the majority's opinion in *Vance* it is that its approach is workable and the dissent's (and EEOC's) is not. But note Justice Ginsburg's critique. Both the majority and the dissent criticize each other's tests for vagueness. But isn't Title VII riddled with general standards whose application is intensely fact-specific? One example is the definition of harassment itself; a second is the standard for actionable retaliation. See page 476. Is there a simpler way to approach the liability question? *See* Samuel R. Bagenstos, *Formalism and Employer Liability Under Title VII*, 2014 U. CHI. LEGAL F. 145 (urging Congress not merely to change the definition of supervisor, as Justice Ginsburg urged in *Vance*, but to make employers liable for any severe or pervasive harassment in the workplace).

Page 392, add after Grossman cite in Note 3, *Bullet-Proofing or Real Structural Change?*:

Linda Hamilton Krieger, Rachel Kahn Best, & Lauren B. Edelman, *When "Best Practices" Win, Employees Lose: Symbolic Compliance and Judicial Inference in Federal Equal Employment Opportunity Cases*, 40 LAW & SOC. INQUIRY 843 (2015);

Page 393, add to end of carryover paragraph in carryover Note 4, *Prong 1(b):*
Reasonable Steps to Correct Harassment:

See also Pryor v. United Air Lines, Inc., 791 F.3d 488 (4th Cir. 2015) (since the reasonableness of an employer's response depends on the seriousness of the underlying conduct, the airline's reaction to complaints of anonymous racist death threats could be found neither prompt nor reasonably calculated to end the harassment when its supervisors did not call police nor take other efforts to prevent a recurrence).

Page 393, add before *Cherry* **cite in carryover Note 4,** *Prong 1(b): Reasonable Steps to Correct Harassment:*

Smith v. Rock-Tenn Servs., 813 F.3d 298 (6th Cir. 2016) (a reasonable jury could have concluded that total inaction for ten days, where the employer knew about the contact and had warned the harasser that further complaints would result in termination, was unreasonable); *Nichols v. Tri-Nat'l Logistics, Inc.*, 809 F.3d 981, 987 (8th Cir. 2016) (a trucking company's response to a complaint by a female long-haul truck driver about her co-driver's conduct could be found to be inadequate when she was left in the harasser's company and denied permission to take truck to a motel where she could stay overnight);

Page 394, add after *Green* **cite in carryover paragraph of carryover Note 4,** *Prong 1(b): Reasonable Steps to Correct Harassment***:**

But even lesser discipline may suffice. *See Williams-Boldware v. Denton County*, 741 F.3d 635 (5th Cir. 2014) (the employer satisfied its obligations by promptly investigating, reprimanding the harasser, requiring him to undergo training, and ensuring that plaintiff was not supervised by the harasser's wife, which resulted in no further harassment).

Page 394, add to end of carryover Note 4, *Prong 1(b) Reasonable Steps to Correct Harassment***:**

See also Orton-Bell v. Indiana, 759 F.3d 768, 777 (7th Cir. 2014) (when the woman engaged in a sexual relationship was not treated as well as the man, the differences between them did not bar a finding of sex discrimination; he had far more seniority, which put him in a position to know better than she; the relationship threatened to compromise his work more than it did hers; and he had had a previous work affair).

5. Special Problems in Applying Title VII, Section 1981, and the ADEA

Page 395, add before *Taylor* cite in second full paragraph of carryover Note 6, *Prong 2, Did the Employee Act Unreasonably?*:

Debord v. Mercy Health Sys. of Kansas, Inc., 737 F.3d 642 (10th Cir. 2013) (plaintiff's Facebook post describing her supervisor as a "snake" who "needs to keep his creepy hands to himself," falls short of a complaint of harassment to her employer when it "was not in accordance with Mercy's otherwise flexible reporting system for sexual harassment complaints");

Page 397, add before *May* citation in last full paragraph:

Freeman v. Dal-Tile Corp., 750 F.3d 413 (4th Cir. 2014) (an employer is liable under Title VII for third parties creating a hostile work environment if the employer knew or should have known of the harassment and failed to take appropriate remedial action);

Page 397, add after *May* citation in second full paragraph:

If adequate corrective action is taken immediately, there can be no negligence liability. *Chaib v. Indiana*, 744 F.3d 974, 985-86 (7th Cir. 2014); *Summa v. Hofstra Univ.*, 708 F.3d 115 (2d Cir. 2013).

Page 397, add before *Bombaci* cite in third full paragraph:

Stewart v. Rise, Inc., 791 F.3d 849, 862 (8th Cir. 2015) (reports to supervisors "need not each reference a prohibited animus"; when many reports expressly included such references, those "that lacked facial animus or express explanations cannot be quarantined and viewed in isolation"; nor is there any requirement that reports be written rather than oral);

Page 398, add at end of last full paragraph:

See also Dallan F. Flake, *Employer Liability for Nonemployee Discrimination*, http://papers.ssrn.com/sol3/papers.cfm?abstract_id=2780677.

Page 399, add before see generally cite in carryover paragraph:

See Stewart v. Rise, Inc., 791 F.3d 849 (8th Cir. June 30, 2015) (harassment of supervisor by subordinates, when coupled with failure of higher level decisionmakers to either discipline the harassers or allow the supervisor to do so is actionable).

Page 400, add at end of last full paragraph:

See also Booth v. Pasco Cnty., 757 F.3d 1198, 1214 (11th Cir. 2014) (upholding a jury verdict against a First Amendment challenge when the speech in question was "part and parcel" of retaliation and the jury found a union liable not merely for notifying its members of a charge of discrimination but for publishing a "'call for reprisal').

D. Discrimination on Account of Religion

Page 406, add at end of carryover Note 2, *Knowledge*:

A similar problem arises with respect to the duty to accommodate. In *Adeyeye v. Heartland Sweeteners, LLC*, 721 F.3d 444, 450-51 (7th Cir. 2013), the court held that, even though plaintiff's religious beliefs and practices were not as familiar as others closer to the modern American mainstream, plaintiff's request for leave to attend his father's funeral gave sufficient notice of the religious nature of the request when it referred to a "funeral ceremony," a "funeral rite," and animal sacrifice and described his participation as "compulsory" and that the spiritual consequence of his absence would be his own and family members' deaths. You will shortly encounter the Supreme Court's recent decision in *EEOC v. Abercrombie & Fitch Stores, Inc.*, where the Court addressed the knowledge question. Ask yourself whether Judge Posner is wrong or whether *Reed* is still good law. Could the employer's action be justified because Reed was refusing to perform his duties and did not explain the basis for his objection so that an accommodation could be considered? Or does *Abercrombie* mean that, once the employer has reason to believe that an employee has a religious objection to some work rule, it can't take an adverse action. That can't be right, can it?

Page 407, add at end of Note 5, *Sincerity*:

See also Adeyeye v. Heartland Sweeteners, LLC, 721 F.3d 444, 451-52 (7th Cir. 2013) (although a son's desire to attend his father's funeral merely out of filial duty would not be entitled to an accommodation, plaintiff's evidence was sufficient to show his desire to participate stemmed from his own personally and sincerely held religious beliefs); *Tagore v. United States*, 735 F.3d 324, 328 (5th Cir. 2013) (despite arguments that a slightly shorter blade length would satisfy plaintiff's religion, there was a genuine issue of material fact on the sincerity of Tagore's practice of wearing a kirpan with a 3-inch blade).

5. Special Problems in Applying Title VII, Section 1981, and the ADEA

Page 408, add before *Grossman* cite in carryover Note 6, *Justifying Religious Discrimination*:

Fields v. City of Tulsa, 753 F.3d 1000 (10th Cir. 2014) (punishment of a police captain for refusal to participate in an event hosted by an Islamic Society did not violate his Free Exercise rights since he could have obeyed the order without compromising his beliefs by ordering subordinates to attend; there was no Establishment Clause violation because no informed, reasonable observer would have perceived the situation as governmental endorsement of Islam);

Page 409, add at end of paragraph after extract:

See also Telfair v. Fed. Express Corp., 567 F. App'x 681 (11th Cir. 2014) (employer's offer to transfer employees to lower-paid positions when shift reassignments would have required them to work on their Sabbath was a reasonable accommodation, thus pretermitting any need to explore any further accommodations).

Page 409, add before *EEOC v. Geo Group* citation in last paragraph:

Yeager v. FirstEnergy Generation Corp., 777 F.3d 362, 363 (6th Cir. 2015) (an employer need accommodate an employee's religious beliefs by violating a federal statute, such as the requirement that employers provide the social security numbers of their workers); *Tagore v. United States*, 735 F.3d 324, 329-30 (5th Cir. 2013) (a Sikh fired because she could not enter her IRS workplace because her kirpan violated federal office security rules need not be accommodated by being allowed to work from her home or being assigned to work at other federal buildings with lower security requirements because that would impose more than "de minimis" costs on the employer);

Page 409, add in last line after closed parenthesis:

But see Davis v. Fort Bend Cnty., 765 F.3d 480, 489 (5th Cir. 2014) (2-1) (no showing of undue hardship when plaintiff obtained a competent volunteer to work her shift); *Adeyeye v. Heartland Sweeteners, LLC*, 721 F.3d 444, 455-56 (7th Cir. 2013) (employer failed to show that allowing worker to take several weeks of unpaid leave would have caused it an undue hardship when it expected high turnover of workers in the relevant job categories in any event).

Page 410, add at the end of carryover paragraph:

In the next principal case, the Supreme Court essentially eliminated the duty of reasonable accommodation as a separate theory of liability under Title VII.

Instead, it folded any such duty into the general duty not to discriminate on the basis of religion — including discrimination against any practice or observance. The obvious question is what, if anything, this recasting will do to the rights of employees and the obligations of employers. We'll explore this in the Notes following the case.

EEOC v. ABERCROMBIE & FITCH STORES, INC.
135 S. Ct. 2028 (2105)

JUSTICE SCALIA delivered the opinion of the Court.

Title VII of the Civil Rights Act of 1964 prohibits a prospective employer from refusing to hire an applicant in order to avoid accommodating a religious practice that it could accommodate without undue hardship. The question presented is whether this prohibition applies only where an applicant has informed the employer of his need for an accommodation.

I

We summarize the facts in the light most favorable to the Equal Employment Opportunity Commission (EEOC), against whom the Tenth Circuit granted summary judgment. Respondent Abercrombie & Fitch Stores, Inc., operates several lines of clothing stores, each with its own "style." Consistent with the image Abercrombie seeks to project for each store, the company imposes a Look Policy that governs its employees' dress. The Look Policy prohibits "caps" — a term the Policy does not define — as too informal for Abercrombie's desired image.

Samantha Elauf is a practicing Muslim who, consistent with her understanding of her religion's requirements, wears a headscarf. She applied for a position in an Abercrombie store, and was interviewed by Heather Cooke, the store's assistant manager. Using Abercrombie's ordinary system for evaluating applicants, Cooke gave Elauf a rating that qualified her to be hired; Cooke was concerned, however, that Elauf's headscarf would conflict with the store's Look Policy.

Cooke sought the store manager's guidance to clarify whether the headscarf was a forbidden "cap." When this yielded no answer, Cooke turned to Randall Johnson, the district manager. Cooke informed Johnson that she believed Elauf wore her headscarf because of her faith. Johnson told Cooke that Elauf's headscarf would violate the Look Policy, as would all other headwear, religious or otherwise, and directed Cooke not to hire Elauf. . . .

II

[Subsections 42 U.S.C. §2000e–2(a)(1) and (2)], often referred to as the "disparate treatment" (or "intentional discrimination") provision and the "disparate impact" provision, are the only causes of action under Title VII. The word "religion" is defined to "includ[e] all aspects of religious observance and practice, as well as belief, unless an employer demonstrates that he is unable to reasonably accommodate to" a "religious observance or practice without undue hardship on the conduct of the employer's business." §2000e(j).[1]

Abercrombie's primary argument is that an applicant cannot show disparate treatment without first showing that an employer has "actual knowledge" of the applicant's need for an accommodation. We disagree. Instead, an applicant need only show that his need for an accommodation was a motivating factor in the employer's decision.[2]

The disparate-treatment provision forbids employers to: (1) "fail . . . to hire" an applicant (2) "because of" (3) "such individual's . . . religion" (which includes his religious practice). Here, of course, Abercrombie (1) failed to hire Elauf. The parties concede that (if Elauf sincerely believes that her religion so requires) Elauf's wearing of a headscarf is (3) a "religious practice." All that remains is whether she was not hired (2) "because of" her religious practice.

The term "because of" appears frequently in antidiscrimination laws. It typically imports, at a minimum, the traditional standard of but-for causation. *University of Tex. Southwestern Medical Center* v. *Nassar* [reproduced in this Supplement at p. 107]. Title VII relaxes this standard, however, to prohibit even making a protected characteristic a "motivating factor" in an employment decision. 42 U.S. C. §2000e–2(m). "Because of" in §2000e–2(a)(1) links the forbidden consideration to each of the verbs preceding it; an individual's actual religious practice may not be a motivating factor in failing to hire, in refusing to hire, and so on.

It is significant that §2000e–2(a)(1) does not impose a knowledge requirement. As Abercrombie acknowledges, some antidiscrimination statutes do. For example, the Americans with Disabilities Act of 1990 defines discrimination to include an employer's failure to make "reasonable accommodations to the *known* physical or mental limitations" of an applicant. §12112(b)(5)(A) (emphasis added). Title VII contains no such limitation.

---

1. For brevity's sake, we will in the balance of this opinion usually omit reference to the §2000e(j) "undue hardship" defense to the accommodation requirement, discussing the requirement as though it is absolute.

2. The concurrence mysteriously concludes that it is not the plaintiff's burden to prove failure to accommodate. But of course that *is* the plaintiff's burden, if failure to hire "because of" the plaintiff's "religious practice" is the gravamen of the complaint. Failing to hire for that reason is *synonymous* with refusing to accommodate the religious practice. To accuse the employer of the one is to accuse him of the other. If he is willing to "accommodate" — which means nothing more than allowing the plaintiff to engage in her religious practice despite the employer's normal rules to the contrary — adverse action "because of" the religious practice is not shown. "The clause that begins with the word 'unless,'" as the concurrence describes it, "has no function except to place upon the employer the burden of establishing an "undue hardship" defense. The concurrence provides no example, not even an unrealistic hypothetical one, of a claim of failure to hire because of religious practice that does not say the employer refused to permit ("failed to accommodate") the religious practice. In the nature of things, there cannot be one.

Instead, the intentional discrimination provision prohibits certain *motives*, regardless of the state of the actor's knowledge. Motive and knowledge are separate concepts. An employer who has actual knowledge of the need for an accommodation does not violate Title VII by refusing to hire an applicant if avoiding that accommodation is not his *motive*. Conversely, an employer who acts with the motive of avoiding accommodation may violate Title VII even if he has no more than an unsubstantiated suspicion that accommodation would be needed.

Thus, the rule for disparate-treatment claims based on a failure to accommodate a religious practice is straightforward: An employer may not make an applicant's religious practice, confirmed or otherwise, a factor in employment decisions. For example, suppose that an employer thinks (though he does not know for certain) that a job applicant may be an orthodox Jew who will observe the Sabbath, and thus be unable to work on Saturdays. If the applicant actually requires an accommodation of that religious practice, and the employer's desire to avoid the prospective accommodation is a motivating factor in his decision, the employer violates Title VII.

Abercrombie urges this Court to adopt the Tenth Circuit's rule "allocat[ing] the burden of raising a religious conflict." This would require the employer to have actual knowledge of a conflict between an applicant's religious practice and a work rule. The problem with this approach is the one that inheres in most incorrect interpretations of statutes: It asks us to add words to the law to produce what is thought to be a desirable result. That is Congress's province. We construe Title VII's silence as exactly that: silence. Its disparate-treatment provision prohibits actions taken with the *motive* of avoiding the need for accommodating a religious practice. A request for accommodation, or the employer's certainty that the practice exists, may make it easier to infer motive, but is not a necessary condition of liability.[3]

Abercrombie argues in the alternative that a claim based on a failure to accommodate an applicant's religious practice must be raised as a disparate-impact claim, not a disparate-treatment claim. We think not. That might have been true if Congress had limited the meaning of "religion" in Title VII to religious *belief*—so that discriminating against a particular religious *practice* would not be disparate treatment though it might have disparate impact. In fact, however, Congress defined "religion," for Title VII's purposes, as "includ[ing] all aspects of religious observance and practice, as well as belief." 42 U.S.C. §2000e(j). Thus, religious practice is one of the protected characteristics that cannot be accorded disparate treatment and must be accommodated.

---

3. While a knowledge requirement cannot be added to the motive requirement, it is arguable that the motive requirement itself is not met unless the employer at least suspects that the practice in question is a religious practice—*i.e.*, that he cannot discriminate "because of" a "religious practice" unless he knows or suspects it to be a religious practice. That issue is not presented in this case, since Abercrombie knew—or at least suspected—that the scarf was worn for religious reasons. The question has therefore not been discussed by either side, in brief or oral argument. It seems to us inappropriate to resolve this unargued point by way of dictum, as the concurrence would do.

Nor does the statute limit disparate-treatment claims to only those employer policies that treat religious practices less favorably than similar secular practices. Abercrombie's argument that a neutral policy cannot constitute "intentional discrimination" may make sense in other contexts. But Title VII does not demand mere neutrality with regard to religious practices — that they be treated no worse than other practices. Rather, it gives them favored treatment, affirmatively obligating employers not "to fail or refuse to hire or discharge any individual . . . because of such individual's" "religious observance and practice." An employer is surely entitled to have, for example, a no-headwear policy as an ordinary matter. But when an applicant requires an accommodation as an "aspec[t] of religious . . . practice," it is no response that the subsequent "fail[ure] . . . to hire" was due to an otherwise-neutral policy. Title VII requires otherwise-neutral policies to give way to the need for an accommodation. . . .

JUSTICE ALITO, concurring in the judgment.

This case requires us to interpret a provision of Title VII of the Civil Rights Act of 1964 that prohibits an employer from taking an adverse employment action (refusal to hire, discharge, etc.) "against any individual . . . because of such individual's . . . religion." 42 U.S.C. §2000e-2(a). Another provision states that the term "religion" "includes all aspects of religious observance and practice, as well as belief, unless an employer demonstrates that he is unable to reasonably accommodate to an employee's or prospective employee's religious observance or practice without undue hardship on the conduct of the employer's business." §2000e(j). When these two provisions are put together, the following rule (expressed in somewhat simplified terms) results: An employer may not take an adverse employment action against an applicant or employee because of any aspect of that individual's religious observance or practice unless the employer demonstrates that it is unable to reasonably accommodate that observance or practice without undue hardship.

[The concurrence rejected the Tenth Circuit's requirement that applicants must inform employers of their religious practices that conflict with a work requirement and their need for a reasonable accommodation for them. While it interpreted the statute] to require proof that Abercrombie knew that Elauf wore the headscarf for a religious reason, the evidence of Abercrombie's knowledge is sufficient to defeat summary judgment.

The opinion of the Court states that "§2000e–2(a)(1) does not impose a knowledge requirement," but then reserves decision on the question whether it is a condition of liability that the employer know or suspect that the practice he refuses to accommodate is a religious practice, n. 3, but in my view, the answer to this question, which may arise on remand, is obvious. I would hold that an employer cannot be held liable for taking an adverse action because of an employee's religious practice unless the employer knows that the employee engages in the practice for a religious reason. If §2000e–2(a)(1) really "does not impose a knowledge requirement," it would be irrelevant in this case whether Abercrombie had any inkling that Elauf is a Muslim or that she wore the headscarf for a religious reason. That would be very strange.

The scarves that Elauf wore were not articles of clothing that were designed or marketed specifically for Muslim women. Instead, she generally purchased her scarves at ordinary clothing stores. In this case, the Abercrombie employee who interviewed Elauf had seen her wearing scarves on other occasions, and for reasons that the record does not make clear, came to the (correct) conclusion that she is a Muslim. But suppose that the interviewer in this case had never seen Elauf before. Suppose that the interviewer thought Elauf was wearing the scarf for a secular reason. Suppose that nothing else about Elauf made the interviewer even suspect that she was a Muslim or that she was wearing the scarf for a religious reason. If "§2000e–2(a)(1) does not impose a knowledge requirement," Abercrombie would still be liable. The EEOC, which sued on Elauf's behalf, does not adopt that interpretation, and it is surely wrong.

The statutory text does not compel such a strange result. It is entirely reasonable to understand the prohibition against an employer's taking an adverse action because of a religious practice to mean that an employer may not take an adverse action because of a practice that the employer knows to be religious. . . . This interpretation makes sense of the statutory provisions. Those provisions prohibit intentional discrimination, which is blameworthy conduct, but if there is no knowledge requirement, an employer could be held liable without fault. The prohibition of discrimination because of religious practices is meant to force employers to consider whether those practices can be accommodated without undue hardship. See §2000e(j). But the "no-knowledge" interpretation would deprive employers of that opportunity. For these reasons, an employer cannot be liable for taking adverse action because of a religious practice if the employer does not know that the practice is religious.

A plaintiff need not show, however, that the employer took the adverse action because of the religious nature of the practice. Cf. (Thomas, J., concurring in part and dissenting in part). Suppose, for example, that an employer rejected all applicants who refuse to work on Saturday, whether for religious or nonreligious reasons. Applicants whose refusal to work on Saturday was known by the employer to be based on religion will have been rejected because of a religious practice.

This conclusion follows from the reasonable accommodation requirement imposed by §2000e(j). If neutral work rules (e.g., every employee must work on Saturday, no employee may wear any head covering) precluded liability, there would be no need to provide that defense, which allows an employer to escape liability for refusing to make an exception to a neutral work rule if doing so would impose an undue hardship.

This brings me to a final point. Under the relevant statutory provisions, an employer's failure to make a reasonable accommodation is not an element that the plaintiff must prove. I am therefore concerned about the Court's statement that it "*is* the plaintiff's burden [to prove failure to accommodate]." n. 2. This blatantly contradicts the language of the statutes. As I noted at the beginning, when §2000e–2(a) and §2000e(j) are combined, this is the result:

It shall be an unlawful employment practice for an employer . . . to fail or refuse to hire . . . any individual . . . because of [any aspect of] such individual's . . . religious . . . practice . . . *unless an employer demonstrates that he is unable to reasonably accommodate to [the] employee's or prospective employee's religious . . . practice . . . without undue hardship on the conduct of the employer's business.*" (Emphasis added.)

The clause that begins with the term "unless" unmistakably sets out an employer defense. If an employer chooses to assert that defense, it bears both the burden of production and the burden of persuasion. A plaintiff, on the other hand, must prove the elements set out prior to the "unless" clause, but that portion of the rule makes no mention of accommodation. Thus, a plaintiff need not plead or prove that the employer wished to avoid making an accommodation or could have done so without undue hardship. If a plaintiff shows that the employer took an adverse employment action because of a religious observance or practice, it is then up to the employer to plead and prove the defense. The Court's statement subverts the statutory text, and in close cases, the Court's reallocation of the burden of persuasion may be decisive.

JUSTICE THOMAS, concurring in part and dissenting in part.

I agree with the Court that there are two — and only two — causes of action under Title VII of the Civil Rights Act of 1964 as understood by our precedents: a disparate-treatment (or intentional-discrimination) claim and a disparate-impact claim. Our agreement ends there. Unlike the majority, I adhere to what I had thought before today was an undisputed proposition: Mere application of a neutral policy cannot constitute "intentional discrimination." Because the Equal Employment Opportunity Commission (EEOC) can prevail here only if Abercrombie engaged in intentional discrimination, and because Abercrombie's application of its neutral Look Policy does not meet that description, I would affirm the judgment of the Tenth Circuit.

I . . .

I would hold that Abercrombie's conduct did not constitute "intentional discrimination." Abercrombie refused to create an exception to its neutral Look Policy for Samantha Elauf's religious practice of wearing a headscarf. In doing so, it did not treat religious practices less favorably than similar secular practices, but instead remained neutral with regard to religious practices. To be sure, the *effects* of Abercrombie's neutral Look Policy, absent an accommodation, fall more harshly on those who wear headscarves as an aspect of their faith. But that is a classic case of an alleged disparate impact. It is not what we have previously understood to be a case of disparate treatment because Elauf received the *same* treatment from Abercrombie as any other applicant who appeared unable to comply with the company's Look Policy. Because I cannot classify Abercrombie's conduct as "intentional discrimination," I would affirm.

II

A

. . . [T]he majority expands the meaning of "intentional discrimination" to include a refusal to give a religious applicant "favored treatment." But contrary to the majority's assumption, this novel theory of discrimination is not commanded by the relevant statutory text.

Title VII makes it illegal for an employer "to fail or refuse to hire . . . any individual . . . because of such individual's . . . religion." §2000e-2(a)(1). And as used in Title VII, "[t]he term 'religion' includes all aspects of religious observance and practice, as well as belief, unless an employer demonstrates that he is unable to reasonably accommodate to an employee's or prospective employee's religious observance or practice without undue hardship on the conduct of the employer's business." §2000e(j). With this gloss on the definition of "religion" in §2000e-2(a) (1), the majority concludes that an employer may violate Title VII if he "refuse[s] to hire . . . any individual . . . because of such individual's . . . religious . . . practice" (unless he has an "undue hardship" defense).

But inserting the statutory definition of religion into §2000e-2(a) does not answer the question whether Abercrombie's refusal to hire Elauf was "because of her religious practice." At first glance, the phrase "because of such individual's religious practice" could mean one of two things. Under one reading, it could prohibit taking an action because of the religious nature of an employee's particular practice. Under the alternative reading, it could prohibit taking an action because of an employee's practice that *happens* to be religious.

The distinction is perhaps best understood by example. Suppose an employer with a neutral grooming policy forbidding facial hair refuses to hire a Muslim who wears a beard for religious reasons. Assuming the employer applied the neutral grooming policy to all applicants, the motivation behind the refusal to hire the Muslim applicant would not be the religious nature of his beard, but its existence. Under the first reading, then, the Muslim applicant would lack an intentional-discrimination claim, as he was not refused employment "because of" the religious nature of his practice. But under the second reading, he would have such a claim, as he was refused employment "because of" a practice that happens to be religious in nature.

One problem with the second, more expansive reading is that it would punish employers who have no discriminatory motive. If the phrase "because of such individual's religious practice" sweeps in any case in which an employer takes an adverse action because of a practice that happens to be religious in nature, an employer who had no idea that a particular practice was religious would be penalized. That strict-liability view is plainly at odds with the concept of intentional discrimination. Surprisingly, the majority leaves the door open to this strict-liability theory, reserving the question whether an employer who does not even "suspec[t]" that the practice in question is a religious practice" can nonetheless be punished for *intentional* discrimination.

For purposes of today's decision, however, the majority opts for a compromise, albeit one that lacks a foothold in the text and fares no better under our precedents. The majority construes §2000e-2(a)(1) to punish employers who refuse to accommodate applicants under neutral policies when they act "with the motive of avoiding accommodation." But an employer who is aware that strictly applying a neutral policy will have an adverse effect on a religious group, and applies the policy anyway, is not engaged in intentional discrimination, at least as that term has traditionally been understood. As the Court explained many decades ago, "'Discriminatory purpose'"—*i.e.*, the purpose necessary for a claim of intentional discrimination—demands "more than . . . awareness of consequences. It implies that the decisionmaker . . . selected or reaffirmed a particular course of action at least in part 'because of,' not merely 'in spite of,' its adverse effects upon an identifiable group." *Personnel Administrator of Mass.* v. *Feeney* [reproduced at p. 146].

I do not dispute that a refusal to accommodate can, in some circumstances, constitute intentional discrimination. If an employer declines to accommodate a particular religious practice, yet accommodates a similar secular (or other denominational) practice, then that may be proof that he has "treated a particular person less favorably than others because of [a religious practice]."*Ricci*; see also, *e.g.*, *Dixon* v. *Hallmark Cos.*, 627 F. 3d 849, 853 (CA11 2010) (addressing a policy forbidding display of "religious items" in management offices). But merely refusing to create an exception to a neutral policy for a religious practice cannot be described as treating a particular applicant "less favorably than others." The majority itself appears to recognize that its construction requires something more than equal treatment. ("Title VII does not demand mere neutrality with regard to religious practices," but instead "gives them favored treatment"). But equal treatment is not disparate treatment, and that basic principle should have disposed of this case.

B

The majority's novel theory of intentional discrimination is also inconsistent with the history of this area of employment discrimination law. As that history shows, cases arising out of the application of a neutral policy absent religious accommodations have traditionally been understood to involve only disparate-impact liability. . . .

[The dissent argued that the Supreme Court's first accommodation case, *Trans World Airlines, Inc.* v. *Hardison*, 432 U.S. 63 (1977), did not view failure to accommodate as intentional discrimination, and that lower courts] following *Hardison* likewise did not equate a failure to accommodate with intentional discrimination. To the contrary, many lower courts, including the Tenth Circuit below, wrongly assumed that Title VII creates a freestanding failure-to-accommodate claim distinct from either disparate treatment or disparate impact. That assumption appears to have grown out of statements in our cases suggesting that Title VII's definitional provision concerning religion created an independent duty. See, *e.g., Ansonia Bd. of Ed.* v. *Philbrook*, 479 U.S. 60, 63, n. 1 (1986) ("The reasonable accommodation duty was incorporated into the statute, somewhat awkwardly, in the definition of religion"). But in doing so, the lower courts correctly recognized that a failure-to-accommodate claim based on the application of a neutral policy is not a disparate-treatment claim. See, *e.g., Reed* v. *International Union, United Auto, Aerospace and Agricultural Implement Workers of Am.*, 569 F. 3d 576, 579–580 (CA6 2009); *Chalmers* v. *Tulon Co. of Richmond*, 101 F.3d 1012, 1018 (CA4 1996).

At least before we granted a writ of certiorari in this case, the EEOC too understood that merely applying a neutral policy did not automatically constitute intentional discrimination giving rise to a disparate-treatment claim. For example, the Commission explained in a recent compliance manual, "A religious accommodation claim is distinct from a disparate treatment claim, in which the question is whether employees are treated equally." EEOC Compliance Manual §12–IV, p. 46 (2008). Indeed, in asking us to take this case, the EEOC dismissed one of Abercrombie's supporting authorities as "a case addressing intentional discrimination, not religious accommodation." Once we granted certiorari in this case, however, the EEOC altered course and advanced the intentional-discrimination theory now adopted by the majority. The Court should have rejected this eleventh-hour request to expand our understanding of "intentional discrimination" to include merely applying a religion-neutral policy

* * *

The Court today rightly puts to rest the notion that Title VII creates a free-standing religious-accommodation claim, but creates in its stead an entirely new form of liability: the disparate-treatment-based-on-equal-treatment claim. Because I do not think that Congress' 1972 redefinition of "religion" also redefined "intentional discrimination," I would affirm the judgment of the Tenth Circuit. I respectfully dissent from the portions of the majority's decision that take the contrary view.

NOTES

1. *Revealing Religion.* You might not be able to tell from the opinions, but *Abercrombie* in the Tenth Circuit was all about whether an employee should have to ask for an accommodation or a prospective employer should have to ask whether an accommodation was needed. That was because Abercrombie didn't "know," although it suspected, that Elauf's attire was an expression of her religion. The Tenth Circuit majority contended that, unless the employee raised the issue, the employer should not inquire into religious beliefs. Given the result in the case, what would you advise an employer to do where the facts are more ambiguous as to whether a basis for rejection is religion-related? By the way, notice that the ADA deals with the question of employer knowledge by limiting the duty of accommodation to the *known* limitations of the employee, thus addressing the Tenth Circuit's issue in that context by often putting the burden of revealing her disability on the worker.

2. *What Duty to Accommodate?* We haven't yet studied the Americans with Disabilities Act, but you should know that there are three theories of discrimination under that statute—disparate treatment, disparate impact, and failure to reasonably accommodate a disability unless such accommodation poses an undue hardship. Sound familiar? But the *Abercrombie* majority rejects the third theory as a separate cause of action under Title VII for religious discrimination cases: "the 'disparate treatment' (or 'intentional discrimination') provision and the 'disparate impact' provision, are the only causes of action under Title VII." That explains Justice Thomas's dissent: he concurs in the rejection of a "freestanding" accommodation theory, finding that, absent a disparate impact claim, the employer can be liable only for disparate treatment, and Abercrombie treated everyone the same — no headwear was allowed for anyone. But wouldn't a third theory of discrimination – a failure to accommodate claim — be both statutorily based and fill the gap between the disparate treatment and disparate impact theories? Why did no justice support such an approach?

3. *One and the Same.* For the majority, the duty to accommodate is wrapped up in the duty not to intentionally discriminate. Look at footnote 2: "Failing to hire [because of plaintiff's religious practice] is *synonymous* with refusing to accommodate the religious practice. To accuse the employer of the one is to accuse him of the other." Justice Scalia then goes on to lambaste Justice Alito's concurrence for not providing any example, "not even an unrealistic hypothetical one, of a claim of failure to hire because of religious practice that does not say the employer refused to permit ("failed to accommodate") the religious practice. In the nature of things, there cannot be one."

That can't be right, can it? Suppose an employer is revolted by animal sacrifice and for that reason refuses to hire a practitioner of Santeria. The would-be employee requires no accommodation—at least no workplace accommodation. This would seem to be plain vanilla discrimination, unaffected by the accommodation notion. Or maybe the majority believes that hiring an animal-killer whose conduct is religious-based is an accommodation of a policy of not hiring those who kill animals? Plus, of course, where discrimination simpliciter is concerned, the undue hardship defense disappears — if there is a defense, it is bona fide occupational qualification.

But saying that the duty not to discriminate is arguably broader than the duty to reasonably accommodate doesn't invalidate Scalia's point that denying employment in order to avoid the duty to accommodate is discrimination on the basis of religion. But he also makes clear that when the disparate treatment claim is based on a failure to accommodate (or to avoid accommodation), the plaintiff bears the burden of proving the accommodation was reasonable.

4. *The Holding.* Whatever the analysis, the Court's holding is "straightforward" and employee-friendly: "An employer may not make an applicant's religious practice, confirmed or otherwise, a factor in employment decisions." But where does employer knowledge fit in? In other words, what does it mean to "make an applicant's religious practice . . . a factor"? The Court writes: "Abercrombie's primary argument is that an applicant cannot show disparate treatment without first showing that an employer has 'actual knowledge' of the applicant's need for an

accommodation. We disagree. Instead, an applicant need only show that his need for an accommodation was a motivating factor in the employer's decision."

Do you understand how a plaintiff could show a motivating factor without showing actual knowledge? Does the Court's footnote 3 help? The majority doesn't reach the question of whether Abercrombie knew or at least suspected that Elauf's scarf was worn for religious reasons. Notice that Justice Alito's concurrence views any possible liability without employer knowledge as "very strange." Does the majority's opinion suggest that an employer is liable if it applies a neutral work-place rule to reject an applicant with no reason to believe that there is a religious basis to the "issue" the applicant poses? If that's correct, it has to be disparate impact, right? But does it follow there's necessarily an impact from such rules? For example, are most of those who would be excluded by a no-beard rule Muslim?

But the majority also finds that the employer must be *motivated* by the religion (or suspected religion) of the applicant to be liable. How can that be true if it doesn't "know" about that religion? Is this all a convoluted way of saying that "know" has a very low threshold here? After all, the Court writes that an employer who acts on the basis of "no more than an unsubstantiated suspicion" may be liable. Does that in effect put the employer to the choice of inquiring further or not rejecting the applicant for reasons which may have a religious basis? By the way, what happens when an employer takes an adverse action against an employee because of a misperception about her religion? See Dallan F. Flake, *Religious Discrimination Based on Employer Misperception*, 2016 WISC. L. REV. 87.

Whatever the Court meant about knowledge, problems in deciding what constitutes discrimination on the basis of religion remain. A remarkable case is *Nobach v. Woodland Village Nursing Center*, 799 F.3d 374 (5th Cir. 2015), which held that firing an employee for refusing to pray the rosary with a patient did not constitute discrimination on account of religion when there was no evidence that plaintiff ever advised anyone that such prayer was against her religion or that anyone involved in the discharge suspected that her refusal was motivated by a religious belief. One might have thought that the religious basis of the objection was apparent from the act.

5. *Where Did Undue Hardship Go?* Suppose, however, that the accommodation would pose an undue hardship? And, remember, "undue hardship" means only more than de minimis costs under Title VII. Could it be that not hiring Ms. Elauf would be a violation even if Abercrombie had the hardship defense? Maybe the answer is yes: that would at least have given the applicant the opportunity to choose. But if the applicant chose not to comply with a work rule that the employer was not required to change, should the employer be liable? Is this where motivating factor/same decision anyway comes into play — Abercrombie would violate the statute by taking Elauf's religion into account, but not owe her damages because she would never have been employed for failure to follow the Look policy?

6. *Back to Accommodation?* In any event, the majority seems to recognize this — sort of — when it writes that "Title VII does not demand mere neutrality with regard to religious practices. . . . Rather, it gives them favored treatment. . . ." At this point, one might expect the majority to cite the duty of accommodation. Instead, it speaks of "affirmatively obligating employers not 'to fail or refuse to

hire or discharge any individual . . . because of such individual's" "religious observance and practice.'" This is consistent with the Court's theme of no third theory of discrimination, but it creates a special variety of disparate treatment. You might think back to the Court's other effort in this direction in the same term in *Young v. UPS*, reproduced at p. 43 of this Supplement.

7. *Justices Alito's Concurrence.* His proposed rule is that "An employer may not take an adverse employment action against an applicant or employee because of any aspect of that individual's religious observance or practice unless the employer demonstrates that it is unable to reasonably accommodate that observance or practice without undue hardship." How different is that from the majority?

8. *Justice Thomas's Dissent.* The core of the Thomas position is that equal treatment can't violate Title VII's disparate treatment theory. He's not alone in that belief—that's precisely why the ADA creates a separate reasonable accommodation provision and why Title VII requires accommodation for religious practice and observance, even though the *Abercrombie* majority folds that duty into the disparate treatment paradigm. But for Thomas, does Title VII's reasonable accommodation language provide only for disparate impact liability? Why would such a provision be necessary?

Page 413.   Add at end of Note 1, *Central to Religion or Merely Religious?*;

Indeed, sincerity may be critical to whether an activity is found to be "religious" in the first place. *Davis v. Fort Bend Cnty.*, 765 F.3d 480, 486-87 (5th Cir. 2014) (2-1) (the fact that others might view an activity as only a social commitment is irrelevant if the employee sincerely viewed it as religious).

Page 414, delete Note 4; replace with:

4. *Accommodation or Discrimination? Wilson* was analyzed as a failure-to-accommodate case rather than a plain old discrimination case. That seems incorrect in light of *Abercrombie & Fitch*, since only the discrimination theory is available. So suppose the court focused on the discrimination claim: does she prevail because the employer targeted her religious practices? Is the only defense a BFOQ? Or is undue hardship a defense to a discrimination claim, too? In other words, is the employer entitled to raise the accommodation issue—that it could not reasonably accommodate plaintiff's religious beliefs without undue hardship—as a defense to an individual disparate treatment case? In a pre-*Abercrombie* case, *Brown v. Polk County*, 61 F.3d 650 (8th Cir. 1995) (en banc), the plaintiff made a straightforward claim that he was terminated because of his religion. The employer then raised accommodation as a defense: it argued that, because the plaintiff never explicitly asked for accommodation of his religious activities, he could not claim the protections of Title VII. The court seemed to accept this approach. While it held against the defendant on the facts, it did suggest that the employer could prevail

if it could show that any accommodation of the plaintiff's religious expression was an undue hardship. *Id.* at 655.

Page 416, add at end of carryover 7, Too Extreme to Accommodate?

See Dallan F. Flake, *Bearing Burdens: Religious Accommodations That Adversely Affect Coworker Morale*, 76 OHIO ST. L.J. 169, 173 (2015) (harm to employee morale from an accommodation should be accepted as sufficient to prove undue hardship 'without requiring further proof of how lowered morale hurts an employer's business, and allowing an employer to establish undue hardship based on the reasonable likelihood an accommodation will harm morale.")

Page 417, add after *Id.* cite after extract:

See also Ockletree v. Franciscan Health Sys., 317 P.3d 1009 (Wash. 2014) (exemption from the state antidiscrimination law for religious nonprofits was constitutional under both the federal and Washington constitutions).

Page 428, add at end of Note 3, *Who's A Minister?*:

In the wake of *Hosanna Tabor*, the Sixth Circuit in *Cannata v. Catholic Diocese of Austin*, 700 F.3d 169 (5th Cir. 2012), held that, although plaintiff was neither ordained nor formally trained in religion, his role as Music Director for the church's liturgy and his playing the piano at Mass brought him within the ministerial exception. *See also Conlon v. Intervarsity Christian Fellowship/USA*, 777 F.3d 829 (6th Cir. 2015) (a "religious group," although not a "church," could claim the ministerial exception even though not tied to a particular denomination; the exception applies when a formal title and religious function are both present). *But see Kant v. Lexington Theological Seminary*, 26 S.W.3d 587 (Ky. 2014) (holding a Jewish professor at a Christian seminary not to be a minister and thus able to pursue a contract claim for discharge in violation of his tenure contract).

Page 429, add after second sentence of first full paragraph of carryover Note 4, *A Law-Free Zone?*

But see Conlon v. Intervarsity Christian Fellowship/USA, 777 F.3d 829, 836 (6th Cir. 2015) ("The ministerial exception is a structural limitation imposed on the government by the Religion Clauses, a limitation that can never be waived.").

Page 429, add before *Potter* cite in second paragraph of Note 5, *The Religious Freedom Restoration Act*:

Tagore v. United States, 735 F.3d 324, 330-32 (5th Cir. 2013) (under RFRA, while the government has a compelling interest in protecting federal buildings, the claimed need for uniformity of security rules may not satisfy the "least restrictive means" test for strict scrutiny in light of numerous exceptions to the general rule);

Page 429, add at the end of Note 5, *The Religious Freedom Restoration Act*:

In *Burwell v. Hobby Lobby Stores, Inc.*, 134 S. Ct. 2751 (2014), a divided Court held that RFRA barred application of government regulations under the Affordable Care Act that would have required two for-profit corporations to either provide comprehensive health insurance for their workers or, in the alternative, to pay a tax. Comprehensive insurance included contraceptive coverage, which was objectionable on religious grounds to the individuals who controlled the two closely-held corporations subject to the mandate.

The majority opinion, authored by Justice Alito and joined by the Chief Justice and Justices Scalia, Thomas, and Kennedy, found RFRA violated by this application of the regulations. Although there had been considerable question over whether the statute reached corporations in the first place or whether such entities could "exercise religion," the majority found that RFRA protects the religious interests of "persons" who direct closely-held corporations, even if the corporations as such are for profit and not explicitly religious:

> Congress provided protection for [owners of close corporations] by employing a familiar legal fiction: It included corporations within RFRA's definition of "persons." But it is important to keep in mind that the purpose of this fiction is to provide protection for human beings.

Id. at 2768. The fact that the corporations were for-profit did not mean that their owners could not simultaneously pursue their religious beliefs through the corporate form.

Second, the majority had "little trouble" determining that ACA imposed substantial burdens on the plaintiffs. One of the plaintiff companies would have to pay as much as $475 million per year if it offered non-compliant health insurance. *Id.* at 2776. Even assuming the employer chose to pay the $2000 per employee tax rather than provide insurance itself, the burden would be $26 million for the largest corporate plaintiff. *Id.* The majority both denigrated and claimed that it would not reach the argument that this tax would be less than the cost of providing health insurance in the first place. Neither did the majority pause long over the contention that providing required coverage had too "attenuated" a connection to the religious beliefs of the controlling individuals given the reality that any use of the objectionable contraceptives would require the actions of multiple other actors (insurers, doctors, employees):

This argument dodges the question that RFRA presents (whether the HHS mandate imposes a substantial burden on the ability of the objecting parties to conduct business in accordance with their *religious beliefs*) and instead addresses a very different question that the federal courts have no business addressing (whether the religious belief asserted in a RFRA case is reasonable).

Id. at 2778.

Applying the statute's language, the majority assumed, without deciding, that providing health insurance with contraceptive coverage furthered a compelling governmental interest. Nevertheless, the majority held that the ACA scheme violated RFRA by not using the least restrictive means of pursuing that objective. The Court flirted with the idea that government payment for such coverage was itself a viable less restrictive alternative, *id.* at 2780 ("The most straightforward way of doing this would be for the Government to assume the cost of providing the four contraceptives at issue to any women who are unable to obtain them under their health-insurance policies due to their employers' religious objections."), but ultimately found a less dramatic alternative available, one which the government already employed for religious nonprofits:

> Under that accommodation, the organization can self-certify that it opposes providing coverage for particular contraceptive services. If the organization makes such a certification, the organization's insurance issuer or third-party administrator must "[e]xpressly exclude contraceptive coverage from the group health insurance coverage provided in connection with the group health plan" and "[p]rovide separate payments for any contraceptive services required to be covered" without imposing "any cost-sharing requirements . . . on the eligible organization, the group health plan, or plan participants or beneficiaries."

Id. at 2782. HHS had essentially viewed this as a win-win-win for religious nonprofits: no need for payment by religious objectors, contraception without additional cost for female employees, and cost savings for insurance companies since contraception coverage cost less than pregnancy and child birth. For the majority, this possibility, while not necessarily suitable for all RFRA objections, was a less restrictive alternative for close corporations like the plaintiffs whose owners did not wish to be complicit in what they viewed as sinful. *See also Holt v. Hobbs*, 135 S. Ct. 853 (2015) (finding in a RLUIPA suit that a prison's no beard policy was not the least restrictive means to ensure the state's compelling interest in prison security).

The principal dissent authored by Justice Ginsburg, who was joined entirely by Justice Sotomayor and in most part by Justices Breyer and Kagan, parted company with the majority on most points. Most importantly, the dissent viewed RFRA as not reaching the case before the Court. Although for-profit corporations might be "persons" within the meaning of the statute, they could not, as such, exercise religion: "the Court forgets that religious organizations exist to serve a community of believers. For-profit corporations do not fit that bill." *Id.* at 2796.

Given the blurring of the for-profit/nonprofit line, the dissent was very concerned about the potential reach of the majority opinion. Although Justice Alito had thought it "unlikely" that "corporate giants" would be able to assert plausible

RFRA claims, he did not rule out that possibility, *id.* at 2774, and the dissent thought the majority's language "extends to corporations of any size, public or private." *Id.* at 2797. Accordingly, it believed a large number of potential religious objectors would appear raising a great number of claims for "alternatives" under a great number of federal statutes. Citing prior cases, for example, it suggested claims for exemptions from the wage and hour laws and antidiscrimination statutes, *id.* at 2802. The majority, however, explicitly rejected this argument:

> The principal dissent raises the possibility that discrimination in hiring, for example on the basis of race, might be cloaked as religious practice to escape legal sanction. Our decision today provides no such shield. The Government has a compelling interest in providing an equal opportunity to participate in the workforce without regard to race, and prohibitions on racial discrimination are precisely tailored to achieve that critical goal.

Id. at 2783 (cross reference omitted).

Further, it may be that Justice Kennedy will provide another backstop. Although he joined the Alito opinion, thus ensuring a majority, his separate concurrence seemed to stress that the majority's opinion did not require the government to "create an additional program." *Id.* at 2786. Rather, all HHS needed to do was extend the accommodation already provided religious nonprofits to for profit companies with religious objections. That was a very different matter from a situation "in which it is more difficult and expensive to accommodate a governmental program to countless religious claims." *Id.* at 2787.

Hobby Lobby was by no means the end of the dispute concerning the intersection of the Affordable Care Act and RFRA. In *Zubik v. Burwell*, 136 S. Ct. 1557 (2016), the Court sent back a number of cases for reconsideration as to how the objections of religiously-affiliated organizations could be reconciled with the employer notice requirements of the ACA.

E. *National Origin and Alienage Discrimination*

Page 442, add before *Hernandez* cite in Note 2, *National Origin Under Title VII*:

Vill. of Freeport v. Barrella, 814 F.3d 594, 606-07 (2d Cir. 2016) ("Hispanics" constitute a race for purposes of both §1981 and Title VII: "discrimination based on ethnicity, including Hispanicity or lack thereof, constitutes racial discrimination under Title VII"; accordingly, discrimination against an Italian American in favor of a Hispanic is actionable even though both are white).

Page 442, add new paragraph at end of Note 2, *National Origin Discrimination Under Title VII*:

Claims are sometimes made that foreign corporations operating in the United States discriminate against individuals of American national origin. Although there may be treaty-based exceptions allowing this, see Note 11, Exemptions, p. 322, courts have recognized this theory. *See Brown v. Daikin Am.*, 756 F.3d 219 (2d Cir. 2014) (holding that a complaint stated a claim of national origin and race discrimination when plaintiff's employment with a New York-based wholly-owned subsidiary of a Japanese corporation was terminated).

Page 446, add before first *Yuracko* cite in last paragraph:

Zachary A. Kramer, *The New Sex Discrimination*, 63 DUKE L.J. 891, 893 (2014) (arguing that "sex discrimination law has not kept pace with the lived experience of discrimination" since modern sex discrimination targets men and women who do not conform to workplace norms; the appropriate approach to this reality is "religious discrimination law, which offers a dynamic conception of identity and a greater array of different theories of discrimination.");

F. Union Liability

Page 449, add at end of second full paragraph:

See Wells v. Chrysler Group LLC, 559 F. App'x 512 (6th Cir. 2014) (union's duty not to discriminate and its duty of fair representation when predicated on failure to process racial grievances were essentially the same but neither was violated when the union failed to pursue a meritless grievance on behalf of the plaintiff); *Green v. AFT/ Ill. Fed'n of Teachers Local 604*, 740 F.3d 1104 (7th Cir. 2014) (regardless of the absence of any duty of fair representation for state employees, failure of union to process black plaintiff's grievance or when it would have done so were he white would violate Title VII); *Stuart v. Local 727, Int'l Bhd. of Teamsters*, 771 F.3d 1014 (7th Cir. 2014) (a union's failure to refer a woman for employment on the basis of her sex would be actionable under Title VII).

G. Age Discrimination

Page 450, add at end of second full paragraph:

Cf. EEOC v. Baltimore Cnty., 747 F.3d 267 (4th Cir. 2010) (discriminatory for a retirement plan to require two new-hires, each with the same number of years until retirement age, to pay different contributions).

5. Special Problems in Applying Title VII, Section 1981, and the ADEA

Page 451, add before *Kannady* cite in carryover paragraph:

Sadie v. City of Cleveland, 718 F.3d 596, 601 (6th Cir. 2013) (joining other circuits in rejecting interpreting "subterfuge" to "nullify the exemption for the mandatory retirement of police and fire officers. . . . The Act allows state and local governments to terminate police and fire officers on the basis of their age pursuant to mandatory-retirement.");

Page 451, add at end of section 2, Bona Fide Employee Benefit Plans:

See also Fulghum v. Embarq Corp., 785 F.3d 395 (10th Cir. 2015) (reduction of life insurance benefits was based on a reasonable factor other than age when the employer presented unrebutted evidence that the change in employee life insurance benefits was motivated by a desire to reduce costs and bring life insurance benefits in line with those provided by other companies; its reduction of health benefits for Medicare-eligible retirees was permissible in light of an EEOC regulation so providing).

6   *Retaliation*

Page 457, add before *Hatmaker* cite in *Note 1, Broader Protection Under the Participation Clause*:

Benes v. A.B. Data, Ltd., 724 F.3d 752, 753 (7th Cir. 2013) (misconduct during mediation of a discrimination claim is a legitimate reason for discharging an employee; in addition, the threat of discharge for barging into employer's room during EEOC-sponsored mediation of his sex discrimination claim and telling employer to take its proposal and "shove it up your ass" would not deter a reasonable employee from engaging in protected conduct), discussed by Charles A. Sullivan, *Taking Civility Too Far*, Workplace Prof Blog, http://lawprofessors.typepad.com/laborprof_blog/2013/08/taking-civility-too-far.html.

Page 458, add after first sentence of second paragraph of Note 2, *Participation Conduct or Opposition Conduct?*:

See Long v. Ala. Dep't of Human Res., No. 15-10856, 2016 U.S. App. LEXIS 9773, at *31-32 (11th Cir. May 31, 2016) (evidence sufficient to raise an inference of retaliation when the investigation that led to plaintiff's termination began shortly after his deposition and entailed a computer search using terms suggesting hostility for that testimony).

Page 458, add after *Jute* cite in Note 2, *Participation Conduct or Opposition Conduct?*:

See also Rodríguez-Vives v. P.R. Firefighters Corps of P.R., 743 F.3d 278 (1st Cir. 2014) (a prior suit challenging sex discrimination under the Equal Protection Clause constitutes protected activity within the opposition clause of Title VII).

6. Retaliation

Page 458, add a new Note 2A

2A. *Rejecting Sexual Advances as Protected?* Is rejecting a sexual harasser protected conduct? By itself, it is not participation conduct, but the first precedential decision on the subject held it to be protected opposition even if the employee did nothing further in the way of complaint. *EEOC v. New Breed Logistics*, 783 F.3d 1057, 1067 (6th Cir. 2015) ("a demand that a supervisor cease his/her harassing conduct constitutes protected activity covered by Title VII"). *Contra Frank v. Harris County*, 118 F. App'x 799, 804 (5th Cir. 2004).

Page 458, add before *O'Leary* cite in second paragraph of Note 3, *Retaliation and the* Ellerth *Affirmative Defense*:

See Boyer-Liberto v. Fontainebleau Corp., 786 F.3d 264 (4th Cir. 2015) (en banc) ("rather than encourage the early reporting vital to achieving Title VII's goal of avoiding harm, [too strict a standard] deters harassment victims from speaking up by depriving them of their statutory entitlement to protection from retaliation.").

Page 463, add in Note 1, *The Managerial Exception* after Modesitt cite:

Congress, however, has amended the WPA to eliminate such a defense. Whistle-blower Protection Enhancement Act of 2012, Pub. L. No 112-199.

Page 463, add at the end of Note 1, *The Managerial Exception*:

See generally Deborah L. Brake, *Retaliation in the EEO Office*, 50 TULSA L. REV. 1, 2 (2014); Deborah L. Brake, *Tortifying Retaliation: Protected Activity at the Intersection of Fault, Duty, and Causation*, 75 OHIO ST. L. REV. 6 (2014).

However, the manager rule has taken somewhat of a beating in two recent decisions. *See DeMasters v. Carilion Clinic*, 796 F.3d 409, 413 (4th Cir. 2015) (finding that the manager rule "has no place in Title VII jurisprudence"); *Littlejohn v. City of New York*, 795 F.3d 297 (2d Cir. 2015) (while merely reporting or investigating other workers' complaints is not by itself protected activity, an employee is protected, even if her job responsibilities involve investigating complaints of discrimination, when she "actively 'supports' other employees in asserting their Title VII rights or personally 'complains' or is 'critical' about 'discriminatory practices'").

Page 463, add at end of Note 3, *What Counts as Opposing?*:

And what about not signing a release? In *EEOC v. Allstate Ins. Co.*, 778 F.3d 444, 451-53 (3d Cir. 2015), the employer required terminated employees to release discrimination claims in order to be considered for engagement as independent contractors. The court held such refusal was not opposition conduct since employees might refuse to sign to preserve any number of claims, not merely discrimination claims.

Page 463, add new Note 4:

4. *Reasonable Belief.* We have seen that a reasonable belief in the illegality of the conduct opposed is generally required under the opposition clause. After *Crawford*, is that still true when an employee answers questions in an internal investigation? *See EEOC v. Rite Way Serv.*, 819 F.3d. 235(5th Cir. 2016) (even a plaintiff who is merely acting as a third party witness to questions about possible discrimination must have a reasonable belief in the conduct's illegality to be protected from retaliation). If not, is *Crawford's* protection nearly as broad as might first appear? *See generally* Deborah L. Brake, *Retaliation in an EEO World*, 89 INDIANA L.J. 115 (2014) (by deciding *Crawford* under the opposition clause rather than the participation clause, the Court left witnesses still subject to the requirement that their answers reflect a reasonable belief in illegality).

Page 467, add at end of Note 2, *Restricting Standing to Those Within the Zone of Interests*:

In *Underwood v. Dep't of Fin. Servs. Fla.*, 518 F. App'x 637 (11th Cir. 2013), the court recognized that *Thompson* bars employers from retaliating against such employees by firing someone with whom the employee has a close personal relationship, but nevertheless held that Title VII does not make it unlawful for an employer to retaliate against one of its own employees, who did not engage in protected conduct, because that employee's spouse, who was a non-employee, filed a discrimination charge against a different employer.

Page 469, add at end of carryover paragraph:

Ernest F. Lidge, III, *The Necessity of Expanding Protection from Retaliation for Employees Who Complain About Hostile Environment Harassment*, 53 U. LOUISVILLE L. REV. 39 (2014) Matthew W. Green Jr., *What's So Reasonable About Reasonableness? Rejecting a Case Law-Centered Approach to Title VII's Reasonable Belief Doctrine*, 62 KAN. L. REV. 759, 763-64 (2014).

Page 469, add at the end of second full paragraph:

See also Cooper v. N.Y. State Dep't of Labor, 819 F.3d 678, 681 (2d Cir. 2016) (The conduct opposed, "amendment of internal procedures in a manner that would permit political considerations to influence the evaluation of discrimination claims," is neither an unlawful employment practice under Title VII nor could be reasonably believed to be one).

Page 469, add at end of last full paragraph:

Clark v. Cache Valley Elec. Co., 573 F. App'x 693 (10th Cir. 2014) (although a human resources complaint included conclusory statements about discrimination, nothing supported a reasonable, good faith belief in gender discrimination as opposed to favoritism towards a female employee resulting from her sexual relationship with a supervisor); *Kelly v. Howard I. Shapiro & Assocs. Consulting Eng'rs, P.C.*, 716 F.3d 10 (2d Cir. 2013) (plaintiff's complaints about "paramour preference" did not suggest that she was being discriminated against because of her sex despite the accusations of "sexual favoritism" and the continual repetition of the words "discrimination" and "harassment").

Page 470, add at end of carryover paragraph:

Deborah L. Brake, *Retaliation in an EEO World*, 89 INDIANA L.J. 115 (2014) (the confluence of broader nondiscrimination corporate policies with the requirement that complaints be aimed at what is reasonably viewed to be illegal discrimination puts employees at risk when they reasonably believe there is a violation of a policy but do not reasonably believe there is a violation of a statute, including complaints about harassment not reasonably believed to be severe or pervasive; lack of affirmative action; and discrimination against unprotected groups, such as gays).

Page 470, add at end of second full paragraph:

An interesting recent example of the reach of participation protection is *Greengrass v. Int'l Monetary Sys., Ltd.*, 776 F.3d 481 (7th Cir. 2015), which held that an employer's naming of a female employee's charge to the EEOC in a required SEC filing could be actionable retaliation if done with the requisite intent to retaliate. While identification of those bringing claims is mandatory when the claim would be material to investors, there was reason to believe that the employer identified her with intent to retaliate because of it inconsistent treatment of similar matters in its SEC filings. *See Protected Conduct vs. Protected Conduct?*, posting of Charles A. Sullivan to Workplace Prof, http://lawprofessors.typepad.com/laborprof_blog/2015/02/protected-conduct-vs-protected-conduct.html.

Page 475, complete Prenkert citation:

91 N.C. L. REV. 889 (2013).

Page 483, add before see generally cite in Note 4, *Employer Liability:*

See Spencer v. Schmidt Elec. Co., 576 F. App'x 442, 455 (5th Cir. 2014) ("It would violate common law agency principles to say that Schmidt should be held liable for the conduct of foremen, who were not empowered by Schmidt to represent the company's interests on site. Because [the foremen's] actions cannot be attributed to the employer, Schmidt cannot be held liable under Title VII for the intimidation, even if it was in retaliation for Spencer's engaging in protected activity.").

Page 483, add before *Bhatti* **cite in Note 5,** *What Counts as Materially Adverse?:*

Brandon v. Sage Corp., 808 F.3d 266, 271 (5th Cir. 2015) (while not rejecting "the possibility that a realistic, drastic pay cut threat might deter someone from supporting a discrimination charge," such a threat by someone outside plaintiff's chain of command made to "a reasonably high placed" employee who was familiar with the organization would not have dissuaded that person from engaging in protected activity); *Wheat v. Fla. Parish Juvenile Justice Comm'n*, 811 F.3d 702 (5th Cir. 2016) (submissions that show correctional officer was assigned to janitorial duties does not, without further detail about those duties, suffice to establish a triable issue of a materially adverse action); *AuBuchon v. Geithner*, 743 F.3d 638, 644-45 (8th Cir. 2014) (no unlawful retaliation when sexual harassment allegations against plaintiff never resulted in harm and other alleged acts constituted only petty slights or minor annoyances);

Page 483, add before *Benuzzi* **cite in Note 5,** *What Counts as Materially Adverse?:*

Planadeball v. Wyndham Vacation Resorts, Inc., 793 F.3d 169 (1st Cir. 2015) ("a reasonable juror could thus infer that these multiple, consecutive threats. . . . could dissuade a reasonable employee from making or supporting a charge of discrimination."); *Laster v. City of Kalamazoo*, 746 F.3d 714, 732 (6th Cir. 2014) ("Facing heightened scrutiny, receiving frequent reprimands for breaking selectively enforced policies, being disciplined more harshly than similarly situated peers, and forced to attend a pre-termination hearing based on unfounded allegations of wrongdoing might well have dissuaded a reasonable worker from making or supporting a charge of discrimination.");

Page 484, add before Lidge cite in carryover Note 5, *What Counts as Materially Adverse?:*

Sandra F. Sperino, *Retaliation and the Reasonable Person*, 67 FLA. L. REV. 2031 (2016) (challenging lower courts' application of the *Burlington Northern* standard for adverse employment actions both on theoretical grounds and in view of an empirical study revealing that subjects viewed various employer responses as more likely to discourage reporting than do many court decisions);

Page 485, delete entire section F, Causation; replace with the following:

F. Causation

University of Texas Southwestern Medical Center v. Nassar
133 S. Ct. 2517 (2013)

Justice KENNEDY delivered the opinion of the Court.

. . . Title VII is central to the federal policy of prohibiting wrongful discrimination in the Nation's workplaces and in all sectors of economic endeavor. This opinion discusses the causation rules for two categories of wrongful employer conduct prohibited by Title VII. The first type is called, for purposes of this opinion, status-based discrimination. The term is used here to refer to basic workplace protection such as prohibitions against employer discrimination on the basis of race, color, religion, sex, or national origin, in hiring, firing, salary structure, promotion and the like. The second type of conduct is employer retaliation on account of an employee having opposed, complained of, or sought remedies for, unlawful workplace discrimination.

An employee who alleges status-based discrimination under Title VII need not show that the causal link between injury and wrong is so close that the injury would not have occurred but for the act. So-called but-for causation is not the test. It suffices instead to show that the motive to discriminate was one of the employer's motives, even if the employer also had other, lawful motives that were causative in the employer's decision. This principle is the result of an earlier case from this Court, *Price Waterhouse v. Hopkins* [reproduced at p. 68] and an ensuing statutory amendment by Congress that codified in part and abrogated in part the holding in *Price Waterhouse*, see §§2000e-2(m), 2000e-5(g)(2)(B). The question the Court must answer here is whether that lessened causation standard is applicable to claims of unlawful employer retaliation under §2 000e-3(a).

[The Court then cited *Gross v. FBL Financial Services, Inc.*, reproduced at p. 91, as concluding] that the ADEA requires proof that the prohibited criterion was the but-for cause of the prohibited conduct. The holding and analysis of that decision are instructive here.

I

Petitioner, the University of Texas Southwestern Medical Center (University), is an academic institution within the University of Texas system. The University specializes in medical education for aspiring physicians, health professionals, and scientists. Over the years, the University has affiliated itself with a number of healthcare facilities including, as relevant in this case, Parkland Memorial Hospital (Hospital). As provided in its affiliation agreement with the University, the Hospital permits the University's students to gain clinical experience working in its facilities. The agreement also requires the Hospital to offer empty staff physician posts to the University's faculty members, and, accordingly, most of the staff physician positions at the Hospital are filled by those faculty members.

Respondent is a medical doctor of Middle Eastern descent who specializes in internal medicine and infectious diseases. In 1995, he was hired to work both as a member of the University's faculty and a staff physician at the Hospital. He left both positions in 1998 for additional medical education and then returned in 2001 as an assistant professor at the University and, once again, as a physician at the Hospital.

In 2004, Dr. Beth Levine was hired as the University's Chief of Infectious Disease Medicine. In that position Levine became respondent's ultimate (though not direct) superior. Respondent alleged that Levine was biased against him on account of his religion and ethnic heritage, a bias manifested by undeserved scrutiny of his billing practices and productivity, as well as comments that "'Middle Easterners are lazy.'" On different occasions during his employment, respondent met with Dr. Gregory Fitz, the University's Chair of Internal Medicine and Levine's supervisor, to complain about Levine's alleged harassment. Despite obtaining a promotion with Levine's assistance in 2006, respondent continued to believe that she was biased against him. So he tried to arrange to continue working at the Hospital without also being on the University's faculty. After preliminary negotiations with the Hospital suggested this might be possible, respondent resigned his teaching post in July 2006 and sent a letter to Dr. Fitz (among others), in which he stated that the reason for his departure was harassment by Levine. That harassment, he asserted, "'stems from . . . religious, racial and cultural bias against Arabs and Muslims.'" After reading that letter, Dr. Fitz expressed consternation at respondent's accusations, saying that Levine had been "publicly humiliated by th[e] letter" and that it was "very important that she be publicly exonerated."

Meanwhile, the Hospital had offered respondent a job as a staff physician, as it had indicated it would. On learning of that offer, Dr. Fitz protested to the Hospital, asserting that the offer was inconsistent with the affiliation agreement's requirement that all staff physicians also be members of the University faculty. The Hospital then withdrew its offer.

[Nassar sued claiming both status-based discrimination claim and retaliation and won a jury verdict on both claims. The Fifth Circuit vacated his discrimination verdict because of insufficient evidence to support constructive discharge, but it affirmed as to the finding of retaliation for Dr. Fitz's efforts to prevent the University from hiring him because retaliation claims] require only a showing that retaliation was a motivating factor for the adverse employment action, rather than its but-for cause. It further held that the evidence supported a finding that Dr. Fitz was motivated, at least in part, to retaliate against respondent for his complaints against Levine. . . .

II

A

This case requires the Court to define the proper standard of causation for Title VII retaliation claims. Causation in fact — i.e., proof that the defendant's conduct did in fact cause the plaintiff's injury — is a standard requirement of any tort claim, see Restatement of Torts §9 (1934) (definition of "legal cause"); §431, Comment a (same); §279, and Comment c (intentional infliction of physical harm); §280 (other intentional torts); §281(c) (negligence). This includes federal statutory claims of workplace discrimination. *Hazen Paper Co. v. Biggins* [reproduced at p.11].

In the usual course, this standard requires the plaintiff to show "that the harm would not have occurred" in the absence of — that is, but for — the defendant's conduct. Restatement of Torts §431, Comment a (negligence); §432(1), and Comment a (same); see §279, and Comment c (intentional infliction of bodily harm); §280 (other intentional torts); Restatement (Third) of Torts: Liability for Physical and Emotional Harm §27, and Comment b (2010) (noting the existence of an exception for cases where an injured party can prove the existence of multiple, independently sufficient factual causes, but observing that "cases invoking the concept are rare"). See also Restatement (Second) of Torts §432(1) (1963 and 1964) (negligence claims); §870, Comment l (intentional injury to another); cf. §435A, and Comment a (legal cause for intentional harm). It is thus textbook tort law that an action "is not regarded as a cause of an event if the particular event would have occurred without it." W. Keeton, D. Dobbs, R. Keeton & D. Owen, Prosser and Keeton on Law of Torts 265 (5th ed. 1984). This, then, is the background against which Congress legislated in enacting Title VII, and these are the default rules it is presumed to have incorporated, absent an indication to the contrary in the statute itself.

B

Since the statute's passage in 1964, it has prohibited employers from discriminating against their employees on any of seven specified criteria. Five of them — race, color, religion, sex, and national origin — are personal characteristics and are set forth in §2000e-2. (As noted at the outset, discrimination based on these five characteristics is called status-based discrimination in this opinion.) And then there is a point of great import for this case: The two remaining categories of wrongful employer conduct — the employee's opposition to employment discrimination, and the employee's submission of or support for a complaint that alleges employment discrimination — are not wrongs based on personal traits but rather types of protected employee conduct. These latter two categories are covered by a separate, subsequent section of Title VII, §2000e-3(a).

[The Court traced the history of §2000e-2(m) in the 1991 Civil Rights Act, which "codified the burden-shifting and lessened-causation framework of *Price Waterhouse* in part but also rejected it to a substantial degree." It described this provision as "a lessened causation standard." Similarly, it quoted §2000e-5(g)(2) as allowing an employer to limit remedies by showing that it "would have taken the same action in the absence of the impermissible motivating factor."]

So, in short, the 1991 Act substituted a new burden-shifting framework for the one endorsed by *Price Waterhouse*. Under that new regime, a plaintiff could obtain declaratory relief, attorney's fees and costs, and some forms of injunctive relief based solely on proof that race, color, religion, sex, or nationality was a motivating factor in the employment action; but the employer's proof that it would still have taken the same employment action would save it from monetary damages and a reinstatement order. See *Gross*.

[The Court then reviewed its decision in *Gross*, "[c]oncentrating first and foremost" on that opinion's reading of "*because of*" to indicate "but-for" causation. *Gross* declined to adopt the interpretation endorsed by the plurality and concurring opinions in *Price Waterhouse*. It] holds two insights for the present case. The first is textual and concerns the proper interpretation of the term "because" as it relates to the principles of causation underlying both §623(a) and §2000e-3(a). The second is the significance of Congress' structural choices in both Title VII itself and the law's 1991 amendments. These principles do not decide the present case but do inform its analysis, for the issues possess significant parallels.

III

A

[§704(a)], like the statute at issue in *Gross*, makes it unlawful for an employer to take adverse employment action against an employee "because" of certain criteria.

Given the lack of any meaningful textual difference between the text in this statute and the one in *Gross*, the proper conclusion here, as in *Gross*, is that Title VII retaliation claims require proof that the desire to retaliate was the but-for cause of the challenged employment action.

The principal counterargument offered by respondent and the United States relies on their different understanding of the motivating-factor section, which—on its face—applies only to status discrimination, discrimination on the basis of race, color, religion, sex, and national origin. In substance, they contend that: (1) retaliation is defined by the statute to be an unlawful employment practice; (2) §2000e-2(m) allows unlawful employment practices to be proved based on a showing that race, color, religion, sex, or national origin was a motivating factor for—and not necessarily the but-for factor in—the challenged employment action; and

(3) the Court has, as a matter of course, held that "retaliation for complaining about race discrimination is 'discrimination based on race.'"

There are three main flaws in this reading of §2000e-2(m). The first is that it is inconsistent with the provision's plain language. It must be acknowledged that because Title VII defines "unlawful employment practice" to include retaliation, the question presented by this case would be different if §2000e-2(m) extended its coverage to all unlawful employment practices. As actually written, however, the text of the motivating-factor provision, while it begins by referring to "unlawful employment practices," then proceeds to address only five of the seven prohibited discriminatory actions—actions based on the employee's status, i.e., race, color, religion, sex, and national origin. This indicates Congress' intent to confine that provision's coverage to only those types of employment practices. The text of §2000e-2(m) says nothing about retaliation claims. Given this clear language, it would be improper to conclude that what Congress omitted from the statute is nevertheless within its scope.

The second problem with this reading is its inconsistency with the design and structure of the statute as a whole. See *Gross*. Just as Congress' choice of words is presumed to be deliberate, so too are its structural choices. When Congress wrote the motivating-factor provision in 1991, it chose to insert it as a subsection within §2000e-2, which contains Title VII's ban on status-based discrimination, and says nothing about retaliation. . . .

[Further, another portion of the 1991 Act expressly references all unlawful employment actions, suggesting deliberateness in omitting retaliation claims from §2000e-2(m).]

The third problem with respondent's and the Government's reading of the motivating-factor standard is in its submission that this Court's decisions interpreting federal antidiscrimination law have, as a general matter, treated bans on status-based discrimination as also prohibiting retaliation. In support of this proposition, both respondent and the United States rely upon decisions in which this Court has "read [a] broadly worded civil rights statute . . . as including an antiretaliation remedy." *CBOCS West, Inc. v. Humphries*, 553 U.S. 442, 452-453 (2008). In *CBOCS*, for example, the Court held that 42 U.S.C. §1981—which declares that all persons "shall have the same right . . . to make and enforce contracts . . . as is enjoyed by white citizens"—prohibits not only racial discrimination but also retaliation against those who oppose it. And in *Gómez-Pérez v. Potter*, 553 U.S. 474 (2008), the Court likewise read a bar on retaliation into the broad wording of the federal-employee provisions of the ADEA. See also *Jackson v. Birmingham Bd. of Ed.*, 544 U.S. 167, 173, 179 (2005) (20 U.S.C. §1681(a) (Title IX)); *Sullivan v. Little Hunting Park, Inc.*, 396 U.S. 229, 235, n. 3, 237 (1969) (42 U.S.C. §1982).

These decisions are not controlling here. It is true these cases do state the general proposition that Congress' enactment of a broadly phrased antidiscrimination statute may signal a concomitant intent to ban retaliation against individuals who oppose that discrimination, even where the statute does not refer to retaliation in so many words. What those cases do not support, however, is the quite different rule that every reference to race, color, creed, sex, or nationality in an antidiscrimination statute is to be treated as a synonym for "retaliation." For one thing, §2000e-2(m) is not itself a substantive bar on discrimination. Rather, it is a rule that establishes the causation standard for proving a violation defined elsewhere in Title VII. The cases cited by respondent and the Government do not address rules of this sort, and those precedents are of limited relevance here.

The approach respondent and the Government suggest is inappropriate in the context of a statute as precise, complex, and exhaustive as Title VII. As noted, the laws at issue in *CBOCS*, *Jackson*, and *Gómez-Pérez* were broad, general bars on discrimination. In interpreting them the Court concluded that by using capacious language Congress expressed the intent to bar retaliation in addition to status-based discrimination. See *Gómez-Pérez*. In other words, when Congress' treatment of the subject of prohibited discrimination was both broad and brief, its omission of any specific discussion of retaliation was unremarkable.

If Title VII had likewise been phrased in broad and general terms, respondent's argument might have more force. But that is not how Title VII was written, which makes it incorrect to infer that Congress meant anything other than what the text does say on the subject of retaliation. . . .

This fundamental difference in statutory structure renders inapposite decisions which treated retaliation as an implicit corollary of status-based discrimination.

Text may not be divorced from context. In light of Congress' special care in drawing so precise a statutory scheme, it would be improper to indulge respondent's suggestion that Congress meant to incorporate the default rules that apply only when Congress writes a broad and undifferentiated statute.

[The Court found confirmation of its holding in Congress' approach to the ADA, which included an express antiretaliation provision despite "seven paragraphs of detailed description of the practices that would constitute the prohibited discrimination." That law,] "which speaks in clear and direct terms to the question of retaliation, rebuts the claim that Congress must have intended to use the phrase 'race, color, religion, sex, or national origin' as the textual equivalent of 'retaliation.'" . . .

B

The proper interpretation and implementation of §2000e-3(a) and its causation standard have central importance to the fair and responsible allocation of resources in the judicial and litigation systems. This is of particular significance because claims of retaliation are being made with ever-increasing frequency. . . .

In addition lessening the causation standard could also contribute to the filing of frivolous claims, which would siphon resources from efforts by employer, administrative agencies, and courts to combat workplace harassment. Consider in this regard the case of an employee who knows that he or she is about to be fired for poor performance, given a lower pay grade, or even just transferred to a different assignment or location. To forestall that lawful action, he or he might be tempted to make an unfounded charge of racial, sexual, or religious discrimination; then, when the unrelated employment action comes, the employee could allege that it is retaliation. If respondent were to prevail in his argument here, that claim could be established by a lessened causation standard, all in order to prevent the undesired change in employment circumstances. Even if the employer could escape judgment after trial, the lessened causation standard would make it far more difficult to dismiss dubious claims at the summary judgment stage. *Cf. Vance v. Ball State Univ.* [reproduced in this Supplement at p. 64]. It would be inconsistent with the structure and operation of Title VII to so raise the costs, both financial and reputational, on an employer whose actions were not in fact the result of any discriminatory or retaliatory intent. Yet there would be a significant risk of that consequence if respondent's position were adopted here.

The facts of this case also demonstrate the legal and factual distinctions between status-based and retaliation claims, as well as the importance of the correct standard of proof. Respondent raised both claims in the District Court. The alleged wrongdoer differed in each: In respondent's status-based discrimination claim, it was his indirect supervisor, Dr. Levine. In his retaliation claim, it was the Chair of Internal Medicine, Dr. Fitz. The proof required for each claim differed, too. For the status-based claim, respondent was required to show instances of racial slurs, disparate treatment, and other indications of nationality-driven animus by Dr. Levine. Respondent's retaliation claim, by contrast, relied on the theory that Dr. Fitz was committed to exonerating Dr. Levine and wished to punish respondent for besmirching her reputation. Separately instructed on each type of claim, the jury returned a separate verdict for each, albeit with a single damages award. And the Court of Appeals treated each claim separately, too, finding insufficient evidence on the claim of status-based discrimination.

If it were proper to apply the motivating-factor standard to respondent's retaliation claim, the University might well be subject to liability on account of Dr. Fitz's alleged desire to exonerate Dr. Levine, even if it could also be shown that the terms of the affiliation agreement precluded the Hospital's hiring of respondent and that the University would have sought to prevent respondent's hiring in order to honor that agreement in any event. That result would be inconsistent with both the text and purpose of Title VII.

[Based on the textual and structural indications, the Court concludes that] Title VII retaliation claims must be proved according to traditional principles of but-for causation, not the lessened causation test stated in §2000e-2(m). This requires proof that the unlawful retaliation would not have occurred in the absence of the alleged wrongful action or actions of the employer.

IV

[The majority rejected arguments for *Skidmore v. Swift & Co.*, 323 U.S. 134 (1944), deference to the EEOC's guidance manual, which endorsed a motivating factor analysis. Since *Skidmore* deference depends on the "persuasive force" of the agency interpretation, it was unavailable when the EEOC's rationale was unconvincing.]

Respondent's final argument . . . is that even if §2000e-2(m) does not control the outcome in this case, the standard applied by *Price Waterhouse* should control instead. That assertion is incorrect. First, this position is foreclosed by the 1991 Act's amendments to Title VII. . . . Given the careful balance of lessened causation and reduced remedies Congress struck in the 1991 Act, there is no reason to think that the different balance articulated by *Price Waterhouse* somehow survived that legislation's passage. Second, even if this argument were still available, it would be inconsistent with the *Gross* Court's reading (and the plain textual meaning) of the word "because" as it appears in both §623(a) and §2000e-3(a). For these reasons, the rule of *Price Waterhouse* is not controlling here. . . .

Justice GINSBURG, with whom Justice BREYER, Justice SOTOMAYOR, and Justice KAGAN join, dissenting.

. . . In so reining in retaliation claims, the Court misapprehends what our decisions teach: Retaliation for complaining about discrimination is tightly bonded to the core prohibition and cannot be disassociated from it. Indeed, this Court has explained again and again that "retaliation in response to a complaint about [proscribed] discrimination is discrimination" on the basis of the characteristic Congress sought to immunize against adverse employment action. *Jackson v. Birmingham Bd. of Ed.*

The Court shows little regard for the trial judges who will be obliged to charge discrete causation standards when a claim of discrimination "because of," e.g., race is coupled with a claim of discrimination "because" the individual has complained of race discrimination. And jurors will puzzle over the rhyme or reason for the dual standards. Of graver concern, the Court has seized on a provision, §2000e-2(m), adopted by Congress as part of an endeavor to strengthen Title VII, and turned it into a measure reducing the force of the ban on retaliation. . . .

II

This Court has long acknowledged the symbiotic relationship between proscriptions on discrimination and proscriptions on retaliation. Antidiscrimination provisions, the Court has reasoned, endeavor to create a workplace where individuals are not treated differently on account of race, ethnicity, religion, or sex. See *Burlington Northern* [*& S.F.R. Co. v. White*, reproduced at p. 476]. Antiretaliation provisions "see[k] to secure that primary objective by preventing an employer from interfering . . . with an employee's efforts to secure or advance enforcement of [antidiscrimination] guarantees." Ibid. As the Court has comprehended, "Title VII depends for its enforcement upon the cooperation of employees who are willing to file complaints and act as witnesses." Id. "'[E]ffective enforcement,'" therefore, can "'only be expected if employees . . . [feel] free to approach officials with their grievances.'" See also *Crawford* [*v. Metropolitan Government of Nashville and Davidson Cty.*, discussed at p. 459].

Adverting to the close connection between discrimination and retaliation for complaining about discrimination, this Court has held, in a line of decisions unbroken until today, that a ban on discrimination encompasses retaliation. In *Sullivan v. Little Hunting Park, Inc.*, 396 U.S. 229, 237 (1969), the Court determined that 42 U.S.C. §1982, which provides that "[a]ll citizens of the United States shall have the same right . . . as is enjoyed by white citizens . . . to inherit, purchase, lease, sell, hold, and convey real and personal property," protected a white man who suffered retaliation after complaining of discrimination against his black tenant. *Jackson v. Birmingham Board of Education* [a Title IX case] elaborated on that holding in the context of sex discrimination. "Retaliation against a person because [he] has complained of sex discrimination," the Court found it inescapably evident, "is another form of intentional sex discrimination." . . .

Gómez-Pérez v. Potter, 553 U.S. 474 887 (2008), was similarly reasoned. . . . See also *CBOCS West, Inc. v. Humphries*, 553 U.S. 442, 447-457 (2008) (retaliation for race discrimination constitutes discrimination based on race under 42 U.S.C. §1981). There is no sound reason in this case to stray from the decisions in *Sullivan*, *Jackson*, *Gómez-Pérez*, and *CBOCS West*.

III

A

[The dissent reviewed the history of §703(m), stressing that "[a]mong the decisions found inadequately protective" by Congress in 1991 was *Price Waterhouse v. Hopkins*, which "endorsed the plurality's conclusion [there] that, to be actionable under Title VII, discrimination must be a motivating factor in, but need not be the but-for cause of, an adverse employment action. Congress disagreed with the Court, however, insofar as the *Price Waterhouse* decision allowed an employer to escape liability by showing that the same action would have been taken regardless of improper motive," and therefore added §703(m) and §706(g)(2)(B).]

B

There is scant reason to think that, despite Congress' aim to "restore and strengthen . . . laws that ban discrimination in employment," Congress meant to exclude retaliation claims from the newly enacted "motivating factor" provision. Section 2000e-2(m) provides that an "unlawful employment practice is established" when the plaintiff shows that a protected characteristic was a factor driving "any employment practice." Title VII, in §2000e-3(a), explicitly denominates retaliation, like status-based discrimination, an "unlawful employment practice." Because "any employment practice" necessarily encompasses practices prohibited under §2000e-3(a), §2000e-2(m), by its plain terms, covers retaliation.

Notably, when it enacted §2000e-2(m), Congress did not tie the new provision specifically to §§2000e-2(a)-(d), which proscribes discrimination "because of" race, color, religion, gender, or national origin. Rather, Congress added an entirely new provision to codify the causation standard, one encompassing "any employment practice." §2000e-2(m).

Also telling, §2000e-2(m) is not limited to situations in which the complainant's race, color, religion, sex, or national origin motivates the employer's action. In contrast, Title VII's substantive antidiscrimination provisions refer to the protected characteristics of the complaining party. Congress thus knew how to limit Title VII's coverage to victims of status-based discrimination when it was so minded. It chose, instead, to bring within §2000e-2(m) "any employment practice." To cut out retaliation from §2000e-2(m)'s scope, one must be blind to that choice.

C

[The dissent reviewed the EEOC's position on the question and stated that the agency position "merits respect" under *Skidmore v. Swift & Co.*, 323 U.S. 134, 140 (1944); *Federal Express Corp. v. Holowecki*, 552 U.S. 389, 399 (2008).] If the breadth of §2000e-2(m) can be deemed ambiguous (although I believe its meaning is plain), the provision should be construed to accord with the EEOC's well-reasoned and longstanding guidance.

IV

The Court draws the opposite conclusion, ruling that retaliation falls outside the scope of §2000e-2(m). In so holding, the Court ascribes to Congress the unlikely purpose of separating retaliation claims from discrimination claims, thereby undermining the Legislature's effort to fortify the protections of Title VII. None of the reasons the Court offers in support of its restrictive interpretation of §2000e-2(m) survives inspection.

A

[The Court acknowledges that "the text of the motivating-factor provision . . . begins by referring to unlawful employment practices," a term that undeniably includes retaliation. While it goes on to reference as "motivating factors only the status-based consideration, the Court errs in viewing retaliation as a protected activity entirely discrete from status-based discrimination. This vision] of retaliation as a separate concept runs up against precedent. Until today, the Court has been clear eyed on just what retaliation is: a manifestation of status-based discrimination. As *Jackson* explained in the context of sex discrimination, "retaliation is discrimination 'on the basis of sex' because it is an intentional response to the nature of the complaint: an allegation of sex discrimination."

[The dissent criticized the majority's distinction of *Jackson* and other cases as not involving "a detailed statutory scheme." It t] is strange logic indeed to conclude that when Congress homed in on retaliation and codified the proscription, as it did in Title VII, Congress meant protection against that unlawful employment practice to have less force than the protection available when the statute does not mention retaliation. It is hardly surprising, then, that our jurisprudence does not support the Court's conclusion. . . .

116

V

A

[The dissent found the majority's reliance on *Gross v. FBL Financial Services, Inc.* misplaced.] the employer prevailed in *Gross* because, according to the Court, the ADEA's antidiscrimination prescription is not like Title VII's. But the employer prevails again in Nassar's case, for there is no "meaningful textual difference," between the ADEA's use of "because" and the use of the same word in Title VII's retaliation provision. What sense can one make of this other than "heads the employer wins, tails the employee loses"? . . .

B

The Court's decision to construe §2000e-3(a) to require but-for causation in line with *Gross* is even more confounding in light of *Price Waterhouse*. . . . It is wrong to revert to *Price Waterhouse*, the Court says, because the 1991 Civil Rights Act's amendments to Title VII abrogated that decision.

This conclusion defies logic. . . . Shut from the Court's sight is a legislative record replete with statements evincing Congress' intent to strengthen antidiscrimination laws and thereby hold employers accountable for prohibited discrimination. It is an odd mode of statutory interpretation that divines Congress' aim in 1991 by looking to a decision of this Court, *Gross*, made under a different statute in 2008, while ignoring the overarching purpose of the Congress that enacted the 1991 Civil Rights Act.

C

The Court shows little regard for trial judges who must instruct juries in Title VII cases in which plaintiffs allege both status-based discrimination and retaliation. Nor is the Court concerned about the capacity of jurors to follow instructions conforming to today's decision. Causation is a complicated concept to convey to juries in the best of circumstances. Asking jurors to determine liability based on different standards in a single case is virtually certain to sow confusion. That would be tolerable if the governing statute required double standards, but here, for the reasons already stated, it does not.

VI

A

The Court's assertion that the but-for cause requirement it adopts necessarily follows from §2000e-3(a)'s use of the word "because" fails to convince. Contrary to the Court's suggestion, the word "because" does not inevitably demand but-for causation to the exclusion of all other causation formulations. When more than one factor contributes to a plaintiff's injury, but-for causation is problematic. See, e.g., 1 Restatement (Third) of Torts §27, Comment a, p. 385 (2005) (noting near universal agreement that the but-for standard is inappropriate when multiple sufficient causes exist) (hereinafter Restatement Third); Restatement of Torts §9, Comment b, p. 18 (1934) (legal cause is a cause that is a "substantial factor in bringing about the harm").

When an event is "overdetermined," i.e., when two forces create an injury each alone would be sufficient to cause, modern tort law permits the plaintiff to prevail upon showing that either sufficient condition created the harm. Restatement Third §27, at 376-377. In contrast, under the Court's approach (which it erroneously calls "textbook tort law"), a Title VII plaintiff alleging retaliation cannot establish liability if her firing was prompted by both legitimate and illegitimate factors.

Today's opinion rehashes arguments rightly rejected in *Price Waterhouse*. . . .

B

As the plurality and concurring opinions in *Price Waterhouse* indicate, a strict but-for test is particularly ill suited to employment discrimination cases. Even if the test is appropriate in some tort contexts, "it is an entirely different matter to determine a 'but-for' relation when . . . consider[ing], not physical forces, but the mind-related characteristics that constitute motive." *Gross* (Breyer, J., dissenting). . . .

NOTES

1. *Two Insights and a Default Principle.* Although the *Nassar* Court stated that *Gross* did "not decide the present case," the "insights" of the earlier opinion came close to doing so: first, its reading of "because" seems to set the default principle for other statutes; second, "Congress' structural choices in both Title VII itself and the law's 1991 amendments" are significant. Needless to say, both "insights" cut strongly against motivating factor causation for §704(a) cases since that provision used the word "because" and §703(m) does not explicitly refer to retaliation. *See generally* Michael J. Zimmer, *Hiding the Statute in Plain View: University of Texas Southwestern Medical Center v. Nassar*, 14 NEV. L.J. 705 (2014) (critiquing the court for its methodology, including abandoning the plain meaning approach to statutory interpretation it purported to use in *Gross*). *See also* Lawrence D. Rosenthal, *A Lack of "Motivation," or Sound Legal Reasoning? Why Most Courts Are Not Applying Either* Price Waterhouse*'s or the 1991 Civil Rights Act's Motivating-Factor Analysis to Title VII Retaliation Claims in a Post-*Gross *World*, 64 ALA. L. REV. 1067 (2013).

2. *Retaliation Is Discrimination?* The path to avoiding this result, of course, was the argument that prior case law had treated a ban on discrimination to necessarily

include a ban on retaliation for opposing such discrimination. *E.g., CBOCS West, Inc. v. Humphries*, 553 U.S. 442, 452-453 (2008). Are you persuaded by the Court's effort to distinguish them—that the earlier cases show that "a broadly phrased antidiscrimination statute may signal a concomitant intent to ban retaliation" but that such an inference should not be drawn in a more detailed statute? What's the relevance of the fact that "§2000e-2(m) is not itself a substantive bar on discrimination. Rather, it is a rule that establishes the causation standard for proving a violation defined elsewhere in Title VII." And does that single sentence put to rest the dispute in the lower courts as to whether there is a single claim of discrimination? See pp. 86-87, Note 11, *Is a §703(m) Case Different from a §703(a) Case?*, and Note 14, *Has* Desert Palace *Trumped* McDonnell Douglas?

3. *Employees Gaming the System.* Although the Court's opinion seems to reach its result without relying on policy considerations, Part IIB stresses both the large number of retaliation claims and the risks of employees filing charges in order to "forestall" an employer's lawful adverse action. While this is a logical possibility, do you think it's a serious problem? Even if so, should the majority have been concerned, given proof problems, about the "false negatives" a stricter standard of causation will produce even when retaliation is the but-for cause of an adverse action? Is that what the Ginsburg dissent was saying? *See generally* Sandra F. Sperino & Suja A. Thomas, *Fakers and Floodgates*, 10 STAN. J. C.R. & C.L. 223 (2014) (finding no empirical support for a problem of Title VII lawsuits beyond the growth in EEOC charges and certainly no evidence of a significant number of spurious retaliation claims); Kerri Lynn Stone, *Reality's Bite*, 28 J. CIV. RTS. & ECON. DEV. 227 (2015). *But see* David Sherwyn, Michael Heise & Zev J. Eigen, *Experimental Evidence that Retaliation Claims are Unlike Other Employment Discrimination Claims*, 44 SETON HALL L. REV. 455 (2014) (justifying a stricter standard of proof for retaliation claims in part to encourage employers to try to assist struggling workers by reducing the risk of a successful retaliation suit).

4. *What About §706(g)?* In one passage, the majority suggests that applying the motivating-factor standard to Dr. Nassar's retaliation claim might well subject the University "to liability on account of Dr. Fitz's alleged desire to exonerate Dr. Levine, even if it could also be shown that the terms of the affiliation agreement precluded the Hospital's hiring of respondent and that the University would have sought to prevent respondent's hiring in order to honor that agreement in any event." It goes on: "That result would be inconsistent with the both the text and purpose of Title VII." But is it? The University would be liable but, given the same decision defense, would not be subject to damages in this scenario. What's inconsistent with a declaratory judgment or even an injunction relating to the retaliation?

5. *Really?* The Court rejected the argument that, even if §703(m) did not govern this case, *Price Waterhouse* should control. Its basic response was that the 1991 Act's amendments displaced the *Price Waterhouse* burden-shifting framework: But, as the dissent stressed, Congress intended to give burden shifting *more* bite in the '91 Amendments. How could the Court have read them to implicitly cut back on the pre-existing regime? *See generally* Stephen M. Rich, *A Matter of Perspective: Textualism, Stare Decisis, and Federal Employment Discrimination Law*, 87 S. CAL. L. REV. 1197, 1199 (2014).

6. *But-for Does Not Mean Sole Cause.* While *Nassar* undoubtedly increased plaintiff's burden, it did not render such cases impossible to prove. *Kwan v. Andalex Grp. LLC*, 737 F.3d 834 (2d Cir. 2013), stressed that "'but-for' causation does not require proof that retaliation was the only cause of the employer's action, but only that the adverse action would not have occurred in the absence of the retaliatory motive." That is because traditional tort principles establish that "a plaintiff's injury can have multiple "but-for" causes, each one of which may be sufficient to support liability." *Id.* at 834 n.5, citing, inter alia, Fowler v. Harper etal., 4 Harper, James and Grayon Torts §20.2 (3d ed. 2007).

7. Gross/Nassar *and Other Antidiscrimination Statutes*. *Desert Palace* and *Gross* create separate analytic regimes for Title VII and the ADEA, and *Nassar* holds that even Title VII does not have a single motivating factor standard. But what about other laws? *See Ford v. Mabus*, 629 F.3d 198 (D.C. Cir. 2010) (in a federal employee suit under ADEA §633a, plaintiffs need show only that age was a factor in the employer's decision in order to prevail as to liability); *see also Palmquist v. Shinseki*, 689 F.3d 66, 73-74 (1st Cir. 2012) (while the Rehabilitation Act borrows its remedial scheme from Title VII, it does not borrow the causation standard set out in §2000e-2(m); instead, the Rehabilitation Act borrows the causation standard from the ADA, which uses very similar causation language to the ADEA and therefore should be construed the same way).

Some have argued that *Gross* will not apply to ADA cases because that statute incorporates Title VII procedures and remedies by reference. *See* Melissa Hart, *Procedural Extremism: The Supreme Court's 2008-2009 Employment and Labor Cases*, 13 Emp. Rts. & Emp. Pol'y J. 253 (2009). *See also* Catherine T. Struve, *Shifting Burdens: Discrimination Law Through the Lens of Jury Instruction*, 51 B.C. L. Rev. 279 (2010). There is also legislative history of the Civil Rights Act of 1991 to this effect: "Similarly, mixed motive cases involving disability under the ADA should be interpreted consistent with the prohibition against all intentional discrimination in Section 5 of this Act." H.R. Rep. No. 102-40 (II), at 4, 1991 U.S.C.C.A.N. 694, 697 (1991). But the early returns suggest that this incorporation theory will not suffice. *Lewis v. Humboldt Acquisition Corp.*, 681 F.3d 312 (6th Cir. 2012); *Serwatka v. Rockwell Automation, Inc.*, 591 F.3d 957 (7th Cir. 2010).

8. *Employer Knowledge*. As noted in the cases earlier studied in this chapter, a retaliation claim requires protected conduct, an adverse action, and a causal link between the two. Some courts also add a fourth requirement: employer knowledge of the employee's protected activity. *See, e.g., Gordon v. New York City Bd. of Educ.*, 232 F.3d 111 (2d Cir. 2000). Others consider employer knowledge as embraced within the causation element. Either way, knowledge seems necessary, a point that *Breeden* made clear. If an employer does not know an employee has engaged in protected conduct, it can't have fired her because of it. *But see EEOC v. Abercrombie & Fitch Stores, Inc.*, reproduced at p. 84 of this supplement.

In some retaliation cases, however, the knowledge requirement might be satisfied by the principles announced in *Staub v. Proctor Hospital*, reproduced at p. 54. *See Zamora v. City of Houston*, 798 F.3d 326 (5th Cir. 2015) (joining the circuits that have addressed the question to hold that cat's paw analysis remains a viable theory of causation for retaliation claims). *See also Goodsite v. Norfolk S. Ry.*,

573 F. App'x 572 (6th Cir. 2014) (assuming the cat's paw theory applied to a retaliation claim, plaintiff's claim failed because there was no evidence that the decisionmaker was influenced by the allegedly biased supervisor).

9. *Temporal Proximity*. Plaintiffs often rely on timing as evidence of causation. When an adverse action follows closely on the heels of protected conduct, it is not a difficult inferential leap to conclude the one may have been caused by the other. But how close in time must the adverse act and the protected conduct be? *Breeden* might be read to hold that the plaintiff always loses on a summary judgment motion where the employer has denied retaliation and the plaintiff's only evidence of causation is that the adverse employment action occurred three months or more after the decisionmaker learned of the protected activity. *See Tyler v. Univ. of Ark. Bd. of Trs.*, 628 F.3d 980, 986-87 (8th Cir. 2011) ("Generally, 'more than a temporal connection is required to present a genuine factual issue on retaliation,' and only in cases where the temporal proximity is very close can the plaintiff rest on it exclusively); *El Sayed v. Hilton Hotels Corp.*, 627 F.3d 931, 933 (2d Cir. 2010) ("The temporal proximity of events may give rise to an inference of retaliation for the purposes of establishing a prima facie case of retaliation under Title VII, but without more, such temporal proximity is insufficient to satisfy appellant's burden to bring forward some evidence of pretext"). *But see Pinkerton v. Colo. Dept. of Transp.*, 563 F.3d 1052 (10th Cir. 2009) (termination within a few days of verification of the complaint plaintiff filed with employer, together with evidence that employer's reasons for firing plaintiff may not have been credible, held sufficient); *Mickey v. Zeidler Tool & Die Co.*, 516 F.3d 516 (6th Cir. 2008) (termination the day employer received notice of EEOC charge sufficed). *See generally* Troy B. Daniels & Richard A. Bales, *Plus at Pretext: Resolving the Split Regarding the Sufficiency of Temporal Proximity Evidence in Title VII Retaliation Cases*, 44 GONZ. L. REV. 493 (2008/2009).

9. *Back to Direct Evidence*. Although, as the previous Note suggests, it certainly remains possible to win a retaliation case by circumstantial evidence "direct evidence" became more important in light of *Nassar's* holding. *Compare Lors v. Dean*, 746 F.3d 857 (8th Cir. 2014) (summary judgment on ADA retaliation claim granted when temporal proximity of discharge during appeal of a challenge to a transfer was not direct evidence of retaliation, "team leader's" statements indicating retaliatory intent were not made by decisionmaker, and discharge letter, albeit referring to his continuing challenge to the transfer, specifically disclaimed retaliatory intent), *with Willis v. Cleco Corp.*, 749 F.3d 314, 323 (5th Cir. 2014) (overturning summary judgment on retaliation claim of an HR representative for reporting racially hostile statements in light of affidavit stating that the HR General Manager stated that he was "very pissed" with Willis for reporting the conversation with Cooper and that "[i]f we have to find a reason, Ed [Taylor] and I have decided; we are going to terminate that nigger Greg Willis for reporting me and trying to burn my ass").

10. What happens if an employer mistakenly believes an employee has engaged in protected conduct and demotes the employee based on the mistaken belief? The Supreme Court faced this question in a case involving a First Amendment claim, holding that it is the employer's motive that matters, and

thus a claim could be stated even if the employee had not actually engaged in conduct protected by the First Amendment. *Heffernan v. City of Paterson*, 136 S. Ct. 1412 (2016). Whether this reasoning will be imported into retaliation claims under Title VII and other employment discrimination statutes remains to be seen.

7 *Disability Discrimination*

Page 487, add before *Henny* cite in first full paragraph:

Brumfield v. City of Chicago, 735 F.3d 619 (7th Cir. 2013) (employment discrimination can be challenged only under Title I, not Title II, of the ADA); *Elwell v. Okla. ex rel. Bd. of Regents of the Univ. of Okla.*, 693 F.3d 1303 (10th Cir. 2012) (same);

Page 489, add at end of first full paragraph:

After several years of court decisions, the empirical evidence seems to suggest that courts are far more ready to find a disability than under the original ADA. *See generally* Stephen F. Befort, *An Empirical Analysis of Case Outcomes Under the ADA Amendments Act*, 70 WASH. & LEE L. REV. 2027 (2013) (the empirical evidence so far reveals more decisions on the "qualified" issue, fewer dismissals for the plaintiff not being disabled, and more plaintiff success in surviving various motions); Nicole B. Porter, *The New ADA Backlash*, 82 TENN. L. REV. 1 (2014 (empirical study showing courts are generally following the ADAAA's command to be more receptive to claims of disability; however, while they are receptive to physical reasonable accommodations addressing actual functions of a job, there are signs of backlash when it comes to requests for accommodations that "relate to structural norms in the workplace"). A more doctrinal analysis of this phenomenon in the courts is found in Michelle A. Travis, *Disqualifying Universality Under the Americans with Disabilities Act Amendments Act*, 2015 MICH. ST. L. REV. 1689.

Page 489, add at end of first full paragraph:

Nicole Buonocore Porter, *Special Treatment Stigma after the ADA Amendments Act*, 43 PEPP. L. REV. 213 (2016) (considering implications of the ADAAA, including the possibility that the expansion of accommodation will reduce the stigma of special treatment suffered by many accommodated disabled individuals).

Page 497, add after *Korn* cite at end of first paragraph of Note 2(b), *Voluntary Conditions*:

Bearing out Professor Korn's prediction, the first post-ADAAA circuit level decision went the other way. *Morriss v. BNSF Ry. Co.*, 817 F.3d 1104, 1109 (8th Cir. 2016), held, that, with regard to actual disability and even after the ADAAA, "for obesity, even morbid obesity, to be considered a physical impairment, it must result from an underlying physiological disorder or condition" As for "regarded as" liability, plaintiff could prevail only by showing that his employer "perceived his obesity to be a condition that met the definition of 'physical impairment.' The ADA does not prohibit discrimination based on a perception that a physical characteristic — as opposed to a physical impairment — may eventually lead to a physical impairment as defined under the Act. Instead, the plain language of the ADA prohibits actions based on an existing impairment or the perception of an existing impairment." *Id.* at 1113.

Page 498, add before *Chamberlain* cite in carryover Note 2(c), *Temporary Impairments*:

In *Summers v. Altarum Inst., Corp.*, 740 F.3d 325, 329-30 (4th Cir. 2014), plaintiff had a serious but temporary injury, one that left him unable to walk for seven months despite surgery, pain medication, and physical therapy. The court held he could be disabled within the meaning of the amended ADA: EEOC regulations providing that a short-term impairment may qualify if sufficiently severe were entitled to deference under *Chevron*, and the possibility that plaintiff could have gotten to work in a wheelchair was irrelevant since mitigating measures should not be considered.

Page 498, add before *Horgan* cite in second paragraph of carryover Note 2(c), *Temporary Impairments*:

Mazzeo v. Color Resolutions Int'l, LLC, 746 F.3d 1264 (11th Cir. 2014) (given the ADAAA, evidence of disc herniation problems, which had existed for years and were serious enough to require surgery, substantially limited plaintiff's ability to walk, bend, sleep, and lift more than ten pounds established a *prima facie* case of disability); *Gogos v. AMS Mech. Sys., Inc.*, 737 F.3d 1170, 1173 (7th Cir. 2013) (an episode of a blood-pressure spike and vision loss may be covered disabilities when both problems may be "episodic" manifestations of a longstanding blood-pressure condition; despite their short duration, they could substantially impair two major life activities, circulatory function and eyesight, and, in any event, plaintiff's chronic blood-pressure condition could also qualify as a disability);

Page 498, add at end of page a new paragraph (e) to carryover Note 2, *Is There an Impairment?*:

(e) The Need for Medical Evidence. In *Felkins v. City of Lakewood,* 774 F.3d 647, 652 (10th Cir. 2014), plaintiff failed to produce any medical testimony that she had avascular necrosis. This proved fatal to her claim of actual disability. While her declarations were admissible in describing her injuries and symptoms, they were inadmissible "insofar as they diagnose her condition or state how that condition causes limitations on major life activities," both of which require an expert witness. Implementing regulations under the ADAAA, 29 C.F.R. §1630.2(j)(1)(v), were read to allow lay testimony as to plaintiff's performance of major life activities compared to others but not as to whether any limitation were caused by a particular disease.

Page 499, add before Roberts cite in first paragraph of Note 3, *Meet GINA*:

Mark A. Rothstein, Jessica Roberts, & Tee L. Guidotti, *Limiting Occupational Medical Evaluations Under the Americans with Disabilities Act and the Genetic Information Nondiscrimination Act,* 41 AM. J. L. & MED. 523, 551-59 (2015) (empirical study of GINA filings and court suits);

Page 506, add before *Thomas* cite near end of carryover Note 2, *Substantially Limits*:

In Cannon v. Jacobs Field Servs. N. Am., 813 F.3d 586 (5th Cir. 2016), plaintiff's shoulder injury, which prevented him from lifting his right arm above shoulder level and caused considerable difficulty in lifting, pushing, or pulling, was ample evidence of a disability under the ADAAA, which views lifting as a major life activity; *Jacobs v. N.C. Admin. Office of the Courts,* 780 F.3d 562, 573-74 (4th Cir. 2015) (since a "person need not live as a hermit in order to be 'substantially limited' in interacting with others, plaintiff's social anxiety disorder may be a protected disability even though she endured social situations, at least when they caused her 'intense anxiety.'");

Page 507, add before *see generally* cite in first line.

See also Surtain v. Hamlin Terrace Found., 789 F.3d 1239 (11th Cir. 2015) (finding an ADA complaint insufficiently plead when plaintiff alleged only that the employer knew that plaintiff had visited a doctor for unknown health issues, and that the doctor had concluded that she could not return to work until further notice; this was not sufficient to conclude "that the employer believed her to be suffering from a disability—not just any medical condition, but one that substantially limited a major life activity").

Page 515, add at end of carryover Note 2, *Substantially Limited in Ability to Work:*

Carothers v. Cnty. of Cook, 808 F.3d 1140, 1147-48 (7th Cir. 2015) (even if plaintiff's anxiety disorder was "exacerbated by exposure to and interactions with teenagers," and therefore limited performance of her job duties of interacting with juvenile detainees, that was merely a "single specific job" at a juvenile correctional center and did not establish that plaintiff could not engage in a broad class of positions);

In a case with potential significance as one of the first post-ADAAA decisions dealing with "substantially limited," the Ninth Circuit in *Weaving v. City of Hillsboro*, 763 F.3d 1106, 1112 (9th Cir. 2014) (2-1), overturned a jury verdict and held that plaintiff's ADHD did not substantially limit his ability to work or to interact with others. He was not limited in his ability to work compared to "most people in the general population" because the evidence showed he was in many respects a skilled police officer since he had developed compensatory mechanisms to deal with his ADHD impediments. As for the activity of interacting with others, his ADHD "may well have limited his ability to *get along* with others, [b]ut that is not the same as a substantial limitation on the ability to *interact* with others."

Page 520, add at end of Note 1, *A Truncated Inquiry*:

Nevertheless, there must be a finding of impairment, not merely lesser physical capacity. *See Fischer v. Minneapolis Pub. Sch.*, 792 F.3d 985, 989 (8th Cir. 2015) ("MPs's belief that Fischer was capable of performing the physical labor of a medium strength worker is not equivalent to a belief that Fischer suffered a physical impairment such as a physiological disorder, cosmetic disfigurement, anatomical loss, or disease.").

Page 520, add at end of Note 2, *Proof of Causation Required*:

See also Kelleher v. Wal-Mart Stores, Inc., 817 F.3d 624 (8th Cir. 2016) (transfer of a disabled person to a new position on the night shift was not an adverse employment action because it did not materially change the terms or conditions of her employment and was less physically strenuous than her prior position). Assuming such an action, the plaintiff must still show that her disability caused the adverse action. That will be easiest when the plaintiff has "direct evidence." *See Rodriguez v. Eli Lilly & Co.*, 820 F3d 759 (5th Cir. 2016) (direct evidence requires proximity in time to the adverse employment action by an individual with authority over that action and related to it; the conversation in question about plaintiff's PTSD was more than six months before his termination and thus failed the proximity requirement).

Page 521, add before see generally cite in Note 3, *"Regarded as" Claims and Stereotyping"*:

But see Coursey v. Univ. of Md. E. Shore, 577 F. App'x 167 (4th Cir. 2014) (an employer's request for a medical evaluation of its employee is not, by itself, sufficient to show that the employer regarded the employee as disabled for purposes of the ADA).

Page 523, add before *Jones* cite in first line after last extract:

Harris v. Reston Hosp. Ctr., LLC, 523 F. App'x 938, 947 (4th Cir. 2013) (plaintiff's "extensive absences and physical incapacity — regardless of their precise causes — would significantly interfere with, if not wholly negate, her ability to perform the essential functions of a surgical floor nurse"); *Majors v. GE Elec. Co.*, 714 F.3d 527 (7th Cir. 2013) (because plaintiff was permanently unable to lift more than twenty pounds, she could not perform an essential function of the auditor position without accommodation and to have another worker lift heavy objects for her is not a reasonable accommodation);

Page 523, add at end of page after *Rosebough* cite:

Rorrer v. City of Stow, 743 F.3d 1025 (6th Cir. 2014) (district court erred in finding no genuine dispute as to whether driving a fire apparatus was an essential function of a firefighter position given no evidence that the department utilized national guidelines so providing and the certifying physician did not rely on them in determining plaintiff's unfitness); *Samson v. Fed. Express Corp.*, 746 F.3d 1196 (11th Cir. 2014) (fact issue as to whether test-driving a truck was an essential function of a Technician position; while several factors suggested yes, including Fed Ex's judgment and job description, many licensed drivers in the terminal could perform that function and the incumbent Technician spent little time doing it); *McMillan v. City of New York*, 711 F.3d 120 (2d Cir. 2013) (while arrival on time might be essential for many, perhaps most jobs, it may not have been an essential requirement of the plaintiff's position given past approval of his late arrivals and the employer's flex-time policy);

Page 533, add at end of second paragraph in Note 1, *The Employer's Judgment*:

See generally Michelle A. Travis, *Disqualifying Universality Under the Americans with Disabilities Act Amendments Act,* 2015 MICH. ST. L. REV. 1689.

Page 533, add before *Carmona* cite in last paragraph of Note 1, *The Employer's Judgment*:

Shell v. Smith, 789 F.3d 715(7th Cir. 2015) (despite a job description that stated that a mechanic's helper may occasionally have to drive a bus, the employer's actual practice of not requiring plaintiff to do so for 12 years created a jury question as to whether driving was an essential function);

Page 534, add at end of Note 2, *Burden of Proof*:

Contra Hawkins v. Schwan's Home Serv., 778 F.3d 877, 879 (10th Cir. 2015) (while the employer may have a burden of production with respect to essential functions, plaintiff failed to carry his burden of persuasion to establish that driving a truck was not essential, even though he had performed his work for more than two years without driving a truck; he was therefore unqualified when he lacked DOT certification)

Page 534, add before *Turner* cite in Note 3, *Defining the Term*:

Rorrer v. City of Stow, 743 F.3d 1025 (6th Cir. 2014) (genuine issue of material fact existed as to reasonable accommodations, including allowing plaintiff to continue working as a firefighter without driving fire apparatus during an emergency since a factfinder could determine that that was a marginal function that could have been easily performed by others);

Page 534, add before *Samper* cite in Note 4, *Attendance as an Essential Job Function*:

EEOC v. Ford Motor Co., 782 F.3d 753 (6th Cir. 2015) (en banc) (regular and predictable on-site attendance was essential for the employee's resale buyer position when technological shifts failed to make this position one that could be performed by proposed telecommuting for up to four days per week); *Taylor-Novotny v. Health Alliance Med. Plans, Inc.,* 772 F.3d 478, 489-90 (7th Cir. 2014) (plaintiff "has not established that regular attendance was not required of someone in her position"; "the fact that her employer allowed for work from home did not mean that punctuality and regular attendance were not essential functions of her position");

7. Disability Discrimination

Page 535, add before *Cehrs* cite in carryover Note 4, *Attendance as an Essential Job Function*:

See Solomon v. Vilsack, 763 F.3d 1 (D.C. Cir. 2014) (a "maxiflex" schedule, one that allows an employee to vary the number of hours worked on a given workday or the number of hours each week, is not a per se unreasonable accommodation under the Rehabilitation Act);

Page 535, add at end of Note 5, *Accommodations that Impact Others*:

See also Hill v. Walker, 737 F.3d 1209, 1217 (8th Cir. 2013) (plaintiff, a social worker, was not otherwise qualified when removing her from particularly stressful cases to accommodate her anxiety would "wreak havoc" with management of the agency).

Page 536, add at end of Note 7, *Essential Even If Infrequent*:

See also Adair v. City of Muskogee, No. 15-7067, 2016 U.S. App. LEXIS 9636, at *30 (10th Cir. May 26, 2016) (plaintiff not otherwise qualified: although his position as HazMat Director did not require him to lift, "he is still a firefighter and can be called to the scene to respond to a fire with hazardous materials," which required lifting); *Scruggs v. Pulaski Cnty.*, 817 F.3d 1087, 1092-93 (8th Cir. 2016) (the ability to lift 40 pounds is an essential function of juvenile detention officer job, despite not being often required; the job exists largely to protect juveniles being supervised from harming themselves and others, and plaintiff conceded that the job sometimes required her to lift detainees off the ground and to restrain juveniles, all of whom weigh more than 40 pounds); *Minnihan v. Mediacom Communs. Corp.*, 779 F.3d 803, 812-13 (8th Cir. 2015) (driving was an essential function of a cable installer's job even absent specific evidence of time actually spent driving and accommodating plaintiff's limitations would have required co-workers to assume additional duties and work extra hours).

Page 537, add at end of carryover paragraph:

See also Smith v. Clark Cnty. Sch. Dist., 727 F.3d 950 (9th Cir. 2013) (while the *Cleveland* standard also applies to statements in applications for state and private disability benefits and FMLA leave, there was no inherent conflict between plaintiff's representations and her ADA claim since impairments may change over time; and such schemes do not address whether an individual could perform the job with a reasonable accommodation).

Page 537, add after third sentence in third paragraph:

See Feist v. Louisiana, Dep't of Justice, Office of the Atty. Gen., 730 F.3d 450 (5th Cir. 2013) (since the ADA requires employers to "mak[e] existing facilities used by employees readily accessible to and usable by individuals with disabilities," the district court erred in requiring a nexus between the requested accommodation and the essential functions of plaintiff's position).

Page 545, add at the end of Note 1, *Is There a Vacancy?*

See Dunderdale v. United Airlines, Inc., 807 F.3d 849, 851 (7th Cir. 2015) (while plaintiff could perform his job with an accommodation, reassignment was not required either to a position violating the seniority system or to positions not shown to be vacant).

Page 549, add at end of Note 3, *When Is a Position Vacant?*:

See also Turner v. City of Paris, Ky., 534 F. App'x 299, 303 (6th Cir. 2013) (a position is not vacant if it is not currently so or will be vacant within "a short period of time," perhaps a week; plaintiff failed to establish that a prospective retirement was sufficient imminent to satisfy that standard). Such determinations can be very fact-sensitive. *See Feldman v. Olin Corp.*, 692 F.3d 748, 754-756 (7th Cir. 2012) (genuine issue of material fact as to whether straight-time positions were open during plaintiff's seven month lay-off).

Page 549, add new Note 4:

4. *Transfer for Treatment?* Suppose an employee is able to perform the essential functions of her job despite her disability. May she demand a transfer to a vacant position in order to obtain better treatment of her disability? *Sanchez v. Vilsack*, 695 F.3d 1174, 1182 (10th Cir. 2012), held that "a transfer accommodation for medical care or treatment is not per se unreasonable, even if an employee is able to perform the essential functions of her job without it."

Page 553, add before *Theilig* cite in carryover Note 1, *The Essential Job Function Inquiry*:

EEOC v. LHC Grp., Inc., 773 F.3d 688 (5th Cir. 2014) (while driving was an essential function of the Field Nurse position, there were factual disputes about whether it was an essential function of the Team Leader position); *Kauffman v. Petersen Health Care VII, LLC*, 769 F.3d 958, 964 (7th Cir. 2014) (reversing summary judgment for a nursing home because of dispute as to whether pushing wheelchairs for residents was an essential job function of a hairdresser and, if so, whether medical restrictions on plaintiff could be reasonably accommodated);

Page 553, add at end of carryover Note 1, *The Essential Job Function Inquiry.*

What do you think of the argument that the employer's having provided accommodation should have no relevance to the issue of whether it is reasonable to continue the accommodation? The issue of whether an employer must continue to provide an accommodation once it starts has been often litigated. Rather than focusing on the statute itself, the courts seem concerned with the disincentives to accommodation that would follow from holding that providing an accommodation established its reasonableness and the absence of undue hardship. *See generally* Nicole Buonocore Porter, *Withdrawn Accommodations*, 63 DRAKE L. REV. 885 (2015).

Page 553, add at end of Note 1, *The Essential Job Function Inquiry*:

See also Keith v. County of Oakland, 703 F.3d 918 (6th Cir. 2013) (genuine issue of material fact as to deaf lifeguard's ability to perform the essential function of communication while working at a wave pool given his visual scanning techniques and use of whistle and physical gestures).

Page 554, add a new bullet to carryover Note 3, *Forms of Reasonable Accommodation*:

Spurling v. C & M Fine Pack, Inc., 739 F.3d 1055, 1061-62 (7th Cir. 2014) (claim stated when further medical testing and prescription medication to control plaintiff's narcolepsy were obvious possibilities that should have been explored in the interactive process);

Page 554, add at end of carryover Note 3, *Forms of Reasonable Accommodation*:

On the other hand, courts have not been sympathetic with employees who demand preferred accommodations when, in the court's judgment, the offered accommodation would suffice. *Bunn v. Khoury Enters.*, 753 F.3d 656 (7th Cir. 2014) (once an employer provided a reasonable accommodation, it had discharged its obligations under the law, whether or not it engaged in the interactive process to explore other possible accommodations); *Yovtcheva v. City of Phila. Water Dep't*, 518 F. App'x 116 (3d Cir. 2013) (city did not need to transfer an asthmatic city chemist or use a solvent to which she was not sensitive when it offered her a reasonable accommodation by a partial-face respirator which she refused to attempt to use due to a panic attack she had suffered while using a full-face device).

Page 554, add after first sentence of Note 4, *Attendance Policies and the Duty of Reasonable Accommodation***:**

See also Agee v. Mercedes-Benz U.S. Int'l, Inc., No. 15-11747, 2016 U.S. App. LEXIS 6944, at *14 (11th Cir. Mar. 30, 2016) (ability to work a flexible schedule and overtime was an essential job function of an automobile assembly plant in view of fluctuating production requirements, and job description when employment application, and employee handbook stated that overtime was job requirement).

Page 555, add before Befort cite in carryover paragraph in carryover Note 4. *Attendance Policies and the Duty of Reasonable Accommodation***:**

Hwang v. Kan. State Univ., 753 F.3d 1159, 1161 (10th Cir. 2014) ("an employee who isn't capable of working for [more than six months] isn't an employee capable of performing a job's essential functions" since requiring an employer to keep a job open for such an extensive period is not a reasonable accommodation even in a university where sabbaticals often exceed that period). Stacy A. Hickox & Joseph M. Guzman, *Leave as an Accommodation: When Is Enough, Enough?*, 62 CLEV. ST. L. REV. 437 (2014);

Page 559, before last sentence of carryover Note 1, *Facially Discriminatory?***:**

Yarberry v. Gregg Appliances, Inc., 625 F. App'x 729, 738 (6th Cir. 2015) (plaintiff's nonviolent but disruptive misconduct was a valid reason for discharge, even if related to his disability); *Bailey v. Real Time Staffing Servs., Inc.*, 543 F. App'x 520 (6th Cir. 2013) (summary judgment against plaintiff proper when he was fired for testing positive for marijuana; although plaintiff argued that the result was caused by HIV medication, there was no evidence that the employer knew that the test was false or of his HIV condition).

Page 559, add after Palmer citation in Note 3, *Essential Job Functions:*

Even less dramatic difficulties in working with others have resulted in a finding that the individual was not otherwise qualified when such interactions were essential to the position. *Walz v. Ameriprise Fin., Inc.*, 779 F.3d 842, 845-46 (8th Cir. 2015) (where plaintiff's bipolar disorder prevented her from working well with others, she could not perform the essential functions of the job without accommodation, and she failed to request any accommodation that might allow her to do so).

7. Disability Discrimination

Page 562, add before *EEOC v.   Convergys* citation in carryover paragraph:

Snapp v. United Transp. Union, 547 F. App'x 824, 826 (9th Cir. 2013) (a job application and a letter from plaintiff's physician referring to his ongoing disability and need for accommodations created a fact question as to notification); *Dinse v. Carlisle Foodservice Products Inc.*, 541 F. App'x 885, 890 (10th Cir. 2013) ("More is required to trigger an employer's duty to engage in the interactive process than mere awareness that the employee is disabled; specifically, the employee must make an adequate request for a reasonable accommodation for the disability.");

Page 562, add at end of carryover paragraph:

However, the accommodation must be requested in a timely fashion. *See Schaffhauser v. UPS*, 794 F.3d 899, 905 (8th Cir. 2015) (request for an accommodation based on a treatment for a medical condition that contributed to an inappropriate remark came too late when it attempted to deflect otherwise appropriate discipline for that remark)

Page 562, add before *McBride* citation in first full paragraph:

Stern v. St. Anthony's Health Ctr., 788 F. 3d 276 (7th Cir. 2015) (failure to engage in the interactive process not independently actionable when plaintiff's cognitive difficulties prevented him from performing the essential functions of chief psychologist given the sensitive nature of the position and the potential safety and liability risks);

Page 561, add before Timmons cite in second full paragraph:

Stephen F. Befort, *Accommodating an Employee's Commute to Work Under the ADA: Reasonable, Preferential or Both?*, 63 Drake L. Rev. 749 (2015).

Page 562, add before *Whelan* cite in last paragraph:

EEOC v. Kohl's Dep't Stores, Inc., 774 F.3d 127, 133-34 (1st Cir. 2014) (when an employer initiates an interactive dialogue, the employee must engage in a good-faith effort to work out potential solutions); *Ward v. McDonald*, 762 F.3d 24, 32 (D.C. Cir. 2014) (when plaintiff resigned during the interactive process, she short-circuited the process and no reasonable juror could have found that the employer, rather than plaintiff, was responsible for the breakdown).

Page 564, add at end of first full paragraph:

See also Reyazuddin v. Montgomery Cnty., 789 F.3d 407, 418 (4th Cir. 2015) (summary judgment when "the district court reduced a multi-factor analysis to a single factor–cost–that the court believed was simply too much for the County to bear. But while cost is important, it cannot be viewed in isolation. Rather, it is the relative cost, along with other factors, that matters.")

Page 565, add after first sentence of second full paragraph:

Barnett also made clear that plaintiff has the burden of showing that a reasonable accommodation is available. *See Horn v. Knight Facilities Mgmt.-GM*, 556 F. App'x 452, 455 (6th Cir. 2014) (plaintiff, a janitor who developed a sensitivity to cleaning fluids, did not identify a reasonable accommodation).

Page 565, add at end of third full paragraph:

Osborne v. Baxter Healthcare Corp., 798 F.3d 1260, 1278 (10th Cir. 2015), held that, to shift the burden of proof to the employer, plaintiff "must show only that her proposed accommodation is reasonable on its face; that is, it would permit her to perform the essential function at issue — here, donor monitoring. She need not show that the accommodation would eliminate every de minimis health or safety risk that [the employer] can hypothesize." It also held it error for the district court to require plaintiff to show "not only that her proposed accommodation is reasonable on its face, but also that the accommodation would be feasible" for the employer; "how much alarms would cost, when they could be added in the production process, and who would install them" are part of the employer's burden to "identify with specificity . . . why the proposed accommodation constitutes an undue hardship and is thus unreasonable." *Id*. at 1273.

Page 565, add after first sentence in last paragraph:

Even in this setting, issues peculiar to the ADA arise. *See* Craig Robert Senn, *Minimal Relevance: Non-Disabled Replacement Evidence in ADA Discrimination Cases*, 66 BAYLOR L. REV. 64 (2014) (arguing that proof of a nondisabled replacement is neither necessary for a prima facie case nor sufficient to create a fact question as to intent).

Page 565, add at end of page:

See also Cheryl L. Anderson, *The Conundrum of Causation and Reasonable Accommodation Under the ADA*, 82 MISS. L.J. 67, 73 (2013) (cautioning that, after *Gross*, causation could "creep into another aspect of reasonable accommodation analysis — as a requirement that plaintiffs show their disability is a but-for cause of their need for the accommodation").

Page 573, add at the end of carryover Note 1, *Individualized Medical Inquiry*:

At least one court, however, has watered down the necessary showing by requiring only that the employer show a reasonable belief as to direct threat. *EEOC v. Beverage Distribs. Co., LLC*, 780 F.3d 1018, 1019 (10th Cir. 2015).

Page 574, add before Korn cite in Note 5, *Direct Threat and Mental Illness*:

Susan D. Carle, *Analyzing Social Impairments Under Title I of the Americans with Disabilities Act*, U.C. DAVIS L. REV. (forthcoming), *available at* http://ssrn.com/abstract=2749179.

Page 585, add at end of carryover paragraph:

See James v. City of Costa Mesa, 700 F.3d 394 (9th Cir. 2012) (since the ADA defines "illegal drug use" by reference to federal, rather than state, law, plaintiffs' medical marijuana use was not protected by the ADA regardless of its legality under California law).

Courts have been permissive as to how employers may deal with individuals who are intoxicated on the job. *See Clifford v. Cnty. of Rockland*, 528 F. App'x 6 (2d Cir. 2013) ("having conceded that termination was a permissible response to on-the-job intoxication, Clifford can hardly charge the County with having failed to afford her a reasonable accommodation when, instead of pursuing termination after the May 13th incident, it agreed to a suspension that afforded her the opportunity to return to work on a showing that she posed no serious risk of relapse). *See also Ostrowski v. Con-Way Freight, Inc.*, 543 F. App'x 128 (3d Cir. 2013) ("employers do not violate the ADA merely by entering into return-to-work agreements that impose employment conditions different from those of other employees, such as barring an employee from consuming alcohol; because the agreement was valid, plaintiff's violation of its terms was a legitimate, non-discriminatory reason for termination).

Page 585, add before *Mauerhan* cite in first full paragraph:

Jarvela v. Crete Carrier Corp., 776 F.3d 822, 830 (11th Cir. 2015) ("a seven-day-old diagnosis is 'current' under governing DOT regulations such that plaintiff was unqualified to drive a commercial motor vehicle); *Shirley v. Precision Castparts Corp.*, 726 F.3d 675, 680-81 (5th Cir. 2013) (plaintiff not within the §12114(b) safe harbor for participating in a supervised rehabilitation program when he, although voluntarily entering an in-patient facility, refused to complete the program and insisted on remaining an opiate pain reliever);

Page 587, add before *Kroll* cite near end of first paragraph:

Bates v. Dura Auto. Sys., Inc., 767 F.3d 566 (6th Cir. 2014) (2-1) (fact question as to whether a company's testing program for drug use, including certain prescription drugs, qualified as "medical examination" or, alternatively, as a disability inquiry; if so, it was not justified by job relation or business necessity);

Page 588, add before *Ward* cite in second full paragraph:

Wright v. Ill. Dep't of Children & Family Servs., 798 F.3d 513 (7th Cir. 2015) (jury question as to whether a fitness for duty examination was consistent with business necessity when, contrary to its practice, the employer continued to assign children's cases to plaintiff pending the examination);

Page 588, add before Ward cite in second paragraph:

Some courts, however, limit standing to assert such claims to qualified disabled individuals. *Wetherbee v. Southern Co.*, 754 F.3d 901, 904 (11th Cir. 2014) (an individual seeking relief for violation of §12112(d)(3)(C), allowing the use of results of post-offer medical examinations "in accordance with this subchapter," must demonstrate that she is a qualified individual with a disability since a violation of that provision "occurs when information is used in violation of some other provision of the ADA"). In any event, the use of such tests has generated considerable litigation and divergent results. Some courts have been deferential to employers. *E.g., Michael v. City of Troy Police Dep't*, 808 F.3d 304, 309 (6th Cir. 2015) (even in the face of conflicting medical opinions about whether the plaintiff could safely perform the job of policeman, a city was entitled to rely on an objectively reasonable medical opinion that he was unfit for duty, especially when coupled with non-medical evidence of plaintiff's unusual conduct that raised grave concerns about his judgment); *Owusu-Ansah v. Coca-Cola Co.*, 715 F.3d 1306, 1312 (11th Cir. 2013) ("Coca-Cola had a reasonable, objective concern about Mr.Owusu-Ansah's mental state, which affected job performance and potentially threatened the safety of its other employees.");

Page 588, add before *Brown* cite towards end of last full paragraph:

Kroll v. White Lake Ambulance Auth., 763 F.3d 619, 625 (6th Cir. 2014) (while plaintiff's conduct might have justified disciplinary proceedings, it "could not support the conclusion that Kroll was experiencing an emotional or psychological problem that interfered with her ability to perform her job functions," thus justifying its demand that she submit to psychological evaluation);

Page 588, add at end of last full paragraph:

The ADA also requires employers to treat certain information confidentially, but not all health information an employer obtains from its workers is protected. *See EEOC v. Thrivent Fin. for Lutherans*, 700 F.3d 1044 (7th Cir. 2012) (an inquiry into the reasons for an employee's absence was not a "medical inquiry" within the meaning of §12112(d)(4)(B) and thus the employer had no need to treat the response, which revealed a history of migraine headaches, as a confidential medical record).

Page 589, add at end of first full paragraph:

The EEOC issued its final rule on Title I and Wellness programs on May 17, 2016, https://www.eeoc.gov/laws/regulations/qanda-ada-wellness-final-rule.cfma. While its details are complicated, the rule would permit employers to offer incentives up to 30% of the total cost of employee-only coverage to promote participation in a wellness program and/or for achieving health outcomes. The rule describes what qualifies as a wellness program, defines what it means for a program to be voluntary, and addresses the confidentiality of medical information obtained through the program.

**Page 591, add at the beginning of second paragraph of
5. Protected Relationships:**

Graziadio v. Culinary Inst. of Am., 817 F.3d 415, 432 (2d Cir. 2016), recognized three kinds of association claims: adverse actions caused by (1) "expense," because the employer believes her association with a disabled person will generate insurance costs; (2) "disability by association," triggered by employer fears that the employee may contract or is genetically predisposed to develop the disability of the associated person; and (3) "distraction," instances in which the employer fears that the employee will be inattentive at work due to the disability of the disabled person.

8 *Procedures for Enforcing the Antidiscrimination Laws*

Page 601, add at end of carryover sentence:

The EEOC has since revised its Intake Questionnaire to require claimants to check a box to request that the EEOC take remedial action. When "Box 2" is checked, an employee "unquestionably files a charge of discrimination." *Hildebrand v. Allegheny Cnty.*, 757 F.3d 99, 113 (3d Cir. 2014).

Page 601, add at end of first paragraph in subsection b, *When Does a Violation "Occur"?*:

See Begolli v. Home Depot U.S.A., Inc., 701 F.3d 1158 (7th Cir. 2012) (the requirement of a timely charge is a kind of statute of limitations, which means that any fact issue relevant to timeliness must be decided by a jury, not a judge at a preliminary hearing).

Page 608, add before "the only limitation" in Note 2, *The Contaminated Environment Exception*:

See also Mandel v. M&Q Packaging Corp., 706 F.3d 157, 167 (3d Cir. 2013) (plaintiff may proceed under a continuing violation theory since she "alleged at least one act that falls within the statute of limitations (i.e., Bachert calling her a 'bitch' during a meeting), and many of the acts that occurred prior to the applicable limitations period involved similar conduct by the same individuals, suggesting a persistent, ongoing pattern").

Page 609, add at end of carryover Note 2, *The Contaminated Environment Exception*:

But see Maliniak v. City of Tucson, 607 F. App'x 626 (9th Cir. 2015) (entire pattern of harassment actionable because "it was not unreasonable for a jury to conclude that the truck sign incident was related to the earlier bathroom incidents, and that all incidents were therefore part of the same actionable hostile work environment claim)"); *Moll v. Telesector Res. Grp., Inc.*, 760 F.3d 198, 203-04 (2d Cir. 2014) (district court erred in refusing to consider "both sexually overt and facially sex-neutral incidents" in assessing whether plaintiff alleged a timely sex-based hostile work environment claim).

Page 609, add at end of Note 3, *Other Pre-Fair Pay Act Exceptions*:

Outside of these situations, the courts have not been ready to identify continuing violations. *E.g., Ayala v. Shinseki*, 780 F.3d 52, 58 (1st Cir. 2015) (transfer to small, windowless room and being stripped of all her duties were not a continuing violation because plaintiff should have known that she had been subjected to adverse employment actions and should have filed promptly).

Page 610, add before *Shuler* cite in third line:

Davis v. Bombardier Transp. Holdings (USA), Inc., 794 F.3d 266, 269 (2d Cir. 2015) ("the Ledbetter Act does not encompass a claim of a discriminatory demotion decision that results in lower wages where, as here, the plaintiff has not offered any proof that the compensation itself was set in a discriminatory manner.").

Page 611, add at the end of Note 8. *Summarizing Current Individual Disparate Treatment Law:*

A failure to timely challenge one discrete act of discrimination, however, will not bar a challenge to a later act that is timely charged. *Stuart v. Local 727, Int'l Bhd. of Teamsters*, 771 F.3d 1014, 1018 (7th Cir. 2014) (a rule that time barred a plaintiff who has been repeatedly discriminated against by her employer from challenging later instances of discrimination when she failed to file a charge within 300 days of the first such act would be "absurd").

Page 612, add new principal case and Notes:

Green v. Brennan
136 S. Ct. 1769 (2016)

JUSTICE SOTOMAYOR delivered the opinion of the Court.

Title VII of the Civil Rights Act of 1964 prohibits employers from discriminating on the basis of race, color, religion, sex, or national origin, or retaliating against their employees for opposing or seeking relief from such discrimination. Before a federal civil servant can sue his employer for violating Title VII, he must, among other things, "initiate contact" with an Equal Employment Opportunity counselor at his agency "within 45 days of the date of the matter alleged to be discriminatory." 29 CFR §1614.105(a)(1) (2015).

If an employee claims he has been fired for discriminatory reasons, the "matter alleged to be discriminatory" includes the discharge itself and the 45-day limitations period begins running only after the employee is fired.

We address here when the limitations period begins to run for an employee who was not fired, but resigns in the face of intolerable discrimination—a "constructive" discharge. We hold that, in such circumstances, the "matter alleged to be discriminatory" includes the employee's resignation, and that the 45-day clock for a constructive discharge begins running only after the employee resigns.

I

We recite the following facts in the light most favorable to petitioner Marvin Green, against whom the District Court entered summary judgment. Green is a black man who worked for the Postal Service for 35 years. In 2008, he was serving as the postmaster for Englewood, Colorado when he applied for a promotion to the vacant postmaster position in nearby Boulder. He was passed over. Shortly thereafter, Green complained he was denied the promotion because of his race.

Green's relations with his supervisors crumbled following his complaint. Tensions peaked on December 11, 2009, when two of Green's supervisors accused him of intentionally delaying the mail—a criminal offense. They informed Green that the Postal Service's Office of the Inspector General (OIG) was investigating the charge and that OIG agents had arrived to interview him as part of their investigation. After Green met with the OIG agents, his supervisors gave him a letter reassigning him to off-duty status until the matter was resolved. Even though the OIG agents reported to Green's supervisors that no further investigation was warranted, the supervisors continued to represent to Green that "the OIG is all over this" and that the "criminal" charge "could be a life changer."

On December 16, 2009, Green and the Postal Service signed an agreement whose meaning remains disputed. Relevant here, the Postal Service promised not to pursue criminal charges in exchange for Green's promise to leave his post in Englewood. The agreement also apparently gave Green a choice: effective March 31, 2010, he could either retire or report for duty in Wamsutter, Wyoming—population 451—at a salary considerably lower than what he earned in his Denver suburb. Green chose to retire and submitted his resignation to the Postal Service on February 9, 2010, effective March 31.

On March 22—41 days after submitting his resignation paperwork to the Postal Service on February 9, but 96 days after signing the settlement agreement on December 16—Green contacted an Equal Employment Opportunity (EEO) counselor to report an unlawful constructive discharge. He contended that his supervisors had threatened criminal charges and negotiated the resulting agreement in retaliation for his original complaint.[1] He alleged that the choice he had been given effectively forced his resignation in violation of Title VII.

[The district court granted summary judgment against Green for failure to act in a timely fashion, and the Tenth Circuit affirmed.]

II

Before a federal civil servant can sue his employer in court for discriminating against him in violation of Title VII, he must first exhaust his administrative remedies. 42 U. S. C. §2000e-16(c). To exhaust those remedies, the Equal Employment Opportunity Commission (EEOC) has promulgated regulations that require, among other things, that a federal employee consult with an EEO counselor prior to filing a discrimination lawsuit. Specifically, he "must initiate contact with a Counselor within 45 days of the date of the matter alleged to be discriminatory or, in the case of personnel action, within 45 days of the effective date of the action." 29 CFR §1614.105(a)(1).[4] The timeliness of Green's claim therefore turns on our interpretation of this EEOC regulation implementing Title VII.

Although we begin our interpretation of the regulation with its text, the text in this case is not particularly helpful. Nowhere does §1614.105 indicate whether a "matter alleged to be discriminatory" in a constructive-discharge claim includes the employee's resignation, as Green contends, or only the employer's discriminatory conduct, as *amica* contends. The word "matter" simply means "an allegation forming the basis of a claim or defense," Black's Law Dictionary 1126 (10th ed. 2014) — a term that could readily apply to a discrimination-precipitated resignation. So the "matter alleged to be discriminatory" could refer to all of the allegations underlying a claim of discrimination, including the employee's resignation, or only to those allegations concerning the employer's discriminatory conduct. We therefore must turn to other canons of interpretation.

The most helpful canon in this context is "the 'standard rule'" for limitations periods. *Graham County Soil & Water Conservation Dist.* v. *United States ex rel. Wilson*, 545 U. S. 409, 418 (2005). Ordinarily, a "'limitations period commences when the plaintiff has a complete and present cause of action.'" *Ibid.* "[A] cause of action does not become 'complete and present' for limitations purposes until the plaintiff can file suit and obtain relief." *Bay Area Laundry and Dry Cleaning Pension Trust Fund* v. *Ferbar Corp. of Cal.*, 522 U. S. 192, 201 (1997). Although the standard rule can be

---

1. We assume without deciding that it is unlawful for a federal agency to retaliate against a civil servant for complaining of discrimination. See *Gomez-Perez* v. *Potter*, 553 U. S. 474, 488, n. 4 (2008).

4. This regulation, applicable to federal employees only, has a statutory analog for private-sector Title VII plaintiffs, who are required to file a charge with the EEOC within 180 or 300 days "after the alleged unlawful employment practice occurred." 42 U.S.C. § 2000e-5(e)(1). Although the language is different, the EEOC treats the federal and private-sector employee limitations periods as identical in operation. See EEOC Compliance Manual: Threshold Issues §2-IV(C)(1), n. 179.

displaced such that the limitations period begins to run before a plaintiff can file a suit, we "will not infer such an odd result in the absence of any such indication" in the text of the limitations period. *Reiter* v. *Cooper*, 507 U. S. 258, 267 (1993).

Applying this default rule, we are persuaded that the "matter alleged to be discriminatory" in a constructive-discharge claim necessarily includes the employee's resignation for three reasons. First, in the context of a constructive-discharge claim, a resignation is part of the "complete and present cause of action" necessary before a limitations period ordinarily begins to run. Second, nothing in the regulation creating the limitations period here, §1614.105, clearly indicates an intent to displace this standard rule. Third, practical considerations confirm the merit of applying the standard rule here. We therefore interpret the term "matter alleged to be discriminatory" for a constructive-discharge claim to include the date Green resigned.

A

The standard rule for limitations periods requires us first to determine what is a "complete and present cause of action" for a constructive-discharge claim. We hold that such a claim accrues only after an employee resigns.

The constructive-discharge doctrine contemplates a situation in which an employer discriminates against an employee to the point such that his "working conditions become so intolerable that a reasonable person in the employee's position would have felt compelled to resign." *Pennsylvania State Police* v. *Suders*, 542 U.S. 129, 141 (2004). When the employee resigns in the face of such circumstances, Title VII treats that resignation as tantamount to an actual discharge. *Id.*

A claim of constructive discharge therefore has two basic elements. A plaintiff must prove first that he was discriminated against by his employer to the point where a reasonable person in his position would have felt compelled to resign. *Id.* But he must also show that he actually resigned. *Ibid.* ("A constructive discharge involves *both* an employee's decision to leave and precipitating conduct . . ." (emphasis added)). In other words, an employee cannot bring a constructive-discharge claim until he is constructively *discharged*. Only after both elements are satisfied can he file suit to obtain relief.

Under the standard rule for limitations periods, the limitations period should begin to run for a constructive-discharge claim only after a plaintiff resigns. At that point — and not before — he can file a suit for constructive discharge. So only at that point — and not before — does he have a "complete and present" cause of action. And only after he has a complete and present cause of action does a limitations period ordinarily begin to run.

In this respect, a claim that an employer constructively discharged an employee is no different from a claim that an employer actually discharged an employee. An ordinary wrongful discharge claim also has two basic elements: discrimination and discharge. See *St. Mary's Honor Center* v. *Hicks*, 509 U.S. 502 (1993), 1 B. Lindemann, P. Grossman, & C. Weirich, Employment Discrimination Law 21-33 (5th ed. 2012) (Lindemann) ("The sine qua non of a discharge case is, of course, a discharge"). The claim accrues when the employee is fired. At that point — and not before — he has a "complete and present cause of action." So at that point — and not before — the limitations period begins to run.

With claims of either constructive discharge or actual discharge, the standard rule thus yields the same result: a limitations period should not begin to run until after the discharge itself. In light of this rule, we interpret the term "matter alleged to be discriminatory" in §1614.105 to refer to all of the elements that make up a constructive-discharge claim — including an employee's resignation.

B

Although the standard rule dictates that a limitations period should commence only after a claim accrues, there is an exception to that rule when the text creating the limitations period clearly indicates otherwise. Nothing in the text of Title VII or the regulation, however, suggests that the standard rule should be displaced here. To the contrary, the language of the regulation confirms our application of the default rule. . . .

C

Finally, we are also persuaded that applying the standard rule for limitations periods to constructive discharge makes a good deal of practical sense. Starting the limitations clock ticking *before* a plaintiff can actually sue for constructive discharge serves little purpose in furthering the goals of a limitations period — and it actively negates Title VII's remedial structure. Cf. *Zipes* v. *Trans World Airlines, Inc.*, 455 U. S. 385, 398 (1982) (holding that the Title VII limitations period should be construed to "honor the remedial purpose of the legislation as a whole without negating the particular purpose of the filing requirement").

This Court has recognized "that the limitations perio[d] should not commence to run so soon that it becomes difficult for a layman to invoke the protection of the civil rights statutes." *Delaware State College* v. *Ricks*, 449 U. S. 250, 262, n. 16 (1980). If the limitations period begins to run following the employer's precipitating discriminatory conduct, but before the employee's resignation, the employee will be forced to file a discrimination complaint after the employer's conduct and later amend the complaint to allege constructive discharge after he resigns. Nothing in the regulation suggests it intended to require a layperson, while making this difficult decision, to follow such a two-step process in order to preserve any remedy if he is constructively discharged.

Moreover, forcing an employee to lodge a complaint before he can bring a claim for constructive discharge places that employee in a difficult situation. An employee who suffered discrimination severe enough that a reasonable person in his shoes would resign might nevertheless force himself to tolerate that discrimination for a period of time. He might delay his resignation until he can afford to leave. Or he might delay in light of other circumstances, as in the case of a teacher waiting until the end of the school year to resign. And, if he feels he must stay for a period of time, he may be reluctant to complain about discrimination while still employed. A complaint could risk termination — an additional adverse consequence that he may have to disclose in future job applications.

III

Amica and the dissent read "matter alleged to be discriminatory" as having a clear enough meaning to displace our reliance on the standard rule for limitations periods. They argue that "matter" is not equivalent to "claim" or "cause of action," and that the use of the phrase "matter alleged to be discriminatory" is a sufficiently clear statement that the standard claim accrual rule should not apply. According to *amica* and the dissent, "matter" refers only to the discriminatory acts of the Postal Service, not Green's resignation.

We disagree. There is nothing inherent in the phrase "matter alleged to be discriminatory" that clearly limits it to employer conduct. Rather, as discussed above, the term can reasonably be interpreted to include the factual basis for a claim. Green is not alleging just that the Postal Service discriminated against him. He claims that the discrimination left him no choice but to resign.

Amica and the dissent dispute that a constructive discharge is a separate claim. According to *amica* and the dissent, the constructive-discharge doctrine merely allows a plaintiff to expand any underlying discrimination claim to include the damages from leaving his job, thereby increasing his available remedies. See 1 Lindemann 21-49 (constructive discharge allows plaintiff to seek backpay, front pay, or reinstatement). In support of this argument, *amica* and the dissent emphasize this Court's statement in *Suders* that "[u]nder the constructive discharge doctrine, an employee's reasonable decision to resign because of unendurable working conditions is assimilated to a formal discharge *for remedial purposes*." (emphasis added); see also *id.* ("[A] constructive discharge is functionally the same as an actual termination in damages-enhancing respects").

But the Court did not hold in *Suders* that a constructive discharge is tantamount to a formal discharge for remedial purposes exclusively. To the contrary, it expressly held that constructive discharge is a claim distinct from the underlying discriminatory act. *Id.* (holding that a hostile-work-environment claim is a "lesser included component" of the "*graver* claim of hostile-environment constructive discharge"). This holding was no mere dictum. See *id.* ("[A] claim for constructive discharge lies under Title VII"). We see no reason to excise an employee's resignation from his constructive-discharge claim for purposes of the limitations period.

The concurrence sets out a theory that there are two kinds of constructive discharge for purposes of the limitations period: constructive discharge "claims" where the employer "makes conditions intolerable *with the specific discriminatory intent of forcing the employee to resign*," and constructive discharge "damages" where the employer does not intend to force the employee to quit, but the discriminatory conditions of employment are so intolerable that the employee quits anyway. (ALITO, J., concurring in judgment). According to the concurrence, the limitations period does not begin to run until an employee resigns under the "claim" theory of constructive discharge, but begins at the last discriminatory act before resignation under the "damages" theory.

This sometimes-a-claim-sometimes-not theory of constructive discharge is novel and contrary to the constructive discharge doctrine. The whole point of allowing an employee to claim "constructive" discharge is that in circumstances of discrimination so intolerable that a reasonable person would resign, we treat the employee's resignation as though the employer actually fired him. *Suders.*[6] We do not also require an employee to come forward with proof—proof that would often be difficult to allege plausibly—that not only was the discrimination so bad that he had to quit, but also that his quitting was his employer's plan all along.

Amica and the dissent also argue that their interpretation is more consistent with this Court's prior precedent on when the limitations period begins to run for discrimination claims. Under their interpretation, Green's resignation was not part of the discriminatory "matter," but was instead the mere inevitable consequence of the Postal Service's discriminatory conduct, and therefore cannot be used to extend the limitations period [citing, inter alia, *Ledbetter* v. *Goodyear Tire & Rubber Co., Delaware State College* v. *Ricks; United Air Lines, Inc.* v. *Evans*]. Similarly, the concurrence argues these cases require that an act done with discriminatory intent must occur within the limitations period.

But these cases are consistent with the standard rule that a limitations period begins to run after a claim accrues, not after an inevitable consequence of that claim. In *Ricks,* for example, the Court considered the discrimination claim of a college faculty member who was denied tenure and given a 1-year "terminal" contract for his last year teaching. The plaintiff's claim accrued—and he could have sued—when the college informed him he would be denied tenure and gave him "explicit notice that his employment would end" when his 1-year contract expired. The Court held that the limitations period began to run on that date, and not after his 1-year contract expired. That final year of teaching was merely an

---

6. The concurrence suggests that its theory is consistent with statements in the *Suders* opinion that constructive discharge is akin to an actual discharge "'for remedial purposes'" and in "'damages-enhancing respects.'" This ignores the more obvious explanation for this qualification: The Court was distinguishing between the merits of a claim of constructive discharge generally, where resignation is imputed as a discriminatory act of the employer, and the affirmative defense available to an employer in a hostile work environment claim specifically, which allows an employer to defend against a hostile work environment claim in certain circumstances if it took no "'official act'" against the employee. The Court in *Suders* recognized that it would be bizarre to always impute resignation as an "official act" of the employer in a constructive discharge hostile work environment case and prohibit the employer from relying on the no-"official-act" defense, because it would make it easier to prove the "graver" claim of a constructive discharge hostile work environment than to prove a hostile work environment claim. Thus, the Court declined to hold that resignation in a constructive discharge case was categorically an "official act" in all instances. In other words, the Court sought a measure of parity between constructive discharge and ordinary discrimination—parity that we extend to the limitations period here.

inevitable consequence of the tenure denial the plaintiff claimed was discriminatory.

Green's resignation, by contrast, is not merely an inevitable consequence of the discrimination he suffered; it is an essential part of his constructive-discharge claim. That is, Green could not sue for constructive discharge until he actually resigned. Of course, Green could not resign and then wait until the consequences of that resignation became most painful to complain. For example, he could not use the date of the expiration of his health insurance after his resignation to extend the limitations period. But the "inevitable consequence" principle of *Ricks, Ledbetter,* and *Evans* does not change the focus of the limitations period, which remains on the claim of discrimination itself. See *Lewis* v. *Chicago*, 560 U. S. 205, 214 (2010) (holding *Evans* and its progeny "establish only that a Title VII plaintiff must show a present violation within the limitations period" (internal quotation marks omitted)); *National Railroad Passenger Corporation* v. *Morgan* (holding limitations period for hostile-work-environment claim runs from the last act composing the claim).[7] For a constructive discharge, the claim does not exist until the employee resigns.

Finally, *amica* contends that her interpretation of the regulation better advances the EEOC's goal of promoting conciliation for federal employees through early, informal contact with an EEO counselor. The dissent suggests that our holding will make a discrimination victim the master of his complaint, permitting him to "'exten[d] the limitation[s period] indefinitely'" by waiting to resign. The concurrence claims that an employee who relies on the limitations period in waiting to resign is "doubly out of luck" if his otherwise-meritorious discrimination claim is time barred and he cannot show the discrimination was so intolerable that it amounted to a constructive discharge.

These concerns are overblown. *Amica* may be right that it is more difficult to achieve conciliation after an employee resigns. But the same is true for a federal civil servant who is fired by his agency for what the employee believes to be a discriminatory purpose. And neither decision is necessarily permanent — a resignation or a termination may be undone after an employee contacts a counselor. Conciliation, while important, does not warrant treating a constructive discharge different from an actual discharge for purposes of the limitations period.

As for the dissent's fear, we doubt that a victim of employment discrimination will continue to work in an intolerable environment merely because he can thereby extend the limitations period for a claim of constructive discharge. If anything, a plaintiff who wishes to prevail on the merits of his constructive discharge claim has

---

7. The dissent relies on *Morgan*'s other holding that, unlike a hostile-work-environment claim that may comprise many discriminatory acts, discrete claims of discrimination based on independent discriminatory acts cannot be aggregated to extend the limitations period. But this just proves the point: The analysis for the limitations period turns on the nature of the specific legal claim at issue. In *Morgan*, the Court noted that even if a claim of discrimination based on a single discriminatory act is time barred, that same act could still be used as part of the basis for a hostile-work-environment claim, so long as one other act that was part of that same hostile-work-environment claim occurred within the limitations period.

the opposite incentive. A claim of constructive discharge requires proof of a causal link between the allegedly intolerable conditions and the resignation. See 1 Lindemann 21-45, and n. 106.

And as for the concurrence's double-loser concern, no plaintiff would be well advised to delay pursuing what he believes to be a meritorious non-constructive-discharge-discrimination claim on the ground that a timely filed constructive discharge claim could resuscitate other time-lapsed claims. The 45-day limitations period begins running on any separate underlying claim of discrimination when that claim accrues, regardless of whether the plaintiff eventually claims constructive discharge. The limitations-period analysis is always conducted claim by claim.

IV

Our decision that a resignation triggers the limitations period for a constructive-discharge claim raises the question of when precisely an employee resigns. Here, Green and the Government agree that an employee resigns when he gives his employer definite notice of his intent to resign. If an employee gives "two weeks' notice" — telling his employer he intends to leave after two more weeks of employment — the limitations period begins to run on the day he tells his employer, not his last day at work.

We agree. A notice rule flows directly from this Court's precedent. In *Ricks* and *Chardon* v. *Fernandez*, 454 U. S. 6 (1981) the Court explained that an ordinary wrongful-discharge claim accrues — and the limitations period begins to run — when the employer notifies the employee he is fired, not on the last day of his employment. Likewise, here, we hold that a constructive-discharge claim accrues — and the limitations period begins to run — when the employee gives notice of his resignation, not on the effective date of that resignation.

One factual issue remains: when exactly Green gave the Postal Service notice of his resignation. The Government argues that Green resigned on December 16, 2009 — when he signed the settlement agreement — and that his claim is therefore still time barred. Green argues that he did not resign until February 9, 2010 — when he submitted his retirement paperwork — and that his claim is therefore timely. We need not resolve this issue. Having concluded that the limitations period for Green's constructive-discharge claim runs from the date he gave notice of his resignation, we leave it to the Tenth Circuit to determine when this in fact occurred. . . .

JUSTICE ALITO, concurring in the judgment.

In its pursuit of a bright-line limitations rule for constructive discharge claims, the Court loses sight of a bedrock principle of our Title VII cases: An act done with discriminatory intent must have occurred within the limitations period. We have repeatedly held that the time to pursue an employment discrimination claim starts running when a discriminatory act occurs, and that a fresh limitations period does not start upon the occurrence of a later nondiscriminatory act — even if that later act carries forward the effects of the earlier discrimination. [citing *United Air Lines, Inc.*

v. *Evans; Delaware State College* v. *Ricks; Chardon* v. *Fernandez; Lorance* v. *AT&T Technologies, Inc.; National Railroad Passenger Corporation* v. *Morgan; Ledbetter* v. *Goodyear Tire & Rubber Co.*] Without mentioning this consistent line of precedent, the Court categorically declares that the limitations period for constructive discharge cases starts upon the employee's resignation, no matter when the last discriminatory act occurred. This effectively disposes of the discriminatory-intent requirement.

Rather than jettison our precedent, I would hold that the limitations period for constructive discharge claims — like all other employment discrimination claims — starts running upon a discriminatory act of the employer. But I would also hold that an employee's resignation can, in many cases, be considered a discriminatory act of the employer. This is so where an employer subjects an employee to intolerable working conditions *with the discriminatory intent to force the employee to resign.* In these circumstances, the employee's consequent resignation is tantamount to an intentional termination by the employer, and so gives rise to a fresh limitations period just as a conventional termination would. Absent such intent, however, the resignation is not an independent discriminatory act but merely a delayed consequence of earlier discrimination. The resignation may be a basis for enhancing damages in a claim brought on the underlying discrimination, but it cannot restart the limitations clock.

In this case, Green presented sufficient evidence that the Postal Service intended to force him to resign when it presented him with a settlement agreement requiring that he either retire or transfer to a distant post office for much less pay. Accordingly, the 45-day window for him to initiate counseling opened when he gave the Postal Service notice of his resignation. . . .

JUSTICE THOMAS, dissenting . . .

Today, the majority holds that a "matter alleged to be discriminatory" [within the meaning of §1614.105(a)] includes a matter that is not "discriminatory" at all: a federal employee's decision to quit his job. The majority reaches this conclusion by adopting an atextual reading of the regulation that expands the constructive-discharge doctrine. Consistent with the text of the regulation and history of the constructive-discharge doctrine, I would hold that only an employer's actions may constitute a "matter alleged to be discriminatory." Because the only employer action alleged to be discriminatory here took place more than 45 days before petitioner Marvin Green contacted EEOC, his claims are untimely. I therefore respectfully dissent. . . .

In the context of employment discrimination, only an employer can discriminate against — or apply unjustifiable differential treatment to — an employee. An employee cannot plausibly be said to discriminate against himself. It therefore makes no sense to say that an employee's act of quitting constitutes an action in which he was treated in a differential manner that lacked a sound justification.

And, it does not make any more sense to say that an employee's decision to quit is itself "discriminatory" simply because it may result from antecedent discriminatory conduct. As two of our precedents — *National Railroad Passenger Corporation* v. *Morgan* and *Delaware State College* v. *Ricks* — illustrate, the "matter alleged to be discriminatory" is the *reason* the employee quit, and not the quitting itself. . . .

148

The majority's error is not merely one of regulatory misinterpretation. By misreading the regulation, the majority expands the constructive-discharge doctrine beyond its original bounds. In particular, the majority cements the (mistaken) notion that constructive discharge is an independent cause of action—and not a mere counterdefense—by unjustifiably focusing on an employee's response to an employer's conduct. In doing so, the majority exacerbates the problems that *Pennsylvania State Police* v. *Suders* first created in adopting a capacious definition of "constructive

[The dissent repeated Justice Thomas's dissent in *Suders* itself, but noted that that decision] at least retained some focus on an employer's conduct. The Court in *Suders* explained that whether to "assimilat[e]" a constructive discharge "to a formal discharge for remedial purposes" entailed an "objective" inquiry that focused on the "working conditions" themselves. And, it held that an employer could raise certain affirmative defenses to stave off liability when no official action forced an employee to resign.

Today, the majority goes even further than *Suders* in eviscerating the limitations on the constructive-discharge doctrine. The majority's rule transforms constructive discharge into a claim focused on the employee's conduct, instead of the employer's. Green does not allege that, after he signed the settlement agreement, any other act—by a supervisor or even a co-worker—occurred or otherwise immediately precipitated his decision to quit. The majority's holding—that Green's claim accrued when he resigned—must rest then on Green's own subjective feelings about the forced settlement. By ignoring the date on which an employer's discriminatory act occurred and instead focusing only on an employee's subjective response to that discriminatory act, the majority dispenses with the function of an employer's conduct. The effect of the majority's analysis, then, is that constructive discharge no longer involves any sort of objective inquiry. . . .

NOTES

1. *Federal Employees.* The principal case involved a federal employee suit, which is subject to somewhat different time limits and administrative procedures than are suits against private or state and local government employers. As indicated, a federal employee has 45 days to "initiate contact" with an agency EEO counselor rather than 180/300 days for filing a charge with the EEOC. See footnote 4. However, while *Green* itself involved only 29 C.F.R. §1614.105(a)(1), its reasoning seems likely to be applied to private sector VII suits. Certainly, that is how Justice Alito reads it: "The majority, for its part, seems to agree that the same rules should apply in the federal and private sectors." While an omitted part of Justice Thomas's dissent focused heavily on the language of the regulation, it seems unlikely he would argue for a different result in the private sector since he also relies heavily on Supreme Court precedents taking a narrow approach to the 180/300 day time limit.

2. *The Holding.* The majority's holding is straightforward: "the . . . clock for a constructive discharge begins running only after the employee resigns." To the

extent there's a twist on this, it is the Court's statement that the employee's notice of resignation, not his last day of work, is the operative point. The concurrence agrees – sometimes. Justice Alito would allow such suits where the employer specifically intended the employee's resignation, and he apparently thinks that that would often be easy to prove when the conditions for a constructive discharge were met. See footnote 7. But, if so, is the game worth the candle? That is, are the complications of a bifurcated constructive discharge liability structure justified? Or is the concurrence is driven more by a sense that the majority's rule imposes liability for an act not intended to be discriminatory (the resignation), even if that acts is caused by a prior discriminatory acts?

3. *The Dissent.* If Justice Alito offers a halfway house, Justice Thomas would reject any employer liability for an employee's act – the resignation. For him, a charge (or initiating counseling) would have to occur within the relevant time from the employer's discriminatory act, however long that was before the resignation. His opinion faults the majority for having time limits turn on "an employee's subjective response to that discriminatory act." But doesn't constructive discharge require the employee to be objectively reasonable in finding continued work intolerable?

4. *Adverse Employment Action.* Although the Court didn't focus on it, it seems clear that it thought the transfer to a lower-paying position in a distant state was a plausible basis for constructive discharge. Given the elevated standard for that, does *Green* cast doubt on some of the cases finding that "lateral transfers" aren't sufficiently adverse to be actionable? Or are the facts in *Green* so extreme as to be of little use in more typical cases?

5. *Intent to Bring About Resignation?* Although most courts viewed *Suders* as having retired any requirement that, for constructive discharge that the employer must have specifically intended the employee's resignation, some cases continued to apply that rule. After *Green*, such a position is no longer sustainable, if it ever was. Indeed, Justice Alito explicitly regards "damage enhancement" cases as a subspecies of constructive discharge.

Page 612, add at end of Note on State Deferral Requirements:

While a state filing is necessary in order to bring a Title VII suit, it will typically also satisfy any state exhaustion requirements. A subsequent suit (whether in state or federal court), then, can assert both federal and state claims, and state law may be more generous than federal law in a number of respects. *See generally* Sandra F. Sperino, *Revitalizing State Employment Discrimination Law*, 20 GEO. MASON L. REV. 545, 546 (2013).

Page 613, add at end of *Tolling and Estoppel* subsection:

In *Menominee Indian Tribe of Wis. v. United States*, 136 S. Ct. 750, 755-56 (2016), a decision not involving the antidiscrimination laws, the Supreme Court held that equitable tolling of a federal statute of limitations turns on two elements, first, whether the party has been pursuing his rights diligently and, second, whether extraordinary circumstances prevent timely filing, which requires that the circumstances that caused the delay "are both extraordinary and beyond [the litigant's] control." This seems a more rigorous standard than the already stringent requirements adopted by the lower courts for employment discrimination suits. But *Menominee Indian Tribe* involved tolling the time to bring court suit and the cases discussed in this section involve tolling charge filing periods. In short, the impact of the new decision on Title VII and related statutes remains to be seen.

Page 614, add at end of carryover paragraph:

This authority, at least insofar as it reaches damages claims at law, may have been undercut by *Petrella v. MGM*, 134 S. Ct. 1962, 1975 n.16 (2014), holding that laches cannot preclude a legal claim for damages brought within a governing statute of limitations although the doctrine can be invoked to limit otherwise appropriate injunctive relief. The Court read *Morgan* as not to the contrary since it at most held that laches may "limit the continuing violation doctrine's potential to rescue *untimely* claims, not claims accruing separately within the limitations period." (emphasis in original). However, *Petrella*'s application to backpay (as opposed to damages) is unclear: since backpay is an equitable remedy, laches may apply to limit recovery.

Other Potential Defenses. A recent Second Circuit opinion raised a possible futility defense to exhausting administrative remedies. *Fowlkes v. Ironworkers Local 40*, 790 F.3d 378, 386 (2d Cir. 2015), wrote that plaintiff "may have a colorable argument that filing a charge alleging discrimination based on his transgender status would have been futile." That was because, at the time she filed her complaint in 2011, "the EEOC had developed a consistent body of decisions that did not recognize Title VII claims based on the complainant's transgender status." *Id.* Only in 2012, did the agency alter its position. "Thus, Fowlkes's failure to exhaust could potentially be excused on the grounds that, in 2011, the EEOC had 'taken a firm stand' against recognizing his Title VII discrimination claims." *Id.* The court also noted that, as we will explore at p. 617, his second charge might be "reasonably related" to an earlier charge, which might also be a basis for excusing the failure to exhaust administrative remedies.

Page 615, add after *But see* in second full paragraph:

Cf. Loubriel v. Fondo Del Seguro Del Estado, 694 F.3d 139, 144 (1st Cir. 2012) (while the continuing violation doctrine may toll the limitations period for filing charge with the EEOC, it does not apply to extend the ninety day filing period for court suit);

Page 618, add before *Richter* cite in carryover paragraph:

Williams v. Milwaukee Health Servs., 562 F. App'x 523 (7th Cir. 2014) (plaintiff's ADA claim failed because the charge she filed with the EEOC did not mention disability discrimination)

Page 618, add at end of carryover paragraph:

Angela D. Morrison, *Misconstruing Notice in EEOC Administrative Processing & Conciliation*, 14 NEV. L.J. 785 (2014) (arguing that courts have mistakenly conflated the requirement of notice in charges of discrimination with notice for purposes of litigation).

Special problems arise when a plaintiff claims to have been retaliated against on the basis of a filed EEOC charge. Some courts find that such retaliation can be challenged as within the scope of the original charge. *Hentosh v. Old Dominion Univ.*, 767 F.3d 413 (4th Cir. 2014) (plaintiff may raise a retaliation claim based on the filing of a charge of discrimination without filing a separate retaliation change since a court has jurisdiction over those claims "reasonably related to" the allegations in the administrative charge even if the charge was untimely, since timely filing is not jurisdictional). But other courts are not so liberal. *See generally* Lawrence D. Rosenthal, *To File or Not to File (Again): The Post-*Morgan *Circuit Split Over the Duty to File an Amended or Second EEOC Charge of Claims of Post-charge Employer Retaliation*, 66 BAYLOR L. REV. 531 (2104).

Page 619, add after *Hayes* cite in second full paragraph:

Matusick v. Erie County Water Auth., 739 F.3d 51 (2d Cir. 2014) (preclusion principles barred relitigation of whether plaintiff actually engaged in misconduct as found in a prior administrative proceeding but did not bar a jury from determining that one of the reasons for his discharge was his romantic relationship with an African American); *Adams v. FedEx Ground Package Sys., Inc.*, 546 F. App'x 772, 775 (10th Cir. 2013) (issue preclusion by prior arbitration agreement barred subsequent suit on discrimination claims, despite contention that plaintiff lacked a full and fair opportunity to litigate her claims because of limited discovery in the arbitration proceedings when plaintiff herself demanded arbitration and did not move to vacate the award).

Page 621, add after first full paragraph:

The Supreme Court has since revisited the issue of class arbitration. Its more significant decision was *American Express Co. v. Italian Colors Restaurant*, 133 S. Ct. 2304, 2307 (2013), which found that a contractual waiver of class arbitration is enforceable under the Federal Arbitration Act even when the plaintiff's cost of individually arbitrating a federal statutory claim exceeds the potential recovery. *Italian Colors* involved suit by retailers against American Express, but there is little doubt that it would reach employment cases. In *Oxford Health Plans LLC v. Sutter*, 133 S. Ct. 2064 (2013), the Court upheld an arbitrator's decision that the parties had agreed to class arbitration. Despite the fact that the *Concepcion* Court had stressed the tension between arbitration and any class procedures, *Oxford Health* found that the arbitrator had grounded his decision in the parties' agreement, and proper respect for entrusting such decisions to arbitrators in the first place required enforcing that decision. Most recently, in *DIRECTV, Inc. v. Imburgia*, 136 S. Ct. 463 (2015), the Court again held that class action waivers in arbitration agreements are enforceable under the FAA and that state courts cannot invalidate such provisions on grounds that would not be applicable to any other contract.

Page 621, delete last two sentences of second full paragraph; replace with:

This aspect of *D.R. Horton* was rejected on review by the Fifth Circuit, 737 F.3d 344 (5th Cir. 2013), and other appellate courts have also found the argument unpersuasive. *Owen v. Bristol Care, Inc.*, 702 F.3d 1050, 1052 (8th Cir. 2013); *Sutherland v. Ernst & Young LLP*, 726 F.3d 290, 297 n.8 (2d Cir. 2013). *See also Johnmohammadi v. Bloomingdale's*, 755 F.3d 1072 (9th Cir. 2014) (by failing to return an opt-out form that would have excluded arbitration, plaintiff agreed to not pursue class relief; not requiring such an agreement as a condition of employment rendered inapposite possible objections under the Norris-LaGuardia and National Labor Relations Acts). However, the Seventh Circuit recently looked to *Horton* to invalidate a bar on class relief for employees, *Lewis v. Epic Sys. Corp.*, No. 15-2997, 2016 U.S. App. LEXIS 9638, at *22 (7th Cir. May 26, 2016), thus creating a circuit split. The issue is currently being briefed in a number of other circuits. *See generally* Charles A. Sullivan & Timothy P. Glynn, *Horton Hatches the Egg: Concerted Action Includes Concerted Dispute Resolution*, 64 ALA. L. REV. 1013 (2013).

Page 633, add at end of Note 3, *No More Disparate Treatment Class Actions?*:

The threat to systemic disparate treatment class actions has led to calls for increased EEOC focus on systemic cases. *See* Angela D. Morrison, *Duke-Ing Out Pattern or Practice After* Wal-Mart*: The EEOC As Fist*, 63 AM. U. L. REV. 87 (2013); Joseph A. Seiner, *Weathering* Wal-Mart, 89 NOTRE DAME L. REV. 1343 (2014). *But see* Michael C. Harper, *Class-Based Adjudication of Title VII Claims in the Age of the Roberts Court*, 95 B.U.L. REV. 1099, 1101 (2015) (The *Wal-Mart* Court's applications of Rule 23, while unfavorable to plaintiffs, were predictable and did not substantially modify any well-established Title VII law. Rule 23 still affords plaintiffs the flexibility to utilize class actions to press a broad range of systemic disparate treatment and impact claims). Michael Selmi & Sylvia Tsakos *Employment Discrimination Class Actions After* Wal-Mart v. Dukes, 48 AKRON L. REV. 803

(2015) ("*Wal-Mart* did not fundamentally change the class action landscape; rather, courts will likely continue to approach class action claims much as they did before the case was decided."); Joseph A. Seiner, *The Issue Class*, 56 B.C. L. REV. 121 (2015).

Page 634, add at end of Note 6, *Retreating from* Watson's *Approval of Disparate Impact*:

In any event, disparate impact class actions may still survive where the challenged policy is objective. In *Stockwell v. City & County of San Francisco*, 749 F.3d 1107, 1116 (9th Cir. 2014), the plaintiffs challenged a decision to abandon an examination as a basis for certain assignments, arguing that it created a disparate impact based on age. The court reversed the lower court's denial of class certification: "the officers are all challenging a single policy they contend has adversely affected them. The question whether the policy has an impermissible disparate impact on the basis of age necessarily has a single answer." The court stressed that in doing so it did not necessarily "approve of the statistical showing the officers have made as adequate to make out their merits case." Rather, it was merely "identifying a common question sufficient for Rule 23(a)(2) purposes," which did not pass on the defendant's arguments challenging the plaintiff's statistical analysis or any other defense the City may offer. *Id.* "The defects the City has identified may well exist, but they go to the merits of this case, or to the predominance question. . . ." *Id.*

Page 636, add at end of carryover paragraph:

Despite *Wal-Mart's* disapproval of "Trial by Formula," *Tyson Foods, Inc. v. Bouaphakeo*, 136 S. Ct 1036 (2016), approved expert proof of average times for donning and doffing in an FLSA class action despite the argument that individual questions as to remedy meant that those questions predominated. The Court viewed such statistical proof as admissible in an individual case to establish each worker's harm and, accordingly, admissible in a class case. It found the employer's reliance on *Wal-Mart* for "the broad proposition that a representative sample is an impermissible means of establishing classwide liability" to be misplaced. In that case, there was *no* common question, whereas in *Bouaphakeo* there were common questions and only the issue of the relationship of those questions to individual questions. The rejected proof in *Wal-Mart* was an effort to "overcome[e] this absence of a common policy," *id.* at 1048, and it was this "Trial by Formula" the Court there held contrary to the Rules Enabling Act because it enlarged the class members' substantive rights. The Court explained why its result in *Bouaphakeo* was consistent with *Wal-Mart*:

> The underlying question in *Wal-Mart*, as here, was whether the sample at issue could have been used to establish liability in an individual action. Since the Court held that

the employees were not similarly situated, none of them could have prevailed in an individual suit by relying on depositions detailing the ways in which other employees were discriminated against by their particular store managers. By extension, if the employees had brought 1 1/2 million individual suits, there would be little or no role for representative evidence. Permitting the use of that sample in a class action, therefore, would have violated the Rules Enabling Act by giving plaintiffs and defendants different rights in a class proceeding than they could have asserted in an individual action.

In contrast, the study here could have been sufficient to sustain a jury finding as to hours worked if it were introduced in each employee's individual action. While the experiences of the employees in *Wal-Mart* bore little relationship to one another, in this case each employee worked in the same facility, did similar work, and was paid under the same policy. . . . [U]nder these circumstances the experiences of a subset of employees can be probative as to the experiences of all of them.

Id.

Page 637, add at end of first full paragraph:

See also Davis v. Cintas Corp., 717 F.3d 476, 489 (6th Cir. 2013) (affirming a district court's denial of certification because the named plaintiff failed to show that the class of women "who failed to obtain employment at many places, over a long time, under a largely subjective hiring system, shared a common question of law or fact").

However, other recent cases reject the more extreme negative interpretations of *Wal-Mart*. In *Scott v. Family Dollar Stores, Inc.*, 733 F.3d 105, 114 (4th Cir. 2013) (2-1), the Fourth Circuit read *Wal-Mart* as limited to discretionary decisions by lower-level employees; when "high-level personnel exercise discretion, [the] resulting decisions affect a much larger group, and depending on their rank in the corporate hierarchy, all the employees in the company." *Id.* at 113-14. In other words, *Wal-Mart*" did not set out a per se rule against class certification where subjective decision-making or discretion is alleged. Rather, . . . *Wal-Mart* directs courts to examine whether 'all managers [] exercise discretion in a common way with[] some common direction.' Thus, to satisfy commonality, a plaintiff must demonstrate that the exercise of discretion is tied to a specific employment practice, and that the 'subjective practice at issue affected the class in a uniform manner.'" *Id.* at 113. The dissent of Judge Wilkerson complained that majority opinion has "drained [*Wal-Mart*] of meaning." *Id.* at 119. *See also Brown v. Nucor Corp.*, 785 F.3d 895 (4th Cir. 2015) (reversing decertification of plant-wide disparate treatment and disparate impact class action by black steel workers in light of statistical and substantial anecdotal evidence of discrimination in promotion decisions in multiple departments).

And in *Chicago Teachers Union, Local No. 1 v. Bd. of Educ. of Chi.*, 797 F.3d 426, (7th Cir. 2015), the court found that "a company-wide practice is appropriate for class challenge even where some decisions in the chain of acts challenged as discriminatory can be exercised by local managers with discretion—at least where the class at issue is affected in a common manner, such as where there is a uniform policy or process applied to all. . . . In short, subjective, discretionary decisions can be the source of a common claim if they are, for example, the outcome of employment practices or policies controlled by higher-level directors, if all decision-makers exercise discretion in a common way because of a company policy or practice, or if all decision-makers act together as one unit."

Page 637, add before *Modesitt* cite in last full paragraph:

David Freeman Engstrom, *Agencies As Litigation Gatekeepers*, 123 YALE L.J. 616 (2013) (arguing for dismantling the EEOC's administrative charge resolution process as adding "strikingly little gatekeeper value"); Margo Schlanger & Pauline T. Kim, *The Equal Employment Opportunity Commission and Structural Reform of the American Workplace*, 91 WASH. U. L. REV. 1519 (2014) (EEOC structural relief "appears primarily aimed at forcing firms to implement what are commonly accepted as good and rational human resources practices" rather than transforming culture and norms); Pauline T. Kim, *Addressing Systemic Discrimination: Public Enforcement and the Role of the EEOC*, 95 B. U. L. REV. 1133 (2015). *See also* Stephanie Bornstein, *Rights in Recession: Towards Administrative Antidiscrimination Law*, 33 YALE L. & POL'Y REV. 119 (2014).

Page 638, add after *CRST* citation in carryover paragraph:

Because of the importance of conciliation to the enforcement of the modern antidiscrimination laws, defendants in EEOC suits sometimes also claimed that the suit should be dismissed because the agency failed to conciliate. Although the argument had mixed success in the lower courts, the Supreme Court's recent decision in *Mach Mining, LLC v. EEOC*, 135 S. Ct. 1645 (2015), should resolve most issues. While the Court did recognize that judicial review of EEOC conciliation efforts was appropriate, it simultaneously framed the scope of review as exceedingly narrow. It is limited to whether the EEOC informed the employer about the specific allegation, including "what the employer has done and which employees (or what class of employees) have suffered as a result," and whether the agency "tr[ied] to engage the employer in some form of discussion (whether written or oral), so as to give the employer an opportunity to remedy the allegedly discriminatory practice." *Id.* at 1656. The Court was firm that "[j]udicial review of those requirements (and nothing else) ensures that the Commission complies with the statute." *Id.* Finally, should a court determine the EEOC had failed to satisfy these minimal standards, "the appropriate remedy is to order the EEOC to undertake the mandated efforts to obtain voluntary compliance." *Id. See also EEOC v. Bass Pro Outdoor World, L.L.C.*, 2016 U.S. App. LEXIS 11031 (5th Cir. June 17, 2016) (conciliation requirements were satisfied in a §706 pattern and practice suit when the EEOC informed the employer of the class it had allegedly discriminated against and months of negotiation followed; similarly, investigation requirements were satisfied by the EEOC relying on statistical and anecdotal evidence in such a suit rather than evidence about specific aggrieved individuals); *EEOC v. Sterling Jewelers Inc.*, 801 F.3d 96 (2d Cir. 2015) (although *Mach Mining* did not address the EEOC's obligation to investigate, judicial review of an EEOC investigation is similarly limited to whether the agency conducted an investigation, not its sufficiency). *Cf. CRST Van Expedited, Inc. v. EEOC*, 136 S. Ct. 1642 (2016) (considering award of attorneys' fees to defendant based largely on the EEOC's failure to investigate before bring suit).

Page 638, add in carryover paragraph before *Fed. Express* cite:

See also EEOC v. Aerotek, Inc., 815 F.3d 328, 334 (7th Cir. 2016) (upholding enforcement of EEOC administrative subpoena seeking staffing agency's client information in investigation of possible age discrimination; the agency's initial review of the employer database revealed hundreds of age-based discriminatory job requests by clients, and EEOC was entitled to further information to determine if other clients also made similar discriminatory requests when production did not impose an undue hardship).

Page 638, add at end of carryover paragraph:

There is also a developing jurisprudence concernly the proper procedures for an EEOC pattern and practice suit. *See EEOC v. Bass Pro Outdoor World, L.L.C.*, No. 15-20078, 2016 U.S. App. LEXIS 11031, at *15 (5th Cir. June 17, 2016) ("Congress did not prohibit the EEOC from bringing pattern or practice suits under Section 706 and, in turn, from carrying them to trial with sequential determinations of liability and damages in a bifurcated framework" under the *Teamsters* framework); *Serrano v. Cintas Corp.*, 699 F.3d 884 (6th Cir. 2012) (reversing a district court holding that the EEOC could not bring a pattern-and-practice claim on the basis of an individual charge under §706 of the statute but only on the basis of a pattern-or-practice suit under §707 (although the court also found that the agency had failed to properly plead the pattern-or-practice claim)).

Page 639, add after *Lapides* cite in second full paragraph:

But see Stroud v. McIntosh, 722 F.3d 1294, 1300-01 (11th Cir. 2013) (although removal to federal court waives state immunity to a federal forum, it does not waive immunity from liability under a federal statute); *contra Bd. of Regents of the Univ. of Wis. Sys. v. Phoenix Int'l Software, Inc.*, 653 F.3d 448, 461 (7th Cir. 2011) (a state's removal to federal court waives immunity); *see also Pettigrew v. Oklahoma ex rel. Oklahoma Dep't of Pub. Safety*, 722 F.3d 1209, 1211 (10th Cir. 2013) (an agreement settling a Title VII suit waived the state's "Eleventh Amendment" right not to be sued in federal court since there was no reasonable construction of its enforcement provisions except as a waiver).

Page 641, add after *Gomez-Perez* cite:

(ADEA). Most lower courts have held that retaliation is also illegal under Title VII. *E.g., Diggs v. HUD*, 670 F.3d 1353, 1357 (Fed. Cir. 2011), although the Supreme Court avoided deciding that question in *Green v. Brennan*, 136 S. Ct. 1769, 1774 n. 1 (2016)

9   *Judicial Relief*

Page 648, add before "See also" in second paragraph:

In *EEOC v. KarenKim, Inc.*, 698 F.3d 92 (2d Cir. 2012), the court found it an abuse of discretion for the district court to decline to order injunctive relief to ensure that an individual found responsible for egregious acts of sexual harassment against multiple female employees could not continue his harassing conduct. A concurring opinion by Judge Katzmann agreed, but also argued, that "the most natural way to practically effectuate the Supreme Court's guidance that Title VII grants courts with 'not merely the power' but 'the duty' to remedy violations of the Act through injunctive relief would be to shift the burden of proving the appropriateness of such relief onto the defendant-employer once liability under the Act is established. *Id.* at 103.

Page 650, add and end of carryover paragraph:

Equitable relief is sometimes ordered even when the harm seems mostly monetary but does not fall easily into other categories of recovery. *See Trainor v. HEI Hospitality, LLC*, 699 F.3d 19, 36 (1st Cir. 2012) (affirming injunction allowing plaintiff to continue vesting in three investment funds, akin to pension plans, designed for senior executives as though he were still employed by HEI, despite contractual provisions limiting participation to those still employed by the defendant).

Page 654, add before Secunda cite in Note 5, *Is Each Victim Entitled to Full Relief?*:

See also Howe v. City of Akron, 801 F.3d 718, 752 (6th Cir. 2015) (no decision on whether the lost-chance method of calculating back pay is appropriate in this case).

Page 656, add at end of carryover paragraph:

See also Howe v. City of Akron, 801 F.3d 718, 746 (6th Cir. 2015) ("step increases are among the types of compensation that a district court must consider when calculating the back-pay award in order to make the plaintiff whole").

In one case, the court even thought that backpay could even be based on what another employer would have paid plaintiff but for the discrimination. *See Szeinbach v. Ohio State Univ.*, 820 F.3d 814, 824 (6th Cir. 2016) ("the district court erred in determining that any amount of back pay had to be based on a comparison between what Szeinbach actually earned while being subjected to OSU's discrimination and what she would have earned at OSU in the absence of discrimination. Instead, the district court should have considered the possibility that employment opportunities with third-party employers might have affected the proper calculation of back pay.").

In any event, prejudgment interest must be added to the backpay award. *Howe v. City of Akron*, 801 F.3d 718 (6th Cir. 2015).

Page 656, add after *Wellborn* cite in first full paragraph under "a. The Backpay Period":

See also Howe v. City of Akron, 801 F.3d 718, 746 (6th Cir. 2015) (the district court erred both in concluding that that the injury to the plaintiffs did not accrue until the eligibility list expired and in using the same start date for each plaintiff when it should have calculated each plaintiff's backpay from the date no more than two years before he or she filed a charge with the EEOC).

Page 656, add before last sentence on the page:

See also Zisumbo v. Ogden Reg'l Med. Ctr., 801 F.3d 1185, 1207 (10th Cir. 2015) (not an abuse of discretion for the district court to end backpay upon the plaintiff's conviction for a misdemeanor assault unconnected with work because the defendant would have terminated him for that conviction).

Page 663, add at end of Note 2, *After-Acquired Evidence Rule*:

A remaining question is, where front pay is involved, can an employee's conduct after discharge affect her right to recovery? *See* Holly G. Eubanks, Note, *Expanding the After-Acquired Evidence Defense to Include Post-Termination Misconduct*, 89 CHI.-KENT L. REV. 823 (2014).

Page 666, add after *King* cite in Note 1, *Front Pay as an Alternative to Reinstatement*:

Cf. Olivares v. Brentwood Indus., 822 F.3d 426 (8th Cir. 2016) (while front pay is normally appropriate where reinstatement is denied, an award must rest on sufficient proof, which plaintiff failed to adduce).

Page 666, add at end of Note 1, *Front Pay as an Alternative to Reinstatement*:

See also Barrett v. Salt Lake Cnty., 754 F.3d 864 (10th Cir. 2014) (affirming district court decision to provide plaintiff the pay he would have earned had he not been demoted when reinstatement would have required removing his replacement and rejecting defendant's claim that this remedy resulted in a "windfall" of more pay for less work).

Page 666, add at end of Note 2, *"Liquidated Damages" and Front Pay*:

See also Trainor v. HEI Hospitality, LLC, 699 F.3d 19, 31 (1st Cir. 2012) (award of front pay not inconsistent with multiplied damages under state law since the purpose of a front pay award is to help to make a plaintiff whole while multiplication of damages under the relevant state law was punitive in nature).

Page 670, delete Note 1; replace with the following:

1. Proving Mental Distress. Damages for mental distress can be recovered only when actual injury is proved; such injury cannot be presumed merely from a civil rights violation. *Carey v. Piphus*, 435 U.S. 247 (1978). As in *Turic*, many decisions have upheld awards for distress, humiliation, or anxiety based only on the testimony of the plaintiff and other lay persons. *E.g., Bennett v. Riceland Foods, Inc.*, 721 F.3d 546, 552 (8th Cir. 2013) (compensatory damage award for emotional distress may be based on a plaintiff's own testimony; medical or other expert evidence is not required); *Farfaras v. Citizens Bank & Trust*, 433 F.3d 558, 566 (7th Cir. 2006) (upholding $100,000 pain and suffering award since medical testimony not necessary to prove emotional injury in a Title VII case). *But see Miller v. Raytheon Co.*, 716 F.3d 138 (5th Cir. 2013) (upholding remittitur of mental anguish award from $1 million to $100,000 because the claim was premised solely on the testimony of plaintiff and his wife); *Trainor v. HEI Hospitality, LLC*, 699 F.3d 19, 32 (1st Cir. 2012) ($500,000 award was grossly excessive where there was no evidence of medical treatment or counseling). And at least one court seems to think that expert testimony of a medically cognizable injury is necessary. *Price v. City of Charlotte*, 93 F.3d 1241 (4th Cir. 1996).

Commentators have urged more judicial openness to recovery for emotional distress. *See generally* Scott A. Moss & Peter H. Huang, *How the New Economics Can Improve Employment Discrimination Law, and How Economics Can Survive the Demise of the "Rational Actor,"* 51 WM. & MARY L. REV. 183 (2009); Zachary A. Kramer, *After Work,* 95 CAL. L. REV. 627, 629 (2007). *See also* Jessica L. Roberts, *Rethinking Employment Discrimination Harms,* 91 IND. L.J. 393 (2016) (arguing for an expanded notion of actionable harm under the antidiscrimination laws in order to deal with stereotype threat). One obstacle to plaintiff's pursuing such recovery is that any privacy interests in a patient's treatment for mental distress are waived if the plaintiff seeks damages for such harm. *Fisher v. Sw. Bell Tel. Co.,* 361 F. App'x 974 (10th Cir. 2010).

Page 676, add at end of first sentence in Note 2a, *Defendant's State of Mind*:

See May v. Chrysler Group LLC, 716 F.3d 963 (7th Cir. 2013) (reinstating jury verdict for punitive damages in light of protracted period in which the employer did little or nothing to deal with continuing, egregious instances of racial harassment); *EEOC v. Autozone, Inc.,* 707 F.3d 824 (7th Cir. 2013) (upholding an award of punitive damages since a jury could find that the employer acted with reckless indifference to the employee's rights by not responding to multiple requests for accommodation despite ADA training of the relevant managers and a company procedure regarding accommodations); *Trickey v. Kaman Indus. Techs. Corp.,* 705 F.3d 788 (8th Cir. 2013) (punitive damages award of $500,000 supported by evidence that manager sabotaged older employee's performance improvement plan).

Page, 677, replace *Vance* cite in Note 3(a) with:

Vance v. Ball State University, 133 S. Ct. 2434 (2013), reproduced at p. 64 of this Supplement.

Page 679, add near end of Note 9, *Substantive Due Process* before *Zhang* cite:

Turley v. ISG Lackawanna, Inc., 774 F.3d 140, 165 (2d Cir. 2014) (overturning a $5 million punitive damages award where compensatory damages were set at $1.3 million; not merely was there a four-to-one ratio of punishment to compensation but the compensatory award was "for intangible — and therefore immeasurable — emotional damages. Imposing extensive punitive damages on top of such an award stacks one attempt to monetize highly offensive behavior, which effort is necessarily to some extent visceral, upon another.");

9. Judicial Relief

Page 679, add near end of Note 9, *Substantive Due Process* **after** *Sealy* **cite:**

EEOC v. Autozone, Inc., 707 F.3d 824 (7th Cir. 2013) (upholding a punitive damages award against a due process attack given (1) the reprehensibility of the defendant's conduct; (2) a 2:1 ratio of punitive to compensatory damages, and less than a 1:1 ratio if backpay is added; and (3) the statutory cap). *But see Arizona v. ASARCO, LLC*, 733 F.3d 882, 888-90 (9th Cir. 2013) (an award with a ratio of $300,000 to $1 of punitive damages to nominal damages for very reprehensible conduct was excessive even though its amount mirrored the statutory cap; the court, however, approved a remittitur of $125,000);

Page 680, add at end of Note 10, *Compensatory and Punitive Damages in ADA Actions***:**

Mark C. Weber, *Accidentally On Purpose: Intent In Disability Discrimination Law*, 56 B. C. L. REV. 1417, 1428 (2015) (no requirement of intent for a reasonable accommodation claim although the employer has a limited affirmative defense to compensatory damages by showing good faith efforts to make such an accommodation).

Page 681, add before *Loveless* **cite in first full paragraph:**

See also Miller v. Raytheon Co., 716 F.3d 138, 146 (5th Cir. 2013) (affirming an award of liquidated damages since following facially neutral RIF procedures does not insulate an employer from a willful violation finding when considerable evidence suggested that "Raytheon went out of its way to avoid rehiring Miller, in contravention of its usual procedures, and to obscure the reasons for its decisions").

Page 681, add before *see generally* **cite at end of last full paragraph:**

But see Miller v. Raytheon Co., 716 F.3d 138 (5th Cir. 2013) (when an ADEA claim warranted liquidated damages and a state claim capped punitive damages, the court should not award both but rather the higher amount).

Page 686, add after *L. B. Foster* **cite in first paragraph of Note 2,** *When Is a Prevailing Defendant Entitled to Attorneys' Fees?***:**

See also EEOC v. Peoplemark, Inc., 732 F.3d 584 (6th Cir. 2013) (no abuse of discretion in award of attorneys' fees against EEOC; while the agency's case was not groundless when filed due to incorrect company official's statements about a supposed policy of denying jobs to applicants with felony records, the Commission should have discontinued its case when discovery clearly belied those statements by establishing that no such policy existed).

Page 686, add at end of first paragraph of Note 2, *When Is a Prevailing Defendant Entitled to Attorneys' Fees?*:

Autry v. Fort Bend Indep. Sch. Dist., 704 F.3d 344, 349-50 (5th Cir. 2013) (finding abuse of discretion to award defendant attorneys' fees when plaintiff's claim, though unsuccessful, was not "frivolous, unreasonable or without foundation").

Page 687, add at end of carryover Note 3, *What Does "Prevail" Mean?*:

Even when a plaintiff prevails on one claim, she may not recover fees for unsuccessful claims, although the successful and unsuccessful claims may be so intertwined that it will not be an abuse of discretion for the district court to give full recovery. *See Waldo v. Consumers Energy Co.*, 726 F.3d 802, 823 (6th Cir. 2013) (refusing to find an abuse of discretion when the trial court did not reduce an attorney fee award even though plaintiff prevailed on only one of seven claims since the claims were all related and focused on a common core of facts evidencing how plaintiff's male co-workers sexually harassed her); *Trainor v. HEI Hospitality, LLC*, 699 F.3d 19 (1st Cir. 2012) (no abuse of discretion by district court in not deducting hours pursuing plaintiff's unsuccessful age discrimination claim when it was inextricably intertwined with his retaliation claim, which was successful).

Most of these cases have considered whether a plaintiff prevailed. In contrast, *CRST Van Expedited, Inc. v. EEOC*, 136 S. Ct. 1642 (2016), decided what it means for a defendant to "prevail" beyond the *Christiansburg* standard of frivolousness. Consistent with the holding of *Fox v. Vice*, 563 U. S. 826, (2011), as to prevailing plaintiffs, see Note 2 above, the Court held a prevailing defendant could recover with respect to some claims, even if it did not win on all claims. More importantly, it rejected the argument that, to be prevailing, a defendant must have obtained a ruling on the merits of the claim on which it was successful. Rather, "[t]he congressional policy regarding the exercise of district court discretion in the ultimate decision whether to award fees does not distinguish between merits-based and non-merits-based judgments," 1565. ct at 1652, since the purpose of the fee-shifting provision was to spare defendants from the costs of frivolous litigation. "Congress must have intended that a defendant could recover fees expended in frivolous, unreasonable, or groundless litigation when the case is resolved in the defendant's favor, whether on the merits or not." *Id.* The Court remanded for consideration of the EEOC's argument that "a defendant must obtain a preclusive judgment in order to prevail." *Id.* at 1653.

Page 688, add before *See generally* **in carryover Note 4,** *Rule 68*:

See also Sanchez v. Prudential Pizza, Inc., 709 F.3d 689 (7th Cir. 2013) (in the Rule 68 context, any ambiguity is resolved against the offeror because of the difficult position such an offer creates for the offeree; thus, a plaintiff who accepted a Rule 68 offer may nevertheless recover attorneys' fees and costs even though the offer stated it included "all of Plaintiff's claims for relief" when it failed to explicitly specify costs or fees). *Cf. Diaz v. Jiten Hotel Mgmt.*, 704 F.3d 150, 154 (1st Cir. 2012) (rejecting a district court's reliance on plaintiffs' rejection of a settlement offer that was much larger than her ultimate recovery in reducing a fee award; given Rule 68, which "already provide[s] the defendant with a mechanism to make the plaintiff '"think very hard" about whether continued litigation is worthwhile' such that the judge-made prophylactic ruling in this case is unnecessary."). *Contra McKelvey v. Sec'y of United States Army*, 768 F.3d 491 (6th Cir. 2014) (a court may consider, among other factors, plaintiff's rejection of a substantial settlement offer in its decision to reduce the lodestar attorneys' fees award by 50%; Rule 68 is no barrier to doing so since it requires fee reductions in some situations whereas the fee statute simply permits them when appropriate). *Cf. Campbell-Ewald Co. v. Gomez*, 136 S. Ct. 663 (2016) (unaccepted Rule 68 offer a legal nullity and therefore does not affect plaintiff's standing to sue).

Page 692, add at the end of Note 7, *The Legal Work That Counts*:

But see Maner v. Linkan LLC, 602 F. App'x 489 (11th Cir. 2015) (no abuse of discretion for trial court to exclude attorney time working on plaintiff's application for state unemployment benefits since, given the absence of preclusive effect of unreviewed administrative decisions on Title VII claims, these hours were not "necessary" or "related" to the federal litigation); *Barrett v. Salt Lake County*, 754 F.3d 854 (10th Cir. 2014) (successful plaintiff entitled to attorneys' fees for his court proceedings but not for those incurred in an internal grievance process).

Page 693, add before *Eshelman* **cite in last paragraph:**

EEOC v. Beverage Distribs. Co., LLC, 780 F.3d 1018 (10th Cir. 2015) (the district court did not err in awarding a tax offset); *EEOC v. Northern Star Hospitality, Inc.*, 777 F.3d 898 (7th Cir. 2015) (allowing a gross-up of the monetary award to compensate plaintiff from being pushed into a higher tax bracket than had his wages had been paid at a regularly scheduled basis);

Page 694, add at end of carryover paragraph:

In light of these rules, efforts to structure settlements to maximize tax savings can be difficult. *See Ahmed v. Comm'r*, 498 F. App'x 919 (11th Cir. 2012) (a settlement of a discrimination suit was taxable even though it reflected harms other than back-pay when the settlement did not allocate any portion of the payment to compensate the taxpayer for physical injuries; even though plaintiff had suffered a heart attack, the settlement document did not specifically reference that harm).

Page 695, add before *see generally* cite in last paragraph:

Slater v. U.S. Steel Corp., 820 F.3d 193 (11th Cir. 2016) (even when the bankruptcy court sought to prosecute a discrimination case against the bankrupt's former employer, the court affirmed dismissal of the suit on the basis of judicial estoppel for failure of the plaintiff to disclose the claim in the bankruptcy filing); *Jones v. Bob Evans Farms, Inc.*, 811 F.3d 1030 (8th Cir. 2016) (plaintiff judicially estopped from suing by its failure to disclose the suit in bankruptcy proceedings which could have given him an unfair advantage in that proceeding since the bankruptcy court might have made any proceeds available to unsecured creditors). *But see Spaine v. Cmty. Contacts, Inc.*, 756 F.3d 542, 548 (7th Cir. 2014) (no judicial estoppel when the failure to disclose a discrimination claim in bankruptcy was cured by oral disclosure to the trustee and no sufficient proof of intentional concealment); *Ah Quin v. Cnty. of Kauai Dep't of Transp.*, 733 F.3d 2676 (9th Cir. 2013) (judicial estoppel of lawsuit for plaintiff's failure to reveal her claim as an asset in a bankruptcy filing is inappropriate where the omission was "inadvertent or mistaken, as those terms are commonly understood" rather than stemming from an intent to conceal);

10 Managing Risks in Employment Discrimination Disputes

Page 699, add after *Penn Plaza* cite in first full paragraph:

See also Boaz v. FedEx Customer Info. Servs., Inc., 725 F.3d 603, 606 (6th Cir. 2013) (an employment agreement that purported to reduce the statute of limitations for EPA claims from two years to six months operates as a waiver of her rights under the FLSA and is therefore invalid).

Page 699, add at end of first full paragraph:

See also EEOC v. Allstate Ins. Co., 778 F.3d 444, 451-53 (3d Cir. 2015) (rejecting EEOC challenge to employer's requiring terminated employees to release discrimination claims in order to be considered for engagement as independent contractors; a new business relationship with the employer provided consideration similar to that given in more typical severance agreements).

Page 702, add at end of Note 3, *Beyond Minimum Conditions*:

Yassan v. J.P. Morgan Chase & Co., 708 F.3d 963, 975 (7th Cir. 2013) (under New York law, release of a claim unknown at the time of signing is enforceable, and that is true even if there is fraud in obtaining the release; "No matter what prior representations Chase had made about its reasons for terminating Yassan, Chase was forthcoming with Yassan about the terms of the release-severance package deal, which plaintiff had ample opportunity to review before he signed.").

Page 713, add at end of page:

Nevertheless, there remains some bite to the requirement that a union cannot waive individual rights unless it does so clearly. *See Ibarra v. UPS*, 695 F.3d

354, 358 (5th Cir. 2012) (an arbitration clause in a collective bargaining agreement did not clearly and unmistakably waive union members' right to pursue statutory claims in court when the agreement did not specifically identify Title VII or state that statutory discrimination claims shall be subject to its grievance procedure but merely created a contract right to be free of discrimination).

Page 714, add at end of first paragraph of carryover Note 1, *Arbitration Uber Alles*:

In a powerful but limited executive order, President Obama barred the use of mandatory predispute arbitration provisions in the employment agreements of contractors who have more than $1 million in federal contracts. Fair Pay and Safe Workplaces Executive Order, July 31, 2014, http://www.whitehouse.gov/the-press-office/2014/07/31/executive-order-fair-pay-and-safe-workplaces.

Page 715, add at end of Note 4, *Duty of Fair Representation*:

See generally Michael Z. Green, *Reading* Ricci *and* Pyett *to Provide Racial Justice Through Union Arbitration*, 87 IND. L.J. 367 (2012) (any union decision not to process a claim should also make clear that the employee will be allowed a forum to effectively vindicate the claim).

Page 716, add before see generally cite in carryover Note 5, *Reviewing Arbitration Awards* before *see generally*:

See Wachovia Sec., LLC v. Brand, 671 F.3d 472, 480 (4th Cir. 2012) (manifest disregard standard survived *Hall Street* as an independent ground for vacatur); *Dewan v. Walia*, 544 F. App'x 230 (4th Cir. 2013) (2-1) (arbitration award vacated because it is the product of manifest disregard of the law since the arbitrator found a release valid but nevertheless awarded the employee damages on released claims).

Page 716, add before *Moses* citation in carryover Note 5, *Reviewing Arbitration Awards*:

See also In re Wal-Mart Wage & Hour Emp't Practices Litig. v. Class Counsel & Party to Arbitration, 737 F.3d 1262, 1267 (9th Cir. 2013) ("[j]ust as the text of the FAA compels the conclusion that the grounds for vacatur of an arbitration award may not be supplemented, it also compels the conclusion that these grounds are not waivable, or subject to elimination by contract," thus rendering a non-appealability clause invalid).

Page 723, add before *Mathews* cite in Note 1, *Who Decides Whether an Agreement is Valid?*:

Opalinski v. Robert Half Int'l, Inc., 761 F.3d 326, 329 (3d Cir. 2014) (since classwide arbitration is a question of arbitrability, it was presumptively a matter for the court; silence in the agreement as to the availability of classwide arbitration left the presumption unrebutted).

Page 724, delete Note 2; replace with:

2. *Finding an Agreement.* As *Hergenreder* reminds us, employers seeking to enforce an arbitration agreement must at least establish offer, acceptance, and consideration. Bickford failed to make sure its workers all signed its form, and thus failed on the formation test. Ironically, the disclaimers in the employee handbook (designed to protect Bickford from other kinds of liability) prevented it from getting the arbitral forum it desired. *See also Campbell v. Gen. Dynamics Gov't Sys. Corp.,* 407 F.3d 546, 556-58 (1st Cir. 2005) (no enforceable arbitration agreement where policy distributed via hyperlink in e-mail notification and employee did not reply to message). *But see Davis v. Nordstrom, Inc.* 755 F.3d 1089 (9th Cir. 2014) (modification of employee handbook requiring class action waiver was valid when the employer did not try to enforce it during the 30 day notice period it provided; employer had no duty to specifically inform employees that continued work constituted acceptance of the modification); *Hardin v. First Cash Fin. Servs.,* 465 F.3d 470 (10th Cir. 2006) (employee's continuing to work constituted agreement to employer's dispute resolution program despite her expressly rejecting program and stating that her continued employment would not serve as consent). Should the manner in which the employer establishes and communicates its arbitration policy matter in assessing contract enforceability? If most employees simply sign whatever documents the employer places before them in the application process, why is it any more objectionable to bind them to a handbook or e-mail arbitration policy?

Like all contracts, agreements to arbitrate require consideration or a consideration substitute, and some employers have failed to satisfy that requirement. *See, e.g., Nelson v. Watch House Int'l, L.L.C.,* 815 F.3d 190 (5th Cir. 2016) (employer's reservation of power to unilaterally make changes to an arbitration agreement effective immediately renders the agreement illusory and thus unenforceable under Texas law); *Scudiero v. Radio One of Texas II, L.L.C.,* 547 F. App'x 429, 432 (5th Cir. 2013) (no error in denying a motion to compel when the arbitration provision was "not a separate, stand-alone contract" but rather contained in an employee handbook, which reserved to the employer the right to unilaterally change, thus rendering the employer's promise to arbitrate was illusory and unenforceable); *Saylor v. Ryan's Family Steak Houses,* 613 S.E.2d 924 (W. Va. 2005) ("meager" promise to review employment application insufficient consideration to support applicant's promise to submit all disputes to arbitration). *Contra Hill v. PeopleSoft USA, Inc.,* 412 F.3d 540, 543-44 (4th Cir. 2005) (arbitration agreement not illusory due to lack of consideration because employer reserved right to change without notice). *See generally* Richard A. Bales, *Contract Formation Issues in Employment Arbitration*, 44 BRANDEIS L.J. 415 (2006).

Some courts have required arbitration agreements to bind both parties in order for there to be consideration, *see Goins v. Ryan's Family Steakhouses, Inc.*, 181 F. App'x 435 (5th Cir. 2006) (refusing to compel arbitration because the employer was not bound to arbitrate disputes), perhaps to provide incentives to the employer to ensure that the arbitral process is fair. *See* Cynthia Estlund, *Rebuilding the Law of the Workplace in an Era of Self-Regulation*, 105 COLUM. L. REV. 319, 436 (2005). However, this is contrary to normal consideration analysis, and most courts have rejected this theory. *Oblix v. Winiecki*, 374 F.3d 488, 491 (7th Cir. 2004) (that the employer "did not promise to arbitrate all of its potential claims is neither here nor there. [Plaintiff] does not deny that the arbitration clause is supported by consideration—her salary").

As to the statute of frauds, the FAA itself requires the agreement to arbitrate to be in writing in order to be enforceable. 9 U.S.C. §2. However, unlike normal statutes of frauds, the writing need not be signed by the party to be charged. *Tillman v. Macy's, Inc.*, 735 F.3d 453, 455 (6th Cir. 2013) ("Macy's provided sufficient notice of its offer to enter into an arbitration agreement," through a video, informational brochure and separate mailings to her home; the plaintiff "accepted by continuing her employment with Macy's and not returning either of the two opt-out forms provided to her"; the absence of a written agreement to arbitrate signed by the employee was not determinative).

Page 725, add after *Stolt-Nielsen* cite in Note 4, *Class Actions and Arbitration*:

But see Oxford Health Plans LLC v. Sutter, 133 S. Ct. 2064 (2013) (upholding arbitrator's decision finding parties had agreed to class arbitration even though the contract did not explicitly refer to such a proceeding).

Page 726, add a new Note 8:

8. *Waiver of Arbitration*: Even where an arbitration agreement is valid and enforceable, the parties may expressly or implicitly waive arbitration; the latter occurs most obviously by not moving to stay court proceedings in a timely manner. *See Messina v. N. Cent. Distrib.*, 821 F.3d 1047 (8th Cir. 2016) (an employer waived its right to arbitration by proceeding in court, including removing the case to federal court, filing an answer, participating in a pretrial hearing, filing a scheduling report which recommended a trial date and discovery deadlines, and filing a motion to transfer venue, all to the prejudice of plaintiff); *Cole v. Jersey City Med. Ctr.*, 72 A.3d 224, 235 (N.J. 2013) ("Liberty waived its right to arbitrate during the course of litigation. Liberty engaged in all of the usual litigation procedures for twenty-one months and, only on the eve of trial, invoked its right to arbitrate."). *See generally* Thomas J. Lilly, Jr., *Participation in Litigation as a Waiver of the Contractual Right to Arbitrate: Toward a Unified Theory*, 92 NEB. L. REV. 86, 88-89 (2013).

Statutes

Age Discrimination in Employment Act*

29 U.S.C. §§621–633a

§621 [§2]. Statement of Findings and Purpose

(a) The Congress hereby finds and declares that—

(1) in the face of rising productivity and affluence, older workers find themselves disadvantaged in their efforts to retain employment, and especially to regain employment when displaced from jobs;

(2) the setting of arbitrary age limits regardless of potential for job performance has become a common practice, and certain otherwise desirable practices may work to the disadvantage of older persons;

(3) the incidence of unemployment, especially long-term unemployment with resultant deterioration of skill, morale, and employer acceptability is, relative to the younger ages, high among older workers; their numbers are great and growing; and their employment problems grave;

(4) the existence in industries affecting commerce, of arbitrary discrimination in employment because of age, burdens commerce and the free flow of goods in commerce.

(b) It is therefore the purpose of this chapter to promote employment of older persons based on their ability rather than age; to prohibit arbitrary age discrimination in employment; to help employers and workers find ways of meeting problems arising from the impact of age on employment.

§622 [§3]. Education and Research Program

(a) The Secretary of Labor shall undertake studies and provide information to labor unions, management, and the general public concerning the needs and abilities of older workers, and their potentials for continued employment and contribution to the economy. In order to achieve the purposes of this chapter, the

---

* The functions of the Secretary of Labor and the Civil Service Commission, referred to in this Act, were transferred to the Equal Employment Opportunity Commission by Reorg. Plan No. 1, Feb. 23, 1978, 44 Fed. Reg. 1053.

Secretary of Labor shall carry on a continuing program of education and information, under which he may, among other measures—

(1) undertake research, and promote research, with a view to reducing barriers to the employment of older persons, and the promotion of measures for utilizing their skills;

(2) publish and otherwise make available to employers, professional societies, the various media of communication, and other interested persons the findings of studies and other materials for the promotion of employment;

(3) foster through the public employment service system and through cooperative effort the development of facilities of public and private agencies for expanding the opportunities and potentials of older persons;

(4) sponsor and assist State and community informational and educational programs.

(b) Not later than six months after the effective date of this chapter, the Secretary shall recommend to the Congress any measures he may deem desirable to change the lower or upper age limits set forth in section 631 of this title.

§623 [§4]. Prohibition of Age Discrimination

(a) *Employment practices*. It shall be unlawful for an employer—

(1) to fail or refuse to hire or to discharge any individual or otherwise discriminate against any individual with respect to his compensation, terms, conditions, or privileges of employment, because of such individual's age;

(2) to limit, segregate, or classify his employees in any way which would deprive or tend to deprive any individual of employment opportunities or otherwise adversely affect his status as an employee, because of such individual's age; or

(3) to reduce the wage rate of any employee in order to comply with this chapter.

(b) *Employment agency practices*. It shall be unlawful for an employment agency to fail or refuse to refer for employment, or otherwise to discriminate against, any individual because of such individual's age, or to classify or refer for employment any individual on the basis of such individual's age.

(c) *Labor organization practices*. It shall be unlawful for a labor organization—

(1) to exclude or to expel from its membership, or otherwise to discriminate against, any individual because of his age;

(2) to limit, segregate, or classify its membership, or to classify or fail to refuse to refer for employment any individual, in any way which would deprive or tend to deprive any individual of employment opportunities, or would limit such employment opportunities or otherwise adversely affect his status as an employee or as an applicant for employment, because of such individual's age;

(3) to cause or attempt to cause an employer to discriminate against an individual in violation of this section.

(d) *Opposition to unlawful practices; participation in investigations, proceedings, or litigation*. It shall be unlawful for any employer to discriminate against any of his employees or applicants for employment, for an employment agency to discriminate against any individual, or for a labor organization to discriminate against any member thereof or applicant for membership, because such individual, member, or applicant for membership, has opposed any practice made unlawful by this section, or because such individual, member, or applicant for membership has made a charge, testified, assisted, or participated in any manner in an investigation, proceeding, or litigation under this Act.

(e) *Printing or publication of notice or advertisement indicating preference, limitation, etc.* It shall be unlawful for an employer, labor organization, or employment agency to print or publish, or cause to be printed or published, any notice or advertisement relating to employment by such an employer or membership in or any classification or referral for employment by such a labor organization, or relating to any classification or referral for employment by such an employment agency, indicating any preference, limitation, specification, or discrimination, based on age.

(f) *Lawful practices; age an occupational qualification; other reasonable factors; seniority system; employee benefit plan; discharge or discipline for good cause.* It shall not be unlawful for an employer, employment agency, or labor organization —

(1) to take any action otherwise prohibited under subsection (a), (b), (c), or (e) of this section where age is a bona fide occupational qualification reasonably necessary to the normal operation of the particular business, or where the differentiation is based on reasonable factors other than age or where such practices involve an employee in a workplace in a foreign country, and compliance with such subsections would cause such employer, or a corporation controlled by such employer, to violate the laws of the country in which such workplace is located;

(2) to take any action otherwise prohibited under subsection (a), (b), (c), or (e) of this section —

(A) to observe the terms of a bona fide seniority system that is not intended to evade the purposes of this Act, except that no such seniority system shall require or permit the involuntary retirement of any individual specified by section 12(a) because of the age of such individual; or

(B) to observe the terms of a bona fide employee benefit plan —

(i) where, for each benefit or benefit package, the actual amount of payment made or cost incurred on behalf of an older worker is no less than that made or incurred on behalf of a younger worker, as permissible under section 1625.10, title 29, Code of Federal Regulations; or

(ii) that is a voluntary early retirement incentive plan consistent with the relevant purpose or purposes of this Act.

Notwithstanding clause (i) or (ii) of subparagraph (B), no such employee benefit plan or voluntary early retirement incentive plan shall excuse the failure to hire any individual, and no such employee benefit plan shall require or permit the involuntary retirement of any individual specified by section 12 (a), because of the age of such individual. An employer, employment agency, or labor organization acting under subparagraph (A), or under clause (i) or

(ii) of subparagraph (B), shall have the burden of proving that such actions are lawful in any civil enforcement proceeding brought under this Act; or

(3) to discharge or otherwise discipline an individual for good cause.

(g) [Deleted]

(h) *Foreign practices.*

(1) If an employer controls a corporation whose place of incorporation is in a foreign country, any practice by such corporation prohibited under this section shall be presumed to be such practice by such employer.

(2) The prohibitions of this section shall not apply where the employer is a foreign person not controlled by an American employer.

(3) For the purpose of this subsection the determination of whether an employer controls a corporation shall be based upon the—

(A) interrelation of operations,

(B) common management,

(C) centralized control of labor relations, and

(D) common ownership or financial control, of the employer and the corporation.

(i) *Employee pension benefit plans; cessation or reduction of benefit accrual or of allocation to employee account; distribution of benefits after attainment of normal retirement age; compliance; highly compensated employees.*

(1) Except as otherwise provided in this subsection, it shall be unlawful for an employer, an employment agency, a labor organization, or any combination thereof to establish or maintain an employee pension benefit plan which requires or permits—

(A) in the case of a defined benefit plan, the cessation of an employee's benefit accrual, or the reduction of the rate of an employee's benefit accrual, because of age, or

(B) in the case of a defined contribution plan, the cessation of allocations to an employee's account, or the reduction of the rate at which amounts are allocated to an employee's account, because of age.

(2) Nothing in this section shall be construed to prohibit an employer, employment agency, or labor organization from observing any provision of an employee pension benefit plan to the extent that such provision imposes (without regard to age) a limitation on the amount of benefits that the plan provides or a limitation on the number of years of service or years of participation which are taken into account for purposes of determining benefit accrual under the plan.

(3) In the case of an employee who, as of the end of any plan year under a defined benefit plan, has attained normal retirement age under such plan—

(A) if distribution of benefits under such plan with respect to such employee has commenced as of the end of such plan year, then any requirement of this subsection for continued accrual of benefits under such plan with respect to such employee during such plan year shall be treated as satisfied to the extent of the actuarial equivalent of inservice distribution of benefits, and

(B) if distribution of benefits under such plan with respect to such employee has not commenced as of the end of such year in accordance with section 1056(a)(3) of this title [Employee Retirement Income Security Act of 1974] and section 401(a)(14)(C) of title 26 [Internal Revenue Code of 1986], and the payment of benefits under such plan with respect to such employee is not suspended during such plan year pursuant to section 1053 (a)(3)(B) of this title [Employee Retirement Income Security Act of 1974] or section 411(a)(3)(B) of title 26 [Internal Revenue Code of 1986], then any requirement of this subsection for continued accrual of benefits under such plan with respect to such employee during such plan year shall be treated as satisfied to the extent of any adjustment in the benefit payable under the plan during such plan year attributable to the delay in the distribution of benefits after the attainment of normal retirement age.

The provisions of this paragraph (3) shall apply in accordance with regulations of the Secretary of the Treasury. Such regulations shall provide for the application of the preceding provisions of this paragraph to all employee pension benefit plans subject to this subsection and may provide for the application of such provisions in the case of any such employee, with respect to any period of time within a plan year.

(4) Compliance with the requirements of this subsection with respect to an employee pension benefit plan shall constitute compliance with the requirements of this section relating to benefit accrual under such plan.

(5) Paragraph (1) shall not apply with respect to any employee who is a highly compensated employee (within the meaning of section 414(q) of title 26 [Internal Revenue Code of 1986]) to the extent provided in regulations prescribed by the Secretary of Treasury for the purposes of precluding discrimination in favor of highly compensated employees within the meaning of subchapter D of chapter I of title 26.

(6) A plan shall not be treated as failing to meet the requirements of paragraph (1) solely because the subsidized portion of any early retirement benefit is disregarded in determining benefit accruals.

(7) Any regulations prescribed by the Secretary of the Treasury pursuant to clause (v) of section 411(b)(1)(H) of title 26 and subparagraphs (C) and (D) of section 411(b)(2) of such title 26 shall apply with respect to the requirements of this subsection in the same manner and to the same extent as such regulations apply with respect to the requirements of such section 411(b)(1)(H) and 411(b)(2) of title 26.

(8) A plan shall not be treated as failing to meet the requirements of this section solely because such plan provides a normal retirement age described in section 1002(24)(B) of this title [Employee Retirement Income Security Act of 1974] and section 411(a)(8)(B) of title 26. [Internal Revenue Code of 1986.]

(9) For purposes of this subsection—

(A) The terms "employee pension benefit plan," "defined benefit plan," "defined contribution plan," and "normal retirement age" have the meanings provided such terms in section 1002 of this title. [Employee Retirement Income Security Act of 1974.]

(B) The term "compensation" has the meaning provided by section 414(s) of title 26. [Internal Revenue Code of 1986.]

(j) Employment as firefighter or law enforcement officer. It shall not be unlawful for an employer which is a State, a political subdivision of a State, an agency or instrumentality of a State or a political subdivision of a State, or an interstate agency to fail or refuse to hire or to discharge any individual because of such individual's age if such action is taken —

(1) with respect to the employment of an individual as a firefighter or as a law enforcement officer, the employer has complied with section 3(d)(2) of the Age Discrimination in Employment Amendments of 1996 if the individual was discharged after the date described in such section, and the individual has attained —

(A) the age of hiring or retirement, respectively, in effect under applicable State or local law on March 3, 1983; or

(B)(i) if the individual was not hired, the age of hiring in effect on the date of such failure or refusal to hire under applicable State or local law enacted after September 30, 1996; or

(ii) if applicable State or local law was enacted after September 30, 1996, and the individual was discharged, the higher of —

(I) the age of retirement in effect on the date of such discharge under such law; and

(II) age 55; and

(2) pursuant to a bona fide hiring or retirement plan that is not a subterfuge to evade the purposes of this chapter.

(k) Seniority system or employee benefit plan; compliance. A seniority system of employee benefit plan shall comply with this Act regardless of the date of adoption of such system or plan.

(*l*) *Lawful practices; minimum age as condition of eligibility for retirement benefits; deduction from severance pay; reduction of long term disability benefits.* Notwithstanding clause (i) or (ii) of subsection (f)(2)(B) —

(1)(A) It shall not be a violation of subsection (a), (b), (c), or (e) solely because —

(i) an employee pension benefit plan (as defined in section 3(2) of the Employee Retirement Income Security Act of 1974) provides for the attainment of a minimum age as a condition of eligibility for normal or early retirement benefits; or

(ii) a defined benefit plan (as defined in section 3(35) of such Act) provides for —

(I) payments that constitute the subsidized portion of an early retirement benefit; or

(II) social security supplements for plan participants that commence before the age and terminate at the age (specified by the plan) when participants are eligible to receive reduced or unreduced old-age insurance benefits under title II of the Social Security Act and that do not exceed such old-age insurance benefits.

(B) A voluntary early retirement incentive plan that—
    (i) is maintained by—
        (I) a local educational agency (as defined in section 7801 of Title 20), or
        (II) an education association which principally represents employees of 1 or more agencies described in subclause (I) and which is described in section 501(c)(5) or (6) of Title 26 and exempt from taxation under section 501(a) of Title 26, and
    (ii) makes payments or supplements described in subclauses (I) and (II) of subparagraph (A)(ii) in coordination with a defined benefit plan (as so defined) maintained by an eligible employer described in section 457(e)(1)(A) of Title 26 or by an education association described in clause (i)(II),

shall be treated solely for purposes of subparagraph (A)(ii) as if it were a part of the defined benefit plan with respect to such payments or supplements. Payments or supplements under such a voluntary early retirement incentive plan shall not constitute severance pay for purposes of paragraph (2).

(2)(A) It shall not be a violation of subsection (a), (b), (c), or (e) solely because following a contingent event unrelated to age—
    (i) the value of any retiree health benefits received by an individual eligible for an immediate pension;
    (ii) the value of any additional pension benefits that are made available solely as a result of the contingent event unrelated to age and following which the individual is eligible for not less than an immediate and unreduced pension, are deducted from severance pay made available as a result of the contingent event unrelated to age; or
    (iii) the values described in both clauses (i) and (ii).

(B) For an individual who receives immediate pension benefits that are actuarially reduced under subparagraph (A)(i), the amount of the deduction available pursuant to subparagraph (A)(i) shall be reduced by the same percentage as the reduction in the pension benefits.

(C) For purposes of this paragraph, severance pay shall include that portion of supplemental unemployment compensation benefits that—
    (i) constitutes additional benefits of up to 52 weeks;
    (ii) has the primary purpose and effect of continuing benefits until an individual becomes eligible for an immediate and unreduced pension; and
    (iii) is discontinued once the individual becomes eligible for an immediate and unreduced pension.

(D) For purposes of this paragraph and solely in order to make the deduction authorized under this paragraph, the term "retiree health benefits" means benefits provided pursuant to a group health plan covering retirees, for which (determined as of the contingent event unrelated to age)—

(i) the package of benefits provided by the employer for the retirees who are below age 65 is at least comparable to benefits provided under title XVIII of the Social Security Act;

(ii) the package of benefits provided by the employer for the retirees who are age 65 and above is at least comparable to that offered under a plan that provides a benefit package with one-fourth the value of benefits provided under title XVIII of such Act; or

(iii) the package of benefits provided by the employer is as described in clauses (i) and (ii).

(E)(i) If the obligation of the employer to provide retiree health benefits is of limited duration, the value for each individual shall be calculated as a rate of $3,000 per year for benefit years before age 65, and $750 per year for benefit years beginning at age 65 and above.

(ii) If the obligation of the employer to provide retiree health benefits is of unlimited duration, the value for each individual shall be calculated at a rate of $48,000 for individuals below age 65, and $24,000 for individuals age 65 and above.

(iii) The values described in clauses (i) and (ii) shall be calculated based on the age of the individual as of the date of the contingent event unrelated to age. The values are effective on the date of enactment of this subsection, and shall be adjusted on an annual basis, with respect to a contingent event that occurs subsequent to the first year after the date of enactment of this subsection, based on the medical component of the Consumer Price Index for all urban consumers published by the Department of Labor.

(iv) If an individual is required to pay a premium for retiree health benefits, the value calculated pursuant to this subparagraph shall be reduced by whatever percentage of the overall premium the individual is required to pay.

(F) If an employer that has implemented a deduction pursuant to subparagraph (A) fails to fulfill the obligation described in subparagraph (E), any aggrieved individual may bring an action for specific performance of the obligation described in subparagraph (E). The relief shall be in addition to any other remedies provided under Federal or State law.

(3) It shall not be a violation of subsection (a), (b), (c) or (e) solely because an employer provides a bona fide employee benefit plan or plans under which long-term disability benefits received by an individual are reduced by any pension benefits (other than those attributable to employee contributions) —

(A) paid to the individual that the individual voluntarily elects to receive; or

(B) for which an individual who has attained the later of age 62 or normal retirement age is eligible.

(m) *Voluntary retirement incentive plans*

Notwithstanding subsection (f)(2)(b), it shall not be a violation of subsection (a), (b), (c) or (e) solely because a plan of an institution of higher education (as defined in section 1001 of title 20) offers employees who are serving under a contract of unlimited tenure (or similar arrangement providing for unlimited tenure) supplemental benefits upon voluntary retirement that are reduced or eliminated on the basis of age, if—

(1) such institution does not implement with respect to such employees any age-based reduction or cessation of benefits that are not such supplemental benefits, except as permitted by other provisions of this chapter;

(2) such supplemental benefits are in addition to any retirement or severance benefits which have been offered generally to employees serving under a contract of unlimited tenure (or similar arrangement providing for unlimited tenure), independent of any early retirement or exit-incentive plan, within the preceding 365 days; and

(3) any employee who attains the minimum age and satisfies all non-age-based conditions for receiving a benefit under the plan has an opportunity lasting not less than 180 days to elect to retire and to receive the maximum benefit that could then be elected by a younger but otherwise similarly situated employee, and the plan does not require retirement to occur sooner than 180 days after such election.

§624 [§5]. Study by Secretary of Labor; Reports to President and Congress; Scope of Study; Implementation of Study; Transmittal Date of Reports

(a)(1) The Secretary of Labor is directed to undertake an appropriate study of institutional and other arrangements giving rise to involuntary retirement, and report his findings and any appropriate legislative recommendations to the President and to the Congress. Such study shall include—

(A) an examination of the effect of the amendment made by section 3(a) of the Age Discrimination in Employment Act Amendments of 1978 [amending 29 USCS §631] in raising the upper age limitation established by section 12(a) of this Act [29 USCS §631(a)] to 70 years of age;

(B) a determination of the feasibility of eliminating such limitation;

(C) a determination of the feasibility of raising such limitation above 70 years of age; and

(D) an examination of the effect of the exemption contained in section 12(c) [29 USCS §631(c)], relating to certain executive employees, and the exemption contained in section 12(d) [29 USCS §631(d)], relating to tenured teaching personnel.

(2) The Secretary may undertake the study required by paragraph (1) of this subsection directly or by contract or other arrangement.

(b) The report required by subsection (a) of this section shall be transmitted to the President and to the Congress as an interim report not later than January 1, 1981, and in final form not later than January 1, 1982.

§625 [§6]. Administration

The Secretary shall have the power —

(a) to make delegations, to appoint such agents and employers, and to pay for technical assistance on a fee-for-service basis, as he deems necessary to assist him in the performance of his functions under this chapter;

(b) to cooperate with regional, State, local, and other agencies, and to co-operate with and furnish technical assistance to employers, labor organizations, and employment agencies to aid in effectuating the purposes of this chapter.

§626. Recordkeeping, Investigation, and Enforcement

(a) *Attendance of witnesses; investigations, inspections, records, and homework regulations.* The Secretary shall have the power to make investigations and require the keeping of records necessary or appropriate for the administration of this Act in accordance with the powers and procedures provided in sections 9 and 11 of the Fair Labor Standards Act of 1938, as amended (29 U.S.C. 209 and 211).

(b) *Enforcement; prohibition of age discrimination under fair labor standards; unpaid minimum wages and unpaid overtime compensation; liquidated damages; judicial relief; conciliation, conference, and persuasion.* The provisions of this Act shall be enforced in accordance with the powers, remedies, and procedures provided in sections 11(b), 16 (except for subsection (a) thereof), and 17 of the Fair Labor Standards Act of 1938, as amended (29 U.S.C. 211(b), 216, 217), and subsection (c) of this section. Any act prohibited under section 4 of this Act [29 USCS §623] shall be deemed to be a prohibited act under section 15 of the Fair Labor Standards Act of 1938, as amended (29 U.S.C. 215). Amounts owing to a person as a result of a violation of this Act shall be deemed to be unpaid minimum wages or unpaid overtime compensation for purposes of sections 16 and 17 of the Fair Labor Standards Act of 1938, as amended (29 U.S.C. 216, 217): *Provided,* That liquidated damages shall be payable only in cases of willful violations of this Act. In any action brought to enforce this Act the court shall have jurisdiction to grant such legal or equitable relief as may be appropriate to effectuate the purposes of this Act, including without limitation judgments compelling employment, reinstatement or promotion, or enforcing the liability for amounts deemed to be unpaid minimum wages or unpaid overtime compensation under this section. Before instituting any action under this section, the Secretary shall attempt to eliminate the discriminatory practice or practices alleged, and to effect voluntary compliance with the requirements of this Act through informal methods of conciliation, conference, and persuasion.

(c) *Civil actions; persons aggrieved; jurisdiction; judicial relief; termination of individual action upon commencement of action by Secretary; jury trial.*

(1) Any person aggrieved may bring a civil action in any court of competent jurisdiction for such legal or equitable relief as will effectuate the purposes of this Act: *Provided,* That the right of any person to bring such action shall terminate upon the commencement of an action by the Secretary to enforce the right of such employee under this Act.

(2) In an action brought under paragraph (1), a person shall be entitled to a trial by jury of any issue of fact in any such action for recovery of amounts

owing as a result of a violation of this Act, regardless of whether equitable relief is sought by any party in such action.

(d)(1) *Filing of charge with Secretary; timeliness; conciliation, conference, and persuasion.* No civil action may be commenced by an individual under this section until 60 days after a charge alleging unlawful discrimination has been filed with the Secretary. Such a charge shall be filed —

 (A) within 180 days after the alleged unlawful practice occurred; or

 (B) in a case to which section 14(b) [29 USCS §633(b)] applies, within 300 days after the alleged unlawful practice occurred, or within 30 days after receipt by the individual of notice of termination of proceedings under State law, whichever is earlier.

(2) Upon receiving such a charge, the Secretary shall promptly notify all persons named in such charge as prospective defendants in the action and shall promptly seek to eliminate any alleged unlawful practice by informal methods of conciliation, conference, and persuasion; and

(3) For purposes of this section, an unlawful practice occurs, with respect to discrimination in compensation in violation of this Act, when a discriminatory compensation decision or other practice is adopted, when a person becomes subject to a discriminatory compensation decision or other practice, or when a person is affected by application of a discriminatory compensation decision or other practice, including each time wages, benefits, or other compensation is paid, resulting in whole or in part from such a decision or other practice.

(e) Section 10 of the Portal-to-Portal Act of 1947 [29 USCS §259] shall apply to actions under this Act. If a charge filed with the Commission under this Act is dismissed or the proceedings of the Commission are otherwise terminated by the Commission, the Commission shall notify the person aggrieved. A civil action may be brought under this section by a person defined in section 11(a) [29 USCS §630(a)] against the respondent named in the charge within 90 days after the date of the receipt of such notice.

(f) *Waiver.*

 (1) An individual may not waive any right or claim under this Act unless the waiver is knowing and voluntary. Except as provided in paragraph (2), a waiver may not be considered knowing and voluntary unless at a minimum —

 (A) the waiver is part of an agreement between the individual and the employer that is written in a manner calculated to be understood by such individual, or by the average individual eligible to participate;

 (B) the waiver specifically refers to rights or claims arising under this Act;

 (C) the individual does not waive rights or claims that may arise after the date the waiver is executed;

 (D) the individual waives rights or claims only in exchange for consideration in addition to anything of value to which the individual already is entitled;

 (E) the individual is advised in writing to consult with an attorney prior to executing the agreement;

(F)(i) the individual is given a period of at least 21 days within which to consider the agreement; or

(ii) if a waiver is requested in connection with an exit incentive or other employment termination program offered to a group or class of employees, the individual is given a period of at least 45 days within which to consider the agreement;

(G) the agreement provides that for a period of at least 7 days following the execution of such agreement, the individual may revoke the agreement, and the agreement shall not become effective or enforceable until the revocation period has expired;

(H) if a waiver is requested in connection with an exit incentive or other employment termination program offered to a group or class of employees, the employer (at the commencement of the period specified in subparagraph (F)) informs the individual in writing in a manner calculated to be understood by the average individual eligible to participate, as to—

(i) any class, unit, or group of individuals covered by such program, any eligibility factors for such program, and any time limits applicable to such program; and

(ii) the job titles and ages of all individuals eligible or selected for the program, and the ages of all individuals in the same job classification or organizational unit who are not eligible or selected for the program.

(2) A waiver in settlement of a charge filed with the Equal Employment Opportunity Commission, or an action filed in court by the individual or the individual's representative, alleging age discrimination of a kind prohibited under section 4 or 15 [29 USCS §623 or 633a] may not be considered knowing and voluntary unless at a minimum—

(A) subparagraphs (A) through (E) of paragraph (1) have been met; and

(B) the individual is given a reasonable period of time within which to consider the settlement agreement.

(3) In any dispute that may arise over whether any of the requirements, conditions, and circumstances set forth in subparagraph (A), (B), (C), (D), (E), (F), (G), or (H) of paragraph (1), or subparagraph (A) or (B) of paragraph (2), have been met, the party asserting the validity of a waiver shall have the burden of proving in a court of competent jurisdiction that a waiver was knowing and voluntary pursuant to paragraph (1) or (2).

(4) No waiver agreement may affect the Commission's rights and responsibilities to enforce this Act. No waiver may be used to justify interfering with the protected right of an employee to file a charge or participate in an investigation or proceeding conducted by the Commission.

§627 [§8]. Notices to Be Posted

Every employer, employment agency, and labor organization shall post and keep posted in conspicuous places upon its premises a notice to be prepared or approved by the Secretary setting forth information as he deems appropriate to effectuate the purposes of this chapter.

§628 [§9]. Rules and Regulations; Exemptions

In accordance with the provisions of subchapter II of chapter 5 of title 5, United States Code, the Secretary may issue such rules and regulations as he may consider necessary or appropriate for carrying out this chapter, and may establish such reasonable exemptions to and from any or all provisions of this chapter as it may find necessary and proper in the public interest.

§629 [§10]. Criminal Penalties

Whoever shall forcibly resist, oppose, impede, intimidate, or interfere with a duly authorized representative of the Secretary while he is engaged in the performance of duties under this Act shall be punished by a fine of not more than $500 or by imprisonment for not more than one year, or by both: *Provided, however,* That no person shall be imprisoned under this section except when there has been a prior conviction hereunder.

§630 [§11]. Definitions

For the purposes of this Act —

(a) The term "person" means one or more individuals, partnerships, associations, labor organizations, corporations, business trusts, legal representatives, or any organized groups of persons.

(b) The term "employer" means a person engaged in an industry affecting commerce who has twenty or more employees for each working day in each of twenty or more calendar weeks in the current or preceding calendar year: Provided, that prior to June 30, 1968, employers having fewer than fifty employees shall not be considered employers. The term also means (1) any agent of such a person, and (2) a State or political subdivision of a State and any agency or instrumentality of a State or a political subdivision of a State, and any interstate agency but such term does not include the United States, or a corporation wholly owned by the Government of the United States.

(c) The term "employment agency" means any person regularly undertaking with or without compensation to procure employees for an employer and includes an agent of such a person; but shall not include an agency of the United States.

(d) The term "labor organization" means a labor organization engaged in an industry affecting commerce, and any agent of such an organization, and includes any organization of any kind, any agency, or employee representation committee, group, association, or plan so engaged in which employees participate and which exists for the purpose, in whole or in part, of dealing with employers concerning grievances, labor disputes, wages, rates of pay, hours, or other terms or conditions of employment, and any conference, general committee, joint or system board, or joint council so engaged which is subordinate to a national or international labor organization.

(e) A labor organization shall be deemed to be engaged in an industry affecting commerce if (1) it maintains or operates a hiring hall or hiring office which procures employees for an employer or procures for employees opportunities to work for an employer, or (2) the number of its members (or, where it is a labor organization composed of other labor organizations or their representatives, if the aggregate number of the members of such other labor organization) is fifty or more prior to July 1, 1968, or twenty-five or more on or after July 1, 1968, and such labor organization —

(1) is the certified representative of employees under the provisions of the National Labor Relations Act, as amended, or the Railway Labor Act, as amended; or

(2) although not certified, is a national or international labor organization or a local labor organization recognized or acting as the representative of employees of an employer or employers engaged in an industry affecting commerce; or

(3) has chartered a local labor organization or subsidiary body which is representing or actively seeking to represent employees of employers within the meaning of paragraph (1) or (2); or

(4) has been chartered by a labor organization representing or actively seeking to represent employees within the meaning of paragraph (1) or (2) as to local or subordinate body through which such employees may enjoy membership or become affiliated with such labor organization; or

(5) is a conference, general committee, joint or system board or joint council subordinate to a national or international labor organization, which includes a labor organization engaged in an industry affecting commerce within the meaning of any of the preceding paragraphs of this subsection.

(f) The term "employee" means any individual employed by an employer except that the term "employee" shall not include any person elected to public office in any State or political subdivision of any State by the qualified voters thereof, or any person chosen by such officer to be on such officer's personal staff, or an appointee on the policy-making level or an immediate adviser with respect to the exercise of the constitutional or legal powers of the office. The exemption set forth in the preceding sentence shall not include employees subject to the civil service laws of a State government, governmental agency, or political subdivision. The term "employee" includes any individual who is a citizen of the United States employed by an employer in a workplace in a foreign country.

(g) The term "commerce" means trade, traffic, commerce, transportation, transmission, or communication among the several States, or between a State and any place outside thereof; or within the District of Columbia, or a possession of the United States, or between points in the same State but through a point outside thereof.

(h) The term "industry affecting commerce" means any activity, business, or industry in commerce or in which a labor dispute would hinder or obstruct commerce or the free flow of commerce and includes any activity or industry "affecting commerce" within the meaning of the Labor-Management Reporting and Disclosure Act of 1959.

(i) The term "State" includes a State of the United States, the District of Columbia, Puerto Rico, the Virgin Islands, American Samoa, Guam, Wake Island, the Canal Zone, and Outer Continental Shelf Lands defined in the Outer Continental Shelf Lands Act.

(j) The term "firefighter" means an employee, the duties of whose position are primarily to perform work directly connected with the control and extinguishment of fires or the maintenance and use of firefighting apparatus and equipment, including an employee engaged in this activity who is transferred to a supervisory or administrative position.

(k) The term "law enforcement officer" means an employee, the duties of whose position are primarily the investigation, apprehension, or detention of individuals suspected or convicted of offenses against the criminal laws of a State, including an employee engaged in this activity who is transferred to a supervisory or administration position. For the purpose of this subsection, "detention" includes the duties of employees assigned to individuals incarcerated in any penal institution.

(*l*) The term "compensation, terms, conditions, or privileges of employment" encompasses all employee benefits, including such benefits provided pursuant to a bona fide employee benefit plan.

§631 [§12]. Age Limits

(a) *Individuals at least 40 years of age*. The prohibitions in this Act shall be limited to individuals who are at least 40 years of age.

(b) *Employees or applicants for employment in Federal Government*. In the case of any personnel action affecting employers or applicants for employment which is subject to the provisions of section 633a of this title, the prohibitions established in section 633a of this title shall be limited to individuals who are at least 40 years of age.

(c) *Bona fide executives or high policymakers*. (1) Nothing in this chapter shall be construed to prohibit compulsory retirement of any employee who has attained 65 years of age, and who, for the two-year period immediately before retirement, is employed in a bona fide executive or a high policymaking position, if such employee is entitled to an immediate nonforfeitable annual retirement benefit from a pension, profit-sharing, savings, or deferred compensation plan, or any combination of such plans, of the employer of such employee, which equals, in aggregate, at least $44,000.

(2) In applying the retirement benefit test of paragraph (1) of this subsection, if any such retirement benefits is in a form other than a straight life annuity (with no ancillary benefits), or if employees contribute to any such plan or make rollover contributions, such benefit shall be adjusted in accordance with regulations prescribed by the Equal Employment Opportunity Commission, after consultation with the Secretary of the Treasury, so that the benefit is the equivalent of a straight life annuity (with no ancillary benefits) under a plan to which employees do not contribute and under which no rollover contributions are made.

§633 [§14]. Federal-State Relationship

(a) *Federal action superseding State action*. Nothing in this chapter shall affect the jurisdiction of any agency of any State performing like functions with regard to discriminatory employment practices on account of age except that upon commencement of an action under this Act such action shall supersede any State action.

(b) *Limitation of Federal Action upon commencement of State proceedings*. In the case of an alleged unlawful practice occurring in a State which has a law prohibiting discrimination in employment because of age and establishing or authorizing a State authority to grant or seek relief from such discriminatory practice, no suit may be brought under section 626 of this title before the expiration of sixty days after proceedings have been commenced under the State law, unless such proceedings have been earlier terminated: *Provided*, That such sixty- day period shall be extended to one hundred and twenty days during the first year after the effective date of such State law. If any requirement for the commencement of such proceedings is imposed by a State authority other than a requirement of the filing of a written and signed statement of the facts upon which the proceedings is based, the proceeding shall be deemed to have been commenced for the purposes of this subsection at the time such statement is sent by registered mail to the appropriate State authority.

§633a [§14a]. Nondiscrimination on Account of Age in Federal Government Employment

(a) *Federal agencies affected*. All personnel actions affecting employees or applicants for employment who are at least 40 years of age (except personnel actions with regard to aliens employed outside the limits of the United States) in military departments as defined in section 102 of title 5, in executive agencies as defined in section 105 of title 5, (including employees and applicants for employment who are paid from non-appropriated funds), in the United States Postal Service and the Postal Rate Commission, in those units in the government of the District of Columbia having positions in the competitive service, and in those units of the legislative and judicial branches of the Federal Government having positions in the competitive service, and in the Library of Congress shall be made free from any discrimination based on age.

(b) *Enforcement by Civil Service Commission and by Librarian of Congress in the Library of Congress; remedies; rules, regulations, orders, and instructions of Commission: compliance by Federal agencies; powers and duties of Commission; notification of final action on complaint of discrimination; exemptions: bona fide occupational qualification*. Except as otherwise provided in this subsection, the Civil Service Commission is authorized to enforce the provisions of subsection (a) of this section through appropriate remedies, including reinstatement of hiring of employees with or without backpay, as will effectuate the policies of this section. The Civil Service Commission shall issue such rules, regulations, orders, and instructions as it deems necessary and appropriate to carry out its responsibilities under this section. The Civil Service Commission shall—

(1) be responsible for the review and evaluation of the operation of all agency programs designed to carry out the policy of this section, periodically obtaining and publishing (on at least a semiannual basis) progress reports from each department, agency, or unit referred to in subsection (a) of this section;

(2) consult with and solicit the recommendations of interested individuals, groups, and organizations relating to non-discrimination in employment on account of age; and

(3) provide for the acceptance and processing of complaints of discrimination in Federal employment on account of age.

The head of each such department, agency, or unit shall comply with such rules, regulations, orders, and instructions of the Civil Service Commission which shall include a provision that an employee or applicant for employment shall be notified of any final action taken on any complaint or discrimination filed by him thereunder. Reasonable exemptions to the provisions of this section may be established by the Commission but only when the Commission has established a maximum age requirement on the basis of a determination that age is a bona fide occupational qualification necessary to the performance of the duties of the position. With respect to employment in the Library of Congress, authorities granted in this subsection to the Equal Employment Opportunity Commission shall be exercised by the Librarian of Congress.

(c) *Civil actions; jurisdiction; relief.* Any person aggrieved may bring a civil action in any Federal district court of competent jurisdiction for such legal or equitable relief as will effectuate the purposes of this chapter.

(d) *Notice to Commission; time of notice; Commission notification of prospective defendants; Commission elimination of unlawful practices.* When the individual has not filed a complaint concerning age discrimination with the Commission, no civil action may be commenced by any individual under this section until the individual has given the Commission not less than thirty days' notice of an intent to file such action. Such notice shall be filed within one hundred and eighty days after the alleged unlawful practice occurred. Upon receiving a notice of intent to sue, the Commission shall promptly notify all persons named therein as prospective defendants in the action and take any appropriate action to assure the elimination of any unlawful practice.

(e) *Duty of Government agency or official.* Nothing contained in this section shall relieve any Government agency or official of the responsibility to assure nondiscrimination on account of age in employment as required under any provision of Federal law.

(f) *Applicability of Statutory provisions to personnel action of Federal departments, etc.* Any personnel action of any department, agency, or other entity referred to in subsection (a) of this section shall not be subject to, or affected by, any provision of this chapter, other than the provisions of sections 626(d)(3) and 631(b) of this title and the provisions of this section.

(g) *Study and report to President and Congress by Civil Service Commission; scope.* (1) The Civil Service Commission shall undertake a study relating to the effects of the amendments made to this section by the Age Discrimination in Employment Act Amendments of 1978, and the effects of section 631(b) of this title.

(2) The Civil Service Commission shall transmit a report to the President and to the Congress containing the findings of the Commission resulting from the study of the Commission under paragraph (1) of this subsection. Such report shall be transmitted no later than January 1, 1980.

Americans with Disabilities Act

*Table of Contents, Title I, Title II, and Title V
42 U.S.C. §§12101–12102, 12111–12117, 12131–12134,
12201–12213 [Pub. L. No. 101–336, 104 Stat. 327 (1990),
as amended by the Civil Rights Act of 1991, Pub. L. No.
102–166, 105 Stat. 1071 (1991)]*

TABLE OF CONTENTS

Subtitle B—Actions Applicable to Public Transportation Provided by Public Entities Considered Discriminatory

Part I—Public Transportation Other Than by Aircraft or Certain Rail Operations

Part III—Public Transportation by Intercity and Commuter Rail

TITLE III—PUBLIC ACCOMMODATIONS AND SERVICES OPERATED BY PRIVATE ENTITIES [omitted]

TITLE V—MISCELLANEOUS PROVISIONS

§12101 [§2]. Findings and Purposes

(a) *Findings.* — The Congress finds that —

(1) physical or mental disabilities in no way diminish a person's right to fully participate in all aspects of society, yet many people with physical or mental disabilities have been precluded from doing so because of discrimination; others who have a record of a disability or are regarded as having a disability also have been subjected to discrimination;

(2) historically, society has tended to isolate and segregate individuals with disabilities, and, despite some improvements, such forms of discrimination against individuals with disabilities continue to be a serious and pervasive social problem;

(3) discrimination against individuals with disabilities persists in such critical areas as employment, housing, public accommodations, education, transportation, communication, recreation, institutionalization, health services, voting, and access to public services;

(4) unlike individuals who have experienced discrimination on the basis of race, color, sex, national origin, religion, or age, individuals who have experienced discrimination on the basis of disability have often had no legal recourse to redress such discrimination;

(5) individuals with disabilities continually encounter various forms of discrimination, including outright intentional exclusion, the discriminatory effects of architectural, transportation, and communication barriers, overprotective rules and policies, failure to make modifications to existing facilities and practices, exclusionary qualification standards and criteria, segregation, and relegation to lesser services, programs, activities, benefits, jobs, or other opportunities;

(6) census data, national polls, and other studies have documented that people with disabilities, as a group, occupy an inferior status in our society, and are severely disadvantaged socially, vocationally, economically, and educationally;

(7) the Nation's proper goals regarding individuals with disabilities are to assure equality of opportunity, full participation, independent living, and economic self-sufficiency for such individuals; and

(8) the continuing existence of unfair and unnecessary discrimination and prejudice denies people with disabilities the opportunity to compete on an equal basis and to pursue those opportunities for which our free society is justifiably famous, and costs the United States billions of dollars in unnecessary expenses resulting from dependency and nonproductivity.

(b) *Purpose.* — It is the purpose of this Act —

(1) to provide a clear and comprehensive national mandate for the elimination of discrimination against individuals with disabilities;

(2) to provide clear, strong, consistent, enforceable standards addressing discrimination against individuals with disabilities;

(3) to ensure that the Federal Government plays a central role in enforcing the standards established in this Act on behalf of individuals with disabilities; and

(4) to invoke the sweep of congressional authority, including the power to enforce the fourteenth amendment and to regulate commerce, in order to address the major areas of discrimination faced day-to-day by people with disabilities.

§12102 [§3]. Definition of Disability

As used in this Act:

(1) Disability. — The term "disability" means, with respect to an individual —

(A) a physical or mental impairment that substantially limits one or more of the major life activities of such individual;

(B) a record of such an impairment; or

(C) being regarded as having such an impairment (as described in paragraph (3)).

(2) Major life activities. —

(A) In general. — For purposes of paragraph (1), major life activities include, but are not limited to, caring for oneself, performing manual tasks, seeing, hearing, eating, sleeping, walking, standing, lifting, bending, speaking, breathing, learning, reading, concentrating, thinking, communicating, and working.

(B) Major bodily functions. — For purposes of paragraph (1), a major life activity also includes the operation of a major bodily function, including but not limited to, functions of the immune system, normal cell growth, digestive, bowel, bladder, neurological, brain, respiratory, circulatory, endocrine, and reproductive functions.

(3) Regarded as having such an impairment. — For purposes of paragraph (1)(C):

(A) An individual meets the requirement of "being regarded as having such an impairment" if the individual establishes that he or she has been subjected to an action prohibited under this Act because of an actual or perceived physical or mental impairment whether or not the impairment limits or is perceived to limit a major life activity.

(B) Paragraph (1)(C) shall not apply to impairments that are transitory and minor. A transitory impairment is an impairment with an actual or expected duration of 6 months or less.

(4) Rules of construction regarding the definition of disability. — The definition of "disability" in paragraph (1) shall be construed in accordance with the following:

(A) The definition of disability in this Act shall be construed in favor of broad coverage of individuals under this Act, to the maximum extent permitted by the terms of this Act.

(B) The term "substantially limits" shall be interpreted consistently with the findings and purposes of the ADA Amendments Act of 2008.

(C) An impairment that substantially limits one major life activity need not limit other major life activities in order to be considered a disability.

(D) An impairment that is episodic or in remission is a disability if it would substantially limit a major life activity when active.

(E)(i) The determination of whether an impairment substantially limits a major life activity shall be made without regard to the ameliorative effects of mitigating measures such as —

(I) medication, medical supplies, equipment, or appliances, low-vision devices (which do not include ordinary eyeglasses or contact lenses), prosthetics including limbs and devices, hearing aids and cochlear implants or other implantable hearing devices, mobility devices, or oxygen therapy equipment and supplies;

(II) use of assistive technology;

(III) reasonable accommodations or auxiliary aids or services; or

(IV) learned behavioral or adaptive neurological modifications.

(ii) The ameliorative effects of the mitigating measures of ordinary eyeglasses or contact lenses shall be considered in determining whether an impairment substantially limits a major life activity.

(iii) As used in this subparagraph —

(I) the term "ordinary eyeglasses or contact lenses" means lenses that are intended to fully correct visual acuity or eliminate refractive error; and

(II) the term "low-vision devices" means devices that magnify, enhance, or otherwise augment a visual image.

§12103 [§4]. Additional Definitions

As used in this Act:

(1) Auxiliary aids and services. — The term "auxiliary aids and services" includes —

(A) qualified interpreters or other effective methods of making aurally delivered materials available to individuals with hearing impairments;

(B) qualified readers, taped texts, or other effective methods of making visually delivered materials available to individuals with visual impairments;

(C) acquisition or modification of equipment or devices; and

(D) other similar services and actions.

(2) State.—The term "State" means each of the several States, the District of Columbia, the Commonwealth of Puerto Rico, Guam, American Samoa, the Virgin Islands of the United States, the Trust Territory of the Pacific Islands, and the Commonwealth of the Northern Mariana Islands.

TITLE I—EMPLOYMENT

§12111 [§101]. Definitions

As used in this title:

(1) Commission.—The term "Commission" means the Equal Employment Opportunity Commission established by section 705 of the Civil Rights Act of 1964 (42 U.S.C. 2000e-4).

(2) Covered Entity.—The term "covered entity" means an employer, employment agency, labor organization, or joint labor-management committee.

(3) Direct Threat.—The term "direct threat" means a significant risk to the health or safety of others that cannot be eliminated by reasonable accommodation.

(4) Employee.—The term "employee" means an individual employed by an employer. With respect to employment in a foreign country, such term includes an individual who is a citizen of the United States.

(5) Employer.—

(A) In general.—The term "employer" means a person engaged in an industry affecting commerce who has 15 or more employees for each working day in each of 20 or more calendar weeks in the current or preceding calendar years, and any agent of such person, except that, for two years following the effective date of this title, an employer means a person engaged in an industry affecting commerce who has 25 or more employees for each working day in each of 20 or more calendar weeks in the current or preceding year, and any agent of such person.

(B) Exceptions.—The term "employer" does not include—

(i) the United States, a corporation wholly owned by the government of the United States, or an Indian tribe; or

(ii) a bona fide private membership club (other than a labor organization) that is exempt from taxation under section 501(c) of the Internal Revenue Code of 1986.

(6) Illegal Use of Drugs.—

(A) In general.—The term "illegal use of drugs" means the use of drugs, the possession or distribution of which is unlawful under the

Controlled Substances Act (21 U.S.C. 812). Such term does not include the use of a drug taken under supervision by a licensed health care professional, or other uses authorized by the Controlled Substances Act or other provisions of Federal law.

(B) Drugs. — The term "drug" means a controlled substance, as defined in schedules I through V of section 202 of the Controlled Substances Act.

(7) Person, etc. — The terms "person," "labor organization," "employment agency," "commerce," and "industry affecting commerce," shall have the same meaning given such terms in section 701 of the Civil Rights Act of 1964 (42 U.S.C. 2000e).

(8) Qualified individual. The term "qualified individual" means an individual who, with or without reasonable accommodation, can perform the essential functions of the employment position that such individual holds or desires. For the purposes of this title, consideration shall be given to the employer's judgment as to what functions of a job are essential, and if an employer has prepared a written description before advertising or interviewing applicants for the job, this description shall be considered evidence of the essential functions of the job.

(9) Reasonable accommodation. The term "reasonable accommodation" may include

(A) making existing facilities used by employees readily accessible to and usable by individuals with disabilities; and

(B) job restructuring, part-time or modified work schedule, reassignment to a vacant position, acquisition or modification of equipment or devices, appropriate adjustment or modifications of examinations, training materials or policies, the provision of qualified readers or interpreters, and other similar accommodations for individuals with disabilities.

(10) Undue hardship. —

(A) In general. — The term "undue hardship" means an action requiring significant difficulty or expense, when considered in light of the factors set forth in subparagraph (B).

(B) Factors to be considered. — In determining whether an accommodation would impose an undue hardship on a covered entity, factors to be considered include —

(i) the nature and cost of the accommodation needed under this Act;

(ii) the overall financial resources of the facility or facilities involved in the provision of the reasonable accommodation; the number of persons employed at such facility; the effect on expenses and resources, or the impact otherwise of such accommodation upon the operation of the facility;

(iii) the overall financial resources of the covered entity; the overall size of the business of a covered entity with respect to the number of its employees; the number, type, and location of its facilities; and

(iv) the type of operation or operations of the covered entity, including the composition, structure, and functions of the workforce of such entity; the geographic separateness, administrative, or fiscal relationship of the facility or facilities in question to the covered entity.

§12112 [§102]. *Discrimination*

(a) *General rule.* — No covered entity shall discriminate against a qualified individual on the basis of disability in regard to job application procedures, the hiring, advancement, or discharge of employees, employee compensation, job training and other terms, conditions, and privileges of employment.

(b) *Construction.* — As used in subsection (a), the term "discriminate against a qualified individual on the basis of disability" includes —

(1) limiting, segregating, or classifying a job applicant or employee in a way that adversely affects the opportunities or status of such applicant or employee because of the disability of such applicant or employee;

(2) participating in a contractual or other arrangement or relationship that has the effect of subjecting a covered entity's qualified applicant or employee with a disability to the discrimination prohibited by this title (such relationship includes a relationship with an employment or referral agency, labor union, an organization providing fringe benefits to an employee of the covered entity, or an organization providing training and apprenticeship programs);

(3) utilizing standards, criteria, or methods of administration —

(A) that have the effect of discrimination on the basis of disability; or

(B) that perpetuate the discrimination of others who are subject to common administrative control;

(4) excluding or otherwise denying equal jobs or benefits to a qualified individual because of the known disability of an individual with whom the qualified individual is known to have a relationship or association;

(5)(A) not making reasonable accommodations to the known physical or mental limitations of an otherwise qualified individual with a disability who is an applicant or employee, unless such covered entity can demonstrate that the accommodation would impose an undue hardship on the operation of the business of such covered entity; or

(B) denying employment opportunities to a job applicant or employee who is an otherwise qualified individual with a disability, if such denial is based on the need of such covered entity to make reasonable accommodation to the physical or mental impairments of the employee or applicant;

(6) using qualification standards, employment tests or other selection criteria that screen out or tend to screen out an individual with a disability or a class of individuals with disabilities unless the standard, test or other selection criteria, as used by the covered entity, is shown to be job-related for the position in question and is consistent with business necessity; and

(7) failing to select and administer tests concerning employment in the most effective manner to ensure that, when such test is administered to a job applicant or employee who has a disability that impairs sensory, manual, or

speaking skills, such test results accurately reflect the skills, aptitude, or whatever other factor of such applicant or employee that such test purports to measure, rather than reflecting the impaired sensory, manual, or speaking skills of such employee or applicant (except where such skills are the factors that the test purports to measure).

(c) *Covered entities in foreign countries.*—

(1) *In general.*—It shall not be unlawful under this section for a covered entity to take any action that constitutes discrimination under this section with respect to an employee in a workplace in a foreign country if compliance with this section would cause such covered entity to violate the law of the foreign country in which such workplace is located.

(2) *Control of corporation.*—

(A) *Presumption.*—If an employer controls a corporation whose place of incorporation is a foreign country, any practice that constitutes discrimination under this section and is engaged in by such corporation shall be presumed to be engaged in by such employer.

(B) *Exception.*—This section shall not apply with respect to the foreign operations of an employer that is a foreign person not controlled by an American employer.

(C) *Determination.*—For purposes of this paragraph, the determination of whether an employer controls a corporation shall be based on—

(i) the interrelation of operations;

(ii) the common management;

(iii) the centralized control of labor relations; and

(iv) the common ownership or financial control, of the employer and the corporation.

(d) *Medical examinations and inquiries.*—

(1) *In general.*—The prohibition against discrimination as referred to in subsection (a) shall include medical examinations and inquiries.

(2) *Preemployment.*—

(A) *Prohibited examination or inquiry.*—Except as provided in paragraph (3), a covered entity shall not conduct a medical examination or make inquiries of a job applicant as to whether such applicant is an individual with a disability or as to the nature or severity of such disability.

(B) *Acceptable inquiry.*—A covered entity may make preemployment inquiries into the ability of an applicant to perform job-related functions.

(3) *Employment entrance examination.*—A covered entity may require a medical examination after an offer of employment has been made to a job applicant and prior to the commencement of the employment duties of such applicant, and may condition an offer of employment on the results of such examination, if—

(A) all entering employees are subjected to such an examination regardless of disability;

(B) information obtained regarding the medical condition or history of the applicant is collected and maintained on separate forms and in separate medical files and is treated as a confidential medical record, except that—

    (i) supervisors and managers may be informed regarding necessary restrictions on the work or duties of the employee and necessary accommodations;

    (ii) first aid and safety personnel may be informed, when appropriate, if the disability might require emergency treatment; and

    (iii) government officials investigating compliance with this Act shall be provided relevant information on request; and

(C) the results of such examination are used only in accordance with this title.

(4) *Examination and inquiry.*—

    (A) *Prohibited examinations and inquiries.*—A covered entity shall not require a medical examination and shall not make inquiries of an employee as to whether such employee is an individual with a disability or as to the nature or severity of the disability, unless such examination or inquiry is shown to be job-related and consistent with business necessity.

    (B) *Acceptable examinations and inquiries.*—A covered entity may conduct voluntary medical examinations, including voluntary medical histories, which are part of an employee health program available to employees at that work site. A covered entity may make inquiries into the ability of an employee to perform job-related functions.

    (C) *Requirement.*—Information obtained under subparagraph (B) regarding the medical condition or history of any employee are subject to the requirements of subparagraphs (B) and (C) of paragraph (3).

§12113 [§103]. Defenses

(a) *In General.*— It may be a defense to a charge of discrimination under this Act that an alleged application of qualification standards, tests, or selection criteria that screen out or tend to screen out or otherwise deny a job or benefit to an individual with a disability has been shown to be job-related and consistent with business necessity, and such performance cannot be accomplished by reasonable accommodation, as required under this title.

(b) *Qualification Standards.* The term "qualification standards" may include a requirement that an individual shall not pose a direct threat to the health or safety of other individuals in the workplace.

(c) *Qualification Standards and Tests Related to Uncorrected Vision.*— Notwithstanding section 3(4)(E)(ii), a covered entity shall not use qualification standards, employment tests, or other selection criteria based on an individual's uncorrected vision unless the standard, test, or other selection criteria, as used by the covered entity, is shown to be job-related for the position in question and consistent with business necessity.

(d) *Religious Entities.*

(1) *In general.* This title shall not prohibit a religious corporation, association, educational institution, or society from giving preference in

employment to individuals of a particular religion to perform work connected with the carrying on by such corporation, association, educational institution, or society of its activities.

(2) *Religious tenets requirements.* Under this title, a religious organization may require that all applicants and employees conform to the religious tenets of such organization.

(e) List of Infectious and Communicable Diseases.

(1) *In general.* The Secretary of Health and Human Services, not later than 6 months after the date of enactment of this Act [enacted July 26, 1990], shall

(A) review all infectious and communicable diseases which may be transmitted through handling the food supply;

(B) publish a list of infectious and communicable diseases which are transmitted through handling the food supply;

(C) publish the methods by which such diseases are transmitted; and

(D) widely disseminate such information regarding the list of diseases and their modes of transmissability [transmissibility] to the general public. Such list shall be updated annually.

(2) *Applications.* — In any case in which an individual has an infectious or communicable disease that is transmitted to others through the handling of food, that is included on the list developed by the Secretary of Health and Human Services under paragraph (1), and which cannot be eliminated by reasonable accommodation, a covered entity may refuse to assign or continue to assign such individual to a job involving food handling.

(3) *Construction.* — Nothing in this Act shall be construed to preempt, modify, or amend any State, county, or local law, ordinance, or regulation applicable to food handling which is designed to protect the public health from individuals who pose a significant risk to the health or safety of others, which cannot be eliminated by reasonable accommodation, pursuant to the list of infectious or communicable diseases and the modes of transmissability [transmissibility] published by the Secretary of Health and Human Services.

§12114 [§104]. Illegal Use of Drugs and Alcohol

(a) *Qualified Individual With a Disability.* For purposes of this title, a qualified individual with a disability shall not include any employee or applicant who is currently engaging in the illegal use of drugs, when the covered entity acts on the basis of such use.

(b) *Rules of Construction.* Nothing in subsection (a) shall be construed to exclude as a qualified individual with a disability an individual who

(1) has successfully completed a supervised drug rehabilitation program and is no longer engaging in the illegal use of drugs, or has otherwise been rehabilitated successfully and is no longer engaging in such use;

(2) is participating in a supervised rehabilitation program and is no longer engaging in such use; or

(3) is erroneously regarded as engaging in such use, but is not engaging in such use; except that it shall not be a violation of this Act for a covered

entity to adopt or administer reasonable policies or procedures, including but not limited to drug testing, designed to ensure that an individual described in paragraph (1) or (2) is no longer engaging in the illegal use of drugs.

(c) *Authority of Covered Entity.* A covered entity

(1) may prohibit the illegal use of drugs and the use of alcohol at the workplace by all employees;

(2) may require that employees shall not be under the influence of alcohol or be engaging in the illegal use of drugs at the workplace;

(3) may require that employees behave in conformance with the requirements established under the Drug-Free Workplace Act of 1988 (41 U.S.C. 701 et seq.);

(4) may hold an employee who engages in the illegal use of drugs or who is an alcoholic to the same qualification standards for employment or job performance and behavior that such entity holds other employees, even if any unsatisfactory performance or behavior is related to the drug use or alcoholism of such employee; and

(5) may, with respect to Federal regulations regarding alcohol and the illegal use of drugs, require that

(A) employees comply with the standards established in such regulations of the Department of Defense, if the employees of the covered entity are employed in an industry subject to such regulations, including complying with regulations (if any) that apply to employment in sensitive positions in such an industry, in the case of employees of the covered entity who are employed in such positions (as defined in the regulations of the Department of Defense);

(B) employees comply with the standards established in such regulations of the Nuclear Regulatory Commission, if the employees of the covered entity are employed in an industry subject to such regulations, including complying with such regulations (if any) that apply to employment in sensitive positions in such an industry, in the case of employees of the covered entity who are employed in such positions (as defined in the regulations of the Nuclear Regulatory Commission); and

(C) employees comply with the standards established in such regulations of the Department of Transportation, if the employees of the covered entity are employed in a transportation industry subject to such regulations, including complying with such regulations (if any) that apply to employment in sensitive positions in such an industry, in the case of employees of the covered entity who are employed in such positions (as defined in the regulations of the Department of Transportation).

(d) *Drug Testing.*

(1) *In general.* For purposes of this title, a test to determine the illegal use of drugs shall not be considered a medical examination.

(2) *Construction.* Nothing in this title shall be constructed to encourage, prohibit, or authorize the conducting of drug testing for the illegal use of drugs by job applicants or employees or making employment decisions based on such test results.

(e) *Transportation Employees*. Nothing in this title shall be construed to encourage, prohibit, restrict, or authorize the otherwise lawful exercise by entities subject to the jurisdiction of the Department of Transportation of authority to —

(1) test employees of such entities in, and applicants for, positions involving safety-sensitive duties for the illegal use of drugs and for on-duty impairment by alcohol; and

(2) remove such persons who test positive for illegal use of drugs and on-duty impairment by alcohol pursuant to paragraph (1) from safety-sensitive duties in implementing subsection (c).

§12115 [§105]. Posting Notices

Every employer, employment agency, labor organization, or joint labor-management committee covered under this title shall post notices in an accessible format to applicants, employees, and members describing the applicable provisions of this Act, in the manner prescribed by section 711 of the Civil Rights Act of 1964 (42 U.S.C. 2000e-10).

§12116 [§106]. Regulations

Not later than 1 year after the date of enactment of this Act, the Commission shall issue regulations in an accessible format to carry out this title in accordance with subchapter II of chapters of title 5, United States Code.

§12117 [§107]. Enforcement

(a) *Powers, Remedies, and Procedures.* — The powers, remedies, and procedures set forth in sections 705, 706, 707, 709, and 710 of the Civil Rights Act of 1964 (42 U.S.C. 2000e-4, 2000e-5, 2000e-6, 2000e-8, and 2000e-9) shall be the powers, remedies, and procedures this title provides to the Commission, to the Attorney General, or to any person alleging discrimination on the basis of disability in violation of any provision of this Act, or regulations promulgated under section 106, concerning employment.

(b) *Coordination.* — The agencies with enforcement authority for actions which allege employment discrimination under this title and under the Rehabilitation Act of 1973 shall develop procedures to ensure that administrative complaints filed under this title and under the Regulations Act of 1973 are dealt with in a manner that avoids duplication of effort and prevents imposition of inconsistent or conflicting standards for the same requirements under this title and the Rehabilitation Act of 1973. The Commission, the Attorney General, and the Office of Federal Contract Compliance Programs shall establish such coordinating mechanisms (similar to provisions contained in the joint regulations promulgated by the Commission and the Attorney General at part 42 of title 28 and part 1691 of title 29, Code of Federal Regulations, and the Memorandum of Understanding between the Commission and the Office of Federal Contact Compliance Programs dated January 16, 1981 (46 Fed. Reg. 7435, January 23, 1981)) in regulations implementing this title and Rehabilitation Act of 1973 not later than 18 months after the date of enactment of this Act.

TITLE II — PUBLIC SERVICE

§12131 [§201]. *Definitions*

As used in this title:

(1) *Public entity*. The term "public entity" means

(A) any State or local government;

(B) any department, agency, special purpose district, or other instrumentality of a State or States or local government; and

(C) the National Railroad Passenger Corporation, and any commuter authority (as defined in section 502(8) of Title 45).

(2) *Qualified individual with a disability*. The term "qualified individual with a disability" means an individual with a disability who, with or without reasonable modifications to rules, policies, or practices, the removal of architectural, communication, or transportation barriers, or the provision of auxiliary aids and services, meets the essential eligibility requirements for the receipt of services or the participation in programs or activities provided by a public entity.

§12132 [§202]. *Discrimination*

Subject to the provisions of this subchapter, no qualified individual with a disability shall, by reason of such disability, be excluded from participation in or be denied the benefits of the services, programs, or activities of a public entity, or be subjected to discrimination by any such entity.

§12133 [§203]. *Enforcement*

The remedies, procedures, and rights set forth in section 794a of Title 29 shall be the remedies, procedures, and rights this subchapter provides to any person alleging discrimination on the basis of disability in violation of section 12132 of this title.

§12134 [§204]. *Regulations*

(a) *In General*. Not later than 1 year after July 26, 1990, the Attorney General shall promulgate regulations in an accessible format that implement this part. Such regulations shall not include any matter within the scope of the authority of the Secretary of Transportation under section 12143, 12149, or 12164 of this title.

(b) *Relationship to Other Regulations*. Except for "program accessibility, existing facilities," and "communications," regulations under subsection (a) of this section shall be consistent with this chapter and with the coordination regulations under part 41 of title 28, Code of Federal Regulations (as promulgated by the Department of Health, Education, and Welfare on January 13, 1978), applicable to recipients of Federal financial assistance under section 794 of Title 29. With respect to "program accessibility, existing facilities," and "communications," such regulations shall be consistent with regulations and analysis as in part 39 of title 28 of the Code of Federal Regulations, applicable to federally conducted activities under such section 794 of Title 29.

(c) *Standards*. Regulations under subsection (a) of this section shall include standards applicable to facilities and vehicles covered by this part, other than facilities, stations, rail passenger cars, and vehicles covered by part B of this subchapter. Such standards shall be consistent with the minimum guidelines and requirements issued by the Architectural and Transportation Barriers Compliance Board in accordance with section 12204(a) of this title.

TITLE V — MISCELLANEOUS PROVISIONS

§12201 [§501]. Construction

(a) *In General*. Except as otherwise provided in this Act, nothing in this Act shall be construed to apply a lesser standard than the standards applied under title V of the Rehabilitation Act of 1973; (29 U.S.C. 790 et seq.) or the regulations issued by Federal agencies pursuant to such title.

(b) *Relationship to Other Laws*. Nothing in this Act shall be construed to invalidate or limit the remedies, rights, and procedures of any Federal law or law of any State or political subdivision of any State or jurisdiction that provides greater or equal protection for the rights of individuals with disabilities than are afforded by this Act. Nothing in this Act shall be construed to preclude the prohibition of, or the imposition of restrictions on, smoking in places of employment covered by title I, in transportation covered by title II or III, or in places of public accommodation covered by title III.

(c) *Insurance*. Titles I through IV of this Act shall not be construed to prohibit or restrict

(1) an insurer, hospital or medical service company, health maintenance organization, or any agent, or entity that administers benefit plans, or similar organizations from underwriting risks, classifying risks, or administering such risks that are based on or not inconsistent with State law; or

(2) a person or organization covered by this Act from establishing, sponsoring, observing or administering the terms of a bona fide benefit plan that are based on underwriting risks, classifying risks, or administering such risks that are based on or not inconsistent with State law; or

(3) a person or organization covered by this Act from establishing, sponsoring, observing or administering the terms of a bona fide benefit plan that is not subject to State laws that regulate insurance.

Paragraphs (1), (2), and (3) shall not be used as a subterfuge to evade the purposes of titles I and III.

(d) *Accommodations and Services*. Nothing in this Act shall be construed to require an individual with a disability to accept an accommodation, aid, service, opportunity, or benefit which such individual chooses not to accept.

(e) *Benefits Under State Worker's Compensation Laws*. — Nothing in this Act alters the standards for determining eligibility for benefits under State worker's compensation laws or under State and Federal disability benefit programs.

(f) *Fundamental Alteration*. — Nothing in this Act alters the provision of section 302(b)(2)(A)(ii) [*42 U.S.C. 12182(b)(2)(A)(ii)*], specifying that reasonable modifications in policies, practices, or procedures shall be required, unless an entity can demonstrate that making such modifications in policies, practices, or procedures, including academic requirements in postsecondary education, would fundamentally alter the nature of the goods, services, facilities, privileges, advantages, or accommodations involved.

(g) *Claims of No Disability.*—Nothing in this Act shall provide the basis for a claim by an individual without a disability that the individual was subject to discrimination because of the individual's lack of disability.

(h) *Reasonable accommodations and modifications.* A covered entity under title I [*42 U.S.C. 12111* et seq.], a public entity under title II [*42 U.S.C. 12131* et seq.], and any person who owns, leases (or leases to), or operates a place of public accommodation under title III [*42 U.S.C. 12181* et seq.], need not provide a reasonable accommodation or a reasonable modification to policies, practices, or procedures to an individual who meets the definition of disability in section 3(1) [*42 U.S.C. 12102(1)*] solely under subparagraph (C) of such section.

§12202 [§502]. State Immunity

A State shall not be immune under the eleventh amendment to the Constitution of the United States from an action in Federal or State court of competent jurisdiction for a violation of this Act. In any action against a State for a violation of the requirements of this Act, remedies (including remedies both at law and in equity) are available for such a violation to the same extent as such remedies are available for such a violation in an action against any public or private entity other than a State.

§12203 [§503]. Prohibition against Retaliation and Coercion

(a) *Retaliation.* No person shall discriminate against any individual because such individual has opposed any act or practice made unlawful by this Act or because such individual made a charge, testified, assisted, or participated in any manner in an investigation, proceeding, or hearing under this Act.

(b) *Interference, Coercion, or Intimidation.* It shall be unlawful to coerce, intimidate, threaten, or interfere with any individual in the exercise or enjoyment of, or on account of his or her having exercised or enjoyed, or on account of his or her having aided or encouraged any other individual in the exercise or enjoyment of, any right granted or protected by this Act.

(c) *Remedies and Procedures.* The remedies and procedures available under sections 107, 203, and 308 of this Act shall be available to aggrieved persons for violations of subsections (a) and (b), with respect to title I, title II and title III, respectively.

§12204 [§504]. Regulations by the Architectural and Transportation Barriers Compliance Board

(a) *Issuance of Guidelines.* Not later than 9 months after the date of enactment of this Act, the Architectural and Transportation Barriers Compliance Board shall issue minimum guidelines that shall supplement the existing Minimum Guidelines and Requirements for Accessible Design for purposes of titles II and III of this Act.

(b) *Contents of Guidelines*. The supplemental guidelines issued under subsection (a) shall establish additional requirements, consistent with this Act, to ensure that buildings, facilities, rail passenger cars, and vehicles are accessible, in terms of architecture and design, transportation, and communication, to individuals with disabilities.

(c) *Qualified Historic Properties*.

(1) *In general.*— The supplemental guidelines issued under subsection (a) shall include procedures and requirements for alterations that will threaten or destroy the historic significance of qualified historic buildings and faculties as defined in 4.17(1)(a) of the Uniform Federal Accessibility Standards.

(2) *Sites eligible for listing in national register.*—With respect to alterations of buildings, or facilities that are eligible for listing in the National Register of Historic Places under the National Historic Preservation Act (16 U.S.C. 470 et seq.), the guidelines described in paragraph (1) shall, at a minimum, maintain the procedures and requirements established in 4.17(1) and (2) of the Uniform Federal Accessibility Standards.

(3) *Other sites.*—With respect to alterations of buildings or facilities designated as historic under State or local law, the guidelines described in paragraph (1) shall establish procedures equivalent to those established by 4.17(1)(b) and (c) of the Uniform Federal Accessibility Standards, and shall require, at a minimum, compliance with the requirements established in 4.17(2) of such standards.

§12205 [§505]. Attorney's Fees

In any action or administrative proceeding commenced pursuant to this Act, the court or agency, in its discretion, may allow the prevailing party, other than the United States, a reasonable attorney's fee, including litigation expenses, and costs, and the United States shall be liable for the foregoing the same as a private individual.

§12205a [§506]. Rule of Construction Regarding Regulatory Authority

The authority to issue regulations granted to the Equal Employment Opportunity Commission, the Attorney General, and the Secretary of Transportation under this chapter includes the authority to issue regulations implementing the definitions of disability in section 12102 [§3] of this title (including rules of construction) and the definitions in section 12103 [§4] of this title, consistent with the ADA Amendments Act of 2008.

§12206 [§507]. Technical Assistance

(a) *Plan for Assistance*.

(1) *In general.* Not later than 180 days after the date of enactment of this Act, the Attorney General, in consultation with the Chair of the Equal Employment Opportunity Commission, the Secretary of Transportation, the

Chair of the Architectural and Transportation Barriers Compliance Board, and the Chairman of the Federal Communications Commission, shall develop a plan to assist entities covered under this Act, and other Federal agencies, in understanding the responsibility of such entities and agencies under this Act.

(2) *Publication of plan*. The Attorney General shall publish the plan referred to in paragraph (1) for public comment in accordance with subchapter II of chapter 5 of title 5, United States Code (commonly known as the Administrative Procedure Act).

(b) *Agency and Public Assistance*. The Attorney General may obtain the assistance of other Federal agencies in carrying out subsection (a), including the National Council on Disability, the President's Committee on Employment of People with Disabilities, the Small Business Administration, and the Department of Commerce.

(c) *Implementation*.

(1) *Rendering assistance*. Each federal agency that has responsibility under paragraph (2) for implementing this Act may render technical assistance to individuals and institutions that have rights or duties under the respective title or titles for which such agency has responsibility.

(2) *Implementation of titles*.

(A) *Title I*. The Equal Employment Opportunity Commission and the Attorney General shall implement the plan for assistance developed under subsection (a), for title I.

(B) *Title II*.

(i) *Subtitle A*. The Attorney General shall implement such plan for assistance for subtitle A of title II.

(ii) *Subtitle B*. The Secretary of Transportation shall implement such plan for assistance for subtitle B of title II.

(C) *Title III*. The Attorney General, in coordination with the Secretary of Transportation and the Chair of the Architectural Transportation Barriers Compliance Board, shall implement such plan for assistance for title III, except for section 304, the plan for assistance for which shall be implemented by the Secretary of Transportation.

(D) *Title IV*. The Chairman of the Federal Communications Commission, in coordination with the Attorney General, shall implement such plan for assistance for title IV.

(3) *Technical assistance manuals*. Each Federal agency that has responsibility under paragraph (2) for implementing this Act shall, as part of its implementation responsibilities, ensure the availability and provision of appropriate technical assistance manuals to individuals or entities with rights or duties under this Act no later than six months after applicable final regulations are published under titles I, II, III, and IV.

(d) *Grants and Contracts*.

(1) *In general*. Each Federal agency that has responsibility under subsection (c)(2) for implementing this Act may make grants or award contracts to effectuate the purposes of this section. Such grants and contracts may be awarded to individuals, institutions not organized for profit and no part of

the net earnings of which inures to the benefit of any private shareholder or individual (including educational institutions), and associations representing individuals who have rights or duties under this Act. Contracts may be awarded to entities organized for profit, but such entities may not be the recipients of grants described in this paragraph.

(2) *Dissemination of information.* Such grants and contracts, among other uses, may be designed to ensure wide dissemination of information about the rights and duties established by this Act and to provide information and technical assistance about techniques for effective compliance with this Act.

(e) *Failure to Receive Assistance.* An employer, public accommodation, or other entity covered under this Act shall not be excused from compliance with the requirements of this Act because of any failure to receive technical assistance under this section, including any failure in the development or dissemination of any technical assistance manual authorized by this section.

§12207 [§508]. Federal Wilderness Areas

(a) *Study.* The National Council on Disability shall conduct a study and report on the effect that wilderness designations and wilderness land management practices have on the ability of individuals with disabilities to use and enjoy the National Wilderness Preservation System as established under the Wilderness Act (16 U.S.C. 1131 et seq.).

(b) *Submission of Report.* Not later than 1 year after the enactment of this Act, the National Council on Disability shall submit the report required under sub-section (a) to Congress.

(c) *Specific Wilderness Access.*

(1) *In general.* Congress reaffirms that nothing in the Wilderness Act is to be construed as prohibiting the use of a wheelchair in a wilderness area by an individual whose disability requires use of a wheelchair, and consistent with the Wilderness Act no agency is required to provide any form of special treatment or accommodation, or to construct any facilities or modify any conditions of lands within a wilderness area in order to facilitate such use.

(2) *Definition.* For purposes of paragraph (1), the term "wheelchair" means a device designated solely for use by a mobility-impaired person for locomotion, that is suitable for use in an indoor pedestrian area.

§12208 [§509]. Transvestites

For the purposes of this Act, term "disabled" or "disability" shall not apply to an individual solely because that individual is a transvestite.

§12209 [§510]. Instrumentalities of the Congress

The General Accounting Office [Government Accountability Office], the Government Printing Office, and the Library of Congress shall be covered as follows:

(1) *In general.* The rights and protections under this Act shall, subject to paragraph (2), apply with respect to the conduct of each instrumentality of the Congress.

(2) *Establishment of remedies and procedures by instrumentalities.* The chief official of each instrumentality of the Congress shall establish remedies and procedures to be utilized with respect to the rights and protections provided pursuant to paragraph (1).

(3) *Report to Congress.* The chief official of each instrumentality of the Congress shall, after establishing remedies and procedures for purposes of paragraph (2), submit to the Congress a report describing the remedies and procedures.

(4) *Definition of instrumentalities.* For purposes of this section, the term "instrumentality of the Congress" means the following: the General Accounting Office [Government Accountability Office], the Government Printing Office, and the Library of Congress.

(5) *Enforcement of employment rights.* The remedies and procedures set forth in section 717 of the Civil Rights Act of 1964 (42 U.S.C. 2000e-16) shall be available to any employee of an instrumentality of the Congress who alleges a violation of the rights and protections under sections 102 through 104 of this Act [42 USCS §§12112-12114] that are made applicable by this section, except that the authorities of the Equal Employment Opportunity Commission shall be exercised by the chief official of the instrumentality of the Congress.

(6) *Enforcement of rights to public services and accommodations.* The remedies and procedures set forth in section 717 of the Civil Rights Act of 1964 (42 U.S.C. 2000e-16) shall be available to any qualified person with a disability who is a visitor, guest, or patron of an instrumentality of Congress and who alleges a violation of the rights and protections under sections 201 through 230 or section 302 or 303 of this Act [42 USCS §§12131-12150 or §12182 or §12183] that are made applicable by this section, except that the authorities of the Equal Employment Opportunity Commission shall be exercised by the chief official of the instrumentality of the Congress.

(7) *Construction.* Nothing in this section shall alter the enforcement procedures for individuals with disabilities provided in the General Accounting Office Personnel Act of 1980 and regulations promulgated pursuant to that Act.

§12210 [§511]. *Illegal Use of Drugs*

(a) *In General.* For purposes of this Act, the term "individual with a disability" does not include an individual who is currently engaging in the illegal use of drugs, when the covered entity acts on the basis of such use.

(b) *Rules of Construction.* Nothing in subsection (a) shall be construed to exclude as an individual with a disability an individual who

(1) has successfully completed a supervised drug rehabilitation program and is no longer engaging in the illegal use of drugs, or has otherwise been rehabilitated successfully and is no longer engaging in such use;

(2) is participating in a supervised rehabilitation program and is no longer engaging in such use; or

(3) is erroneously regarded as engaging in such use, but is not engaging in such use; except that it shall not be a violation of this Act for a covered entity to adopt or administer reasonable policies or procedures, including but not limited to drug testing, designed to ensure that an individual described in paragraph (1) or (2) is no longer engaging in the illegal use of drugs; however, nothing in this section shall be construed to encourage, prohibit, restrict, or authorize the conducting of testing for illegal use of drugs.

(c) *Health and Other Services.* Notwithstanding subsection (a) and section 512(b)(3), an individual shall not be denied health services, or services provided in connection with drug rehabilitation, on the basis of the current illegal use of drugs if the individual is otherwise entitled to such services.

(d) *Definition of Illegal Use of Drugs.*

(1) *In general.* The term "illegal use of drugs" means the use of drugs, the possession or distribution of which is unlawful under the Controlled Substances Act (21 U.S.C. 812). Such term does not include the use of a drug taken under supervision by a licensed health care professional, or other uses authorized by the Controlled Substances Act or other provisions of Federal law.

(2) *Drugs.* The term "drug" means a controlled substance, as defined in schedules I through IV of section 202 of the Controlled Substances Act.

§12211 [§512]. Definitions

(a) *Homosexuality and Bisexuality.* For purposes of the definition of "disability" in section 3(2), homosexuality and bisexuality are not impairments and as such are not disabilities under this Act.

(b) *Certain Conditions.* Under this Act, the term "disability" shall not include

(1) transvestism, transsexualism, pedophilia, exhibitionism, voyeurism, gender identity disorders not resulting from physical impairments, or other sexual behavior disorders;

(2) compulsive gambling, kleptomania, or pyromania; or

(3) psychoactive substance use disorders resulting from current illegal use of drugs.

§12212 [§514]. Alternative Means of Dispute Resolution

Where appropriate and to the extent authorized by law, the use of alternative means of dispute resolution, including settlement negotiations, conciliation, facilitation, mediation, factfinding, minitrials, and arbitration, is encouraged to resolve disputes arising under this Act.

§12213 [§515]. Severability

Should any provision in this Act be found to be unconstitutional by a court of law, such provision shall be severed from the remainder of the Act, and such action shall not affect the enforceability of the remaining provisions of the Act.

ADA Amendments Act of 2008

Pub. L. No. 110-325; 122 Stat. 3553

[Editors' Note: The ADA Amendments Act of 2008, as its title suggests, amended the American with Disabilities Act. The amendments have been incorporated in the ADA. The ADAAA, however, is reproduced for convenience of reference.]

Be it enacted by the Senate and House of Representatives of the United States of America in Congress assembled,

Sec. 1. Short Title

This Act may be cited as the "ADA Amendments Act of 2008".

Sec. 2. Findings and Purposes

(a) *Findings.* — Congress finds that —

(1) in enacting the Americans with Disabilities Act of 1990 (ADA), Congress intended that the Act "provide a clear and comprehensive national mandate for the elimination of discrimination against individuals with disabilities" and provide broad coverage;

(2) in enacting the ADA, Congress recognized that physical and mental disabilities in no way diminish a person's right to fully participate in all aspects of society, but that people with physical or mental disabilities are frequently precluded from doing so because of prejudice, antiquated attitudes, or the failure to remove societal and institutional barriers;

(3) while Congress expected that the definition of disability under the ADA would be interpreted consistently with how courts had applied the definition of a handicapped individual under the Rehabilitation Act of 1973, that expectation has not been fulfilled;

(4) the holdings of the Supreme Court in *Sutton v. United Air Lines, Inc., 527 U.S. 471 (1999)* and its companion cases have narrowed the broad scope of protection intended to be afforded by the ADA, thus eliminating protection for many individuals whom Congress intended to protect;

(5) the holding of the Supreme Court in *Toyota Motor Manufacturing, Kentucky, Inc. v. Williams, 534 U.S. 184 (2002)* further narrowed the broad scope of protection intended to be afforded by the ADA;

(6) as a result of these Supreme Court cases, lower courts have incorrectly found in individual cases that people with a range of substantially limiting impairments are not people with disabilities;

(7) in particular, the Supreme Court, in the case of *Toyota Motor Manufacturing, Kentucky, Inc. v. Williams, 534 U.S. 184 (2002)*, interpreted the term "substantially limits" to require a greater degree of limitation than was intended by Congress; and

(8) Congress finds that the current Equal Employment Opportunity Commission ADA regulations defining the term "substantially limits" as "significantly restricted" are inconsistent with congressional intent, by expressing too high a standard.

(b) *Purposes.* — The purposes of this Act are —

(1) to carry out the ADA's objectives of providing "a clear and comprehensive national mandate for the elimination of discrimination" and "clear, strong, consistent, enforceable standards addressing discrimination" by reinstating a broad scope of protection to be available under the ADA;

(2) to reject the requirement enunciated by the Supreme Court in *Sutton v. United Air Lines, Inc., 527 U.S. 471 (1999)* and its companion cases that whether an impairment substantially limits a major life activity is to be determined with reference to the ameliorative effects of mitigating measures;

(3) to reject the Supreme Court's reasoning in *Sutton v. United Air Lines, Inc., 527 U.S. 471 (1999)* with regard to coverage under the third prong of the definition of disability and to reinstate the reasoning of the Supreme Court in *School Board of Nassau County v. Arline, 480 U.S. 273 (1987)* which set forth a broad view of the third prong of the definition of handicap under the Rehabilitation Act of 1973;

(4) to reject the standards enunciated by the Supreme Court in *Toyota Motor Manufacturing, Kentucky, Inc. v. Williams, 534 U.S. 184 (2002)*, that the terms "substantially" and "major" in the definition of disability under the ADA "need to be interpreted strictly to create a demanding standard for qualifying as disabled," and that to be substantially limited in performing a major life activity under the ADA "an individual must have an impairment that prevents or severely restricts the individual from doing activities that are of central importance to most people's daily lives";

(5) to convey congressional intent that the standard created by the Supreme Court in the case of *Toyota Motor Manufacturing, Kentucky, Inc. v. Williams, 534 U.S. 184 (2002)* for "substantially limits", and applied by lower courts in numerous decisions, has created an inappropriately high level of limitation necessary to obtain coverage under the ADA, to convey that it is the intent of Congress that the primary object of attention in cases brought under the ADA should be whether entities covered under the ADA have complied with their obligations, and to convey that the question of whether an individual's impairment is a disability under the ADA should not demand extensive analysis; and

(6) to express Congress' expectation that the Equal Employment Opportunity Commission will revise that portion of its current regulations that defines the term "substantially limits" as "significantly restricted" to be consistent with this Act, including the amendments made by this Act.

Sec. 3. Codified Findings

Section 2(a) of the Americans with Disabilities Act of 1990 (*42 U.S.C. 12101*) is amended —

(1) by amending paragraph (1) to read as follows:

"(1) physical or mental disabilities in no way diminish a person's right to fully participate in all aspects of society, yet many people with physical or mental disabilities have been precluded from doing so because of discrimination; others who have a record of a disability or are regarded as having a disability also have been subjected to discrimination;";

(2) by striking paragraph (7); and

(3) by redesignating paragraphs (8) and (9) as paragraphs (7) and (8), respectively.

Sec. 4. Disability Defined and Rules of Construction

(a) *Definition of Disability.* — Section 3 of the Americans with Disabilities Act of 1990 (*42 U.S.C. 12102*) is amended to read as follows:

"Sec. 3. DEFINITION OF DISABILITY.

"As used in this Act:

"(1) *Disability.* — The term 'disability' means, with respect to an individual —

"(A) a physical or mental impairment that substantially limits one or more major life activities of such individual;

"(B) a record of such an impairment; or

"(C) being regarded as having such an impairment (as described in paragraph (3)).

"(2) *Major life activities.* —

"(A) *In general.* — For purposes of paragraph (1), major life activities include, but are not limited to, caring for oneself, performing manual tasks, seeing, hearing, eating, sleeping, walking, standing, lifting, bending, speaking, breathing, learning, reading, concentrating, thinking, communicating, and working.

"(B) *Major bodily functions.* — For purposes of paragraph (1), a major life activity also includes the operation of a major bodily function, including but not limited to, functions of the immune system, normal cell growth, digestive, bowel, bladder, neurological, brain, respiratory, circulatory, endocrine, and reproductive functions.

"(3) *Regarded as having such an impairment.* — For purposes of paragraph (1)(C):

"(A) An individual meets the requirement of 'being regarded as having such an impairment' if the individual establishes that he or she has been subjected to an action prohibited under this Act because of an actual or perceived physical or mental impairment whether or not the impairment limits or is perceived to limit a major life activity.

"(B) Paragraph (1)(C) shall not apply to impairments that are transitory and minor. A transitory impairment is an impairment with an actual or expected duration of 6 months or less.

"(4) *Rules of construction regarding the definition of disability.*—The definition of 'disability' in paragraph (1) shall be construed in accordance with the following:

"(A) The definition of disability in this Act shall be construed in favor of broad coverage of individuals under this Act, to the maximum extent permitted by the terms of this Act.

"(B) The term 'substantially limits' shall be interpreted consistently with the findings and purposes of the ADA Amendments Act of 2008.

"(C) An impairment that substantially limits one major life activity need not limit other major life activities in order to be considered a disability.

"(D) An impairment that is episodic or in remission is a disability if it would substantially limit a major life activity when active."

"(E)(i) The determination of whether an impairment substantially limits a major life activity shall be made without regard to the ameliorative effects of mitigating measures such as—

"(I) medication, medical supplies, equipment, or appliances, low-vision devices (which do not include ordinary eyeglasses or contact lenses), prosthetics including limbs and devices, hearing aids and cochlear implants or other implantable hearing devices, mobility devices, or oxygen therapy equipment and supplies;

"(II) use of assistive technology;

"(III) reasonable accommodations or auxiliary aids or services; or

"(IV) learned behavioral or adaptive neurological modifications.

"(ii) The ameliorative effects of the mitigating measures of ordinary eyeglasses or contact lenses shall be considered in determining whether an impairment substantially limits a major life activity.

"(iii) As used in this subparagraph—

"(I) the term 'ordinary eyeglasses or contact lenses' means lenses that are intended to fully correct visual acuity or eliminate refractive error; and

"(II) the term 'low-vision devices' means devices that magnify, enhance, or otherwise augment a visual image.".

(b) *Conforming Amendment.*—The Americans with Disabilities Act of 1990 (*42 U.S.C. 12101* et seq.) is further amended by adding after section 3 the following:

"Sec. 4. ADDITIONAL DEFINITIONS.

"As used in this Act:

"(1) *Auxiliary aids and services.*—The term 'auxiliary aids and services' includes—

"(A) qualified interpreters or other effective methods of making aurally delivered materials available to individuals with hearing impairments;

"(B) qualified readers, taped texts, or other effective methods of making visually delivered materials available to individuals with visual impairments;

"(C) acquisition or modification of equipment or devices; and

"(D) other similar services and actions.

"(2) *State.* — The term 'State' means each of the several States, the District of Columbia, the Commonwealth of Puerto Rico, Guam, American Samoa, the Virgin Islands of the United States, the Trust Territory of the Pacific Islands, and the Commonwealth of the Northern Mariana Islands.".

(c) *Amendment to the Table of Contents.* — The table of contents contained in section 1(b) of the Americans with Disabilities Act of 1990 is amended by striking the item relating to section 3 and inserting the following items:

"Sec. 3. Definition of disability.

"Sec. 4. Additional definitions.".

Sec. 5. Discrimination on the Basis of Disability

(a) *On the Basis of Disability.* — Section 102 of the Americans with Disabilities Act of 1990 (*42 U.S.C. 12112*) is amended —

(1) in subsection (a), by striking "with a disability because of the disability of such individual" and inserting "on the basis of disability"; and

(2) in subsection (b) in the matter preceding paragraph (1), by striking "discriminate" and inserting "discriminate against a qualified individual on the basis of disability".

(b) *Qualification Standards and Tests Related to Uncorrected Vision.* — Section 103 of the Americans with Disabilities Act of 1990 (*42 U.S.C. 12113*) is amended by redesignating subsections (c) and (d) as subsections (d) and (e), respectively, and inserting after subsection (b) the following new subsection:

"(c) *Qualification Standards and Tests Related to Uncorrected Vision.* — Notwithstanding section 3(4)(E)(ii), a covered entity shall not use qualification standards, employment tests, or other selection criteria based on an individual's uncorrected vision unless the standard, test, or other selection criteria, as used by the covered entity, is shown to be job-related for the position in question and consistent with business necessity.".

(c) *Conforming Amendments.* —

(1) Section 101(8) of the Americans with Disabilities Act of 1990 (*42 U.S.C. 12111(8)*) is amended —

(A) in the paragraph heading, by striking "with a disability"; and

(B) by striking "with a disability" after "individual" both places it appears.

(2) Section 104(a) of the Americans with Disabilities Act of 1990 (*42 U.S.C. 12114(a)*) is amended by striking "the term 'qualified individual with a disability' shall" and inserting "a qualified individual with a disability shall".

Sec. 6. Rules of Construction

(a) Title V of the Americans with Disabilities Act of 1990 (*42 U.S.C. 12201* et seq.) is amended —

(1) by adding at the end of section 501 the following:

"(e) *Benefits Under State Worker's Compensation Laws.* — Nothing in this Act alters the standards for determining eligibility for benefits under State worker's compensation laws or under State and Federal disability benefit programs.

"(f) *Fundamental Alteration.* — Nothing in this Act alters the provision of section 302(b)(2)(A)(ii), specifying that reasonable modifications in policies, practices, or procedures shall be required, unless an entity can demonstrate that making such modifications in policies, practices, or procedures, including academic requirements in postsecondary education, would fundamentally alter the nature of the goods, services, facilities, privileges, advantages, or accommodations involved.

"(g) *Claims of No Disability.* — Nothing in this Act shall provide the basis for a claim by an individual without a disability that the individual was subject to discrimination because of the individual's lack of disability.

"(h) *Reasonable Accommodations and Modifications.* — A covered entity under title I, a public entity under title II, and any person who owns, leases (or leases to), or operates a place of public accommodation under title III, need not provide a reasonable accommodation or a reasonable modification to policies, practices, or procedures to an individual who meets the definition of disability in section 3(1) solely under subparagraph (C) of such section.";

(2) by redesignating section 506 through 514 as sections 507 through 515, respectively, and adding after section 505 the following:

"Sec. 506. RULE OF CONSTRUCTION REGARDING REGULATORY AUTHORITY.

"The authority to issue regulations granted to the Equal Employment Opportunity Commission, the Attorney General, and the Secretary of Transportation under this Act includes the authority to issue regulations implementing the definitions of disability in section 3 (including rules of construction) and the definitions in section 4, consistent with the ADA Amendments Act of 2008."; and

(3) in section 511 (as redesignated by paragraph (2)) (*42 U.S.C. 12211*), in subsection (c), by striking "511(b)(3)" and inserting "512(b)(3)".

(b) The table of contents contained in section 1(b) of the Americans with Disabilities Act of 1990 is amended by redesignating the items relating to sections 506 through 514 as the items relating to sections 507 through 515, respectively, and by inserting after the item relating to section 505 the following new item:

"Sec. 506. *Rule of construction regarding regulatory authority.*".

Sec. 7. Conforming Amendments

Section 7 of the Rehabilitation Act of 1973 (*29 U.S.C. 705*) is amended —
    (1) in paragraph (9)(B), by striking "a physical" and all that follows through "major life activities", and inserting "the meaning given it in section 3 of the Americans with Disabilities Act of 1990 (*42 U.S.C. 12102*)"; and
    (2) in paragraph (20)(B), by striking "any person who" and all that follows through the period at the end, and inserting "any person who has a disability as defined in section 3 of the Americans with Disabilities Act of 1990 (*42 U.S.C. 12102*).".

Sec. 8. Effective Date

This Act and the amendments made by this Act shall become effective on January 1, 2009.

Civil Rights Act of 1991

Pub. L. No. 102–166, 105 Stat. 1071

[Editors' Note: The Civil Rights Act of 1991 amended a variety of other statutes, most notably Title VII and 42 U.S.C. §1981. These amendments have been incorporated in the relevant statutes as they are reproduced elsewhere in this Supplement. The core provisions of the 1991 Act, however, are reproduced here for convenience of reference. Where the text of the statute does not so indicate, brackets after the title specify where the sections are codified or noted in the U.S.C.]

Be it enacted by the Senate and House of Representatives of the United States of America in Congress assembled,

Sec. 1. Short Title [42 U.S.C. 1981 note]

This Act may be cited as the "Civil Rights Act of 1991."

Sec. 2. Findings [42 U.S.C. 1981 note]

The Congress finds that—

(1) additional remedies under Federal law are needed to deter unlawful harassment and intentional discrimination in the workplace;

(2) the decision of the Supreme Court in *Wards Cove Packing Co. v. Atonio*, 490 U.S. 642 (1989) has weakened the scope and effectiveness of Federal civil rights protections; and

(3) legislation is necessary to provide additional protections against unlawful discrimination in employment.

Sec. 3. Purposes [42 U.S.C. 1981 note]

The purposes of this Act are—

(1) to provide appropriate remedies for intentional discrimination and unlawful harassment in the workplace;

(2) to codify the concepts of "business necessity" and "job related" enunciated by the Supreme Court in *Griggs v. Duke Power Co.*, 401 U.S. 424

(1971), and in the other Supreme Court decisions prior to *Wards Cove Packing Co. v. Atonio*, 490 U.S. 642 (1989);

(3) to confirm statutory authority and provide statutory guidelines for the adjudication of disparate impact suits under title VII of the Civil Rights Act of 1964 (42 U.S.C. 2000e et seq.); and

(4) to respond to recent decisions of the Supreme Court by expanding the scope of relevant civil rights statutes in order to provide adequate protection to victims of discrimination.

TITLE I — FEDERAL CIVIL RIGHTS REMEDIES

Sec. 101. Prohibition Against All Racial Discrimination in the Making and Enforcement of Contracts

Section 1977 of the Revised Statutes (42 U.S.C. 1981) is amended —

(1) by inserting "(a)" before "All persons within"; and

(2) by adding at the end the following new subsections:

(b) For purposes of this section, the term "make and enforce contracts" includes the making, performance, modification, and termination of contracts, and the enjoyment of all benefits, privileges, terms, and conditions of the contractual relationship.

(c) The rights protected by this section are protected against impairment by nongovernmental discrimination and impairment under color of State law.

Sec. 102. Damages in Cases of Intentional Discrimination

The Revised Statutes are amended by inserting after section 1977 (42 U.S.C. 1981) the following new section:

Sec. 1977A [42 U.S.C. 1981a]. Damages in Cases of Intentional Discrimination in Employment

(a) Right of Recovery —

(1) *Civil rights.* — In an action brought by a complaining party under section 706 or 717 of the Civil Rights Act of 1964 (42 U.S.C. 2000e-5) against a respondent who engaged in unlawful intentional discrimination (not an employment practice that is unlawful because of its disparate impact) prohibited under section 703, 704, or 717 of the Act (42 U.S.C. 2000e-2 or 2000e-3), and provided that the complaining party cannot recover under section 1977 of the Revised Statutes (42 U.S.C. 1981), the complaining party may recover compensatory and punitive damages as allowed in subsection (b), in addition to any relief authorized by section 706(g) of the Civil Rights Act of 1964, from the respondent.

(2) *Disability.* — In an action brought by a complaining party under the powers, remedies, and procedures set forth in section 706 or 717 of the Civil Rights Act of 1964 (as provided in section 107(a) of the Americans with

Disabilities Act of 1990 (42 U.S.C. 12117(a)), and section 505(a)(1) of the Rehabilitation Act of 1973 (29 U.S.C. 794a(a)(1)), respectively) against a respondent who engaged in unlawful intentional discrimination (not an employment practice that is unlawful because of its disparate impact) under section 501 of the Rehabilitation Act of 1973 (29 U.S.C. 791) and the regulations implementing section 501, or who violated the requirements of section 501 of the Act or the regulations implementing section 501 concerning the provision of a reasonable accommodation, or section 102 of the Americans with Disabilities Act of 1990 (42 U.S.C. 12112), or committed a violation of section 102(b)(5) of the Act, against an individual, the complaining party may recover compensatory and punitive damages as allowed in subsection (b), in addition to any relief authorized by section 706(g) of the Civil Rights Act of 1964, from the respondent.

(3) *Reasonable accommodation and good faith effort.* — In cases where a discriminatory practice involves the provision of a reasonable accommodation pursuant to section 102(b)(5) of the Americans with Disabilities Act of 1990 or regulations implementing section 501 of the Rehabilitation Act of 1973, damages may not be awarded under this section where the covered entity demonstrates good faith efforts, in consultation with the person with the disability who has informed the covered entity that accommodation is needed, to identify and make a reasonable accommodation that would provide such individual with an equally effective opportunity and would not cause an undue hardship on the operation of the business.

(b) *Compensatory and Punitive Damages.* —

(1) *Determination of punitive damages.* A complaining party may recover punitive damages under this section against a respondent (other than a government, government agency or political subdivision) if the complaining party demonstrates that the respondent engaged in a discriminatory practice or discriminatory practices with malice or with reckless indifference to the federally protected rights of an aggrieved individual.

(2) *Exclusions from compensatory damages.* — Compensatory damages awarded under this section shall not include backpay, interest on backpay, or any other type of relief authorized under section 706(g) of the Civil Rights Act of 1964.

(3) *Limitations.* — The sum of the amount of compensatory damages awarded under this section for future pecuniary losses, emotional pain, suffering, inconvenience, mental anguish, loss of enjoyment of life, and other non-pecuniary losses, and the amount of punitive damages awarded under this section, shall not exceed, for each complaining party —

(A) in the case of a respondent who has more than 14 and fewer than 101 employees in each of 20 or more calendar weeks in the current or preceding calendar year, $50,000;

(B) in the case of a respondent who has more than 100 and fewer than 201 employees in each of 20 or more calendar weeks in the current or preceding calendar year, $100,000; and

(C) in the case of a respondent who has more than 200 and fewer than 501 employees in each of 20 or more calendar weeks in the current or preceding calendar year, $200,000; and

(D) in the case of a respondent who has more than 500 employees in each of 20 or more calendar weeks in the current or preceding calendar year, $300,000.

(4) *Construction.* Nothing in this section shall be construed to limit the scope of, or the relief available under, section 1977 of the Revised Statutes (42 U.S.C. 1981).

(c) *Jury Trial.* — If a complaining party seeks compensatory or punitive damages under this section —

(1) any party may demand a trial by jury; and

(2) the court shall not inform the jury of the limitations described in subsection (b)(3).

(d) *Definitions.* — As used in this section:

(1) *Complaining party.* — The term "complaining party" means —

(A) in the case of a person seeking to bring an action under subsection (a)(1), the Equal Employment Opportunity Commission, the Attorney General, or a person who may bring an action or proceeding under title VII of the Civil Rights Act of 1964 (42 U.S.C. 2000e et seq.); or

(B) in the case of a person seeking to bring an action under subsection (a)(2), the Equal Employment Opportunity Commission, the Attorney General, a person who may bring an action or proceeding under section 505(a)(1) of the Rehabilitation Act of 1973 (29 U.S.C. 794a(a)(1)), or a person who may bring an action or proceeding under title I of the Americans with Disabilities Act of 1990 (42 U.S.C. 12010 et seq.).

(2) *Discriminatory practice.* — The term "discriminatory practice" means the discrimination described in paragraph (1), or the discrimination or the violation described in paragraph (2), of subsection (a).

Sec. 103. Attorney's Fees

The last sentence of section 722 of the Revised Statutes (42 U.S.C. 1988) is amended by inserting, "1977A" after "1977." [42 U.S.C. 1981a]

Sec. 104. Definitions

Section 701 of the Civil Rights Act of 1964 (42 U.S.C. 2000e) is amended by adding at the end the following new subsections:

(*l*) The term "complaining party" means the Commission, the Attorney General, or a person who may bring an action or proceeding under this title.

(m) The term "demonstrates" means meets the burdens of production and persuasion.

(n) The term "respondent" means an employer, employment agency, labor organization, joint labor-management committee controlling apprenticeship or other training or retraining program, including an on-the-job training program, or Federal entity subject to section 717.

Sec. 105. Burden of Proof in Disparate Impact Cases

(a) Section 703 of the Civil Rights Act of 1964 (42 U.S.C. 2000e-2) is amended by adding at the end the following new subsection:

(k)(1)(A) An unlawful employment practice based on disparate impact is established under this title only if—

(i) a complaining party demonstrates that a respondent uses a particular employment practice that causes a disparate impact on the basis of race, color, religion, sex, or national origin and the respondent fails to demonstrate that the challenged practice is job related for the position in question and consistent with business necessity; or

(ii) the complaining party makes the demonstration described in subparagraph (C) with respect to an alternative employment practice and the respondent refuses to adopt such alternative employment practices.

(B)(i) With respect to demonstrating that a particular employment practice causes a disparate impact as described in subparagraph (A)(i), the complaining party shall demonstrate that each particular challenged employment practice causes a disparate impact, except that if the complaining party can demonstrate to the court that the elements of a respondent's decisionmaking process are not capable of separation for analysis, the decisionmaking process may be analyzed as one employment practice.

(ii) If the respondent demonstrates that a specific employment practice does not cause the disparate impact, the respondent shall not be required to demonstrate that such practice is required by business necessity.

(C) The demonstration referred to by subparagraph (A)(ii) shall be in accordance with the law as it existed on June 4, 1989, with respect to the concept of "alternative employment practice."

(2) A demonstration that an employment practice is required by business necessity may not be used as a defense against a claim of intentional discrimination under this title.

(3) Notwithstanding any other provision of this title, a rule barring the employment of an individual who currently and knowingly uses or possesses a controlled substance, as defined in schedules I and II of section 102(6) of the Controlled Substances Act (21 U.S.C. 802(6)), other than the use or possession of a drug taken under the supervision of a licensed health care professional, or any other use or possession authorized by the Controlled Substances Act or any other provision of Federal law, shall be considered an unlawful employment practice under this title only if such rule is adopted or applied with an intent to discriminate because of race, color, religion, sex, or national origin.

(b) No statements other than the interpretive memorandum appearing at Vol. 137 Congressional Record S 15276 (daily ed. Oct. 25, 1991) shall be considered legislative history of, or relied upon in any way as legislative history in construing or applying, any provision of this Act that relates to *Wards Cove* — Business necessity/cumulation/alternative business practice.

Sec. 106. Prohibition Against Discriminatory Use of Test Scores

Section 703 of the Civil Rights Act of 1964 (42 U.S.C. 2000e-2) (as amended by section 105) is further amended by adding at the end the following new subsection:

(1) It shall be an unlawful employment practice for a respondent, in connection with the selection or referral of applicants or candidates for employment or promotion, to adjust the scores of, use different cutoff scores for, or otherwise alter the results of, employment related tests on the basis of race, color, religion, sex, or national origin.

Sec. 107. Clarifying Prohibition Against Impermissible Consideration of Race, Color, Religion, Sex, or National Origin in Employment Practices

(a) *In General.* — Section 703 of the Civil Rights Act of 1964 (42 U.S.C. 2000e-2) (as amended by sections 105 and 106) is further amended by adding at the end the following new subsection:

(m) Except as otherwise provided in this title, an unlawful employment practice is established when the complaining party demonstrates that race, color, religion, sex, or national origin was a motivating factor for any employment practice, even though other factors also motivated the practice.

(b) *Enforcement Provisions.* — Section 706(g) of such Act (42 U.S.C. 2000e-5(g)) is amended —

(1) by designating the first through third sentences as paragraph (1);

(2) by designating the fourth sentence as paragraph (2)(A) and indenting accordingly; and

(3) by adding at the end the following new subparagraph:

(B) On a claim in which an individual proves a violation under section 703(m) and a respondent demonstrates that the respondent would have taken the same action in the absence of the impermissible motivating factor, the court —

(i) may grant declaratory relief, injunctive relief (except as provided in clause (ii)), and attorney's fees and costs demonstrated to be directly attributable only to the pursuit of a claim under section 703(m); and

(ii) shall not award damages or issue an order requiring any admission, reinstatement, hiring, promotion, or payment, described in subparagraph (A).

Sec. 108. Facilitating Prompt and Orderly Resolution of Challenges to Employment Practices Implementing Litigated or Consent Judgments or Orders

Section 703 of the Civil Rights Act of 1964 (42 U.S.C. 2000e-2) (as amended by sections 105, 106, and 107 of this title) is further amended by adding at the end the following new subsection:

(n)(1)(A) Notwithstanding any other provision of law, and except as provided in paragraph (2), an employment practice that implements and is within the scope of a litigated or consent judgment or order that resolves a claim of employment discrimination under the Constitution or Federal civil rights laws may not be challenged under the circumstances described in subparagraph (B).

(B) A practice described in subparagraph (A) may not be challenged in a claim under the Constitution or Federal civil rights laws —

(i) by a person who, prior to the entry of the judgment or order described in subparagraph (A), had —

(I) actual notice of the proposed judgment or order sufficient to apprise such person that such judgment or order might adversely affect the interests and legal rights of such person and that an opportunity was available to present objections to such judgment or order by a future date certain; and

(II) a reasonable opportunity to present objections to such judgment or order; or

(ii) by a person whose interests were adequately represented by another person who had previously challenged the judgment or order on the same legal grounds and with a similar factual situation, unless there has been an intervening change in law or fact.

(2) Nothing in this subsection shall be construed to —

(A) alter the standards for intervention under rule 24 of the Federal Rules of Civil Procedure or apply to the rights of parties who have successfully intervened pursuant to such rule in the proceeding in which the parties intervened;

(B) apply to the rights of parties to the action in which a litigated or consent judgment or order was entered, or of members of a class represented or sought to be represented in such action, or of members of a group on whose behalf relief was sought in such action by the Federal Government;

(C) prevent challenges to a litigated or consent judgment or order on the ground that such judgment or order was obtained through collusion or fraud, or is transparently invalid or was entered by a court lacking subject matter jurisdiction; or

(D) authorize or permit the denial to any person of the due process of law required by the Constitution.

(3) Any action not precluded under this subsection that challenges an employment consent judgment or order described in paragraph (1) shall be brought in the court, and if possible before the judge, that entered such judgment or order. Nothing in this subsection shall preclude a transfer of such action pursuant to section 1404 of title 28, United States Code.

Sec. 109. *Protection of Extraterritorial Employment*

(a) *Definition of Employee.* — Section 701(f) of the Civil Rights Act of 1964 (42 U.S.C. 2000e(f)) and section 101(4) of the Americans with Disabilities Act of 1990

(42 U.S.C. 12111(4)) are each amended by adding at the end the following: "With respect to employment in a foreign country, such term includes an individual who is a citizen of the United States."

(b) *Exemption.* —

(1) Civil Rights Act of 1964. — Section 702 of the Civil Rights Act of 1964 (42 U.S.C. 2000e-1) is amended —

(A) by inserting "(a)" after "Sec. 702."; and

(B) by adding at the end the following:

(b) It shall not be unlawful under section 703 or 704 for an employer (or a corporation controlled by an employer), labor organization, employment agency, or joint labor-management committee controlling apprenticeship or other training or retraining (including on-the-job training programs) to take any action otherwise prohibited by such section, with respect to an employee in a workplace in a foreign country if compliance with such section would cause such employer (or such corporation), such organization, such agency, or such committee to violate the law of the foreign country in which such workplace is located.

(c)(1) If an employer controls a corporation whose place of incorporation is a foreign country, any practice prohibited by section 703 or 704 engaged in by such corporation shall be presumed to be engaged in by such employer.

(2) Sections 703 and 704 shall not apply with respect to the foreign operations of an employer that is a foreign person not controlled by an American employer.

(3) For purposes of this subsection, the determination of whether an employer controls a corporation shall be based on —

(A) the interrelation of operations;

(B) the common management;

(C) the centralized control of labour relations; and

(D) the common ownership or financial control, of the employer and the corporation.

(2) Americans with Disabilities Act of 1990. — Section 102 of the Americans with Disabilities Act of 1990 (42 U.S.C. 12112) is amended —

(A) by redesignating subsection (c) as subsection (d); and

(B) by inserting after subsection (b) the following new subsection:

(c) Covered Entities in Foreign Countries. —

(1) *In general.* — It shall not be unlawful under this section for a covered entity to take any action that constitutes discrimination under this section with respect to an employee in a workplace in a foreign country if compliance with this section would cause such covered entity to violate the law of the foreign country in which such workplace is located.

(2) *Control of corporation.* —

(A) *Presumption.* — If an employer controls a corporation whose place of incorporation is a foreign country, any practice that constitutes discrimination under this section and is engaged in by such corporation shall be presumed to be engaged in by such employer.

(B) *Exception.* — This section shall not apply with respect to the foreign operations of an employer that is a foreign person not controlled by an American employer.

(C) *Determination.* — For purposes of this paragraph, the determination of whether an employer controls a corporation shall be based on —

(i) the interrelation of operations;

(ii) the common management;

(iii) the centralized control of labor relations; and

(iv) the common ownership or financial control, of the employer and the corporation.

(c) *Application of Amendments.* — The amendments made by this section shall not apply with respect to conduct occurring before the date of the enactment of this Act.

Sec. 110. *Technical Assistance Training Institute*

(a) *Technical Assistance.* — Section 705 of the Civil Rights Act of 1964 (42 U.S.C. 2000e-4) is amended by adding at the end the following new subsection:

(j)(1) The Commission shall establish a Technical Assistance Training Institute, through which the Commission shall provide technical assistance and training regarding the laws and regulations enforced by the Commission.

(2) An employer or other entity covered under this title shall not be excused from compliance with the requirements of this title because of any failure to receive technical assistance under this subsection.

(3) There are authorized to be appropriated to carry out this subsection such sums as may be necessary for fiscal year 1992.

(b) *Effective Date.* — The amendment made by this section shall take effect on the date of the enactment of this Act.

Sec. 111. *Education and Outreach*

Section 705(h) of the Civil Rights Act of 1964 (42 U.S.C. 2000e-4(h)) is amended —

(1) by inserting "(1)" after "(h)"; and

(2) by adding at the end the following new paragraph:

(2) In exercising its powers under this title, the Commission shall carry out educational and outreach activities (including dissemination of information in languages other than English) targeted to —

(A) individuals who historically have been victims of employment discrimination and have not been equitably served by the Commission; and

(B) individuals on whose behalf the Commission has authority to enforce any other law prohibiting employment discrimination, concerning rights and obligations under this title or such law, as the case may be.

Sec. 112. Expansion of Right to Challenge Discriminatory Seniority Systems

Section 706(e) of the Civil Rights Act of 1964 (42 U.S.C. 2000e-5(e)) is amended—
> (1) by inserting "(1)" before "A charge under this section"; and
> (2) by adding at the end the following new paragraph:
>> (2) For purposes of this section, an unlawful employment practice occurs, with respect to a seniority system that has been adopted for an intentionally discriminatory purpose in violation of this title (whether or not the discriminatory purpose is apparent on the face of the seniority provision), when the seniority system is adopted, when an individual becomes subject to the seniority system, or when a person aggrieved is injured by the application of the seniority system or provision of the system.

Sec. 113. Authorizing Award of Expert Fees

(a) *Revised Statutes.*—Section 722 of the Revised Statutes [42 U.S.C. 1988] is amended—
> (1) by designating the first and second sentences as subsections (a) and (b), respectively, and indenting accordingly; and
> (2) by adding at the end the following new subsection:
>> (c) In awarding an attorney's fee under subsection (b) in any action or proceeding to enforce a provision of sections 1977 or 1977A of the Revised Statutes, the court, in its discretion, may include expert fees as part of the attorney's fee.

(b) *Civil Rights Act of 1964.*—Section 706(k) of the Civil Rights Act of 1964 (42 U.S.C. 2000e-5(k)) is amended by inserting "(including expert fees)" after "attorney's fee."

Sec. 114. Providing for Interest and Extending the Statute of Limitations in Actions Against the Federal Government

Section 717 of the Civil Rights Act of 1964 (42 U.S.C. 2000e-16) is amended—
> (1) in subsection (c), by striking "thirty days" and inserting "90 days"; and
> (2) in subsection (d), by inserting before the period, "and the same interest to compensate for delay in payment shall be available as in cases involving nonpublic parties."

Sec. 115. Notice or Limitations Period Under the Age Discrimination in Employment Act of 1967

Section 7(e) of the Age Discrimination in Employment Act of 1967 (29 U.S.C. 626(e)) is amended—
> (1) by striking paragraph (2);
> (2) by striking the paragraph designation in paragraph (1);
> (3) by striking "Sections 6 and" and inserting "Section"; and
> (4) by adding at the end the following: If a charge filed with the Commission under this Act is dismissed or the proceedings of the Commission are

otherwise terminated by the Commission, the Commission shall notify the person aggrieved. A civil action may be brought under this section by a person defined in section 11(a) against the respondent named in the charge within 90 days after the date of the receipt of such notice.

Sec. 116. *Lawful Court-Ordered Remedies, Affirmative Action, and Conciliation Agreements Not Affected*

Nothing in the amendments made by this title shall be construed to affect court-ordered remedies, affirmative action, or conciliation agreements, that are in accordance with the law.

Sec. 117. *Coverage of House of Representatives and the Agencies of the Legislative Branch [2 U.S.C. 601]*

(a) *Coverage of the House of Representatives.*—

(1) *In general.*—Notwithstanding any provision of title VII of the Civil Rights Act of 1964 (42 U.S.C. 2000e et seq.) or of other law, the purposes of such title shall, subject to paragraph (2), apply in their entirety to the House of Representatives.

(2) *Employment in the House.*—

(A) *Application.*—The rights and protections under title VII of the Civil Rights Act of 1964 (42 U.S.C. 2000e et seq.) shall, subject to paragraph (B), apply with respect to any employee in an employment position in the House of Representatives and any employing authority of the House of Representatives.

(B) *Administration.*—

(i) *In general.*—In the administration of this paragraph, the remedies and procedures made applicable pursuant to the resolution described in clause (ii) shall apply exclusively.

(ii) *Resolution.*—The resolution referred to in clause (i) is the Fair Employment Practices Resolution (House Resolution 558 of the One Hundredth Congress, as agreed to October 4, 1988), as incorporated into the Rules of the House of Representatives of the One Hundred Second Congress as Rule LI, or any other provision that continues in effect the provisions of such resolution.

(C) *Exercise of rulemaking power.*—The provisions of subpara- graph (B) are enacted by the House of Representatives as an exercise of the rulemaking power of the House of Representatives, with full recognition of the right of the House to change its rules, in the same manner, and to the same extent as in the case of any other rule of the House.

(b) *Instrumentalities of Congress.*—

(1) *In general.*—The rights and protections under this title and title VII of the Civil Rights Act of 1964 (42 U.S.C. 2000e et seq.) shall, subject to paragraph (2), apply with respect to the conduct of each instrumentality of the Congress.

(2) *Establishment of remedies and procedures by instrumentalities.* — The chief official of each instrumentality of the Congress shall establish remedies and procedures to be utilized with respect to the rights and protections provided pursuant to paragraph (1). Such remedies and procedures shall apply exclusively, except for the employees who are defined as Senate employees, in section 301(c)(1).

(3) *Report to Congress.* — The chief official of each instrumentality of the Congress shall, after establishing remedies and procedures for purposes of paragraph (2), submit to the Congress a report describing the remedies and procedures.

(4) *Definition of instrumentalities.* — For purposes of this section, instrumentalities of the Congress include the following: the Architect of the Capitol, the Congressional Budget Office, the General Accounting Office, the Government Printing Office, the Office of Technology Assessment, and the United States Botanic Garden.

(5) *Construction.* — Nothing in this section shall alter the enforcement procedures for individuals protected under section 71 of title VII for the Civil Rights Act of 1964 (42 U.S.C. 2000e-16).

Sec. 118. *Alternative Means of Dispute Resolution*
[42 U.S.C. 1981 note]

Where appropriate and to the extent authorized by law, the use of alternative means of dispute resolution, including settlement negotiations, conciliation, facilitation, mediation, factfinding, minitrials, and arbitration, is encouraged to resolve disputes arising under the Acts or provisions of Federal law amended by this title.

... TITLE IV — GENERAL PROVISIONS

Sec. 401. *Severability [42 U.S.C. 1981 note]*

If any provision of this Act, or an amendment made by this Act, or the application of such provision to any person or circumstances is held to be invalid, the remainder of this Act and the amendments made by this Act, and the application of such provision to other persons and circumstances, shall not be affected.

Sec. 402. *Effective Date [42 V.S.C. 1981 note]*

(a) *General.* — Except as otherwise specifically provided, this Act and the amendments made by this Act shall take effect upon enactment.

(b) *Certain Disparate Impact Cases.* — Notwithstanding any other provision of this Act, nothing in this Act shall apply to any disparate impact cases for which a complaint was filed before March 1, 1975, and for which an initial decision was rendered after October 30, 1983.

Congressional Accountability Act

2 U.S.C. §§1301–1302, 1311–1313, 1317, 1361

Sec. 1301. Definitions

Except as otherwise specifically provided in this chapter, as used in this chapter.

(1) *Board*. The term "Board" means the Board of Directors of the Office of Compliance.

(2) *Chair*. The term "Chair" means the Chair of the Board of Directors of the Office of Compliance.

(3) *Covered employee*. The term "covered employee" means any employee of

       (A) the House of Representatives;

       (B) the Senate;

       (C) the Capitol Guide Service;

       (D) the Capitol Police;

       (E) the Congressional Budget Office;

       (F) the Office of the Architect of the Capitol;

       (G) the Office of the Attending Physician;

       (H) the Office of Compliance; or

       (I) the Office of Technology Assessment.

(4) *Employee*. The term "employee" includes an applicant for employment and a former employee.

(5) *Employee of the Office of the Architect of the Capitol*. The term "employee of the Office of the Architect of the Capitol" includes any employee of the Office of the Architect of the Capitol, the Botanic Garden.

(6) *Employee of the Capitol Police*. The term "employee of the Capitol Police" includes any member or officer of the Capitol Police.

(7) *Employee of the House of Representatives*. The term "employee of the House of Representatives" includes an individual occupying a position the pay for which is disbursed by the Clerk of the House of Representatives, or another official designated by the House of Representatives, or any employment position in an entity that is paid with funds derived from the clerk-hire allowance

of the House of Representatives but not any such individual employed by any entity listed in subparagraphs (C) through (I) of paragraph (3).

(8) *Employee of the Senate*. The term "employee of the Senate" includes any employee whose pay is disbursed by the Secretary of the Senate, but not any such individual employed by any entity listed in subparagraphs (C) through (I) of paragraph (3).

(9) Employing office. The term "employing office" means

(A) the personal office of a Member of the House of Representatives or of a Senator;

(B) a committee of the House of Representatives or the Senate or a joint committee;

(C) any other office headed by a person with the final authority to appoint, hire, discharge, and set the terms, conditions, or privileges of the employment of an employee of the House of Representatives or the Senate; or

(D) the Office of Congressional Accessibility Services, the United States Capitol Police, the Congressional Budget Office, the Office of the Architect of the Capitol, the Office of Attending Physician, the Office of Compliance, and the Office of Technology Assessment.

(10) *Executive Director*. The term "Executive Director" means the Executive Director of the Office of Compliance.

(11) *General Counsel*. The term "General Counsel" means the General Counsel of the Office of Compliance.

(12) *Office*. The term "Office" means the Office of Compliance.

Sec. 1302. *Application of Laws*

(a) *Laws Made Applicable*. The following laws shall apply, as prescribed by this chapter, to the legislative branch of the Federal Government:

(1) The Fair Labor Standards Act of 1938 (29 U.S.C. 201 et seq.).

(2) Title VII of the Civil Rights Act of 1964 (42 U.S.C. 2000e et seq.).

(3) The Americans with Disabilities Act of 1990 (42 U.S.C. 12101 et seq.).

(4) The Age Discrimination in Employment Act of 1967 (29 U.S.C. 621 et seq.).

(5) The Family and Medical Leave Act of 1993 (29 U.S.C. 2611 et seq.).

(6) The Occupational Safety and Health Act of 1970 (29 U.S.C. 651 et seq.).

(7) Chapter 71 (relating to Federal service labor-management relations) of Title 5.

(8) The Employee Polygraph Protection Act of 1988 (29 U.S.C. 2001 et seq.).

(9) The Worker Adjustment and Retraining Notification Act (29 U.S.C. 2101 et seq.).

(10) The Rehabilitation Act of 1973 (29 U.S.C. 701 et seq.).

(11) Chapter 43 (relating to veterans' employment and reemployment) of Title 38.

(b) *Laws Which May Be Made Applicable*.

(1) *In general*. The Board shall review provisions of Federal law (including regulations) relating to (A) the terms and conditions of employment (including hiring, promotion, demotion, termination, salary, wages, overtime compensation, benefits, work assignments or reassignments, grievance and disciplinary procedures, protection from discrimination in personnel actions, occupational health and safety, and family and medical and other leave) of employees, and (B) access to public services and accommodations.

(2) *Board report*. Beginning on December 31, 1996, and every 2 years thereafter, the Board shall report on (A) whether or to what degree the provisions described in paragraph (1) are applicable or inapplicable to the legislative branch, and (B) with respect to provisions inapplicable to the legislative branch, whether such provisions should be made applicable to the legislative branch. The presiding officers of the House of Representatives and the Senate shall cause each such report to be printed in the Congressional Record and each such report shall be referred to the committees of the House of Representatives and the Senate with jurisdiction.

(3) *Reports of congressional committees*. Each report accompanying any bill or joint resolution relating to terms and conditions of employment or access to public services or accommodations reported by a committee of the House of Representatives or the Senate shall

(A) describe the manner in which the provisions of the bill or joint resolution apply to the legislative branch; or

(B) in the case of a provision not applicable to the legislative branch, include a statement of the reasons the provision does not apply.

On the objection of any Member, it shall not be in order for the Senate or the House of Representatives to consider any such bill or joint resolution if the report of the committee on such bill or joint resolution does not comply with the provisions of this paragraph. This paragraph may be waived in either House by majority vote of that House.

Sec. 1311. *Rights and Protections under Title VII of the Civil Rights Act of 1964, the Age Discrimination in Employment Act of 1967, the Rehabilitation Act of 1973, and Title I of the Americans with Disabilities Act of 1990*

(a) *Discriminatory Practices Prohibited*. All personnel actions affecting covered employees shall be made free from any discrimination based on

(1) race, color, religion, sex, or national origin, within the meaning of section 703 of the Civil Rights Act of 1964 (42 U.S.C. 2000e-2);

(2) age, within the meaning of section 15 of the Age Discrimination in Employment Act of 1967 (29 U.S.C. 633a); or

(3) disability, within the meaning of section 501 of the Rehabilitation Act of 1973 (29 U.S.C. 791) and sections 102 through 104 of the Americans with Disabilities Act of 1990 (42 U.S.C. 12112-12114).

(b) *Remedy*.
    (1) *Civil rights*. The remedy for a violation of subsection (a)(1) shall be
        (A) such remedy as would be appropriate if awarded under section 706(g) of the Civil Rights Act of 1964 (42 U.S.C. 2000e-5(g)); and
        (B) such compensatory damages as would be appropriate if awarded under section 1977 of the Revised Statutes (42 U.S.C. 1981), or as would be appropriate if awarded under sections 1977A(a)(1), 1977A(b)(2), and, irrespective of the size of the employing office, 1977A(b)(3)(D) of the Revised Statutes (42 U.S.C. 1981a(a)(1), 1981a(b)(2), and 1981a(b)(3)(D)).
    (2) *Age discrimination*. The remedy for a violation of subsection (a)(2) shall be
        (A) such remedy as would be appropriate if awarded under section 15(c) of the Age Discrimination in Employment Act of 1967 (29 U.S.C. 633a(c)); and
        (B) such liquidated damages as would be appropriate if awarded under section 7(b) of such Act (29 U.S.C. 626(b)).
        In addition, the waiver provisions of section 7(f) of such Act (29 U.S.C. 626(f)) shall apply to covered employees.
    (3) *Disabilities discrimination*. The remedy for a violation of subsection (a)(3) shall be
        (A) such remedy as would be appropriate if awarded under section 505(a)(1) of the Rehabilitation Act of 1973 (29 U.S.C. 794a(a)(1)) or section 107(a) of the Americans with Disabilities Act of 1990 (42 U.S.C. 12117(a)); and
        (B) such compensatory damages as would be appropriate if awarded under sections 1977A(a)(2), 1977A(a)(3), 1977A(b)(2), and, irrespective of the size of the employing office, 1977A(b)(3)(D) of the Revised Statutes (42 U.S.C. 1981a(a)(2), 1981a(a)(3), 1981a(b)(2), and 1981a(b)(3)(D)).
(c) [Omitted.]
(d) *Effective Date*. This section shall take effect 1 year after the date of the enactment of this Act [enacted Jan. 23, 1995].

Sec. 1312. Rights and Protections under the Family and Medical Leave Act of 1993

(a) *Family and Medical Leave Rights and Protections Provided*.
    (1) *In general*. The rights and protections established by sections 101 through 105 of the Family and Medical Leave Act of 1993 (29 U.S.C. 2611 through 2615) shall apply to covered employees.
    (2) *Definition*. For purposes of the application described in paragraph (1)
        (A) the term "employer" as used in the Family and Medical Leave Act of 1993 means any employing office, and
        (B) the term "eligible employee" as used in the Family and Medical Leave Act of 1993 means a covered employee who has been employed in

any employing office for 12 months and for at least 1,250 hours of employment during the previous 12 months.

(b) *Remedy.* The remedy for a violation of subsection (a) shall be such remedy, including liquidated damages, as would be appropriate if awarded under paragraph (1) of section 107(a) of the Family and Medical Leave Act of 1993 (29 U.S.C. 2617(a)(1)).

(c) [Omitted.]

(d) *Regulations.*

(1) *In general.* The Board shall, pursuant to section 304 [2 U.S.C. §1384], issue regulations to implement the rights and protections under this section.

(2) *Agency regulations.* The regulations issued under paragraph (1) shall be the same as substantive regulations promulgated by the Secretary of Labor to implement the statutory provisions referred to in subsection (a) except insofar as the Board may determine, for good cause shown and stated together with the regulation, that a modification of such regulations would be more effective for the implementation of the rights and protections under this section.

(e) *Effective Date.*

(1) In general. Subsections (a) and (b) shall be effective 1 year after the date of the enactment of this Act [enacted Jan. 23, 1995].

(2) *General Accounting Office and Library of Congress.* Subsection (c) shall be effective 1 year after transmission to the Congress of the study under section 230 [2 U.S.C. §1371].

Sec. 1313. *Rights and Protections under the Fair Labor Standards Act of 1938 [Equal Pay Act]*

(a) *Fair Labor Standards.*

(1) *In general.* The rights and protections established by subsections (a)(1) and (d) of section 6, section 7, and section 12(c) of the Fair Labor Standards Act of 1938 (29 U.S.C. 206(a)(1) and (d), 207, 212(c)) shall apply to covered employees.

(2) *Interns.* For the purposes of this section, the term "covered employee" does not include an intern as defined in regulations under subsection (c).

(3) *Compensatory time.* Except as provided in regulations under subsection (c)(3) and in subsection (c)(4), covered employees may not receive compensatory time in lieu of overtime compensation.

(b) *Remedy.* The remedy for a violation of subsection (a) shall be such remedy, including liquidated damages, as would be appropriate if awarded under section 16(b) of the Fair Labor Standards Act of 1938 (29 U.S.C. 216(b)).

(c) *Regulations to Implement Section.*

(1) *In general.* The Board shall, pursuant of section 304 [2 U.S.C. §1384], issue regulations to implement this section.

(2) *Agency regulations.* Except as provided in paragraph (3), the regulations issued under paragraph (1) shall be the same as substantive regulations promulgated by the Secretary of Labor to implement the statutory provisions

referred to in subsection (a) except insofar as the Board may determine, for good cause shown and stated together with the regulation, that a modification of such regulations would be more effective for the implementation of the rights and protections under this section.

(3) *Irregular work schedules.* The Board shall issue regulations for covered employees whose work schedules directly depend on the schedule of the House of Representatives or the Senate that shall be comparable to the provisions in the Fair Labor Standards Act of 1938 [29 U.S.C. §§201 et seq.] that apply to employees who have irregular work schedules.

(4) *Law enforcement.* Law enforcement personnel of the Capitol Police who are subject to the exemption under section 7(k) of the Fair Labor Standards Act of 1938 (29 U.S.C. 207(k)) may elect to receive compensatory time off in lieu of overtime compensation for hours worked in excess of the maximum for their work period.

(d) [Omitted.]

(e) *Effective Date.* Subsections (a) and (b) shall be effective 1 year after the date of the enactment of this Act [enactment Jan. 23, 1995].

Sec. 1317. *Prohibition of Intimidation or Reprisal*

(a) *In General.* It shall be unlawful for an employing office to intimidate, take reprisal against, or otherwise discriminate against, any covered employee because the covered employee has opposed any practice made unlawful by this Act, or because the covered employee has initiated proceedings, made a charge, or testified, assisted, or participated in any manner in a hearing or other proceeding under this Act.

(b) *Remedy.* The remedy available for violation of subsection (a) shall be such legal or equitable remedy as may be appropriate to redress a violation of subsection (a).

Sec. 1361. *Generally Applicable Remedies and Limitations*

(a) *Attorney's Fees.* If a covered employee, with respect to any claim under this Act, or a qualified person with a disability, with respect to any claim under section 210 [2 U.S.C. §1331], is a prevailing party in any proceeding under section 405, 406, 407, or 408 [2 U.S.C. §§1405, 1406, 1407, or 1408], the hearing officer, Board, or court, as the case may be, may award attorney's fees, expert fees, and any other costs as would be appropriate if awarded under section 706(k) of the Civil Rights Act of 1964 (42 U.S.C. 2000e-5(k)).

(b) *Interest.* In any proceeding under section 405, 406, 407, or 408 [2 U.S.C. §§1405, 1406, 1407, or 1408], the same interest to compensate for delay in payment shall be made available as would be appropriate if awarded under section 717(d) of the Civil Rights Act of 1964 (42 U.S.C. 2000e-16(d)).

(c) *Civil Penalties and Punitive Damages.* No civil penalty or punitive damages may be awarded with respect to any claim under this Act.

(d) *Exclusive Procedure.*

(1) In general. Except as provided in paragraph (2), no person may commence an administrative or judicial proceeding to seek a remedy for the rights and protections afforded by this Act except as provided in this Act.

(2) *Veterans.* A covered employee under section 206 [2 U.S.C. §1316] may also utilize any provisions of chapter 43 of title 38, United States Code [38 U.S.C. §§4301 et seq.], that are applicable to that employee.

(e) *Scope of Remedy.* Only a covered employee who has undertaken and completed the procedures described in sections 402 and 403 [2 U.S.C. §§1402, 1403] may be granted a remedy under part A of this title [2 U.S.C. §§1311 et seq.]

(f) *Construction.*

(1) *Definitions and exemption.* Except where inconsistent with definitions and exemptions provided in this Act, the definitions and exemptions in the laws made applicable by this Act shall apply under this Act.

(2) *Size limitations.* Notwithstanding paragraph (1), provisions in the laws made applicable under this Act (other than the Worker Adjustment and Retraining Notification Act [29 U.S.C. §§2101 et seq.]) determining coverage based on size, whether expressed in terms of numbers of employees, amount of business transacted, or other measure, shall not apply in determining coverage under this Act.

(3) *Executive branch enforcement.* This Act shall not be construed to authorize enforcement by the executive branch of this Act.

Equal Pay Act

29 U.S.C. §206(d)

§206. Minimum Wage . . .

(d) *Prohibition of sex discrimination.*

(1) [§3] No employer having employees subject to any provisions of this section shall discriminate, within any establishment in which such employees are employed, between employees on the basis of sex by paying wages to employees in such establishment at a rate less than the rate at which he pays wages to employees of the opposite sex in such establishment and for equal work on jobs the performance of which requires equal skill, effort, and responsibility, and which are performed under similar working conditions, except where such payment is made pursuant to (i) a seniority system; (ii) a merit system; (iii) a system which measures earnings by quantity or quality of production; or (iv) a differential based on any other factor other than sex: *Provided,* That an employer who is paying a wage rate differential in violation of this subsection shall not, in order to comply with the provisions of this subsection, reduce the wage rate of any employee.

(2) No labor organization, or its agents, representing employees of an employer having employees subject to any provisions of this section shall cause or attempt to cause such an employer to discriminate against an employee in violation of paragraph (1) of this subsection.

(3) For purposes of administration and enforcement, any amounts owing to any employee which have been withheld in violation of this subsection shall be deemed to be unpaid minimum wages or unpaid overtime compensation under this chapter.

(4) As used in this subsection, the term "labor organization" means any organization of any kind, or any agency or employee representation committee or plan, in which employees participate and which exists for the purpose, in whole or in part, of dealing with employers concerning grievances, labor disputes, wages, rates of pay, hours of employment, or conditions of work.

Fair Labor Standards Act

29 U.S.C. §§207(r), 216 and 217

§207(r)(1) An employer shall provide —

    (A) a reasonable break time for an employee to express breast milk for her nursing child for 1 year after the child's birth each time such employee has need to express the milk; and

    (B) a place, other than a bathroom, that is shielded from view and free from intrusion from coworkers and the public, which may be used by an employee to express breast milk.

(2) An employer shall not be required to compensate an employee receiving reasonable break time under paragraph (1) for any work time spent for such purpose.

(3) An employer that employs less than 50 employees shall not be subject to the requirements of this subsection, if such requirements would impose an undue hardship by causing the employer significant difficulty or expense when considered in relation to the size, financial resources, nature, or structure of the employer's business.

(4) Nothing in this subsection shall preempt a State law that provides greater protections to employees than the protections provided for under this subsection.

§216 [§16]. Penalties

(a) *Fines and Imprisonment.* Any person who willfully violates any of the provisions of section 215 of this title shall upon conviction thereof be subject to a fine of not more than $10,000, or to imprisonment for not more than six months, or both. No person shall be imprisoned under this subsection except for an offense committed after the conviction of such person for a prior offense under this subsection.

(b) *Damages; Right of Action; Attorney's Fees and Costs; Termination of Right of Action.* Any employer who violates the provisions of section 206 or section 207 of this title shall be liable to the employee or employees affected in the amount of their unpaid minimum wages, or their unpaid overtime compensation, as the case may be, and in an additional equal amount as liquidated damages. Any employer who violates the provisions of section 215(a)(3) of this title shall be liable for such legal or equitable relief as may be appropriate to effectuate the purposes of section 215(a)(3) of this title, including without limitation employment, reinstatement, promotion, and the payment of wages lost and an additional equal amount as liquidated damages. An action to recover the liability prescribed in either of the preceding sentences may be maintained against any employer (including a public agency) in any Federal or State court of competent jurisdiction by any one or more employees for and in behalf of himself or themselves and other employees similarly situated. No employee shall be a party plaintiff to any such action unless he gives his consent in writing to become such a party and such consent is filed in the court in which such action is brought. The court in such action shall, in addition to any judgment awarded to the plaintiff or plaintiffs, allow a reasonable attorney's fee to be paid by the defendant, and costs of the action. The right provided by this subsection to bring an action by or on behalf of any employee, and the right of any employee to become a party plaintiff to any such action, shall terminate upon the filing of a complaint by the Secretary of Labor in an action under section 217 of this title in which (1) restraint is sought of any further delay in the payment of unpaid minimum wages, or the amount of unpaid overtime compensation, as the case may be, owing to such employee under section 206 or section 207 of this title by an employer liable therefor under the provisions of this subsection or (2) legal or equitable relief is sought as a result of alleged violations of section 215(a)(3) of this title.

(c) *Payment of Wages and Compensation; Waiver of Claims; Actions by the Secretary; Limitation of Actions.* — The Secretary is authorized to supervise the payment of the unpaid minimum wages or the unpaid overtime compensation owing to any employee or employees under section 206 or 207 of this title, and the agreement of any employee to accept such payment shall upon payment in full constitute a waiver by such employee of any right he may have under subsection (b) of this section to such unpaid minimum wages or unpaid overtime compensation and an additional equal amount as liquidated damages. The Secretary may bring an action in any court of competent jurisdiction to recover the amount of the unpaid minimum wages or overtime compensation and an equal amount as liquidated damages. The right provided by subsection (b) of this section to bring an action by or on behalf of any employee to recover the liability specified in the first sentence of such subsection and of any employee to become a party plaintiff to any such action shall terminate upon the filing of a complaint by the Secretary in an action under this subsection in which a recovery is sought of unpaid minimum wages or unpaid overtime compensation under sections 206 or 207 of this title or liquidated or other damages provided by this subsection owing to such employee by an employer liable under the provisions of subsection (b) of this section, unless such action is dismissed without prejudice on motion of the Secretary. Any sums thus recovered by the Secretary of Labor on behalf of an employee pursuant to this subsection shall be held in a special deposit account and shall be paid, on order of the Secretary of Labor, directly to the employee or employees affected. Any such sums not paid to an employee because of inability to do so within a period of three years shall be covered into the Treasury of the United States as miscellaneous receipts. In determining when an action is commenced by the Secretary of Labor under this subsection for the purposes of the statutes of limitations provided in section 255(a) of this title, it shall be considered to be commenced in the case of any individual claimant on the date when the complaint is filed if he is specifically named as a party plaintiff in the complaint, or if his name did not so appear, on the subsequent date on which his name is added as a party plaintiff in such action. . . .

§217 [§17]. *Injunction Proceedings*

The district courts, together with the United States District Court for the District of the Canal Zone, the District Court of the Virgin Islands, and the District Court of Guam shall have jurisdiction for cause shown, to restrain violations of section 215 of this title, including in the case of violations of section 215(a)(2) of this title the restraint of any withholding of payment of minimum wages or overtime compensation found by the court to be due to employees under this chapter (except sums which employees are barred from recovering, at the time of the commencement of the action to restrain the violations, by virtue of the provisions of section 255 of this title).

Family and Medical Leave Act of 1993

29 U.S.C §§2601, 2611–2619, 2651–2654

§2601. Findings and Purposes

(a) *Findings*. Congress finds that—

(1) the number of single-parent households and two-parent households in which the single parent or both parents work is increasing significantly;

(2) it is important for the development of children and the family unit that fathers and mothers be able to participate in early childrearing and the care of family members who have serious health conditions;

(3) the lack of employment policies to accommodate working parents can force individuals to choose between job security and parenting;

(4) there is inadequate job security for employees who have serious health conditions that prevent them from working for temporary periods;

(5) due to the nature of the roles of men and women in our society, the primary responsibility for family caretaking often falls on women, and such responsibility affects the working lives of women more than it affects the working lives of men; and

(6) employment standards that apply to one gender only have serious potential for encouraging employers to discriminate against employees and applicants for employment who are of that gender.

(b) *Purposes*. It is the purpose of this Act—

(1) to balance the demands of the workplace with the needs of families, to promote the stability and economic security of families, and to promote national interests in preserving family integrity;

(2) to entitle employees to take reasonable leave for medical reasons, for the birth or adoption of a child, and for the care of a child, spouse, or parent who has a serious health condition;

(3) to accomplish the purposes described in paragraphs (1) and (2) in a manner that accommodates the legitimate interests of employers;

(4) to accomplish the purposes described in paragraphs (1) and (2) in a manner that, consistent with the Equal Protection Clause of the Fourteenth

Amendment, minimizes the potential for employment discrimination on the basis of sex by ensuring generally that leave is available for eligible medical reasons (including maternity-related disability) and for compelling family reasons, on a gender-neutral basis; and

(5) to promote the goal of equal employment opportunity for women and men, pursuant to such clause.

TITLE I—GENERAL REQUIREMENTS FOR LEAVE

§2611. *Definitions*

As used in this subchapter:

(1) *Commerce*. The terms "commerce" and "industry or activity affecting commerce" means any activity, business, or industry in commerce or in which a labor dispute would hinder or obstruct commerce or the free flow of commerce, and include "commerce" and any "industry affecting commerce," as defined in paragraphs (1) and (3) of section 142 of this title.

(2) *Eligible employee*.

(A) *In general*. The term "eligible employee" means an employee who has been employed—

(i) for at least 12 months by the employer with respect to whom leave is requested under section 2612 of this title; and

(ii) for at least 1,250 hours of service with such employer during the previous 12-month period.

(B) *Exclusions*. The term "eligible employee" does not include—

(i) any Federal officer or employee covered under subchapter V of chapter 63 of Title 5; or

(ii) any employee of an employer who is employed at a worksite at which such employer employs less than 50 employees if the total number of employees employed by that employer within 75 miles of that worksite is less than 50.

(C) *Determination*. For purposes of determining whether an employee meets the hours of service requirement specified in subparagraph (A)(ii), the legal standards established under section 207 of this title shall apply.

(D) *Airline flight crews*.

(i) *Determination*. For purposes of determining whether an employee who is a flight attendant or flight crewmember (as such terms are defined in regulations of the Federal Aviation Administration) meets the hours of service requirement specified in subparagraph (A)(ii), the employee will be considered to meet the requirement if—

(I) the employee has worked or been paid for not less than 60 percent of the applicable total monthly guarantee, or the equivalent, for the previous 12- month period, for or by the employer with respect to whom leave is requested under section 2612 of this title; and

(II) the employee has worked or been paid for not less than 504 hours (not counting personal commute time or time spent on vacation leave or medical sick leave) during the previous 12-month period, for or by that employer.

(ii) *File.* Each employer of an employee described in clause (i) shall maintain on file with the Secretary (in accordance with such regulations as the Secretary may prescribe) containing information specifying the applicable monthly guarantee with respect to each category of employee to which such guarantee applies.

(iii) *Definition.* In this subparagraph, the term "applicable monthly guarantee" means—

(I) for an employee described in clause (i) other than an employee on reserve status, the minimum number of hours for which an employer as agreed to schedule such employee for any given month; and

(II) for an employee described in clause (i) who is on reserve status, the number of hours for which an employer has agreed to pay such employee on reserve status for any given month, as established in this applicable collective bargaining agreement or, if none exists, in the employer's policies.

(3) *Employ; Employee; State.* The terms "employ," "employee," and "State" have the same meanings given such terms in subsections (c), (e), and (g) of section 209 of this title.

(4) *Employer.*

(A) *In general.* The term "employer"—

(i) means any person engaged in commerce or in any industry or activity affecting commerce who employs 50 or more employees for each working day during each of 20 or more calendar workweeks in the current or preceding calendar year;

(ii) includes—

(I) any person who acts, directly or indirectly, in the interest of an employer to any of the employees of such employer; and

(II) any successor in interest of an employer;

(iii) includes any "public agency," as defined in section 203(x) of this title; and

(iv) includes the Government Accountability Office and the Library of Congress.

(B) *Public agency.* For purposes of subparagraph (A)(iii), a public agency shall be considered to be a person engaged in commerce or in an industry or activity affecting commerce.

(5) *Employment benefits.* The term "employment benefits" means all benefits provided or made available to employees by an employer, including group life insurance, health insurance, disability insurance, sick leave, annual leave, educational benefits, and pensions, regardless of whether such benefits

are provided by a practice or written policy of an employer or through an "employee benefit plan," as defined in section 1002(3) of this title.

(6) *Health care provider.* The term "health care provider" means—

    (A) a doctor of medicine or osteopathy who is authorized to practice medicine or surgery (as appropriate) by the State in which the doctor practices; or

    (B) any other person determined by the Secretary to be capable of providing health care services.

(7) *Parent.* The term "parent" means the biological parent of an employee or an individual who stood in loco parentis to an employee when the employee was a son or daughter.

(8) *Person.* The term "person" has the same meaning given such term in section 203(a) of this title.

(9) *Reduced leave schedule.* The term "reduced leave schedule" means a leave schedule that reduces the usual number of hours per workweek, or hours per workday, of an employee.

(10) *Secretary.* The term "Secretary" means the Secretary of Labor.

(11) *Serious health conditions.* The term "serious health condition" means an illness, injury, impairment, or physical or mental condition that involves—

    (A) inpatient care in a hospital, hospice, or residential medical care facility; or

    (B) continuing treatment by a health care provider.

(12) *Son or daughter.* The term "son or daughter" means a biological, adopted, or foster child, a stepchild, a legal ward, or a child of a person standing in loco parentis, who is—

    (A) under 18 years of age; or

    (B) 18 years of age or older and incapable of self-care because of a mental or physical disability.

(13) *Spouse.* The term "spouse" means a husband or wife, as the case may be.

(14) *Covered Active Duty.* The term "covered active duty" means—

    (A) in the case of a member of a regular component of the Armed Forces, a duty during the deployment of the member with the Armed Forced to a fireogn country; and

    (B) in the case of a member of a reserve component of the Armed Forced, duty during the deployment of the member with the Armed Forced to a foreign country under a call or order to active duty under a provision of law referred to in section 101(a)(13)(B) of Title 10.

(15) *Covered Servicemember.* The term "covered servicemember" means—

    (A) a member of the Armed Forces (including a member of the National Guard or Reserves) who is undergoing medical treatment, recuperation, or therapy, is otherwise in outpatient status, or is otherwise on the temporary disability retired list, for a serious injury or illness; or

(B) a veteran who is undergoing medical treatment, recuperation or therapy, for a serious injury or illness and who was a member of the Armed Forced (including a member of the National Guard of reserves) at any time during the period of 5 years preceding the date on which the veteran undergoes that medical treatment, recuperation or therapy.

(16) *Outpatient Status.* The term "outpatient status", with respect to a covered servicemember, means the status of a member of the Armed Forces assigned to —

(A) a military medical treatment facility as an outpatient; or

(B) a unit established for the purpose of providing command and control of members of the Armed Forces receiving medical care as outpatients.

(17) *Next of Kin.* — The term "next of kin," used with respect to an individual, means the nearest blood relative of that individual.

(18) *Serious Injury or Illness.* The term "serious injury or illness," —

(A) in the case of a member of the Armed Forces (including a member of the National Guard or Reserves) means an injury or illness that was incurred by the member in line of duty on active duty in the Armed Forces (or existed before the beginning of the member's active duty and was aggravated by service in line of duty on active duty in the Armed Forces) and that may render the member medically unfit to perform the duties of the member's office, grade, rank, or rating; and

(B) in the case of a veteran who was a member of the Armed Forces (including a member of the National Guard or Reserves) at any time during a period described in paragraph 15(B), means a qualifying (as defined by the Secretary of Labor) injury or illness that was incurred by the member in line of duty on active duty in the Armed Forces (or existed before the beginning of the member's duty and was aggravated by service in line of duty on active duty in the Armed Forces) and that manifested itself before or after the member became a veteran.

(19) *Veteran.* The term "veteran" has the meaning given the term in section 101 of Title 38.

§2612. Leave Requirement

(a) *In General.*

(1) *Entitlement to leave.* Subject to section 2613, an eligible employee shall be entitled to a total of 12 workweeks of leave during any 12-month period for one or more of the following:

(A) Because of the birth of a son or daughter of the employee and in order to care for such son or daughter.

(B) Because of the placement of a son or daughter with the employee for adoption or foster care.

(C) In order to care for the spouse, or a son, daughter, or parent, of the employee, if such spouse, son, daughter, or parent has a serious health condition.

(D) Because of a serious health condition that makes the employee unable to perform the functions of the position of such employee.

(E) Because of any qualifying exigency (as the Secretary shall, by regulation, determine) arising out of the fact that the spouse, or a son, daughter, or parent of the employee is on covered active duty (or has been notified of an impending call or order to covered active duty) in the Armed Forces.

(2) *Expiration of entitlement.* The entitlement to leave under subparagraphs (A) and (B) of paragraph (1) for a birth or placement of a son or daughter shall expire at the end of the 12-month period beginning on the date of such birth or placement.

(3) *Servicemember Family Leave.* — Subject to section 2613, an eligible employee who is the spouse, son, daughter, parent, or next of kin of a covered servicemember shall be entitled to a total of 26 workweeks of leave during a 12-month period to care for the servicemember. The leave described in this paragraph shall only be available during a single 12-month period.

(4) *Combined Leave Total.* — During the single 12-month period described in paragraph (3), an eligible employee shall be entitled to a combined total of 26 workweeks of leave under paragraphs (1) and (3). Nothing in this paragraph shall be construed to limit the availability of leave under paragraph (1) during any other 12-month period.

(5) *Calculation of leave for airline flight crews.* The Secretary may provide, by regulation, a method for calculating the leave described in paragraph (1) with respect to employees described in section 2611(2)(D) of this title.

(b) *Leave Taken Intermittently or on a Reduced Leave Schedule.*

(1) *In general.* Leave under subparagraph (A) or (B) of subsection (a)(1) of this section shall not be taken by an employee intermittently or on a reduced leave schedule unless the employee and the employer of the employee agree otherwise. Subject to paragraph (2), subsection (e)(2) of this section, and subsection (b)(5) or (f) (as appropriate) of section 2613 of this title, leave under subparagraph (C) or (D) of subsection (a)(1) of this section or under subsection (a)(3) of this section may be taken intermittently or on a reduced leave schedule when medically necessary. Subject to subsection (e)(3) of this section and section 2613(f) of this title, leave under subsection (a)(1)(E) of this section may be taken intermittently or on a reduced leave schedule. The taking of leave intermittently or on a reduced leave schedule pursuant to this paragraph shall not result in a reduction in the total amount of leave to which the employee is entitled under subsection (a) of this section beyond the amount of leave actually taken.

(2) *Alternative position.* If an employee requests intermittent leave, or leave on a reduced leave schedule, under subparagraph (C) or (D) of subsection (a)(1) of this section or under subsection (a)(3) of this section, that is foreseeable based on planned medical treatment, the employer may require such employee to transfer temporarily to an available alternative position offered by the employer for which the employee is qualified and that —

(A) has equivalent pay and benefits; and

(B) better accommodates recurring periods of leave than the regular employment position of the employee.

(c) *Unpaid Leave Permitted.* Except as provided in subsection (d) of this section, leave granted under subsection (a) may consist of unpaid leave. Where an employee is otherwise exempt under regulations issued by the Secretary pursuant to section 213(a)(1) of this title, the compliance of an employer with this subchapter by providing unpaid leave shall not affect the exempt status of the employee under such section.

(d) *Relationship to Paid Leave.*

(1) *Unpaid leave.* If an employer provides paid leave for fewer than 12 workweeks (or 26 workweeks in the case of leave provided under subsection (a)(3) of this section), the additional weeks of leave necessary to attain the 12 workweeks (or 26 workweeks, as appropriate) of leave required under this subchapter may be provided without compensation.

(2) *Substitution of paid leave.*

(A) *In general.* An eligible employee may elect, or an employee may require the employee, to substitute any of the accrued paid vacation leave, personal leave, or family leave of the employee for leave provided under subparagraph (A), (B), (C), or (E) of subsection (a)(1) of this section, for any part of the 12-week period of such leave under such subsection.

(B) *Serious health condition.* An eligible employee may elect, or an employer may require the employee, to substitute any of the accrued paid vacation leave, personal leave, or medical or sick leave of the employee for leave provided under subparagraph (C) or (D) of subsection (a)(1) of this section for any part of the 12-week period of such leave under such subsection, except that nothing in this subchapter shall require an employer to provide paid sick leave or paid medical leave in any situation in which such employer would not normally provide any such paid leave. An eligible employee may elect, or an employer may require the employee, to substitute any of the accrued paid vacation leave, personal leave, family leave, or medical or sick leave of the employee for leave provided under subsection (a)(3) of this section for any part of the 26-week period of such leave under such subsection, except that nothing in this subchapter requires an employer to provide paid sick leave or paid medical leave in any situation in which the employer would not normally provide any such paid leave.

(e) *Foreseeable Leave.*

(1) *Requirement of notice.* In any case in which the necessity for leave under subparagraph (A) or (B) of subsection (a)(1) of this section is foreseeable based on an expected birth or placement, the employee shall provide the employer with not less than 30 days' notice, before the date the leave is to begin, or the employee's intention to take leave under such subparagraph, except that if the date of the birth or placement requires leave to begin in less than 30 days, the employee shall provide such notice as is practicable.

(2) *Duties of employee.* In any case in which the necessity for leave under subparagraph (C) or (D) of subsection (a)(1) of this section is foreseeable based on planned medical treatment, the employee—

    (A) shall make a reasonable effort to schedule the treatment so as not to disrupt unduly the operations of the employer, subject to the approval of the health care provider of the employee or the health care provider of the son, daughter, spouse, or parent, or covered servicemember of the employee, as appropriate; and

    (B) shall provide the employer with not less than 30 days' notice, before the date the leave is to begin, of the employee's intention to take leave under such subparagraph, except that if the date of the treatment requires leave to begin in less than 30 days, the employee shall provide such notice as is practicable.

(3) *Notice for Leave Due to Covered Active Duty of Family Member.* In any case in which the necessity for leave under subsection (a)(1)(E) of this section is foreseeable, whether because the spouse, or a son, daughter, or parent, of the employee is on active duty, or because of notification of an impending call or order to active duty, the employee shall provide such notice to the employer as is reasonable and practicable.

(f) *Spouses Employed by Same Employer.*

(1) *In General.* In any case in which a husband and wife entitled to leave under subsection (a) are employed by the same employer, the aggregate number of workweeks of leave to which both may be entitled may be limited to 12 workweeks during any 12-month period, if such leave is taken—

    (A) under subparagraph (A) or (B) of subsection (a)(1) of this section; or

    (B) to care for a sick parent under subparagraph (C) of such subsection.

(2) *Servicemember Family Leave.*

    (A) *In General.* The aggregate number of workweeks of leave to which both husband and wife may be entitled under subsection (a) may be limited to 26 workweeks during the single 12-month period described in subsection (a)(3) of this section if the leave is—

        (i) leave under subsection (a)(3) of this section; or

        (ii) a combination of leave under subsection (a)(3) and leave described in paragraph (1).

    (B) *Both Limitations Applicable.* If the leave taken by the husband and wife includes leave described in paragraph (1), the limitation in paragraph (1) shall apply to the leave described in paragraph (1).

§2613. *Certification*

(a) *In General.* An employer may require that a request for leave under subparagraph (C) or (D) of paragraph (1) or paragraph (3) of section 2612(a) of this title be supported by a certification issued by the health care provider of the eligible employee or of the son, daughter, spouse, or parent of the employee, or of the next of kin of an individual in the case of leave taken under such paragraph

(3), as appropriate. The employee shall provide, in a timely manner, a copy of such certificate to the employer.

(b) *Sufficient Certification.* Certification provided under subsection (a) shall be sufficient if it states —

(1) the date on which the serious health condition commenced;

(2) the probable duration of the condition;

(3) the appropriate medical facts within the knowledge of the health care provider regarding the condition;

(4)(A) for purposes of leave under section 2612(a)(1)(C) of this title, a statement that the eligible employee is needed to care for the son, daughter, spouse, or parent and an estimate of the amount of time that such employee is needed to care for the son, daughter, spouse, or parent; and

(B) for purposes of leave under section 2612(a)(1)(D) of this title, a statement that the employee is unable to perform the functions of the position of the employee;

(5) in the case of certification for intermittent leave, or leave on a reduced leave schedule, for planned medical treatment, the dates on which such treatment is expected to be given and the duration of such treatment;

(6) in the case of certification for intermittent leave, or leave on a reduced leave schedule, under section 2612(a)(1)(D) of this title, a statement of the medical necessity for the intermittent leave or leave on a reduced leave schedule, and the expected duration of the intermittent leave or reduced leave schedule; and

(7) in the case of certification for intermittent leave, or leave on a reduced leave schedule, under section 2612(a)(1)(C) of this title, a statement that the employee's intermittent leave or leave on a reduced leave schedule is necessary for the care of the son, daughter, parent, or spouse who has a serious health condition, or will assist in their recovery, and the expected duration and schedule of the intermittent leave or reduced leave schedule.

(c) *Second Opinion.*

(1) *In general.* In any case in which the employer has reason to doubt the validity of the certification provided under subsection (a) of this section for leave under subparagraph (C) or (D) of section 2612(a)(1) of this title, the employer may require, at the expense of the employer, that the eligible employee obtain the opinion of a second health care provider designated or approved by the employer concerning any information certified under subsection (b) of this section for such leave.

(2) *Limitation.* A health care provider designated or approved under paragraph (1) shall not be employed on a regular basis by the employer.

(d) *Resolution of Conflicting Opinions.*

(1) *In general.* In any case in which the second opinion described in subsection (c) of this section differs from the opinion in the original certification provided under subsection (a) of this section, the employer may require, at the expense of the employer, that the employee obtain the opinion

of a third health care provider designated or approved jointly by the employer and the employee concerning the information certified under subsection (b).

(2) *Finality*. The opinion of the third health care provider concerning the information certified under subsection (b) of this section shall be considered to be final and shall be binding on the employer and the employee.

(e) *Subsequent Recertification*. The employer may require that the eligible employee obtain subsequent recertification on a reasonable basis.

(f) *Certification Related to Active Duty or Call to Active Duty*. An employer may require that a request for leave under section 2612(a)(1)(E) of this title be supported by a certification issued at such time and in such manner as the Secretary may by regulation prescribe. If the Secretary issues a regulation requiring such certification, the employee shall provide, in a timely manner, a copy of such certification to the employer.

§2614. Employment and Benefits Protection

(a) *Restoration to Position*.

(1) *In general*. Except as provided in subsection (b) of this section, any eligible employee who takes leave under section 2612 of this title for the intended purpose of the leave shall be entitled, on return from such leave —

    (A) to be restored by the employer to the position of employment held by the employee when the leave commenced; or

    (B) to be restored to an equivalent position with equivalent employment benefits, pay, and other terms and conditions of employment.

(2) *Loss of benefits*. The taking of leave under section 2612 of this title shall not result in the loss of any employment benefit accrued prior to the date on which the leave commenced.

(3) *Limitations*. Nothing in this section shall be construed to entitle any restored employee to —

    (A) the accrual of any seniority or employment benefits during any period of leave; or

    (B) any right, benefit, or position of employment other than any right, benefit, or position to which the employee would have been entitled had the employee not taken the leave.

(4) *Certification*. As a condition of restoration under paragraph (1) for an employee who has taken leave under section 2612(a)(1)(D) of this title, the employer may have a uniformly applied practice or policy that requires each such employee to receive certification from the health care provider of the employee that the employee is able to resume work, except that nothing in this paragraph shall supersede a valid State or local law or a collective bargaining agreement that governs the return to work of such employees.

(5) *Construction*. Nothing in this subsection shall be construed to prohibit an employer from requiring an employee on leave under section 2612 to

report periodically to the employer on the status and intention of the employee to return to work.

(b) *Exemption Concerning Certain Highly Compensated Employees.*

(1) *Denial of restoration.* An employer may deny restoration under subsection (a) of this section to any eligible employee described in paragraph (2) if—

(A) such denial is necessary to prevent substantial and grievous economic injury to the operations of the employer;

(B) the employer notifies the employee of the intent of the employer to deny restoration on such basis at the time the employer determines that such injury would occur; and

(C) in any case in which the leave has commenced, the employee elects not to return to employment after receiving such notice.

(2) *Affected employees.* An eligible employee described in paragraph (1) is a salaried eligible employee who is among the highest paid 10 percent of the employees employed by the employer within 75 miles of the facility at which the employee is employed.

(c) *Maintenance of Health Benefits.*

(1) *Coverage.* Except as provided in paragraph (2), during any period that an eligible employee takes leave under section 2612 of this title, the employer shall maintain coverage under any "group health plan" (as defined in section 5000(b)(1) of the Title 26) for the duration of such leave at the level and under the conditions coverage would have been provided if the employee had continued in employment continuously for the duration of such leave.

(2) *Failure to return from leave.* The employer may recover the premium that the employer paid for maintaining coverage for the employee under such group health plan during any period of unpaid leave under section 1262 of this title if—

(A) the employee fails to return from leave under section 2612 of this title after the period of leave to which the employee is entitled has expired; and

(B) the employee fails to return to work for a reason other than–

(i) the continuation, recurrence, or onset of a serious health condition that entitles the employee to leave under subparagraph (C) or (D) of section 2612(a)(1) of this title or under section 2612(a)(3) of this title; or

(ii) other circumstances beyond the control of the employee.

(3) *Certification.*

(A) *Issuance.* An employer may require that a claim that an employee is unable to return to work because of the continuation, recurrence, or onset of the serious health condition described in paragraph (2)(B)(i) be supported by —

(i) a certification issued by the health care provider of the son, daughter, spouse, or parent of the employee, as appropriate, in the case of an employee unable to return to work because of a condition specified in section 2612(a)(1)(C) of this title;

(ii) a certification issued by the health care provider of the eligible employee, in the case of an employee unable to return to work because of a condition specified in section 2612(a)(1)(D) of this title; or

(iii) a certification issued by the health care provider of the servicemember being cared for by the employee, in the case of an employee unable to return to work because of a condition specified in section 2612(a)(3) of this title.

(B) *Copy.* The employee shall provide, in a timely manner, a copy of such certification to the employer.

(C) *Sufficiency of certification.*

(i) *Leave due to serious health condition of employee.* The certification described in subparagraph (A)(ii) shall be sufficient if the certification states that a serious health condition prevented the employee from being able to perform the functions of the position of the employee on the date that the leave of the employee expired.

(ii) *Leave due to serious health condition of family member.* The certification described in subparagraph (A)(i) shall be sufficient if the certification states that the employee is needed to care for the son, daughter, spouse, or parent who has a serious health condition on the date that the leave of the employee expired.

§2615. Prohibited Acts

(a) *Interference with rights.*

(1) *Exercise of rights.* It shall be unlawful for any employee to interfere with, restrain, or deny the exercise of or the attempt to exercise, any right provided under this title.

(2) *Discrimination.* It shall be unlawful for any employer to discharge or in any other manner discriminate against any individual for opposing any practice made unlawful by this title.

(b) *Interference With Proceedings or Inquiries.* It shall be unlawful for any person to discharge or in any other manner discriminate against any individual because such individual

(1) has filed any charge, or has instituted or caused to be instituted any proceeding, under or related to this title;

(2) has given, or is about to give, any information in connection with any inquiry or proceeding relating to any right provided under this title; or

(3) has testified, or is about to testify, in any inquiry or proceeding relating to any right provided under this title.

§2616. Investigative Authority

(a) *In General.* To ensure compliance with the provisions of this title, or any regulation or order issued under this title, the Secretary shall have, subject to subsection (c), the investigative authority provided under section 11(a) of the Fair Labor Standards Act of 1938 (29 U.S.C. 211(a)).

(b) *Obligation to Keep and Preserve Records.* Any employer shall make, keep, and preserve records pertaining to compliance with this title in accordance with section 11(c) of the Fair Labor Standards Act of 1938 (29 U.S.C. 211(c)) and in accordance with regulations issued by the Secretary.

(c) *Required Submissions Generally Limited to an Annual Basis.* The Secretary shall not under the authority of this section require any employer or any plan, fund, or program to submit to the Secretary any books or records more than once during any 12-month period, unless the Secretary has reasonable cause to believe there may exist a violation of this title or any regulation or order issued pursuant to this title, or is investigating a charge pursuant to section 107(b).

(d) *Subpoena Powers.* For the purposes of any investigation provided for in this section, the Secretary shall have the subpoena authority provided for under section 9 of the Fair Labor Standards Act of 1938 (29 U.S.C. 209).

§2617. Enforcement

(a) *Civil Action by Employees.*

(1) *Liability.* Any employer who violates section 2615 shall be liable to any eligible employee affected—

(A) for damages equal to

(i) the amount of

(I) any wages, salary, employment benefits, or other compensation denied or lost to such employee by reason of the violation; or

(II) in a case in which wages, salary, employment benefits, or other compensation have not been denied or lost to the employee, any actual monetary losses sustained by the employee as a direct result of the violation, such as the cost of providing care, up to a sum equal to 12 weeks (or 26 weeks, in a case involving leave under section 2612(a)(3) of this title) of wages or salary for the employee;

(ii) the interest on the amount described in clause (i) calculated at the prevailing rate; and

(iii) an additional amount as liquidated damages equal to the sum of the amount described in clause (i) and the interest described in clause (ii), except that if an employer who has violated section 2615 of this title proves to the satisfaction of the court that the act or omission which violated section 2615 of this title was in good faith and that the employer had reasonable grounds for believing that the act or omission was not a violation of section 2615 of this title, such court may, in the discretion of the court, reduce the amount of the liability to the amount and interest determined under clauses (i) and (ii), respectively; and

(B) for such equitable relief as may be appropriate, including employment, reinstatement, and promotion.

(2) *Right of action*. An action to recover the damages or equitable relief prescribed in paragraph (1) may be maintained against any employer (including a public agency) in any Federal or State court of competent jurisdiction by one or more employees for and in behalf of—

(A) the employees; or

(B) the employees and other employees similarly situated.

(3) *Fees and costs*. The court in such an action shall, in addition to any judgment awarded to the plaintiff, allow a reasonable attorney's fee, reasonable expert witness fees, and other costs of the action to be paid by the defendant.

(4) *Limitations*. The right provided by paragraph (2) to bring an action by or on behalf of any employee shall terminate—

(A) on the filing of a complaint by the Secretary in an action under subsection (d) of this section in which restraint is sought of any further delay in the payment of the amount described in paragraph (1)(A) to such employee by an employer responsible under paragraph (1) for the payment; or

(B) on the filing of a complaint by the Secretary in an action under subsection (b) in which a recovery is sought of the damages described in paragraph (1)(A) owing to an eligible employee by an employer liable under paragraph (1), unless the action described in subparagraph (A) or

(B) is dismissed without prejudice on motion of the Secretary.

(b) *Action by the Secretary*.

(1) *Administrative action*. The Secretary shall receive, investigate, and attempt to resolve complaints of violations of section 2615 of this title in the same manner that the Secretary receives, investigates, and attempts to resolve complaints of violations of sections 206 and 207 of this title.

(2) *Civil action*. The Secretary may bring an action in any court of competent jurisdiction to recover the damages described in subsection (a)(1)(A) of this section.

(3) *Sums recovered*. Any sums recovered by the Secretary pursuant to paragraph (2) shall be held in special deposit account and shall be paid, on order of the Secretary, directly to each employee affected. Any such sums not paid to an employee because of inability to do so within a period of 3 years shall be deposited into the Treasury of the United States as miscellaneous receipts.

(c) *Limitations*.

(1) *In general*. Except as provided in paragraph (2), an action may be brought under this section not later than 2 years after the date of the last event constituting the alleged violation for which the action is brought.

(2) *Willful violation*. In the case of such action brought for a willful violation of section 2615 of this title, such action may be brought within 3 years

of the date of the last event constituting the alleged violation for which such action is brought.

(3) *Commencement*. In determining when an action is commenced by the Secretary under this section for the purposes of this subsection, it shall be considered to be commenced on the date when the complaint is filed.

(d) *Action for Injunction by Secretary*. The district courts of the United States shall have jurisdiction, for cause shown, in an action brought by the Secretary—

(1) to restrain violations of section 2615 of this title, including the restraint of any withholding of payment of wages, salary, employment benefits, or other compensation, plus interest, found by the court to be due to eligible employees; or

(2) to award such other equitable relief as may be appropriate, including employment, reinstatement, and promotion.

(e) *Solicitor of Labor*. The Solicitor of Labor may appear for and represent the Secretary on any litigation brought under this section.

(f) *General Accountability Office and Library of Congress*. In the case of the General Accountability Office and the Library of Congress, the authority of the Secretary of Labor under this subchapter shall be exercised respectively by the Comptroller General of the United States and the Librarian of Congress.

§2618. *Special Rules Concerning Employees of Local Educational Agencies*

(a) *Application*.

(1) *In general*. Except as otherwise provided in this section, the rights (including the rights under section 2614 of this title, which shall extend throughout the period of leave of any employee under this section), remedies, and procedures under this subchapter shall apply to—

(A) any "local educational agency" (as defined in section 7801 of Title 20) and an eligible employee of the agency; and

(B) any private elementary or secondary school and an eligible employee of the school.

(2) *Definitions*. For purposes of the application described in paragraph (1):

(A) *Eligible employee*. The term "eligible employee" means an eligible employee of an agency or school described in paragraph (1).

(B) *Employer*. The term "employer" means an agency or school described in paragraph (1).

(b) *Leave Does Not Violate Certain Other Federal Laws*. A local educational agency and a private elementary or secondary school shall not be in violation of the Individuals with Disabilities Education Act (20 U.S.C. 1400 et seq.), section 794 of this title, or title VI of the Civil Rights Act of 1964 (42 U.S.C. 2000d et seq.), solely as a result of an eligible employee of such agency or school exercising the rights of such employee under this subchapter.

(c) *Intermittent Leave or Leave on a Reduced Schedule for Instructional Employees*.

(1) *In general*. Subject to paragraph (2), in any case in which an eligible employee employed principally in an instructional capacity by any such educational agency or school requests leave under subparagraph (C) or (D) of section 2612(a)(1) or under section 2612(a)(3) of this title that is foreseeable

based on planed medical treatment and the employee would be on leave for greater than 20 percent of the total number of working days in the period during which the leave would extend, the agency or school may require that such employee elect either —

(A) to take leave for periods of a particular duration, not to exceed the duration of the planned medical treatment; or

(B) to transfer temporarily to an available alternative position offered by the employer for which the employee is qualified, and that

(i) has equivalent pay and benefits; and

(ii) better accommodates recurring periods of leave than the regular employment position of the employee.

(2) *Application.* The elections described in subparagraphs (A) and (B) or paragraph (1) shall apply only with respect to an eligible employee who complies with section 2612(e)(2) of this title.

(d) *Rules* Applicable to Periods Near the Conclusion of an Academic Term. The following rules shall apply with respect to periods of leave near the conclusion of an academic term in the case of any eligible employee employed principally in an instructional capacity by any such educational agency or school:

(1) *Leave more than 5 weeks prior to end of term.* If the eligible employee begins leave under section 2612 of this title more than 5 weeks prior to the end of the academic term, the agency or school may require the employee to continue taking leave until the end of such term, if —

(A) the leave is of at least 3 weeks duration; and

(B) the return to employment would occur during the 3-week period before the end of such term.

(2) *Leave less than 5 weeks prior to end of term.* If the eligible employee begins leave under subparagraph (A), (B), or (C) of section 2612(a)(1) of this title or under section 2612(a)(3) of this title during the period that commences 5 weeks prior to the end of the academic term, the agency or school may require the employee to continue taking leave until the end of such term, if

(A) the leave is of greater than 2 weeks duration; and

(B) the return to employment would occur during the 2-week period before the end of such term.

(3) *Leave less than 3 weeks prior to end of term.* If the eligible employee begins leave under subparagraph (A), (B), or (C) of section 2612(a)(1) of this title or under section 2612(a)(3) of this title during the period that commenced 3 weeks prior to the end of the academic term and the duration of the leave is greater than 5 working days, the agency or school may require the employee to continue to take leave until the end of such term.

(e) *Restoration to Equivalent Employment Position.* For purposes of determinations under section 2614(a)(1)(B) of this title (relating to the restoration of an eligible employee to an equivalent position), in the case of a local educational agency or a private elementary or secondary school, such determination shall be made on the basis of established school board policies and practices, private school policies and practices, and collective bargaining agreements.

(f) *Reduction of the Amount of Liability*. If a local educational agency or a private elementary or secondary school that has violated this title proves to the satisfaction of the court that the agency, school, or department had reasonable grounds for believing that the underlying act or omission was not a violation of this title, such court may, in the discretion of the court, reduce the amount of the liability provided for under section 2617(a)(1)(A) of this title to the amount and interest determined under clauses (i) and (ii), respectively, of such section.

§2619. Notice

(a) *In General*. Each employer shall post and keep posted, in conspicuous places on the premises of the employer where notices to employees and applicants for employment are customarily posted, a notice, to be prepared or approved by the Secretary, setting forth excerpts from, or summaries of, the pertinent provisions of this title and information pertaining to the filing of a charge.

(b) *Penalty*. Any employer that willfully violates this section may be assessed a civil money penalty not to exceed $100 for each separate offense.

§2651. Effect on Other Laws

(a) *Federal and State Antidiscrimination Laws*. Nothing in this Act or any amendment made by this Act shall be construed to modify or affect any Federal or State law prohibiting discrimination on the basis of race, religion, color, national origin, sex, age, or disability.

(b) State and Local Laws. Nothing in this Act or any amendment made by this Act shall be construed to supersede any provision of any State or local law that provides greater family or medical leave rights than the rights established under this Act or any amendment made by this Act.

§2652. Effect on Existing Employment Benefits

(a) *More Protective*. Nothing in this Act or any amendment made by this Act shall be construed to diminish the obligation of an employer to comply with any collective bargaining agreement or any employment benefit program or plan that provides greater family or medical leave rights to employees than the rights established under this Act or any amendment made by this Act.

(b) *Less Protective*. The rights established for employees under this Act or any amendment made by this Act shall not be diminished by any collective bargaining agreement or any employment benefit program or plan.

§2653. Encouragement of More Generous Leave Policies

Nothing in this Act or any amendment made by this Act shall be construed to discourage employers from adopting or retaining leave policies more generous than any policies that comply with the requirements under this Act or any amendment made by this Act.

§2654. Regulations

The Secretary of Labor shall prescribe such regulations as are necessary to carry out title I and this not later than 120 days after the date of the enactment of this Act [Feb. 5, 1993].

Federal Arbitration Act

9 U.S.C. §§1–16

§1. "Maritime Transactions" and "Commerce" Defined; Exceptions to Operation of Title

"Maritime transaction," as herein defined, means charter parties, bills of lading of water carriers, agreements relating to wharfage, supplies furnished vessels or repairs to vessels, collisions, or any other matters in foreign commerce which, if the subject of controversy, would be embraced within admiralty jurisdiction; "commerce," as herein defined, means commerce among the several States or with foreign nations, or in any Territory of the United States or in the District of Columbia, or between any such Territory and another, or between any such Territory and any State or foreign nation, or between the District of Columbia and any State or Territory or foreign nation, but nothing herein contained shall apply to contracts of employment of seamen, railroad employees, or any other class of workers engaged in foreign or interstate commerce.

§2. Validity, Irrevocability, and Enforcement of Agreements to Arbitrate

A written provision in any maritime transaction or a contract evidencing a transaction involving commerce to settle by arbitration a controversy thereafter arising out of such contract or transaction, or the refusal to perform the whole or any part thereof, or an agreement in writing to submit to arbitration an existing controversy arising out of such a contract, transaction, or refusal, shall be valid, irrevocable, and enforceable, save upon such grounds as exist at law or in equity for the revocation of any contract.

§3. Stay of Proceedings Where Issue Therein Referable to Arbitration

If any suit or proceeding be brought in any of the courts of the United States upon any issue referable to arbitration under an agreement in writing for such arbitration, the court in which such suit is pending, upon being satisfied that the issue involved in such suit or proceeding is referable to arbitration under such an agreement, shall on application of one of the parties stay the trial of the action until such arbitration has been had in accordance with the terms of the agreement, providing the applicant for the stay is not in default in proceeding with such arbitration.

§4. Failure to Arbitrate under Agreement; Petition to United States Court Having Jurisdiction for Order to Compel Arbitration; Notice and Service Thereof; Hearing and Determination

A party aggrieved by the alleged failure, neglect, or refusal of another to arbitrate under a written agreement for arbitration may petition any United States district court which, save for such agreement, would have jurisdiction under Title 28, in a civil action or in admiralty of the subject matter of a suit arising out of the controversy between the parties, for an order directing that such arbitration proceed in the manner provided for in such agreement. Five days' notice in writing of such application shall be served upon the party in default. Service thereof shall be made in the manner provided by the Federal Rules of Civil Procedure. The court shall hear the parties, and upon being satisfied that the making of the agreement for arbitration or the failure to comply therewith is not in issue, the court shall make an order directing the parties to proceed to arbitration in accordance with the terms of the agreement. The hearing and proceedings, under such agreement, shall be within the district in which the petition for an order directing such arbitration is filed. If the making of the arbitration agreement or the failure, neglect, or refusal to perform the same be in issue, the court shall proceed summarily to the trial thereof. If no jury trial be demanded by the party alleged to be in default, or if the matter in dispute is within admiralty jurisdiction, the court shall hear and determine such issue. Where such an issue is raised, the party alleged to be in default may, except in cases of admiralty, on or before the return day of the notice of application, demand a jury trial of such issue, and upon such demand the court shall make an order referring the issue or issues to a jury in the manner provided by the Federal Rules of Civil Procedure, or may specially call a jury for that purpose. If the jury find that no agreement in writing for arbitration was made or that there is no default in proceeding thereunder, the proceeding shall be dismissed. If the jury find that an agreement for arbitration was made in writing and that there is a default in proceeding thereunder, the court shall make an order summarily directing the parties to proceed with the arbitration in accordance with the terms thereof.

§5. Appointment of Arbitrators or Umpire

If in the agreement provision be made for a method of naming or appointing an arbitrator or arbitrators or an umpire, such method shall be followed; but if no method be provided therein, or if a method be provided and any party thereto shall fail to avail himself of such method, or if for any other reason there shall be a lapse in the naming of an arbitrator or arbitrators or umpire, or in filling a vacancy, then upon the application of either party to the controversy the court shall designate and appoint an arbitrator or arbitrators or umpire, as the case may require, who shall act under the said agreement with the same force and effect as if he or they had been specifically named therein; and unless otherwise provided in the agreement the arbitration shall be by a single arbitrator.

§6. *Application Heard as Motion*

Any application to the court hereunder shall be made and heard in the manner provided by law for the making and hearing of motions, except as otherwise herein expressly provided.

§7. *Witnesses Before Arbitrators; Fees; Compelling Attendance*

The arbitrators selected either as prescribed in this title or otherwise, or a majority of them, may summon in writing any person to attend before them or any of them as a witness and in a proper case to bring with him or them any book, record, document, or paper which may be deemed material as evidence in the case. The fees for such attendance shall be the same as the fees of witnesses before masters of the United States courts. Said summons shall issue in the name of the arbitrator or arbitrators, or a majority of them, and shall be signed by the arbitrators, or a majority of them, and shall be directed to the said person and shall be served in the same manner as subpoenas to appear and testify before the court; if any person or persons so summoned to testify shall refuse or neglect to obey said summons, upon petition the United States district court for the district in which such arbitrators, or a majority of them, are sitting may compel the attendance of such person or persons before said arbitrator or arbitrators, or punish said person or persons for contempt in the same manner provided by law for securing the attendance of witnesses or their punishment for neglect or refusal to attend in the courts of the United States.

§8. *Proceedings Begun by Libel in Admiralty and Seizure of Vessel or Property*

If the basis of jurisdiction be a cause of action otherwise justiciable in admiralty, then, notwithstanding anything herein to the contrary, the party claiming to be aggrieved may begin his proceeding hereunder by seizure of the vessel or other property of the other party according to the usual course of admiralty proceedings, and the court shall then have jurisdiction to direct the parties to proceed with the arbitration and shall retain jurisdiction to enter its decree upon the award.

§9. *Award of Arbitrators; Confirmation; Jurisdiction; Procedure*

If the parties in their agreement have agreed that a judgment of the court shall be entered upon the award made pursuant to the arbitration, and shall specify the court, then at any time within one year after the award is made any party to the arbitration may apply to the court so specified for an order confirming the award, and thereupon the court must grant such an order unless the award is vacated, modified, or corrected as prescribed in sections 10 and 11 of this title. If no court is specified in the agreement of the parties, then such application may be made to the United States court in and for the district within which such award was made. Notice of the application shall be served upon the adverse party, and thereupon the court shall have jurisdiction of such party as though he had appeared generally in the proceeding. If the adverse party is a resident of the district within which the award was made, such service shall be made upon the adverse party or his attorney as prescribed by law for service of notice of motion in an action in the same court. If the adverse party shall be a nonresident, then the notice of the application shall be served by the marshal of any district within which the adverse party may be found in like manner as other process of the court.

§10. Same; Vacation; Grounds; Rehearing

(a) In any of the following cases the United States court in and for the district wherein the award was made may make an order vacating the award upon the application of any party to the arbitration—

(1) Where the award was procured by corruption, fraud, or undue means;

(2) Where there was evident partiality or corruption in the arbitrators, or either of them;

(3) Where the arbitrators were guilty of misconduct in refusing to postpone the hearing, upon sufficient cause shown, or in refusing to hear evidence pertinent and material to the controversy; or of any other misbehavior by which the rights of any party have been prejudiced; or

(4) Where the arbitrators exceeded their powers, or so imperfectly executed them that a mutual, final, and definite award upon the subject matter submitted was not made.

(b) If an award is vacated and the time within which the agreement required the award to be made has not expired, the court may, in its discretion, direct a rehearing by the arbitrators.

(c) The United States district court for the district wherein an award was made that was issued pursuant to section 580 of title 5 may make an order vacating the award upon the application of a person, other than a party to the arbitration, who is adversely affected or aggrieved by the award, if the use of arbitration or the award is clearly inconsistent with the factors set forth in section 572 of title 5.

§11. Same; Modification or Correction; Grounds; Order

In either of the following cases the United States court in and for the district wherein the award was made may make an order modifying or correcting the award upon the application of any party to the arbitration—

(a) Where there was an evident material miscalculation of figures or an evident material mistake in the description of any person, thing, or property referred to in the award.

(b) Where the arbitrators have awarded upon a matter not submitted to them, unless it is a matter not affecting the merits of the decision upon the matter submitted.

(c) Where the award is imperfect in matter of form not affecting the merits of the controversy.

The order may modify and correct the award, so as to effect the intent thereof and promote justice between the parties.

§12. Notice of Motions to Vacate or Modify; Service; Stay of Proceedings

Notice of a motion to vacate, modify, or correct an award must be served upon the adverse party or his attorney within three months after the award is filed or delivered. If the adverse party is a resident of the district within which the award was made, such service shall be made upon the adverse party or his attorney as prescribed by law for service of notice of motion in an action in the same court. If the adverse party shall be a nonresident then the notice of the application shall be served by the marshal of any district within which the adverse party may be found in like manner as other process of the court. For the purposes of the motion any judge who might make an order to stay the proceedings in an action brought in the same court may make an order, to be served with the notice of motion, staying the proceedings of the adverse party to enforce the award.

§13. Papers Filed with Order on Motions; Judgment; Docketing; Force and Effect; Enforcement

The party moving for an order confirming, modifying, or correcting an award shall, at the time such order is filed with the clerk for the entry of judgment thereon, also file the following papers with the clerk:

(a) The agreement; the selection or appointment, if any, of an additional arbitrator or umpire; and each written extension of the time, if any, within which to make the award.

(b) The award.

(c) Each notice, affidavit, or other paper used upon an application to confirm, modify, or correct the award, and a copy of each order of the court upon such an application.

The judgment shall be docketed as if it was rendered in an action.

The judgment so entered shall have the same force and effect, in all respects, as, and be subject to all the provisions of law relating to, a judgment in an action; and it may be enforced as if it had been rendered in an action in the court in which it is entered.

§14. Contracts Not Affected

This title shall not apply to contracts made prior to January 1, 1926.

§15. Inapplicability of the Act of State Doctrine

Enforcement of arbitral agreements, confirmation of arbitral awards, and execution upon judgments based on orders confirming such awards shall not be refused on the basis of the Act of State doctrine.

§16. Appeals

(a) An appeal may be taken from

(1) an order—

(A) refusing a stay of any action under section 3 of this title,

(B) denying a petition under section 4 of this title to order arbitration to proceed,

(C) denying an application under section 206 of this title to compel arbitration,

(D) confirming or denying confirmation of an award or partial award, or

(E) modifying, correcting, or vacating an award;

(2) an interlocutory order granting, continuing, or modifying an injunction against an arbitration that is subject to this title; or

(3) a final decision with respect to an arbitration that is subject to this title.

(b) Except as otherwise provided in section 1292(b) of title 28, an appeal may not be taken from an interlocutory order —

(1) granting a stay of any action under section 3 of this title;

(2) directing arbitration to proceed under section 4 of this title;

(3) compelling arbitration under section 206 of this title; or

(4) refusing to enjoin an arbitration that is subject to this title.

42 U.S.C. §1981

§1981. Equal Rights Under the Law*

(a) All persons within the jurisdiction of the United States shall have the same right in every State and Territory to make and enforce contracts, to sue, be parties, give evidence, and to the full and equal benefit of all laws and proceedings for the security of persons and property as is enjoyed by white citizens, and shall be subject to like punishment, pains, penalties, taxes, licences, and exactions of every kind, and to no other.

(b) For purposes of this section, the term "make and enforce contracts" includes the making, performance, modification, and termination of contracts, and the enjoyment of all benefits, privileges, terms, and conditions of the contractual relationship.

(c) The rights protected by this section are protected against impairment by nongovernmental discrimination and impairment under color of State law.

---

* Sections 1981(b), (c) and 1981a were added by the Civil Rights Act of 1991.

42 U.S.C. §1981a

§1981a. Damages in Cases of Intentional Discrimination
        in Employment

(a) *Right of Recovery.*

(1) *Civil rights.* In an action brought by a complaining party under section 42 U.S.C. 2000e-5 or 42 U.S.C. 2000e-16 of the Civil Rights Act of 1964 against a respondent who engaged in unlawful intentional discrimination (not an employment practice that is unlawful because of its disparate impact) prohibited under section 42 U.S.C. 2000e-2, -3, or -16 of the Act, and provided that the complaining party cannot recover under 42 U.S.C. 1981 of the Revised Statutes, the complaining party may recover compensatory and punitive damages as allowed in subsection (b), in addition to any relief authorized by section 2000e-5(g) of the Civil Rights Act of 1964, from the respondent.

(2) *Disability.* In an action brought by a complaining party that the powers, remedies, and procedures set forth in section 2000e-5 or 2000e-16 of the Civil Rights Act of 1964 (as provided in section 42 U.S.C. 12117(a) of the Americans With Disabilities Act of 1990 and section 29 U.S.C. 794a(a)(1) of the Rehabilitation Act of 1973, respectively) against a respondent who engaged in unlawful intentional discrimination (not an employment practice that is unlawful because of its disparate impact) under section 29 U.S.C. 791 of the Rehabilitation Act of 1973 and the regulations implementing section 791, or who violated the requirements of section 791 of the Act or the regulations implementing section 791 concerning the provision of a reasonable accommodation, or section 42 U.S.C. 12112 of the Americans With Disabilities Act, or committed a violation of section 12112(b)(5) of the Act, against an individual, the complaining party may recover compensatory and punitive damages as allowed in subsection (b), in addition to any relief authorized by section 42 U.S.C. 2000e-5(g) of the Civil Rights Act of 1964, from the respondent.

(3) *Reasonable accommodation and good faith effort.* In cases where a discriminatory practice involves the provision of a reasonable accommodation pursuant to section 12112(b)(5) of the Americans With Disabilities Act of 1990 or regulations implementing section 791 of the Rehabilitation Act of 1973, damages may not be awarded under this section where the covered entity demonstrates good faith efforts, in consultation with the person with the disability who has informed the covered entity that accommodation is needed, to identify and make a reasonable accommodation that would provide such individual with an equally effective opportunity and would not cause an undue hardship on the question of the business.

(b) *Compensatory and Punitive Damages.*

(1) *Determination of punitive damages.* A complaining party may recover punitive damages under this section against a respondent (other than a government, government agency or political subdivision) if the complaining party demonstrates that the respondent engaged in a discriminatory practice or discriminatory practices with malice or with reckless indifference to the federally protected rights of an aggrieved individual.

(2) *Exclusions from compensatory damages.* Compensatory damages awarded under this section shall not include backpay, interest on backpay, or any other type of relief authorized under section 2000e-5(g) of the Civil Rights Act of 1964.

(3) *Limitations.* The sum of the amount of compensatory damages awarded under this section for future pecuniary losses, emotional pain, suffering, inconvenience, mental anguish, loss of enjoyment of life, and other non-pecuniary losses, and the amount of punitive damages awarded under this section, shall not exceed, for each complaining party

　　(A) in the case of a respondent who has more than 14 and fewer than 101 employees in each of 20 or more calendar weeks in the current or preceding calendar year, $50,000;

　　(B) in the case of a respondent who has more than 100 and fewer than 201 employees in each of 20 or more calendar weeks in the current or preceding calendar year, $100,000; and

　　(C) in the case of a respondent who has more than 200 and fewer than 501 employees in each of 20 or more calendar weeks in the current or preceding calendar year, $200,000; and

　　(D) in the case of a respondent who has more than 500 employees in each of 20 or more calendar weeks in the current or preceding calendar year, $300,000.

(4) *Construction.* Nothing in this section shall be construed to limit the scope of, or the relief available under, section 1981 of the Revised Statutes (42 U.S.C. 1981).

(c) *Jury Trial.* If a complaining party seeks compensatory or punitive damages under this section.

(1) any party may demand a trial by jury; and

(2) the court shall not inform the jury of the limitation described in subsection (b)(3).

(d) *Definitions.* As used in this section:

(1) *Complaining party.* The term "complaining party" means

(A) in the case of a person seeking to bring an action under subsection (a)(1), the Equal Employment Opportunity Commission, the Attorney General, or a person who may bring an action or proceeding under title VII of the Civil Rights Act of 1964; or

(B) in the case of a person seeking to bring an action under (a)(2), the Equal Employment Opportunity Commission, the Attorney General, a person who may bring an action or proceeding under section 794a(a)(1) of the Rehabilitation Act of 1973 (29 U.S.C. 794a(a)(1)), or a person who may bring an action or proceeding under title I of the Americans With Disabilities Act of 1990.

(2) *Discriminatory practice.* The term "discriminatory practice" means the discrimination described in paragraph (1), or the discrimination or the violation described in paragraph (2), of subsection (a).

42 U.S.C. §1983

§1983. Civil Action for Deprivation of Rights

Every person who, under color of any statute, ordinance, regulation, custom, or usage, of any State or Territory or the District of Columbia, subjects, or causes to be subjected, any citizen of the United States or other person within the jurisdiction thereof to the deprivation of any rights, privileges, or immunities secured by the Constitution and laws, shall be liable to the party injured in an action at law, suit in equity, or other proper proceeding for redress, except that in any action brought against a judicial officer for an act or omission taken in such officer's judicial capacity, injunctive relief shall not be granted unless a declaratory decree was violated or declaratory relief was unavailable. For the purposes of this section, any Act of Congress applicable exclusively to the District of Columbia shall be considered to be a statute of the District of Columbia.

42 U.S.C. §1985(3)

§1985. Conspiracy to Interfere with Civil Rights

(3) *Depriving persons of rights or privileges.* If two or more persons in any State or Territory conspire or go in disguise on the highway or on the premises of another, for the purpose of depriving, either directly or indirectly, any person or class of persons of the equal protection of the laws, or of equal privileges and immunities under the laws; or for the purpose of preventing or hindering the constituted authorities of any State or Territory from giving or securing to all persons within such State or Territory the equal protection of the laws; or if two or more persons conspire to prevent by force, intimidation, or threat, any citizen who is lawfully entitled to vote, from giving his support or advocacy in a legal manner, toward or in favor of the election of any lawfully qualified person as an elector for President or Vice President, or as a Member of Congress of the United States; or to injure any citizen in person or property on account of such support or advocacy; in any case of conspiracy set forth in this section, if one or more persons engaged therein do, or cause to be done, any act in furtherance of the object of such conspiracy, whereby another is injured in his person or property, or deprived of having and exercising any right or privilege of a citizen of the United States, the party so injured or deprived may have an action for the recovery of damages occasioned by such injury or deprivation, against any one or more of the conspirators.

42 U.S.C. §1988

§1988. Proceedings in Vindication of Civil Rights

(a) *Applicability of Statutory and Common Law.* The jurisdiction in civil and criminal matters conferred on the district courts by the provisions of Titles 13, 24, and 70 of the Revised Statutes, for the protection of all persons in the United States in their civil rights, and for their vindication, shall be exercised and enforced in conformity with the laws of the United States, so far as such laws are suitable to carry the same into effect; but in all cases where they are not adapted to the object, or are deficient in the provisions necessary to furnish suitable remedies and punish offences against law, the common law, as modified and changed by the constitution and statutes of the State wherein the court having jurisdiction of such civil or criminal cause is held, so far as the same is not inconsistent with the Constitution and laws of the United States, shall be extended to and govern the said courts in the trial and disposition of the cause, and, if it is of a criminal nature, in the infliction of punishment on the party found guilty.

(b) *Attorney's Fees.* In any action or proceeding to enforce a provision of sections 1981, 1981a, 1982, 1983, 1985, and 1986 of this title [42 U.S.C.], title IX of Public Law 92-318 [20 U.S.C. §§1681 et seq.], the Religious Freedom Restoration Act of 1993 [42 U.S.C. §§2000bb et seq.], the Religious Land Use and Institutionalized Persons Act of 2000 [42 U.S.C. §§2000cc et seq.], title VI of the Civil Rights Act of 1964 [42 U.S.C. §§2000d et seq.], or section 13981 of this title, the court, in its discretion, may allow the prevailing party, other than the United States, a reasonable attorney's fee as part of the costs, except that in any action brought against a judicial officer for an act or omission taken in such officer's judicial capacity such officer shall not be held liable for any costs, including attorney's fees, unless such action was clearly in excess of such officer's jurisdiction.

(c) *Expert Fees.* In awarding an attorney's fee under subsection (b) in any action or proceeding to enforce a provision of sections 1981 or 1981a of this title, the court, in its discretion, may include expert fees as part of the attorney's fee.

References in Text

Title 13 of the Revised Statutes, referred to in subsection (a), was in the original "this Title" meaning title 13 of the Revised Statutes, consisting of R.S. §§530 to 1093. For complete classification of R.S. §§530 to 1093 to the Code, see Tables.

Title 24 of the Revised Statutes, referred to in subsection (a), was in the original "Title 'CIVIL RIGHTS,'" meaning title 24 of the Revised Statutes, consisting of R.S. §§1977 to 1991, which are classified to sections 1981 to 1983, 1985 to 1987, and 1989 to 1994 of this title. For complete classification of R.S. §§1977 to 1991 to the Code, see Tables.

Title 70 of the Revised Statutes, referred to in subsection (a), was in the original "Title 'CRIMES,'" meaning title 70 of the Revised Statutes, consisting of R.S. §§5323 to 5550. For complete classification of R.S. §§5323 to 5550, see Tables.

42 U.S.C. §2000d-7

§2000d-7. Civil Rights Remedies Equalization

(a) *General Provision.*

(1) A State shall not be immune under the Eleventh Amendment of the Constitution of the United States from suit in Federal court for a violation of section 504 of the Rehabilitation Act of 1973 [29 U.S.C.A. §794], title IX of the Education Amendments of 1972 [20 U.S.C.A. §1681 et seq.], the Age Discrimination Act of 1975 [42 U.S.C.A. §6101 et seq.], title VI of the Civil Rights Act of 1964 [42 U.S.C.A. 2000d et seq.], or the provisions of any other Federal statute prohibiting discrimination by recipients of Federal financial assistance.

(2) In a suit against a State for a violation of a statute referred to in paragraph (I), remedies (including remedies both at law and in equity) are available for such a violation to the same extent as such remedies are available for such a violation in the suit against any public or private entity other than a State.

(b) *Effective Date.*

The provisions of subsection (a) of this section shall take effect with respect to violations that occur in whole or in part after October 21, 1986.

Genetic Information Nondiscrimination Act of 2008

Pub. L. No. 110-233, 122 Stat. 881

An Act To prohibit discrimination on the basis of genetic information with respect to health insurance and employment.

Be it enacted by the Senate and House of Representatives of the United States of America in Congress assembled,

Sec. 1. Short Title; Table of Contents

(a) SHORT TITLE. This Act may be cited as the "Genetic Information Nondiscrimination Act of 2008".

(b) TABLE OF CONTENTS. The table of contents of this Act is as follows:

TITLE III — MISCELLANEOUS PROVISIONS
[not reproduced]

Sec. 2. *Findings*

Congress makes the following findings:

(1) Deciphering the sequence of the human genome and other advances in genetics open major new opportunities for medical progress. New knowledge about the genetic basis of illness will allow for earlier detection of illnesses, often before symptoms have begun. Genetic testing can allow individuals to take steps to reduce the likelihood that they will contract a particular disorder. New knowledge about genetics may allow for the development of better therapies that are more effective against disease or have fewer side effects than current treatments. These advances give rise to the potential misuse of genetic information to discriminate in health insurance and employment.

(2) The early science of genetics became the basis of State laws that provided for the sterilization of persons having presumed genetic "defects" such as mental retardation, mental disease, epilepsy, blindness, and hearing loss, among other conditions. The first sterilization law was enacted in the State of Indiana in 1907. By 1981, a majority of States adopted sterilization laws to "correct" apparent genetic traits or tendencies. Many of these State laws have since been repealed, and many have been modified to include essential constitutional requirements of due process and equal protection. However, the current explosion in the science of genetics, and the history of sterilization laws by the States based on early genetic science, compels Congressional action in this area.

(3) Although genes are facially neutral markers, many genetic conditions and disorders are associated with particular racial and ethnic groups and gender. Because some genetic traits are most prevalent in particular groups, members of a particular group may be stigmatized or discriminated against as a result of that genetic information. This form of discrimination was evident

in the 1970s, which saw the advent of programs to screen and identify carriers of sickle cell anemia, a disease which afflicts African Americans. Once again, State legislatures began to enact discriminatory laws in the area, and in the early 1970s began mandating genetic screening of all African Americans for sickle cell anemia, leading to discrimination and unnecessary fear. To alleviate some of this stigma, Congress in 1972 passed the National Sickle Cell Anemia Control Act, which withholds Federal funding from States unless sickle cell testing is voluntary.

(4) Congress has been informed of examples of genetic discrimination in the workplace. These include the use of pre-employment genetic screening at Lawrence Berkeley Laboratory, which led to a court decision in favor of the employees in that case. Norman-Bloodsaw v. Lawrence Berkeley Laboratory (135 F.3d 1260, 1269 (9th Cir. 1998)). Congress clearly has a compelling public interest in relieving the fear of discrimination and in prohibiting its actual practice in employment and health insurance.

(5) Federal law addressing genetic discrimination in health insurance and employment is incomplete in both the scope and depth of its protections. Moreover, while many States have enacted some type of genetic non-discrimination law, these laws vary widely with respect to their approach, application, and level of protection. Congress has collected substantial evidence that the American public and the medical community find the existing patchwork of State and Federal laws to be confusing and inadequate to protect them from discrimination. Therefore Federal legislation establishing a national and uniform basic standard is necessary to fully protect the public from discrimination and allay their concerns about the potential for discrimination, thereby allowing individuals to take advantage of genetic testing, technologies, research, and new therapies.

TITLE II — Prohibiting Employment Discrimination on the Basis of Genetic Information

Sec. 201. *Definitions*

(1) *Commission*. The term "Commission" means the Equal Employment Opportunity Commission as created by section 705 of the Civil Rights Act of 1964 [42 U.S.C. 2000e-4].

(2) *Employee; Employer; Employment Agency; Labor Organization; Member.*

(A) *In General*. The term "employee" means—

(i) an employee (including an applicant), as defined in section 701(f) of the Civil Rights Act of 1964 (42 U.S.C. 2000e(f));

(ii) a State employee (including an applicant) described in section 304(a) of the Government Employee Rights Act of 1991 (42 U.S.C. 2000e-16c(a));

(iii) a covered employee (including an applicant), as defined in section 101 of the Congressional Accountability Act of 1995 (2 U.S.C. 1301);

(iv) a covered employee (including an applicant), as defined in section 411(c) of title 3, United States Code; or

(v) an employee or applicant to which section 717(a) of the Civil Rights Act of 1964 (42 U.S.C. 2000e-16(a)) applies.

(B) *Employer.* The term "employer" means —

(i) an employer (as defined in section 701(b) of the Civil Rights Act of 1964 (42 U.S.C. 2000e(b)));

(ii) an entity employing a State employee described in section 304(a) of the Government Employee Rights Act of 1991;

(iii) an employing office, as defined in section 101 of the Congressional Accountability Act of 1995;

(iv) an employing office, as defined in section 411(c) of title 3, United States Code; or

(v) an entity to which section 717(a) of the Civil Rights Act of 1964 applies.

(C) *Employment Agency; Labor Organization.* The terms "employment agency" and "labor organization" have the meanings given the terms in section 701 of the Civil Rights Act of 1964 (42 U.S.C. 2000e).

(D) *Member.* The term "member", with respect to a labor organization, includes an applicant for membership in a labor organization.

(3) *Family Member.* The term "family member" means, with respect to an individual —

(A) a dependent (as such term is used for purposes of section 701(f)(2) of the Employee Retirement Income Security Act of 1974) of such individual, and

(B) any other individual who is a first-degree, second-degree, third-degree, or fourth-degree relative of such individual or of an individual described in subparagraph (A).

(4) *Genetic Information.*

(A) *In General.* The term "genetic information" means, with respect to any individual, information about —

(i) such individual's genetic tests,

(ii) the genetic tests of family members of such individual, and

(iii) the manifestation of a disease or disorder in family members of such individual.

(B) *Inclusion Of Genetic Services and Participation in Genetic Research.* Such term includes, with respect to any individual, any request for, or receipt of, genetic services, or participation in clinical research which includes genetic services, by such individual or any family member of such individual.

(C) *Exclusions.* The term "genetic information" shall not include information about the sex or age of any individual.

(5) *Genetic Monitoring.* The term "genetic monitoring" means the periodic examination of employees to evaluate acquired modifications to their genetic material, such as chromosomal damage or evidence of increased occurrence of mutations, that may have developed in the course of employment due to exposure to toxic substances in the workplace, in order to identify, evaluate, and respond to the effects of or control adverse environmental exposures in the workplace.

(6) *Genetic Services.* The term "genetic services" means—

(A) a genetic test;

(B) genetic counseling (including obtaining, interpreting, or assessing genetic information); or

(C) genetic education.

(7) *Genetic Test.*

(A) *In General.* The term "genetic test" means an analysis of human DNA, RNA, chromosomes, proteins, or metabolites, that detects genotypes, mutations, or chromosomal changes.

(B) *Exceptions.* The term "genetic test" does not mean an analysis of proteins or metabolites that does not detect genotypes, mutations, or chromosomal changes.

Sec. 202. *Employer Practices*

(a) *Discrimination Based on Genetic Information.* It shall be an unlawful employment practice for an employer—

(1) to fail or refuse to hire, or to discharge, any employee, or otherwise to discriminate against any employee with respect to the compensation, terms, conditions, or privileges of employment of the employee, because of genetic information with respect to the employee; or

(2) to limit, segregate, or classify the employees of the employer in any way that would deprive or tend to deprive any employee of employment opportunities or otherwise adversely affect the status of the employee as an employee, because of genetic information with respect to the employee.

(b) *Acquisition of Genetic Information.* It shall be an unlawful employment practice for an employer to request, require, or purchase genetic information with respect to an employee or a family member of the employee except—

(1) where an employer inadvertently requests or requires family medical history of the employee or family member of the employee;

(2) where—

(A) health or genetic services are offered by the employer, including such services offered as part of a wellness program;

(B) the employee provides prior, knowing, voluntary, and written authorization;

(C) only the employee (or family member if the family member is receiving genetic services) and the licensed health care professional or board certified genetic counselor involved in providing such services receive individually identifiable information concerning the results of such services; and

(D) any individually identifiable genetic information provided under subparagraph (C) in connection with the services provided under subparagraph (A) is only available for purposes of such services and shall not be disclosed to the employer except in aggregate terms that do not disclose the identity of specific employees;

(3) where an employer requests or requires family medical history from the employee to comply with the certification provisions of section 103 of the Family and Medical Leave Act of 1993 (29 U.S.C. 2613) or such requirements under State family and medical leave laws;

(4) where an employer purchases documents that are commercially and publicly available (including newspapers, magazines, periodicals, and books, but not including medical databases or court records) that include family medical history;

(5) where the information involved is to be used for genetic monitoring of the biological effects of toxic substances in the workplace, but only if—

(A) the employer provides written notice of the genetic monitoring to the employee;

(B)(i) the employee provides prior, knowing, voluntary, and written authorization; or

(ii) the genetic monitoring is required by Federal or State law;

(C) the employee is informed of individual monitoring results;

(D) The Monitoring Is in Compliance With

(i) any Federal genetic monitoring regulations, including any such regulations that may be promulgated by the Secretary of Labor pursuant to the Occupational Safety and Health Act of 1970 (29 U.S.C. 651 et seq.), the Federal Mine Safety and Health Act of 1977 (30 U.S.C. 801 et seq.), or the Atomic Energy Act of 1954 (42 U.S.C. 2011 et seq.); or

(ii) State genetic monitoring regulations, in the case of a State that is implementing genetic monitoring regulations under the authority of the Occupational Safety and Health Act of 1970 (29 U.S.C. 651 et seq.); and

(E) the employer, excluding any licensed health care professional or board certified genetic counselor that is involved in the genetic monitoring program, receives the results of the monitoring only in aggregate terms that do not disclose the identity of specific employees; or

(6) where the employer conducts DNA analysis for law enforcement purposes as a forensic laboratory or for purposes of human remains identification, and requests or requires genetic information of such employer's employees, but only to the extent that such genetic information is used for analysis of DNA identification markers for quality control to detect sample contamination.

(c) *Preservation of Protections.* In the case of information to which any of paragraphs (1) through (6) of subsection (b) applies, such information may not be used in violation of paragraph (1) or (2) of subsection (a) or treated or disclosed in a manner that violates section 206.

Sec. 203. *Employment Agency Practices*

(a) *Discrimination Based on Genetic Information.* It shall be an unlawful employment practice for an employment agency—

(1) to fail or refuse to refer for employment, or otherwise to discriminate against, any individual because of genetic information with respect to the individual;

(2) to limit, segregate, or classify individuals or fail or refuse to refer for employment any individual in any way that would deprive or tend to deprive any individual of employment opportunities, or otherwise adversely affect the status of the individual as an employee, because of genetic information with respect to the individual; or

(3) to cause or attempt to cause an employer to discriminate against an individual in violation of this title.

(b) *Acquisition of Genetic Information.* It shall be an unlawful employment practice for an employment agency to request, require, or purchase genetic information with respect to an individual or a family member of the individual except—

(1) where an employment agency inadvertently requests or requires family medical history of the individual or family member of the individual;

(2) where—

(A) health or genetic services are offered by the employment agency, including such services offered as part of a wellness program;

(B) the individual provides prior, knowing, voluntary, and written authorization;

(C) only the individual (or family member if the family member is receiving genetic services) and the licensed health care professional or board certified genetic counselor involved in providing such services receive individually identifiable information concerning the results of such services; and

(D) any individually identifiable genetic information provided under subparagraph (C) in connection with the services provided under subparagraph (A) is only available for purposes of such services and shall not be disclosed to the employment agency except in aggregate terms that do not disclose the identity of specific individuals;

(3) where an employment agency requests or requires family medical history from the individual to comply with the certification provisions of section 103 of the Family and Medical Leave Act of 1993 (29 U.S.C. 2613) or such requirements under State family and medical leave laws;

(4) where an employment agency purchases documents that are commercially and publicly available (including newspapers, magazines, periodicals, and books, but not including medical databases or court records) that include family medical history; or

(5) where the information involved is to be used for genetic monitoring of the biological effects of toxic substances in the workplace, but only if—

(A) the employment agency provides written notice of the genetic monitoring to the individual;

(B)(i) the individual provides prior, knowing, voluntary, and written authorization; or

(ii) the genetic monitoring is required by Federal or State law;

(C) the individual is informed of individual monitoring results;

(D) The Monitoring Is in Compliance With

(i) any Federal genetic monitoring regulations, including any such regulations that may be promulgated by the Secretary of Labor pursuant to the Occupational Safety and Health Act of 1970 (29 U.S.C. 651 et seq.), the Federal Mine Safety and Health Act of 1977 (30 U.S.C. 801 et seq.), or the Atomic Energy Act of 1954 (42 U.S.C. 2011 et seq.); or

(ii) State genetic monitoring regulations, in the case of a State that is implementing genetic monitoring regulations under the authority of the Occupational Safety and Health Act of 1970 (29 U.S.C. 651 et seq.); and

(E) the employment agency, excluding any licensed health care professional or board certified genetic counselor that is involved in the genetic monitoring program, receives the results of the monitoring only in aggregate terms that do not disclose the identity of specific individuals.

(c) *Preservation of Protections.* In the case of information to which any of paragraphs (1) through (5) of subsection (b) applies, such information may not be used in violation of paragraph (1), (2), or (3) of subsection (a) or treated or disclosed in a manner that violates section 206.

Sec. 204. Labor Organization Practices

(a) *Discrimination Based on Genetic Information.* It shall be an unlawful employment practice for a labor organization—

(1) to exclude or to expel from the membership of the organization, or otherwise to discriminate against, any member because of genetic information with respect to the member;

(2) to limit, segregate, or classify the members of the organization, or fail or refuse to refer for employment any member, in any way that would deprive or tend to deprive any member of employment opportunities, or otherwise adversely affect the status of the member as an employee, because of genetic information with respect to the member; or

(3) to cause or attempt to cause an employer to discriminate against a member in violation of this title.

(b) *Acquisition of Genetic Information.* It shall be an unlawful employment practice for a labor organization to request, require, or purchase genetic information with respect to a member or a family member of the member except—

(1) where a labor organization inadvertently requests or requires family medical history of the member or family member of the member;

(2) where—

(A) health or genetic services are offered by the labor organization, including such services offered as part of a wellness program;

(B) the member provides prior, knowing, voluntary, and written authorization;

(C) only the member (or family member if the family member is receiving genetic services) and the licensed health care professional or board certified genetic counselor involved in providing such services receive individually identifiable information concerning the results of such services; and

(D) any individually identifiable genetic information provided under subparagraph (C) in connection with the services provided under subparagraph (A) is only available for purposes of such services and shall not be disclosed to the labor organization except in aggregate terms that do not disclose the identity of specific members;

(3) where a labor organization requests or requires family medical history from the members to comply with the certification provisions of section 103 of the Family and Medical Leave Act of 1993 (29 U.S.C. 2613) or such requirements under State family and medical leave laws;

(4) where a labor organization purchases documents that are commercially and publicly available (including newspapers, magazines, periodicals, and books, but not including medical databases or court records) that include family medical history; or

(5) Where the Information Involved Is To Be Used for Genetic Monitoring of the Biological Effects of Toxic Substances in the Workplace, But Only If

(A) the labor organization provides written notice of the genetic monitoring to the member;

(B)(i) the member provides prior, knowing, voluntary, and written authorization; or

(ii) the genetic monitoring is required by Federal or State law;

(C) the member is informed of individual monitoring results;

(D) The Monitoring Is in Compliance With

(i) any Federal genetic monitoring regulations, including any such regulations that may be promulgated by the Secretary of Labor pursuant to the Occupational Safety and Health Act of 1970 (29 U.S.C. 651 et seq.), the Federal Mine Safety and Health Act of 1977 (30 U.S.C. 801 et seq.), or the Atomic Energy Act of 1954 (42 U.S.C. 2011 et seq.); or

(ii) State genetic monitoring regulations, in the case of a State that is implementing genetic monitoring regulations under the authority of the Occupational Safety and Health Act of 1970 (29 U.S.C. 651 et seq.); and

(E) the labor organization, excluding any licensed health care professional or board certified genetic counselor that is involved in the genetic monitoring program, receives the results of the monitoring only in aggregate terms that do not disclose the identity of specific members.

(c) *Preservation of Protections*. In the case of information to which any of paragraphs (1) through (5) of subsection (b) applies, such information may not be used in violation of paragraph (1), (2), or (3) of subsection (a) or treated or disclosed in a manner that violates section 206.

Sec. 205. *Training Programs*

(a) *Discrimination Based on Genetic Information.* It shall be an unlawful employment practice for any employer, labor organization, or joint labor-management committee controlling apprenticeship or other training or retraining, including on-the-job training programs—

    (1) to discriminate against any individual because of genetic information with respect to the individual in admission to, or employment in, any program established to provide apprenticeship or other training or retraining;

    (2) to limit, segregate, or classify the applicants for or participants in such apprenticeship or other training or retraining, or fail or refuse to refer for employment any individual, in any way that would deprive or tend to deprive any individual of employment opportunities, or otherwise adversely affect the status of the individual as an employee, because of genetic information with respect to the individual; or

    (3) to cause or attempt to cause an employer to discriminate against an applicant for or a participant in such apprenticeship or other training or retraining in violation of this title.

(b) *Acquisition of Genetic Information.* It shall be an unlawful employment practice for an employer, labor organization, or joint labor-management committee described in subsection (a) to request, require, or purchase genetic information with respect to an individual or a family member of the individual except—

    (1) where the employer, labor organization, or joint labor-management committee inadvertently requests or requires family medical history of the individual or family member of the individual;

    (2) where—

        (A) health or genetic services are offered by the employer, labor organization, or joint labor-management committee, including such services offered as part of a wellness program;

        (B) the individual provides prior, knowing, voluntary, and written authorization;

        (C) only the individual (or family member if the family member is receiving genetic services) and the licensed health care professional or board certified genetic counselor involved in providing such services receive individually identifiable information concerning the results of such services; and

        (D) any individually identifiable genetic information provided under subparagraph (C) in connection with the services provided under subparagraph (A) is only available for purposes of such services and shall not be disclosed to the employer, labor organization, or joint labor-management committee except in aggregate terms that do not disclose the identity of specific individuals;

    (3) where the employer, labor organization, or joint labor-management committee requests or requires family medical history from the individual to

comply with the certification provisions of section 103 of the Family and Medical Leave Act of 1993 (29 U.S.C. 2613) or such requirements under State family and medical leave laws;

(4) where the employer, labor organization, or joint labor-management committee purchases documents that are commercially and publicly available (including newspapers, magazines, periodicals, and books, but not including medical databases or court records) that include family medical history;

(5) where the information involved is to be used for genetic monitoring of the biological effects of toxic substances in the workplace, but only if—

(A) the employer, labor organization, or joint labor-management committee provides written notice of the genetic monitoring to the individual;

(B)(i) the individual provides prior, knowing, voluntary, and written authorization; or

(ii) the genetic monitoring is required by Federal or State law;

(C) the individual is informed of individual monitoring results;

(D) The Monitoring Is in Compliance With

(i) any Federal genetic monitoring regulations, including any such regulations that may be promulgated by the Secretary of Labor pursuant to the Occupational Safety and Health Act of 1970 (29 U.S.C. 651 et seq.), the Federal Mine Safety and Health Act of 1977 (30 U.S.C. 801 et seq.), or the Atomic Energy Act of 1954 (42 U.S.C. 2011 et seq.); or

(ii) State genetic monitoring regulations, in the case of a State that is implementing genetic monitoring regulations under the authority of the Occupational Safety and Health Act of 1970 (29 U.S.C. 651 et seq.); and

(E) the employer, labor organization, or joint labor-management committee, excluding any licensed health care professional or board certified genetic counselor that is involved in the genetic monitoring program, receives the results of the monitoring only in aggregate terms that do not disclose the identity of specific individuals; or

(6) where the employer conducts DNA analysis for law enforcement purposes as a forensic laboratory or for purposes of human remains identification, and requests or requires genetic information of such employer's apprentices or trainees, but only to the extent that such genetic information is used for analysis of DNA identification markers for quality control to detect sample contamination.

(c) *Preservation of Protections.* In the case of information to which any of paragraphs (1) through (6) of subsection (b) applies, such information may not be used in violation of paragraph (1), (2), or (3) of subsection (a) or treated or disclosed in a manner that violates section 206.

Sec. 206. Confidentiality of Genetic Information

(a) *Treatment of Information as Part of Confidential Medical Record.* — If an employer, employment agency, labor organization, or joint labor-management committee possesses genetic information about an employee or member, such information shall be maintained on separate forms and in separate medical files and be treated as a confidential medical record of the employee or member. An employer, employment agency, labor organization, or joint labor-management committee shall be considered to be in compliance with the maintenance of information requirements of this subsection with respect to genetic information subject to this subsection that is maintained with and treated as a confidential medical record under section 102(d)(3)(B) of the Americans With Disabilities Act (42 U.S.C. 12112(d)(3)(B)).

(b) *Limitation on Disclosure.*—An employer, employment agency, labor organization, or joint labor-management committee shall not disclose genetic information concerning an employee or member except—

(1) to the employee or member of a labor organization (or family member if the family member is receiving the genetic services) at the written request of the employee or member of such organization;

(2) to an occupational or other health researcher if the research is conducted in compliance with the regulations and protections provided for under part 46 of title 45, Code of Federal Regulations;

(3) in response to an order of a court, except that—

(A) the employer, employment agency, labor organization, or joint labor-management committee may disclose only the genetic information expressly authorized by such order; and

(B) if the court order was secured without the knowledge of the employee or member to whom the information refers, the employer, employment agency, labor organization, or joint labor-management committee shall inform the employee or member of the court order and any genetic information that was disclosed pursuant to such order;

(4) to government officials who are investigating compliance with this title if the information is relevant to the investigation;

(5) to the extent that such disclosure is made in connection with the employee's compliance with the certification provisions of section 103 of the Family and Medical Leave Act of 1993 (29 U.S.C. 2613) or such requirements under State family and medical leave laws; or

(6) to a Federal, State, or local public health agency only with regard to information that is described in section 201(4)(A)(iii) and that concerns a contagious disease that presents an imminent hazard of death or life-threatening illness, and that the employee whose family member or family members is or are the subject of a disclosure under this paragraph is notified of such disclosure.

(c) *Relationship to HIPAA Regulations.*—With respect to the regulations promulgated by the Secretary of Health and Human Services under part C of title XI of the Social Security Act (42 U.S.C. 1320d et seq.) and section 264 of the Health Insurance Portability and Accountability Act of 1996 (42 U.S.C. 1320d-2 note), this title does not prohibit a covered entity under such regulations from any use or disclosure of health information that is authorized for the covered entity under such regulations. The previous sentence does not affect the authority of such Secretary to modify such regulations.

Sec. 207. Remedies and Enforcement

(a) *Employees Covered by Title VII of the Civil Rights Act of 1964.*

(1) *In General.* The powers, procedures, and remedies provided in sections 705, 706, 707, 709, 710, and 711 of the Civil Rights Act of 1964 (42 U.S.C. 2000e-4 et seq.) to the Commission, the Attorney General, or any person, alleging a violation of title VII of that Act (42 U.S.C. 2000e et seq.) shall be the powers, procedures, and remedies this title provides to the Commission, the Attorney General, or any person, respectively, alleging an unlawful employment practice in violation of this title against an employee described in section 201(2)(A)(i), except as provided in paragraphs (2) and (3).

(2) *Costs and Fees.* The powers, remedies, and procedures provided in subsections (b) and (c) of section 722 of the Revised Statutes of the United States (42 U.S.C. 1988), shall be powers, remedies, and procedures this title provides to the Commission, the Attorney General, or any person, alleging such a practice.

(3) *Damages.* The powers, remedies, and procedures provided in section 1977A of the Revised Statutes of the United States (42 U.S.C. 1981a), including the limitations contained in subsection (b)(3) of such section 1977A, shall be powers, remedies, and procedures this title provides to the Commission, the Attorney General, or any person, alleging such a practice (not an employment practice specifically excluded from coverage under section 1977A(a)(1) of the Revised Statutes of the United States).

(b) *Employees Covered by Government Employee Rights Act of 1991.*

(1) *In General.* The powers, remedies, and procedures provided in sections 302 and 304 of the Government Employee Rights Act of 1991 (42 U.S.C. 2000e-16b, 2000e-16c) to the Commission, or any person, alleging a violation of section 302(a)(1) of that Act (42 U.S.C. 2000e-16b(a)(1)) shall be the powers, remedies, and procedures this title provides to the Commission, or any person, respectively, alleging an unlawful employment practice in violation of this title against an employee described in section 201(2)(A)(ii), except as provided in paragraphs (2) and (3).

(2) *Costs and Fees.* The powers, remedies, and procedures provided in subsections (b) and (c) of section 722 of the Revised Statutes of the United States (42 U.S.C. 1988), shall be powers, remedies, and procedures this title provides to the Commission, or any person, alleging such a practice.

(3) *Damages.* The powers, remedies, and procedures provided in section 1977A of the Revised Statutes of the United States (42 U.S.C. 1981a), including the limitations contained in subsection (b)(3) of such section 1977A, shall be powers, remedies, and procedures this title provides to the Commission, or any person, alleging such a practice (not an employment practice specifically excluded from coverage under section 1977A(a)(1) of the Revised Statutes of the United States).

(c) *Employees Covered By Congressional Accountability Act of 1995.*

(1) *In General.* The powers, remedies, and procedures provided in the Congressional Accountability Act of 1995 (2 U.S.C. 1301 et seq.) to the Board (as defined in section 101 of that Act (2 U.S.C. 1301)), or any person, alleging

a violation of section 201(a)(1) of that Act (42 U.S.C. 1311(a)(1)) shall be the powers, remedies, and procedures this title provides to that Board, or any person, alleging an unlawful employment practice in violation of this title against an employee described in section 201(2)(A)(iii), except as provided in paragraphs (2) and (3).

(2) *Costs and Fees.* The powers, remedies, and procedures provided in subsections (b) and (c) of section 722 of the Revised Statutes of the United States (42 U.S.C. 1988), shall be powers, remedies, and procedures this title provides to that Board, or any person, alleging such a practice.

(3) *Damages.* The powers, remedies, and procedures provided in section 1977A of the Revised Statutes of the United States (42 U.S.C. 1981a), including the limitations contained in subsection (b)(3) of such section 1977A, shall be powers, remedies, and procedures this title provides to that Board, or any person, alleging such a practice (not an employment practice specifically excluded from coverage under section 1977A(a)(1) of the Revised Statutes of the United States).

(4) *Other Applicable Provisions.* With respect to a claim alleging a practice described in paragraph (1), title III of the Congressional Accountability Act of 1995 (2 U.S.C. 1381 et seq.) shall apply in the same manner as such title applies with respect to a claim alleging a violation of section 201(a)(1) of such Act (2 U.S.C. 1311(a)(1)).

(d) *Employees Covered by Chapter 5 of Title 3, United States Code.*

(1) *In General.* The powers, remedies, and procedures provided in chapter 5 of title 3, United States Code, to the President, the Commission, the Merit Systems Protection Board, or any person, alleging a violation of section 411(a)(1) of that title, shall be the powers, remedies, and procedures this title provides to the President, the Commission, such Board, or any person, respectively, alleging an unlawful employment practice in violation of this title against an employee described in section 201(2)(A)(iv), except as provided in paragraphs (2) and (3).

(2) *Costs And Fees.* The powers, remedies, and procedures provided in subsections (b) and (c) of section 722 of the Revised Statutes of the United States (42 U.S.C. 1988), shall be powers, remedies, and procedures this title provides to the President, the Commission, such Board, or any person, alleging such a practice.

(3) *Damages.* The powers, remedies, and procedures provided in section 1977A of the Revised Statutes of the United States (42 U.S.C. 1981a), including the limitations contained in subsection (b)(3) of such section 1977A, shall be powers, remedies, and procedures this title provides to the President, the Commission, such Board, or any person, alleging such a practice (not an employment practice specifically excluded from coverage under section 1977A(a)(1) of the Revised Statutes of the United States).

(e) *Employees Covered by Section 717 of the Civil Rights Act of 1964.*

(1) *In General.* The powers, remedies, and procedures provided in section 717 of the Civil Rights Act of 1964 (42 U.S.C. 2000e-16) to the Commission, the Attorney General, the Librarian of Congress, or any person,

alleging a violation of that section shall be the powers, remedies, and procedures this title provides to the Commission, the Attorney General, the Librarian of Congress, or any person, respectively, alleging an unlawful employment practice in violation of this title against an employee or applicant described in section 201(2)(A)(v), except as provided in paragraphs (2) and (3).

(2) *Costs and Fees.* The powers, remedies, and procedures provided in subsections (b) and (c) of section 722 of the Revised Statutes of the United States (42 U.S.C. 1988), shall be powers, remedies, and procedures this title provides to the Commission, the Attorney General, the Librarian of Congress, or any person, alleging such a practice.

(3) *Damages.* The powers, remedies, and procedures provided in section 1977A of the Revised Statutes of the United States (42 U.S.C. 1981a), including the limitations contained in subsection (b)(3) of such section 1977A, shall be powers, remedies, and procedures this title provides to the Commission, the Attorney General, the Librarian of Congress, or any person, alleging such a practice (not an employment practice specifically excluded from coverage under section 1977A(a)(1) of the Revised Statutes of the United States).

(f) *Prohibition Against Retaliation.* No person shall discriminate against any individual because such individual has opposed any act or practice made unlawful by this title or because such individual made a charge, testified, assisted, or participated in any manner in an investigation, proceeding, or hearing under this title. The remedies and procedures otherwise provided for under this section shall be available to aggrieved individuals with respect to violations of this subsection.

(g) *Definition.* In this section, the term "Commission" means the Equal Employment Opportunity Commission.

Sec. 208. *Disparate Impact*

(a) *General Rule.* Notwithstanding any other provision of this Act, "disparate impact", as that term is used in section 703(k) of the Civil Rights Act of 1964 (42 U.S.C. 2000e-2(k)), on the basis of genetic information does not establish a cause of action under this Act.

(b) *Commission.* On the date that is 6 years after the date of enactment of this Act, there shall be established a commission, to be known as the Genetic Nondiscrimination Study Commission (referred to in this section as the "Commission") to review the developing science of genetics and to make recommendations to Congress regarding whether to provide a disparate impact cause of action under this Act.

(c) *Membership.*

(1) *In General.* The Commission shall be composed of 8 members, of which —

(A) 1 member shall be appointed by the Majority Leader of the Senate;

(B) 1 member shall be appointed by the Minority Leader of the Senate;

(C) 1 member shall be appointed by the Chairman of the Committee on Health, Education, Labor, and Pensions of the Senate;

(D) 1 member shall be appointed by the ranking minority member of the Committee on Health, Education, Labor, and Pensions of the Senate;

(E) 1 member shall be appointed by the Speaker of the House of Representatives;

(F) 1 member shall be appointed by the Minority Leader of the House of Representatives;

(G) 1 member shall be appointed by the Chairman of the Committee on Education and Labor of the House of Representatives; and

(H) 1 member shall be appointed by the ranking minority member of the Committee on Education and Labor of the House of Representatives.

(2) *Compensation and Expenses.* The members of the Commission shall not receive compensation for the performance of services for the Commission, but shall be allowed travel expenses, including per diem in lieu of subsistence, at rates authorized for employees of agencies under subchapter I of chapter 57 of title 5, United States Code, while away from their homes or regular places of business in the performance of services for the Commission.

(d) *Administrative Provisions.*

(1) *Location.* The Commission shall be located in a facility maintained by the Equal Employment Opportunity Commission.

(2) *Detail of Government Employees.* Any Federal Government employee may be detailed to the Commission without reimbursement, and such detail shall be without interruption or loss of civil service status or privilege.

(3) *Information from Federal Agencies.* The Commission may secure directly from any Federal department or agency such information as the Commission considers necessary to carry out the provisions of this section. Upon request of the Commission, the head of such department or agency shall furnish such information to the Commission.

(4) *Hearings.* The Commission may hold such hearings, sit and act at such times and places, take such testimony, and receive such evidence as the Commission considers advisable to carry out the objectives of this section, except that, to the extent possible, the Commission shall use existing data and research.

(5) *Postal Services.* The Commission may use the United States mails in the same manner and under the same conditions as other departments and agencies of the Federal Government.

(e) *Report.* Not later than 1 year after all of the members are appointed to the Commission under subsection (c)(1), the Commission shall submit to Congress a report that summarizes the findings of the Commission and makes such recommendations for legislation as are consistent with this Act.

(f) *Authorization of Appropriations.* There are authorized to be appropriated to the Equal Employment Opportunity Commission such sums as may be necessary to carry out this section.

Sec. 209. *Construction*

(a) *In General.* Nothing in this title shall be construed to—

(1) limit the rights or protections of an individual under any other Federal or State statute that provides equal or greater protection to an individual than the rights or protections provided for under this title, including the protections of an individual under the Americans with Disabilities Act of 1990 (42 U.S.C. 12101 et seq.) (including coverage afforded to individuals under section 102 of such Act (42 U.S.C. 12112)), or under the Rehabilitation Act of 1973 (29 U.S.C. 701 et seq.);

(2)(A) limit the rights or protections of an individual to bring an action under this title against an employer, employment agency, labor organization, or joint labor-management committee for a violation of this title; or

(B) provide for enforcement of, or penalties for violation of, any requirement or prohibition applicable to any employer, employment agency, labor organization, or joint labor-management committee subject to enforcement for a violation under—

(i) the amendments made by title I of this Act;

(ii)(I) subsection (a) of section 701 of the Employee Retirement Income Security Act of 1974 as such section applies with respect to genetic information pursuant to subsection (b)(1)(B) of such section;

(II) section 702(a)(1)(F) of such Act; or

(III) section 702(b)(1) of such Act as such section applies with respect to genetic information as a health status-related factor;

(iii)(I) subsection (a) of section 2701 of the Public Health Service Act as such section applies with respect to genetic information pursuant to subsection (b)(1)(B) of such section;

(II) section 2702(a)(1)(F) of such Act; or

(III) section 2702(b)(1) of such Act as such section applies with respect to genetic information as a health status-related factor; or

(iv)(I) subsection (a) of section 9801 of the Internal Revenue Code of 1986 as such section applies with respect to genetic information pursuant to subsection (b)(1)(B) of such section;

(II) section 9802(a)(1)(F) of such Act; or

(III) section 9802(b)(1) of such Act as such section applies with respect to genetic information as a health status-related factor;

(3) apply to the Armed Forces Repository of Specimen Samples for the Identification of Remains;

(4) limit or expand the protections, rights, or obligations of employees or employers under applicable workers' compensation laws;

(5) limit the authority of a Federal department or agency to conduct or sponsor occupational or other health research that is conducted in compliance with the regulations contained in part 46 of title 45, Code of Federal Regulations (or any corresponding or similar regulation or rule);

(6) limit the statutory or regulatory authority of the Occupational Safety and Health Administration or the Mine Safety and Health Administration to promulgate or enforce workplace safety and health laws and regulations; or

(7) require any specific benefit for an employee or member or a family member of an employee or member under any group health plan or health insurance issuer offering group health insurance coverage in connection with a group health plan.

(b) *Genetic Information of a Fetus or Embryo*. Any reference in this title to genetic information concerning an individual or family member of an individual shall —

(1) with respect to such an individual or family member of an individual who is a pregnant woman, include genetic information of any fetus carried by such pregnant woman; and

(2) with respect to an individual or family member utilizing an assisted reproductive technology, include genetic information of any embryo legally held by the individual or family member.

(c) *Relation to Authorities Under Title* I. With respect to a group health plan, or a health insurance issuer offering group health insurance coverage in connection with a group health plan, this title does not prohibit any activity of such plan or issuer that is authorized for the plan or issuer under any provision of law referred to in clauses (i) through (iv) of subsection (a)(2)(B).

Sec. 210. Medical Information That Is Not Genetic Information

An employer, employment agency, labor organization, or joint labor-management committee shall not be considered to be in violation of this title based on the use, acquisition, or disclosure of medical information that is not genetic information about a manifested disease, disorder, or pathological condition of an employee or member, including a manifested disease, disorder, or pathological condition that has or may have a genetic basis.

Sec. 211. Regulations

Not later than 1 year after the date of enactment of this title, the Commission shall issue final regulations to carry out this title.

Sec. 212. Authorization of Appropriations

There are authorized to be appropriated such sums as may be necessary to carry out this title (except for section 208).

Sec. 213. Effective Date

This title takes effect on the date that is 18 months after the date of enactment of this Act.

Immigration Reform and Control Act

8 U.S.C. §1324b

§1324b. Unfair Immigration-Related Employment Practices

(a) *Prohibition of Discrimination Based on National Origin or Citizenship Status.*

(1) *General rule.* It is unfair immigration-related employment practice for a person or other entity to discriminate against any individual (other than an unauthorized alien) with respect to the hiring, or recruitment or referral for a fee, of the individual for employment or the discharging of the individual from employment

   (A) because of such individual's national origin, or

   (B) in the case of a protected individual (as defined in paragraph (3)), because of such individual's citizenship status.

(2) *Exceptions.* Paragraph (1) shall not apply to

   (A) a person or other entity that employs three or fewer employees,

   (B) a person's or entity's discrimination because of an individual's national origin if the discrimination with respect to that person or entity and that individual is covered under section 703 of the Civil Rights Act of 1964, or

   (C) discrimination because of citizenship status which is otherwise required in order to comply with law, regulation, or executive order, or required by Federal, State, or local government contract, or which the Attorney General determines to be essential for an employer to do business with an agency or department of the Federal, State, or local government.

(3) *"Protected individual" defined.* As used in paragraph (1), the term "protected individual" means an individual who

   (A) is a citizen or national of the United States, or

   (B) is an alien who is lawfully admitted for permanent residence, is granted the status of an alien lawfully admitted for temporary residence under section 210(1), 210A(a), or 245A(a)(1), is admitted as a refugee under section 207, or is granted asylum under section 208; but does not include (i) an alien who fails to apply for naturalization within six months of the date the alien first becomes eligible (by virtue of period of lawful permanent residence) to apply for naturalization or, if later, within six months after the date of the enactment of this section and (ii) an alien who has applied on a timely basis, but has not been naturalized as a citizen within 2 years after the date of the application, unless the alien can establish that the alien is actively pursuing naturalization, except that time consumed in the Service's processing the application shall not be counted toward the 2-year period.

(4) *Additional exception providing right to prefer equally qualified citizens.* Notwithstanding any other provision of this section, it is not an unfair immigration-related employment practice for a person or other entity to prefer to hire, recruit, or refer an individual who is a citizen or national of the United States over another individual who is an alien if the two individuals are equally qualified.

(5) *Prohibition of intimidation or retaliation.* It is also an unfair immigration-related employment practice for a person or other entity to intimidate, threaten, coerce, or retaliate against any individual for the purpose of interfering with any right or privilege secured under this section or because the individual intends to file or has filed a charge or a complaint, testified, assisted, or participated in any manner in an investigation, proceeding, or hearing under section. An individual so intimidated, threatened, coerced, or retaliated against shall be considered, for purposes of subsections (d) and (g), to have been discriminated against.

(6) *Treatment of certain documentary practices as employment practices.* A person's or other entity's request, for purposes of satisfying the requirements of section 274A(b) [8 U.S.C. §1324A(b)] of this title, for more or different documents than are required under such section or refusing to honor documents tendered that on their face reasonably appear to be genuine shall be treated as an unfair immigration-related employment practice if made for the purpose or with the intent of discriminating against an individual in violation of paragraph (1).

(b) *Charges of Violations.*

(1) *In general.* Except as provided in paragraph (2), any person alleging that the person is adversely affected directly by an unfair immigration-related employment practice (or a person on that person's behalf) or an officer of the Service alleging that an unfair immigration-related employment practice has occurred or is occurring may file a charge respecting such practice or violation with the Special Counsel (appointed under subsection (c)). Charges shall be in writing under oath or affirmation and shall contain such information as the Attorney General requires. The Special Counsel by certified mail shall serve a notice of the charge (including the date, place, and circumstances of the alleged unfair immigration-related employment practice) on the person or entity involved within 10 days.

(2) *No overlap with EEOC complaints.* No charge may be filed respecting an unfair immigration-related employment practice described in subsection

(a)(1)(A) if a charge with respect to that practice based on the same set of facts has been filed with the Equal Employment Opportunity Commission under title VII of the Civil Rights Act of 1964, unless the charge is dismissed as being outside the scope of such title. No charge respecting an employment practice may be filed with the Equal Employment Opportunity Commission under such title if a charge with respect to such practice based on the same set of facts has been filed under this subsection, unless the charge is dismissed under this section as being outside the scope of this section.

(c) *Special Counsel*.

(1) *Appointment*. The President shall appoint, by and with the advice and consent of the Senate, a Special Counsel for Immigration-Related Unfair Employment Practices (hereinafter in this section referred to as the "Special Counsel") within the Department of Justice to serve for a term of four years. In the case of a vacancy in the office of the Special Counsel the President may designate the officer or employee who shall act as Special Counsel during such vacancy.

(2) *Duties*. The Special Counsel shall be responsible for investigation of charges and issuance of complaints under this section and in respect of the prosecution of all such complaints before administrative law judges and the exercise of certain functions under subsection (j)(1).

(3) *Compensation*. The Special Counsel is entitled to receive compensation at a rate not to exceed the rate now or hereafter provided for grade GS-17 of the General Schedule, under section 5332 of title 5, United States Code.

(4) *Regional offices*. The Special Counsel, in accordance with regulations of the Attorney General, shall establish such regional offices as may be necessary to carry out his duties.

(d) *Investigation of Charges*.

(1) *By special counsel*. The Special Counsel shall investigate each charge received and, within 120 days of the date of the receipt of the charge, determine whether or not there is reasonable cause to believe that the charge is true and whether or not to bring a complaint with respect to the charge before an administrative law judge. The Special Counsel may, on his own initiative, conduct investigations respecting unfair immigration-related employment practices and, based on such an investigation and subject to paragraph (3), file a complaint before such a judge.

(2) *Private actions*. If the Special Counsel, after receiving such a charge respecting an unfair immigration-related employment practice which alleges knowing and intentional discriminatory activity or a pattern or practice of discriminatory activity, has not filed a complaint before an administrative law judge with respect to such charge within such 120-day period, the Special Counsel shall notify the person making the charge of the determination not to file such a complaint during such period and the person making the charge may (subject to paragraph (3)) file a complaint directly before such a judge within 90 days after the date of receipt of the notice. The Special Counsel's failure to file such a complaint within such 120-day period shall not

affect the right of the Special Counsel to investigate the charge or to bring a complaint before an administrative judge during such 90-day period.

(3) *Time limitations on complaints.* No complaint may be filed respecting any unfair immigration-related employment practice occurring more than 180 days prior to the date of the filing of the charge with the Special Counsel. This subparagraph shall not prevent the subsequent amending of a charge or complaint under subsection (e)(1) of this section.

(e) *Hearings.*

(1) *Notice.* Whenever a complaint is made that a person or entity has engaged in or is engaging in any such unfair immigration-related employment practice, an administrative law judge shall have power to issue and cause to be served upon such person or entity a copy of the complaint and a notice of hearing before the judge at a place therein fixed, not less than five days after the serving of the complaint. Any such complaint may be amended by the judge conducting the hearing, upon the motion of the party filing the complaint, in the judge's discretion at any time prior to the issuance of an order based thereon. The person or entity so complained of shall have the right to file an answer to the original or amended complaint and to appear in person or otherwise and give testimony at the place and time fixed in the complaint.

(2) *Judges hearing cases.* Hearings on complaints under this subsection shall be considered before administrative law judges who are specially designated by the Attorney General as having special training respecting employment discrimination and, to the extent practicable, before such judges who only consider cases under this section.

(3) *Complainant as party.* Any person filing a charge with the Special Counsel respecting an unfair immigration-related employment practice shall be considered a party to any complaint before an administrative law judge respecting such practice and any subsequent appeal respecting that complaint. In the discretion of the judge conducting the hearing, any other person may be allowed to intervene in the proceeding and to present testimony.

(f) *Testimony and Authority of Hearing Officers.*

(1) *Testimony.* The testimony taken by the administrative law judge shall be reduced to writing. Thereafter, the judge, in his discretion, upon notice may provide for the taking of further testimony or hear argument.

(2) *Authority of administrative law judges.* In conducting investigations and hearings under this subsection and in accordance with regulations of the Attorney General, the Special Counsel and administrative law judges shall have reasonable access to examine evidence of any person or entity being investigated. The administrative law judges by subpoena may compel the attendance of witnesses and the production of evidence at any designated place or hearing. In case of contumacy or refusal to obey a subpoena lawfully issued under this paragraph and upon application of the administrative law judge, an appropriate district court of the United States may issue an order requiring compliance with such subpoena and any failure to obey such order may be punished by such court as a contempt thereof.

(g) *Determinations.*

(1) *Order.* The administrative law judge shall issue and cause to be served on the parties to the proceeding an order, which shall be final unless appealed as provided under subsection (i).

(2) *Orders finding violations.*

(A) *In general.* If, upon the preponderance of the evidence, an administrative law judge determines that any person or entity named in the complaint has engaged in or is engaging in any such unfair immigration-related employment practice, then the judge shall state his findings of fact and shall issue and cause to be served on such person or entity an order which requires such person or entity to cease and desist from such unfair immigration-related employment practice.

(B) *Contents of order.* Such an order also may require the person or entity

(i) to comply with the requirements of section 274A(b) [8 U.S.C. §1324a(b)] with respect to individuals hired (or recruited or referred for employment for a fee) during a period of up to three years;

(ii) to retain for the period referred to in clause (i) and only for purposes consistent with section 274A(b)(5), the name and address of each individual who applies, in person or in writing, for hiring of an existing position, or for recruiting or referring for a fee, for employment in the United States;

(iii) to hire individuals directly and adversely affected, with or without back pay;

(iv)(I) except as provided in subclauses (III) through (IV), to pay a civil penalty of not less than $250 and not more than $2,000 for each individual discriminated against,

(II) except as provided in subclauses (III) and (IV), in the case of a person or entity previously subject to a single order under this paragraph, to pay a civil penalty of not less than $2,000 and not more than $5,000 for each individual discriminated against,

(III) except as provided in subclause (IV), in the case of a person or entity previously subject to more than one order under this paragraph, to pay a civil penalty of not less than $3,000 and not more than $10,000 for each individual discriminated against, and

(IV) in the case of an unfair immigration-related employment practice described in subsection (a)(6), to pay a civil penalty of not less than $100 and not more than $1,000 for each individual discriminated against;

(v) to post notices to employees about their rights under this section and employers' obligations under section 274A [8 U.S.C. §1324a];

(vi) to educate all personnel involved in hiring and complying with this section or section 274A about the requirements of this section or such section;

(vii) to remove (in an appropriate case) a false performance review or false warning from an employees personnel file; and

(viii) to lift (in an appropriate case) any restrictions on any employee's assignments, work shifts, or movements.

(C) *Limitation on back pay remedy.* In providing a remedy under subparagraph (B)(iii), back pay liability shall not accrue from a date more than two years prior to the date of the filing of a charge with an administrative law judge. Interim earnings or amounts earnable with reasonable diligence by the individual or individuals discriminated against shall operate to reduce the back pay otherwise allowable under such subparagraph. No order shall require the hiring of an individual as an employee or the payment to an individual of any back pay, if the individual was refused employment for any reason other than discrimination on account of national origin or citizenship status.

(D) *Treatment of distinct entities.* In applying this subsection in the case of a person or entity composed of distinct, physically separate subdivisions each of which provides separately for the hiring, recruiting, or referring for employment, without reference to the practices of, and not under the control of or common control with, another subdivision, each such subdivision shall be considered a separate person or entity.

(3) *Orders not finding violations.* If upon the preponderance of the evidence an administrative law judge determines that the person or entity named in the complaint has not engaged and is not engaging in any such unfair immigration-related employment practice, then the judge shall state his findings of fact and shall issue an order dismissing the complaint.

(h) *Awarding of Attorney's Fees.* In any complaint respecting an unfair immigration-related employment practice, an administrative law judge, in the judge's discretion, may allow a prevailing party, other than the United States, a reasonable attorney's fee, if the losing party's argument is without reasonable foundation in law and fact.

(i) *Review of Final Orders.*

(1) *In general.* Not later than 60 days after the entry of such final order, any person aggrieved by such final order may seek a review of such order in the United States court of appeals for the circuit in which the violation is alleged to have occurred or in which the employer resides or transacts business.

(2) Further review. Upon the filing of the record with the court, the jurisdiction of the court shall be exclusive and its judgment shall be final, except that the same shall be subject to review by the Supreme Court of the United States upon writ of certiorari or certification as provided in section 1254 of title 28, United States Code.

(j) *Court Enforcement of Administrative Orders.*

(1) *In general.* If an order of the agency is not appealed under subsection (i)(1), the Special Counsel (or, if the Special Counsel fails to act, the person filing the charge) may petition the United States district court for the district in which a violation of the order is alleged to have occurred, or in which the

respondent resides or transacts business, for the enforcement of the order of the administrative law judge, by filing in such court a written petition praying that such order be enforced.

(2) *Court enforcement order.* Upon the filing of such petition, the court shall have jurisdiction to make and enter a decree enforcing the order of the administrative law judge. In such a proceeding, the order of the administrative law judge shall not be subject to review.

(3) Enforcement decree in original review. If, upon appeal of an order under subsection (i)(1), the United States court of appeals does not reverse such order, such court shall have the jurisdiction to make and enter a decree enforcing the order of the administrative law judge.

(4) *Awarding of attorney's fees.* In any judicial proceeding under subsection (i) or this subsection, the court, in its discretion, may allow a prevailing party, other than the United States, a reasonable attorney's fee a part of costs but only if the losing party's argument is without reasonable foundation in law and fact.

(k) *Termination Dates.*

(1) This section shall not apply to discrimination in hiring, recruiting, referring, or discharging of individuals occurring after the date of any termination of the provisions of section 274A [8 U.S.C. §1324a], under subsection (1) of that section.

(2) The provisions of this section shall terminate 30 calendar days after receipt of the last report required to be transmitted under section 274A(j) if

(A) the Comptroller General determines, and so reports in such report that

(i) no significant discrimination has resulted, against citizens or nationals of the United States or against any eligible workers seeking employment, from the implementation of section 274A, or

(ii) such section has created an unreasonable burden on employers hiring such workers; and

(B) there has been enacted, within such period of 30 calendar days, a joint resolution stating in substance that the Congress approves the findings of the Comptroller General contained in such report. . . .*

---

* [Editor's Note: Public Law No. 99-603, which enacted these provisions, also provided in §101(b):

(b) No effect on EEOC authority. — Except as may be specifically provided in this section, nothing in this section shall be construed to restrict the authority of the Equal Employment Opportunity Commission to investigate allegations, in writing and under oath or affirmation, of unlawful employment practices, as provided in section 706 of the Civil Rights Act of 1964 or any other authority provided therein.]

Lilly Ledbetter Fair Pay Act of 2009

Pub. L. No. 111-2, 123 Stat. 5

[Editors' Note: The Lilly Ledbetter Fair Pay Act of 2009 amended a number of statutes, most notably Title VII and the ADEA. These amendments have been incorporated in the relevant statutes as they are reproduced in the Supplement. The Fair Pay Act, however, is reproduced here for ease of reference.]

Be it enacted by the Senate and House of Representatives of the United States of America in Congress assembled,

Sec. 1. Short Title

This Act may be cited as the "Lilly Ledbetter Fair Pay Act of 2009".

Sec. 2. Findings

Congress finds the following:

(1) The Supreme Court in *Ledbetter v. Goodyear Tire & Rubber Co., 550 U.S. 618 (2007),* significantly impairs statutory protections against discrimination in compensation that Congress established and that have been bedrock principles of American law for decades. The Ledbetter decision undermines those statutory protections by unduly restricting the time period in which victims of discrimination can challenge and recover for discriminatory compensation decisions or other practices, contrary to the intent of Congress.

(2) The limitation imposed by the Court on the filing of discriminatory compensation claims ignores the reality of wage discrimination and is at odds with the robust application of the civil rights laws that Congress intended.

(3) With regard to any charge of discrimination under any law, nothing in this Act is intended to preclude or limit an aggrieved person's right to introduce evidence of an unlawful employment practice that has occurred outside the time for filing a charge of discrimination.

(4) Nothing in this Act is intended to change current law treatment of when pension distributions are considered paid.

Sec. 3. *Discrimination in Compensation Because of Race, Color, Religion, Sex, or National Origin*

Section 706(e) of the Civil Rights Act of 1964 (*42 U.S.C. 2000e-5(e)*) is amended by adding at the end the following:

"(3)(A) For purposes of this section, an unlawful employment practice occurs, with respect to discrimination in compensation in violation of this title, when a discriminatory compensation decision or other practice is adopted, when an individual becomes subject to a discriminatory compensation decision or other practice, or when an individual is affected by application of a discriminatory compensation decision or other practice, including each time wages, benefits, or other compensation is paid, resulting in whole or in part from such a decision or other practice.

"(B) In addition to any relief authorized by section 1977A of the Revised Statutes (*42 U.S.C. 1981a*), liability may accrue and an aggrieved person may obtain relief as provided in subsection (g)(1), including recovery of back pay for up to two years preceding the filing of the charge, where the unlawful employment practices that have occurred during the charge filing period are similar or related to unlawful employment practices with regard to discrimination in compensation that occurred outside the time for filing a charge.".

Sec. 4. *Discrimination in Compensation Because of Age*

Section 7(d) of the Age Discrimination in Employment Act of 1967 (*29 U.S.C. 626(d)*) is amended—
(1) in the first sentence—
(A) by redesignating paragraphs (1) and (2) as subparagraphs (A) and (B), respectively; and
(B) by striking "(d)" and inserting "(d)(1)";
(2) in the third sentence, by striking "Upon" and inserting the following: "(2) Upon"; and
(3) by adding at the end the following:

"(3) For purposes of this section, an unlawful practice occurs, with respect to discrimination in compensation in violation of this Act, when a discriminatory compensation decision or other practice is adopted, when a person becomes subject to a discriminatory compensation decision or other practice, or when a person is affected by application of a discriminatory compensation decision or other practice, including each time wages, benefits, or other compensation is paid, resulting in whole or in part from such a decision or other practice.".

Sec. 5. *Application to Other Laws*

(a) Americans With Disabilities Act of 1990.—The amendments made by section 3 shall apply to claims of discrimination in compensation brought under title I and section 503 of the Americans with Disabilities Act of 1990 (*42 U.S.C. 12111* et seq., *12203*), pursuant to section 107(a) of such Act (*42 U.S.C. 12117(a)*), which adopts the powers, remedies, and procedures set forth in section 706 of the Civil Rights Act of 1964 (*42 U.S.C. 2000e-5*).

(b) Rehabilitation Act of 1973.—The amendments made by section 3 shall apply to claims of discrimination in compensation brought under sections 501 and 504 of the Rehabilitation Act of 1973 (*29 U.S.C. 791, 794*), pursuant to—

(1) sections 501(g) and 504(d) of such Act (*29 U.S.C. 791(g), 794(d)*), respectively, which adopt the standards applied under title I of the Americans with Disabilities Act of 1990 for determining whether a violation has occurred in a complaint alleging employment discrimination; and

(2) paragraphs (1) and (2) of section 505(a) of such Act (*29 U.S.C. 794a(a)*) (as amended by subsection (c)).

(c) Conforming Amendments.—

(1) Rehabilitation act of 1973.—Section 505(a) of the Rehabilitation Act of 1973 (*29 U.S.C. 794a(a)*) is amended—

(A) in paragraph (1), by inserting after "(*42 U.S.C. 2000e-5 (f)* through (k))" the following: "(and the application of section 706(e)(3) (*42 U.S.C. 2000e-5(e)(3)*) to claims of discrimination in compensation)"; and

(B) in paragraph (2), by inserting after "1964" the following: "(*42 U.S.C. 2000d* et seq.) (and in subsection (e)(3) of section 706 of such Act (*42 U.S.C. 2000e-5*), applied to claims of discrimination in compensation)".

(2) Civil rights act of 1964.—Section 717 of the Civil Rights Act of 1964 (*42 U.S.C. 2000e-16*) is amended by adding at the end the following:

"(f) Section 706(e)(3) shall apply to complaints of discrimination in compensation under this section.".

(3) Age discrimination in employment act of 1967.—Section 15(f) of the Age Discrimination in Employment Act of 1967 (*29 U.S.C. 633a(f)*) is amended by striking "of section" and inserting "of sections 7(d)(3) and".

Sec. 6. Effective Date

This Act, and the amendments made by this Act, take effect as if enacted on May 28, 2007 and apply to all claims of discrimination in compensation under title VII of the Civil Rights Act of 1964 (*42 U.S.C. 2000e* et seq.), the Age Discrimination in Employment Act of 1967 (*29 U.S.C. 621* et seq.), title I and section 503 of the Americans with Disabilities Act of 1990, and sections 501 and 504 of the Rehabilitation Act of 1973, that are pending on or after that date.

National Labor Relations Act

29 U.S.C. §§151-169

§151. Findings and Declaration of Policy

The denial by some employers of the right of employees to organize and the refusal by some employees to accept the procedure of collective bargaining lead to strikes and other forms of industrial strife or unrest, which have the intent or the necessary effect of burdening or obstructing commerce by (a) impairing the efficiency, safety, or operation of the instrumentalities of commerce; (b) occurring in the current of commerce; (c) materially affecting, restraining, or controlling the flow of raw materials or manufactured or processed goods from or into the channels of commerce, or the prices of such materials or goods in commerce; or (d) causing diminution of employment and wages in such volume as substantially to impair or disrupt the market for goods flowing from or into the channels of commerce.

The inequality of bargaining power between employees who do not possess full freedom of association or actual liberty of contract, and employers who are organized in the corporate or other forms of ownership association substantially burdens and affects the flow of commerce, and tends to aggravate recurrent business depressions, by depressing wage rates and the purchasing power of wage earners in industry and by preventing the stabilization of competitive wage rates and working conditions within and between industries.

Experience has proved that protection of law of the right of employees to organize and bargain collectively safeguards commerce from injury, impairment, or interruption, and promotes the flow of commerce by removing certain recognized sources of industrial strife and unrest, by encouraging practices fundamental to the friendly adjustment of industrial disputes arising out of differences as to wages, hours, or other working conditions, and by restoring equality of bargaining power between employers and employees.

Experience has further demonstrated that certain practices by some labor organizations, their offices, and members have the intent or the necessary effect of burdening or obstructing commerce by preventing the free flow of goods in such commerce through strikes and other forms of industrial unrest or through concerted activities which impair the interest of the public in the free flow of such commerce. The elimination of such practices is a necessary condition to the assurance of the rights herein guaranteed.

It is hereby declared to be the policy of the United States to eliminate the causes of certain substantial obstructions to the free flow of commerce and to mitigate and eliminate these obstructions when they have occurred by encouraging the practice and procedure of collective bargaining and by protecting the exercise by workers of full freedom of association, self-organization, and designation of representatives of their own choosing, for the purpose of negotiating the terms and conditions of their employment or other mutual aid or protection.

§152. *Definitions*

When used in this subchapter

(1) The term "person" includes one or more individuals, labor organizations, partnerships, associations, corporations, legal representatives, trustees, trustees in cases under Title 11, or receivers.

(2) The term "employer" includes any person acting as an agent of an employer, directly or indirectly, but shall not include the United States or any wholly owned Government corporation, or any Federal Reserve Bank, or any State or political subdivision thereof, or any person subject to the Railway Labor Act [45 U.S.C.A. §151 et seq.], as amended from time to time, or any labor organization (other than when acting as an employer), or anyone acting in the capacity of officer or agent of such labor organization.

(3) The term "employee" shall include any employer, and shall not be limited to the employees of a particular employer, unless this subchapter explicitly states otherwise, and shall include any individual whose work has ceased as a consequence of, or in connection with, any current labor dispute or because of any unfair labor practice, and who has not obtained any other regular and substantially equivalent employment, but shall not include any individual employed as an agricultural laborer, or in the domestic service of any family or person at his home, or any individual employed by his parent or spouse, or any individual employed as a supervisor, or any individual employed by an employer subject to the Railway Labor Act, as amended from time to time, or by any other person who is not an employer as herein defined.

(4) The term "representatives" includes any individual or labor organization.

(5) The term "labor organization" means any organization of any kind, or any agency or employee representation committee or plan, in which employees participate and which exists for the purpose, in whole or in part, of dealing with employers concerning grievances, labor disputes, wages, rates of pay, hours of employment, or conditions of work.

(6) The term "commerce" means trade, tariff, commerce, transportation, or communication among the several States, or between the District of

Columbia or any Territory of the United States and any State or other Territory, or between any foreign country and any State, Territory, or the District of Columbia, or within the District of Columbia or any Territory, or between points in the same State but through any other State or any Territory or the District of Columbia or any foreign country.

(7) The term "affecting commerce" means in commerce, or burdening or obstructing commerce or the free flow of commerce, or having led or tending to lead to a labor dispute burdening or obstructing commerce or the free flow of commerce.

(8) The term "unfair labor practice" means any unfair labor practice listed in section 158 of this title.

(9) The term "labor dispute" includes any controversy concerning terms, tenure or conditions of employment, or concerning the association or representation of persons in negotiating, fixing, maintaining, changing, or seeking to arrange terms or conditions of employment, regardless of whether the disputants stand in the proximate relation of employer and employee.

(10) The term "National Labor Relations Board" means the National Labor Relations Board provided for in section 153 of this title.

(11) The term "supervisor" means any individual having authority, in the interest of the employer, to hire, transfer, suspend, lay off, recall, promote, discharge, assign, reward, or discipline other employees, or responsibly to direct them, or to adjust their grievances, or effectively to recommend such action, if in connection with the foregoing the exercise of such authority is not of a merely routine or clerical nature, but requires the use of independent judgment.

(12) The term "professional employee" means

(A) any employee engaged in work (i) predominately intellectual and varied in character as opposed to routine mental, manual, mechanical, or physical work; (ii) involving the consistent exercise of discretion and judgment in its performance; (iii) of such a character that the output produced or the result accomplished cannot be standardized in relation to a given period of time; (iv) requiring knowledge of an advanced type in a field of science or learning customarily acquired by a prolonged course of specialized intellectual instruction and study in an institution of higher learning or a hospital, as distinguished from a general academic education or from an apprenticeship or from training in the performance of routine mental, manual, or physical processes; or

(B) any employee, who (i) has completed the courses of specialized intellectual instruction and study described in clause (iv) of paragraph (A), and (ii) is performing related work under the supervision of a professional person to qualify himself to become a professional employee as defined in paragraph (A).

(13) In determining whether any person is acting as an "agent" of another person so as to make such other person responsible for his acts, the question of whether the specific acts performed were actually authorized or subsequently ratified shall not be controlling.

(14) The term "health care institution" shall include any hospital, convalescent hospital, health maintenance organization, health clinic, nursing home, extended care facility, or other institution devoted to the care of sick, infirm, or aged person.

§153. National Labor Relations Board

(a) *Creation, composition, appointment, and tenure; Chairman; removal of members.* The National Labor Relations Board (hereinafter called the "Board") created by this subchapter prior to its amendment by the Labor Management Relations Act, 1947, is continued as an agency of the United States, except that the Board shall consist of five instead of three members, appointed by the President by and with the advice and consent of the Senate. Of the two additional members so provided for, one shall be appointed for a term of five years and the other for a term of two years. Their successors, and the successors of the other members, shall be appointed for terms of five years each, excepting that any individual chosen to fill a vacancy shall be appointed only for the unexpired term of the member whom he shall succeed. The President shall designate one member to serve as Chairman of the Board. Any member of the Board may be removed by the President, upon notice and hearing, for neglect of duty or malfeasance in office, but for no other cause.

(b) *Delegation of powers to members and regional directors; review and stay of actions of regional directors; quorum; seal.* The Board is authorized to delegate to any group of three or more members any or all of the powers which it may itself exercise. The Board is also authorized to delegate to its regional directors its powers under section 159 of this title to determine the unit appropriate for the purpose of collective bargaining, to investigate and provide for hearings, and determine whether a question of representation exists, and to direct an election or take a secret ballot under subsection (c) or (e) of section 159 of this title and certify the results thereof, except that upon the filing of a request therefor with the Board by any interested person, the Board may review any action of a regional director delegated to him under this paragraph, but such a review shall not, unless specifically ordered by the Board, operate as a stay of any action taken by the regional director. A vacancy in the Board shall not impair the right of the remaining members to exercise all of the powers of the Board, and three members of the Board shall, at all times, constitute a quorum of the Board, except that two members shall constitute a quorum of any group designated pursuant to the first sentence hereof. The Board shall have an official seal which shall be judicially noticed.

(c) *Annual reports to Congress and the President.* The Board shall at the close of each fiscal year make a report in writing to Congress and to the President summarizing significant case activities and operations for that fiscal year.

(d) *General Counsel; appointment and tenure; powers and duties; vacancy.* There shall be a General Counsel of the Board who shall be appointed by the President, by and with the advice and consent of the Senate, for a term of four years. The General Counsel of the Board shall exercise general supervision over all attorneys employed by the Board (other than administrative law judges and legal assistants to Board members) and over the officers and employees in the regional offices. He shall have final authority, on behalf of the Board, in respect of the investigation of charges and issuance of complaints under section 160 of this title, and in respect of the prosecution of such complaints before the Board, and shall have such other duties as the Board may prescribe or as may be provided by law. In case of a vacancy in the office of the General Counsel the President is authorized to designate the officer or employee who shall act as General Counsel during such vacancy, but no person or persons so designated shall so act (1) for more than forty days when the Congress is in session unless a nomination to fill such vacancy shall have been submitted to the Senate, or (2) after the adjournment sine die of the session of the Senate in which such nomination was submitted.

§154. National Labor Relations Board; Eligibility for Reappointment; Officers and Employees; Payment of Expenses

(a) Each member of the Board and the General Council of the Board shall be eligible for reappointment, and shall not engage in any other business, vocation, or employment. The Board shall appoint an executive secretary, and such attorneys, examiners, and regional directors, and such other employees as it may from time to time find necessary for the proper performance of its duties. The Board may not employ any attorneys for the purpose of reviewing transcripts of hearings or preparing drafts of opinions except that any attorney employed for assignment as a legal assistant to any Board member may for such Board member review such transcripts and prepare such drafts. No administrative law judge's report shall be reviewed, either before or after its publication, by any person other than a member of the Board or his legal assistant and no administrative law judge shall advise or consult with the Board with respect to exceptions taken to his findings, rulings, or recommendations. The Board may establish or utilize such regional, local, or other agencies, and utilize such voluntary and uncompensated services, as may from time to time be needed. Attorneys appointed under this section may, at the direction of the Board, appear for and represent the Board in any case in court. Nothing in this subchapter shall be construed to authorize the Board to appoint individuals for the purpose of conciliation or mediation, or for economic analysis.

(b) All of the expenses of the Board, including all necessary traveling and subsistence expenses outside the District of Columbia incurred by the members or employees of the Board under its orders, shall be allowed and paid on the presentation of itemized vouchers therefor approved by the Board or by any individual it designates for that purpose.

§155. National Labor Relations Board; Principal Office, Conducting Inquiries Throughout Country; Participation in Decisions or Inquiries Conducted by Member

The principal office of the Board shall be in the District of Columbia, but it may meet and exercise any or all of its powers at any other place. The Board may, by one or more of its members or by such agents or agencies as it may designate, prosecute any inquiry necessary to its functions in any part of the United States. A member who participates in such an inquiry shall not be disqualified from subsequently participating in a decision of the Board in the same case.

§156. National Labor Relations Board; Rules and Regulations

The Board shall have authority from time to time to make, amend, and rescind, in the manner prescribed by the Administrative Procedure Act, such rules and regulations as may be necessary to carry out the provisions of this subchapter.

§157. Right of Employees as to Organization, Collective Bargaining, etc.

Employees shall have the right to self-organization, to form, join, or assist labor organizations, to bargain collectively through representatives of their own choosing, and to engage in other concerted activities for the purpose of collective bargaining or other mutual aid or protection, and shall also have the right to refrain from any or all of such activities except to the extent that such right may be affected by an agreement requiring membership in a labor organization as a condition of employment as authorized in section 158(a)(3) of this title.

§158. Unfair Labor Practices

(a) *Unfair labor practices by employer*. It shall be an unfair labor practice for an employer

(1) to interfere with, restrain, or coerce employees in the exercise of the rights guaranteed in section 157 of this title;

(2) to dominate or interfere with the formation or administration of any labor organization or contribute financial or other support to it: Provided, That subject to rules and regulations made and published by the Board pursuant to section 156 of this title, an employer shall not be prohibited from permitting employees to confer with him during working hours without loss of time or pay;

(3) by discrimination in regard to hire or tenure of employment or any term or condition of employment to encourage or discourage membership in any labor organization: Provided, That nothing in this subchapter, or in any other statute of the United States, shall preclude an employer from making an agreement with a labor organization (not established, maintained, or assisted by any action defined in this subsection as an unfair labor practice) to require as a condition of employment membership therein on or after the thirtieth day following the beginning of such employment or the effective date of such agreement, whichever is the later, (i) if such labor organization is the representative of the employees as provided in section 159(a) of this title, in the appropriate collective-bargaining unit covered by such agreement when made, and (ii) unless following an election held as provided in section 159(e) of this title within one year preceding the effective date of such agreement, the Board shall have certified that at least a majority of the

employees eligible to vote in such election have voted to rescind the authority of such labor organization to make such an agreement: Provided further, That no employer shall justify any discrimination against an employee for nonmembership in a labor organization (A) if he has reasonable grounds for believing that such membership was not available to the employee on the same terms and conditions generally applicable to other members, or (B) if he has reasonable grounds for believing that membership was denied or terminated for reasons other than the failure of the employee to tender the periodic dues and the initiation fees uniformly required as a condition of acquiring or retaining membership.

(4) to discharge or otherwise discriminate against an employee because he has filed charges or given testimony under this subchapter.

(5) to refuse to bargain collectively with the representatives of his employees, subject to the provisions of section 159(a) of this title.

(b) *Unfair labor practices by labor organization.* It shall be an unfair labor practice for a labor organization or its agents

(1) to restrain or coerce (A) employees in the exercise of the rights guaranteed in section 157 of this title: Provided, That this paragraph shall not impair the right of a labor organization to prescribe its own rules with respect to the acquisition or retention of membership therein; or (B) an employer in the selection of his representatives for the purposes of collective bargaining or the adjustment of grievances;

(2) to cause or attempt to cause an employer to discriminate against an employee in violation of subsection (a)(3) of this section or to discriminate against an employee with respect to whom membership in such organization has been denied or terminated on some ground other than his failure to tender the periodic dues and the initiation fees uniformly required as a condition of acquiring or retaining membership;

(3) to refuse to bargain collectively with an employer, provided it is the representative of his employees subject to the provisions of section 159(a) of this title;

(4)(i) to engage in, or to induce or encourage any individual employed by any person engaged in commerce or in an industry affecting commerce to engage in, a strike or a refusal in the course of his employment to use, manufacture, process, transport, or otherwise handle or work on any goods, articles, materials, or commodities or to perform any services; or (ii) to threaten, coerce, or restrain any person engaged in commerce or in an industry affecting commerce, where in either case an object thereof is

(A) forcing or requiring any employer or self-employed person to join any labor or employer organization or to enter into any agreement which is prohibited by subsection (e) of this section;

(B) forcing or requiring any person to cease using, selling, handling, transporting, or otherwise dealing in the products of any other producer, processor, or manufacturer, or to cease doing business with any other person, or forcing or requiring any other employer to recognize or bargain with a labor organization as the representative of his employees unless such labor organization has been certified as the representative of such employees under the provisions of section 159 of this title: Provided, That nothing contained in this clause (B) shall be construed to make unlawful, where not otherwise unlawful, any primary strike or primary picketing;

(C) forcing or requiring any employer to recognize or bargain with a particular labor organization as the representative of his employees if another labor organization has been certified as the representative of such employees under the provisions of section 159 of this title;

(D) forcing or requiring any employer to assign particular work to employees in a particular labor organization or in a particular trade, craft, or class rather than to employees in another labor organization or in another trade, craft, or class, unless such employer is failing to conform to an order or certification of the Board determining the bargaining representative for employees performing such work: Provided, That nothing contained in this subsection shall be construed to make unlawful a refusal by any person to enter upon the premises of any employer (other than his own employer), if the employees of such employer are engaged in a strike ratified or approved by a representative of such employees whom such employer is required to recognize under this subchapter: Provided further, That for the purposes of this paragraph (4) only, nothing contained in such paragraph shall be construed to prohibit publicity, other than picketing, for the purpose of truthfully advising the public, including consumers and members of a labor organization, that a product or products are produced by an employer with whom the labor organization has a primary dispute and are distributed by another employer, as long as such publicity does not have an effect of inducing any individual employed by any person other than the primary employer in the course of his employment to refuse to pick up, deliver, or transport any goods, or not to perform any services, at the establishment of the employer engaged in such distribution;

(5) to require of employees covered by an agreement authorized under subsection (a)(3) of this section the payment, as a condition precedent to becoming a member of such organization, of a fee in an amount which the Board finds excessive or discriminatory under all the circumstances. In making such a finding, the Board shall consider, among other relevant factors, the practices and customs of labor organizations in the particular industry, and the wages currently paid to the employees affected;

(6) to cause or attempt to cause an employer to pay or deliver or agree to pay or deliver any money or other thing of value, in the nature of an exaction, for services which are not performed or not to be performed; and

(7) to picket or cause to be picketed, or threaten to picket or cause to be picketed, any employer where an object thereof is forcing or requiring an employer to recognize or bargain with a labor organization as the representative of his employees, or forcing or requiring the employees of an employer to accept or select such labor organization as their collective

bargaining representative, unless such labor organization is currently certified as the representative of such employees:

(A) where the employer has lawfully recognized in accordance with this subchapter any other labor organization and a question concerning representation may not appropriately be raised under section 159(c) of this title.

(B) where within the preceding twelve months a valid election under section 159(c) of this title has been conducted, or

(C) where such picketing has been conducted without a petition under section 159(c) of this title being filed within a reasonable period of time not to exceed thirty days from the commencement of such picketing: Provided, That when such a petition has been filed the Board shall forthwith, without regard to the provisions of section 159(c)(1) of this title or the absence of a showing of a substantial interest on the part of the labor organization, direct an election in such unit as the Board finds to be appropriate and shall certify the results thereof: Provided further, That nothing in this subparagraph (C) shall be construed to prohibit any picketing or other publicity for the purpose of truthfully advising the public (including consumers) that an employer does not employ members of, or have a contact with, a labor organization, unless an effect of such picketing is to induce any individual employed by any other person in the course of his employment, not to pickup, deliver or transport any goods or not to perform any services.

Nothing in this paragraph (7) shall be construed to permit any act which should otherwise be an unfair labor practice under this subsection.

(c) *Expression of views without threat of reprisal or force or promise of benefit.* The expressing of any views, argument, or opinion, or the dissemination thereof, whether in written, printed, graphic, or visual form, shall not constitute or be evidence of an unfair labor practice under any of the provisions of this subchapter, if such expression contains no threat of reprisal or force or promise of benefit.

(d) *Obligation to bargain collectively.* For the purposes of this section, to bargain collectively is the performance of the mutual obligation of the employer and the representative of the employees to meet at reasonable times and confer in good faith with respect to wages, hours, and other terms and conditions of employment, or the negotiation of an agreement, or any question arising thereunder, and the execution of a written contract incorporating any agreement reached if requested by either party, but such obligation does not compel either party to agree to a proposal or require the making of a concession: Provided, That where there is in effect a collective-bargaining contract covering employees in an industry affecting commerce, the duty to bargain collectively shall also mean that no party to such contract shall terminate or modify such contract, unless the party desiring such termination or modification

(1) serves a written notice upon the other party to the contract of the proposed termination or modification sixty days prior to the expiration date thereof, or in the event such contract contains no expiration date, sixty days prior to the time it is proposed to make such termination or modification;

(2) offers to meet and confer with the other party for the purpose of negotiating a new contract or a contract containing the proposed modifications;

(3) notifies the Federal Mediation and Conciliation Service within thirty days after such notice of the existence of a dispute, and simultaneously therewith notifies any State or Territorial agency established to mediate and conciliate disputes within the State or Territory where the dispute occurred, provided no agreement has been reached by that time; and

(4) continues in full force and effect, without resorting to strike or lockout, all the terms and conditions of the existing contract for a period of sixty days after such notice is given or until the expiration date of such contract, whichever occurs later.

The duties imposed upon employers, employees, and labor organizations by paragraphs (2) to (4) of this subsection shall become inapplicable upon an intervening certification of the Board, under which the labor organization or individual, which is a party to the contract, has been superseded as or ceased to be the representative of the employees subject to the provisions of section 159(a) of this title, and the duties so imposed shall not be construed as requiring either party to discuss or agree to any modification of the terms and conditions contained in a contract for a fixed period, if such modification is to become effective before such terms and conditions can be reopened under the provisions of the contract. Any employee who engages in a strike within any notice period specified in this subsection, or who engages in any strike within the appropriate period specified in subsection (g) of this section, shall lose his status as an employee of the employer engaged in the particular labor dispute, for the purposes of sections 158, 159 and 160 of this title, but such loss of status for such employee shall terminate if and when he is reemployed by such employer. Whenever the collective bargaining involves employees of a health care institution, the provisions of this subsection shall be modified as follows:

(A) The notice of paragraph (1) of this subsection shall be ninety days; the notice of paragraph (3) of this subsection shall be sixty days; and the contract period of paragraph (4) of this subsection shall be ninety days.

(B) Where the bargaining is for an initial agreement following certification or recognition, at least thirty days' notice of the existence of a dispute shall be given by the labor organization to the agencies set forth in paragraph (3) of this subsection.

(C) After notice is given to the Federal Mediation and Conciliation Service under either clause (A) or (B) of this sentence, the Service shall promptly communicate with the parties and use its best efforts, by mediation and conciliation, to bring them to agreement. The parties shall participate fully and promptly in such meetings as may be undertaken by the Service for the purpose of aiding in a settlement of the dispute.

(e) *Enforceability of contract or agreement to boycott any other employer; exception.* It shall be an unfair labor practice for any labor organization and any employer to enter into any contract or agreement, express or implied, whereby such employer ceases or refrains or agrees to cease or refrain from handling, using, selling, transporting or otherwise dealing with any other person, and any contract or agreement entered into heretofore or hereafter containing such an agreement shall be to such extent unenforceable and void: Provided, That nothing in this subsection shall apply to an agreement between a labor organization and an employer in the construction industry relating to the contracting or sub-contracting of work to be done at the site of the construction, alteration, painting, or repair of a building, structure, or other work: Provided further, That for the purposes of this subsection and subsection (b)(4)(B) of this section the terms "any employer," "any person engaged in commerce or an industry affecting commerce," and "any person" when used in relation to the terms "any other producer, processor, or manufacturer," "any other employer," or "any other person" shall not include persons in the relation of a jobber, manufacturer, contractor, or subcontractor working on the goods or premises of the jobber or manufacturer or performing parts of an integrated process of production in the apparel and clothing industry: Provided further, That nothing in this subchapter shall prohibit the enforcement of any agreement which is within the foregoing exception.

(f) *Agreement covering employees in the building and construction industry.* It shall not be an unfair labor practice under subsections (a) and (b) of this section for an employer engaged primarily in the building and construction industry to make an agreement covering employees engaged (or who, upon their employment, will be engaged) in the building and construction industry with a labor organization of which building and construction employees are members (not established, maintained, or assisted by any action defined in subsection (a) of this section as an unfair labor practice) because (1) the majority status of such labor organization has not been established under the provisions of section 159 of this title prior to the making of such agreement, or (2) such agreement requires as a condition of employment, membership in such labor organization after the seventh day following the beginning of such employment or the effective date of the agreement, whichever is later, or (3) such agreement requires the employer to notify such labor organization of opportunities for employment with such employer, or gives such labor organization an opportunity to refer qualified applicants for such employment, or (4) such agreement specifies minimum training or experience qualifications for employment or provides for priority in opportunities for employment based upon length of service with such employer, in the industry or in the particular geographical area: Provided, That nothing in this subsection shall set aside the final proviso to subsection (a)(3) of this section: Provided further, That any agreement which would be invalid, but for clause (1) of this subsection, shall not be a bar to a petition filed pursuant to section 159(c) or 159(e) of this title.

(g) *Notification of intention to strike or picket at any health care institution.* A labor organization before engaging in any strike, picketing, or other concerted refusal to work at any health care institution shall, not less than ten days prior to such action, notify the institution in writing and the Federal Mediation and Conciliation Service of that intention, except that in the case of bargaining for an initial agreement following certification or recognition the notice required by this subsection shall not be given until the expiration of the period specified in clause (B) of the last sentence of subsection (d) of this section. The notice shall state the date and time that such action will commence. The notice, once given, may be extended by the written agreement of both parties.

§159. Representatives and Elections

(a) *Exclusive representatives; employees' adjustment of grievances directly with employer.* Representatives designated or selected for the purposes of collective bargaining by the majority of the employees in a unit appropriate for such purposes, shall be the exclusive representatives of all the employees in such unit for the purposes of collective bargaining in respect of rates of pay, wages, hours of employment, or other conditions of employment. Provided, That any individual employee or a group of employees shall have the right at any time to present grievances to their employer and to have such grievances adjusted, without the intervention of the bargaining representative, as long as the adjustment is not inconsistent with the terms of a collective-bargaining contract or agreement then in effect: Provided further, That the bargaining representative has been given opportunity to be present as such adjustment.

(b) *Determination of bargaining unit by Board.* The Board shall decide in each case whether, in order to assure to employees the fullest freedom in exercising the rights guaranteed by this subchapter, the unit appropriate for purposes of collective bargaining shall be the employer unit, craft unit, plant unit, or subdivision thereof: Provided, That the Board shall not (1) decide that any unit is appropriate for such purposes if such unit includes both professional employees and employees who are not professional employees unless a majority of such professional employees vote for inclusion in such unit; or (2) decide that any craft unit is inappropriate for such purposes on the ground that a different unit has been established by a prior Board determination, unless a majority of the employees in the proposed craft unit vote against separate representation or (3) decide that any unit is appropriate for such purposes if it includes, together with other employees, any individual employed as a guard to enforce against employees and other persons rules to protect property of the employer or to protect the safety of persons on the employer's premises; but no labor organization shall be certified as the representative of employees in a bargaining unit of guards if such organization admits to membership, or is affiliated directly or indirectly with an organization which admits to membership, employees other than guards.

(c) *Hearings on questions affecting commerce; rules and regulations.*

(1) Whenever a petition shall have been filed, in accordance with such regulations as may be prescribed by the Board

(A) by an employee or group of employees or any individual or labor organization acting in their behalf alleging that a substantial number of employees (i) wish to be represented for collective bargaining and that their employer declines to recognize their representative as the representative defined in subsection (a) of this section, or (ii) assert that the individual or labor organization, which has been certified or is being currently recognized by their employer as the bargaining representative, is no longer a representative as defined in subsection (a) of this section; or

(B) by an employer, alleging that one or more individuals or labor organizations have presented to him a claim to be recognized as the representative defined in subsection (a) of this section; the Board shall investigate such petition and if it has reasonable cause to believe that a question of representation affecting commerce exists shall provide for an appropriate hearing upon due notice. Such hearing may be conducted by an officer or employee of the regional office, who shall not make any recommendations with respect thereto. If the Board finds upon the record of such hearing that such a question of representation exists, it shall direct an election by secret ballot and shall certify the results thereof.

(2) In determining whether or not a question of representation affecting commerce exists, the same regulations and rules of decision shall apply irrespective of the identity of the persons filing the petition or the kind of relief sought and in no case shall the Board deny a labor organization a place on the ballot by reason of an order with respect to such labor organization or its predecessor not issued in conformity with section 160(c) of this title.

(3) No election shall be directed in any bargaining unit or any subdivision within which in the preceding twelve-month period, a valid election shall have been held. Employees engaged in an economic strike who are not entitled to reinstatement shall be eligible to vote under such regulations as the Board shall find are consistent with the purposes and provisions of this subchapter in any election conducted within twelve months after the commencement of the strike. In any election where none of the choices on the ballot receives a majority, a run-off shall be conducted, the ballot providing for a selection between the two choices receiving the largest and second largest number of valid votes cast in the election.

(4) Nothing in this section shall be construed to prohibit the waiving of hearings by stipulation for the purposes of a consent election in conformity with regulations and rules of decision of the Board.

(5) In determining whether a unit is appropriate for the purposes specified in subsection (b) of this section the extent to which the employees have organized shall not be controlling.

(d) *Petition for enforcement or review; transcript.* Whenever an order of the Board made pursuant to section 160(c) of this title is based in whole or in part upon facts certified following an investigation pursuant to subsection (c) of this section and there is a petition for the enforcement or review of such order, such certification and the record of such investigation shall be included in the transcript of the entire record required to be filed under subsection (e) or (f) of section 160 of this title, and thereupon the decree of the court enforcing, modifying, or setting aside in whole or in part the order of the Board shall be made and entered upon the pleadings, testimony, and proceedings set forth in such transcript.

(e) *Secret ballot; limitation of elections.*

(1) Upon the filing with the Board, by 30 per centum or more of the employees in a bargaining unit covered by an agreement between their employer and a labor organization made pursuant to section 158(a)(3) of this title, of a petition alleging they desire that such authority be rescinded, the Board shall take a secret ballot of the employees in such unit and certify the results thereof to such labor organization and to the employer.

(2) No election shall be conducted pursuant to this subsection in any bargaining unit or any subdivision within which, in the preceding twelve-month period, a valid election shall have been held.

§160. *Prevention of Unfair Labor Practices*

(a) *Powers of Board generally.* The Board is empowered, as hereinafter provided, to prevent any person from engaging in any unfair labor practice (listed in section 158 of this title) affecting commerce. This power shall not be affected by any other means of adjustment or prevention that has been or may be established by agreement, law, or otherwise: Provided, That the Board is empowered by agreement with any agency of any State or Territory to cede to such agency jurisdiction over any cases in any industry (other than mining, manufacturing, communications, and transportation except where predominantly local in character) even though such cases may involved labor disputes affecting commerce, unless the provision of the State or Territorial statute applicable to the determination of such cases by such agency is inconsistent with the corresponding provision of this subchapter or has received a construction inconsistent therewith.

(b) *Complaint and notice of hearing; answer; court rules of evidence applicable.* Whenever it is charged that any person has engaged in or is engaging in any such unfair labor practice, the Board, or any agent or agency designated by the Board for such purposes, shall have power to issue and cause to be served upon such person a complaint stating the charges in that respect, and containing a notice of hearing before the Board or a member thereof, or before a designated agent or agency, at a place therein fixed, not less than five days after the serving of said complaint: Provided, That no complaint shall issue based upon any unfair labor practice occurring more than six months prior to the filing of the charge with the Board and the service of a copy thereof upon the person against whom such charge is made, unless the person aggrieved thereby was prevented from filing such charge by reason of service in the armed forces, in which event the six-month period shall be computed from the day of his discharge. Any such complaint may be amended by the member, agent, or agency conducting the hearing or the Board in its discretion at any time prior to the issuance of an order based thereon. The person so complained of shall have the right to file an answer to the original or amended complaint and to appear in person or otherwise and give testimony at the place and time fixed in the complaint. In the discretion of the member, agent, or agency conducting the hearing or the Board, any other person may be allowed to intervene in the said proceeding and to present testimony. Any such proceeding shall, so far as practicable, be conducted in accordance with the rules of evidence applicable in the district courts of the United States under the rules of civil procedure for the district courts of the United States, adopted by the Supreme Court of the United States pursuant to section 2072 of Title 28.

(c) *Reduction of testimony to writing; findings and orders of Board.* The testimony taken by such member, agent, or agency or the Board shall be reduced to writing and filed with the Board. Thereafter, in its discretion, the Board upon notice may take further testimony or hear argument. If upon the preponderance of the testimony taken the Board shall be of the opinion that any person named in the complaint has engaged in or is engaging in any such unfair labor practice, then the Board shall state its findings of fact and shall issue and cause to be served on such person an order requiring such person to cease and desist from such unfair labor practice, and to take such affirmative action including reinstatement of employees with or without back pay, as will effectuate the policies of this subchapter: Provided, That where an order directs reinstatement of an employee, back pay may be required of the employer or labor organization, as the case may be, responsible for the discrimination suffered by him: And provided further, That in determining whether a complaint shall issue alleging a violation of subsection (a)(1) or (a)(2) of section 158 of this title, and in deciding such cases, the same regulations and rules of decision shall apply irrespective of whether or not the labor organization affected is affiliated with a labor organization national or international in scope. Such an order may further require such person to make reports from time to time showing the extent to which it has complied with the order. If upon the preponderance of the testimony taken the Board shall not be of the opinion that the person named in the complaint has engaged in or is engaging in any such unfair labor practice, then the Board shall state its findings of fact and shall issue an order dismissing the said complaint. No order of the Board shall require the reinstatement of any individual as an employee who has been suspended or discharged, or the payment to him of any back pay, if such individual was suspended or discharged for cause. In case the evidence is presented before a member of the Board, or before an administrative law judge or judges thereof, such member, or such judge; or judges as the case may be, shall issue and cause to be served on the parties to the proceeding a proposed report, together with a recommended order, which shall be filed with the Board, and if no exceptions are filed within twenty days after service thereof upon such parties, or within such further period as the Board may authorize, such recommended order shall become the order of the Board and become effective as therein prescribed.

(d) *Modification of findings or orders prior to filing record in court.* Until the record in a case shall have been filed in a court, as hereinafter provided, the Board may at any time upon reasonable notice and in such manner as it shall deem proper, modify or set aside, in whole or in part, any finding or order made or issued by it.

(e) *Petition to court for enforcement of order; proceedings; review of judgment.* The Board shall have power to petition any court of appeals of the United States, or if all the courts of appeals to which application may be made are in vacation, any district court of the United States, within any circuit or district, respectively, wherein the unfair labor practice in question occurred or wherein such person resides or transacts business, for the enforcement of such order and for appropriate temporary relief or restraining order, and shall file in the court the record in the proceedings, as provided in section 2112 of Title 28. Upon the filing of such petition, the court shall cause notice thereof to be served upon such person, and thereupon shall have jurisdiction of the proceeding and of the question determined therein, and shall have power to grant such temporary relief or restraining order as it deems just and proper, and to make and enter a decree enforcing, modifying, and enforcing as so modified, or setting aside in whole or in part the order of the Board. No objection that has not been urged before the Board, its member, agent, or agency, shall be considered by the court, unless the failure or neglect to urge such objection shall be excused because of extraordinary circumstances. The findings of the Board with respect to questions of fact if supported by substantial evidence on the record considered as a whole shall be conclusive. If either party shall apply to the court for leave to adduce additional evidence and shall show to the satisfaction of the court that such additional evidence is material and that there were reasonable grounds for the failure to adduce such evidence in the hearing before the Board, its member, agent, or agency, the court may order such additional evidence to be taken before the Board, its member, agent, or agency, and to be made a part of the record. The Board may modify its findings as to the facts or make new findings by reason of additional evidence so taken and filed, and it shall file such modified or new findings, which findings with respect to questions of fact if supported by substantial evidence on the record considered as a whole shall be conclusive, and shall file its recommendations, if any, for the modification or setting aside of its original order. Upon the filing of the record with it the jurisdiction of the court shall be exclusive and its judgment and decree shall be final, except that the same shall be subject to review by the appropriate United States court of appeals if application was made to the district court as here in above provided, and by the Supreme Court of the United States upon writ of certiorari or certification as provided in section 1254 of Title 28.

(f) *Review of final order of Board on petition to court.* Any person aggrieved by a final order of the Board granting or denying in whole or in part the relief sought may obtain a review of such order in any United States court of appeals in the circuit wherein the unfair labor practice in question was alleged to have been engaged in or wherein such person resides or transacts business, or in the United States Court of Appeals for the District of Columbia, by filing in such a court a written petition praying that the order of the Board be modified or set aside. A copy of such petition shall be forthwith transmitted by the clerk of the court to the Board, and thereupon the aggrieved party shall file in the court the record in the proceeding, certified by the Board, as provided in section 2112 of Title 28. Upon the filing of such petition, the court shall proceed in the same manner as in the case of an application by the Board under subsection (e) of this section, and shall have the same jurisdiction to grant to the Board such temporary relief or restraining order as it deems just and proper, and in like manner to make and enter a decree enforcing, modifying, and enforcing as so modified, or setting aside in whole or in part the order of the Board; the findings of the Board with respect to questions of fact if supported by substantial evidence on the record considered as a whole shall in like manner be conclusive.

(g) *Institution of court proceedings as stay of Board's order.* The commencement of proceedings under subsection (e) or (f) of this section shall not, unless specifically ordered by the court, operate as a stay of the Board's order.

(h) *Jurisdiction of courts unaffected by limitations prescribed in sections 101 to 115 of this title.* When granting appropriate temporary relief or a restraining order, or making and entering a decree enforcing, modifying, and enforcing as so modified, or setting aside in whole or in part an order of the Board, as provided in this section, the jurisdiction of courts sitting in equity shall not be limited by sections 101 to 115 of this title.

(i) Repealed. Pub. L. 98-620, Title IV, §402(31), Nov. 8, 1984, 98 Stat. 3360

(j) *Injunctions.* The Board shall have power, upon issuance of a complaint as provided in subsection (b) of this section charging that any person has engaged in or is engaging in an unfair labor practice, to petition any United States district court, within any district wherein the unfair labor practice in question is alleged to have occurred or wherein such person resides or transacts business, for appropriate temporary relief or restraining order. Upon the filing of any such petition the court shall cause notice thereof to be served upon such person, and thereupon shall have jurisdiction to grant to the Board such temporary relief or restraining order as it deems just and proper.

(k) *Hearings on jurisdictional strikes.* Whenever it is charged that any person has engaged in an unfair labor practice within the meaning of paragraph (4)(D) of section 158(b) of this title, the Board is empowered and directed to hear and determine the dispute out of which such unfair labor practice shall have arisen, unless, within ten days after notice that such charge has been filed, the parties to such dispute submit to the Board satisfactory evidence that they have adjusted, or agreed upon methods for the voluntary adjustment of, the dispute. Upon compliance by the parties to the dispute with the decision of the Board or upon such voluntary adjustment of the dispute, such charge shall be dismissed.

(l) *Boycotts and strikes to force recognition of uncertified labor organizations, injunctions; notice; service of process.* Whenever it is charged that any person has engaged in an unfair labor practice within the meaning of paragraph (4)(A), (B), or (C) of section 158(b) of this title, or section 158(e) of this title or section 158(b)(7) of this title, the preliminary investigation of such charge shall be made forthwith and given priority over all other cases except cases of like character in the office where it is filed or to which it is referred. If, after such investigation, the officer or regional attorney to whom the matter may be referred has reasonable cause to believe such charge is true and that a complaint should issue, he shall, on behalf of the Board, petition any United States district court within any district where the unfair labor practice in question has occurred, is alleged to have occurred, or wherein such person resides or transacts business, for appropriate injunctive relief pending the final adjudication of the Board with respect to such matter. Upon the filing of such petition the district court shall have jurisdiction to grant such injunctive relief or temporary restraining order as it deems just and proper, notwithstanding any other provision of law: Provided further, That no temporary restraining order shall be issued without notice unless a petition alleges that substantial and irreparable injury to the charging party will be unavoidable and such temporary restraining order shall be effective for no longer than five days and will become void at the expiration of such period: Provided further, That such officer or regional attorney shall not apply for any restraining order under section 158(b)(7) of this title if a charge against the employer under section 158(a)(2) of this title has been filed and after the preliminary investigation, he has reasonable cause to believe that such charge is true and that a complaint should issue. Upon filing of any such petition the courts shall cause notice thereof to be served upon any person involved in the charge and such person, including the charging party, shall be given an opportunity to appear by counsel and present any relevant testimony: Provided further, That for the purposes of this subsection district courts shall be deemed to have jurisdiction of a labor organization (1) in the district in which such organization maintains its principal office, or (2) in any district in which its duly authorized officers or agents are engaged in promoting or protecting the interests of employee members. The service of legal process upon such officer or agent shall constitute service upon the labor organization and make such organization a party to the suit. In situations where such relief is appropriate the procedure specified herein shall apply to charges with respect to section 158(b)(4)(D) of this title.

(m) *Priority of cases.* Whenever it is charged that any person has engaged in an unfair labor practice within the meaning of subsection (a)(3) or (b)(2) of section 158 of this title, such charge shall be given priority over all other cases except cases of like character in the office where it is filed or to which it is referred and cases given priority under subsection (1) of this section.

§161. *Investigatory Powers of Board*

For the purpose of all hearings and investigations, which, in the opinion of the Board, are necessary and proper for the exercise of the powers vested in it by sections 159 and 160 of this title

(1) *Documentary evidence; summoning witnesses and taking testimony.* The Board, or its duly authorized agents or agencies, shall at all reasonable times have access to, for the purpose of examination, and the right to copy any evidence of any person being investigated or proceeded against that relates to any matter under investigation or in question. The Board, or any member thereof, shall upon application of any party to such proceedings, forthwith issue to such party subpoenas requiring the attendance and testimony of witnesses or the production of any evidence in such proceeding or investigation requested in such application. Within five days after the service of a subpoena on any person requiring the production of evidence in his possession or under his control, such person may petition the Board to revoke, and the Board shall revoke, such subpoena if in its opinion the evidence whose production is required does not relate to any matter under investigation, or any matter in question in such proceedings, or if in its opinion such subpoena does not describe with sufficient particularity the evidence whose production is required. Any member of the Board, or any agent or agency designated by the Board for such purposes, may administer oaths and affirmations, examine witnesses, and receive evidence. Such attendance of witnesses and the production of such

evidence may be required from any place in the United States or any Territory or possession thereof, at any designated place of hearing.

(2) *Court aid in compelling production of evidence and attendance of witnesses.* In case of contumacy or refusal to obey a subpoena issued to any person, any district court of the United States or the United States courts of any Territory or possession, within the jurisdiction of which the inquiry is carried on or within the jurisdiction of which said person guilty of contumacy or refusal to obey is found or resides or transacts business, upon application by the Board shall have jurisdiction to issue to such person an order requiring such person to appear before the Board, its member, agent, or agency, there to produce evidence if so ordered, or there to give testimony touching the matter under investigation or in question; and any failure to obey such order of the court may be punished by said court as a contempt thereof.

(3) Repealed. Pub. L. 91-452, Title II, §234, Oct. 15, 1970, 84 Stat. 930.

(4) *Process, service and return; fees of witnesses.* Complaints, orders, and other process and papers of the Board, its member, agent, or agency, may be served either personally or by registered or certified mail or by telegraph or by leaving a copy thereof at the principal office or place of business of the person required to be served. The verified return by the individual so serving the same setting forth the manner of such service shall be proof of the same, and the return post office receipt or telegraph receipt therefor when registered or certified and mailed or when telegraphed as aforesaid shall be proof of service of the same. Witnesses summoned before the Board, its member, agent, or agency, shall be paid the same fees and mileage that are paid witnesses in the courts of the United States, and witnesses whose depositions are taken and the persons taking the same shall severally be entitled to the same fees as are paid for like services in the courts of the United States.

(5) *Process, where served.* All process of any court to which application may be made under this subchapter may be served in the judicial district wherein the defendant or other person required to be served resides or may be found.

(6) *Information and assistance from departments.* The several departments and agencies of the Government, when directed by the President, shall furnish the Board, upon its request, all records, papers, and information in their possession relating to any matter before the Board.

§162. *Offenses and Penalties*

Any person who shall willfully resist, prevent, impede, or interfere with any member of the Board or any of its agents or agencies in the performance of duties pursuant to this subchapter shall be punished by a fine of not more than $5,000 or by imprisonment for not more than one year, or both.

§163. *Right to Strike Preserved*

Nothing in this subchapter, except as specifically provided for herein, shall be construed so as either to interfere with or impede or diminish in any way the right to strike, or to affect the limitations or qualifications on that right.

§164. Construction of Provisions

(a) *Supervisors as union members.* Nothing herein shall prohibit any individual employed as a supervisor from becoming or remaining a member of a labor organization, but no employer subject to this subchapter shall be compelled to deem individuals defined herein as supervisors as employees for the purpose of any law, either national or local, relating to collective bargaining.

(b) *Agreements requiring union membership in violation of State law.* Nothing in this subchapter shall be construed as authorizing the execution or application of agreements requiring membership in a labor organization as a condition of employment in any State or Territory in which such execution or application is prohibited by State or Territorial law.

(c) *Power of Board to decline jurisdiction of labor disputes; assertion of jurisdiction by State and Territorial courts.*

(1) The Board, in its discretion, may, by rule of decision or by published rules adopted pursuant to subchapter II of chapter 5 of Title 5, decline to assert jurisdiction over any labor dispute involving any class or category of employers, where, in the opinion of the Board, the effect of such labor dispute on commerce is not sufficiently substantial to warrant the exercise of its jurisdiction: Provided, That the Board shall not decline to assert jurisdiction over any labor dispute over which it would assert jurisdiction under the standards prevailing upon August 1, 1959.

(2) Nothing in this subchapter shall be deemed to prevent or bar any agency or the courts of any State or Territory (including the Commonwealth of Puerto Rico, Guam, and the Virgin Islands), from assuming and asserting jurisdiction over labor disputes over which the Board declines, pursuant to paragraph (1) of this subsection, to assert jurisdiction.

§165. Conflict of Laws

Wherever the application of the provisions of section 672 of Title 11 conflicts with the application of the provisions of this subchapter, this subchapter shall prevail: Provided, That in any situation where the provisions of this subchapter cannot be validly enforced, the provisions of such other Acts shall remain in full force and effect.

§166. Separability

If any provision of this subchapter, or the application of such provision to any person or circumstances, shall be held invalid, the remainder of this subchapter, or the application of such provision to persons or circumstances other than those as to which it is held invalid, shall not be affected thereby.

§167. Short Title of Subchapter

This subchapter may be cited as the "National Labor Relations Act."

§168. *Validation of Certificates and Other Board Actions*

No petition entertained, no investigation made, no election held, and no certification issued by the National Labor Relations Board, under any of the provisions of section 159 of this title, shall be invalid by reason of the failure of the Congress of Industrial Organizations to have complied with the requirements of section 159(f), (g), or (h) of this title prior to December 22, 1949, or by reason of the failure of the American Federation of Labor to have complied with the provisions of section 159(f), (g), or (h) of this title prior to November 7, 1947: Provided, That no liability shall be imposed under any provision of this chapter upon any person for failure to honor any election or certificate referred to above, prior to October 22, 1951: Provided, however, That this proviso shall not have the effect of setting aside or in any way affecting judgments or decrees heretofore entered under section 160(e) or (f) of this title and which have become final.

§169. *Employees with Religious Convictions; Payment of Dues and Fees*

Any employee who is a member of and adheres to established and traditional tenets or teachings of a bona fide religion, body, or sect which has historically held conscientious objections to joining or financially supporting labor organization shall not be required to join or financially support any labor organization as a condition of employment; except that such employee may be required in a contract between such employees' employer and a labor organization in lieu of periodic dues and initiation fees, to pay sums equal to such dues and initiation fees to a nonreligious, nonlabor organization charitable fund exempt from taxation under section 501(c)(3) of Title 26, chosen by such employee from a list of at least three such funds, designated in such contract or if the contract fails to designate such funds, then to any such fund chosen by the employee. If such employee who holds conscientious objections pursuant to this section requests the labor organization to use the grievance-arbitration procedure on the employee's behalf, the labor organization is authorized to charge the employee for the reasonable cost of using such procedure.

Portal-to-Portal Act

29 U.S.C. §§255, 256, 260

§255 [§6]. Statute of Limitations

Any action commenced on or after May 14, 1947, to enforce any cause of action for unpaid minimum wages, unpaid overtime compensation, or liquidated damages, under the Fair Labor Standards Act of 1938, as amended, the Walsh-Healey Act, or the Bacon-Davis Act—

(a) if the cause of action accrues on or after May 14, 1947—may be commenced within two years after the cause of action accrued, and every such action shall be forever barred unless commenced within two years after the cause of action accrued, except that a cause of action arising out of a willful violation may be commenced within three years after the cause of action accrued. . . .

§256 [§7]. Determination of Commencement of Future Actions

In determining when an action is commenced for the purposes of section 255 of this title, an action commenced on or after May 14, 1947 under the Fair Labor Standards Act of 1938, as amended, the Walsh-Healey Act, or the Bacon-Davis Act, shall be considered to be commenced on the date when the complaint is filed; except that in the case of a collective or class action instituted under the Fair Labor Standards Act of 1938, as amended, or the Bacon-Davis Act, it shall be considered to be commenced in the case of any individual claimant—

(a) on the date when the complaint is filed, if he is specifically named as a party plaintiff in the complaint and his written consent to become a party plaintiff is filed on such date in the court in which the action is brought; or

(b) if such written consent was not so filed or if his name did not so appear—on the subsequent date on which such written consent is filed in the court in which the action was commenced.

§260 [§11]. Liquidated Damages

In any action commenced prior to or on or after May 14, 1947 to recover unpaid minimum wages, unpaid overtime compensation, or liquidated damages, under the Fair Labor Standards Act of 1938, as amended, if the employer shows to the satisfaction of the court that the act or omission giving rise to such action was in good faith and that he had reasonable grounds for believing that his act or omission was not a violation of the Fair Labor Standards Act of 1938, as amended, the court may, in its sound discretion, award no liquidation damages or award any amount thereof not to exceed the amount specified in section 216 of this title.

Rehabilitation Act of 1973

29 U.S.C. §§705, 791, 793, 794, 794a

§705. Definitions

For the purposes of this chapter: . . .

(6) *Construction; cost of construction.*

    (A) *Construction.* The term "construction" means

        (i) the construction of new buildings;

        (ii) the acquisition, expansion, remodeling, alteration, and renovation of existing buildings; and

        (iii) initial equipment of buildings described in clauses (i) and (ii).

    (B) *Cost of construction.* The term "cost of construction" includes architects' fees and the cost of acquisition of land in connection with construction but does not include the cost of offsite improvements. . . .

(9) *Disability.* The term "disability" means

    (A) except as otherwise provided in subparagraph (B), a physical or mental impairment that constitutes or results in a substantial impediment to employment; or

    (B) for purposes of sections 701, 711, and 712 of this title and subchapters II, IV, V, and VII of this chapter [29 U.S.C.A. §760 et seq., and 796 et seq.], the meaning given it in section 12102 of Title 42.

(10) *Drug and illegal use of drugs.*

    (A) *Drug.* The term "drug" means a controlled substance, as defined in schedules I through V of section 202 of the Controlled Substances Act [21 U.S.C. 812].

    (B) *Illegal use of drugs.* The term "illegal use of drugs" means the use of drugs, the possession or distribution of which is unlawful under the Controlled Substances Act. Such term does not include the use of a drug taken under supervision by a licensed health care professional, or other uses authorized by the Controlled Substances Act or other provisions of Federal law. . . .

(20) Individual with a disability.

(A) *In general.* Except as otherwise provided in subparagraph (B), the term "individual with a disability" means any individual who

(i) has a physical or mental impairment which for such individual constitutes or results in a substantial impediment to employment; and

(ii) can benefit in terms of an employment outcome from vocational rehabilitation services provided pursuant to subchapter I, II, or VI [29 U.S.C.S. §§720 et seq., 771 et seq., or 795 et seq.].

(B) *Certain programs; limitations on major life activities.* Subject to subparagraphs (C), (D), (E), and (F), the term "individual with a disability" means, for purposes of sections 701, 711 and 712 of this title and subchapters I, IV, V and VII of this Act [29 U.S.C.S §760 et seq., 790 et seq.], any person who has a disability in section 12102 of Title 42.

(C) *Rights and advocacy provisions.*

(i) *In general; exclusion of individuals engaging in drug use.* For purposes of title V [29 U.S.C.S. §§790 et seq.], the term "individual with a disability" does not include an individual who is currently engaging in the illegal use of drugs, when a covered entity acts on the basis of such use.

(ii) *Exception for individuals no longer engaging in drug use.* Nothing in clause (i) shall be construed to exclude as an individual with a disability an individual who

(I) has successfully completed a supervised drug rehabilitation program and is no longer engaging in the illegal use of drugs, or has otherwise been rehabilitated successfully and is no longer engaging in such use;

(II) is participating in a supervised rehabilitation program and is no longer engaging in such use; or

(III) is erroneously regarded as engaging in such use, but is not engaging in such use;

except that it shall not be a violation of this chapter [29 U.S.C.A. § 720 et seq.] for a covered entity to adopt or administer reasonable policies or procedures, including but not limited to drug testing, designed to ensure that an individual described in subclause (I) or (II) is no longer engaging in the illegal use of drugs.

(iii) *Exclusion for certain services.* Notwithstanding clause (i), for purposes of programs and activities providing health services and services provided under titles I, II, and III [29 U.S.C.S. §§720 et seq., 760 et seq., 771 et seq.], an individual shall not be excluded from the benefits of such programs or activities on the basis of his or her current illegal use of drugs if he or she is otherwise entitled to such services.

(iv) *Disciplinary action.* For purposes of programs and activities providing educational services, local educational agencies may take disciplinary action pertaining to the use or possession of illegal drugs or alcohol against any student who is an individual with a disability and who currently is engaging in the illegal use of drugs or in the use of alcohol to the same extent that such disciplinary action is taken against students who are not individuals with disabilities. Furthermore, the due process procedures at section 104.36 of title 34, Code of Federal Regulations (or any corresponding similar regulation or ruling) shall not apply to such disciplinary actions.

(v) *Employment; exclusions of alcoholics.* For purposes of sections 793 and 794 of this title as such sections relate to employment, the term "individual with a disability" does not include any individual who is an alcoholic whose current use of alcohol prevents such individual from performing the duties of the job in question or whose employment, by reasons of such current alcohol abuse, would constitute a direct threat to property or the safety of others.

(D) *Employment; exclusion of individuals with certain diseases or infections.* For the purposes of sections 793 and 794 of this title, as such sections relate to employment, such term does not include an individual who has a currently contagious disease or infection and who, by reason of such disease or infection, would constitute a direct threat to the health or safety of other individuals or who, by reasons of the currently contagious disease or infection, is unable to perform the duties of the job.

(E) *Rights provisions; exclusion of individuals on basis of homosexuality or bisexuality.* For the purposes of sections 791, 793 and 794 of this title —

(i) for purposes of the application of subparagraph (B) to such sections, the term "impairment" does not include homosexuality or bisexuality; and

(ii) therefore the term "individual with a disability" does not include an individual on the basis of homosexuality or bisexuality.

(F) *Rights provisions; exclusion of individuals on basis of certain disorders.* For the purposes of sections 791, 793 and 794 of this title, the term "individual with a disability" does not include an individual on the basis of

(i) transvestism, transsexualism, pedophilia, exhibitionism, voyeurism, gender identity disorders not resulting from physical impairments, or other sexual behavior disorders;

(ii) compulsive gambling, kleptomania, or pyromania; or

(iii) psychoactive substance use disorders resulting from current illegal use of drugs.

(G) *Individuals with disabilities.* The term "individuals with disabilities" means more than one individual with a disability.

§791 [§501]. *Employment of Individuals with Handicaps . . .*

(b) *Federal Agencies; Affirmative Action Program Plan.* Each department, agency, and instrumentality (including the United States Postal Service and the Postal Regulatory Commission) in the executive branch and the Smithsonian Institution shall, within one hundred and eighty days of September 26, 1973, submit to the

Equal Employment Opportunity Commission and to the Committee an affirmative action program plan for the hiring, placement, and advancement of individuals with disabilities in such department, agency, or instrumentality. Such plan shall include a description of the extent to which and methods whereby the special needs of employees who are individuals with disabilities are being met. Such plan shall be updated annually, and shall be reviewed annually and approved by the Commission, if the Commission determines, after consultation with the Committee, that such plan provides sufficient assurances, procedures and commitments to provide adequate hiring, placement, and advancement opportunities for individuals with disabilities. . . .

(g) *Standards used in determining violation of section.* The standards used to determine whether this section has been violated in a complaint alleging non-affirmative action employment discrimination under this section shall be the standards applied under title I of the Americans with Disabilities Act of 1990 (42 U.S.C. §§12111 et seq.) and the provisions of sections 501 through 504, and 510, of the Americans with Disabilities Act of 1990 (42 U.S.C. §§12201-12204 and §12210), as such sections relate to employment.

§793 [§503]. Employment Under Federal Contracts

(a) *Amount of Contracts or Subcontracts; Provision for Employment and Advancement of Qualified Individuals with Handicaps; Regulations.* Any contract in excess of $10,000 entered into by any Federal department or agency for the procurement of personal property and nonpersonal services (including construction) for the United States shall contain a provision requiring that, in employing persons to carry out such contract the party contracting with the United States shall take affirmative action to employ and advance in employment qualified individuals with handicaps as defined in section 706(7) of this title. The provisions of this section shall apply to any subcontract in excess of $10,000 entered into by a prime contractor in carrying out any contract for the procurement of personal property and nonpersonal services (including construction) for the United States. The President shall implement the provisions of this section by promulgating regulations within ninety days after September 26, 1973.

(b) *Administrative. Enforcement; Complaints; Investigation; Department Action.* If any individual with handicaps believes any contractor has failed or refuses to comply with the provisions of his contract with the United States, relating to employment of individuals with handicaps, such individual may file a complaint with the Department of Labor. The Department shall promptly investigate such complaint and shall take such action thereon as the facts and circumstances warrant, consistent with the terms of such contract and the laws and regulations applicable thereto. . . .

§794 [§504]. Nondiscrimination Under Federal Grants and Programs; Promulgation of Rules and Regulations

(a) *Promulgation of rules and regulations.* No otherwise qualified individual with a disability in the United States, as defined in section 705(20) of this title, shall,

Rehabilitation Act of 1973 §794 [§504]

solely by reason of her or his disability, be excluded from the participation in, be denied the benefits of, or be subjected to discrimination under any program or activity receiving Federal financial assistance or under any program or activity conducted by any Executive agency or by the United States Postal Service. The head of each such agency shall promulgate such regulations as may be necessary to carry out the amendments to this section made by the Rehabilitation, Comprehensive Services, and Developmental Disabilities Act of 1978. Copies of any proposed regulation shall be submitted to appropriate authorizing committees of the Congress, and such regulation may take effect no earlier than the thirtieth day after the date on which such regulation is so submitted to such committees.

(b) *"Program or activity" defined.* For the purposes of this section, the term "program or activity" means all of the operations of—

(1)(A) a department, agency, special purpose district, or other instrumentality of a State or of a local government; or

(B) the entity of such State or local government that distributes such assistance and each such department or agency (and each other State or local government entity) to which the assistance is extended, in the case of assistance to a State or local government;

(2)(A) a college, university, or other postsecondary institution, or a public system of higher education; or

(B) a local educational agency (as defined in section 7801 of Title 20), system of vocational education, or other school system;

(3)(A) an entire corporation, partnership, or other private organization, or an entire sole proprietorship—

(i) if assistance is extended to such corporation, partnership, private organization, or sole proprietorship as a whole; or

(ii) which is principally engaged in the business of providing education, health care, housing, social services, or parks and recreation; or

(B) the entire plant or other comparable, geographically separate facility to which Federal financial assistance is extended, in the case of any other corporation, partnership, private organization, or sole proprietorship; or

(4) any other entity which is established by two or more of the entities described in paragraph (1), (2), or (3); any part of which is extended Federal financial assistance.

(c) *Significant structural alterations by small providers; exception.* Small providers are not required by subsection (a) of this section to make significant structural alterations to their existing facilities for the purpose of assuring program accessibility, if alternative means of providing the services are available. The terms used in this subsection shall be construed with reference to the regulations existing on March 22, 1988.

(d) *Standards used in determining violation of section.* The standards used to determine whether this section has been violated in a complaint alleging employment discrimination under this section shall be the standards applied under title I of the Americans with Disabilities Act of 1990 [42 U.S.C. §§12111 et seq.]

and the provisions of sections 501 through 504, and 510, of the Americans with Disabilities Act of 1990 [42 U.S.C. §§12201-12204 and 12210], as such sections relate to employment.

§794a [§505]. Remedies and Attorney Fees

(a)(1) The remedies, procedures, and rights set forth in section 717 of the Civil Rights Act of 1964 [42 U.S.C. §2000e-16], including the application of sections 706(f) through 706(k) [42 U.S.C. §2000e-5(f)-(k)] and the application of section 706(e)(3) [42 U.S.C. §2000e-5(e)(3)] to claims of discrimination in compensation shall be available, with respect to any complaint under section 791 of this title, to any employee or applicant for employment aggrieved by the final disposition of such complaint, or by the failure to take final action on such complaint. In fashioning an equitable or affirmative action remedy under such section, a court may take into account the reasonableness of the cost of any necessary work place accommodation, and the availability of alternatives therefor or other appropriate relief in order to achieve an equitable and appropriate remedy.

(2) The remedies, procedures, and rights set forth in title VI of the Civil Rights Act of 1964 [42 U.S.C. §2000d et seq.] (and in subsection (e)(3) of section 706 of such act [42 U.S.C. §2000e-5], applied to claims of discrimination in compensation) shall be available to any person aggrieved by any act or failure to act by any recipient of Federal assistance or Federal provider of such assistance under section 794 of this title.

(b) In any action or proceeding to enforce or charge a violation of a provision of this subchapter, the court, in its discretion, may allow the prevailing party, other than the United States, a reasonable attorney's fee as part of the costs.

Religious Freedom Restoration Act

42 U.S.C. §2000bb

§2000bb. Congressional Findings and Declaration of Purposes

(a) *Findings.* The Congress finds that—

(1) the framers of the Constitution, recognizing free exercise of religion as an unalienable right, secured its protection in the First Amendment to the Constitution;

(2) laws "neutral" toward religion may burden religious exercise as surely as laws intended to interfere with religious exercise;

(3) governments should not substantially burden religious exercise without compelling justification;

(4) in Employment Division v. Smith, 494 U.S. 872 (1990) the Supreme Court virtually eliminated the requirement that the government justify burdens on religious exercise imposed by laws neutral toward religion; and

(5) the compelling interest test as set forth in prior Federal court rulings is a workable test for striking sensible balances between religious liberty and competing prior governmental interests.

(b) *Purposes.* The purposes of this chapter are—

(1) to restore the compelling interest test as set forth in Sherbert v. Verner, 374 U.S. 398 (1963) and Wisconsin v. Yoder, 406 U.S. 205 (1972) and to guarantee its application in all cases where free exercise of religion is substantially burdened; and

(2) to provide a claim or defense to persons whose religious exercise is substantially burdened by government.

§2000bb-1. Free Exercise of Religion Protected

(a) *In general.* Government shall not substantially burden a person's exercise of religion even if the burden results from a rule of general applicability, except as provided in subsection (b) of this section.

(b) *Exception.* Government may substantially burden a person's exercise of religion only if it demonstrates that application of the burden to the person —

    (1) is in furtherance of a compelling governmental interest; and

    (2) is the least restrictive means of furthering that compelling governmental interest.

(c) *Judicial relief.* A person whose religious exercise has been burdened in violation of this section may assert that violation as a claim or defense in a judicial proceeding and obtain appropriate relief against a government. Standing to assert a claim or defense under this section shall be governed by the general rules of standing under article III of the Constitution.

§2000bb-2. Definitions

As used in this chapter —

    (1) the term "government" includes a branch, department, agency, instrumentality, and official (or other person acting under color of law) of the United States, or of a covered entity;

    (2) the term "covered entity" means the District of Columbia, the Commonwealth of Puerto Rico, and each territory and possession of the United States;

    (3) the term "demonstrates" means meets the burdens of going forward with the evidence and of persuasion; and

    (4) the term "exercise of religion" means religious exercise, as defined in section 2000cc-5 of this title.

§2000bb-3. Applicability

(a) *In general.* This chapter applies to all Federal law, and the implementation of that law, whether statutory or otherwise, and whether adopted before or after November 16, 1993.

(b) *Rule of construction.* Federal statutory law adopted after November 16, 1993 is subject to this chapter unless such law explicitly excludes such application by reference to this chapter.

(c) *Religious belief unaffected.* Nothing in this chapter shall be construed to authorize any government to burden any religious belief.

§2000bb-4. Establishment Clause Unaffected

Nothing in this chapter shall be construed to affect, interpret, or in any way address that portion of the First Amendment prohibiting laws respecting the establishment of religion (referred to in this section as the "Establishment Clause"). Granting government funding, benefits, or exemptions, to the extent permissible under the Establishment Clause, shall not constitute a violation of this chapter. As used in this section, the term "granting", used with respect to government funding, benefits, or exemptions, does not include the denial of government funding, benefits, or exemptions.

Residual Statute of Limitations

28 U.S.C. §1658

§1658. Time Limitations on the Commencement of Civil Actions Arising under Acts of Congress

(a) Except as otherwise provided by law, a civil action arising under an Act of Congress enacted after the date of the enactment of this section [December 1, 1990] may not be commenced later than 4 years after the cause of action accrues.

(b) Notwithstanding subsection (a), a private right of action that involves a claim of fraud, deceit, manipulation, or contrivance in contravention of a regulatory requirement concerning the securities laws, as defined in section 3(a)(47) of the Securities Exchange Act of 1934 [15 U.S.C. §78c(a)(47)], may be brought not later than the earlier of—

> (1) 2 years after the discovery of the facts constituting the violation; or
>
> (2) 5 years after such violation.

Title VI of the Civil Rights Act of 1964

42 U.S.C. §§2000d, 2000d-1, 2000d-3, 2000d-4(a)

§2000d [§601]. Nondiscrimination in Federally Assisted Programs

No person in the United States shall, on the ground of race, color, or national origin, be excluded from participation in, be denied the benefits of, or be subjected to discrimination under any program or activity receiving Federal financial assistance.

§2000d-1 [§602]. Federal Authority and Financial Assistance to Programs or Activities by way of Grant, Loan, or Contract Other than Contract of Insurance or Guaranty; Rules and Regulations; Approved by President; Compliance with Requirements; Reports to Congressional Committees; Effective Date of Administrative Action.

Each federal department and agency which is empowered to extend Federal financial assistance to any program or activity, by way of grant, loan, or contract other than a contract of insurance or guaranty, is authorized and directed to effectuate the provisions of section 2000d of this title with respect to such program or activity by issuing rules, regulations, or orders of general applicability which shall be consistent with achievement of the objectives of the statute authorizing the financial assistance in connection with which the action is taken. No such rule, regulation, or order shall become effective unless and until approved by the President. Compliance with any requirement adopted pursuant to this section may be affected (1) by the termination of or refusal to grant or to continue assistance under such program or activity to any recipient as to whom there has been an express finding on the record, after opportunity for hearing, of a failure to comply with such requirement, but such termination or refusal shall be limited to the particular political entity, or part thereof, or other recipient as to whom such a finding has been made and shall be limited in its effect to the particular program, or part thereof, in which such noncompliance has been so found, or (2) by any other means authorized by law: *Provided, however,* That no such action shall be taken until the department or agency concerned has advised the appropriate person or persons of the failure to comply with the requirement and has determined that compliance cannot be secured by voluntary means. In the case of any action terminating, or refusing to grant or continue, assistance because of failure to comply with a requirement, imposed pursuant to this section, the head of the Federal department or agency shall file with the committees of the House and Senate having legislative jurisdiction over the program or activity involved a full written report of the circumstances and the grounds for such action. No such action shall become effective until thirty days have elapsed after the filing of such report.

§2000d-3 [§604]. Construction of Provisions Not to Authorize Administrative Action with Respect to Employment Practices Except Where Primary Objective of Federal Financial Assistance Is to Provide Employment.

Nothing contained in this subchapter shall be construed to authorize action under this subchapter by any department or agency with respect to any employment practice of any employer, employment agency, or labor organization except where a primary objective of the Federal financial assistance is to provide employment.

§2000d-4(a) [§606]. Interpretation of "Program or Activity"

For the purposes of this title, the term "program or activity" and the term "program" mean all of the operations of—

(1)(A) a department, agency, special purpose district, or other instrumentality of a State or a local government; or

(B) the entity of such State or local government that distributes such assistance and each such department or agency (and each other State or local government entity) to which the assistance is extended, in the case of assistance to a State or local government;

(2)(A) a college, university, or other postsecondary institution, or a public system of higher education; or

(B) a local educational agency (as defined in section 7801 of Title 20), system of vocational education, or other school system;

(3)(A) an entire corporation, partnership, or other private organization, or an entire sole proprietorship—

(i) if assistance is extended to such corporation, partnership, private organization, or sole proprietorship as a whole; or

(ii) which is principally engaged in the business of providing education, health care, housing, social services, or parks and recreation; or

(B) the entire plant or other comparable, geographically separate facility to which Federal financial assistance is extended, in the case of any other corporation, partnership, private organization, or sole proprietorship; or

(4) any other entity which is established by two or more of the entities described in paragraph (1), (2), or (3); any part of which is extended Federal financial assistance.

Title VII of the Civil Rights Act of 1964

42 U.S.C. §§2000e–2000e-17

TITLE VII

§2000e [§701]. Equal Employment Opportunity Definitions

For the purposes of this title —

(a) The term "person" includes one or more individuals, governments, governmental agencies, political subdivisions, labor unions, partnerships, associations, corporations, legal representatives, mutual companies, joint-stock companies, trusts, unincorporated organizations, trustees, trustees in bankruptcy, or receivers.

(b) The term "employer" means a person engaged in an industry affecting commerce who has fifteen or more employees for each working day in each of twenty or more calendar weeks in the current or preceding calendar year, and any agent of such a person, but such term does not include (1) the United States, a corporation wholly owned by the Government of the United States, an Indian tribe, or any department or agency of the District of Columbia subject by statute to procedures of the competitive service (as defined in section 2102 of title 5 of the United States Code), or (2) a bona fide private membership club (other than a labor organization) which is exempt from taxation under section 501(c) of the Internal Revenue Code of 1954, except that, during the first year after the date of enactment of the Equal Employment Opportunity Act of 1972, persons having fewer than twenty-five employees (and their agents) shall not be considered employers.

(c) The term "employment agency" means any person regularly undertaking with or without compensation to procure employees for an employer or to procure for employees opportunities to work for an employer and includes an agent of such a person.

(d) The term "labor organization" means a labor organization engaged in an industry affecting commerce, and any agent of such an organization, and includes any organization of any kind, any agency, or employee representation committee, group, association, or plan so engaged in which employees participate and which exists for the purpose, in whole or in part, of dealing with employees concerning grievances, labor disputes, wages, rates of pay, hours, or other terms or conditions of employment, and any conference, general committee, joint or system board, or joint council so engaged which is subordinate to a national or international labor organization.

(e) A labor organization shall be deemed to be engaged in an industry affecting commerce if (1) it maintains or operates a hiring hall or hiring office which procures employees for an employer or produces for employees opportunities to work for an employer, or (2) the number of its members (or, where it is a labor organization composed of other labor organizations or their representatives, if the aggregate number of the members of such labor organization) is (A) twenty-five or more during the first year after the date of enactment of the Equal Employment Opportunity Act of 1972, or (B) fifteen or more thereafter, and such labor organization —

(1) is the certified representative of employees under the provisions of the National Labor Relations Act, as amended, or the Railway Labor Act, as amended;

(2) although not certified, is a national or international labor organization or a local labor organization recognized or acting as the representative of employees of an employer or employers engaged in an industry affecting commerce; or

(3) has chartered a local labor organization or subsidiary body which is representing or actively seeking to represent employees of employers within the meaning of paragraph (1) or (2); or

(4) has been chartered by a labor organization representing or actively seeking to represent employees within the meaning of paragraph (1) or (2) as the local or subordinate body through which such employees may enjoy membership or become affiliated with such labor organization; or

(5) is a conference, general committee, joint or system board, or joint council subordinate to a national or international labor organization, which includes a labor organization engaged in an industry affecting commerce within the meaning of any of the preceding paragraphs of this subsection.

(f) The term "employee" means an individual employed by an employer, except that term "employee" shall not include any person elected to public office in any State or political subdivision of any State by the qualified voters thereof, or any person chosen by such officer to be on such officer's personal staff, or an appointee on the policy making level or an immediate adviser with respect to the exercise of the constitutional or legal powers of the office. The exemption set forth in the preceding sentence shall not include employees subject to the civil service laws of a State government, governmental agency, or political subdivision. With respect to employment in a foreign country, such term includes an individual who is a citizen of the United States.

(g) The term "commerce" means trade, traffic, commerce, transportation, transmission, or communication among the several States; or between a State and any place outside thereof; or within the District of Columbia, or a possession of the United States; or between points in the same State but through a point outside thereof.

(h) The term "industry affecting commerce" means any activity, business, or industry in commerce or in which a labor dispute would hinder or obstruct commerce or the free flow of commerce and includes any activity or industry "affecting commerce" within the meaning of the Labor-Management Reporting and Disclosure Act of 1959, and further includes any governmental industry, business, or activity.

(i) The term "State" includes a State of the United States, the District of Columbia, Puerto Rico, the Virgin Islands, American Samoa, Guam, Wake Island, the Canal Zone, and Outer Continental Shelf lands defined in the Outer Continental Shelf Lands Act.

(j) The term "religion" includes all aspects of religious observance and practice, as well as belief, unless an employer demonstrates that he is unable to reasonably accommodate to an employee's or prospective employee's religious observance or practice without undue hardship on the conduct of the employer's business.

(k) The terms "because of sex" or "on the basis of sex" includes, but are not limited to, because of or on the basis of pregnancy, childbirth or related medical conditions; and women affected by pregnancy, childbirth, or related medical conditions shall be treated the same for all employment-related purposes, including receipt of benefits under fringe benefit programs, as other persons not so affected but similar in their ability or inability to work, and nothing in section 2000e-2(h) of this title shall be interpreted to permit otherwise. This subsection shall not require an employer to pay for health insurance benefits for abortion, except where the life of the mother would be endangered if the fetus were carried to term, or except where medical complications have arisen from an abortion: Provided, That nothing herein shall preclude an employer from providing abortion benefits or otherwise affect bargaining agreements in regard to abortion.

(l) The term "complaining party" means the Commission, the Attorney General, or a person who may bring an action or proceeding under this title.

(m) The term "demonstrates" means meets the burdens of production and persuasion.

(n) The term "respondent" means an employer, employment agency, labor organization, joint labor-management committee controlling apprenticeship or other training or retraining program, including an on-the-job training program, or Federal entity subject to section 2000e-16 of this title.

§2000e-1 [§702]. Application to Foreign and Religious Employment

(a) *Inapplicability of subchapter to certain aliens and employees of religious entities.* This subchapter shall not apply to an employer with respect to the employment of aliens outside any State, or to a religious corporation, association, educational institution, or society with respect to the employment of individuals of a particular religion to perform work connected with the carrying on by such corporation, association, educational institution, or society of its activities.

(b) *Compliance with statute as violative of foreign law*. It shall not be unlawful under section 2000e-2 or 2000e-3 of this title for any employer (or a corporation controlled by an employer), labor organization, employment agency, or joint labor-management committee controlling apprenticeship or other training or retraining (including on-the-job training programs) to take any action otherwise prohibited by such section, with respect to an employee in a workplace in a foreign country if compliance with such section would cause such employer (or such corporation), such organization, such agency, or such committee to violate the law of the foreign country in which such workplace is located.

(c) *Control of corporation incorporated in a foreign country*.

(1) If an employer controls a corporation whose place of incorporation is a foreign country, any practice prohibited by section 2000e-2 or 2000e-3 of this title engaged in such corporation shall be presumed to be engaged in such employer.

(2) Sections 2000e-2 and 2000e-3 of this title shall not apply with respect to the foreign operations of an employer that is a foreign person not controlled by an American employer.

(3) For purposes of this subsection, the determination of whether an employer controls a corporation shall be based on—

(A) the interrelation of operations;

(B) the common management;

(C) the centralized control of labor relations; and

(D) the common ownership or financial control, of the employer and the corporation.

§2000e-2 [§703]. *Discrimination Because of Race, Color, Religion, Sex, or National Origin*

(a) *Employer practices*. It shall be an unlawful employment practice for an employer—

(1) to fail or refuse to hire or to discharge any individual, or otherwise to discriminate against any individual with respect to his compensation, terms, conditions, or privileges of employment, because of such individual's race, color, religion, sex, or national origin; or

(2) to limit, segregate, or classify his employees or applicants for employment in any way which would deprive or tend to deprive any individual of employment opportunities or otherwise adversely affect his status as an employee, because of such individual's race, color, religion, sex, or national origin.

(b) *Employment agency practices*. It shall be an unlawful employment practice for an employment agency to fail or refuse to refer for employment, or otherwise to discriminate against, any individual because of his race, color, religion, sex, or national origin, or to classify or refer for employment any individual on the basis of his race, color, religion, sex, or national origin.

(c) *Labor organization practices*. It shall be an unlawful employment practice for a labor organization —

(1) to exclude or to expel from its membership, or otherwise to discriminate against, any individual because of his race, color, religion, sex, or national origin;

(2) to limit, segregate, or classify its membership or applicants for membership or to classify or fail to refuse to refer for employment any individual, in any way which would deprive or tend to deprive any individual of employment opportunities, or would limit such employment opportunities or otherwise adversely affect his status as an employee or as an applicant for employment, because of such individual's race, color, religion, sex, or national origin; or

(3) to cause or attempt to cause an employer to discriminate against an individual in violation of this section.

(d) *Training programs*. It shall be an unlawful employment practice for any employer, labor organization, or joint labor-management committee controlling apprenticeship or other training or retraining, including on-the-job training programs, to discriminate against any individual because of his race, color, religion, sex, or national origin in admission to, or employment in, any program established to provide apprenticeship or other training.

(e) *Business or enterprises with personnel qualified on basis of religion, sex, or national origin; educational institutions with personnel of particular religion*. Notwithstanding any other provision of this title, (1) it shall not be an unlawful employment practice for an employer to hire and employ employees, for an employment agency to classify; or refer for employment any individual, for a labor organization to classify its membership or to classify or refer for employment any individual, or for an employer, labor organization, or joint labor-management committee controlling apprenticeship or other training or retraining programs to admit or employ any individual in any such program, on the basis of his religion, sex, or national origin in those certain instances where religion, sex, or national origin is a bona fide occupational qualification reasonably necessary to the normal operation of that particular business or enterprise, and (2) it shall not be an unlawful employment practice for a school, college, university, or other educational institution or institution of learning to hire and employ employees of a particular religion if such school, college, university, or other educational institution or institution of learning is, in whole or in substantial part, owned, supported, controlled, or managed by a particular religion or by a particular religious corporation, association, or society, or if the curriculum of such school, college, university, or other educational institution or institution of learning is directed toward the propagation of a particular religion.

(f) *Members of Communist Party or Communist-action or Communist-front organizations*. As used in this title, the phrase "unlawful employment practice" shall not be deemed to include any action or measure taken by an employer, labor organization, joint labor-management committee, or employment agency with respect to an individual who is a member of the Communist Party of the United States or of any other organization required to register as a Communist-action or

Communist-front organization by final order of the Subversive Activities Control Board pursuant to the Subversive Activities Control Act of 1950.

(g) *National security.* Notwithstanding any other provision of this title, it shall not be an unlawful employment practice for an employee to fail or refuse to hire and employ any individual for any position, for an employer to discharge an individual from any position, or for an employment agency to fail or refuse to refer any individual for employment in any position, or for a labor organization to fail or refuse to refer any individual for employment in any position, if—

(1) the occupancy of such position, or access to the premises in or upon which any part of the duties of such position is performed or is to be performed, is subject to any requirement imposed in the interest of the national security of the United States under any security program in effect pursuant to or administered under any statute of the United States or any Executive Order of the President; and

(2) such individual has not fulfilled or has ceased to fulfill that requirement.

(h) *Seniority or merit system; quantity or quality of production; ability test; compensation based on sex and authorized by minimum wage provisions.* Notwithstanding any other provision of this title, it shall not be an unlawful employment practice for an employer to apply different standards of compensation, or different terms, conditions, or privileges of employment pursuant to a bona fide seniority or merit system, or a system which measures earnings by quantity or quality or production or to employees who work in different locations, provided that such differences are not the result of an intention to discriminate because of race, color, religion, sex, or national origin; nor shall it be an unlawful employment practice for an employer to give and to act upon the results of any professionally developed ability test provided that such test, its administration or action upon the results is not designed, intended, or used to discriminate because of race, color, religion, sex, or national origin. It shall not be an unlawful employment practice under this title for any employer to differentiate upon the basis of sex in determining the amount of the wages or compensation paid to employees of such employer if such differentiation is authorized by the provisions of Section 6(d) of the Fair Labor Standards Act of 1938 as amended (29 U.S.C. 206(d)).

(i) *Businesses or enterprises extending preferential treatment to Indians.* Nothing contained in this title shall apply to any business or enterprise on or near an Indian reservation with respect to any publicly announced employment practice of such business or enterprise under which a preferential treatment is given to any individual because he is an Indian living on or near a reservation.

(j) *Preferential treatment not to be granted on account of existing number or percentage imbalance.* Nothing contained in this title shall be interpreted to require any employer, employment agency, labor organization, or joint labor-management committee subject to this title to grant preferential treatment to any individual or to any group because of the race, color, religion, sex, or national origin of such individual or group on account of an imbalance which may exist with respect to the total number of percentage of persons of any race, color, religion, sex, or national origin employed by any employer, referred or classified for employment by any employment agency or labor organization, admitted to membership or classified by any labor organization, or admitted to, or employed in, any apprenticeship or other training program, in comparison with the total number or percentage of persons of such race, color, religion, sex, or national origin in any community, State, section, or other area, or in the available work force in any community, State, section, or other area.

(k) *Burden of proof in disparate impact cases.*

(1)(A) An unlawful employment practice based on disparate impact is established under this title only if—

(i) a complaining party demonstrates that a respondent uses a particular employment practice that causes a disparate impact on the basis of race, color, religion, sex, or national origin and the respondent fails to demonstrate that the challenged practice is job related for the position in question and consistent with business necessity; or

(ii) the complaining party makes the demonstration described in subparagraph (C) with respect to an alternative employment practice and the respondent refuses to adopt such alternative employment practice.

(B)(i) With respect to demonstrating that a particular employment practice causes a disparate impact as described in subparagraph (A)(i), the complaining party shall demonstrate that each particular challenged employment practice causes a disparate impact, except that if the complaining party can demonstrate to the court that the elements of a respondent's decision making process are not capable of separation for analysis, the decision making process may be analyzed as one employment practice.

(ii) If the respondent demonstrates that a specific employment practice does not cause the disparate impact, the respondent shall not be required to demonstrate that such practice is required by business necessity.

(C) The demonstration referred to by subparagraph (A)(ii) shall be in accordance with the law as it existed on June 4, 1989, with respect to the concept of "alternative employment practice."

(2) A demonstration that an employment practice is required by business necessity may not be used as a defense against a claim of intentional discrimination under this title.

(3) Notwithstanding any other provision of this title, a rule barring the employment of an individual who currently and knowingly uses or possesses a controlled substance, as defined in schedules I and II of section 102(6) of the Controlled Substances Act (21 U.S.C. 802(6)), other than the use or possession of a drug taken under the supervision of a licensed health care professional, or any other use or possession authorized by the Controlled Substances Act or any other provision of Federal law, shall be considered an unlawful employment practice under this title only if such rule is adopted or

applied with an intent to discriminate because of race, color, religion, sex, or national origin.

(l) *Prohibition of discriminatory use of test scores.* It shall be an unlawful employment practice for a respondent, in connection with the selection or referral of applicants or candidates for employment or promotion, to adjust the scores of, use different cutoff scores for, or otherwise alter the results of, employment related tests on the basis of race, color, religion, sex, or national origin.

(m) *Impermissible consideration of race, color, religion, sex, or national origin in employment practices.* Except as otherwise provided in this title, an unlawful employment practice is established when the complaining party demonstrates that race, color, religion, sex, or national origin was a motivating factor for any employment practice, even though other factors also motivated the practice.

(n) *Resolution of challenges to employment practices implementing litigated or consent judgment or orders.*

(1)(A) Notwithstanding any other provision of law, and except as provided in paragraph (2), an employment practice that implements and is within the scope of a litigated or consent judgment or order that resolves a claim of employment discrimination under the Constitution or Federal civil rights laws may not be challenged under the circumstances described in subparagraph (B).

(B) A practice described in paragraph (A) may not be challenged in a claim under the Constitution or Federal civil rights laws —

(i) by a person who, prior to the entry of the judgment or order described in subparagraph (A), had —

(I) actual notice of the proposed judgment or order sufficient to apprise such person that such judgment or order might adversely affect the interests and legal rights of such person and that an opportunity was available to present objections to such judgment or order by a future date certain; and

(II) a reasonable opportunity to present objections to such judgment or order; or

(ii) by a person whose interests were adequately represented by another person who had previously challenged the judgment or order on the same legal grounds and with a similar factual situation, unless there has been an intervening change in law or fact.

(2) Nothing in this subsection shall be construed to —

(A) alter the standards for intervention under Rule 24 of the Federal Rules of Civil Procedure or apply to the rights of parties who have successfully intervened pursuant to such rule in the proceeding in which the parties intervened;

(B) apply to the rights of parties to the action in which a litigated or consent judgment or order was entered, or of members of a class represented or sought to be represented in such action, or of members of a group on whose behalf relief was sought in such action by the Federal Government;

(C) prevent challenges to a litigated or consent judgment or order on the ground that such judgment or order was obtained through collusion or fraud, or is transparently invalid or was entered by a court lacking subject matter jurisdiction; or

(D) authorize or permit the denial to any person of the due process of law required by the Constitution.

(3) Any action not precluded under this subsection that challenges an employment consent judgment or order described in paragraph (1) shall be brought in the court, and if possible before the judge, that entered such judgment or order. Nothing in this subsection shall preclude a transfer of such action pursuant to section 1404 of Title 28, United States Code.

§2000e-3 [§704]. Other Unlawful Employment Practices

(a) *Discrimination for making charges, testifying, assisting, or participating in enforcement proceedings.* It shall be an unlawful employment practice for an employer to discriminate against any of his employees or applicants for employment, for an employment agency or joint labor-management committee controlling apprenticeship or other training or retraining, including on-the-job training programs, to discriminate against any individual, or for a labor organization to discriminate against any member thereof or applicant for membership, because he has opposed any practice, made an unlawful employment practice by this title, or because he has made a charge, testified, assisted, or participated in any manner in an investigation, proceeding, or hearing under this title.

(b) *Printing or publication of notices or advertisements indicating prohibited preference, specification, or discrimination; occupational qualification exception.* It shall be an unlawful employment practice for an employer, labor organization; employment agency, or joint labor-management committee controlling apprenticeship or other training or retraining, including on-the-job training programs, to print or cause to be printed or published any notice or advertisement relating to employment by such a labor organization, or relating to any classification or referral for employment by such an employment agency, or relating to admission to, or employment in, any program established to provide apprenticeship or other training by such a joint labor-management committee indicating any preference, limitation, specification, or discrimination, based on race, color, religion, sex, or national origin, except that such a notice or advertisement may indicate a preference, limitation, specification, or discrimination based on religion, sex, or national origin when religion, sex, or national origin is a bona fide occupational qualification for employment.

§2000e-4 [§705]. Equal Employment Opportunity Commission

(a) *Creation; composition; political representation; Chairman and Vice Chairman; compensation of personnel.* There is hereby created a Commission to be known as the Equal Employment Opportunity Commission, which shall be composed of five members, not more than three of whom shall be members of the same political party. Members of the Commission shall be appointed by the President by and with the advice and consent of the Senate for a term of five years. Any individual chosen to fill a vacancy shall be appointed only for the unexpired term of the member whom he shall succeed, and all members of the Commission shall continue to serve until their successors are appointed and qualified, except that no such member of the Commission shall continue to serve (1) for more than sixty days when the Congress is in session unless a nomination to fill such vacancy shall have been submitted to the Senate, or (2) after the adjournment sine die of the session of the Senate in which such nomination was submitted. The President shall designate one member to serve as Chairman of the Commission, and one member to serve as Vice Chairman. The Chairman shall be responsible on behalf of the Commission for the administrative operations of the Commission, and, except as provided in subsection (b), shall appoint, in accordance with the provisions of title 5, United States Code, governing appointments in the competitive service, such officers, agents, attorneys, hearing examiners, and employees as he deems necessary to assist it in the performance of its functions and to fix their compensation in accordance with the provisions of chapter 51 and subchapter III of chapter 53 of title 5, United States Code, relating to classification and General Schedule pay rates: Provided, That assignment, removal, and compensation of hearing examiners shall be in accordance with sections 3105, 3344, 5372, and 7521 of title 5, United States Code.

(b) *General Counsel; appointment; term; duties; representation by attorneys and Attorney General.*

(1) There shall be a General Counsel of the Commission appointed by the President, by and with the advice and consent of the Senate, for a term of four years. The General Counsel shall have responsibility for the conduct of litigation as provided in sections 706 and 707 of this title. The General Counsel shall have such other duties as the Commission may prescribe or as may be provided by law and shall concur with the Chairman of the Commission on the appointment and supervision of regional attorneys. The General Counsel of the Commission on the effective date of this Act shall continue in such position and perform the functions specified in this subsection until a successor is appointed and qualified.

(2) Attorneys appointed under this section may, at the direction of the Commission, appear for and represent the Commission in any case in court, provided that the Attorney General shall conduct all litigation to which the commission is a party in the Supreme Court pursuant to this title.

(c) *Exercise of power during vacancy; quorum.* A vacancy in the Commission shall not impair the right of the remaining members to exercise all the powers of the Commission and three members thereof shall constitute a quorum.

(d) *Seal; judicial notice.* The commission shall have an official seal which shall be judicially noticed.

(e) *Reports to Congress and to President.* The Commission shall at the middle and at the close of each fiscal year report to the Congress and to the President concerning the action it has taken; the names, salaries, and duties of all individuals in its employ and the moneys it has disbursed; and shall make such further reports on the cause of and means of eliminating discrimination and such recommendations for further legislation as may appear desirable.

(f) *Principal and other office.* The principal office of the Commission shall be in or near the District of Columbia, but it may meet or exercise any or all its powers at any other place. The Commission may establish such regional or state offices as it deems necessary to accomplish the purpose of this title.

(g) *Power of Commission.* The Commission shall have power—

(1) to cooperate with and, with their consent, utilize regional, state, local, and other agencies, both public and private, and individuals;

(2) to pay to witnesses whose depositions are taken or who are summoned before the Commission or any of its agents the same witness and mileage fees as are paid to witnesses in the courts of the United States;

(3) to furnish to persons subject to this title such technical assistance as they may request to further their compliance with this title or an order issued thereunder;

(4) upon the request of (i) any employer, whose employees or some of them, or (ii) any labor organization, whose members or some of them, refuse or threaten to refuse to cooperate in effectuating the provisions of this title, to assist in such effectuation by conciliation or such other remedial action as is provided by this title;

(5) to make such technical studies as are appropriate to effectuate the purposes and policies of this title and to make the results of such studies available to the public;

(6) to intervene in a civil action brought under section 706 by an aggrieved party against a respondent other than a government, governmental agency or political subdivision.

(h) *Cooperation with other departments and agencies in performance of educational or promotional activities; outreach activities.*

(1) The Commission shall, in any of its educational or promotional activities, cooperate with other departments and agencies in the performance of such educational and promotional activities.

(2) In exercising its powers under this title, the Commission shall carry out educational and outreach activities (including dissemination of information in languages other than English) targeted to—

(A) individuals who historically have been victims of employment discrimination and have not been equitably served by the Commission; and

(B) individuals on whose behalf the Commission has authority to enforce any other law prohibiting employment discrimination, concerning rights and obligations under this title or such law, as the case may be.

(i) *Personnel subject to political activity restrictions.* All officers, agents, attorneys and employees of the Commission, including the members of the Commission, shall be subject to the provisions of section 9 of the act of August 2, 1939, as amended (Hatch Act), notwithstanding any exemption contained in such section.

(j) *Technical Assistance Training Institute.*

(1) The Commission shall establish a Technical Assistance Training Institute, through which the Commission shall provide technical assistance and training regarding the laws and regulations enforced by the Commission.

(2) An employer or other entity covered under this title shall not be excused from compliance with the requirements of this title because of any failure to receive technical assistance under this subsection.

(3) There are authorized to be appropriated to carry out this subsection such sums as may be necessary for fiscal year 1992.

§2000e-5 [§706]. *Prevention of Unlawful Employment Practices*

(a) *Power of Commission to prevent unlawful employment practices.* The Commission is empowered, as hereinafter provided, to prevent any person from engaging in any unlawful employment practice as set forth in section 703 or 704 of this title.

(b) *Charges by persons aggrieved or member of Commission of unlawful employment practices by employers, etc.; filing; allegations; notice to respondent; contents of notice; investigation by Commission; contents of charges; prohibition on disclosure of charges; determination of reasonable cause; conference, conciliation, and persuasion for elimination of unlawful practices; prohibition on disclosure of informal endeavors to end unlawful practices; use of evidence in subsequent proceedings; penalties for disclosure of information; time for determination of reasonable cause.* Whenever a charge is filed by or on behalf of a person claiming to be aggrieved, or by a member of the Commission, alleging that an employer, employment agency, labor organization, or joint labor-management committee controlling apprenticeship or other training or retraining including on-the-job training programs, has engaged in an unlawful employment practice, the Commission shall serve a notice of the charge (including the date, place and circumstances of the alleged unlawful employment practice) on such employer, employment agency, labor organization, or joint labor-management committee (hereinafter referred to as the "respondent") within ten days and shall make an investigation thereof. Charges shall be in writing under oath or affirmation and shall contain such information and be in such form as the Commission requires. Charges shall not be made public by the Commission. If the Commission determines after such investigation that there is not reasonable cause to believe that the charge is true, it shall dismiss the charge and promptly notify the person claiming to be aggrieved and the respondent of its action. In determining whether reasonable cause exists, the Commission shall accord substantial weight to final findings and orders made by the State or local authorities in proceedings commenced under State or local law pursuant to the requirements of subsections (c) and (d). If the Commission determines after such investigation that there is reasonable cause to believe that the charge is true, the Commission shall endeavor to eliminate any such alleged unlawful employment practice by informal methods of conference, conciliation, and persuasion. Nothing said or done during and as a part of such informal endeavors may be made public by the Commission, its officers or employees, or used as evidence in a subsequent proceeding without the written consent of the persons concerned. Any person who makes public information in violation of this subsection shall be fined not more than $1,000 or imprisoned for not more than one year, or both. The Commission shall make its determination on reasonable cause as promptly as possible and, so far as practicable, not later than one hundred and twenty days from the filing of the charge or, where applicable under subsection (c) or (d), from the date upon which the Commission is authorized to take action with respect to the charge.

(c) *State or local enforcement proceedings; notification of state or local authority; time for filing charges with Commission; commencement of proceedings.* In the case of an alleged unlawful employment practice occurring in a State, or political subdivision of a State, which as a State or local law prohibiting the unlawful employment practice alleged and establishing or authorizing a State or local authority to grant or seek relief from such practice or to institute criminal proceedings with respect thereto upon receiving notice thereof, no charge may be filed under subsection (a) [Probably should be subsection (b)] by the person aggrieved before the expiration of sixty days after proceedings have been commenced under the State or local law, unless such proceedings have been earlier terminated, provided that such sixty-day period shall be extended to one hundred and twenty days during the first year after the effective date of such State or local law. If any requirement for the commencement of such proceedings is imposed by a State or local authority other than requirement of the filing of a written and signed statement of the facts upon which the proceeding is based, the proceeding shall be deemed to have been commenced for the purposes of this subsection at the time such statement is sent by registered mail to the appropriate State or local authority.

(d) *State or local enforcement proceedings; notification of state or local authority; time for action on charges by Commission.* In the case of any charge filed by a member of the Commission alleging an unlawful employment practice occurring in a State or political subdivision of a State which has a State or local law prohibiting the practice alleged and establishing or authorizing a State or local authority to grant or seek relief from such practice or to institute criminal proceedings with respect thereto upon receiving notice thereof, the Commission shall, before taking any action with respect to such charge, notify the appropriate State or local officials and, upon request, afford them a reasonable time, but not less than sixty days (provided that such sixty-day period shall be extended to one hundred and twenty days during the first year after the effective day of such State or local law), unless a shorter period is requested, to act under such State or local law to remedy the practice alleged.

(e) *Time for filing charges; time for service of notice of charge; filing of charge by Commission with state or local agency; seniority system.*

(1) A charge under this section shall be filed within one hundred and eighty days after alleged the unlawful employment practice occurred and notice of the charge (including the date, place and circumstances of the alleged unlawful employment practice) shall be served upon the person against whom such charge is made within ten days thereafter, except that in a case of an unlawful employment practice with respect to which the person aggrieved has initially instituted proceedings with a State or local agency with authority to grant or seek relief from such practice or to institute criminal proceedings with respect thereto upon receiving notice thereof, such charge shall be filed

by or on behalf of the person aggrieved within three hundred days after the alleged unlawful employment practice occurred, or within thirty days after receiving notice that the State or local agency has terminated the proceedings under the State or local law, whichever is earlier, and a copy of such charge shall be filed by the Commission with the State or local agency.

(2) For purposes of this section, an unlawful employment practice occurs, with respect to a seniority system that has been adopted for an intentionally discriminatory purpose in violation of this title (whether or not that discriminatory purpose is apparent on the face of the seniority provision), when the seniority system is adopted, when an individual becomes subject to the seniority system, or when a person aggrieved is injured by the application of the seniority system or provision of the system.

(3)(A) For purposes of this section, an unlawful employment practice occurs, with respect to discrimination in compensation in violation of this title, when a discriminatory compensation decision or other practice is adopted, when an individual becomes subject to a discriminatory compensation decision or other practice, or when an individual is affected by application of a discriminatory compensation decision or other practice, including each time wages, benefits, or other compensation is paid, resulting in whole or in part from such a decision or other practice.

(B) In addition to any relief authorized by section 1977A of the Revised Statutes (*42 U.S.C. 1981a*), liability may accrue and an aggrieved person may obtain relief as provided in subsection (g)(1), including recovery of back pay for up to two years preceding the filing of the charge, where the unlawful employment practices that have occurred during the charge filing period are similar or related to unlawful employment practices with regard to discrimination in compensation that occurred outside the time for filing a charge.

(f) *Civil action by Commission, Attorney General, or person aggrieved; preconditions; procedure; appointment of attorney; payment of fees, costs, or security; intervention; stay of Federal proceedings; action for appropriate temporary or preliminary relief pending final disposition of charge; jurisdiction and venue of United States courts; designation of judge to hear and determine case; assignment of case for hearing; expedition of case; appointment of master.*

(1) If within thirty days after a charge is filed with the Commission or within thirty days after expiration of any period of reference under subsections (c) or (d), the Commission has been unable to secure from the respondent a conciliation agreement acceptable to the Commission, the Commission may bring a civil action against any respondent not a government, governmental agency, or political subdivision named in the charge. In the case of a respondent which is a government, governmental agency, or political subdivision, if the Commission has been unable to secure from the respondent a conciliation agreement acceptable to the Commission, the Commission shall take no further action and shall refer the case to the Attorney General who may bring civil action against such respondent in the appropriate United States district court. The person or persons aggrieved shall have the right to

intervene in a civil action brought by the Commission or the Attorney General in a case involving a government, governmental agency, or political subdivision. If a charge filed with the Commission pursuant to subsection (b) is dismissed by the Commission, or if within one hundred and eighty days from the filing of such charge or the expiration of any period of reference under subsections (c) or (d), whichever is later, the Commission has not filed a civil action under this section or the Attorney General has not filed a civil action in a case involving a government, governmental agency, or political subdivision, or the Commission has not entered into a conciliation agreement to which the person aggrieved is a party, the Commission, or the Attorney General in a case involving a government, governmental agency, or political subdivision, shall so notify the person aggrieved and within ninety days after the giving of such notice a civil action may be brought against the respondent named in the charge (A) by the person claiming to be aggrieved or (B) if such charge was filed by a member of the Commission, by any person whom the charge alleged was aggrieved by the alleged unlawful employment practice. Upon application by the complainant and in such circumstances as the court may deem just, the court may appoint an attorney for such complainant and may authorize the commencement of the action without the payment of fees, costs, or security. Upon timely application, the court may, in its discretion, permit the Commission, or the Attorney General in a case involving a government, governmental agency, or political subdivision, to intervene in such civil action upon certification that the case is of general public importance. Upon request, the court may, in its discretion, stay further proceedings for not more than sixty days pending the termination of State or local proceedings described in subsections (c) or (d) of this section or further efforts of the Commission to obtain voluntary compliance.

(2) Whenever a charge is filed with the Commission and the Commission concludes on the basis of a preliminary investigation that prompt judicial action is necessary to carry out the purpose of this Act, the Commission, or the Attorney General in a case involving a government, governmental agency, or political subdivision, may bring an action for appropriate temporary or preliminary relief pending final disposition of such charge. Any temporary restraining order or order granting preliminary or temporary relief shall be issued in accordance with rule 65 of the Federal Rules of Civil Procedure. It shall be the duty of a court having jurisdiction over proceedings under this section to assign cases for hearing at the earliest practicable date and to cause such cases to be in every way expedited.

(3) Each United States district court and each United States court of a place subject to the jurisdiction of the United States shall have jurisdiction of actions brought under this title. Such an action may be brought in any judicial district in the State in which the unlawful employment practice is alleged to have been committed, in the judicial district in which the employment records relevant to such practice are maintained and administered, or in the judicial district in which the aggrieved person would have worked but for the alleged unlawful employment practice, but if the respondent is not found

within any such district, such an action may be brought within the judicial district in which the respondent has his principal office. For purposes of sections 1404 and 1406 of title 28 of the United States Code, the judicial district in which the respondent has his principal office shall in all cases be considered a district in which the action might have been brought.

(4) It shall be the duty of the chief judge of the district (or in his absence, the acting chief judge) in which the case is pending immediately to designate a judge in such district to hear and determine the case. In the event that no judge in the district is available to hear and determine the case, the chief judge of the district, or the acting chief judge, as the case may be, shall certify this fact to the chief judge of the circuit (or in his absence, the acting chief judge) who shall then designate a district or circuit judge of the circuit to hear and determine the case.

(5) It shall be the duty of the judge designated pursuant to this subsection to assign the case for hearing at the earliest practicable date and to cause the case to be in every way expedited. If such judge has not scheduled the case for trial within one hundred and twenty days after issue has been joined that judge may appoint a master pursuant to rule 53 of the Federal Rules of Civil Procedure.

(g) *Injunctions; appropriate affirmative action; accrual of back pay; reduction of back pay; limitations on judicial orders.*

(1) If the court finds that the respondent has intentionally engaged in or is intentionally engaging in an unlawful employment practice charged in the complaint, the court may enjoin the respondent from engaging in such unlawful employment practice, and order such affirmative action as may be appropriate, which may include, but is not limited to, reinstatement or hiring of employees, with or without back pay (payable by the employer, employment agency, or labor organization, as the case may be, responsible for the unlawful employment practice), or any other equitable relief as the court deems appropriate. Back pay liability shall not accrue from a date more than two years prior to the filing of a charge with the Commission. Interim earnings or amounts earnable with reasonable diligence by the person or persons discriminated against shall operate to reduce the back pay otherwise allowable.

(2)(A) No order of the court shall require the admission or reinstatement of an individual as a member of a union, or the hiring, reinstatement, or promotion of an individual as an employee, or the payment to him of any back pay, if such individual was refused admission, suspended, or expelled, or was refused employment or advancement or was suspended or discharged for any reason other than discrimination on account of race, color, religion, sex, or national origin or in violation of section 704(a).

(B) On a claim in which an individual proves a violation under section 703(m) and a respondent demonstrates that the respondent would have taken the same action in the absence of the impermissible motivating factor, the court—

(i) may grant declaratory relief, injunctive relief (except as provided in clause (ii)), and attorney's fees and costs demonstrated to be directly attributable only to the pursuit of a claim under section 703(m); and

    (ii) shall not award damages or issue an order requiring any admission, reinstatement, hiring, promotion, or payment, described in subparagraph (A).

(h) *Provisions of chapter 6 of title 29 not applicable to civil actions for presentation of unlawful employment practices.* The provisions of the Act entitled "An Act to amend the judicial Code and to define and limit the jurisdiction of courts sitting in equity, and for other purposes," approved March 23, 1932 (29 U.S.C. 101- 115), shall not apply with respect to civil actions brought under this section.

(i) *Proceedings by Commission to compel compliance with judicial orders.* In any case in which an employer, employment agency, or labor organization fails to comply with an order of a court issued in a civil action brought under this section the Commission may commence proceedings to compel compliance with such order.

(j) *Appeals.* Any civil action brought under this section and any proceedings brought under subsection (j) shall be subject to appeal as provided in sections 1291 and 1292, title 28, United States Code.

(k) *Attorney's fees; liability of Commission and United States for costs.* In any action or proceeding under this title the court, in its discretion, may allow the prevailing party, other than the Commission or the United States, a reasonable attorney's fee (including expert fees) as part of the costs, and the Commission and the United States shall be liable for costs the same as a private person.

§2000e-6 [§707]. Suits by the Attorney General

(a) *Complaint.* Whenever the Attorney General has reasonable cause to believe that any person or group of persons is engaged in a pattern or practice of resistance to the full enjoyment of any of the rights secured by this title, and that the pattern or practice is of such a nature and is intended to deny the full exercise of the rights herein described, the Attorney General may bring a civil action in the appropriate district court of the United States by filing with it a complaint (1) signed by him (or in his absence the Acting Attorney General), (2) setting forth facts pertaining to such pattern or practice, and (3) requesting such relief, including an application for a permanent or temporary injunction, restraining order or other order against the person or persons responsible for such pattern or practice, as he deems necessary to insure the full enjoyment of the rights herein described.

(b) *Jurisdiction; hearing and determination.* The district courts of the United States shall have and shall exercise jurisdiction of proceedings instituted pursuant to this section, and in any such proceeding the Attorney General may file with the clerk of such court a request that a court of three judges be convened to hear and determine the case. Such request for the Attorney General shall be accompanied by a certificate that, in the opinion, the case is of general public importance. A copy of the certificate and request for a three-judge court shall be immediately furnished by such clerk to the chief judge of the circuit (or in his absence, the presiding circuit judge of the circuit) in which the case is pending. Upon receipt of such request it shall be the duty of the chief judge of the circuit or the presiding circuit judge, as the case may be, to designate immediately three judges in such circuit, of whom at least one shall be a circuit judge and another of whom shall be a district judge of the court in which the proceeding was instituted, to hear and determine such case, and it shall be the duty of the judges so designated to assign the case for hearing at the earliest practicable date, to participate in the hearing and determination thereof, and to cause the case to be in every way expedited. An appeal from the final judgment of such court will lie to the Supreme Court.

In the event the Attorney General fails to file such a request in any such proceeding, it shall be the duty of the chief judge of the district (or in his absence, the acting chief judge) in which the case is pending immediately to designate a judge in such district to hear and determine the case. In the event that no judge in the district is available to hear and determine the case, the chief judge of the district, or the acting chief judge, as the case may be, shall certify this fact to the chief judge of the circuit (or in his absence, the acting chief judge) who shall then designate a district or circuit judge of the circuit to hear and determine the case.

It shall be the duty of the judge designated pursuant to this section to assign the case for hearing at the earliest practicable date and to cause the case to be in every way expedited.

(c) *Transfer of functions to Commission.* Effective two years after the date of enactment of the Equal Employment Opportunity Act of 1972, the functions of the Attorney General under this section shall be transferred to the Commission, together with such personnel, property, records, and unexpended balances of appropriations, allocations, and other funds employed, used, held, available or to be made available in connection with such functions unless the President submits, and neither House or Congress vetoes, a reorganization plan pursuant to chapter 9 of title 5, United States Code, inconsistent with the provisions of this subsection. The Commission shall carry out such functions in accordance with subsections (d) and (e) of this section.

(d) *Transfer of functions, etc., not to affect suits commenced pursuant to this section prior to date of transfer.* Upon the transfer of functions provided for in subsection (c) of this section, in all suits commenced pursuant to this section prior to the date of such transfer, proceedings shall continue without abatement, all court orders and decrees shall remain in effect, and the Commission shall be substituted as a party for the United States of America, the Attorney General, or the Acting Attorney General, as appropriate.

(e) *Investigation and action by Commission pursuant to filing of charge of discrimination; procedure.* Subsequent to the date of enactment of the Equal Employment Opportunity Act of 1972, the Commission shall have authority to investigate and act on a charge of a pattern or practice of discrimination, whether filed by or on behalf of a person claiming to be aggrieved or by a member of the Commission. All such actions shall be conducted in accordance with the procedures set forth in section 706 of this Act.

§2000e-7 [§708]. *Effect on State Laws*

Nothing in this title shall be deemed to exempt or relieve any person from any liability, duty, penalty, or punishment provided by any present or future law or any State or political subdivision of a State, other than any such law which purports to require or permit the doing of any act which would be an unlawful employment practice under this title.

§2000e-8 [§709]. Investigations

(a) *Access to evidence.* In connection with any investigation of a charge filed under section 706 [42 USCS §2000e-5], the Commission or its designated representative shall at all reasonable times have access to, for the purposes of examination, and the right to copy any evidence of any person being investigated or proceeded against that relates to unlawful employment practice covered by this title [42 USCS §§2000e et seq.] and is relevant to the charge under investigation.

(b) *Cooperation with State and local agencies.* The Commission may cooperate with State and local agencies charged with the administration of State fair employment practices laws and, with the consent of such agencies, may, for the purpose of carrying out its functions and duties under this title and within the limitation of funds appropriated specifically for such purpose, engage in and contribute to the cost of research and other projects of mutual interest undertaken by such agencies, and utilize the services of such agencies and their employees, and, notwithstanding any other provision of law, pay by advance or reimbursement such agencies and their employees for services rendered to assist the Commission in carrying out this title. In furtherance of such cooperative efforts, the commission may enter into written agreements with such State or local agencies and such agreements may include provisions under which the Commission shall refrain from processing a charge in any cases or class of cases specified in such agreements or under which the Commission shall relieve any person or class of persons in such State or locality from requirements imposed under this section. The Commission shall rescind any such agreement whenever it determines that the agreement no longer serves the interests of effective enforcement of this title.

(c) *Recordkeeping; reports.* Every employer, employment agency, and labor organization subject to this title shall (1) make and keep such records relevant to the determinations of whether unlawful employment practices have been or are being committed, (2) preserve such records for such periods, and (3) make such reports therefrom as the Commission shall prescribe by regulation or order, after public hearing, as reasonable, necessary, or appropriate for the enforcement of this title or the regulations or orders thereunder. The Commission shall, by regulation, require each employer, labor organization, and joint labor-management committee subject to this title which controls an apprenticeship or other training program to maintain such records as are reasonably necessary to carry out the purposes of this title, including, but not limited to, a list of applicants who wish to participate in such program, including the chronological order in which applications were received, and to furnish to the Commission upon request, a detailed description of the manner in which persons are selected to participate in the apprenticeship or other training program. Any employer, employment agency, labor organization, or joint labor-management committee which believes that the application to it of any regulation or order issued under this section would result in undue hardship may apply to the Commission for an exemption from the application of such regulation or order, and, if such application for an exemption is denied, bring a civil action in the United States district court for the district where such records are kept. If the Commission or the court, as the case may be, finds that the application of the regulation or order to the employer, employment agency, or labor organization in question would impose an undue hardship, the Commission or the court, as the case may be, may grant appropriate relief. If any person required to comply with the provisions of this subsection fails or refuses to do so, the United States district court for the district in which such person is found, resides, or transacts business, shall, upon application of the Commission, or the Attorney General in a case involving a government, governmental agency, or political subdivision, have jurisdiction to issue to such person an order requiring him to comply.

(d) *Coordination with State and Federal agencies; availability of information.* In prescribing requirements pursuant to subsection (c) of this section, the Commission shall consult with other interested State and Federal agencies and shall endeavor to coordinate its requirements with those adopted by such agencies. The Commission shall furnish upon request and without cost to any State or local agency charged with the administration of a fair employment practice law information obtained pursuant to subsection (c) of this section from any employer, employment agency, labor organization, or joint labor-management committee subject to the jurisdiction of such agency. Such information shall be furnished on condition that it not be made public by the recipient agency prior to the institution of a proceeding under State or local law involving such information. If this condition is violated by a recipient agency, the Commission may decline to honor subsequent requests pursuant to this subsection.

(e) *Disclosure of information; penalty.* It shall be unlawful for any officer or employee of the Commission to make public in any manner whatever any information obtained by the Commission pursuant to its authority under this section prior to the institution of any proceeding under this title involving such information. Any officer or employee of the Commission who shall make public in any manner whatever any information in violation of this subsection shall be guilty of a misdemeanor and, upon conviction thereof, shall be fined not more than $1,000, or imprisoned not more than one year.

§2000e-9 [§710]. Conduct of Hearings and Investigations Pursuant to Section 161 of Title 29

For the purpose of all hearings and investigations conducted by the Commission or its duly authorized agents or agencies, section 11 of the National Labor Relations Act (49 Stat. 455; 29 U.S.C. 161) shall apply.

§2000e-10 [§711]. Posting of Notices; Penalties

(a) Every employer, employment agency and labor organization, as the case may be, shall post and keep posted in conspicuous places upon its premises where notices to employees, applicants for employment and members are customarily posted a notice to be prepared or approved by the Commission setting forth excerpts from or, summaries of, the pertinent provisions of this title and information pertinent to the filing of a complaint.

(b) A willful violation of this section shall be punishable by a fine of not more than $100 for each separate offense.

§2000e-11 [§712]. Veterans' Special Rights or Preference

Nothing contained in this title shall be construed to repeal or modify any Federal, State, territorial, or local law creating special rights or preference for veterans.

§2000e-12 [§713]. Rules and Regulations

(a) The Commission shall have authority from time to time to issue, amend, or rescind suitable procedural regulations to carry out the provisions of this title. Regulations issued under this section shall be in conformity with the standards and limitations of the Administrative Procedure Act.

(b) In any action or proceeding based on any alleged unlawful employment practice, no person shall be subject to any liability or punishment for or on account of (1) the commission by such person of an unlawful employment practice if he pleads and proves that the act of omission complained of was in good faith, in conformity with, and in reliance on any written interpretation or opinion of the Commission, or (2) the failure of such person to publish and file any information required by any provision of this title if he pleads and proves that he failed to publish and file such information in good faith, in conformity with the instructions of the Commission issued under this title regarding the filing of such information. Such a defense, if established, shall be a bar to the action or proceeding, notwithstanding that (A) after such act or omission, such interpretation or opinion is modified or rescinded or is determined by judicial authority to be invalid or of no legal effect, or (B) after publishing or filing the description and annual reports, such publication or filing is determined by judicial authority not to be in conformity with the requirements of this title.

§2000e-13 [§714]. Forcibly Resisting the Commission or Its Representatives

The provisions of sections 111 and 1114, title 18, United States Code, shall apply to officers, agents, and employees of the Commission in the performance of their official duties. Notwithstanding the provisions of sections 111 and 1114 of title 18, United States Code, whoever in violation of the provisions of section 1114 of such title kills a person while engaged in or on account of the performance of his official functions under this Act shall be punished by imprisonment for any term of years or for life.

§2000e-14 [§715]. Equal Employment Opportunity Coordinating Council

The Equal Employment Opportunity Commission shall have the responsibility for developing and implementing agreements, policies and practices designed to maximize effort, promote efficiency, and eliminate conflict, competition, duplication and inconsistency among the operations, functions and jurisdictions of the various departments, agencies and branches of the Federal Government responsible for the implementation and enforcement of equal employment opportunity legislation, orders, and policies. On or before October 1 of each year, the Equal Employment Opportunity Commission shall transmit to the President and to the Congress a report of its activities, together with such recommendations for legislative or administrative changes as it concludes are desirable to further promote the purposes of this section.

§2000e-16 [§717]. *Nondiscrimination in Federal Government Employment*

(a) *Discrimination prohibited.* All personnel actions affecting employees or applicants for employment (except with regard to aliens employed outside the limits of the United States) in military departments as defined in section 102 of title 5, United States Code, in executive agencies (other than the General Accounting Office) as defined in section 105 of title 5, United States Code (including employees and applicants for employment who are paid from nonappropriated funds), in the United States Postal Service and the Postal Rate Commission, in those units of the Government of the District of Columbia having positions in the competitive service, and in those units of the legislative and judicial branches of the Federal Government having positions in the competitive service, and in the Library of Congress shall be made free from any discrimination based on race, color, religion, sex, or national origin.

(b) *Role of Equal Employment Opportunity Commission; compliance of departments and agencies with rules and regulations.* Except as otherwise provided in this subsection, the Equal Employment Opportunity Commission shall have authority to enforce the provisions of subsection (a) of this section through appropriate remedies, including reinstatement or hiring of employees with or without back pay, as will effectuate the policies of this section, and shall issue such rules, regulations, orders and instructions as it deems necessary and appropriate to carry out its responsibilities under this section. The Equal Employment Opportunity Commission shall—

(1) be responsible for the annual review and approval of a national and regional equal employment opportunity plan which each department and agency and each appropriate unit referred to in subsection (a) of this section shall submit in order to maintain an affirmative program of equal employment opportunity for all such employees and applicants for employment;

(2) be responsible for the review and evaluation of the operation of all agency equal employment opportunity programs, periodically obtaining and publishing (on at least a semiannual basis) progress reports from each such department, agency, or unit; and

(3) consult with and solicit the recommendations of interested individuals, groups, and organizations relating to equal employment opportunity.

The head of each such department, agency, or unit shall comply with such rules, regulations, orders, and instructions which shall include a provision that an employee or applicant for employment shall be notified of any final action taken on any complaint of discrimination filed by him thereunder. The plan submitted by each department, agency, and unit shall include, but not be limited to—

(1) provision for the establishment of training and education programs designed to promote a maximum opportunity for employees to advance so as to perform at their highest potential; and

(2) a description of the qualifications in terms of training and experience relating to equal employment opportunity for the principal and operating officials of each such department, agency, or unit responsible for carrying out the equal employment opportunity program and of the allocation of personnel and resources proposed by such department, agency, or unit to carry out its equal employment opportunity program.

With respect to employment in the Library of Congress, authorities granted in this subsection to the Equal Employment Opportunity Commission shall be exercised by the Librarian of Congress.

(c) *Civil action by party aggrieved.* Within 90 days of receipt of notice of final action taken by a department, agency, or unit referred to in subsection 717(a), or by the Equal Employment Opportunity Commission upon an appeal from a decision or order of such department, agency, or unit on a complaint of discrimination based on race, color, religion, sex, or national origin, brought pursuant to subsection (a) of this section, Executive Order 11478 or any succeeding executive orders, or after one hundred and eighty days from the filing of the initial charge with the department, agency, or unit or with the Equal Employment Opportunity Commission on appeal from a decision or order of such department, agency, or unit, an employee or applicant for employment, if aggrieved by the final disposition of his complaint, or by the failure to take final action on his complaint, may file a civil action as provided in section 706, in which civil action the head of the department, agency, or unit, as appropriate, shall be the defendant.

(d) *Application of certain provisions.* The provisions of section 706(f) through (k), as applicable, shall govern civil actions brought hereunder and the same interest to compensate for delay in payment shall be available as in cases involving nonpublic parties.

(e) *Continuing responsibilities of agencies and officials to assure nondiscrimination.* Nothing contained in this Act shall relieve any Government agency or official of its or his primary responsibility to assure nondiscrimination in employment as required by the Constitution and statutes or of its or his responsibilities under Executive Order 11478 relating to equal employment opportunity in the Federal Government.

(f) Section 706(e)(3) shall apply to complaints of discrimination in compensation under this section.

§2000e-16a. Government Employee Rights Act of 1991

(a) *Short title.* This title may be cited as the "Government Employee Rights Act of 1991."

(b) *Purpose.* The purpose of this title is to provide procedures to protect the rights of certain government employees, with respect to their public employment, to be free of discrimination on the basis of race, color, religion, sex, national origin, age, or disability.

(c) *Definition.* For purposes of this title, the term "violation" means a practice that violates section 302(a) of this title [42 USCS §2000e-16b(a)].

§2000e-16b. Discriminatory Practices Prohibited

(a) *Practices.* All personnel actions affecting the Presidential appointees described in section 303 [2 USCS §1219] or the State employees described in section 304 [42 USCS §2000e-16c] shall be made free from any discrimination based on —

(1) race, color, religion, sex, or national origin, within the meaning of section 717 of the Civil Rights Act of 1964 (42 U.S.C. 2000e-16);

(2) age, within the meaning of section 15 of the Age Discrimination in Employment Act of 1967 (29 U.S.C. 633a); or

(3) disability, within the meaning of section 501 of the Rehabilitation Act of 1973 (29 U.S.C. 791) and sections 102 through 104 of the Americans with Disabilities Act of 1990 (42 U.S.C. 12112-14).

(b) *Remedies.* The remedies referred to in sections 303(a)(1) and 304(a) [2 USCS 1219(a)(1) and 42 USCS §2000e-16c(a)] —

(1) may include, in the case of a determination that a violation of subsection (a)(1) or (a)(3) has occurred, such remedies as would be appropriate if awarded under sections 706(g), 706(k), and 717(d) of the Civil Rights Act of 1964 (42 U.S.C. 2000e-5(g), 2000e-5(k), 2000e-16(d)), and such compensatory damages as would be appropriate if awarded under section 1977 or sections 1977A(a) and 1977A(b)(2) of the Revised Statutes (42 U.S.C. 1981 and 1981a(a) and (b)(2));

(2) may include, in the case of a determination that a violation of subsection (a)(2) has occurred, such remedies as would be appropriate if awarded under section 15(c) of the Age Discrimination in Employment Act of 1967 (29 U.S.C. 633a(c)); and

(3) may not include punitive damages.

§2000e-16c. Coverage of Previously Exempt State Employees

(a) *Application.* The rights, protections, and remedies provided pursuant to section 302 [42 USCS §2000e-16b] shall apply with respect to employment of any individual chosen or appointed, by a person elected to public office in any State or political subdivision of any State by the qualified voters thereof—

(1) to be a member of the elected official's personal staff;

(2) to serve the elected official on the policymaking level; or

(3) to serve the elected official as an immediate advisor with respect to the exercise of the constitutional or legal powers of the office.

(b) *Enforcement by administrative action.*

(1) In general. Any individual referred to in subsection (a) may file a complaint alleging a violation, not later than 180 days after the occurrence of the alleged violation, with the Equal Employment Opportunity Commission, which, in accordance with the principles and procedures set forth in sections 554 through 557 of title 5, United States Code, shall determine whether a violation has occurred and shall set forth its determination in a final order. If

the Equal Employment Opportunity Commission determines that a violation has occurred, the final order shall also provide for appropriate relief.

(2) *Referral to state and local authorities.*

(A) Application. Section 706(d) of the Civil Rights Act of 1964 (42 U.S.C. 2000e-5(d)) shall apply with respect to any proceeding under this section.

(B) Definition. For purposes of the application described in subparagraph (A), the term "any charge filed by a member of the Commission alleging an unlawful employment practice" means a complaint filed under this section.

(c) *Judicial review.* Any party aggrieved by a final order under subsection (b) may obtain a review of such order under chapter 158 of title 28, United States Code [28 USCS §§2341 et seq.]. For the purpose of this review, the Equal Employment Opportunity Commission shall be an "agency" as that term is used in chapter 158 of title 28, United States Code [28 USCS §§2341 et seq.].

(d) *Standard of review.* To the extent necessary to decision and when presented, the reviewing court shall decide all relevant questions of law and interpret constitutional and statutory provisions. The court shall set aside a final order under subsection (b) if it is determined that the order was —

(1) arbitrary, capricious, an abuse of discretion, or otherwise not consistent with law;

(2) not made consistent with required procedures; or

(3) unsupported by substantial evidence.

In making the foregoing determinations, the court shall review the whole record or those parts of it cited by a party, and due account shall be taken of the rule of prejudicial error.

(e) *Attorney's fees.* If the individual referred to in subsection (a) is the prevailing party in a proceeding under this subsection, attorney's fees may be allowed by the court in accordance with the standards prescribed under section 706(k) of the Civil Rights Act of 1964 (42 U.S.C. 2000e-5(k)).

§2000e-17 [§718]. Special Provision with Respect to Denial, Termination and Suspension of Government Contract

No Government contract, or portion thereof, with any employer, shall be denied, withheld, terminated, or suspended, by any agency or officer of the United States under any equal employment opportunity law or order, where such employer has an affirmative action plan which has previously been accepted by the Government for the same facility within the past twelve months without first according such employer full hearing and adjudication under the provisions of title 5, United States Code, section 554, and the following pertinent sections: Provided, That if such employer has deviated substantially from such previously agreed to affirmative action plan, this section shall not apply: Provided further, That for the purposes of this section an affirmative action plan shall be deemed to have been accepted by the Government at the time the appropriate compliance agency has accepted such plan unless within forty-five days thereafter the Office of Federal Contract Compliance has disapproved such plan.

Title IX of the Education Amendments of 1972

20 U.S.C. §§1681–1688

TITLE IX

§1681. Sex

(a) *Prohibition Against Discrimination; Exceptions.* — No person in the United States shall, on the basis of sex, be excluded from participation in, be denied the benefits of, or be subjected to discrimination under any education program or activity receiving Federal financial assistance, except that:

(1) Classes of educational institutions subject to prohibition. — In regard to admissions to educational institutions, this section shall apply only to institutions of vocational education, professional education, and graduate higher education, and to public institutions of undergraduate higher education;

(2) Educational institutions commencing planned change in admissions. — In regard to admissions to educational institutions, this section shall not apply (A) for one year from June 23, 1972, nor for six years after June 23, 1972, in the case of an educational institution which has begun the process of changing from being an institution which admits only students of one sex to being an institution which admits students of both sexes, but only if it is carrying out a plan for such a change which is approved by the Secretary of Education or (B) for seven years from the date an educational institution begins the process of changing from being an institution which admits students of only one sex to being an institution which admits students of both sexes, but only if it is carrying out a plan for such a change which is approved by the Secretary of Education, whichever is the later;

(3) Educational institutions of religious organizations with contrary religious tenets. — This section shall not apply to an educational institution which is controlled by a religious organization if the application of this subsection would not be consistent with the religious tenets of such organization;

(4) Educational institutions training individuals for military services or merchant marine. — This section shall not apply to an educational institution

whose primary purpose is the training of individuals for the military services of the United States, or the merchant marine;

(5) Public educational institutions with traditional and continuing admissions policy. — In regard to admissions this section shall not apply to any public institution of undergraduate higher education which is an institution that traditionally and continually from its establishment has had a policy of admitting only students of one sex;

(6) Social fraternities or sororities; voluntary youth service organizations. This section shall not apply to membership practices —

(A) of a social fraternity or social sorority which is exempt from taxation under section 501(a) of Title 26, the active membership of which consists primarily of students in attendance at an institution of higher education, or

(B) of the Young Men's Christian Association, Young Women's Christian Association, Girl Scouts, Boy Scouts, Camp Fire Girls, and voluntary youth service organizations which are so exempt, the membership of which has traditionally been limited to persons of one sex and principally to persons of less than nineteen years of age;

(7) Boy or Girl conferences. — This section shall not apply to —

(A) any program or activity of the American Legion undertaken in connection with the organization or operation of any Boys State conference, Boys Nation conference, Girls State conference, or Girls Nation conference; or

(B) any program or activity of any secondary school or educational institution specifically for —

(i) the promotion of any Boys State conference, Boys Nation conference, Girls State conference, or Girls Nation conference; or

(ii) the selection of students to attend any such conference;

(8) Father-son or mother-daughter activities at educational institutions. — This section shall not preclude father-son or mother-daughter activities at an educational institution, but if such activities are provided for students of one sex, opportunities for reasonably comparable activities shall be provided for students of the other sex; and

(9) Institution of higher education scholarship awards in "beauty" pageants. — This section shall not apply with respect to any scholarship or other financial assistance awarded by an institution of higher education to any individual because such individual has received such award in any pageant in which the attainment of such award is based upon a combination of factors related to the personal appearance, poise, and talent of such individual and in which participation is limited to individuals of one sex only, so long as such pageant is in compliance with other nondiscrimination provisions of Federal law.

(b) *Preferential or Disparate Treatment Because of Imbalance in Participation or Receipt of Federal Benefits; Statistical Evidence of Imbalance.* — Nothing contained in subsection (a) of this section shall be interpreted to require any educational institution to grant preferential or disparate treatment to the members of one sex on account of an imbalance which may exist with respect to the total number or percentage of persons of that sex participating in or receiving the benefits of any federally supported program or activity, in comparison with the total number of percentage of persons of that sex in any community, State, section, or other area: Provided, that this subsection shall not be construed to prevent the consideration in any hearing or proceeding under this chapter of statistical evidence tending to show that such an imbalance exists with respect to the participation in, or receipt of the benefits of, any such program or activity by the members of one sex.

(c) *"Educational Institution" Defined.* — For purposes of this chapter an educational institution means any public or private preschool, elementary, or secondary school, or any institution of vocational, professional, or higher education, except that in the case of an educational institution composed of more than one school, college, or department which are administratively separate units, such term means each such school, college, or department.

§1682. *Federal Administrative Enforcement; Report to Congressional Committees*

Each Federal department and agency which is empowered to extend Federal financial assistance to any education program or activity, by way of grant, loan, or contract other than contract of insurance or guaranty, is authorized and directed to effectuate the provisions of section 1681 of this title with respect to such program or activity by issuing rules, regulations, or orders of general applicability which shall be consistent with achievement of the objectives of the statute authorizing the financial assistance in connection with which the action is taken. No such rule, regulation, or order shall become effective unless and until approved by the President. Compliance with any requirement adopted pursuant to this section may be effected (1) by the termination of or refusal to grant or to continue assistance under such program or activity to any recipient as to whom there has been an express finding on the record, after opportunity for hearing, of a failure to comply with such requirement, but such termination or refusal shall be limited to the particular political entity, or part thereof, or other recipient as to whom such a finding has been made, and shall be limited in its effect to the particular program, or part thereof, in which such noncompliance has been so found, or (2) by any other means authorized by law: Provided, however, that no such action shall be taken until the department or agency concerned has advised the appropriate person or persons of the failure to comply with the requirement and has determined that compliance cannot be secured by voluntary means. In the case of any action terminating, or refusing to grant or continue, assistance because of failure to comply with a requirement imposed pursuant to this section, the head of the Federal department or agency shall file with the committees of the House and Senate having legislative jurisdiction over the program or activity involved a full written report of the circumstances and the grounds for such action. No such action shall become effective until thirty days have elapsed after the filing of such report.

§1683. Judicial Review

Any department or agency action taken pursuant to section 1682 of this title shall be subject to such judicial review as may otherwise be provided by law for similar action taken by such department or agency on other grounds. In the case of action, not otherwise subject to judicial review, terminating or refusing to grant or to continue financial assistance upon a finding of failure to comply with any requirement imposed pursuant to section 1682 of this title, any person aggrieved (including any State or political subdivision thereof and any agency of either) may obtain judicial review of such action in accordance with chapter 7 of Title 5, and such action shall not be deemed committed to unreviewable agency discretion within the meaning of section 701 of that title.

§1684. Blindness or Visual Impairment; Prohibition Against Discrimination

No person in the United States shall, on the ground of blindness or severely impaired vision, be denied admission in any course of study by a recipient of Federal financial assistance for any education program or activity, but nothing herein shall be construed to require any such institution to provide any special services to such person because of his blindness or visual impairment.

§1685. Authority Under Other Laws Unaffected

Nothing in this chapter shall add to or detract from any existing authority with respect to any program or activity under which Federal financial assistance is extended by way of a contract of insurance or guaranty.

§1686. Interpretation With Respect to Living Facilities

Notwithstanding anything to the contrary contained in this chapter, nothing contained herein shall be construed to prohibit any educational institution receiving funds under this Act, from maintaining separate living facilities for the different sexes.

§1687. Interpretation of "Program or Activity"

For the purposes of this chapter, the term "program or activity" and "program" mean all of the operation of—

(1)(A) a department, agency, special purpose district, or other instrumentality of a State or of a local government; or

(B) the entity of such State or local government that distributes such assistance and each such department or agency (and each other State or local government entity) to which the assistance is extended, in the case of assistance to a State or local government;

(2)(A) a college, university, or other postsecondary institution, or a public system of higher education; or

(B) a local educational agency (as defined in section 7801 of this title), system of vocational education, or other school system;

(3)(A) an entire corporation, partnership, or other private organization, or an entire sole proprietorship—

(i) if assistance is extended to such corporation, partnership, private organization, or sole proprietorship as a whole; or

(ii) which is principally engaged in the business of providing education, health care, housing, social services, or parks and recreation; or

(B) the entire plant or other comparable, geographically separate facility to which Federal financial assistance is extended, in the case of any other corporation, partnership, private organization, or sole proprietorship; or

(4) any other entity which is established by two or more of the entities described in paragraph (1), (2), or (3); any part of which is extended Federal financial assistance, except that such term does not include any operation of an entity which is controlled by a religious organization if the application of section 1681 of this title to such operation would not be consistent with the religious tenets of such organization.

§1688. *Neutrality With Respect to Abortion*

Nothing in this chapter shall be construed to require or prohibit any person, or public or private entity, to provide or pay for any benefit or service, including the use of facilities, related to an abortion. Nothing in this section shall be construed to permit a penalty to be imposed on any person or individual because such person or individual is seeking or has received any benefit or service related to a legal abortion.

Regulations

Regulations to Implement the Equal Employment Provisions of the Americans with Disabilities Act

29 C.F.R. Part 1630

§1630.1 Purpose, applicability, and construction

(a) Purpose. The purpose of this part is to implement title I of the Americans with Disabilities Act (ADA), as amended by the ADA Amendments Act of 2008 (ADAAA or Amendments Act), 42 U.S.C. 12101, et seq., requiring equal employment opportunities for individuals with disabilities. The ADA as amended, and these regulations, are intended to provide a clear and comprehensive national mandate for the elimination of discrimination against individuals with disabilities, and to provide clear, strong, consistent, enforceable standards addressing discrimination.

(b) Applicability. This part applies to "covered entities" as defined at §1630.2(b).

(c) Construction—

(1) In general. Except as otherwise provided in this part, this part does not apply a lesser standard than the standards applied under title V of the Rehabilitation Act of 1973 (29 U.S.C. 790-794a, as amended), or the regulations issued by Federal agencies pursuant to that title.

(2) Relationship to other laws. This part does not invalidate or limit the remedies, rights, and procedures of any Federal law or law of any State or political subdivision of any State or jurisdiction that provides greater or equal protection for the rights of individuals with disabilities than is afforded by this part.

(3) State workers' compensation laws and disability benefit programs. Nothing in this part alters the standards for determining eligibility for benefits under State workers' compensation laws or under State and Federal disability benefit programs.

(4) Broad coverage. The primary purpose of the ADAAA is to make it easier for people with disabilities to obtain protection under the ADA. Consistent with the Amendments Act's purpose of reinstating a broad scope of protection under the ADA, the definition of "disability" in this part shall be

construed broadly in favor of expansive coverage to the maximum extent permitted by the terms of the ADA. The primary object of attention in cases brought under the ADA should be whether covered entities have complied with their obligations and whether discrimination has occurred, not whether the individual meets the definition of disability. The question of whether an individual meets the definition of disability under this part should not demand extensive analysis.

§1630.2 Definitions

(a) Commission means the Equal Employment Opportunity Commission established by section 705 of the Civil Rights Act of 1964 (42 U.S.C. 2000e-4).

(b) Covered Entity means an employer, employment agency, labor organization, or joint labor management committee.

(c) Person, labor organization, employment agency, commerce and industry affecting commerce shall have the same meaning given those terms in section 701 of the Civil Rights Act of 1964 (42 U.S.C. 2000e).

(d) State means each of the several States, the District of Columbia, the Commonwealth of Puerto Rico, Guam, American Samoa, the Virgin Islands, the Trust Territory of the Pacific Islands, and the Commonwealth of the Northern Mariana Islands.

(e) Employer—

(1) In general. The term employer means a person engaged in an industry affecting commerce who has 15 or more employees for each working day in each of 20 or more calendar weeks in the current or preceding calendar year, and any agent of such person, except that, from July 26, 1992 through July 25, 1994, an employer means a person engaged in an industry affecting commerce who has 25 or more employees for each working day in each of 20 or more calendar weeks in the current or preceding year and any agent of such person.

(2) Exceptions. The term employer does not include—

(i) The United States, a corporation wholly owned by the government of the United States, or an Indian tribe; or

(ii) A bona fide private membership club (other than a labor organization) that is exempt from taxation under section 501(c) of the Internal Revenue Code of 1986.

(f) Employee means an individual employed by an employer.

(g) Definition of "disability."

(1) In general. Disability means, with respect to an individual—

(i) A physical or mental impairment that substantially limits one or more of the major life activities of such individual;

(ii) A record of such an impairment; or

(iii) Being regarded as having such an impairment as described in paragraph (l) of this section. This means that the individual has been subjected to an action prohibited by the ADA as amended because of an actual or perceived impairment that is not both "transitory and minor."

(2) An individual may establish coverage under any one or more of these three prongs of the definition of disability, i.e., paragraphs (g)(1)(i) (the "actual disability" prong), (g)(1)(ii) (the "record of" prong), and/or (g)(1)(iii) (the "regarded as" prong) of this section.

(3) Where an individual is not challenging a covered entity's failure to make reasonable accommodations and does not require a reasonable accommodation, it is generally unnecessary to proceed under the "actual disability" or "record of" prongs, which require a showing of an impairment that substantially limits a major life activity or a record of such an impairment. In these cases, the evaluation of coverage can be made solely under the "regarded as" prong of the definition of disability, which does not require a showing of an impairment that substantially limits a major life activity or a record of such an impairment. An individual may choose, however, to proceed under the "actual disability" and/or "record of" prong regardless of whether the individual is challenging a covered entity's failure to make reasonable accommodations or requires a reasonable accommodation.

Note to paragraph (g): See §1630.3 for exceptions to this definition.

(h) Physical or mental impairment means—

(1) Any physiological disorder or condition, cosmetic disfigurement, or anatomical loss affecting one or more body systems, such as neurological, musculoskeletal, special sense organs, respiratory (including speech organs), cardiovascular, reproductive, digestive, genitourinary, immune, circulatory, hemic, lymphatic, skin, and endocrine; or

(2) Any mental or psychological disorder, such as an intellectual disability (formerly termed "mental retardation"), organic brain syndrome, emotional or mental illness, and specific learning disabilities.

(i) Major life activities—

(1) In general. Major life activities include, but are not limited to:

(i) Caring for oneself, performing manual tasks, seeing, hearing, eating, sleeping, walking, standing, sitting, reaching, lifting, bending, speaking, breathing, learning, reading, concentrating, thinking, communicating, interacting with others, and working; and

(ii) The operation of a major bodily function, including functions of the immune system, special sense organs and skin; normal cell growth; and digestive, genitourinary, bowel, bladder, neurological, brain, respiratory, circulatory, cardiovascular, endocrine, hemic, lymphatic, musculoskeletal, and reproductive functions. The operation of a major bodily function includes the operation of an individual organ within a body system.

(2) In determining other examples of major life activities, the term "major" shall not be interpreted strictly to create a demanding standard for disability. ADAAA Section 2(b)(4) (Findings and Purposes). Whether an activity is a "major life activity" is not determined by reference to whether it is of "central importance to daily life."

(j) Substantially limits—

(1) Rules of construction. The following rules of construction apply when determining whether an impairment substantially limits an individual in a major life activity:

(i) The term "substantially limits" shall be construed broadly in favor of expansive coverage, to the maximum extent permitted by the terms of the ADA. "Substantially limits" is not meant to be a demanding standard.

(ii) An impairment is a disability within the meaning of this section if it substantially limits the ability of an individual to perform a major life activity as compared to most people in the general population. An impairment need not prevent, or significantly or severely restrict, the individual from performing a major life activity in order to be considered substantially limiting. Nonetheless, not every impairment will constitute a disability within the meaning of this section.

(iii) The primary object of attention in cases brought under the ADA should be whether covered entities have complied with their obligations and whether discrimination has occurred, not whether an individual's impairment substantially limits a major life activity. Accordingly, the threshold issue of whether an impairment "substantially limits" a major life activity should not demand extensive analysis.

(iv) The determination of whether an impairment substantially limits a major life activity requires an individualized assessment. However, in making this assessment, the term "substantially limits" shall be interpreted and applied to require a degree of functional limitation that is lower than the standard for "substantially limits" applied prior to the ADAAA.

(v) The comparison of an individual's performance of a major life activity to the performance of the same major life activity by most people in the general population usually will not require scientific, medical, or statistical analysis. Nothing in this paragraph is intended, however, to prohibit the presentation of scientific, medical, or statistical evidence to make such a comparison where appropriate.

(vi) The determination of whether an impairment substantially limits a major life activity shall be made without regard to the ameliorative effects of mitigating measures. However, the ameliorative effects of ordinary eyeglasses or contact lenses shall be considered in determining whether an impairment substantially limits a major life activity.

(vii) An impairment that is episodic or in remission is a disability if it would substantially limit a major life activity when active.

(viii) An impairment that substantially limits one major life activity need not substantially limit other major life activities in order to be considered a substantially limiting impairment.

(ix) The six-month "transitory" part of the "transitory and minor" exception to "regarded as" coverage in §1630.15(f) does not apply to the definition of "disability" under paragraphs (g)(1)(i) (the "actual disability" prong) or (g)(1)(ii) (the "record of" prong) of this section. The effects of an impairment lasting or expected to last fewer than six months can be substantially limiting within the meaning of this section.

(2) Non-applicability to the "regarded as" prong. Whether an individual's impairment "substantially limits" a major life activity is not relevant to coverage under paragraph (g)(1)(iii) (the "regarded as" prong) of this section.

(3) Predictable assessments —

(i) The principles set forth in paragraphs (j)(1)(i) through (ix) of this section are intended to provide for more generous coverage and application of the ADA's prohibition on discrimination through a framework that is predictable, consistent, and workable for all individuals and entities with rights and responsibilities under the ADA as amended.

(ii) Applying the principles set forth in paragraphs (j)(1)(i) through (ix) of this section, the individualized assessment of some types of impairments will, in virtually all cases, result in a determination of coverage under paragraphs (g)(1)(i) (the "actual disability" prong) or (g)(1)(ii) (the "record of" prong) of this section. Given their inherent nature, these types of impairments will, as a factual matter, virtually always be found to impose a substantial limitation on a major life activity. Therefore, with respect to these types of impairments, the necessary individualized assessment should be particularly simple and straightforward.

(iii) For example, applying the principles set forth in paragraphs (j)(1)(i) through (ix) of this section, it should easily be concluded that the following types of impairments will, at a minimum, substantially limit the major life activities indicated: Deafness substantially limits hearing; blindness substantially limits seeing; an intellectual disability (formerly termed mental retardation) substantially limits brain function; partially or completely missing limbs or mobility impairments requiring the use of a wheelchair substantially limit musculoskeletal function; autism substantially limits brain function; cancer substantially limits normal cell growth; cerebral palsy substantially limits brain function; diabetes substantially limits endocrine function; epilepsy substantially limits neurological function; Human Immunodeficiency Virus (HIV) infection substantially limits immune function; multiple sclerosis substantially limits neurological function; muscular dystrophy substantially limits neurological function; and major depressive disorder, bipolar disorder, post-traumatic stress disorder, obsessive compulsive disorder, and schizophrenia substantially limit brain function. The types of impairments described in this section may substantially limit additional major life activities not explicitly listed above.

(4) Condition, manner, or duration —

(i) At all times taking into account the principles in paragraphs (j)(1)(i) through (ix) of this section, in determining whether an individual is substantially limited in a major life activity, it may be useful in appropriate cases to consider, as compared to most people in the general population, the condition under which the individual performs the major life activity; the manner in which the individual performs the major life activity; and/or the duration of time it takes the individual to perform the major life activity, or for which the individual can perform the major life activity.

(ii) Consideration of facts such as condition, manner, or duration may include, among other things, consideration of the difficulty, effort, or time required to perform a major life activity; pain experienced when performing a major life activity; the length of time a major life activity can be performed; and/or the way an impairment affects the operation of a major bodily function. In addition, the non-ameliorative effects of mitigating measures, such as negative side effects of medication or burdens associated with following a particular treatment regimen, may be considered when determining whether an individual's impairment substantially limits a major life activity.

(iii) In determining whether an individual has a disability under the "actual disability" or "record of" prongs of the definition of disability, the focus is on how a major life activity is substantially limited, and not on what outcomes an individual can achieve. For example, someone with a learning disability may achieve a high level of academic success, but may nevertheless be substantially limited in the major life activity of learning because of the additional time or effort he or she must spend to read, write, or learn compared to most people in the general population.

(iv) Given the rules of construction set forth in paragraphs (j)(1)(i) through (ix) of this section, it may often be unnecessary to conduct an analysis involving most or all of these types of facts. This is particularly true with respect to impairments such as those described in paragraph (j)(3)(iii) of this section, which by their inherent nature should be easily found to impose a substantial limitation on a major life activity, and for which the individualized assessment should be particularly simple and straightforward.

(5) Examples of mitigating measures — Mitigating measures include, but are not limited to:

(i) Medication, medical supplies, equipment, or appliances, low-vision devices (defined as devices that magnify, enhance, or otherwise augment a visual image, but not including ordinary eyeglasses or contact lenses), prosthetics including limbs and devices, hearing aid(s) and cochlear implant(s) or other implantable hearing devices, mobility devices, and oxygen therapy equipment and supplies;

(ii) Use of assistive technology;

(iii) Reasonable accommodations or "auxiliary aids or services" (as defined by 42 U.S.C. 12103(1));

(iv) Learned behavioral or adaptive neurological modifications; or

(v) Psychotherapy, behavioral therapy, or physical therapy.

(6) Ordinary eyeglasses or contact lenses — defined. Ordinary eyeglasses or contact lenses are lenses that are intended to fully correct visual acuity or to eliminate refractive error.

(k) Has a record of such an impairment —

(1) In general. An individual has a record of a disability if the individual has a history of, or has been misclassified as having, a mental or physical impairment that substantially limits one or more major life activities.

(2) Broad construction. Whether an individual has a record of an impairment that substantially limited a major life activity shall be construed broadly to the maximum extent permitted by the ADA and should not demand extensive analysis. An individual will be considered to have a record of a disability if the individual has a history of an impairment that substantially limited one or more major life activities when compared to most people in the general population, or was misclassified as having had such an impairment. In determining whether an impairment substantially limited a major life activity, the principles articulated in paragraph (j) of this section apply.

(3) Reasonable accommodation. An individual with a record of a substantially limiting impairment may be entitled, absent undue hardship, to a reasonable accommodation if needed and related to the past disability. For example, an employee with an impairment that previously limited, but no longer substantially limits, a major life activity may need leave or a schedule change to permit him or her to attend follow-up or "monitoring" appointments with a health care provider.

(l) "Is regarded as having such an impairment." The following principles apply under the "regarded as" prong of the definition of disability (paragraph (g)(1)(iii) of this section) above:

(1) Except as provided in §1630.15(f), an individual is "regarded as having such an impairment" if the individual is subjected to a prohibited action because of an actual or perceived physical or mental impairment, whether or not that impairment substantially limits, or is perceived to substantially limit, a major life activity. Prohibited actions include but are not limited to refusal to hire, demotion, placement on involuntary leave, termination, exclusion for failure to meet a qualification standard, harassment, or denial of any other term, condition, or privilege of employment

(2) Except as provided in §1630.15(f), an individual is "regarded as having such an impairment" any time a covered entity takes a prohibited action against the individual because of an actual or perceived impairment, even if the entity asserts, or may or does ultimately establish, a defense to such action.

(3) Establishing that an individual is "regarded as having such an impairment" does not, by itself, establish liability. Liability is established under title I of the ADA only when an individual proves that a covered entity discriminated on the basis of disability within the meaning of section 102 of the ADA, 42 U.S.C. 12112.

(m) The term "qualified," with respect to an individual with a disability, means that the individual satisfies the requisite skill, experience, education and other job-related requirements of the employment position such individual holds or desires and, with or without reasonable accommodation, can perform the essential functions of such position. See §1630.3 for exceptions to this definition.

(n) Essential functions —

(1) In general. The term essential functions means the fundamental job duties of the employment position the individual with a disability holds or desires. The term "essential functions" does not include the marginal functions of the position.

(2) A job function may be considered essential for any of several reasons, including but not limited to the following:

(i) The function may be essential because the reason the position exists is to perform that function;

(ii) The function may be essential because of the limited number of employees available among whom the performance of that job function can be distributed; and/or

(iii) The function may be highly specialized so that the incumbent in the position is hired for his or her expertise or ability to perform the particular function.

(3) Evidence of whether a particular function is essential includes, but is not limited to:

(i) The employer's judgment as to which functions are essential;

(ii) Written job descriptions prepared before advertising or interviewing applicants for the job;

(iii) The amount of time spent on the job performing the function;

(iv) The consequences of not requiring the incumbent to perform the function;

(v) The terms of a collective bargaining agreement;

(vi) The work experience of past incumbents in the job; and/or

(vii) The current work experience of incumbents in similar jobs.

(o) Reasonable accommodation.

(1) The term reasonable accommodation means:

(i) Modifications or adjustments to a job application process that enable a qualified applicant with a disability to be considered for the position such qualified applicant desires; or

(ii) Modifications or adjustments to the work environment, or to the manner or circumstances under which the position held or desired is customarily performed, that enable an individual with a disability who is qualified to perform the essential functions of that position; or

(iii) Modifications or adjustments that enable a covered entity's employee with a disability to enjoy equal benefits and privileges of employment as are enjoyed by its other similarly situated employees without disabilities.

(2) Reasonable accommodation may include but is not limited to:

(i) Making existing facilities used by employees readily accessible to and usable by individuals with disabilities; and

(ii) Job restructuring; part-time or modified work schedules; reassignment to a vacant position; acquisition or modifications of equipment or devices; appropriate adjustment or modifications of examinations, training materials, or policies; the provision of qualified readers or interpreters; and other similar accommodations for individuals with disabilities.

(3) To determine the appropriate reasonable accommodation it may be necessary for the covered entity to initiate an informal, interactive process with the individual with a disability in need of the accommodation. This process should identify the precise limitations resulting from the disability and potential reasonable accommodations that could overcome those limitations.

(4) A covered entity is required, absent undue hardship, to provide a reasonable accommodation to an otherwise qualified individual who meets the definition of disability under the "actual disability" prong (paragraph (g)(1)(i) of this section), or "record of" prong (paragraph (g)(1)(ii) of this section), but is not required to provide a reasonable accommodation to an individual who meets the definition of disability solely under the "regarded as" prong (paragraph (g)(1)(iii) of this section).

(p) Undue hardship —

(1) In general. Undue hardship means, with respect to the provision of an accommodation, significant difficulty or expense incurred by a covered entity, when considered in light of the factors set forth in paragraph (p)(2) of this section.

(2) Factors to be considered. In determining whether an accommodation would impose an undue hardship on a covered entity, factors to be considered include:

(i) The nature and net cost of the accommodation needed under this part, taking into consideration the availability of tax credits and deductions, and/or outside funding;

(ii) The overall financial resources of the facility or facilities involved in the provision of the reasonable accommodation, the number of persons employed at such facility, and the effect on expenses and resources;

(iii) The overall financial resources of the covered entity, the overall size of the business of the covered entity with respect to the number of its employees, and the number, type and location of its facilities;

(iv) The type of operation or operations of the covered entity, including the composition, structure and functions of the workforce of such entity, and the geographic separateness and administrative or fiscal relationship of the facility or facilities in question to the covered entity; and

(v) The impact of the accommodation upon the operation of the facility, including the impact on the ability of other employees to perform their duties and the impact on the facility's ability to conduct business.

(q) Qualification standards means the personal and professional attributes including the skill, experience, education, physical, medical, safety and other requirements established by a covered entity as requirements which an individual must meet in order to be eligible for the position held or desired.

(r) Direct Threat means a significant risk of substantial harm to the health or safety of the individual or others that cannot be eliminated or reduced by reasonable accommodation. The determination that an individual poses a "direct threat" shall be based on an individualized assessment of the individual's present ability to safely perform the essential functions of the job. This assessment shall be based on a reasonable medical judgment that relies on the most current medical knowledge and/or on the best available objective evidence. In determining whether an individual would pose a direct threat, the factors to be considered include:

(1) The duration of the risk;

(2) The nature and severity of the potential harm;

(3) The likelihood that the potential harm will occur; and

(4) The imminence of the potential harm.

§1630.3 Exceptions to the definitions of "Disability" and "Qualified Individual with a Disability"

(a) The terms disability and qualified individual with a disability do not include individuals currently engaging in the illegal use of drugs, when the covered entity acts on the basis of such use.

(1) Drug means a controlled substance, as defined in schedules I through V of Section 202 of the Controlled Substances Act (21 U.S.C 812)

(2) Illegal use of drugs means the use of drugs the possession or distribution of which is unlawful under the Controlled Substances Act, as periodically updated by the Food and Drug Administration. This term does not include the use of a drug taken under the supervision of a licensed health care professional, or other uses authorized by the Controlled Substances Act or other provisions of Federal law.

(b) However, the terms disability and qualified individual with a disability may not exclude an individual who:

(1) Has successfully completed a supervised drug rehabilitation program and is no longer engaging in the illegal use of drugs, or has otherwise been rehabilitated successfully and is no longer engaging in the illegal use of drugs; or

(2) Is participating in a supervised rehabilitation program and is no longer engaging in such use; or

(3) Is erroneously regarded as engaging in such use, but is not engaging in such use.

(c) It shall not be a violation of this part for a covered entity to adopt or administer reasonable policies or procedures, including but not limited to drug testing, designed to ensure that an individual described in paragraph (b) (1) or (2) of this section is no longer engaging in the illegal use of drugs. (See §1630.16(c) Drug testing).

(d) Disability does not include:

(1) Transvestism, transsexualism, pedophilia, exhibitionism, voyeurism, gender identity disorders not resulting from physical impairments, or other sexual behavior disorders;

(2) Compulsive gambling, kleptomania, or pyromania; or

(3) Psychoactive substance use disorders resulting from current illegal use of drugs.

(e) Homosexuality and bisexuality are not impairments and so are not disabilities as defined in this part.

§1630.4 Discrimination prohibited

(a) In general—

(1) It is unlawful for a covered entity to discriminate on the basis of disability against a qualified individual in regard to:

(i) Recruitment, advertising, and job application procedures;

(ii) Hiring, upgrading, promotion, award of tenure, demotion, transfer, layoff, termination, right of return from layoff, and rehiring;

(iii) Rates of pay or any other form of compensation and changes in compensation;

(iv) Job assignments, job classifications, organizational structures, position descriptions, lines of progression, and seniority lists;

(v) Leaves of absence, sick leave, or any other leave;

(vi) Fringe benefits available by virtue of employment, whether or not administered by the covered entity;

(vii) Selection and financial support for training, including: apprenticeships, professional meetings, conferences and other related activities, and selection for leaves of absence to pursue training;

(viii) Activities sponsored by a covered entity, including social and recreational programs; and

(ix) Any other term, condition, or privilege of employment.

(2) The term discrimination includes, but is not limited to, the acts described in §§1630.4 through 1630.13 of this part.

(b) Claims of no disability. Nothing in this part shall provide the basis for a claim that an individual without a disability was subject to discrimination because of his lack of disability, including a claim that an individual with a disability was granted an accommodation that was denied to an individual without a disability.

§1630.5 Limiting, segregating, and classifying

It is unlawful for a covered entity to limit, segregate, or classify a job applicant or employee in a way that adversely affects his or her employment opportunities or status on the basis of disability.

§1630.6 Contractual or other arrangements

(a) In general. It is unlawful for a covered entity to participate in a contractual or other arrangement or relationship that has the effect of subjecting the covered entity's own qualified applicant or employee with a disability to the discrimination prohibited by this part.

(b) Contractual or other arrangement defined. The phrase contractual or other arrangement or relationship includes, but is not limited to, a relationship with an employment or referral agency; labor union, including collective bargaining agreements; an organization providing fringe benefits to an employee of the covered entity; or an organization providing training and apprenticeship programs.

(c) Application. This section applies to a covered entity, with respect to its own applicants or employees, whether the entity offered the contract or initiated the relationship, or whether the entity accepted the contract or acceded to the relationship. A covered entity is not liable for the actions of the other party or parties to the contract which only affect that other party's employees or applicants.

§1630.7 Standards, criteria, or methods of administration

It is unlawful for a covered entity to use standards, criteria, or methods of administration, which are not job- related and consistent with business necessity, and:

(a) That have the effect of discriminating on the basis of disability; or

(b) That perpetuate the discrimination of others who are subject to common administrative control.

§1630.8 Relationship or association with an individual with a disability

It is unlawful for a covered entity to exclude or deny equal jobs or benefits to, or otherwise discriminate against, a qualified individual because of the known disability of an individual with whom the qualified individual is known to have a family, business, social or other relationship or association.

§1630.9 Not making reasonable accommodation

(a) It is unlawful for a covered entity not to make reasonable accommodation to the known physical or mental limitations of an otherwise qualified applicant or employee with a disability, unless such covered entity can demonstrate that the accommodation would impose an undue hardship on the operation of its business.

(b) It is unlawful for a covered entity to deny employment opportunities to an otherwise qualified job applicant or employee with a disability based on the need of such covered entity to make reasonable accommodation to such individual's physical or mental impairments.

(c) A covered entity shall not be excused from the requirements of this part because of any failure to receive technical assistance authorized by section 507 of the ADA, including any failure in the development or dissemination of any technical assistance manual authorized by that Act.

(d) An individual with a disability is not required to accept an accommodation, aid, service, opportunity or benefit which such qualified individual chooses not to accept. However, if such individual rejects a reasonable accommodation, aid, service, opportunity or benefit that is necessary to enable the individual to perform the essential functions of the position held or desired, and cannot, as a result of that rejection, perform the essential functions of the position, the individual will not be considered qualified.

(e) A covered entity is required, absent undue hardship, to provide a reasonable accommodation to an otherwise qualified individual who meets the definition of disability under the "actual disability" prong (§1630.2(g)(1)(i)), or "record of" prong (§1630.2(g)(1)(ii)), but is not required to provide a reasonable accommodation to an individual who meets the definition of disability solely under the "regarded as" prong (§1630.2(g)(1)(iii)).

§1630.10 Qualification standards, tests, and other selection criteria

(a) In general. It is unlawful for a covered entity to use qualification standards, employment tests or other selection criteria that screen out or tend to screen out an individual with a disability or a class of individuals with disabilities, on the basis of disability, unless the standard, test, or other selection criteria, as used by the covered entity, is shown to be job related for the position in question and is consistent with business necessity.

(b) Qualification standards and tests related to uncorrected vision. Notwithstanding §1630.2(j)(1)(vi) of this part, a covered entity shall not use qualification standards, employment tests, or other selection criteria based on an individual's uncorrected vision unless the standard, test, or other selection criterion, as used by the covered entity, is shown to be job related for the position in question and is consistent with business necessity. An individual challenging a covered entity's application of a qualification standard, test, or other criterion based on uncorrected vision need not be a person with a disability, but must be adversely affected by the application of the standard, test, or other criterion.

§1630.11 Administration of tests

It is unlawful for a covered entity to fail to select and administer tests concerning employment in the most effective manner to ensure that, when a test is administered to a job applicant or employee who has a disability that impairs sensory, manual or speaking skills, the test results accurately reflect the skills, aptitude, or whatever other factor of the applicant or employee that the test purports to measure, rather than reflecting the impaired sensory, manual, or speaking skills of such employee or applicant (except where such skills are the factors that the test purports to measure).

§1630.12 Retaliation and coercion

(a) Retaliation. It is unlawful to discriminate against any individual because that individual has opposed any act or practice made unlawful by this part or because that individual made a charge, testified, assisted, or participated in any manner in an investigation, proceeding, or hearing to enforce any provision contained in this part.

(b) Coercion, interference or intimidation. It is unlawful to coerce, intimidate, threaten, harass or interfere with any individual in the exercise or enjoyment of, or because that individual aided or encouraged any other individual in the exercise of, any right granted or protected by this part.

§1630.13 Prohibited medical examination and inquiries

(a) Pre-employment examination or inquiry. Except as permitted by §1630.14, it is unlawful for a covered entity to conduct a medical examination of an applicant or to make inquiries as to whether an applicant is an individual with a disability or as to the nature or severity of such disability.

(b) Examination or inquiry of employees. Except as permitted by §1630.14, it is unlawful for a covered entity to require a medical examination of an employee or to make inquiries as to whether an employee is an individual with a disability or as to the nature or severity of such disability.

§1630.14 Class 1-D-E: Exemption of certain members of a reserve component or student taking military training

In Class 1-D-E shall be placed any registrant who:

(a) Is a student enrolled in an officer procurement program at a military college the curriculum of which is approved by the Secretary of Defense; or

(b) Has been enlisted in the Delayed Entry Program (DEP) at least ten days prior to his scheduled induction date; or

(c) Has been transferred to a reserve component of the Army, Navy, Air Force, Marine Corps or Coast Guard after a period of extended active duty, which was not for training only.

§1630.15 Defenses

Defenses to an allegation of discrimination under this part may include, but are not limited to, the following:

(a) Disparate treatment charges. It may be a defense to a charge of disparate treatment brought under §§1630.4 through 1630.8 and 1630.11 through 1630.12 that the challenged action is justified by a legitimate, nondiscriminatory reason.

(b) Charges of discriminatory application of selection criteria—

(1) In general. It may be a defense to a charge of discrimination, as described in §1630.10, that an alleged application of qualification standards, tests, or selection criteria that screens out or tends to screen out or otherwise denies a job or benefit to an individual with a disability has been shown to be job-related and consistent with business necessity, and such performance

cannot be accomplished with reasonable accommodation, as required in this part.

(2) Direct threat as a qualification standard. The term "qualification standard" may include a requirement that an individual shall not pose a direct threat to the health or safety of the individual or others in the workplace. (See §1630.2(r) defining direct threat.)

(c) Other disparate impact charges. It may be a defense to a charge of discrimination brought under this part that a uniformly applied standard, criterion, or policy has a disparate impact on an individual with a disability or a class of individuals with disabilities that the challenged standard, criterion or policy has been shown to be job-related and consistent with business necessity, and such performance cannot be accomplished with reasonable accommodation, as required in this part.

(d) Charges of not making reasonable accommodation. It may be a defense to a charge of discrimination, as described in §1630.9, that a requested or necessary accommodation would impose an undue hardship on the operation of the covered entity's business.

(e) Conflict with other federal laws. It may be a defense to a charge of discrimination under this part that a challenged action is required or necessitated by another Federal law or regulation, or that another Federal law or regulation prohibits an action (including the provision of a particular reasonable accommodation) that would otherwise be required by this part.

(f) Claims based on transitory and minor impairments under the "regarded as" prong. It may be a defense to a charge of discrimination by an individual claiming coverage under the "regarded as" prong of the definition of disability that the impairment is (in the case of an actual impairment) or would be (in the case of a perceived impairment) "transitory and minor." To establish this defense, a covered entity must demonstrate that the impairment is both "transitory" and "minor." Whether the impairment at issue is or would be "transitory and minor" is to be determined objectively. A covered entity may not defeat "regarded as" coverage of an individual simply by demonstrating that it subjectively believed the impairment was transitory and minor; rather, the covered entity must demonstrate that the impairment is (in the case of an actual impairment) or would be (in the case of a perceived impairment) both transitory and minor. For purposes of this section, "transitory" is defined as lasting or expected to last six months or less.

(g) Additional defenses. It may be a defense to a charge of discrimination under this part that the alleged discriminatory action is specifically permitted by §1630.14 or §1630.16.

§1630.16 Specific activities permitted

(a) Religious entities. A religious corporation, association, educational institution, or society is permitted to give preference in employment to individuals of a particular religion to perform work connected with the carrying on by that corporation, association, educational institution, or society of its activities. A religious entity may require that all applicants and employees conform to the religious tenets of such organization. However, a religious entity may not discriminate against a qualified individual, who satisfies the permitted religious criteria, on the basis of his or her disability.

(b) Regulation of alcohol and drugs. A covered entity:

(1) May prohibit the illegal use of drugs and the use of alcohol at the workplace by all employees;

(2) May require that employees not be under the influence of alcohol or be engaging in the illegal use of drugs at the workplace;

(3) May require that all employees behave in conformance with the requirements established under the Drug-Free Workplace Act of 1988 (41 U.S.C. 701 et seq.);

(4) May hold an employee who engages in the illegal use of drugs or who is an alcoholic to the same qualification standards for employment or job performance and behavior to which the entity holds its other employees, even if any unsatisfactory performance or behavior is related to the employee's drug use or alcoholism;

(5) May require that its employees employed in an industry subject to such regulations comply with the standards established in the regulations (if any) of the Departments of Defense and Transportation, and of the Nuclear Regulatory Commission, regarding alcohol and the illegal use of drugs; and

(6) May require that employees employed in sensitive positions comply with the regulations (if any) of the Departments of Defense and Transportation and of the Nuclear Regulatory Commission that apply to employment in sensitive positions subject to such regulations.

(c) Drug testing—

(1) General policy. For purposes of this part, a test to determine the illegal use of drugs is not considered a medical examination. Thus, the administration of such drug tests by a covered entity to its job applicants or employees is not a violation of §1630.13 of this part. However, this part does not encourage, prohibit, or authorize a covered entity to conduct drug tests of job applicants or employees to determine the illegal use of drugs or to make employment decisions based on such test results.

(2) Transportation employees. This part does not encourage, prohibit, or authorize the otherwise lawful exercise by entities subject to the jurisdiction of the Department of Transportation of authority to:

(i) Test employees of entities in, and applicants for, positions involving safety sensitive duties for the illegal use of drugs or for on-duty impairment by alcohol; and

(ii) Remove from safety-sensitive positions persons who test positive for illegal use of drugs or on-duty impairment by alcohol pursuant to paragraph (c)(2)(i) of this section.

(3) Confidentiality. Any information regarding the medical condition or history of any employee or applicant obtained from a test to determine the illegal use of drugs, except information regarding the illegal use of drugs, is subject to the requirements of §1630.14(b) (2) and (3) of this part.

(d) Regulation of smoking. A covered entity may prohibit or impose restrictions on smoking in places of employment. Such restrictions do not violate any provision of this part.

(e) Infectious and communicable diseases; food handling jobs—

(1) In general. Under title I of the ADA, section 103(d)(1), the Secretary of Health and Human Services is to prepare a list, to be updated annually, of infectious and communicable diseases which are transmitted through the handling of food. (Copies may be obtained from Center for Infectious Diseases, Centers for Disease Control, 1600 Clifton Road, NE., Mailstop C09, Atlanta, GA 30333.) If an individual with a disability is disabled by one of the infectious or communicable diseases included on this list, and if the risk of transmitting the disease associated with the handling of food cannot be eliminated by reasonable accommodation, a covered entity may refuse to assign or continue to assign such individual to a job involving food handling. However, if the individual with a disability is a current employee, the employer must consider whether he or she can be accommodated by reassignment to a vacant position not involving food handling.

(2) Effect on State or other laws. This part does not preempt, modify, or amend any State, county, or local law, ordinance or regulation applicable to food handling which:

(i) Is in accordance with the list, referred to in paragraph (e)(1) of this section, of infectious or communicable diseases and the modes of transmissibility published by the Secretary of Health and Human Services; and

(ii) Is designed to protect the public health from individuals who pose a significant risk to the health or safety of others, where that risk cannot be eliminated by reasonable accommodation.

(f) Health insurance, life insurance, and other benefit plans—

(1) An insurer, hospital, or medical service company, health maintenance organization, or any agent or entity that administers benefit plans, or similar organizations may underwrite risks, classify risks, or administer such risks that are based on or not inconsistent with State law.

(2) A covered entity may establish, sponsor, observe or administer the terms of a bona fide benefit plan that are based on underwriting risks, classifying risks, or administering such risks that are based on or not inconsistent with State law.

(3) A covered entity may establish, sponsor, observe, or administer the terms of a bona fide benefit plan that is not subject to State laws that regulate insurance.

(4) The activities described in paragraphs (f) (1), (2), and (3) of this section are permitted unless these activities are being used as a subterfuge to evade the purposes of this part.

Interpretive Guidance on Title I of the Americans with Disabilities Act

Appendix to Part 1630

INTRODUCTION

The Americans with Disabilities Act (ADA) is a landmark piece of civil rights legislation signed into law on July 26, 1990, and amended effective January 1, 2009. See 42 U.S.C. 12101 et seq., as amended. In passing the ADA, Congress recognized that "discrimination against individuals with disabilities continues to be a serious and pervasive social problem" and that the "continuing existence of unfair and unnecessary discrimination and prejudice denies people with disabilities the opportunity to compete on an equal basis and to pursue those opportunities for which our free society is justifiably famous, and costs the United States billions of dollars in unnecessary expenses resulting from dependency and nonproductivity." 42 U.S.C. 12101(a)(2), (8). Discrimination on the basis of disability persists in critical areas such as housing, public accommodations, education, transportation, communication, recreation, institutionalization, health services, voting, access to public services, and employment. 42 U.S.C. 12101(a)(3). Accordingly, the ADA prohibits discrimination in a wide range of areas, including employment, public services, and public accommodations.

Title I of the ADA prohibits disability-based discrimination in employment. The Equal Employment Opportunity Commission (the Commission or the EEOC) is responsible for enforcement of title I (and parts of title V) of the ADA. Pursuant to the ADA as amended, the EEOC is expressly granted the authority and is expected to amend these regulations. 42 U.S.C. 12205a. Under title I of the ADA, covered entities may not discriminate against qualified individuals on the basis of disability in regard to job application procedures, the hiring, advancement or discharge of employees, employee compensation, job training, or other terms, conditions, and privileges of employment. 42 U.S.C. 12112(a). For these purposes, "discriminate" includes (1) limiting, segregating, or classifying a job applicant or employee in a way that adversely affects the opportunities or status of the applicant or employee; (2) participating in a contractual or other arrangement or relationship that has the effect of subjecting a covered entity's qualified applicants or employees to discrimination; (3) utilizing standards, criteria, or other methods of administration that have the effect of discrimination on the basis of disability; (4) not making reasonable accommodation to the known physical or mental limitations of an otherwise qualified individual with a disability, unless the covered entity can demonstrate that the accommodation would impose an undue hardship on the operation of the business of the covered entity; (5) denying employment opportunities to a job applicant or employee who is otherwise qualified, if such denial is based on the need to make reasonable accommodation; (6) using qualification standards, employment tests or other selection criteria that screen out or tend to screen out an individual with a disability or a class of individuals with disabilities unless the standard, test or other selection criterion is shown to be job related for the position in question and is consistent with business necessity; and (7) subjecting applicants or employees to prohibited medical inquiries or examinations. See 42 U.S.C. 12112(b), (d).

As with other civil rights laws, individuals seeking protection under these anti-discrimination provisions of the ADA generally must allege and prove that they are members of the "protected class."[1] Under the ADA, this typically means they have to show that they meet the statutory definition of "disability." 2008 House Judiciary Committee Report at 5. However, "Congress did not intend for the threshold question of disability to be used as a means of excluding individuals from coverage." Id.

In the original ADA, Congress defined "disability" as (1) a physical or mental impairment that substantially limits one or more major life activities of an individual; (2) a record of such an impairment; or (3) being regarded as having such an impairment. 42 U.S.C. 12202(2). Congress patterned these three parts of the definition of disability—the "actual," "record of," and "regarded as" prongs—after the definition of "handicap" found in the Rehabilitation Act of 1973. 2008 House Judiciary Committee Report at 6. By doing so, Congress intended that the relevant case law developed under the Rehabilitation Act would be generally applicable to the term "disability" as used in the ADA. H.R. Rep. No. 485 part 3, 101st Cong., 2d Sess. 27 (1990) (1990 House Judiciary Report or House Judiciary Report); see also S. Rep. No. 116, 101st Cong., 1st Sess. 21 (1989) (1989 Senate Report or Senate Report); H.R. Rep. No. 485 part 2, 101st Cong., 2d Sess. 50 (1990) (1990 House Labor Report or House Labor Report). Congress expected that the definition of disability and related terms, such as "substantially limits" and "major life activity," would be interpreted under the ADA "consistently with how courts had applied the definition of a handicapped individual under the Rehabilitation Act"—i.e., expansively and in favor of broad coverage. ADA Amendments Act of 2008 (ADAAA or Amendments Act) at Section 2(a)(1)-(8) and (b)(1)-(6) (Findings and Purposes); see also Senate Statement of the Managers to Accompany S. 3406 (2008 Senate Statement of Managers) at 3 ("When Congress passed the ADA in 1990, it adopted the functional definition of disability from section 504 of the Rehabilitation Act of 1973, in part, because after 17 years of development through case law the requirements of the definition were well understood. Within this framework, with its generous and inclusive definition of disability, courts treated the determination of disability as a threshold issue but focused primarily on whether unlawful discrimination had occurred."); 2008 House Judiciary Committee Report at 6 & n.6 (noting that courts had interpreted this Rehabilitation Act definition "broadly to include persons with a wide range of physical and mental impairments").

That expectation was not fulfilled. ADAAA Section 2(a)(3). The holdings of several Supreme Court cases sharply narrowed the broad scope of protection Congress originally intended under the ADA, thus eliminating protection for many individuals whom Congress intended to protect. Id. For example, in Sutton v. United Air Lines, Inc., 527 U.S. 471 (1999), the Court ruled that whether an impairment substantially limits a major life activity is to be determined with reference to the ameliorative effects of mitigating measures. In Sutton, the Court also adopted a restrictive reading of the meaning of being "regarded as" disabled under the ADA's definition of disability. Subsequently, in Toyota Motor Mfg., Ky., Inc. v. Williams, 534 U.S. 184 (2002), the Court held that the terms "substantially" and "major" in the definition of disability "need to be interpreted strictly to create a demanding standard for qualifying as disabled" under the ADA, and that to be substantially limited in performing a major life activity under the ADA, "an individual must have an impairment that prevents or severely restricts the individual from doing activities that are of central importance to most people's daily lives."

As a result of these Supreme Court decisions, lower courts ruled in numerous cases that individuals with a range of substantially limiting impairments were not individuals with disabilities, and thus not protected by the ADA. See 2008 Senate Statement of Managers at 3 ("After the Court's decisions in Sutton that impairments must be considered in their mitigated state and in Toyota that there must be a demanding standard for qualifying as disabled, lower courts more often found that an individual's impairment did not constitute a disability. As a result, in too many cases, courts would never reach the question whether discrimination had occurred."). Congress concluded that these rulings imposed a greater degree of limitation and expressed a higher standard than it had originally intended, and coupled with the EEOC's 1991 ADA regulations which had defined the term "substantially limits" as "significantly restricted," unduly precluded many individuals from being covered under the ADA. Id. — ("[t]hus, some 18 years later we are faced with a situation in which physical or mental impairments that would previously have been found to constitute disabilities are not considered disabilities under the Supreme Court's narrower standard" and "[t]he resulting court decisions contribute to a legal environment in which individuals must demonstrate an inappropriately high degree of functional limitation in order to be protected from discrimination under the ADA").

Consequently, Congress amended the ADA with the Americans with Disabilities Act Amendments Act of 2008. The ADAAA was signed into law on September 25, 2008, and became effective on January 1, 2009. This legislation is the product of extensive bipartisan efforts, and the culmination of collaboration and coordination between legislators and stakeholders, including representatives of the disability, business, and education communities. See Statement of Representatives Hoyer and Sensenbrenner, 154 Cong. Rec. H8294-96 (daily ed. Sept. 17, 2008) (Hoyer-Sensenbrenner Congressional Record Statement); Senate Statement of Managers at 1. The express purposes of the ADAAA are, among other things:

(1) To carry out the ADA's objectives of providing "a clear and comprehensive national mandate for the elimination of discrimination" and "clear, strong, consistent, enforceable standards addressing discrimination" by reinstating a broad scope of protection under the ADA;

(2) To reject the requirement enunciated in Sutton and its companion cases that whether an impairment substantially limits a major life activity is to be determined with reference to the ameliorative effects of mitigating measures;

(3) To reject the Supreme Court's reasoning in Sutton with regard to coverage under the third prong of the definition of disability and to reinstate the reasoning of the Supreme Court in School Board of Nassau County v. Arline, 480 U.S. 273 (1987), which set forth a broad view of the third prong of the definition of handicap under the Rehabilitation Act of 1973;

(4) To reject the standards enunciated by the Supreme Court in Toyota that the terms "substantially" and "major" in the definition of disability under the ADA "need to be interpreted strictly to create a demanding standard for qualifying as disabled," and that to be substantially limited in performing a major life activity under the ADA "an individual must have an impairment that prevents or severely restricts the individual from doing activities that are of central importance to most people's daily lives";

(5) To convey congressional intent that the standard created by the Supreme Court in Toyota for "substantially limits," and applied by lower courts in numerous decisions, has created an inappropriately high level of limitation necessary to obtain coverage under the ADA;

(6) To convey that it is the intent of Congress that the primary object of attention in cases brought under the ADA should be whether entities covered under the ADA have complied with their obligations, and to convey that the question of whether an individual's impairment is a disability under the ADA should not demand extensive analysis; and

(7) To express Congress' expectation that the EEOC will revise that portion of its current regulations that defines the term "substantially limits" as "significantly restricted" to be consistent with the ADA as amended.

ADAAA Section 2(b). The findings and purposes of the ADAAA "give[ ] clear guidance to the courts and * * * [are] intend[ed] to be applied appropriately and consistently." 2008 Senate Statement of Managers at 5.

The EEOC has amended its regulations to reflect the ADAAA's findings and purposes. The Commission believes that it is essential also to amend its appendix to the original regulations at the same time, and to reissue this interpretive guidance as amended concurrently with the issuance of the amended regulations. This will help to ensure that individuals with disabilities understand their rights, and to facilitate and encourage compliance by covered entities under this part.

Accordingly, this amended appendix addresses the major provisions of this part and explains the major concepts related to disability-based employment discrimination. This appendix represents the Commission's interpretation of the issues addressed within it, and the Commission will be guided by this appendix when resolving charges of employment discrimination.

NOTE ON CERTAIN TERMINOLOGY USED

The ADA, the EEOC's ADA regulations, and this appendix use the term "disabilities" rather than the term "handicaps" which was originally used in the Rehabilitation Act of 1973, 29 U.S.C. 701-796. Substantively, these terms are equivalent. As originally noted by the House Committee on the Judiciary, "[t]he use of the term 'disabilities' instead of the term 'handicaps' reflects the desire of the Committee to use the most current terminology. It reflects the preference of persons with disabilities to use that term rather than 'handicapped' as used in previous laws, such as the Rehabilitation Act of 1973 * * *." 1990 House Judiciary Report at 26-27; see also 1989 Senate Report at 21; 1990 House Labor Report at 50-51.

In addition, consistent with the Amendments Act, revisions have been made to the regulations and this Appendix to refer to "individual with a disability" and "qualified individual" as separate terms, and to change the prohibition on discrimination to "on the basis of disability" instead of prohibiting discrimination against a qualified individual "with a disability because of the disability of such individual." "This ensures that the emphasis in questions of disability discrimination is properly on the critical inquiry of whether a qualified person has been discriminated against on the basis of disability, and not unduly focused on the preliminary question of whether a particular person is a 'person with a disability.'" 2008 Senate Statement of Managers at 11.

The use of the term "Americans" in the title of the ADA, in the EEOC's regulations, or in this Appendix as amended is not intended to imply that the ADA only applies to United States citizens. Rather, the ADA protects all qualified individuals with disabilities, regardless of their citizenship status or nationality, from discrimination by a covered entity.

Finally, the terms "employer" and "employer or other covered entity" are used interchangeably throughout this Appendix to refer to all covered entities subject to the employment provisions of the ADA.

The Equal Employment Opportunity Commission (the Commission or EEOC) is responsible for enforcement of title I of the Americans with Disabilities Act (ADA), 42 U.S.C. 12101 et seq. (1990), which prohibits employment discrimination on the basis of disability. The Commission believes that it is essential to issue interpretive guidance concurrently with the issuance of this part in order to ensure that qualified individuals with disabilities understand their rights under this part and to facilitate and encourage compliance by covered entities. This appendix represents the Commission's interpretation of the issues discussed, and the Commission will be guided by it when resolving charges of employment discrimination. The appendix addresses the major provisions of this part and explains the major concepts of disability rights.

The terms "employer" or "employer or other covered entity" are used interchangeably throughout the appendix to refer to all covered entities subject to the employment provisions of the ADA.

Section 1630.1 Purpose, Applicability and Construction

Section 1630.1(a) Purpose

The express purposes of the ADA as amended are to provide a clear and comprehensive national mandate for the elimination of discrimination against individuals with disabilities; to provide clear, strong, consistent, enforceable standards addressing discrimination against individuals with disabilities; to ensure that the Federal Government plays a central role in enforcing the standards articulated in the ADA on behalf of individuals with disabilities; and to invoke the sweep of congressional authority to address the major areas of discrimination faced day-to-day by people with disabilities. 42 U.S.C. 12101(b). The EEOC's ADA regulations are intended to implement these Congressional purposes in simple and straightforward terms.

Section 1630.1(b) Applicability

The EEOC's ADA regulations as amended apply to all "covered entities" as defined at §1630.2(b). The ADA defines "covered entities" to mean an employer, employment agency, labor organization, or joint labor-management committee. 42 U.S.C. 12111(2). All covered entities are subject to the ADA's rules prohibiting discrimination. 42 U.S.C. 12112.

Section 1630.1(c) Construction

The ADA must be construed as amended. The primary purpose of the Amendments Act was to make it easier for people with disabilities to obtain protection under the ADA. See Joint Hoyer-Sensenbrenner Statement on the Origins of the ADA Restoration Act of 2008, H.R. 3195 (reviewing provisions of H.R. 3195 as revised following negotiations between representatives of the disability and business communities) (Joint Hoyer-Sensenbrenner Statement) at 2. Accordingly, under the ADA as amended and the EEOC's regulations, the definition of "disability" "shall be construed in favor of broad coverage of individuals under [the ADA], to the maximum extent permitted by the terms of [the ADA]." 42 U.S.C. 12102(4)(A); see also 2008 Senate Statement of Managers at 3 ("The ADA Amendments Act * * * reiterates that Congress intends that the scope of the [ADA] be broad and inclusive."). This construction is also intended to reinforce the general rule that civil rights statutes must be broadly construed to achieve their remedial purpose. Id. at 2; see also 2008 House Judiciary Committee Report at 19 (this rule of construction "directs courts to construe the definition of 'disability' broadly to advance the ADA's remedial purposes" and thus "brings treatment of the ADA's definition of disability in line with treatment of other civil rights laws, which should be construed broadly to effectuate their remedial purposes").

The ADAAA and the EEOC's regulations also make clear that the primary object of attention in cases brought under the ADA should be whether entities covered under the ADA have complied with their obligations, not—whether the individual meets the definition of disability. ADAAA Section 2(b)(5). This means, for example, examining whether an employer has discriminated against an employee, including whether an employer has fulfilled its obligations with respect to providing a "reasonable accommodation" to an individual with a disability; or whether an employee has met his or her responsibilities under the ADA with respect to engaging in the reasonable accommodation "interactive process." See also 2008 Senate Statement of Managers at 4 ("[L]ower court cases have too often turned solely on the question of whether the plaintiff is an individual with a disability rather than the merits of discrimination claims, such as whether adverse decisions were impermissibly made by the employer on the basis of disability, reasonable accommodations were denied, or qualification standards were unlawfully discriminatory."); 2008 House Judiciary Committee Report at 6 ("An individual who does not qualify as disabled * * * does not meet th[e] threshold question of coverage in the protected class and is therefore not permitted to attempt to prove his or her claim of discriminatory treatment.").

Further, the question of whether an individual has a disability under this part "should not demand analysis." ADAAA Section 2(b)(5). See also House Education and Labor Committee Report at 9 ("The Committee intends that the establishment of coverage under the ADA should not be overly complex nor difficult. * * *").

In addition, unless expressly stated otherwise, the standards applied in the ADA are intended to provide at least as much protection as the standards applied under the Rehabilitation Act of 1973.

The ADA does not preempt any Federal law, or any State or local law, that grants to individuals with disabilities protection greater than or equivalent to that provided by the ADA. This means that the existence of a lesser standard of protection to individuals with disabilities under the ADA will not provide a defense to failing to meet a higher standard under another law. Thus, for example, title I of the ADA would not be a defense to failing to prepare and maintain an affirmative action program under section 503 of the Rehabilitation Act. On the other hand, the existence of a lesser standard under another law will not provide a defense to failing to meet a higher standard under the ADA. See 1990 House Labor Report at 135; 1990 House Judiciary Report at 69-70.

This also means that an individual with a disability could choose to pursue claims under a State discrimination or tort law that does not confer greater substantive rights, or even confers fewer substantive rights, if the potential available remedies would be greater than those available under the ADA and this part. The ADA does not restrict an individual with a disability from pursuing such claims in addition to charges brought under this part. 1990 House Judiciary Report at 69-70.

The ADA does not automatically preempt medical standards or safety requirements established by Federal law or regulations. It does not preempt State, county, or local laws, ordinances or regulations that are consistent with this part and designed to protect the public health from individuals who pose a direct threat to the health or safety of others that cannot be eliminated or reduced by reasonable accommodation. However, the ADA does preempt inconsistent requirements established by State or local law for safety or security sensitive positions. See 1989 Senate Report at 27; 1990 House Labor Report at 57.

This also means that an individual with a disability could choose to pursue claims under a State discrimination or tort law that does not confer greater substantive rights, or even confers fewer substantive rights, if the potential available remedies would be greater than those available under the ADA and this part. The ADA does not restrict an individual with a disability from pursuing such claims in addition to charges brought under this part. 1990 House Judiciary Report at 69-70.

The ADA does not automatically preempt medical standards or safety requirements established by Federal law or regulations. It does not preempt State, county, or local laws, ordinances or regulations that are consistent with this part and designed to protect the public health from individuals who pose a direct threat to the health or safety of others that cannot be eliminated or reduced by reasonable accommodation. However, the ADA does preempt inconsistent requirements established by State or local law for safety or security sensitive positions. See 1989 Senate Report at 27; 1990 House Labor Report at 57.

An employer allegedly in violation of this part cannot successfully defend its actions by relying on the obligation to comply with the requirements of any State or local law that imposes prohibitions or limitations on the eligibility of individuals with disabilities who are qualified to practice any occupation or profession. For example, suppose a municipality has an ordinance that prohibits individuals with tuberculosis from teaching school children. If an individual with dormant tuberculosis challenges a private school's refusal to hire him or her on the basis of the tuberculosis, the private school would not be able to rely on the city ordinance as a defense under the ADA.

Paragraph (c)(3) is consistent with language added to section 501 of the ADA by the ADA Amendments Act. It makes clear that nothing in this part is intended to alter the determination of eligibility for benefits under state workers' compensation laws or Federal and State disability benefit programs. State workers' compensation laws and Federal disability benefit programs, such as programs that provide payments to veterans with service-connected disabilities and the Social Security Disability Insurance program, have fundamentally different purposes than title I of the ADA.

Sections 1630.2(a)-(f) Commission, Covered Entity, etc.

The definitions section of part 1630 includes several terms that are identical, or almost identical, to the terms found in title VII of the Civil Rights Act of 1964. Among these terms are "Commission," "Person," "State," and "Employer." These terms are to be given the same meaning under the ADA that they are given under title VII. In general, the term "employee" has the same meaning that it is given under title VII. However, the ADA's definition of "employee" does not contain an exception, as does title VII, for elected officials and their personal staffs. It should further be noted that all State and local governments are covered by title II of the ADA whether or not they are also covered by this part. Title II, which is enforced by the Department of Justice, became effective on January 26, 1992. See 28 CFR part 35.

The term "covered entity" is not found in title VII. However, the title VII definitions of the entities included in the term "covered entity" (e.g., employer, employment agency, labor organization, etc.) are applicable to the ADA.

Section 1630.2(g) Disability

In addition to the term "covered entity," there are several other terms that are unique to the ADA as amended. The first of these is the term "disability." "This definition is of critical importance because as a threshold issue it determines whether an individual is covered by the ADA." 2008 Senate Statement of Managers at 6.

In the original ADA, "Congress sought to protect anyone who experiences discrimination because of a current, past, or perceived disability." 2008 Senate Statement of Managers at 6. Accordingly, the definition of the term "disability" is divided into three prongs: An individual is considered to have a "disability" if that individual (1) has a physical or mental impairment that substantially limits one or more of that person's major life activities (the "actual disability" prong); (2) has a record of such an impairment (the "record of" prong); or (3) is regarded by the covered entity as an individual with a disability as defined in §1630.2(l) (the "regarded as" prong). The ADAAA retained the basic structure and terms of the original definition of disability. However, the Amendments Act altered the interpretation and application of this critical statutory term in fundamental ways. See 2008 Senate Statement of Managers at 1 ("The bill maintains the ADA's inherently functional definition of disability" but "clarifies and expands the definition's meaning and application.").

As noted above, the primary purpose of the ADAAA is to make it easier for people with disabilities to obtain protection under the ADA. See Joint Hoyer-Sensenbrenner Statement at 2. Accordingly, the ADAAA provides rules of construction regarding the definition of disability. Consistent with the congressional intent to reinstate a broad scope of protection under the ADA, the ADAAA's rules of construction require that the definition of "disability" "shall be construed in favor of broad coverage of individuals under [the ADA], to the maximum extent permitted by the terms of [the ADA]." 42 U.S.C. 12102(4)(A). The legislative history of the ADAAA is replete with references emphasizing this principle. See Joint Hoyer-Sensenbrenner Statement at 2 ("[The bill] establishes that the definition of disability must be interpreted broadly to achieve the remedial purposes of the ADA"); 2008 Senate Statement of Managers at 1 (the ADAAA's purpose is to "enhance the protections of the [ADA]" by "expanding the definition, and by rejecting several opinions of the United States Supreme Court that have had the effect of restricting the meaning and application of the definition of disability"); id. (stressing the importance of removing barriers "to construing and applying the definition of disability more generously"); id. at 4 ("The managers have intro-duced the [ADAAA] to restore the proper balance and application of the ADA by clarifying and broadening the definition of disability, and to increase eligibility for the protections of the ADA."); id. ("It is our expectation that because the bill makes the definition of disability more generous, some people who were not covered before will now be covered."); id. (warning that "the definition of dis-ability should not be unduly used as a tool for excluding individuals from the ADA's protections"); id. (this principle "sends a clear signal of our intent that the courts must interpret the definition of disability broadly rather than stringently"); 2008 House Judiciary Committee Report at 5 ("The purpose of the bill is to restore protection for the broad range of individuals with disabilities as originally envisioned by Congress by responding to the Supreme Court's narrow interpre-tation of the definition of disability.").

Further, as the purposes section of the ADAAA explicitly cautions, the "pri-mary object of attention" in cases brought under the ADA should be whether entities covered under the ADA have complied with their obligations. As noted above, this means, for example, examining whether an employer has discrimi-nated against an employee, including whether an employer has fulfilled its obli-gations with respect to providing a "reasonable accommodation" to an individual with a disability; or whether an employee has met his or her responsibilities under the ADA with respect to engaging in the reasonable accommodation "interactive process." ADAAA Section 2(b)(5); see also 2008 Senate Statement of Managers at 4 ("[L]ower court cases have too often turned solely on the question of whether the plaintiff is an individual with a disability rather than the merits of discrimination claims, such as whether adverse decisions were impermissibly made by the em-ployer on the basis of disability, reasonable accommodations were denied, or qualification standards were unlawfully discriminatory."); 2008 House Judiciary Committee Report (criticizing pre-ADAAA court decisions which "prevented individuals that Congress unquestionably intended to cover from ever getting a chance to prove their case"). Accordingly, the threshold coverage question of whether an individual's impairment is a disability under the ADA "should not demand extensive analysis." ADAAA Section 2(b)(5).

Section 1630.2(g)(2) provides that an individual may establish coverage under any one or more (or all three) of the prongs in the definition of disability. However, to be an individual with a disability, an individual is only required to satisfy one prong.

As §1630.2(g)(3) indicates, in many cases it may be unnecessary for an individual to resort to coverage under the "actual disability" or "record of" prongs. Where the need for a reasonable accommodation is not at issue — for example, where there is no question that the individual is "qualified" without a reasonable accommodation and is not seeking or has not sought a reasonable accommodation — it would not be necessary to determine whether the individual is substantially limited in a major life activity (under the actual disability prong) or has a record of a substantially limiting impairment (under the record of prong). Such claims could be evaluated solely under the "regarded as" prong of the definition. In fact, Congress expected the first and second prongs of the definition of disability "to be used only by people who are affirmatively seeking reasonable accommodations * * *" and that "[a]ny individual who has been discriminated against because of an impairment—short of being granted a reasonable accommodation * * *—should be bringing a claim under the third prong of the definition which will require no showing with regard to the severity of his or her impairment." Joint Hoyer-Sensenbrenner Statement at 4. An individual may choose, however, to proceed under the "actual disability" and/or "record of" prong regardless of whether the individual is challenging a covered entity's failure to make reasonable accommodation or requires a reasonable accommodation.

To fully understand the meaning of the term "disability," it is also necessary to understand what is meant by the terms "physical or mental impairment," "major life activity," "substantially limits," "record of," and "regarded as." Each of these terms is discussed below.

Section 1630.2(h) Physical or Mental Impairment

Neither the original ADA nor the ADAAA provides a definition for the terms "physical or mental impairment." However, the legislative history of the Amendments Act notes that Congress "expect[s] that the current regulatory definition of these terms, as promulgated by agencies such as the U.S. Equal Employment Opportunity Commission (EEOC), the Department of Justice (DOJ) and the Department of Education Office of Civil Rights (DOE OCR) will not change." 2008 Senate Statement of Managers at 6. The definition of "physical or mental impairment" in the EEOC's regulations remains based on the definition of the term "physical or mental impairment" found in the regulations implementing section 504 of the Rehabilitation Act at 34 CFR part 104. However, the definition in EEOC's regulations adds additional body systems to those provided in the section 504 regulations and makes clear that the list is non-exhaustive.

It is important to distinguish between conditions that are impairments and physical, psychological, environmental, cultural, and economic characteristics that are not impairments. The definition of the term "impairment" does not include physical characteristics such as eye color, hair color, left-handedness, or height, weight, or muscle tone that are within "normal" range and are not the result of a physiological disorder. The definition, likewise, does not include characteristic predisposition to illness or disease. Other conditions, such as pregnancy, that are not the result of a physiological disorder are also not impairments. However, a pregnancy-related impairment that substantially limits a major life activity is a disability under the first prong of the definition. Alternatively, a pregnancy-related impairment may constitute a "record of" a substantially limiting impairment," or may be covered under the "regarded as" prong if it is the basis for a prohibited employment action and is not "transitory and minor."

The definition of an impairment also does not include common personality traits such as poor judgment or a quick temper where these are not symptoms of a mental or psychological disorder. Environmental, cultural, or economic disadvantages such as poverty, lack of education, or a prison record are not impairments. Advanced age, in and of itself, is also not an impairment. However, various medical conditions commonly associated with age, such as hearing loss, osteoporosis, or arthritis would constitute impairments within the meaning of this part. See 1989 Senate Report at 22-23; 1990 House Labor Report at 51-52; 1990 House Judiciary Report at 28-29.

Section 1630.2(i) Major Life Activities

The ADAAA provided significant new guidance and clarification on the subject of "major life activities." As the legislative history of the Amendments Act explains, Congress anticipated that protection under the ADA would now extend to a wider range of cases, in part as a result of the expansion of the category of major life activities. See 2008 Senate Statement of Managers at 8 n.17.

For purposes of clarity, the Amendments Act provides an illustrative list of major life activities, including caring for oneself, performing manual tasks, seeing, hearing, eating, sleeping, walking, standing, lifting, bending, speaking, breathing, learning, reading, concentrating, thinking, communicating, and working. The ADA Amendments expressly made this statutory list of examples of major life activities non-exhaustive, and the regulations include sitting, reaching, and interacting with others as additional examples. Many of these major life activities listed in the ADA Amendments Act and the regulations already had been included in the EEOC's 1991 now-superseded regulations implementing title I of the ADA and in sub-regulatory documents, and already were recognized by the courts.

The ADA as amended also explicitly defines "major life activities" to include the operation of "major bodily functions." This was an important addition to the statute. This clarification was needed to ensure that the impact of an impairment on the operation of a major bodily function would not be overlooked or wrongly dismissed as falling outside the definition of "major life activities" under the ADA. 2008 House Judiciary Committee Report at 16; see also 2008 Senate Statement of Managers at 8 ("for the first time [in the ADAAA], the category of 'major life activities' is defined to include the operation of major bodily functions, thus better addressing chronic impairments that can be substantially limiting").

The regulations include all of those major bodily functions identified in the ADA Amendments Act's non-exhaustive list of examples and add a number of others that are consistent with the body systems listed in the regulations' definition of "impairment" (at §1630.2(h)) and with the U.S. Department of Labor's non-discrimination and equal employment opportunity regulations implementing section 188 of the Workforce Investment Act of 1998, 29 U.S.C. 2801, et seq. Thus, special sense organs, skin, genitourinary, cardiovascular, hemic, lymphatic, and musculoskeletal functions are major bodily functions not included in the statutory list of examples but included in §1630.2(i)(1)(ii). The Commission has added these examples to further illustrate the non-exhaustive list of major life activities, including major bodily functions, and to emphasize that the concept of major life activities is to be interpreted broadly consistent with the Amendments Act. The regulations also provide that the operation of a major bodily function may include the operation of an individual organ within a body system. This would include, for example, the operation of the kidney, liver, pancreas, or other organs.

The link between particular impairments and various major bodily functions should not be difficult to identify. Because impairments, by definition, affect the functioning of body systems, they will generally affect major bodily functions. For example, cancer affects an individual's normal cell growth; diabetes affects the operation of the pancreas and also the function of the endocrine system; and Human Immunodeficiency Virus (HIV) infection affects the immune system. Likewise, sickle cell disease affects the functions of the hemic system, lymphedema affects lymphatic functions, and rheumatoid arthritis affects musculoskeletal functions.

In the legislative history of the ADAAA, Congress expressed its expectation that the statutory expansion of "major life activities" to include major bodily functions (along with other statutory changes) would lead to more expansive coverage. See 2008 Senate Statement of Managers at 8 n.17 (indicating that these changes will make it easier for individuals to show that they are eligible for the ADA's protections under the first prong of the definition of disability). The House Education and Labor Committee explained that the inclusion of major bodily functions would "affect cases such as U.S. v. Happy Time Day Care Ctr. in which the courts struggled to analyze whether the impact of HIV infection substantially limits various major life activities of a five-year-old child, and recognizing, among other things, that 'there is something inherently illogical about inquiring whether' a five-year-old's ability to procreate is substantially limited by his HIV infection; Furnish v. SVI Sys., Inc, in which the court found that an individual with cirrhosis of the liver caused by Hepatitis B is not disabled because liver function—unlike eating, working, or reproducing—'is not integral to one's daily existence;' and Pimental v. Dartmouth-Hitchcock Clinic, in which the court concluded that the plaintiff's stage three breast cancer did not substantially limit her ability to care for herself, sleep, or concentrate. The Committee expects that the plaintiffs in each of these cases could establish a [substantial limitation] on major bodily functions that would qualify them for protection under the ADA." 2008 House Education and Labor Committee Report at 12. The examples of major life activities (including major bodily functions) in the ADAAA and the EEOC's regulations are illustrative and non-exhaustive, and the absence of a particular life activity or bodily function from the examples does not create a negative implication as to whether an omitted activity or function constitutes a major life activity under the statute. See 2008 Senate Statement of Managers at 8; see also 2008 House Committee on Educ. and Labor Report at 11; 2008 House Judiciary Committee Report at 17.

The Commission anticipates that courts will recognize other major life activities, consistent with the ADA Amendments Act's mandate to construe the definition of disability broadly. As a result of the ADA Amendments Act's rejection of the holding in Toyota Motor Mfg., Ky., Inc. v. Williams, 534 U.S. 184 (2002), whether an activity is a "major life activity" is not determined by reference to whether it is of "central importance to daily life." See Toyota, 534 U.S. at 197 (defining "major life activities" as activities that are of "central importance to most people's daily lives"). Indeed, this holding was at odds with the earlier Supreme Court decision of Bragdon v. Abbott, 524 U.S. 624 (1998), which held that a major life activity (in that case, reproduction) does not have to have a "public, economic or daily aspect." Id. at 639.

Accordingly, the regulations provide that in determining other examples of major life activities, the term "major" shall not be interpreted strictly to create a demanding standard for disability. Cf. 2008 Senate Statement of Managers at 7 (indicating that a person is considered an individual with a disability for purposes of the first prong when one or more of the individual's "important life activities" are restricted) (citing 1989 Senate Report at 23). The regulations also reject the notion that to be substantially limited in performing a major life activity, an individual must have an impairment that prevents or severely restricts the individual from doing "activities that are of central importance to most people's daily lives." Id.; see also 2008 Senate Statement of Managers at 5 n.12.

Thus, for example, lifting is a major life activity regardless of whether an individual who claims to be substantially limited in lifting actually performs activities of central importance to daily life that require lifting. Similarly, the Commission anticipates that the major life activity of performing manual tasks (which was at issue in Toyota) could have many different manifestations, such as performing tasks involving fine motor coordination, or performing tasks involving grasping, hand strength, or pressure. Such tasks need not constitute activities of central importance to most people's daily lives, nor must an individual show that he or she is substantially limited in performing all manual tasks.

Section 1630.2(j) Substantially Limits

In any case involving coverage solely under the "regarded as" prong of the definition of "disability" (e.g., cases where reasonable accommodation is not at issue), it is not necessary to determine whether an individual is "substantially limited" in any major life activity. See 2008 Senate Statement of Managers at 10; id. at 13 ("The functional limitation imposed by an impairment is irrelevant to the third 'regarded as' prong."). Indeed, Congress anticipated that the first and second prongs of the definition of disability would "be used only by people who are affirmatively seeking reasonable accommodations * * *" and that "[a]ny individual who has been discriminated against because of an impairment—short of being granted a reasonable accommodation * * *—should be bringing a claim under the third prong of the definition which will require no showing with regard to the severity of his or her impairment." Joint Hoyer-Sensenbrenner Statement at 4. Of course, an individual may choose, however, to proceed under the "actual disability" and/or "record of" prong regardless of whether the individual is challenging a covered entity's failure to make reasonable accommodations or requires a reasonable accommodation. The concept of "substantially limits" is only relevant in cases involving coverage under the "actual disability" or "record of" prong of the definition of disability. Thus, the information below pertains to these cases only.

Section 1630.2(j)(1) Rules of Construction

It is clear in the text and legislative history of the ADAAA that Congress concluded the courts had incorrectly construed "substantially limits," and disapproved of the EEOC's now-superseded 1991 regulation defining the term to mean "significantly restricts." See 2008 Senate Statement of Managers at 6 ("We do not believe that the courts have correctly instituted the level of coverage we intended to establish with the term 'substantially limits' in the ADA" and "we believe that the level of limitation, and the intensity of focus, applied by the Supreme Court in Toyota goes beyond what we believe is the appropriate standard to create coverage under this law."). Congress extensively deliberated over whether a new term other than "substantially limits" should be adopted to denote the appropriate functional limitation necessary under the first and second prongs of the definition of disability. See 2008 Senate Statement of Managers at 6-7. Ultimately, Congress affirmatively opted to retain this term in the Amendments Act, rather than replace it. It concluded that "adopting a new, undefined term that is subject to widely disparate meanings is not the best way to achieve the goal of ensuring consistent and appropriately broad coverage under this Act." Id. Instead, Congress determined "a better way * * * to express [its] disapproval of Sutton and Toyota (along with the current EEOC regulation) is to retain the words 'substantially limits,' but clarify that it is not meant to be a demanding standard." Id. at 7. To achieve that goal, Congress set forth detailed findings and purposes and "rules of construction" to govern the interpretation and application of this concept going forward. See ADAAA Sections 2-4; 42 U.S.C. 12102(4).

The Commission similarly considered whether to provide a new definition of "substantially limits" in the regulation. Following Congress's lead, however, the Commission ultimately concluded that a new definition would inexorably lead to greater focus and intensity of attention on the threshold issue of coverage than intended by Congress. Therefore, the regulations simply provide rules of construction that must be applied in determining whether an impairment substantially limits (or substantially limited) a major life activity. These are each discussed in greater detail below.

Section 1630.2(j)(1)(ii) Broad Construction; not a Demanding Standard

Section 1630.2(j)(1)(i) states: "The term 'substantially limits' shall be construed broadly in favor of expansive coverage, to the maximum extent permitted by the terms of the ADA. 'Substantially limits' is not meant to be a demanding standard."

Congress stated in the ADA Amendments Act that the definition of disability "shall be construed in favor of broad coverage," and that "the term 'substantially limits' shall be interpreted consistently with the findings and purposes of the ADA Amendments Act of 2008." 42 U.S.C. 12101(4)(A)-(B), as amended. "This is a textual provision that will legally guide the agencies and courts in properly interpreting the term 'substantially limits.'" Hoyer-Sensenbrenner Congressional Record Statement at H8295. As Congress noted in the legislative history of the ADAAA, "[t]o be clear, the purposes section conveys our intent to clarify not only that 'substantially limits' should be measured by a lower standard than that used in Toyota, but also that the definition of disability should not be unduly used as a tool for excluding individuals from the ADA's protections." 2008 Senate Statement of Managers at 5 (also stating that "[t]his rule of construction, together with the rule of construction providing that the definition of disability shall be construed in favor of broad coverage of individuals sends a clear signal of our intent that the courts must interpret the definition of disability broadly rather than stringently"). Put most succinctly, "substantially limits" "is not meant to be a demanding standard." 2008 Senate Statement of Managers at 7.

Section 1630.2(j)(1)(ii)   Significant or Severe Restriction Not Required; Nonetheless, Not Every Impairment Is Substantially Limiting

Section 1630.2(j)(1)(ii) states: "An impairment is a disability within the meaning of this section if it substantially limits the ability of an individual to perform a major life activity as compared to most people in the general population. An impairment need not prevent, or significantly or severely restrict, the individual from performing a major life activity in order to be considered substantially limiting. Nonetheless, not every impairment will constitute a 'disability' within the meaning of this section."

In keeping with the instruction that the term "substantially limits" is not meant to be a demanding standard, the regulations provide that an impairment is a disability if it substantially limits the ability of an individual to perform a major life activity as compared to most people in the general population. However, to be substantially limited in performing a major life activity an individual need not have an impairment that prevents or significantly or severely restricts the individual from performing a major life activity. See 2008 Senate Statement of Managers at 2, 6-8 & n.14; 2008 House Committee on Educ. and Labor Report at 9-10 ("While the limitation imposed by an impairment must be important, it need not rise to the level of severely restricting or significantly restricting the ability to perform a major life activity to qualify as a disability."); 2008 House Judiciary Committee Report at 16 (similarly requiring an "important" limitation). The level of limitation required is "substantial" as compared to most people in the general population, which does not require a significant or severe restriction. Multiple impairments that combine to substantially limit one or more of an individual's major life activities also constitute a disability. Nonetheless, not every impairment will constitute a "disability" within the meaning of this section. See 2008 Senate Statement of Managers at 4 ("We reaffirm that not every individual with a physical or mental impairment is covered by the first prong of the definition of disability in the ADA.")

Section 1630.2(j)(1)(iii)   Substantial Limitation Should Not Be Primary Object of Attention; Extensive Analysis Not Needed

Section 1630.2(j)(1)(iii) states: "The primary object of attention in cases brought under the ADA should be whether covered entities have complied with their obligations, not whether an individual's impairment substantially limits a major life activity. Accordingly, the threshold issue of whether an impairment 'substantially limits' a major life activity should not demand extensive analysis."

Congress retained the term "substantially limits" in part because it was concerned that adoption of a new phrase — and the resulting need for further judicial scrutiny and construction — would not "help move the focus from the threshold issue of disability to the primary issue of discrimination." 2008 Senate Statement of Managers at 7.

This was the primary problem Congress sought to solve in enacting the ADAAA. It recognized that "clearing the initial [disability] threshold is critical, as individuals who are excluded from the definition 'never have the opportunity to have their condition evaluated in light of medical evidence and a determination made as to whether they [are] 'otherwise quali fied.''" 2008 House Judiciary Committee Report at 7; see also id. (expressing concern that "[a]n individual who does not qualify as disabled does not meet th[e] threshold question of coverage in the protected class and is therefore not permitted to attempt to prove his or her claim of discriminatory treatment"); 2008 Senate Statement of Managers at 4 (criticizing pre-ADAAA lower court cases that "too often turned solely on the question of whether the plaintiff is an individual with a disability rather than the merits of discrimination claims, such as whether adverse decisions were impermissibly made by the employer on the basis of disability, reasonable accommodations were denied, or qualification standards were unlawfully discriminatory").

Accordingly, the Amendments Act and the amended regulations make plain that the emphasis in ADA cases now should be squarely on the merits and not on the initial coverage question. The revised regulations therefore provide that an impairment is a disability if it substantially limits the ability of an individual to perform a major life activity as compared to most people in the general population and deletes the language to which Congress objected. The Commission believes that this provides a useful framework in which to analyze whether an impairment satisfies the definition of disability. Further, this framework better reflects Congress's expressed intent in the ADA Amendments Act that the definition of the term "disability" shall be construed broadly, and is consistent with statements in the Amendments Act's legislative history. See 2008 Senate Statement of Managers at 7 (stating that "adopting a new, undefined term" and the "resulting need for further judicial scrutiny and construction will not help move the focus from the threshold issue of disability to the primary issue of discrimination," and finding that "'substantially limits' as construed consistently with the findings and purposes of this legislation establishes an appropriate functionality test of determining whether an individual has a disability" and that "using the correct standard — one that is lower than the strict or demanding standard created by the Supreme Court in Toyota — will make the disability determination an appropriate threshold issue but not an onerous burden for those seeking accommodations or modifications").

Consequently, this rule of construction makes clear that the question of whether an impairment substantially limits a major life activity should not demand extensive analysis. As the legislative history explains, "[w]e expect that courts interpreting [the ADA] will not demand such an extensive analysis over whether a person's physical or mental impairment constitutes a disability." Hoyer-Sensenbrenner Congressional Record Statement at H8295; see id. ("Our goal throughout this process has been to simplify that analysis.")

Section 1630.2(j)(1)(iv) Individualized Assessment Required, But With Lower Standard Than Previously Applied

Section 1630.2(j)(1)(iv) states: "The determination of whether an impairment substantially limits a major life activity requires an individualized assessment. However, in making this assessment, the term 'substantially limits' shall be interpreted and applied to require a degree of functional limitation that is lower than the standard for 'substantially limits' applied prior to the ADAAA."

By retaining the essential elements of the definition of disability including the key term "substantially limits," Congress reaffirmed that not every individual with a physical or mental impairment is covered by the first prong of the definition of disability in the ADA. See 2008 Senate Statement of Managers at 4. To be covered under the first prong of the definition, an individual must establish that an impairment substantially limits a major life activity. That has not changed — nor will the necessity of making this determination on an individual basis. Id. However, what the ADAAA changed is the standard required for making this determination. Id. at 4-5.

The Amendments Act and the EEOC's regulations explicitly reject the standard enunciated by the Supreme Court in Toyota Motor Mfg., Ky., Inc. v. Williams, 534 U.S. 184 (2002), and applied in the lower courts in numerous cases. See ADAAA Section 2(b)(4). That previous standard created "an inappropriately high level of limitation necessary to obtain coverage under the ADA." Id. at Section 2(b)(5). The Amendments Act and the EEOC's regulations reject the notion that "substantially limits" should be interpreted strictly to create a demanding standard for qualifying as disabled. Id. at Section 2(b)(4). Instead, the ADAAA and these regulations establish a degree of functional limitation required for an impairment to constitute a disability that is consistent with what Congress originally intended. 2008 Senate Statement of Managers at 7. This will make the disability determination an appropriate threshold issue but not an onerous burden for those seeking to prove discrimination under the ADA. Id.

Section 1630.2(j)(1)(v) Scientific, Medical, or Statistical Analysis Not Required, But Permissible When Appropriate

Section 1630.2(j)(1)(v) states: "The comparison of an individual's performance of a major life activity to the performance of the same major life activity by most people in the general population usually will not require scientific, medical, or statistical analysis. Nothing in this paragraph is intended, however, to prohibit the presentation of scientific, medical, or statistical evidence to make such a comparison where appropriate."

The term "average person in the general population," as the basis of comparison for determining whether an individual's impairment substantially limits a major life activity, has been changed to "most people in the general population." This revision is not a substantive change in the concept, but rather is intended to conform the language to the simpler and more straightforward terminology used in the legislative history to the Amendments Act. The comparison between the individual and "most people" need not be exacting, and usually will not require scientific, medical, or statistical analysis. Nothing in this subparagraph is intended, however, to prohibit the presentation of scientific, medical, or statistical evidence to make such a comparison where appropriate.

The comparison to most people in the general population continues to mean a comparison to other people in the general population, not a comparison to those similarly situated. For example, the ability of an individual with an amputated limb to perform a major life activity is compared to other people in the general population, not to other amputees. This does not mean that disability cannot be shown where an impairment, such as a learning disability, is clinically diagnosed based in part on a disparity between an individual's aptitude and that individual's actual versus expected achievement, taking into account the person's chronological age, measured intelligence, and age-appropriate education. Individuals diagnosed with dyslexia or other learning disabilities will typically be substantially limited in performing activities such as learning, reading, and thinking when compared to most people in the general population, particularly when the ameliorative effects of mitigating measures, including therapies, learned behavioral or adaptive neurological modifications, assistive devices (e.g., audio recordings, screen reading devices, voice activated software), studying longer, or receiving more time to take a test, are disregarded as required under the ADA Amendments Act.

Section 1630.2(j)(1)(vi) Mitigating Measures

Section 1630.2(j)(1)(vi) states: "The determination of whether an impairment substantially limits a major life activity shall be made without regard to the ameliorative effects of mitigating measures. However, the ameliorative effects of ordinary eyeglasses or contact lenses shall be considered in determining whether an impairment substantially limits a major life activity."

The ameliorative effects of mitigating measures shall not be considered in determining whether an impairment substantially limits a major life activity. Thus, "[w]ith the exception of ordinary eyeglasses and contact lenses, impairments must be examined in their unmitigated state." See 2008 Senate Statement of Managers at 5.

This provision in the ADAAA and the EEOC's regulations "is intended to eliminate the catch-22 that exist[ed] * * * where individuals who are subjected to discrimination on the basis of their disabilities [we]re frequently unable to invoke the ADA's protections because they [we]re not considered people with disabilities when the effects of their medication, medical supplies, behavioral adaptations, or other interventions [we]re considered." Joint Hoyer-Sensenbrenner Statement at 2; see also 2008 Senate Statement of Managers at 9 ("This provision is intended to eliminate the situation created under [prior] law in which impairments that are

mitigated [did] not constitute disabilities but [were the basis for discrimination].").
To the extent cases pre-dating the 2008 Amendments Act reasoned otherwise,
they are contrary to the law as amended. See 2008 House Judiciary Committee
Report at 9 & nn.25, 20-21 (citing, e.g., McClure v. General Motors Corp., 75 F.
App'x 983 (5th Cir. 2003) (court held that individual with muscular dystrophy
who, with the mitigating measure of "adapting" how he performed manual tasks,
had successfully learned to live and work with his disability was therefore not an
individual with a disability); Orr v. Wal-Mart Stores, Inc., 297 F.3d 720 (8th Cir.
2002) (court held that Sutton v. United Air Lines, Inc., 527 U.S. 471 (1999),
required consideration of the ameliorative effects of plaintiff's careful regimen of
medicine, exercise and diet, and declined to consider impact of uncontrolled
diabetes on plaintiff's ability to see, speak, read, and walk); Gonzales v. National
Bd. of Med. Examiners, 225 F.3d 620 (6th Cir. 2000) (where the court found that
an individual with a diagnosed learning disability was not substantially limited
after considering the impact of self-accommodations that allowed him to read and
achieve academic success); McMullin v. Ashcroft, 337 F. Supp. 2d 1281 (D. Wyo.
2004) (individual fired because of clinical depression not protected because of the
successful management of the condition with medication for fifteen years);
Eckhaus v. Consol. Rail Corp., 2003 WL 23205042 (D.N.J. Dec. 24, 2003) (individual fired because of a hearing impairment was not protected because a hearing
aid helped correct that impairment); Todd v. Academy Corp., 57 F. Supp. 2d 448,
452 (S.D. Tex. 1999) (court held that because medication reduced the frequency
and intensity of plaintiff's seizures, he was not disabled)).

An individual who, because of the use of a mitigating measure, has experienced no limitations, or only minor limitations, related to the impairment may
still be an individual with a disability, where there is evidence that in the absence
of an effective mitigating measure the individual's impairment would be substantially limiting. For example, someone who began taking medication for hypertension before experiencing substantial limitations related to the impairment
would still be an individual with a disability if, without the medication, he or she
would now be substantially limited in functions of the cardiovascular or circulatory
system.

Evidence showing that an impairment would be substantially limiting in the
absence of the ameliorative effects of mitigating measures could include evidence
of limitations that a person experienced prior to using a mitigating measure,
evidence concerning the expected course of a particular disorder absent mitigating measures, or readily available and reliable information of other types.
However, we expect that consistent with the Amendments Act's command (and the
related rules of construction in the regulations) that the definition of disability
"should not demand extensive analysis," covered entities and courts will in many
instances be able to conclude that a substantial limitation has been shown without
resort to such evidence.

The Amendments Act provides an "illustrative but non-comprehensive list of
the types of mitigating measures that are not to be considered." See 2008 Senate
Statement of Managers at 9. Section 1630.2(j)(5) of the regulations includes all of
those mitigating measures listed in the ADA Amendments Act's illustrative list of

mitigating measures, including reasonable accommodations (as applied under title I) or "auxiliary aids or services" (as defined by 42 U.S.C. 12103(1) and applied under titles II and III). Since it would be impossible to guarantee comprehensiveness in a finite list, the list of examples of mitigating measures provided in the ADA and the regulations is non-exhaustive. See 2008 House Judiciary Committee Report at 20. The absence of any particular mitigating measure from the list in the regulations should not convey a negative implication as to whether the measure is a mitigating measure under the ADA. See 2008 Senate Statement of Managers at 9.

For example, the fact that mitigating measures include "reasonable accommodations" generally makes it unnecessary to mention specific kinds of accommodations. Nevertheless, the use of a service animal, job coach, or personal assistant on the job would certainly be considered types of mitigating measures, as would the use of any device that could be considered assistive technology, and whether individuals who use these measures have disabilities would be determined without reference to their ameliorative effects. See 2008 House Judiciary Committee Report at 20; 2008 House Educ. & Labor Rep. at 15. Similarly, adaptive strategies that might mitigate, or even allow an individual to otherwise avoid performing particular major life activities, are mitigating measures and also would not be considered in determining whether an impairment is substantially limiting. Id.

The determination of whether or not an individual's impairment substantially limits a major life activity is unaffected by whether the individual chooses to forgo mitigating measures. For individuals who do not use a mitigating measure (including for example medication or reasonable accommodation that could alleviate the effects of an impairment), the availability of such measures has no bearing on whether the impairment substantially limits a major life activity. The limitations posed by the impairment on the individual and any negative (non-ameliorative) effects of mitigating measures used determine whether an impairment is substantially limiting. The origin of the impairment, whether its effects can be mitigated, and any ameliorative effects of mitigating measures in fact used may not be considered in determining if the impairment is substantially limiting. However, the use or non-use of mitigating measures, and any consequences thereof, including any ameliorative and non-ameliorative effects, may be relevant in determining whether the individual is qualified or poses a direct threat to safety.

The ADA Amendments Act and the regulations state that "ordinary eyeglasses or contact lenses" shall be considered in determining whether someone has a disability. This is an exception to the rule that the ameliorative effects of mitigating measures are not to be taken into account. "The rationale behind this exclusion is that the use of ordinary eyeglasses or contact lenses, without more, is not significant enough to warrant protection under the ADA." Joint Hoyer-Sensenbrenner Statement at 2. Nevertheless, as discussed in greater detail below at §1630.10(b), if an applicant or employee is faced with a qualification standard that requires uncorrected vision (as the plaintiffs in the Sutton case were), and the applicant or employee who is adversely affected by the standard brings a challenge under the ADA, an employer will be required to demonstrate that the qualification standard is job related and consistent with business necessity. 2008 Senate Statement of Managers at 9.

The ADAAA and the EEOC's regulations both define the term "ordinary eyeglasses or contact lenses" as lenses that are "intended to fully correct visual acuity or eliminate refractive error." So, if an individual with severe myopia uses eyeglasses or contact lenses that are intended to fully correct visual acuity or eliminate refractive error, they are ordinary eyeglasses or contact lenses, and therefore any inquiry into whether such individual is substantially limited in seeing or reading would be based on how the individual sees or reads with the benefit of the eyeglasses or contact lenses. Likewise, if the only visual loss an individual experiences affects the ability to see well enough to read, and the individual's ordinary reading glasses are intended to completely correct for this visual loss, the ameliorative effects of using the reading glasses must be considered in determining whether the individual is substantially limited in seeing. Additionally, eyeglasses or contact lenses that are the wrong prescription or an outdated prescription may nevertheless be "ordinary" eyeglasses or contact lenses, if a proper prescription would fully correct visual acuity or eliminate refractive error.

Both the statute and the regulations distinguish "ordinary eyeglasses or contact lenses" from "low vision devices," which function by magnifying, enhancing, or otherwise augmenting a visual image, and which are not considered when determining whether someone has a disability. The regulations do not establish a specific level of visual acuity (e.g., 20/20) as the basis for determining whether eyeglasses or contact lenses should be considered "ordinary" eyeglasses or contact lenses. Whether lenses fully correct visual acuity or eliminate refractive error is best determined on a case-by-case basis, in light of current and objective medical evidence. Moreover, someone who uses ordinary eyeglasses or contact lenses is not automatically considered to be outside the ADA's protection. Such an individual may demonstrate that, even with the use of ordinary eyeglasses or contact lenses, his vision is still substantially limited when compared to most people.

Section 1630.2(j)(1)(vii) Impairments That Are Episodic or in Remission

Section 1630.2(j)(1)(vii) states: "An impairment that is episodic or in remission is a disability if it would substantially limit a major life activity when active."

An impairment that is episodic or in remission is a disability if it would substantially limit a major life activity in its active state. "This provision is intended to reject the reasoning of court decisions concluding that certain individuals with certain conditions — such as epilepsy or post traumatic stress disorder — were not protected by the ADA because their conditions were episodic or intermittent." Joint Hoyer-Sensenbrenner Statement at 2-3. The legislative history provides: "This * * * rule of construction thus rejects the reasoning of the courts in cases like Todd v. Academy Corp. [57 F. Supp. 2d 448, 453 (S.D. Tex. 1999)] where the court found that the plaintiff's epilepsy, which resulted in short seizures during which the plaintiff was unable to speak and experienced tremors, was not sufficiently limiting, at least in part because those seizures occurred episodically. It similarly rejects the results reached in cases [such as Pimental v. Dartmouth-Hitchock Clinic, 236 F. Supp. 2d 177, 182-83 (D.N.H. 2002)] where the courts have discounted the impact of an impairment [such as cancer] that may be in remission as too short-lived to be substantially limiting. It is thus expected that individuals with impairments that are episodic or in remission (e.g., epilepsy, multiple sclerosis, cancer) will be able to establish coverage if, when active, the impairment or the manner in which it manifests (e.g., seizures) substantially limits a major life activity." 2008 House Judiciary Committee Report at 19-20.

Other examples of impairments that may be episodic include, but are not limited to, hypertension, diabetes, asthma, major depressive disorder, bipolar disorder, and schizophrenia. See 2008 House Judiciary Committee Report at 19-20. The fact that the periods during which an episodic impairment is active and substantially limits a major life activity may be brief or occur infrequently is no longer relevant to determining whether the impairment substantially limits a major life activity. For example, a person with post-traumatic stress disorder who experiences intermittent flashbacks to traumatic events is substantially limited in brain function and thinking.

Section 1630.2(j)(1)(viii) Substantial Limitation in Only One Major Life Activity Required

Section 1630.2(j)(1)(viii) states: "An impairment that substantially limits one major life activity need not substantially limit other major life activities in order to be considered a substantially limiting impairment."

The ADAAA explicitly states that an impairment need only substantially limit one major life activity to be considered a disability under the ADA. See ADAAA Section 4(a); 42 U.S.C. 12102(4)(C). "This responds to and corrects those courts that have required individuals to show that an impairment substantially limits more than one life activity." 2008 Senate Statement of Managers at 8. In addition, this rule of construction is "intended to clarify that the ability to perform one or more particular tasks within a broad category of activities does not preclude coverage under the ADA." Id. To the extent cases pre-dating the applicability of the 2008 Amendments Act reasoned otherwise, they are contrary to the law as amended. Id. (citing Holt v. Grand Lake Mental Health Ctr., Inc., 443 F. 3d 762 (10th Cir. 2006) (holding an individual with cerebral palsy who could not independently perform certain specified manual tasks was not substantially limited in her ability to perform a "broad range" of manual tasks)); see also 2008 House Judiciary Committee Report at 19 & n.52 (this legislatively corrects court decisions that, with regard to the major life activity of performing manual tasks, "have offset substantial limitation in the performance of some tasks with the ability to perform others" (citing Holt)).

For example, an individual with diabetes is substantially limited in endocrine function and thus an individual with a disability under the first prong of the definition. He need not also show that he is substantially limited in eating to qualify for coverage under the first prong. An individual whose normal cell growth is substantially limited due to lung cancer need not also show that she is substantially limited in breathing or respiratory function. And an individual with HIV infection is substantially limited in the function of the immune system, and therefore is an individual with a disability without regard to whether his or her HIV infection substantially limits him or her in reproduction.

In addition, an individual whose impairment substantially limits a major life activity need not additionally demonstrate a resulting limitation in the ability to perform activities of central importance to daily life in order to be considered an individual with a disability under §1630.2(g)(1)(i) or §1630.2(g)(1)(ii), as cases relying on the Supreme Court's decision in Toyota Motor Mfg., Ky., Inc. v. Williams, 534 U.S. 184 (2002), had held prior to the ADA Amendments Act.

Thus, for example, someone with an impairment resulting in a 20-pound lifting restriction that lasts or is expected to last for several months is substantially limited in the major life activity of lifting, and need not also show that he is unable to perform activities of daily living that require lifting in order to be considered substantially limited in lifting. Similarly, someone with monocular vision whose depth perception or field of vision would be substantially limited, with or without any compensatory strategies the individual may have developed, need not also show that he is unable to perform activities of central importance to daily life that require seeing in order to be substantially limited in seeing.

Section 1630.2(j)(1)(ix) Effects of an Impairment Lasting Fewer Than Six Months Can Be Substantially Limiting

Section 1630.2(j)(1)(ix) states: "The six-month 'transitory' part of the 'transitory and minor' exception to 'regarded as' coverage in §1630.2(l) does not apply to the definition of 'disability' under §1630.2(g)(1)(i) or §1630.2(g)(1)(ii). The effects of an impairment lasting or expected to last fewer than six months can be substantially limiting within the meaning of this section."

The regulations include a clear statement that the definition of an impairment as transitory, that is, "lasting or expected to last for six months or less," only applies to the "regarded as" (third) prong of the definition of "disability" as part of the "transitory and minor" defense to "regarded as" coverage. It does not apply to the first or second prong of the definition of disability. See Joint Hoyer-Sensenbrenner Statement at 3 ("[T]here is no need for the transitory and minor exception under the first two prongs because it is clear from the statute and the legislative history that a person can only bring a claim if the impairment substantially limits one or more major life activities or the individual has a record of an impairment that substantially limits one or more major life activities.").

Therefore, an impairment does not have to last for more than six months in order to be considered substantially limiting under the first or the second prong of the definition of disability. For example, as noted above, if an individual has a back impairment that results in a 20-pound lifting restriction that lasts for several months, he is substantially limited in the major life activity of lifting, and therefore covered under the first prong of the definition of disability. At the same time, "[t]he duration of an impairment is one factor that is relevant in determining whether the impairment substantially limits a major life activity. Impairments that last only for a short period of time are typically not covered, although they may be covered if sufficiently severe." Joint Hoyer-Sensenbrenner Statement at 5.

Section 1630.2(j)(3) Predictable Assessments

As the regulations point out, disability is determined based on an individualized assessment. There is no "per se" disability. However, as recognized in the regulations, the individualized assessment of some kinds of impairments will virtually always result in a determination of disability. The inherent nature of these types of medical conditions will in virtually all cases give rise to a substantial limitation of a major life activity. Cf. Heiko v. Columbo Savings Bank, F.S.B., 434 F.3d 249, 256 (4th Cir. 2006) (stating, even pre-ADAAA, that "certain impairments are by their very nature substantially limiting: the major life activity of seeing, for example, is always substantially limited by blindness"). Therefore, with respect to these types of impairments, the necessary individualized assessment should be particularly simple and straightforward.

This result is the consequence of the combined effect of the statutory changes to the definition of disability contained in the Amendments Act and flows from application of the rules of construction set forth in §§1630.2(j)(1)(i)-(ix) (including the lower standard for "substantially limits"; the rule that major life activities include major bodily functions; the principle that impairments that are episodic or in remission are disabilities if they would be substantially limiting when active; and the requirement that the ameliorative effects of mitigating measures (other than ordinary eyeglasses or contact lenses) must be disregarded in assessing whether an individual has a disability).

The regulations at §1630.2(j)(3)(iii) provide examples of the types of impairments that should easily be found to substantially limit a major life activity. The legislative history states that Congress modeled the ADA definition of disability on the definition contained in the Rehabilitation Act, and said it wished to return courts to the way they had construed that definition. See 2008 House Judiciary Committee Report at 6. Describing this goal, the legislative history states that courts had interpreted the Rehabilitation Act definition "broadly to include persons with a wide range of physical and mental impairments such as epilepsy, diabetes, multiple sclerosis, and intellectual and developmental disabilities * * * even where a mitigating measure—like medication or a hearing aid—might lessen their impact on the individual." Id.; see also id. at 9 (referring to individuals with disabilities that had been covered under the Rehabilitation Act and that Congress intended to include under the ADA—"people with serious health conditions like epilepsy, diabetes, cancer, cerebral palsy, multiple sclerosis, intellectual and developmental disabilities"); id. at n.6 (citing cases also finding that cerebral palsy, hearing impairments, mental retardation, heart disease, and vision in only one eye were disabilities under the Rehabilitation Act); id. at 10 (citing testimony from Rep. Steny H. Hoyer, one of the original lead sponsors of the ADA in 1990, stating that "we could not have fathomed that people with diabetes, epilepsy, heart conditions, cancer, mental illnesses and other disabilities would have their ADA claims denied because they would be considered too functional to meet the definition of disability"); 2008 Senate Statement of Managers at 3 (explaining that "we [we]re faced with a situation in which physical or mental impairments that would previously [under the Rehabilitation Act] have been found to constitute disabilities [we]re not considered disabilities" and citing individuals with impairments such as amputation, intellectual disabilities, epilepsy, multiple sclerosis, diabetes, muscular dystrophy, and cancer as examples).

Of course, the impairments listed in subparagraph 1630.2(j)(3)(iii) may substantially limit a variety of other major life activities in addition to those listed in the regulation. For example, mobility impairments requiring the use of a wheelchair substantially limit the major life activity of walking. Diabetes may substantially limit major life activities such as eating, sleeping, and thinking. Major depressive disorder may substantially limit major life activities such as thinking, concentrating, sleeping, and interacting with others. Multiple sclerosis may substantially limit major life activities such as walking, bending, and lifting.

By using the term "brain function" to describe the system affected by various mental impairments, the Commission is expressing no view on the debate concerning whether mental illnesses are caused by environmental or biological factors, but rather intends the term to capture functions such as the ability of the brain to regulate thought processes and emotions.

Section 1630.2(j)(4) Condition, Manner, or Duration

The regulations provide that facts such as the "condition, manner, or duration" of an individual's performance of a major life activity may be useful in determining whether an impairment results in a substantial limitation. In the legislative history of the ADAAA, Congress reiterated what it had said at the time of the original ADA: "A person is considered an individual with a disability for purposes of the first prong of the definition when [one or more of] the individual's important life activities are restricted as to the conditions, manner, or duration under which they can be performed in comparison to most people." 2008 Senate Statement of Managers at 7 (citing 1989 Senate Report at 23). According to Congress: "We particularly believe that this test, which articulated an analysis that considered whether a person's activities are limited in condition, duration and manner, is a useful one. We reiterate that using the correct standard—one that is lower than the strict or demanding standard created by the Supreme Court in Toyota—will make the disability determination an appropriate threshold issue but not an onerous burden for those seeking accommodations * * *. At the same time, plaintiffs should not be constrained from offering evidence needed to establish that their impairment is substantially limiting." 2008 Senate Statement of Managers at 7.

Consistent with the legislative history, an impairment may substantially limit the "condition" or "manner" under which a major life activity can be performed in a number of ways. For example, the condition or manner under which a major life activity can be performed may refer to the way an individual performs a major life activity. Thus, the condition or manner under which a person with an amputated hand performs manual tasks will likely be more cumbersome than the way that someone with two hands would perform the same tasks.

Condition or manner may also describe how performance of a major life activity affects the individual with an impairment. For example, an individual whose impairment causes pain or fatigue that most people would not experience when performing that major life activity may be substantially limited. Thus, the condition or manner under which someone with coronary artery disease performs the major life activity of walking would be substantially limiting if the individual experiences shortness of breath and fatigue when walking distances that most people could walk without experiencing such effects. Similarly, condition or manner may refer to the extent to which a major life activity, including a major bodily function, can be performed. For example, the condition or manner under which a major bodily function can be performed may be substantially limited when the impairment "causes the operation [of the bodily function] to over-produce or under-produce in some harmful fashion." See 2008 House Judiciary Committee Report at 17.

"Duration" refers to the length of time an individual can perform a major life activity or the length of time it takes an individual to perform a major life activity, as compared to most people in the general population. For example, a person whose back or leg impairment precludes him or her from standing for more than two hours without significant pain would be substantially limited in standing, since most people can stand for more than two hours without significant pain. However, a person who can walk for ten miles continuously is not substantially limited in walking merely because on the eleventh mile, he or she begins to experience pain because most people would not be able to walk eleven miles without experiencing some discomfort. See 2008 Senate Statement of Managers at 7 (citing 1989 Senate Report at 23).

The regulations provide that in assessing substantial limitation and considering facts such as condition, manner, or duration, the non-ameliorative effects of mitigating measures may be considered. Such "non-ameliorative effects" could include negative side effects of medicine, burdens associated with following a particular treatment regimen, and complications that arise from surgery, among others. Of course, in many instances, it will not be necessary to assess the negative impact of a mitigating measure in determining that a particular impairment substantially limits a major life activity. For example, someone with end-stage renal disease is substantially limited in kidney function, and it thus is not necessary to consider the burdens that dialysis treatment imposes.

Condition, manner, or duration may also suggest the amount of time or effort an individual has to expend when performing a major life activity because of the effects of an impairment, even if the individual is able to achieve the same or similar result as someone without the impairment. For this reason, the regulations include language which says that the outcome an individual with a disability is able to achieve is not determinative of whether he or she is substantially limited in a major life activity.

Thus, someone with a learning disability may achieve a high level of academic success, but may nevertheless be substantially limited in the major life activity of learning because of the additional time or effort he or she must spend to read, write, or learn compared to most people in the general population. As Congress emphasized in passing the Amendments Act, "[w]hen considering the condition, manner, or duration in which an individual with a specific learning disability performs a major life activity, it is critical to reject the assumption that an individual who has performed well academically cannot be substantially limited in activities such as learning, reading, writing, thinking, or speaking." 2008 Senate Statement of Managers at 8. Congress noted that: "In particular, some courts have found that students who have reached a high level of academic achievement are not to be considered individuals with disabilities under the ADA, as such individuals may have difficulty demonstrating substantial limitation in the major life activities of learning or reading relative to 'most people.' When considering the condition, manner or duration in which an individual with a specific learning disability performs a major life activity, it is critical to reject the assumption that an individual who performs well academically or otherwise cannot be substantially limited in activities such as learning, reading, writing, thinking, or speaking. As such, the Committee rejects the findings in Price v. National Board of Medical Examiners, Gonzales v. National Board of Medical Examiners, and Wong v. Regents of University of California. The Committee believes that the comparison of individuals with specific learning disabilities to 'most people' is not problematic unto itself, but requires a careful analysis of the method and manner in which an individual's impairment limits a major life activity. For the majority of the population, the basic mechanics of reading and writing do not pose extraordinary lifelong challenges; rather, recognizing and forming letters and words are effortless, unconscious, automatic processes. Because specific learning disabilities are neurologically-based impairments, the process of reading for an individual with a reading disability (e.g. dyslexia) is word-by-word, and otherwise cumbersome, painful, deliberate and slow — throughout life. The Committee expects that individuals with specific learning disabilities that substantially limit a major life activity will be better protected under the amended Act." 2008 House Educ. & Labor Rep. at 10-11.

It bears emphasizing that while it may be useful in appropriate cases to consider facts such as condition, manner, or duration, it is always necessary to consider and apply the rules of construction in §1630.2(j)(1)(i)-(ix) that set forth the elements of broad coverage enacted by Congress. 2008 Senate Statement of Managers at 6. Accordingly, while the Commission's regulations retain the concept of "condition, manner, or duration," they no longer include the additional list of "substantial limitation" factors contained in the previous version of the regulations (i.e., the nature and severity of the impairment, duration or expected duration of the impairment, and actual or expected permanent or long-term impact of or resulting from the impairment).

Finally, "condition, manner, or duration" are not intended to be used as a rigid three-part standard that must be met to establish a substantial limitation. "Condition, manner, or duration" are not required "factors" that must be considered as a talismanic test. Rather, in referring to "condition, manner, or duration," the regulations make clear that these are merely the types of facts that may be considered in appropriate cases. To the extent such aspects of limitation may be useful or relevant to show a substantial limitation in a particular fact pattern, some or all of them (and related facts) may be considered, but evidence relating to each of these facts may not be necessary to establish coverage.

At the same time, individuals seeking coverage under the first or second prong of the definition of disability should not be constrained from offering evidence needed to establish that their impairment is substantially limiting. See 2008 Senate Statement of Managers at 7. Of course, covered entities may defeat a showing of "substantial limitation" by refuting whatever evidence the individual seeking coverage has offered, or by offering evidence that shows an impairment does not impose a substantial limitation on a major life activity. However, a showing of substantial limitation is not defeated by facts related to "condition, manner, or duration" that are not pertinent to the substantial limitation the individual has proffered.

Sections 1630.2(j)(5) and (6) Examples of Mitigating Measures; Ordinary Eyeglasses or Contact Lenses

These provisions of the regulations provide numerous examples of mitigating measures and the definition of "ordinary eyeglasses or contact lenses." These definitions have been more fully discussed in the portions of this interpretive guidance concerning the rules of construction in §1630.2(j)(1).

SUBSTANTIALLY LIMITED IN WORKING

The Commission has removed from the text of the regulations a discussion of the major life activity of working. This is consistent with the fact that no other major life activity receives special attention in the regulation, and with the fact that, in light of the expanded definition of disability established by the Amendments Act, this major life activity will be used in only very targeted situations.

In most instances, an individual with a disability will be able to establish coverage by showing substantial limitation of a major life activity other than working; impairments that substantially limit a person's ability to work usually substantially limit one or more other major life activities. This will be particularly true in light of the changes made by the ADA Amendments Act. See, e.g., Corley v. Dep't of Veterans Affairs ex rel Principi, 218 F. App'x. 727, 738 (10th Cir. 2007) (employee with seizure disorder was not substantially limited in working because he was not foreclosed from jobs involving driving, operating machinery, childcare, military service, and other jobs; employee would now be substantially limited in neurological function); Olds v. United Parcel Serv., Inc., 127 F. App'x. 779, 782 (6th Cir. 2005) (employee with bone marrow cancer was not substantially limited in working due to lifting restrictions caused by his cancer; employee would now be substantially limited in normal cell growth); Williams v. Philadelphia Hous. Auth. Police Dep't, 380 F.3d 751, 763-64 (3d Cir. 2004) (issue of material fact concerning whether police officer's major depression substantially limited him in performing a class of jobs due to restrictions on his ability to carry a firearm; officer would now be substantially limited in brain function).

In the rare cases where an individual has a need to demonstrate that an impairment substantially limits him or her in working, the individual can do so by showing that the impairment substantially limits his or her ability to perform a class of jobs or broad range of jobs in various classes as compared to most people having comparable training, skills, and abilities. In keeping with the findings and purposes of the Amendments Act, the determination of coverage under the law should not require extensive and elaborate assessment, and the EEOC and the courts are to apply a lower standard in determining when an impairment substantially limits a major life activity, including the major life activity of working, than they applied prior to the Amendments Act. The Commission believes that the courts, in applying an overly strict standard with regard to "substantially limits" generally, have reached conclusions with regard to what is necessary to demonstrate a substantial limitation in the major life activity of working that would be inconsistent with the changes now made by the Amendments Act. Accordingly, as used in this section the terms "class of jobs" and "broad range of jobs in various classes" will be applied in a more straightforward and simple manner than they were applied by the courts prior to the Amendments Act.

Demonstrating a substantial limitation in performing the unique aspects of a single specific job is not sufficient to establish that a person is substantially limited in the major life activity of working.

A class of jobs may be determined by reference to the nature of the work that an individual is limited in performing (such as commercial truck driving, assembly line jobs, food service jobs, clerical jobs, or law enforcement jobs) or by reference to job-related requirements that an individual is limited in meeting (for example, jobs requiring repetitive bending, reaching, or manual tasks, jobs requiring repetitive or heavy lifting, prolonged sitting or standing, extensive walking, driving, or working under conditions such as high temperatures or noise levels).

For example, if a person whose job requires heavy lifting develops a disability that prevents him or her from lifting more than fifty pounds and, consequently, from performing not only his or her existing job but also other jobs that would similarly require heavy lifting, that person would be substantially limited in working because he or she is substantially limited in performing the class of jobs that require heavy lifting.

Section 1630.2(k) Record of a Substantially Limiting Impairment

The second prong of the definition of "disability" provides that an individual with a record of an impairment that substantially limits or limited a major life activity is an individual with a disability. The intent of this provision, in part, is to ensure that people are not discriminated against because of a history of disability. For example, the "record of" provision would protect an individual who was treated for cancer ten years ago but who is now deemed by a doctor to be free of cancer, from discrimination based on that prior medical history. This provision also ensures that individuals are not discriminated against because they have been misclassified as disabled. For example, individuals misclassified as having learning disabilities or intellectual disabilities (formerly termed "mental retardation") are protected from discrimination on the basis of that erroneous classification. Senate Report at 23; House Labor Report at 52-53; House Judiciary Report at 29; 2008 House Judiciary Report at 7-8 & n.14. Similarly, an employee who in the past was misdiagnosed with bipolar disorder and hospitalized as the result of a temporary reaction to medication she was taking has a record of a substantially limiting impairment, even though she did not actually have bipolar disorder.

This part of the definition is satisfied where evidence establishes that an individual has had a substantially limiting impairment. The impairment indicated in the record must be an impairment that would substantially limit one or more of the individual's major life activities. There are many types of records that could potentially contain this information, including but not limited to, education, medical, or employment records.

Such evidence that an individual has a past history of an impairment that substantially limited a major life activity is all that is necessary to establish coverage under the second prong. An individual may have a "record of" a substantially limiting impairment — and thus be protected under the "record of" prong of the statute — even if a covered entity does not specifically know about the relevant record. Of course, for the covered entity to be liable for discrimination under title I of the ADA, the individual with a "record of" a substantially limiting impairment must prove that the covered entity discriminated on the basis of the record of the disability.

The terms "substantially limits" and "major life activity" under the second prong of the definition of "disability" are to be construed in accordance with the same principles applicable under the "actual disability" prong, as set forth in §1630.2(j). Individuals who are covered under the "record of" prong will often be covered under the first prong of the definition of disability as well. This is a consequence of the rule of construction in the ADAAA and the regulations providing that an individual with an impairment that is episodic or in remission can be protected under the first prong if the impairment would be substantially limiting when active. See 42 U.S.C. 12102(4)(D); §1630.2(j)(1)(vii). Thus, an individual who has cancer that is currently in remission is an individual with a disability under the "actual disability" prong because he has an impairment that would substantially limit normal cell growth when active. He is also covered by the "record of" prong based on his history of having had an impairment that substantially limited normal cell growth.

Finally, this section of the EEOC's regulations makes it clear that an individual with a record of a disability is entitled to a reasonable accommodation currently needed for limitations resulting from or relating to the past substantially limiting impairment. This conclusion, which has been the Commission's long-standing position, is confirmed by language in the ADA Amendments Act stating that individuals covered only under the "regarded as" prong of the definition of disability are not entitled to reasonable accommodation. See 42 U.S.C. 12201(h). By implication, this means that individuals covered under the first or second prongs are otherwise eligible for reasonable accommodations. See 2008 House

Judiciary Committee Report at 22 ("This makes clear that the duty to accommodate . . . arises only when an individual establishes coverage under the first or second prong of the definition."). Thus, as the regulations explain, an employee with an impairment that previously substantially limited but no longer substantially limits, a major life activity may need leave or a schedule change to permit him or her to attend follow-up or "monitoring" appointments from a health care provider.

Section 1630.2(l) Regarded as Substantially Limited in a Major Life Activity

Coverage under the "regarded as" prong of the definition of disability should not be difficult to establish. See 2008 House Judiciary Committee Report at 17 (explaining that Congress never expected or intended it would be a difficult standard to meet). Under the third prong of the definition of disability, an individual is "regarded as having such an impairment" if the individual is subjected to an action prohibited by the ADA because of an actual or perceived impairment that is not "transitory and minor."

This third prong of the definition of disability was originally intended to express Congress's understanding that "unfounded concerns, mistaken beliefs, fears, myths, or prejudice about disabilities are often just as disabling as actual impairments, and [its] corresponding desire to prohibit discrimination founded on such perceptions." 2008 Senate Statement of Managers at 9; 2008 House Judiciary Committee Report at 17 (same). In passing the original ADA, Congress relied extensively on the reasoning of School Board of Nassau County v. Arline "that the negative reactions of others are just as disabling as the actual impact of an impairment." 2008 Senate Statement of Managers at 9. The ADAAA reiterates Congress's reliance on the broad views enunciated in that decision, and Congress "believe[s] that courts should continue to rely on this standard." Id.

Accordingly, the ADA Amendments Act broadened the application of the "regarded as" prong of the definition of disability. 2008 Senate Statement of Managers at 9-10. In doing so, Congress rejected court decisions that had required an individual to establish that a covered entity perceived him or her to have an impairment that substantially limited a major life activity. This provision is designed to restore Congress's intent to allow individuals to establish coverage under the "regarded as" prong by showing that they were treated adversely because of an impairment, without having to establish the covered entity's beliefs concerning the severity of the impairment. Joint Hoyer-Sensenbrenner Statement at 3.

Thus it is not necessary, as it was prior to the ADA Amendments Act, for an individual to demonstrate that a covered entity perceived him as substantially limited in the ability to perform a major life activity in order for the individual to establish that he or she is covered under the "regarded as" prong. Nor is it necessary to demonstrate that the impairment relied on by a covered entity is (in the case of an actual impairment) or would be (in the case of a perceived impairment) substantially limiting for an individual to be "regarded as having such an impairment." In short, to qualify for coverage under the "regarded as" prong, an individual is not subject to any functional test. See 2008 Senate Statement of Managers at 13 ("The functional limitation imposed by an impairment is irrelevant to the third 'regarded as' prong."); 2008 House Judiciary Committee Report at 17 (that is, "the individual is not required to show that the perceived impairment limits performance of a major life activity"). The concepts of "major life activities" and "substantial limitation" simply are not relevant in evaluating whether an individual is "regarded as having such an impairment."

To illustrate how straightforward application of the "regarded as" prong is, if an employer refused to hire an applicant because of skin graft scars, the employer has regarded the applicant as an individual with a disability. Similarly, if an employer terminates an employee because he has cancer, the employer has regarded the employee as an individual with a disability.

A "prohibited action" under the "regarded as" prong refers to an action of the type that would be unlawful under the ADA (but for any defenses to liability). Such prohibited actions include, but are not limited to, refusal to hire, demotion, placement on involuntary leave, termination, exclusion for failure to meet a qualification standard, harassment, or denial of any other term, condition, or privilege of employment.

Where an employer bases a prohibited employment action on an actual or perceived impairment that is not "transitory and minor," the employer regards the individual as disabled, whether or not myths, fears, or stereotypes about disability motivated the employer's decision. Establishing that an individual is "regarded as having such an impairment" does not, by itself, establish liability. Liability is established only if an individual meets the burden of proving that the covered entity discriminated unlawfully within the meaning of section 102 of the ADA, 42 U.S.C. 12112.

Whether a covered entity can ultimately establish a defense to liability is an inquiry separate from, and follows after, a determination that an individual was regarded as having a disability. Thus, for example, an employer who terminates an employee with angina from a manufacturing job that requires the employee to work around machinery, believing that the employee will pose a safety risk to himself or others if he were suddenly to lose consciousness, has regarded the individual as disabled. Whether the employer has a defense (e.g., that the employee posed a direct threat to himself or coworkers) is a separate inquiry.

The fact that the "regarded as" prong requires proof of causation in order to show that a person is covered does not mean that proving a "regarded as" claim is complex. While a person must show, for both coverage under the "regarded as" prong and for ultimate liability, that he or she was subjected to a prohibited action because of an actual or perceived impairment, this showing need only be made once. Thus, evidence that a covered entity took a prohibited action because of an impairment will establish coverage and will be relevant in establishing liability, although liability may ultimately turn on whether the covered entity can establish a defense.

As prescribed in the ADA Amendments Act, the regulations provide an exception to coverage under the "regarded as" prong where the impairment on which a prohibited action is based is both transitory (having an actual or expected duration of six months or less) and minor. The regulations make clear (at §1630.2(l)(2) and §1630.15(f)) that this exception is a defense to a claim of discrimination. "Providing this exception responds to concerns raised by employer organizations and is reasonable under the 'regarded as' prong of the definition because individuals seeking coverage under this prong need not meet the functional limitation requirement contained in the first two prongs of the definition." 2008 Senate Statement of Managers at 10; see also 2008 House Judiciary Committee Report at 18 (explaining that "absent this exception, the third prong of the definition would have covered individuals who are regarded as having common ailments like the cold or flu, and this exception responds to concerns raised by members of the business community regarding potential abuse of this provision and misapplication of resources on individuals with minor ailments that last only a short period of time"). However, as an exception to the general rule for broad coverage under the "regarded as" prong, this limitation on coverage should be construed narrowly. 2008 House Judiciary Committee Report at 18.

The relevant inquiry is whether the actual or perceived impairment on which the employer's action was based is objectively "transitory and minor," not whether the employer claims it subjectively believed the impairment was transitory and minor. For example, an employer who terminates an employee whom it believes has bipolar disorder cannot take advantage of this exception by asserting that it believed the employee's impairment was transitory and minor, since bipolar disorder is not objectively transitory and minor. At the same time, an employer that terminated an employee with an objectively "transitory and minor" hand wound, mistakenly believing it to be symptomatic of HIV infection, will nevertheless have "regarded" the employee as an individual with a disability, since the covered entity took a prohibited employment action based on a perceived impairment (HIV infection) that is not "transitory and minor."

An individual covered only under the "regarded as" prong is not entitled to reasonable accommodation. 42 U.S.C. 12201(h). Thus, in cases where reasonable accommodation is not at issue, the third prong provides a more straightforward framework for analyzing whether discrimination occurred. As Congress observed in enacting the ADAAA: "[W]e expect [the first] prong of the definition to be used only by people who are affirmatively seeking reasonable accommodations or modifications. Any individual who has been discriminated against because of an impairment — short of being granted a reasonable accommodation or modification — should be bringing a claim under the third prong of the definition which will require no showing with regard to the severity of his or her impairment." Joint Hoyer-Sensenbrenner Statement at 6.

Section 1630.2(l) Regarded as Substantially Limited in a Major Life Activity

If an individual cannot satisfy either the first part of the definition of "disability" or the second "record of" part of the definition, he or she may be able to satisfy the third part of the definition. The third part of the definition provides that an individual who is regarded by an employer or other covered entity as having an impairment that substantially limits a major life activity is an individual with a disability.

There are three different ways in which an individual may satisfy the definition of "being regarded as having a disability":

(1) The individual may have an impairment which is not substantially limiting but is perceived by the employer or other covered entity as constituting a substantially limiting impairment;

(2) The individual may have an impairment which is only substantially limiting because of the attitudes of others toward the impairment; or

(3) The individual may have no impairment at all but is regarded by the employer or other covered entity as having a substantially limiting impairment.

Senate Report at 23; House Labor Report at 53; House Judiciary Report at 29. An individual satisfies the first part of this definition if the individual has an impairment that is not substantially limiting, but the covered entity perceives the impairment as being substantially limiting. For example, suppose an employee has controlled high blood pressure that is not substantially limiting. If an employer reassigns the individual to less strenuous work because of unsubstantiated fears that the individual will suffer a heart attack if he or she continues to perform strenuous work, the employer would be regarding the individual as disabled.

An individual satisfies the second part of the "regarded as" definition if the individual has an impairment that is only substantially limiting because of the attitudes of others toward the condition. For example, an individual may have a prominent facial scar or disfigurement, or may have a condition that periodically causes an involuntary jerk of the head but does not limit the individual's major life activities. If an employer discriminates against such an individual because of the negative reactions of customers, the employer would be regarding the individual as disabled and acting on the basis of that perceived disability. See Senate Report at 24; House Labor Report at 53; House Judiciary Report at 30-31.

An individual satisfies the third part of the "regarded as" definition of "disability" if the employer or other covered entity erroneously believes the individual has a substantially limiting impairment that the individual actually does not have. This situation could occur, for example, if an employer discharged an employee in response to a rumor that the employee is infected with Human Immunodeficiency Virus (HIV). Even though the rumor is totally unfounded and the individual has no impairment at all, the individual is considered an individual with a disability because the employer perceived of this individual as being disabled. Thus, in this example, the employer, by discharging this employee, is discriminating on the basis of disability.

The rationale for the "regarded as" part of the definition of disability was articulated by the Supreme Court in the context of the Rehabilitation Act of 1973 in School Board of Nassau County v. Arline, 480 U.S. 273 (1987). The Court noted that, although an individual may have an impairment that does not in fact substantially limit a major life activity, the reaction of others may prove just as disabling. "Such an impairment might not diminish a person's physical or mental capabilities, but could nevertheless substantially limit that person's ability to work as a result of the negative reactions of others to the impairment." 480 U.S. at 283. The Court concluded that by including "regarded as" in the Rehabilitation Act's definition, "Congress acknowledged that society's accumulated myths and fears about disability and diseases are as handicapping as are the physical limitations that flow from actual impairment." 480 U.S. at 284.

An individual rejected from a job because of the "myths, fears and stereotypes" associated with disabilities would be covered under this part of the definition of disability, whether or not the employer's or other covered entity's perception were shared by others in the field and whether or not the individual's actual physical or mental condition would be considered a disability under the first or second part of this definition. As the legislative history notes, sociologists have identified common attitudinal barriers that frequently result in employers excluding individuals with disabilities. These include concerns regarding productivity, safety, insurance, liability, attendance, cost of accommodation and accessibility, workers' compensation costs, and acceptance by coworkers and customers.

Therefore, if an individual can show that an employer or other covered entity made an employment decision because of a perception of disability based on "myth, fear or stereotype," the individual will satisfy the "regarded as" part of the definition of disability. If the employer cannot articulate a non-discriminatory reason for the employment action, an inference that the employer is acting on the basis of "myth, fear or stereotype" can be drawn.

Section 1630.2(m) Qualified Individual

The ADA prohibits discrimination on the basis of disability against a qualified individual. The determination of whether an individual with a disability is "qualified" should be made in two steps. The first step is to determine if the individual satisfies the prerequisites for the position, such as possessing the appropriate educational background, employment experience, skills, licenses, etc. For example, the first step in determining whether an accountant who is paraplegic is qualified for a certified public accountant (CPA) position is to examine the individual's credentials to determine whether the individual is a licensed CPA. This is sometimes referred to in the Rehabilitation Act caselaw as determining whether the individual is "otherwise qualified" for the position. See Senate Report at 33; House Labor Report at 64-65. (See §1630.9 Not Making Reasonable Accommodation).

The second step is to determine whether or not the individual can perform the essential functions of the position held or desired, with or without reasonable accommodation. The purpose of this second step is to ensure that individuals with disabilities who can perform the essential functions of the position held or desired are not denied employment opportunities because they are not able to perform marginal functions of the position. House Labor Report at 55.

The determination of whether an individual with a disability is qualified is to be made at the time of the employment decision. This determination should be based on the capabilities of the individual with a disability at the time of the employment decision, and should not be based on speculation that the employee may become unable in the future or may cause increased health insurance premiums or workers compensation costs.

Section 1630.2(n) Essential Functions

The determination of which functions are essential may be critical to the determination of whether or not the individual with a disability is qualified. The essential functions are those functions that the individual who holds the position must be able to perform unaided or with the assistance of a reasonable accommodation.

The inquiry into whether a particular function is essential initially focuses on whether the employer actually requires employees in the position to perform the functions that the employer asserts are essential. For example, an employer may state that typing is an essential function of a position. If, in fact, the employer has never required any employee in that particular position to type, this will be evidence that typing is not actually an essential function of the position.

If the individual who holds the position is actually required to perform the function the employer asserts is an essential function, the inquiry will then center around whether removing the function would fundamentally alter that position. This determination of whether or not a particular function is essential will generally include one or more of the following factors listed in part 1630.

The first factor is whether the position exists to perform a particular function. For example, an individual may be hired to proofread documents. The ability to proofread the documents would then be an essential function, since this is the only reason the position exists.

The second factor in determining whether a function is essential is the number of other employees available to perform that job function or among whom the performance of that job function can be distributed. This may be a factor either because the total number of available employees is low, or because of the fluctuating demands of the business operation. For example, if an employer has a relatively small number of available employees for the volume of work to be performed, it may be necessary that each employee perform a multitude of different functions. Therefore, the performance of those functions by each employee becomes more critical and the options for reorganizing the work become more limited. In such a situation, functions that might not be essential if there were a larger staff may become essential because the staff size is small compared to the volume of work that has to be done. See Treadwell v. Alexander, 707 F.2d 473 (11th Cir. 1983).

A similar situation might occur in a larger work force if the workflow follows a cycle of heavy demand for labor intensive work followed by low demand periods. This type of workflow might also make the performance of each function during the peak periods more critical and might limit the employer's flexibility in reorganizing operating procedures. See Dexler v. Tisch, 660 F. Supp. 1418 (D. Conn. 1987).

The third factor is the degree of expertise or skill required to perform the function. In certain professions and highly skilled positions the employee is hired for his or her expertise or ability to perform the particular function. In such a situation, the performance of that specialized task would be an essential function.

Whether a particular function is essential is a factual determination that must be made on a case by case basis. In determining whether or not a particular function is essential, all relevant evidence should be considered. Part 1630 lists various types of evidence, such as an established job description, that should be considered in determining whether a particular function is essential. Since the list is not exhaustive, other relevant evidence may also be presented. Greater weight will not be granted to the types of evidence included on the list than to the types of evidence not listed.

Although part 1630 does not require employers to develop or maintain job descriptions, written job descriptions prepared before advertising or interviewing applicants for the job, as well as the employer's judgment as to what functions are essential are among the relevant evidence to be considered in determining whether a particular function is essential. The terms of a collective bargaining agreement are also relevant to the determination of whether a particular function is essential. The work experience of past employees in the job or of current employees in similar jobs is likewise relevant to the determination of whether a particular function is essential. See H.R. Conf. Rep. No. 101-596, 101st Cong., 2d Sess. 58 (1990) [hereinafter Conference Report]; House Judiciary Report at 33-34. See also Hall v. U.S. Postal Service, 857 F.2d 1073 (6th Cir. 1988).

The time spent performing the particular function may also be an indicator of whether that function is essential. For example, if an employee spends the vast majority of his or her time working at a cash register, this would be evidence that operating the cash register is an essential function. The consequences of failing to require the employee to perform the function may be another indicator of whether a particular function is essential. For example, although a firefighter may not regularly have to carry an unconscious adult out of a burning building, the consequence of failing to require the firefighter to be able to perform this function would be serious.

It is important to note that the inquiry into essential functions is not intended to second guess an employer's business judgment with regard to production standards, whether qualitative or quantitative, nor to require employers to lower such standards. (See §1630.10 Qualification Standards, Tests and Other Selection Criteria). If an employer requires its typists to be able to accurately type 75 words per minute, it will not be called upon to explain why an inaccurate work product, or a typing speed of 65 words per minute, would not be adequate. Similarly, if a hotel requires its service workers to thoroughly clean 16 rooms per day, it will not have to explain why it requires thorough cleaning, or why it chose a 16 room rather than a 10 room requirement. However, if an employer does require ac- curate 75 word per minute typing or the thorough cleaning of 16 rooms, it will have to show that it actually imposes such requirements on its employees in fact, and not simply on paper. It should also be noted that, if it is alleged that the employer intentionally selected the particular level of production to exclude individuals with disabilities, the employer may have to offer a legitimate, non-discriminatory reason for its selection.

Section 1630.2(o) Reasonable Accommodation

An individual with a disability is considered "qualified" if the individual can perform the essential functions of the position held or desired with or without reasonable accommodation. A covered entity is required, absent undue hardship, to provide reasonable accommodation to an otherwise qualified individual with a substantially limiting impairment or a "record of" such an impairment. However, a covered entity is not required to provide an accommodation to an individual who meets the definition of disability solely under the "regarded as" prong.

The legislative history of the ADAAA makes clear that Congress included this provision in response to various court decisions that had held (pre-Amendments Act) that individuals who were covered solely under the "regarded as" prong were eligible for reasonable accommodations. In those cases, the plaintiffs had been found not to be covered under the first prong of the definition of disability "because of the overly stringent manner in which the courts had been interpreting that prong." 2008 Senate Statement of Managers at 11. The legislative history goes on to explain that "[b]ecause of [Congress's] strong belief that accommodating individuals with disabilities is a key goal of the ADA, some members [of Congress] continue to have reservations about this provision." Id. However, Congress ultimately concluded that clarifying that individuals covered solely under the "regarded as" prong are not entitled to reasonable accommodations "is an acceptable compromise given our strong expectation that such individuals would now be covered under the first prong of the definition [of disability], properly applied"). Further, individuals covered only under the third prong still may bring discrimination claims (other than failure-to-accommodate claims) under title I of the ADA. 2008 Senate Statement of Managers at 9-10.

In general, an accommodation is any change in the work environment or in the way things are customarily done that enables an individual with a disability to enjoy equal employment opportunities. There are three categories of reasonable accommodation. These are (1) accommodations that are required to ensure equal opportunity in the application process; (2) accommodations that enable the employer's employees with disabilities to perform the essential functions of the position held or desired; and (3) accommodations that enable the employer's employees with disabilities to enjoy equal benefits and privileges of employment as are enjoyed by employees without disabilities. It should be noted that nothing in this part prohibits employers or other covered entities from providing accommodations beyond those required by this part.

Part 1630 lists the examples, specified in title I of the ADA, of the most common types of accommodation that an employer or other covered entity may be required to provide. There are any number of other specific accommodations that may be appropriate for particular situations but are not specifically mentioned in this listing. This listing is not intended to be exhaustive of accommodation possibilities. For example, other accommodations could include permitting the use of accrued paid leave or providing additional unpaid leave for necessary treatment, making employer provided transportation accessible, and providing reserved parking spaces. Providing personal assistants, such as a page turner for an employee with no hands or a travel attendant to act as a sighted guide to assist a blind employee on occasional business trips, may also be a reasonable accommodation. Senate Report at 31; House Labor Report at 62; House Judiciary Report at 39.

It may also be a reasonable accommodation to permit an individual with a disability the opportunity to provide and utilize equipment, aids or services that an employer is not required to provide as a reasonable accommodation. For example, it would be a reasonable accommodation for an employer to permit an individual who is blind to use a guide dog at work, even though the employer would not be required to provide a guide dog for the employee.

The accommodations included on the list of reasonable accommodations are generally self explanatory. However, there are a few that require further explanation. One of these is the accommodation of making existing facilities used by employees readily accessible to, and usable by, individuals with disabilities. This accommodation includes both those areas that must be accessible for the employee to perform essential job functions, as well as non-work areas used by the employer's employees for other purposes. For example, accessible break rooms, lunch rooms, training rooms, restrooms etc., may be required as reasonable accommodations.

Another of the potential accommodations listed is "job restructuring." An employer or other covered entity may restructure a job by reallocating or redistributing nonessential, marginal job functions. For example, an employer may have two jobs, each of which entails the performance of a number of marginal functions. The employer hires an individual with a disability who is able to perform some of the marginal functions of each job but not all of the marginal functions of either job. As an accommodation, the employer may redistribute the marginal functions so that all of the marginal functions that the individual with a disability can perform are made a part of the position to be filled by the individual with a disability. The remaining marginal functions that the individual with a disability cannot perform would then be transferred to the other position. See Senate Report at 31; House Labor Report at 62.

An employer or other covered entity is not required to reallocate essential functions. The essential functions are by definition those that the individual who holds the job would have to perform, with or without reasonable accommodation, in order to be considered qualified for the position. For example, suppose a security guard position requires the individual who holds the job to inspect identification cards. An employer would not have to provide an individual who is legally blind with an assistant to look at the identification cards for the legally blind employee. In this situation the assistant would be performing the job for the individual with a disability rather than assisting the individual to perform the job. See Coleman v. Darden, 595 F.2d 533 (10th Cir. 1979).

An employer or other covered entity may also restructure a job by altering when and/or how an essential function is performed. For example, an essential function customarily performed in the early morning hours may be rescheduled until later in the day as a reasonable accommodation to a disability that precludes performance of the function at the customary hour. Likewise, as a reasonable accommodation, an employee with a disability that inhibits the ability to write, may be permitted to computerize records that were customarily maintained manually.

Reassignment to a vacant position is also listed as a potential reasonable accommodation. In general, reassignment should be considered only when accommodation within the individual's current position would pose an undue hardship. Reassignment is not available to applicants. An applicant for a position must be qualified for, and be able to perform the essential functions of, the position sought with or without reasonable accommodation.

Reassignment may not be used to limit, segregate, or otherwise discriminate against employees with disabilities by forcing reassignments to undesirable positions or to designated offices or facilities. Employers should reassign the individual to an equivalent position, in terms of pay, status, etc., if the individual is qualified, and if the position is vacant within a reasonable amount of time. A "reasonable amount of time" should be determined in light of the totality of the circumstances. As an example, suppose there is no vacant position available at the time that an individual with a disability requests reassignment as a reasonable accommodation. The employer, however, knows that an equivalent position for which the individual is qualified, will become vacant next week. Under these circumstances, the employer should reassign the individual to the position when it becomes available.

An employer may reassign an individual to a lower graded position if there are no accommodations that would enable the employee to remain in the current position and there are no vacant equivalent positions for which the individual is qualified with or without reasonable accommodation. An employer, however, is not required to maintain the reassigned individual with a disability at the salary of the higher graded position if it does not so maintain reassigned employees who are not disabled. It should also be noted that an employer is not required to promote an individual with a disability as an accommodation. See Senate Report at 31-32; House Labor Report at 63.

The determination of which accommodation is appropriate in a particular situation involves a process in which the employer and employee identify the precise limitations imposed by the disability and explore potential accommodations that would overcome those limitations. This process is discussed more fully in §1630.9 Not Making Reasonable Accommodation.

Section 1630.2(p) Undue Hardship

An employer or other covered entity is not required to provide an accommodation that will impose an undue hardship on the operation of the employer's or other covered entity's business. The term "undue hardship" means significant difficulty or expense in, or resulting from, the provision of the accommodation. The "undue hardship" provision takes into account the financial realities of the particular employer or other covered entity. However, the concept of undue hardship is not limited to financial difficulty. "Undue hardship" refers to any accommodation that would be unduly costly, extensive, substantial, or disruptive, or that would fundamentally alter the nature or operation of the business. See Senate Report at 35; House Labor Report at 67.

For example, suppose an individual with a disabling visual impairment that makes it extremely difficult to see in dim lighting applies for a position as a waiter in a nightclub and requests that the club be brightly lit as a reasonable accommodation. Although the individual may be able to perform the job in bright lighting, the nightclub will probably be able to demonstrate that that particular accommodation, though inexpensive, would impose an undue hardship if the bright lighting would destroy the ambience of the nightclub and/or make it difficult for the customers to see the stage show. The fact that that particular accommodation poses an undue hardship, however, only means that the employer is not required to provide that accommodation. If there is another accommodation that will not create an undue hardship, the employer would be required to provide the alternative accommodation.

An employer's claim that the cost of a particular accommodation will impose an undue hardship will be analyzed in light of the factors outlined in part 1630. In part, this analysis requires a determination of whose financial resources should be considered in deciding whether the accommodation is unduly costly. In some cases the financial resources of the employer or other covered entity in its entirety should be considered in determining whether the cost of an accommodation poses an undue hardship. In other cases, consideration of the financial resources of the employer or other covered entity as a whole may be inappropriate because it may not give an accurate picture of the financial resources available to the particular facility that will actually be required to provide the accommodation. See House Labor Report at 68-69; House Judiciary Report at 40-41; see also Conference Report at 56-57.

If the employer or other covered entity asserts that only the financial resources of the facility where the individual will be employed should be considered, part 1630 requires a factual determination of the relationship between the employer or other covered entity and the facility that will provide the accommodation. As an example, suppose that an independently owned fast food franchise that receives no money from the franchisor refuses to hire an individual with a hearing impairment because it asserts that it would be an undue hardship to provide an interpreter to enable the individual to participate in monthly staff meetings. Since the financial relationship between the franchisor and the franchise is limited to payment of an annual franchise fee, only the financial resources of the franchise would be considered in determining whether or not providing the accommodation would be an undue hardship. See House Labor Report at 68; House Judiciary Report at 40.

If the employer or other covered entity can show that the cost of the accommodation would impose an undue hardship, it would still be required to provide the accommodation if the funding is available from another source, e.g., a State vocational rehabilitation agency, or if Federal, State or local tax deductions or tax credits are available to offset the cost of the accommodation. If the employer or other covered entity receives, or is eligible to receive, monies from an external source that would pay the entire cost of the accommodation, it cannot claim cost as an undue hardship. In the absence of such funding, the individual with a disability requesting the accommodation should be given the option of providing the accommodation or of paying that portion of the cost which constitutes the undue hardship on the operation of the business. To the extent that such monies pay or would pay for only part of the cost of the accommodation, only that portion of the cost of the accommodation that could not be recovered—the final net cost to the entity—may be considered in determining undue hardship. (See §1630.9 Not Making Reasonable Accommodation). See Senate Report at 36; House Labor Report at 69.

Section 1630.2(r) Direct Threat

An employer may require, as a qualification standard, that an individual not pose a direct threat to the health or safety of himself/herself or others. Like any other qualification standard, such a standard must apply to all applicants or employees and not just to individuals with disabilities. If, however, an individual poses a direct threat as a result of a disability, the employer must determine whether a reasonable accommodation would either eliminate the risk or reduce it to an acceptable level. If no accommodation exists that would either eliminate or reduce the risk, the employer may refuse to hire an applicant or may discharge an employee who poses a direct threat. An employer, however, is not permitted to deny an employment opportunity to an individual with a disability merely because of a slightly increased risk. The risk can only be considered when it poses a significant risk, i.e., high probability, of substantial harm; a speculative or remote risk is insufficient. See Senate Report at 27; House Report Labor Report at 56-57; House Judiciary Report at 45.

Determining whether an individual poses a significant risk of substantial harm to others must be made on a case by case basis. The employer should identify the specific risk posed by the individual. For individuals with mental or emotional disabilities, the employer must identify the specific behavior on the part of the individual that would pose the direct threat. For individuals with physical disabilities, the employer must identify the aspect of the disability that would pose the direct threat. The employer should then consider the four factors listed in part 1630:

      (1) The duration of the risk;

      (2) The nature and severity of the potential harm;

      (3) The likelihood that the potential harm will occur; and

      (4) The imminence of the potential harm.

Such consideration must rely on objective, factual evidence—not on subjective perceptions, irrational fears, patronizing attitudes, or stereotypes—about the nature or effect of a particular disability, or of disability generally. See Senate

Report at 27; House Labor Report at 56-57; House Judiciary Report at 45-46. See also Strathie v. Department of Transportation, 716 F.2d 227 (3d Cir. 1983). Relevant evidence may include input from the individual with a disability, the experience of the individual with a disability in previous similar positions, and opinions of medical doctors, rehabilitation counselors, or physical therapists who have expertise in the disability involved and/or direct knowledge of the individual with the disability.

An employer is also permitted to require that an individual not pose a direct threat of harm to his or her own safety or health. If performing the particular functions of a job would result in a high probability of substantial harm to the individual, the employer could reject or discharge the individual unless a reasonable accommodation that would not cause an undue hardship would avert the harm. For example, an employer would not be required to hire an individual, disabled by narcolepsy, who frequently and unexpectedly loses consciousness for a carpentry job the essential functions of which require the use of power saws and other dangerous equipment, where no accommodation exists that will reduce or eliminate the risk.

The assessment that there exists a high probability of substantial harm to the individual, like the assessment that there exists a high probability of substantial harm to others, must be strictly based on valid medical analyses and/or on other objective evidence. This determination must be based on individualized factual data, using the factors discussed above, rather than on stereotypic or patronizing assumptions and must consider potential reasonable accommodations. Generalized fears about risks from the employment environment, such as exacerbation of the disability caused by stress, cannot be used by an employer to disqualify an individual with a disability. For example, a law firm could not reject an applicant with a history of disabling mental illness based on a generalized fear that the stress of trying to make partner might trigger a relapse of the individual's mental illness. Nor can generalized fears about risks to individuals with disabilities in the event of an evacuation or other emergency be used by an employer to disqualify an individual with a disability. See Senate Report at 56; House Labor Report at 73-74; House Judiciary Report at 45. See also Mantolete v. Bolger, 767 F.2d 1416 (9th Cir. 1985); Bentivegna v. U.S. Department of Labor, 694 F.2d 619 (9th Cir. 1982).

Section 1630.3 Exceptions to the Definitions of "Disability" and "Qualified Individual with a Disability"

Section 1630.3(a) through (c) Illegal Use of Drugs

Part 1630 provides that an individual currently engaging in the illegal use of drugs is not an individual with a disability for purposes of this part when the employer or other covered entity acts on the basis of such use. Illegal use of drugs refers both to the use of unlawful drugs, such as cocaine, and to the unlawful use of prescription drugs. Employers, for example, may discharge or deny employment to persons who illegally use drugs, on the basis of such use, without fear of being held liable for discrimination. The term "currently engaging" is not intended to be limited to the use of drugs on the day of, or within a matter of days or weeks before, the employment action in question. Rather, the provision is intended to apply to the illegal use of drugs that has occurred recently enough to indicate that the individual is actively engaged in such conduct. See Conference Report at 64.

Individuals who are erroneously perceived as engaging in the illegal use of drugs, but are not in fact illegally using drugs are not excluded from the definitions of the terms "disability" and "qualified individual with a disability." Individuals who are no longer illegally using drugs and who have either been rehabilitated successfully or are in the process of completing a rehabilitation program are, likewise, not excluded from the definitions of those terms. The term "rehabilitation program" refers to both in-patient and out-patient programs, as well as to appropriate employee assistance programs, professionally recognized self-help programs, such as Narcotics Anonymous, or other programs that provide professional (not necessarily medical) assistance and counseling for individuals who illegally use drugs. See Conference Report at 64; see also House Labor Report at 77; House Judiciary Report at 47.

It should be noted that this provision simply provides that certain individuals are not excluded from the definitions of "disability" and "qualified individual with a disability." Consequently, such individuals are still required to establish that they satisfy the requirements of these definitions in order to be protected by the ADA and this part. An individual erroneously regarded as illegally using drugs, for example, would have to show that he or she was regarded as a drug addict in order to demonstrate that he or she meets the definition of "disability" as defined in this part.

Employers are entitled to seek reasonable assurances that no illegal use of drugs is occurring or has occurred recently enough so that continuing use is a real and ongoing problem. The reasonable assurances that employers may ask applicants or employees to provide include evidence that the individual is participating in a drug treatment program and/or evidence, such as drug test results, to show that the individual is not currently engaging in the illegal use of drugs. An employer, such as a law enforcement agency, may also be able to impose a qualification standard that excludes individuals with a history of illegal use of drugs if it can show that the standard is job-related and consistent with business necessity. (See §1630.10 Qualification Standards, Tests and Other Selection Criteria) See Conference Report at 64.

Section 1630.4 Discrimination Prohibited

Paragraph (a) of this provision prohibits discrimination on the basis of disability against a qualified individual in all aspects of the employment relationship. The range of employment decisions covered by this nondiscrimination mandate is to be construed in a manner consistent with the regulations implementing section 504 of the Rehabilitation Act of 1973.

Paragraph (b) makes it clear that the language "on the basis of disability" is not intended to create a cause of action for an individual without a disability who claims that someone with a disability was treated more favorably (disparate treatment), or was provided a reasonable accommodation that an individual without a disability was not provided. See 2008 House Judiciary Committee Report at 21 (this provision "prohibits reverse discrimination claims by disallowing claims based on the lack of disability"). Additionally, the ADA and this part do not affect laws that may require the affirmative recruitment or hiring of individuals with disabilities, or any voluntary affirmative action employers may undertake on behalf of individuals with disabilities. However, part 1630 is not intended to limit the ability of covered entities to choose and maintain a qualified workforce. Employers can continue to use criteria that are job related and consistent with business necessity to select qualified employees, and can continue to hire employees who can perform the essential functions of the job.

The Amendments Act modified title I's nondiscrimination provision to replace the prohibition on discrimination "against a qualified individual with a disability because of the disability of such individual" with a prohibition on discrimination "against a qualified individual on the basis of disability." As the legislative history of the ADAAA explains: "[T]he bill modifies the ADA to conform to the structure of Title VII and other civil rights laws by requiring an individual to demonstrate discrimination 'on the basis of disability' rather than discrimination 'against an individual with a disability' because of the individual's disability. We hope this will be an important signal to both lawyers and courts to spend less time and energy on the minutia of an individual's impairment, and more time and energy on the merits of the case — including whether discrimination occurred because of the disability, whether an individual was qualified for a job or eligible for a service, and whether a reasonable accommodation or modification was called for under the law." Joint Hoyer-Sensenbrenner Statement at 4; see also 2008 House Judiciary Report at 21 ("This change harmonizes the ADA with other civil rights laws by focusing on whether a person who has been discriminated against has proven that the discrimination was based on a personal characteristic (disability), not on whether he or she has proven that the characteristic exists.").

Section 1630.5 Limiting, Segregating and Classifying

This provision and the several provisions that follow describe various specific forms of discrimination that are included within the general prohibition of §1630.4. The capabilities of qualified individuals must be determined on an individualized, case by case basis. Covered entities are also prohibited from segregating qualified employees into separate work areas or into separate lines of advancement on the basis of their disabilities.

Thus, for example, it would be a violation of this part for an employer to limit the duties of an employee with a disability based on a presumption of what is best for an individual with such a disability, or on a presumption about the abilities of an individual with such a disability. It would be a violation of this part for an employer to adopt a separate track of job promotion or progression for employees with disabilities based on a presumption that employees with disabilities are uninterested in, or incapable of, performing particular jobs. Similarly, it would be a violation for an employer to assign or reassign (as a reasonable accommodation) employees with disabilities to one particular office or installation, or to require that employees with disabilities only use particular employer provided non-work facilities such as segregated break-rooms, lunch rooms, or lounges. It would also be a violation of this part to deny employment to an applicant or employee with a disability based on generalized fears about the safety of an individual with such a disability, or based on generalized assumptions about the absenteeism rate of an individual with such a disability.

In addition, it should also be noted that this part is intended to require that employees with disabilities be accorded equal access to whatever health insurance coverage the employer provides to other employees. This part does not, however, affect pre-existing condition clauses included in health insurance policies offered by employers. Consequently, employers may continue to offer policies that contain such clauses, even if they adversely affect individuals with disabilities, so long as the clauses are not used as a subterfuge to evade the purposes of this part.

So, for example, it would be permissible for an employer to offer an insurance policy that limits coverage for certain procedures or treatments to a specified number per year. Thus, if a health insurance plan provided coverage for five blood transfusions a year to all covered employees, it would not be discriminatory to offer this plan simply because a hemophiliac employee may require more than five blood transfusions annually. However, it would not be permissible to limit or deny the hemophiliac employee coverage for other procedures, such as heart surgery or the setting of a broken leg, even though the plan would not have to provide coverage for the additional blood transfusions that may be involved in these procedures. Likewise, limits may be placed on reimbursements for certain procedures or on the types of drugs or procedures covered (e.g. limits on the number of permitted X-rays or non-coverage of experimental drugs or procedures), but that limitation must be applied equally to individuals with and without disabilities. See Senate Report at 28-29; House Labor Report at 58-59; House Judiciary Report at 36.

Leave policies or benefit plans that are uniformly applied do not violate this part simply because they do not address the special needs of every individual with a disability. Thus, for example, an employer that reduces the number of paid sick leave days that it will provide to all employees, or reduces the amount of medical insurance coverage that it will provide to all employees, is not in violation of this part, even if the benefits reduction has an impact on employees with disabilities in need of greater sick leave and medical coverage. Benefits reductions adopted for discriminatory reasons are in violation of this part. See Alexander v. Choate, 469 U.S. 287 (1985). See Senate Report at 85; House Labor Report at 137. (See also, the discussion at §1630.16(f) Health Insurance, Life Insurance, and Other Benefit Plans).

Section 1630.6 Contractual or Other Arrangements

An employer or other covered entity may not do through a contractual or other relationship what it is prohibited from doing directly. This provision does not affect the determination of whether or not one is a "covered entity" or "employer" as defined in §1630.2.

This provision only applies to situations where an employer or other covered entity has entered into a contractual relationship that has the effect of discriminating against its own employees or applicants with disabilities. Accordingly, it would be a violation for an employer to participate in a contractual relationship that results in discrimination against the employer's employees with disabilities in hiring, training, promotion, or in any other aspect of the employment relationship. This provision applies whether or not the employer or other covered entity intended for the contractual relationship to have the discriminatory effect.

Part 1630 notes that this provision applies to parties on either side of the contractual or other relationship. This is intended to highlight that an employer whose employees provide services to others, like an employer whose employees receive services, must ensure that those employees are not discriminated against on the basis of disability. For example, a copier company whose service representative is a dwarf could be required to provide a stepstool, as a reasonable accommodation, to enable him to perform the necessary repairs. However, the employer would not be required, as a reasonable accommodation, to make structural changes to its customer's inaccessible premises.

The existence of the contractual relationship adds no new obligations under part 1630. The employer, therefore, is not liable through the contractual arrangement for any discrimination by the contractor against the contractors own employees or applicants, although the contractor, as an employer, may be liable for such discrimination.

An employer or other covered entity, on the other hand, cannot evade the obligations imposed by this part by engaging in a contractual or other relationship. For example, an employer cannot avoid its responsibility to make reasonable accommodation subject to the undue hardship limitation through a contractual arrangement. See Conference Report at 59; House Labor Report at 59-61; House Judiciary Report at 36-37.

To illustrate, assume that an employer is seeking to contract with a company to provide training for its employees. Any responsibilities of reasonable accommodation applicable to the employer in providing the training remain with that employer even if it contracts with another company for this service. Thus, if the training company were planning to conduct the training at an inaccessible location, thereby making it impossible for an employee who uses a wheelchair to attend, the employer would have a duty to make reasonable accommodation unless to do so would impose an undue hardship. Under these circumstances, appropriate accommodations might include (1) having the training company identify accessible training sites and relocate the training program; (2) having the training company make the training site accessible; (3) directly making the training site accessible or providing the training company with the means by which to make the site accessible; (4) identifying and contracting with another training company that uses accessible sites; or (5) any other accommodation that would result in making the training available to the employee.

As another illustration, assume that instead of contracting with a training company, the employer contracts with a hotel to host a conference for its employees. The employer will have a duty to ascertain and ensure the accessibility of the hotel and its conference facilities. To fulfill this obligation the employer could, for example, inspect the hotel first-hand or ask a local disability group to inspect the hotel. Alternatively, the employer could ensure that the contract with the hotel specifies it will provide accessible guest rooms for those who need them and that all rooms to be used for the conference, including exhibit and meeting rooms, are accessible. If the hotel breaches this accessibility provision, the hotel may be liable to the employer, under a non-ADA breach of contract theory, for the cost of any accommodation needed to provide access to the hotel and conference, and for any other costs accrued by the employer. (In addition, the hotel may also be independently liable under title III of the ADA). However, this would not relieve the employer of its responsibility under this part nor shield it from charges of discrimination by its own employees. See House Labor Report at 40; House Judiciary Report at 37.

Section 1630.8 Relationship or Association With an Individual With a Disability

This provision is intended to protect any qualified individual, whether or not that individual has a disability, from discrimination because that person is known to have an association or relationship with an individual who has a known disability. This protection is not limited to those who have a familial relationship with an individual with a disability.

To illustrate the scope of this provision, assume that a qualified applicant without a disability applies for a job and discloses to the employer that his or her spouse has a disability. The employer thereupon declines to hire the applicant because the employer believes that the applicant would have to miss work or frequently leave work early in order to care for the spouse. Such a refusal to hire would be prohibited by this provision. Similarly, this provision would prohibit an employer from discharging an employee because the employee does volunteer work with people who have AIDS, and the employer fears that the employee may contract the disease.

This provision also applies to other benefits and privileges of employment. For example, an employer that provides health insurance benefits to its employees for their dependents may not reduce the level of those benefits to an employee simply because that employee has a dependent with a disability. This is true even if the provision of such benefits would result in increased health insurance costs for the employer.

It should be noted, however, that an employer need not provide the applicant or employee without a disability with a reasonable accommodation because that duty only applies to qualified applicants or employees with disabilities. Thus, for example, an employee would not be entitled to a modified work schedule as an accommodation to enable the employee to care for a spouse with a disability. See Senate Report at 30; House Labor Report at 61-62; House Judiciary Report at 38-39.

Section 1630.9 Not Making Reasonable Accommodation

The obligation to make reasonable accommodation is a form of non-discrimination. It applies to all employment decisions and to the job application process. This obligation does not extend to the provision of adjustments or modifications that are primarily for the personal benefit of the individual with a disability. Thus, if an adjustment or modification is job-related, e.g., specifically assists the individual in performing the duties of a particular job, it will be considered a type of reasonable accommodation. On the other hand, if an adjustment or modification assists the individual throughout his or her daily activities, on and off the job, it will be considered a personal item that the employer is not required to provide. Accordingly, an employer would generally not be required to provide an employee with a disability with a prosthetic limb, wheelchair, or eyeglasses. Nor would an employer have to provide as an accommodation any amenity or convenience that is not job-related, such as a private hot plate, hot pot or refrigerator that is not provided to employees without disabilities. See Senate Report at 31; House Labor Report at 62.

It should be noted, however, that the provision of such items may be required as a reasonable accommodation where such items are specifically designed or required to meet job-related rather than personal needs. An employer, for example, may have to provide an individual with a disabling visual impairment with eyeglasses specifically designed to enable the individual to use the office computer monitors, but that are not otherwise needed by the individual outside of the office.

The term "supported employment," which has been applied to a wide variety of programs to assist individuals with severe disabilities in both competitive and non-competitive employment, is not synonymous with reasonable accommodation. Examples of supported employment include modified training materials, restructuring essential functions to enable an individual to perform a job, or hiring an outside professional ("job coach") to assist in job training. Whether a particular form of assistance would be required as a reasonable accommodation must be determined on an individualized, case by case basis without regard to whether that assistance is referred to as "supported employment." For example, an employer, under certain circumstances, may be required to provide modified training materials or a temporary "job coach" to assist in the training of a qualified individual with a disability as a reasonable accommodation. However, an employer would not be required to restructure the essential functions of a position to fit the skills of an individual with a disability who is not otherwise qualified to perform the position, as is done in certain supported employment programs. See 34 CFR part 363. It should be noted that it would not be a violation of this part for an employer to provide any of these personal modifications or adjustments, or to engage in supported employment or similar rehabilitative programs.

The obligation to make reasonable accommodation applies to all services and programs provided in connection with employment, and to all non-work facilities provided or maintained by an employer for use by its employees. Accordingly, the obligation to accommodate is applicable to employer sponsored placement or counseling services, and to employer provided cafeterias, lounges, gymnasiums, auditoriums, transportation and the like.

The reasonable accommodation requirement is best understood as a means by which barriers to the equal employment opportunity of an individual with a disability are removed or alleviated. These barriers may, for example, be physical or structural obstacles that inhibit or prevent the access of an individual with a disability to job sites, facilities or equipment. Or they may be rigid work schedules that permit no flexibility as to when work is performed or when breaks may be taken, or inflexible job procedures that unduly limit the modes of communication that are used on the job, or the way in which particular tasks are accomplished.

The term "otherwise qualified" is intended to make clear that the obligation to make reasonable accommodation is owed only to an individual with a disability who is qualified within the meaning of §1630.2(m) in that he or she satisfies all the skill, experience, education and other job-related selection criteria. An individual with a disability is "otherwise qualified," in other words, if he or she is qualified for a job, except that, because of the disability, he or she needs a reasonable accommodation to be able to perform the job's essential functions.

For example, if a law firm requires that all incoming lawyers have graduated from an accredited law school and have passed the bar examination, the law firm need not provide an accommodation to an individual with a visual impairment who has not met these selection criteria. That individual is not entitled to a reasonable accommodation because the individual is not "otherwise qualified" for the position.

On the other hand, if the individual has graduated from an accredited law school and passed the bar examination, the individual would be "otherwise qualified." The law firm would thus be required to provide a reasonable accommodation, such as a machine that magnifies print, to enable the individual to perform the essential functions of the attorney position, unless the necessary accommodation would impose an undue hardship on the law firm. See Senate Report at 33-34; House Labor Report at 64-65.

The reasonable accommodation that is required by this part should provide the qualified individual with a disability with an equal employment opportunity. Equal employment opportunity means an opportunity to attain the same level of performance, or to enjoy the same level of benefits and privileges of employment as are available to the average similarly situated employee without a disability. Thus, for example, an accommodation made to assist an employee with a disability in the performance of his or her job must be adequate to enable the individual to perform the essential functions of the relevant position. The accommodation, however, does not have to be the "best" accommodation possible, so long as it is sufficient to meet the job-related needs of the individual being accommodated. Accordingly, an employer would not have to provide an employee disabled by a back impairment with a state-of-the art mechanical lifting device if it provided the employee with a less expensive or more readily available device that enabled the employee to perform the essential functions of the job. See Senate

Report at 35; House Labor Report at 66; see also Carter v. Bennett, 840 F.2d 63 (DC Cir. 1988).

Employers are obligated to make reasonable accommodation only to the physical or mental limitations resulting from the disability of the individual with a disability that is known to the employer. Thus, an employer would not be expected to accommodate disabilities of which it is unaware. If an employee with a known disability is having difficulty performing his or her job, an employer may inquire whether the employee is in need of a reasonable accommodation. In general, however, it is the responsibility of the individual with a disability to inform the employer that an accommodation is needed. When the need for an accommodation is not obvious, an employer, before providing a reasonable accommodation, may require that the individual with a disability provide documentation of the need for accommodation. See Senate Report at 34; House Labor Report at 65.

PROCESS OF DETERMINING THE APPROPRIATE REASONABLE ACCOMMODATION

Once the individual with a disability has requested provision of a reasonable accommodation, the employer must make a reasonable effort to determine the appropriate accommodation. The appropriate reasonable accommodation is best determined through a flexible, interactive process that involves both the employer and the individual with a disability. Although this process is described below in terms of accommodations that enable the individual with a disability to perform the essential functions of the position held or desired, it is equally applicable to accommodations involving the job application process, and to accommodations that enable the individual with a disability to enjoy equal benefits and privileges of employment. See Senate Report at 34-35; House Labor Report at 65-67.

When the individual with a disability has requested a reasonable accommodation to assist in the performance of a job, the employer, using a problem solving approach, should:

(1) Analyze the particular job involved and determine its purpose and essential functions;

(2) Consult with the individual with a disability to ascertain the precise job-related limitations imposed by the individual's disability and how those limitations could be overcome with a reasonable accommodation;

(3) In consultation with the individual to be accommodated, identify potential accommodations and assess the effectiveness each would have in enabling the individual to perform the essential functions of the position; and

(4) Consider the preference of the individual to be accommodated and select and implement the accommodation that is most appropriate for both the employee and the employer.

In many instances, the appropriate reasonable accommodation may be so obvious to either or both the employer and the individual with a disability that it may not be necessary to proceed in this step-by-step fashion. For example, if an employee who uses a wheelchair requests that his or her desk be placed on blocks to elevate the desktop above the arms of the wheelchair and the employer complies, an appropriate accommodation has been requested, identified, and provided without either the employee or employer being aware of having engaged in any sort of "reasonable accommodation process."

However, in some instances neither the individual requesting the accommodation nor the employer can readily identify the appropriate accommodation. For example, the individual needing the accommodation may not know enough about the equipment used by the employer or the exact nature of the work site to suggest an appropriate accommodation. Likewise, the employer may not know enough about the individual's disability or the limitations that disability would impose on the performance of the job to suggest an appropriate accommodation. Under such circumstances, it may be necessary for the employer to initiate a more defined problem solving process, such as the step-by-step process described above, as part of its reasonable effort to identify the appropriate reasonable accommodation.

This process requires the individual assessment of both the particular job at issue, and the specific physical or mental limitations of the particular individual in need of reasonable accommodation. With regard to assessment of the job, "individual assessment" means analyzing the actual job duties and determining the true purpose or object of the job. Such an assessment is necessary to ascertain which job functions are the essential functions that an accommodation must enable an individual with a disability to perform.

After assessing the relevant job, the employer, in consultation with the individual requesting the accommodation, should make an assessment of the specific limitations imposed by the disability on the individual's performance of the job's essential functions. This assessment will make it possible to ascertain the precise barrier to the employment opportunity which, in turn, will make it possible to determine the accommodation(s) that could alleviate or remove that barrier.

If consultation with the individual in need of the accommodation still does not reveal potential appropriate accommodations, then the employer, as part of this process, may find that technical assistance is helpful in determining how to accommodate the particular individual in the specific situation. Such assistance could be sought from the Commission, from State or local rehabilitation agencies, or from disability constituent organizations. It should be noted, however, that, as provided in §1630.9(c) of this part, the failure to obtain or receive technical assistance from the Federal agencies that administer the ADA will not excuse the employer from its reasonable accommodation obligation.

Once potential accommodations have been identified, the employer should assess the effectiveness of each potential accommodation in assisting the individual in need of the accommodation in the performance of the essential functions of the position. If more than one of these accommodations will enable the individual to perform the essential functions or if the individual would prefer to provide his or her own accommodation, the preference of the individual with a disability should be given primary consideration. However, the employer providing the accommodation has the ultimate discretion to choose between effective accommodations, and may choose the less expensive accommodation or the accommodation that is easier for it to provide. It should also be noted that the individual's willingness to provide his or her own accommodation does not relieve the employer of the duty to provide the accommodation should the individual for any reason be unable or unwilling to continue to provide the accommodation.

REASONABLE ACCOMMODATION PROCESS ILLUSTRATED

The following example illustrates the informal reasonable accommodation process. Suppose a Sack Handler position requires that the employee pick up fifty pound sacks and carry them from the company loading dock to the storage room, and that a sack handler who is disabled by a back impairment requests a reasonable accommodation. Upon receiving the request, the employer analyzes the Sack Handler job and determines that the essential function and purpose of the job is not the requirement that the job holder physically lift and carry the sacks, but the requirement that the job holder cause the sack to move from the loading dock to the storage room.

The employer then meets with the sack handler to ascertain precisely the barrier posed by the individual's specific disability to the performance of the job's essential function of relocating the sacks. At this meeting the employer learns that the individual can, in fact, lift the sacks to waist level, but is prevented by his or her disability from carrying the sacks from the loading dock to the storage room. The employer and the individual agree that any of a number of potential accommodations, such as the provision of a dolly, hand truck, or cart, could enable the individual to transport the sacks that he or she has lifted.

Upon further consideration, however, it is determined that the provision of a cart is not a feasible effective option. No carts are currently available at the company, and those that can be purchased by the company are the wrong shape to hold many of the bulky and irregularly shaped sacks that must be moved. Both the dolly and the hand truck, on the other hand, appear to be effective options. Both are readily available to the company, and either will enable the individual to relocate the sacks that he or she has lifted. The sack handler indicates his or her preference for the dolly. In consideration of this expressed preference, and because the employer feels that the dolly will allow the individual to move more sacks at a time and so be more efficient than would a hand truck, the employer ultimately provides the sack handler with a dolly in fulfillment of the obligation to make reasonable accommodation.

Section 1630.9(b)

This provision states that an employer or other covered entity cannot prefer or select a qualified individual without a disability over an equally qualified individual with a disability merely because the individual with a disability will require a reasonable accommodation. In other words, an individual's need for an accommodation cannot enter into the employer's or other covered entity's decision regarding hiring, discharge, promotion, or other similar employment decisions, unless the accommodation would impose an undue hardship on the employer. See House Labor Report at 70.

Section 1630.9(d)

The purpose of this provision is to clarify that an employer or other covered entity may not compel the individual with a disability to accept an accommodation, where that accommodation is neither requested nor needed by the individual. However, if a necessary reasonable accommodation is refused, the individual may not be considered qualified. For example, an individual with a visual impairment that restricts his or her field of vision but who is able to read unaided would not be required to accept a reader as an accommodation. However, if the individual were not able to read unaided and reading was an essential function of the job, the individual would not be qualified for the job if he or she refused a reasonable accommodation that would enable him or her to read. See Senate Report at 34; House Labor Report at 65; House Judiciary Report at 71-72.

Section 1630.9(e)

The purpose of this provision is to incorporate the clarification made in the ADA Amendments Act of 2008 that an individual is not entitled to reasonable accommodation under the ADA if the individual is only covered under the "regarded as" prong of the definition of "individual with a disability." However, if the individual is covered under both the "regarded as" prong and one or both of the other two prongs of the definition of disability, the ordinary rules concerning the provision of reasonable accommodation apply.

Section 1630.10 Qualification Standards, Tests, and Other Selection Criteria

Section 1630.10(a)—In General

The purpose of this provision is to ensure that individuals with disabilities are not excluded from job opportunities unless they are actually unable to do the job. It is to ensure that there is a fit between job criteria and an applicant's (or employee's) actual ability to do the job. Accordingly, job criteria that even unintentionally screen out, or tend to screen out, an individual with a disability or a class of individuals with disabilities because of their disability may not be used unless the employer demonstrates that those criteria, as used by the employer, are job related for the position to which they are being applied and are consistent with business necessity. The concept of "business necessity" has the same meaning as the concept of "business necessity" under section 504 of the Rehabilitation Act of 1973.

Selection criteria that exclude, or tend to exclude, an individual with a disability or a class of individuals with disabilities because of their disability but do not concern an essential function of the job would not be consistent with business necessity.

The use of selection criteria that are related to an essential function of the job may be consistent with business necessity. However, selection criteria that are related to an essential function of the job may not be used to exclude an individual with a disability if that individual could satisfy the criteria with the provision of a reasonable accommodation. Experience under a similar provision of the regulations implementing section 504 of the Rehabilitation Act indicates that challenges to selection criteria are, in fact, often resolved by reasonable accommodation.

This provision is applicable to all types of selection criteria, including safety requirements, vision or hearing requirements, walking requirements, lifting requirements, and employment tests. See 1989 Senate Report at 37-39; House Labor Report at 70-72; House Judiciary Report at 42. As previously noted, however, it is not the intent of this part to second guess an employer's business judgment with regard to production standards. See §1630.2(n) (Essential Functions). Consequently, production standards will generally not be subject to a challenge under this provision.

The Uniform Guidelines on Employee Selection Procedures (UGESP) 29 CFR part 1607 do not apply to the Rehabilitation Act and are similarly inapplicable to this part.

Section 1630.10(b) — Qualification Standards and Tests Related to Uncorrected Vision

This provision allows challenges to qualification standards based on uncorrected vision, even where the person excluded by a standard has fully corrected vision with ordinary eyeglasses or contact lenses. An individual challenging a covered entity's application of a qualification standard, test, or other criterion based on uncorrected vision need not be a person with a disability. In order to have standing to challenge such a standard, test, or criterion, however, a person must be adversely affected by such standard, test or criterion. The Commission also believes that such individuals will usually be covered under the "regarded as" prong of the definition of disability. Someone who wears eyeglasses or contact lenses to correct vision will still have an impairment, and a qualification standard that screens the individual out because of the impairment by requiring a certain level of uncorrected vision to perform a job will amount to an action prohibited by the ADA based on an impairment. (See §1630.2(l); Appendix to §1630.2(l).)

In either case, a covered entity may still defend a qualification standard requiring a certain level of uncorrected vision by showing that it is job related and consistent with business necessity. For example, an applicant or employee with uncorrected vision of 20/100 who wears glasses that fully correct his vision may challenge a police department's qualification standard that requires all officers to have uncorrected vision of no less than 20/40 in one eye and 20/100 in the other, and visual acuity of 20/20 in both eyes with correction. The department would then have to establish that the standard is job related and consistent with business necessity.

Section 1630.11 Administration of Tests

The intent of this provision is to further emphasize that individuals with disabilities are not to be excluded from jobs that they can actually perform merely because a disability prevents them from taking a test, or negatively influences the results of a test, that is a prerequisite to the job. Read together with the reasonable accommodation requirement of section 1630.9, this provision requires that employment tests be administered to eligible applicants or employees with disabilities that impair sensory, manual, or speaking skills in formats that do not require the use of the impaired skill.

The employer or other covered entity is, generally, only required to provide such reasonable accommodation if it knows, prior to the administration of the test, that the individual is disabled and that the disability impairs sensory, manual or speaking skills. Thus, for example, it would be unlawful to administer a written employment test to an individual who has informed the employer, prior to the administration of the test, that he is disabled with dyslexia and unable to read. In such a case, as a reasonable accommodation and in accordance with this provision, an alternative oral test should be administered to that individual. By the same token, a written test may need to be substituted for an oral test if the applicant taking the test is an individual with a disability that impairs speaking skills or impairs the processing of auditory information.

Occasionally, an individual with a disability may not realize, prior to the administration of a test, that he or she will need an accommodation to take that particular test. In such a situation, the individual with a disability, upon becoming aware of the need for an accommodation, must so inform the employer or other covered entity. For example, suppose an individual with a disabling visual impairment does not request an accommodation for a written examination because he or she is usually able to take written tests with the aid of his or her own specially designed lens. When the test is distributed, the individual with a disability discovers that the lens is insufficient to distinguish the words of the test because of the unusually low color contrast between the paper and the ink, the individual would be entitled, at that point, to request an accommodation. The employer or other covered entity would, thereupon, have to provide a test with higher contrast, schedule a retest, or provide any other effective accommodation unless to do so would impose an undue hardship.

Other alternative or accessible test modes or formats include the administration of tests in large print or braille, or via a reader or sign interpreter. Where it is not possible to test in an alternative format, the employer may be required, as a reasonable accommodation, to evaluate the skill to be tested in another manner (e.g., through an interview, or through education license, or work experience requirements). An employer may also be required, as a reasonable accommodation, to allow more time to complete the test. In addition, the employer's obligation to make reasonable accommodation extends to ensuring that the test site is accessible. (See §1630.9 Not Making Reasonable Accommodation) See Senate Report at 37-38; House Labor Report at 70-72; House Judiciary Report at 42; see also Stutts v. Freeman, 694 F.2d 666 (11th Cir. 1983); Crane v. Dole, 617 F. Supp. 156 (D.D.C. 1985).

This provision does not require that an employer offer every applicant his or her choice of test format. Rather, this provision only requires that an employer provide, upon advance request, alternative, accessible tests to individuals with disabilities that impair sensory, manual, or speaking skills needed to take the test.

This provision does not apply to employment tests that require the use of sensory, manual, or speaking skills where the tests are intended to measure those skills. Thus, an employer could require that an applicant with dyslexia take a written test for a particular position if the ability to read is the skill the test is designed to measure. Similarly, an employer could require that an applicant complete a test within established time frames if speed were one of the skills for which the applicant was being tested. However, the results of such a test could not be used to exclude an individual with a disability unless the skill was necessary to perform an essential function of the position and no reasonable accommodation was available to enable the individual to perform that function, or the necessary accommodation would impose an undue hardship.

Section 1630.13 Prohibited Medical Examinations and Inquiries

Section 1630.13(a) Pre-employment Examination or Inquiry

This provision makes clear that an employer cannot inquire as to whether an individual has a disability at the pre-offer stage of the selection process. Nor can an employer inquire at the pre-offer stage about an applicant's workers' compensation history.

Employers may ask questions that relate to the applicant's ability to perform job-related functions. However, these questions should not be phrased in terms of disability. An employer, for example, may ask whether the applicant has a driver's license, if driving is a job function, but may not ask whether the applicant has a visual disability. Employers may ask about an applicant's ability to perform both essential and marginal job functions. Employers, though, may not refuse to hire an applicant with a disability because the applicant's disability prevents him or her from performing marginal functions. See Senate Report at 39; House Labor Report at 72-73; House Judiciary Report at 42-43.

Section 1630.13(b) Examination or Inquiry of Employees

The purpose of this provision is to prevent the administration to employees of medical tests or inquiries that do not serve a legitimate business purpose. For example, if an employee suddenly starts to use increased amounts of sick leave or starts to appear sickly, an employer could not require that employee to be tested for AIDS, HIV infection, or cancer unless the employer can demonstrate that such testing is job-related and consistent with business necessity. See Senate Report at 39; House Labor Report at 75; House Judiciary Report at 44.

Section 1630.14 Medical Examinations and Inquiries Specifically Permitted

Section 1630.14(a) Pre-employment Inquiry

Employers are permitted to make pre-employment inquiries into the ability of an applicant to perform job-related functions. This inquiry must be narrowly tailored. The employer may describe or demonstrate the job function and inquire whether or not the applicant can perform that function with or without reasonable accommodation. For example, an employer may explain that the job requires assembling small parts and ask if the individual will be able to perform that function, with or without reasonable accommodation. See Senate Report at 39; House Labor Report at 73; House Judiciary Report at 43.

An employer may also ask an applicant to describe or to demonstrate how, with or without reasonable accommodation, the applicant will be able to perform job-related functions. Such a request may be made of all applicants in the same job category regardless of disability. Such a request may also be made of an applicant whose known disability may interfere with or prevent the performance of a job-related function, whether or not the employer routinely makes such a request of all applicants in the job category. For example, an employer may ask an individual with one leg who applies for a position as a home washing machine repairman to demonstrate or to explain how, with or without reasonable accommodation, he would be able to transport himself and his tools down basement stairs. However, the employer may not inquire as to the nature or severity of the disability. Therefore, for example, the employer cannot ask how the individual lost the leg or whether the loss of the leg is indicative of an underlying impairment.

On the other hand, if the known disability of an applicant will not interfere with or prevent the performance of a job-related function, the employer may only request a description or demonstration by the applicant if it routinely makes such a request of all applicants in the same job category. So, for example, it would not be permitted for an employer to request that an applicant with one leg demonstrate his ability to assemble small parts while seated at a table, if the employer does not routinely request that all applicants provide such a demonstration.

An employer that requires an applicant with a disability to demonstrate how he or she will perform a job-related function must either provide the reasonable accommodation the applicant needs to perform the function or permit the applicant to explain how, with the accommodation, he or she will perform the function. If the job-related function is not an essential function, the employer may not exclude the applicant with a disability because of the applicant's inability to perform that function. Rather, the employer must, as a reasonable accommodation, either provide an accommodation that will enable the individual to perform the function, transfer the function to another position, or exchange the function for one the applicant is able to perform.

An employer may not use an application form that lists a number of potentially disabling impairments and ask the applicant to check any of the impairments he or she may have. In addition, as noted above, an employer may not ask how a particular individual became disabled or the prognosis of the individual's disability. The employer is also prohibited from asking how often the individual will require leave for treatment or use leave as a result of incapacitation because of the disability. However, the employer may state the attendance requirements of the job and inquire whether the applicant can meet them.

An employer is permitted to ask, on a test announcement or application form, that individuals with disabilities who will require a reasonable accommodation in order to take the test so inform the employer within a reasonable established time period prior to the administration of the test. The employer may also request that documentation of the need for the accommodation accompany the request. Requested accommodations may include accessible testing sites, modified testing conditions and accessible test formats. (See §1630.11 Administration of Tests).

Physical agility tests are not medical examinations and so may be given at any point in the application or employment process. Such tests must be given to all similarly situated applicants or employees regardless of disability. If such tests screen out or tend to screen out an individual with a disability or a class of individuals with disabilities, the employer would have to demonstrate that the test is job-related and consistent with business necessity and that performance cannot be achieved with reasonable accommodation. (See §1630.9 Not Making Reasonable Accommodation: Process of Determining the Appropriate Reasonable Accommodation).

As previously noted, collecting information and inviting individuals to identify themselves as individuals with disabilities as required to satisfy the affirmative action requirements of section 503 of the Rehabilitation Act is not restricted by this part. (See §1630.1 (b) and (c) Applicability and Construction).

Section 1630.14(b) Employment Entrance Examination

An employer is permitted to require post-offer medical examinations before the employee actually starts working. The employer may condition the offer of employment on the results of the examination, provided that all entering employees in the same job category are subjected to such an examination, regardless of disability, and that the confidentiality requirements specified in this part are met.

This provision recognizes that in many industries, such as air transportation or construction, applicants for certain positions are chosen on the basis of many factors including physical and psychological criteria, some of which may be identified as a result of post-offer medical examinations given prior to entry on duty. Only those employees who meet the employer's physical and psychological criteria for the job, with or without reasonable accommodation, will be qualified to receive confirmed offers of employment and begin working.

Medical examinations permitted by this section are not required to be job-related and consistent with business necessity. However, if an employer withdraws an offer of employment because the medical examination reveals that the employee does not satisfy certain employment criteria, either the exclusionary criteria must not screen out or tend to screen out an individual with a disability or a class of individuals with disabilities, or they must be job-related and consistent with business necessity. As part of the showing that an exclusionary criteria is job-related and consistent with business necessity, the employer must also demonstrate that there is no reasonable accommodation that will enable the individual with a disability to perform the essential functions of the job. See Conference Report at 59-60; Senate Report at 39; House Labor Report at 73-74; House Judiciary Report at 43.

As an example, suppose an employer makes a conditional offer of employment to an applicant, and it is an essential function of the job that the incumbent be available to work every day for the next three months. An employment entrance examination then reveals that the applicant has a disabling impairment that, according to reasonable medical judgment that relies on the most current medical knowledge, will require treatment that will render the applicant unable to work for a portion of the three month period. Under these circumstances, the employer would be able to withdraw the employment offer without violating this part.

The information obtained in the course of a permitted entrance examination or inquiry is to be treated as a confidential medical record and may only be used in a manner not inconsistent with this part. State workers' compensation laws are not preempted by the ADA or this part. These laws require the collection of information from individuals for State administrative purposes that do not conflict with the ADA or this part. Consequently, employers or other covered entities may submit information to State workers' compensation offices or second injury funds in accordance with State workers' compensation laws without violating this part.

Consistent with this section and with §1630.16(f) of this part, information obtained in the course of a permitted entrance examination or inquiry may be used for insurance purposes described in §1630.16(f).

Section 1630.14(c) Examination of Employees

This provision permits employers to make inquiries or require medical examinations (fitness for duty exams) when there is a need to determine whether an employee is still able to perform the essential functions of his or her job. The provision permits employers or other covered entities to make inquiries or require medical examinations necessary to the reasonable accommodation process described in this part. This provision also permits periodic physicals to determine fitness for duty or other medical monitoring if such physicals or monitoring are required by medical standards or requirements established by Federal, State, or local law that are consistent with the ADA and this part (or in the case of a Federal standard, with section 504 of the Rehabilitation Act) in that they are job-related and consistent with business necessity.

Such standards may include Federal safety regulations that regulate bus and truck driver qualifications, as well as laws establishing medical requirements for pilots or other air transportation personnel. These standards also include health standards promulgated pursuant to the Occupational Safety and Health Act of 1970, the Federal Coal Mine Health and Safety Act of 1969, or other similar statutes that require that employees exposed to certain toxic and hazardous substances be medically monitored at specific intervals. See House Labor Report at 74-75.

The information obtained in the course of such examination or inquiries is to be treated as a confidential medical record and may only be used in a manner not inconsistent with this part.

Section 1630.14(d) Other Acceptable Examinations and Inquiries

Part 1630 permits voluntary medical examinations, including voluntary medical histories, as part of employee health programs. These programs often include, for example, medical screening for high blood pressure, weight control counseling, and cancer detection. Voluntary activities, such as blood pressure monitoring and the administering of prescription drugs, such as insulin, are also permitted. It should be noted, however, that the medical records developed in the course of such activities must be maintained in the confidential manner required by this part and must not be used for any purpose in violation of this part, such as limiting health insurance eligibility. House Labor Report at 75; House Judiciary Report at 43-44.

Section 1630.15 Defenses

The section on defenses in part 1630 is not intended to be exhaustive. However, it is intended to inform employers of some of the potential defenses available to a charge of discrimination under the ADA and this part.

Section 1630.15(a) Disparate Treatment Defenses

The "traditional" defense to a charge of disparate treatment under title VII, as expressed in McDonnell Douglas Corp. v. Green, 411 U.S. 792 (1973), Texas Department of Community Affairs v. Burdine, 450 U.S. 248 (1981), and their progeny, may be applicable to charges of disparate treatment brought under the ADA. See Prewitt v. U.S. Postal Service, 662 F.2d 292 (5th Cir. 1981). Disparate treatment means, with respect to title I of the ADA, that an individual was treated differently on the basis of his or her disability. For example, disparate treatment has occurred where an employer excludes an employee with a severe facial disfigurement from staff meetings because the employer does not like to look at the employee. The individual is being treated differently because of the employer's attitude towards his or her perceived disability. Disparate treatment has also occurred where an employer has a policy of not hiring individuals with AIDS regardless of the individuals' qualifications.

The crux of the defense to this type of charge is that the individual was treated differently not because of his or her disability but for a legitimate non-discriminatory reason such as poor performance unrelated to the individual's disability. The fact that the individual's disability is not covered by the employer's current insurance plan or would cause the employer's insurance premiums or workers' compensation costs to increase, would not be a legitimate nondiscriminatory reason justifying disparate treatment of an individual with a disability. Senate Report at 85; House Labor Report at 136 and House Judiciary Report at 70. The defense of a legitimate nondiscriminatory reason is rebutted if the alleged nondiscriminatory reason is shown to be pretextual.

Section 1630.15(b) and (c) Disparate Impact Defenses

Disparate impact means, with respect to title I of the ADA and this part, that uniformly applied criteria have an adverse impact on an individual with a disability or a disproportionately negative impact on a class of individuals with disabilities. Section 1630.15(b) clarifies that an employer may use selection criteria that have such a disparate impact, i.e., that screen out or tend to screen out an individual with a disability or a class of individuals with disabilities only when they are job-related and consistent with business necessity.

For example, an employer interviews two candidates for a position, one of whom is blind. Both are equally qualified. The employer decides that while it is not essential to the job it would be convenient to have an employee who has a driver's license and so could occasionally be asked to run errands by car. The employer hires the individual who is sighted because this individual has a driver's license. This is an example of a uniformly applied criterion, having a driver's permit, that screens out an individual who has a disability that makes it impossible to obtain a driver's permit. The employer would, thus, have to show that this criterion is job-related and consistent with business necessity. See House Labor Report at 55.

However, even if the criterion is job-related and consistent with business necessity, an employer could not exclude an individual with a disability if the criterion could be met or job performance accomplished with a reasonable accommodation. For example, suppose an employer requires, as part of its application process, an interview that is job-related and consistent with business necessity. The employer would not be able to refuse to hire a hearing impaired applicant because he or she could not be interviewed. This is so because an interpreter could be provided as a reasonable accommodation that would allow the individual to be interviewed, and thus satisfy the selection criterion.

With regard to safety requirements that screen out or tend to screen out an individual with a disability or a class of individuals with disabilities, an employer must demonstrate that the requirement, as applied to the individual, satisfies the "direct threat" standard in §1630.2(r) in order to show that the requirement is job-related and consistent with business necessity.

Section 1630.15(c) clarifies that there may be uniformly applied standards, criteria and policies not relating to selection that may also screen out or tend to screen out an individual with a disability or a class of individuals with disabilities. Like selection criteria that have a disparate impact, non-selection criteria having such an impact may also have to be job-related and consistent with business necessity, subject to consideration of reasonable accommodation.

It should be noted, however, that some uniformly applied employment policies or practices, such as leave policies, are not subject to challenge under the adverse impact theory. "No-leave" policies (e.g., no leave during the first six months of employment) are likewise not subject to challenge under the adverse impact theory. However, an employer, in spite of its "no-leave" policy, may, in appropriate circumstances, have to consider the provision of leave to an employee with a disability as a reasonable accommodation, unless the provision of leave would impose an undue hardship. See discussion at §1630.5 Limiting, Segregating and Classifying, and §1630.10 Qualification Standards, Tests, and Other Selection Criteria.

Section 1630.15(d) Defense To Not Making Reasonable Accommodation

An employer or other covered entity alleged to have discriminated because it did not make a reasonable accommodation, as required by this part, may offer as a defense that it would have been an undue hardship to make the accommodation. It should be noted, however, that an employer cannot simply assert that a needed accommodation will cause it undue hardship, as defined in §1630.2(p), and thereupon be relieved of the duty to provide accommodation. Rather, an employer will have to present evidence and demonstrate that the accommodation will, in fact, cause it undue hardship. Whether a particular accommodation will impose an undue hardship for a particular employer is determined on a case by case basis. Consequently, an accommodation that poses an undue hardship for one employer at a particular time may not pose an undue hardship for another employer, or even for the same employer at another time. Likewise, an accommodation that poses an undue hardship for one employer in a particular job setting, such as a temporary construction worksite, may not pose an undue hardship for another employer, or even for the same employer at a permanent worksite. See House Judiciary Report at 42.

The concept of undue hardship that has evolved under section 504 of the Rehabilitation Act and is embodied in this part is unlike the "undue hardship" defense associated with the provision of religious accommodation under title VII of the Civil Rights Act of 1964. To demonstrate undue hardship pursuant to the ADA and this part, an employer must show substantially more difficulty or expense than would be needed to satisfy the "de minimis" title VII standard of undue hardship. For example, to demonstrate that the cost of an accommodation poses an undue hardship, an employer would have to show that the cost is undue as compared to the employer's budget. Simply comparing the cost of the accommodation to the salary of the individual with a disability in need of the accommodation will not suffice. Moreover, even if it is determined that the cost of an accommodation would unduly burden an employer, the employer cannot avoid making the accommodation if the individual with a disability can arrange to cover that portion of the cost that rises to the undue hardship level, or can otherwise arrange to provide the accommodation. Under such circumstances, the necessary accommodation would no longer pose an undue hardship. See Senate Report at 36; House Labor Report at 68-69; House Judiciary Report at 40-41.

Excessive cost is only one of several possible bases upon which an employer might be able to demonstrate undue hardship. Alternatively, for example, an employer could demonstrate that the provision of a particular accommodation would be unduly disruptive to its other employees or to the functioning of its business. The terms of a collective bargaining agreement may be relevant to this determination. By way of illustration, an employer would likely be able to show undue hardship if the employer could show that the requested accommodation of the upward adjustment of the business' thermostat would result in it becoming unduly hot for its other employees, or for its patrons or customers. The employer would thus not have to provide this accommodation. However, if there were an alternate accommodation that would not result in undue hardship, the employer would have to provide that accommodation.

It should be noted, moreover, that the employer would not be able to show undue hardship if the disruption to its employees were the result of those employees fears or prejudices toward the individual's disability and not the result of the provision of the accommodation. Nor would the employer be able to demonstrate undue hardship by showing that the provision of the accommodation has a negative impact on the morale of its other employees but not on the ability of these employees to perform their jobs.

Section 1630.15(e) Defense—Conflicting Federal Laws and Regulations

There are several Federal laws and regulations that address medical standards and safety requirements. If the alleged discriminatory action was taken in compliance with another Federal law or regulation, the employer may offer its obligation to comply with the conflicting standard as a defense. The employer's defense of a conflicting Federal requirement or regulation may be rebutted by a showing of pretext, or by showing that the Federal standard did not require the discriminatory action, or that there was a nonexclusionary means to comply with the standard that would not conflict with this part. See House Labor Report at 74.

Section 1630.15(f) Claims Based on Transitory and Minor Impairments Under the "Regarded As" Prong

It may be a defense to a charge of discrimination where coverage would be shown solely under the "regarded as" prong of the definition of disability that the impairment is (in the case of an actual impairment) or would be (in the case of a perceived impairment) both transitory and minor. Section 1630.15(f)(1) explains that an individual cannot be "regarded as having such an impairment" if the impairment is both transitory (defined by the ADAAA as lasting or expected to last less than six months) and minor. Section 1630.15(f)(2) explains that the determination of "transitory and minor" is made objectively. For example, an individual who is denied a promotion because he has a minor back injury would be "regarded as" an individual with a disability if the back impairment lasted or was expected to last more than six months. Although minor, the impairment is not transitory. Similarly, if an employer discriminates against an employee based on the employee's bipolar disorder (an impairment that is not transitory and minor), the employee is "regarded as" having a disability even if the employer subjectively believes that the employee's disorder is transitory and minor.

Section 1630.16 Specific Activities Permitted

Section 1630.16(a) Religious Entities

Religious organizations are not exempt from title I of the ADA or this part. A religious corporation, association, educational institution, or society may give a preference in employment to individuals of the particular religion, and may require that applicants and employees conform to the religious tenets of the organization. However, a religious organization may not discriminate against an individual who satisfies the permitted religious criteria because that individual is disabled. The religious entity, in other words, is required to consider individuals with disabilities who are qualified and satisfy the permitted religious criteria on an equal basis with qualified individuals without disabilities who similarly satisfy the religious criteria. See Senate Report at 42; House Labor Report at 76-77; House Judiciary Report at 46.

Section 1630.16(b) Regulation of Alcohol and Drugs

This provision permits employers to establish or comply with certain standards regulating the use of drugs and alcohol in the workplace. It also allows employers to hold alcoholics and persons who engage in the illegal use of drugs to the same performance and conduct standards to which it holds all of its other employees. Individuals disabled by alcoholism are entitled to the same protections accorded other individuals with disabilities under this part. As noted above, individuals currently engaging in the illegal use of drugs are not individuals with disabilities for purposes of part 1630 when the employer acts on the basis of such use.

Section 1630.16(c) Drug Testing

This provision reflects title I's neutrality toward testing for the illegal use of drugs. Such drug tests are neither encouraged, authorized nor prohibited. The results of such drug tests may be used as a basis for disciplinary action. Tests for the illegal use of drugs are not considered medical examinations for purposes of this part. If the results reveal information about an individual's medical condition beyond whether the individual is currently engaging in the illegal use of drugs, this additional information is to be treated as a confidential medical record. For example, if a test for the illegal use of drugs reveals the presence of a controlled substance that has been lawfully prescribed for a particular medical condition, this information is to be treated as a confidential medical record. See House Labor Report at 79; House Judiciary Report at 47.

Section 1630.16(e) Infectious and Communicable Diseases; Food Handling Jobs

This provision addressing food handling jobs applies the "direct threat" analysis to the particular situation of accommodating individuals with infectious or communicable diseases that are transmitted through the handling of food. The Department of Health and Human Services is to prepare a list of infectious and communicable diseases that are transmitted through the handling of food. If an individual with a disability has one of the listed diseases and works in or applies for a position in food handling, the employer must determine whether there is a reasonable accommodation that will eliminate the risk of transmitting the disease through the handling of food. If there is an accommodation that will not pose an undue hardship, and that will prevent the transmission of the disease through the handling of food, the employer must provide the accommodation to the individual. The employer, under these circumstances, would not be permitted to discriminate against the individual because of the need to provide the reasonable accommodation and would be required to maintain the individual in the food handling job.

If no such reasonable accommodation is possible, the employer may refuse to assign, or to continue to assign the individual to a position involving food handling. This means that if such an individual is an applicant for a food handling position the employer is not required to hire the individual. However, if the individual is a current employee, the employer would be required to consider the accommodation of reassignment to a vacant position not involving food handling for which the individual is qualified. Conference Report at 61-63. (See §1630.2(r) Direct Threat).

Section 1630.16(f) Health Insurance, Life Insurance, and Other Benefit Plans

This provision is a limited exemption that is only applicable to those who establish, sponsor, observe or administer benefit plans, such as health and life insurance plans. It does not apply to those who establish, sponsor, observe or administer plans not involving benefits, such as liability insurance plans.

The purpose of this provision is to permit the development and administration of benefit plans in accordance with accepted principles of risk assessment. This provision is not intended to disrupt the current regulatory structure for self-insured employers. These employers may establish, sponsor, observe, or administer the terms of a bona fide benefit plan not subject to State laws that regulate insurance. This provision is also not intended to disrupt the current nature of insurance underwriting, or current insurance industry practices in sales, underwriting, pricing, administrative and other services, claims and similar insurance related activities based on classification of risks as regulated by the States.

The activities permitted by this provision do not violate part 1630 even if they result in limitations on individuals with disabilities, provided that these activities are not used as a subterfuge to evade the purposes of this part. Whether or not these activities are being used as a subterfuge is to be determined without regard to the date the insurance plan or employee benefit plan was adopted.

However, an employer or other covered entity cannot deny an individual with a disability who is qualified equal access to insurance or subject a qualified individual with a disability to different terms or conditions of insurance based on disability alone, if the disability does not pose increased risks. Part 1630 requires that decisions not based on risk classification be made in conformity with non-discrimination requirements. See Senate Report at 84-86; House Labor Report at 136-138; House Judiciary Report at 70-71. See the discussion of §1630.5 Limiting, Segregating and Classifying.

Part 1635 — Genetic Information Nondiscrimination Act of 2008

§1635.1 Purpose

(a) The purpose of this part is to implement Title II of the Genetic Information Nondiscrimination Act of 2008, 42 U.S.C. 2000ff, et seq. Title II of GINA:

(1) Prohibits use of genetic information in employment decision-making;

(2) Restricts employers and other entities subject to Title II of GINA from requesting, requiring, or purchasing genetic information;

(3) Requires that genetic information be maintained as a confidential medical record, and places strict limits on disclosure of genetic information; and

(4) Provides remedies for individuals whose genetic information is acquired, used, or disclosed in violation of its protections.

(b) This part does not apply to actions of covered entities that do not pertain to an individual's status as an employee, member of a labor organization, or participant in an apprenticeship program. For example, this part would not apply to:

(1) A medical examination of an individual for the purpose of diagnosis and treatment unrelated to employment, which is conducted by a health care

professional at the hospital or other health care facility where the individual is an employee; or

(2) Activities of a covered entity carried on in its capacity as a law enforcement agency investigating criminal conduct, even where the subject of the investigation is an employee of the covered entity.

§1635.1 Definitions — General.

(a) Commission means the Equal Employment Opportunity Commission, as established by section 705 of the Civil Rights Act of 1964, 42 U.S.C. 2000e-4.

(b) Covered Entity means an employer, employing office, employment agency, labor organization, or joint labor-management committee.

(c) Employee means an individual employed by a covered entity, as well as an applicant for employment and a former employee. An employee, including an applicant for employment and a former employee, is:

(1) As defined by section 701 of the Civil Rights Act of 1964, 42 U.S.C. 2000e, an individual employed by a person engaged in an industry affecting commerce who has fifteen or more employees for each working day in each of twenty or more calendar weeks in the current or preceding calendar year and any agent of such a person;

(2) As defined by section 304(a) of the Government Employee Rights Act, 42 U.S.C. 2000e-16c(a), a person chosen or appointed by an individual elected to public office by a State or political subdivision of a State to serve as part of the personal staff of the elected official, to serve the elected official on a policy-making level, or to serve the elected official as the immediate advisor on the exercise of the elected official's constitutional or legal powers.

(3) As defined by section 101 of the Congressional Accountability Act, 2 U.S.C. 1301, any employee of the House of Representatives, the Senate, the Capitol Guide Service, the Capitol Police, the Congressional Budget Office, the Office of the Architect of the Capitol, the Office of the Attending Physician, the Office of Compliance, or the Office of Technology Assessment;

(4) As defined by, and subject to the limitations in, section 2(a) of the Presidential and Executive Office Accountability Act, 3 U.S.C. 411(c), any employee of the executive branch not otherwise covered by section 717 of the Civil Rights Act of 1964, 42 U.S.C. 2000e-16, section 15 of the Age Discrimination in Employment Act of 1967, 29 U.S.C. 633a, or section 501 of the Rehabilitation Act of 1973, 29 U.S.C. 791, whether appointed by the President or any other appointing authority in the executive branch, including an employee of the Executive Office of the President;

(5) As defined by, and subject to the limitations in, section 717 of the Civil Rights Act of 1964, 42 U.S.C. 2000e-16, and regulations of the Equal Employment Opportunity Commission at 29 CFR 1614.103, an employee of a federal executive agency, the United States Postal Service and the Postal Rate Commission, the Tennessee Valley Authority, the National Oceanic and Atmospheric Administration Commissioned Corps, the Government Printing

Office, and the Smithsonian Institution; an employee of the federal judicial branch having a position in the competitive service; and an employee of the Library of Congress.

(d) Employer means any person that employs an employee defined in §1635.2(c) of this part, and any agent of such person, except that, as limited by section 701(b)(1) and (2) of the Civil Rights Act of 1964, 42 U.S.C. 2000e(b)(1) and (2), an employer does not include an Indian tribe, or a bona fide private club (other than a labor organization) that is exempt from taxation under section 501(c) of the Internal Revenue Code of 1986.

(e) Employing office is defined in the Congressional Accountability Act, 2 U.S.C. 1301(9), to mean the personal office of a Member of the House of Representatives or of a Senator; a committee of the House of Representatives or the Senate or a joint committee; any other office headed by a person with the final authority to appoint, hire, discharge, and set the terms, conditions, or privileges of the employment of an employee of the House of Representatives or the Senate; or the Capitol Guide Board, the Capitol Police Board, the Congressional Budget Office, the Office of the Architect of the Capitol, the Office of the Attending Physician, the Office of Compliance, and the Office of Technology Assessment.

(f) Employment agency is defined in 42 U.S.C. 2000e(c) to mean any person regularly undertaking with or without compensation to procure employees for an employer or to procure for employees opportunities to work for an employer and includes an agent of such a person.

(g) Joint labor-management committee is defined as an entity that controls apprenticeship or other training or retraining programs, including on-the-job training programs.

(h) Labor organization is defined at 42 U.S.C. 2000e(d) to mean an organization with fifteen or more members engaged in an industry affecting commerce, and any agent of such an organization in which employees participate and which exists for the purpose, in whole or in part, of dealing with employers concerning grievances, labor disputes, wages, rates of pay, hours, or other terms or conditions of employment.

(i) Member includes, with respect to a labor organization, an applicant for membership.

(j) Person is defined at 42 U.S.C. 2000e(a) to mean one or more individuals, governments, governmental agencies, political subdivisions, labor unions, partnerships, associations, corporations, legal representatives, mutual companies, joint-stock companies, trusts, unincorporated organizations, trustees, trustees in cases under title 11, or receivers.

(k) State is defined at 42 U.S.C. 2000e(i) and includes a State of the United States, the District of Columbia, Puerto Rico, the Virgin Islands, American Samoa, Guam, Wake Island, the Canal Zone, and Outer Continental Shelf lands defined in the Outer Continental Shelf Lands Act (43 U.S.C. 1331 et seq.).

§1635.3 Definitions specific to GINA

(a) Family member means with respect to any individual:

(1) A person who is a dependent of that individual as the result of marriage, birth, adoption, or placement for adoption; or

(2) A first-degree, second-degree, third-degree, or fourth-degree relative of the individual, or of a dependent of the individual as defined in §1635.3(a)(1).

(i) First-degree relatives include an individual's parents, siblings, and children.

(ii) Second-degree relatives include an individual's grandparents, grandchildren, uncles, aunts, nephews, nieces, and half-siblings.

(iii) Third-degree relatives include an individual's great-grandparents, great grandchildren, great uncles/aunts, and first cousins.

(iv) Fourth-degree relatives include an individual's great-great-grandparents, great-great-grandchildren, and first cousins once-removed (i.e., the children of the individual's first cousins).

(b) Family medical history. Family medical history means information about the manifestation of disease or disorder in family members of the individual.

(c) Genetic information.

(1) Genetic information means information about:

(i) An individual's genetic tests;

(ii) The genetic tests of that individual's family members;

(iii) The manifestation of disease or disorder in family members of the individual (family medical history);

(iv) An individual's request for, or receipt of, genetic services, or the participation in clinical research that includes genetic services by the individual or a family member of the individual; or

(v) The genetic information of a fetus carried by an individual or by a pregnant woman who is a family member of the individual and the genetic information of any embryo legally held by the individual or family member using an assisted reproductive technology.

(2) Genetic information does not include information about the sex or age of the individual, the sex or age of family members, or information about the race or ethnicity of the individual or family members that is not derived from a genetic test.

(d) Genetic monitoring means the periodic examination of employees to evaluate acquired modifications to their genetic material, such as chromosomal damage or evidence of increased occurrence of mutations, caused by the toxic substances they use or are exposed to in performing their jobs, in order to identify, evaluate, and respond to the effects of, or to control adverse environmental exposures in the workplace.

(e) Genetic services. Genetic services means a genetic test, genetic counseling (including obtaining, interpreting, or assessing genetic information), or genetic education.

(f) Genetic test—

(1) In general. "Genetic test" means an analysis of human DNA, RNA, chromosomes, proteins, or metabolites that detects genotypes, mutations, or chromosomal changes.

(2) Genetic tests include, but are not limited to:

(i) A test to determine whether someone has the BRCA1 or BRCA2 variant evidencing a predisposition to breast cancer, a test to determine whether someone has a genetic variant associated with hereditary non-polyposis colon cancer, and a test for a genetic variant for Huntington's Disease;

(ii) Carrier screening for adults using genetic analysis to determine the risk of conditions such as cystic fibrosis, sickle cell anemia, spinal muscular atrophy, or fragile X syndrome in future offspring;

(iii) Amniocentesis and other evaluations used to determine the presence of genetic abnormalities in a fetus during pregnancy;

(iv) Newborn screening analysis that uses DNA, RNA, protein, or metabolite analysis to detect or indicate genotypes, mutations, or chromosomal changes, such as a test for PKU performed so that treatment can begin before a disease manifests;

(v) Preimplantation genetic diagnosis performed on embryos created using invitro fertilization;

(vi) Pharmacogenetic tests that detect genotypes, mutations, or chromosomal changes that indicate how an individual will react to a drug or a particular dosage of a drug;

(vii) DNA testing to detect genetic markers that are associated with information about ancestry; and

(viii) DNA testing that reveals family relationships, such as paternity.

(3) The following are examples of tests or procedures that are not genetic tests:

(i) An analysis of proteins or metabolites that does not detect genotypes, mutations, or chromosomal changes;

(ii) A medical examination that tests for the presence of a virus that is not composed of human DNA, RNA, chromosomes, proteins, or metabolites;

(iii) A test for infectious and communicable diseases that may be transmitted through food handling;

(iv) Complete blood counts, cholesterol tests, and liver-function tests.

(4) Alcohol and Drug Testing —

(i) A test for the presence of alcohol or illegal drugs is not a genetic test.

(ii) A test to determine whether an individual has a genetic predisposition for alcoholism or drug use is a genetic test.

(g) Manifestation or manifested means, with respect to a disease, disorder, or pathological condition, that an individual has been or could reasonably be diagnosed with the disease, disorder, or pathological condition by a health care professional with appropriate training and expertise in the field of medicine involved. For purposes of this part, a disease, disorder, or pathological condition is not manifested if the diagnosis is based principally on genetic information.

§1635.4 Prohibited practices — in general

(a) It is unlawful for an employer to discriminate against an individual on the basis of the genetic information of the individual in regard to hiring, discharge, compensation, terms, conditions, or privileges of employment.

(b) It is unlawful for an employment agency to fail or refuse to refer any individual for employment or otherwise discriminate against any individual because of genetic information of the individual.

(c) It is unlawful for a labor organization to exclude or to expel from the membership of the organization, or otherwise to discriminate against, any member because of genetic information with respect to the member.

(d) It is an unlawful employment practice for any employer, labor organization, or joint labor-management committee controlling apprenticeship or other training or retraining programs, including on-the-job training programs to discriminate against any individual because of the individual's genetic information in admission to, or employment in, any program established to provide apprenticeship or other training or retraining.

§1635.5 Limiting, segregating, and classifying

(a) A covered entity may not limit, segregate, or classify an individual, or fail or refuse to refer for employment any individual, in any way that would deprive or tend to deprive the individual of employment opportunities or otherwise affect the status of the individual as an employee, because of genetic information with respect to the individual. A covered entity will not be deemed to have violated this section if it limits or restricts an employee's job duties based on genetic information because it was required to do so by a law or regulation mandating genetic monitoring, such as regulations administered by the Occupational and Safety Health Administration (OSHA). See 1635.8(b)(5) and 1635.11(a).

(b) Notwithstanding any language in this part, a cause of action for disparate impact within the meaning of section 703(k) of the Civil Rights Act of 1964, 42 U.S.C. 2000e-2(k), is not available under this part.

§1635.6 Causing a covered entity to discriminate.

A covered entity may not cause or attempt to cause another covered entity, or its agent, to discriminate against an individual in violation of this part, including with respect to the individual's participation in an apprenticeship or other training or retraining program, or with respect to a member's participation in a labor organization.

§1635.7 Retaliation

A covered entity may not discriminate against any individual because such individual has opposed any act or practice made unlawful by this title or because such individual made a charge, testified, assisted, or participated in any manner in an investigation, proceeding, or hearing under this title.

§1635.8 Acquisition of genetic information

(a) General prohibition. A covered entity may not request, require, or purchase genetic information of an individual or family member of the individual, except as specifically provided in paragraph (b) of this section. "Request" includes conducting an Internet search on an individual in a way that is likely to result in a covered entity obtaining genetic information; actively listening to third-party conversations or searching an individual's personal effects for the purpose of obtaining genetic information; and making requests for information about an individual's current health status in a way that is likely to result in a covered entity obtaining genetic information.

(b) Exceptions. The general prohibition against requesting, requiring, or purchasing genetic information does not apply:

(1) Where a covered entity inadvertently requests or requires genetic information of the individual or family member of the individual.

(i) Requests for Medical Information:

(A) If a covered entity acquires genetic information in response to a lawful request for medical information, the acquisition of genetic information will not generally be considered inadvertent unless the covered entity directs the individual and/or health care provider from whom it requested medical information (in writing, or verbally, where the covered entity does not typically make requests for medical information in writing) not to provide genetic information.

(B) If a covered entity uses language such as the following, any receipt of genetic information in response to the request for medical information will be deemed inadvertent: "The Genetic Information Nondiscrimination Act of 2008 (GINA) prohibits employers and other entities covered by GINA Title II from requesting or requiring genetic information of an individual or family member of the individual, except as specifically allowed by this law. To comply with this law, we are asking that you not provide any genetic information when responding to this request for medical information. 'Genetic information' as defined by GINA, includes an individual's family medical history, the results of an individual's or family member's genetic tests, the fact that an individual or an individual's family member sought or received genetic services, and genetic information of a fetus carried by an individual or an individual's family member or an embryo lawfully held by an individual or family member receiving assistive reproductive services."

(C) A covered entity's failure to give such a notice or to use this or similar language will not prevent it from establishing that a particular receipt of genetic information was inadvertent if its request for medical information was not "likely to result in a covered entity obtaining genetic information" (for example, where an overly broad response is received in response to a tailored request for medical information).

(D) Situations to which the requirements of subsection (b)(1)(i) apply include, but are not limited to the following:

(1) Where a covered entity requests documentation to support a request for reasonable accommodation under Federal, State, or local law, as long as the covered entity's request for such documentation is lawful. A request for documentation supporting a request for reasonable accommodation is lawful only when the disability and/or the need for accommodation is not obvious; the documentation is no more than is sufficient to establish that an individual has a disability and needs a reasonable accommodation; and the documentation relates only to the impairment that the individual claims to be a disability that requires reasonable accommodation;

(2) Where an employer requests medical information from an individual as required, authorized, or permitted by Federal, State, or local law, such as where an employee requests leave under the Family and Medical Leave Act (FMLA) to attend to the employee's own serious health condition or where an employee complies with the FMLA's employee return to work certification requirements; or

(3) Where a covered entity requests documentation to support a request for leave that is not governed by Federal, State, or local laws requiring leave, as long as the documentation required to support the request otherwise complies with the requirements of the Americans with Disabilities Act and other laws limiting a covered entity's access to medical information.

(ii) The exception for inadvertent acquisition of genetic information also applies in, but is not necessarily limited to, situations where—

(A) A manager, supervisor, union representative, or employment agency representative learns genetic information about an individual by overhearing a conversation between the individual and others;

(B) A manager, supervisor, union representative, or employment agency representative learns genetic information about an individual by receiving it from the individual or third-parties during a casual conversation, including in response to an ordinary expression of concern that is the subject of the conversation. For example, the exception applies when the covered entity, acting through a supervisor or other official, receives family medical history directly from an individual following a general health inquiry (e.g., "How are you?" or "Did they catch it early?" asked of an employee who was just diagnosed with cancer) or a question as to whether the individual has a manifested condition. Similarly, a casual question between colleagues, or between a supervisor and subordinate, concerning the general well-being of a parent or child would not violate GINA (e.g., "How's your son feeling today?", "Did they catch it early?" asked of an employee whose family member was just diagnosed with cancer, or "Will your daughter be OK?"). However, this exception does not apply where an employer follows up a question concerning a family member's general health with questions that are probing in nature, such as whether other family members have the condition, or whether the individual has been tested for the condition, because the covered entity should know that these questions are likely to result in the acquisition of genetic information;

(C) A manager, supervisor, union representative, or employment agency representative learns genetic information from the individual or a third-party without having solicited or sought the information (e.g., where a manager or supervisor receives an unsolicited email about the health of an employee's family member from a co-worker); or

(D) A manager, supervisor, union representative, or employment agency representative inadvertently learns genetic information from a social media platform which he or she was given permission to access by the creator of the profile at issue (e.g., a supervisor and employee are connected on a social networking site and the employee provides family medical history on his page).

(2) Where a covered entity offers health or genetic services, including such services offered as part of a voluntary wellness program.

(i) This exception applies only where —

(A) The provision of genetic information by the individual is voluntary, meaning the covered entity neither requires the individual to provide genetic information nor penalizes those who choose not to provide it;

(B) The individual provides prior knowing, voluntary, and written authorization, which may include authorization in electronic format. This requirement is only met if the covered entity uses an authorization form that:

(1) Is written so that the individual from whom the genetic information is being obtained is reasonably likely to understand it;

(2) Describes the type of genetic information that will be obtained and the general purposes for which it will be used; and

(3) Describes the restrictions on disclosure of genetic information;

(C) Individually identifiable genetic information is provided only to the individual (or family member if the family member is receiving genetic services) and the licensed health care professionals or board certified genetic counselors involved in providing such services, and is not accessible to managers, supervisors, or others who make employment decisions, or to anyone else in the workplace; and

(D) Any individually identifiable genetic information provided under paragraph (b)(2) of this section is only available for purposes of such services and is not disclosed to the covered entity except in aggregate terms that do not disclose the identity of specific individuals (a covered entity will not violate the requirement that it receive information only in aggregate terms if it receives information that, for reasons outside the control of the provider or the covered entity (such as the small number of participants), makes the genetic information of a particular individual readily identifiable with no effort on the covered entity's part).

(ii) Consistent with the requirements of paragraph (b)(2)(i) of this section, a covered entity may not offer a financial inducement for individuals to provide genetic information, but may offer financial inducements for completion of health risk assessments that include questions about family medical history or other genetic information, provided the covered entity makes clear, in language reasonably likely to be understood by those completing the health risk assessment, that the inducement will be made available whether or not the participant answers questions regarding genetic information. For example:

(A) A covered entity offers $150 to employees who complete a health risk assessment with 100 questions, the last 20 of them concerning family medical history and other genetic information. The instructions for completing the health risk assessment make clear that the inducement will be provided to all employees who respond to the first 80 questions, whether or not the remaining 20 questions concerning family medical history and other genetic information are answered. This health risk assessment does not violate Title II of GINA.

(B) Same facts as the previous example, except that the instructions do not indicate which questions request genetic information; nor does the assessment otherwise make clear which questions must be answered in order to obtain the inducement. This health risk assessment violates Title II of GINA.

(iii) A covered entity may offer financial inducements to encourage individuals who have voluntarily provided genetic information (e.g., family medical history) that indicates that they are at increased risk of acquiring a health condition in the future to participate in disease management programs or other programs that promote healthy lifestyles, and/or to meet particular health goals as part of a health or genetic service. However, to comply with Title II of GINA, these programs must also be offered to individuals with current health conditions and/or to individuals whose lifestyle choices put them at increased risk of developing a condition. For example:

(A) Employees who voluntarily disclose a family medical history of diabetes, heart disease, or high blood pressure on a health risk assessment that meets the requirements of (b)(2)(ii) of this section and employees who have a current diagnosis of one or more of these conditions are offered $150 to participate in a wellness program designed to encourage weight loss and a healthy lifestyle. This does not violate Title II of GINA.

(B) The program in the previous example offers an additional inducement to individuals who achieve certain health outcomes. Participants may earn points toward "prizes" totaling $150 in a single year for lowering their blood pressure, glucose, and cholesterol levels, or for losing weight. This inducement would not violate Title II of GINA.

(iv) Nothing contained in §1635.8(b)(2)(iii) limits the rights or protections of an individual under the Americans with Disabilities Act (ADA), as amended, or other applicable civil rights laws, or under the Health Insurance Portability and Accountability Act (HIPAA), as amended by GINA. For example, if an employer offers a financial inducement for participation in disease management programs or other programs that promote healthy lifestyles and/or require individuals to meet particular health goals, the employer must make reasonable accommodations to the extent required by the ADA, that is, the employer must make "modifications or adjustments that enable a covered entity's employee with a disability to enjoy equal benefits and privileges of employment as are enjoyed by its other similarly situated employees without disabilities" unless "such covered entity can demonstrate that the accommodation would impose an undue hardship on the operation of its business." 29 CFR 1630.2(o)(1)(iii); 29 CFR 1630.9(a). In addition, if the employer's wellness program provides (directly, through reimbursement, or otherwise) medical care (including genetic counseling), the program may constitute a group health plan and must comply with the special requirements for wellness programs that condition rewards on an individual satisfying a standard related to a health factor, including the requirement to provide an individual with a "reasonable alternative (or waiver of the otherwise applicable standard)" under HIPAA, when "it is unreasonably difficult due to a medical condition to satisfy" or "medically inadvisable to attempt to satisfy" the otherwise applicable standard. See section 9802 of the Internal Revenue Code (26 U.S.C. 9802, 26 CFR 54.9802-1 and 54.9802-3T), section 702 of the Employee Retirement Income Security Act of 1974 (ERISA) (29 U.S.C. 1182, 29 CFR 2590.702 and 2590.702-1), and section 2705 of the Public Health Service Act (45 CFR 146.121 and 146.122).

(3) Where the covered entity requests family medical history to comply with the certification provisions of the Family and Medical Leave Act of 1993 (29 U.S.C. 2601 et seq.) or State or local family and medical leave laws, or pursuant to a policy (even in the absence of requirements of Federal, State, or

local leave laws) that permits the use of leave to care for a sick family member and that requires all employees to provide information about the health condition of the family member to substantiate the need for leave.

(4) Where the covered entity acquires genetic information from documents that are commercially and publicly available for review or purchase, including newspapers, magazines, periodicals, or books, or through electronic media, such as information communicated through television, movies, or the Internet, except that this exception does not apply—

(i) To medical databases, court records, or research databases available to scientists on a restricted basis;

(ii) To genetic information acquired through sources with limited access, such as social networking sites and other media sources which require permission to access from a specific individual or where access is conditioned on membership in a particular group, unless the covered entity can show that access is routinely granted to all who request it;

(iii) To genetic information obtained through commercially and publicly available sources if the covered entity sought access to those sources with the intent of obtaining genetic information; or

(iv) To genetic information obtained through media sources, whether or not commercially and publicly available, if the covered entity is likely to acquire genetic information by accessing those sources, such as Web sites and on-line discussion groups that focus on issues such as genetic testing of individuals and genetic discrimination.

(5) Where the covered entity acquires genetic information for use in the genetic monitoring of the biological effects of toxic substances in the workplace. In order for this exception to apply, the covered entity must provide written notice of the monitoring to the individual and the individual must be informed of the individual monitoring results. The covered entity may not retaliate or otherwise discriminate against an individual due to his or her refusal to participate in genetic monitoring that is not required by federal or state law. This exception further provides that such monitoring:

(i) Is either required by federal or state law or regulation, or is conducted only where the individual gives prior knowing, voluntary and written authorization. The requirement for individual authorization is only met if the covered entity uses an authorization form that:

(A) Is written so that the individual from whom the genetic information is being obtained is reasonably likely to understand the form;

(B) Describes the genetic information that will be obtained; and

(C) Describes the restrictions on disclosure of genetic information;

(ii) Is conducted in compliance with any Federal genetic monitoring regulations, including any regulations that may be promulgated by the Secretary of Labor pursuant to the Occupational Safety and Health Act of 1970 (29 U.S.C. 651 et seq.), the Federal Mine Safety and Health Act of 1977 (30 U.S.C. 801 et seq.), or the Atomic Energy Act of 1954 (42 U.S.C. 2011 et seq.); or State genetic monitoring regulations, in the case of a State that is implementing genetic monitoring regulations under the authority of the Occupational Safety and Health Act of 1970 (29 U.S.C. 651 et seq.); and

(iii) Provides for reporting of the results of the monitoring to the covered entity, excluding any licensed health care professional or board certified genetic counselor involved in the genetic monitoring program, only in aggregate terms that do not disclose the identity of specific individuals.

(6) Where an employer conducts DNA analysis for law enforcement purposes as a forensic laboratory or for purposes of human remains identification and requests or requires genetic information of its employees, apprentices, or trainees, but only to the extent that the genetic information is used for analysis of DNA identification markers for quality control to detect sample contamination and is maintained and disclosed in a manner consistent with such use.

(c) Inquiries Made of Family Members Concerning a Manifested Disease, Disorder, or Pathological Condition.

(1) A covered entity does not violate this section when it requests, requires, or purchases information about a manifested disease, disorder, or pathological condition of an employee, member, or apprenticeship program participant whose family member is an employee for the same employer, a member of the same labor organization, or a participant in the same apprenticeship program. For example, an employer will not violate this section by asking someone whose sister also works for the employer to take a post-offer medical examination that does not include requests for genetic information.

(2) A covered entity does not violate this section when it requests, requires, or purchases genetic information or information about the manifestation of a disease, disorder, or pathological condition of an individual's family member who is receiving health or genetic services on a voluntary basis. For example, an employer does not unlawfully acquire genetic information about an employee when it asks the employee's family member who is receiving health services from the employer if her diabetes is under control.

(d) Medical examinations related to employment. The prohibition on acquisition of genetic information, including family medical history, applies to medical examinations related to employment. A covered entity must tell health care providers not to collect genetic information, including family medical history, as part of a medical examination intended to determine the ability to perform a job, and must take additional reasonable measures within its control if it learns that genetic information is being requested or required. Such reasonable measures may depend on the facts and circumstances under which a request for genetic information was made, and may include no longer using the services of a health care professional who continues to request or require genetic information during medical examinations after being informed not to do so.

(e) A covered entity may not use genetic information obtained pursuant to subparagraphs (b) or (c) of this section to discriminate, as defined by §§1635.4, 1635.5, or 1635.6, and must keep such information confidential as required by §1635.9.

§1635.9 Confidentiality

(a) Treatment of genetic information.

(1) A covered entity that possesses genetic information in writing about an employee or member must maintain such information on forms and in medical files (including where the information exists in electronic forms and files) that are separate from personnel files and treat such information as a confidential medical record.

(2) A covered entity may maintain genetic information about an employee or member in the same file in which it maintains confidential medical information subject to section 102(d)(3)(B) of the Americans with Disabilities Act, 42 U.S.C. 12112(d)(3)(B).

(3) Genetic information that a covered entity receives orally need not be reduced to writing, but may not be disclosed, except as permitted by this part.

(4) Genetic information that a covered entity acquires through sources that are commercially and publicly available, as provided by, and subject to the limitations in, 1635.8(b)(4) of this part, is not considered confidential genetic information, but may not be used to discriminate against an individual as described in §§1635.4, 1635.5, or 1635.6 of this part.

(5) Genetic information placed in personnel files prior to November 21, 2009 need not be removed and a covered entity will not be liable under this part for the mere existence of the information in the file. However, the prohibitions on use and disclosure of genetic information apply to all genetic information that meets the statutory definition, including genetic information requested, required, or purchased prior to November 21, 2009.

(b) Exceptions to limitations on disclosure. A covered entity that possesses any genetic information, regardless of how the entity obtained the information (except for genetic information acquired through commercially and publicly available sources), may not disclose it except:

(1) To the employee or member (or family member if the family member is receiving the genetic services) about whom the information pertains upon receipt of the employee's or member's written request;

(2) To an occupational or other health researcher if the research is conducted in compliance with the regulations and protections provided for under 45 CFR part 46;

(3) In response to an order of a court, except that the covered entity may disclose only the genetic information expressly authorized by such order; and if the court order was secured without the knowledge of the employee or member to whom the information refers, the covered entity shall inform the employee or member of the court order and any genetic information that was disclosed pursuant to such order;

(4) To government officials investigating compliance with this title if the information is relevant to the investigation;

(5) To the extent that such disclosure is made in support of an employee's compliance with the certification provisions of section 103 of the Family and Medical Leave Act of 1993 (29 U.S.C. 2613) or such requirements under State family and medical leave laws; or

(6) To a Federal, State, or local public health agency only with regard to information about the manifestation of a disease or disorder that concerns a contagious disease that presents an imminent hazard of death or life-threatening illness, provided that the individual whose family member is the subject of the disclosure is notified of such disclosure.

(c) Relationship to HIPAA Privacy Regulations. Pursuant to §1635.11(d) of this part, nothing in this section shall be construed as applying to the use or disclosure of genetic information that is protected health information subject to the regulations issued pursuant to section 264(c) of the Health Insurance Portability and Accountability Act of 1996.

§1635.10 Enforcement and remedies

(a) Powers and procedures: The following powers and procedures shall apply to allegations that Title II of GINA has been violated:

(1) The powers and procedures provided to the Commission, the Attorney General, or any person by sections 705 through 707 and 709 through 711 of the Civil Rights Act of 1964, 42 U.S.C. 2000e-4 through 2000e-6 and 2000e-8 through 2000e-10, where the alleged discrimination is against an employee defined in 1635.2(c)(1) of this part or against a member of a labor organization;

(2) The powers and procedures provided to the Commission and any person by sections 302 and 304 of the Government Employees Rights Act, 42 U.S.C. 2000e-16b and 2000e-16c, and in regulations at 29 CFR part 1603, where the alleged discrimination is against an employee as defined in §1635.2(c)(2) of this part;

(3) The powers and procedures provided to the Board of Directors of the Office of Compliance and to any person under the Congressional Accountability Act, 2 U.S.C. 1301 et seq. (including the provisions of Title 3 of that act, 2 U.S.C. 1381 et seq.), where the alleged discrimination is against an employee defined in §1635.2(c)(3) of this part;

(4) The powers and procedures provided in 3 U.S.C. 451 et seq., to the President, the Commission, or any person in connection with an alleged violation of section 3 U.S.C. 411(a)(1), where the alleged discrimination is against an employee defined in §1635.2(c)(4) of this part;

(5) The powers and procedures provided to the Commission, the Librarian of Congress, and any person by section 717 of the Civil Rights Act, 42 U.S.C. 2000e-16, where the alleged discrimination is against an employee defined in §1635.2(c)(5) of this part.

(b) Remedies. The following remedies are available for violations of GINA sections 202, 203, 204, 205, 206, and 207(f):

(1) Compensatory and punitive damages as provided for, and limited by, 42 U.S.C. 1981a(a)(1) and (b);

(2) Reasonable attorney's fees, including expert fees, as provided for, and limited by, 42 U.S.C. 1988(b) and (c); and

(3) Injunctive relief, including reinstatement and hiring, back pay, and other equitable remedies as provided for, and limited by, 42 U.S.C. 2000e-5(g).

(c) Posting of Notices.

(1) Every covered entity shall post and keep posted in conspicuous places upon its premises where notices to employees, applicants for employment, and members are customarily posted a notice to be prepared or approved by the Commission setting forth excerpts from or, summaries of, the pertinent provisions of this regulation and information pertinent to the filing of a complaint.

(2) A willful violation of this requirement shall be punishable by a fine of not more than $100 for each separate offense.

§1635.11 Construction

(a) Relationship to other laws, generally. This part does not—

(1) Limit the rights or protections of an individual under any other Federal, State, or local law that provides equal or greater protection to an individual than the rights or protections provided for under this part, including the Americans with Disabilities Act of 1990 (42 U.S.C. 12101 et seq.), the Rehabilitation Act of 1973 (29 U.S.C. 701 et seq.), and State and local laws prohibiting genetic discrimination or discrimination on the basis of disability;

(2) Apply to the Armed Forces Repository of Specimen Samples for the Identification of Remains;

(3) Limit or expand the protections, rights, or obligations of employees or employers under applicable workers' compensation laws;

(4) Limit the authority of a Federal department or agency to conduct or sponsor occupational or other health research in compliance with the regulations and protections provided for under 45 CFR part 46;

(5) Limit the statutory or regulatory authority of the Occupational Safety and Health Administration or the Mine Safety and Health Administration to promulgate or enforce workplace safety and health laws and regulations; or

(6) Require any specific benefit for an employee or member or a family member of an employee or member (such as additional coverage for a particular health condition that may have a genetic basis) under any group health plan or health insurance issuer offering group health insurance coverage in connection with a group health plan.

(b) Relation to certain Federal laws governing health coverage.

(1) General: Nothing in GINA Title II provides for enforcement of, or penalties for, violation of any requirement or prohibition of a covered entity subject to enforcement under:

(i) Amendments made by Title I of GINA.

(ii) Section 701(a) of the Employee Retirement Income Security Act (29 U.S.C. 1181) (ERISA), section 2704(a) of the Public Health Service Act, and section 9801(a) of the Internal Revenue Code (26 U.S.C. 9801(a)), as such sections apply with respect to genetic information pursuant to section 701(b)(1)(B) of ERISA, section 2704(b)(1)(B) of the Public Health Service Act, and section 9801(b)(1)(B) of the Internal Revenue Code, respectively, of such sections, which prohibit a group health plan or a health insurance issuer in the group market from imposing a preexisting condition exclusion based solely on genetic information, in the absence of a diagnosis of a condition;

(iii) Section 702(a)(1)(F) of ERISA (29 U.S.C. 1182(a)(1)(F)), section 2705(a)(6) of the Public Health Service Act, and section 9802(a)(1)(F) of the Internal Revenue Code (26 U.S.C. 9802(a)(1)(F)), which prohibit a group health plan or a health insurance issuer in the group market from discriminating against individuals in eligibility and continued eligibility for benefits based on genetic information; or

(iv) Section 702(b)(1) of ERISA (29 U.S.C. 1182(b)(1)), section 2705(b)(1) of the Public Health Service Act, and section 9802(b)(1) of the Internal Revenue Code (26 U.S.C. 9802(b)(1)), as such sections apply with respect to genetic information as a health status-related factor, which prohibit a group health plan or a health insurance issuer in the group market from discriminating against individuals in premium or contribution rates under the plan or coverage based on genetic information.

(2) Application. The application of paragraph (b)(1) of this section is intended to prevent Title II causes of action from being asserted regarding matters subject to enforcement under Title I or the other genetics provisions for group coverage in ERISA, the Public Health Service Act, and the Internal Revenue Code. The firewall seeks to ensure that health plan or issuer provisions or actions are addressed and remedied through ERISA, the Public Health Service Act, or the Internal Revenue Code, while actions taken by employers and other GINA Title II covered entities are remedied through GINA Title II. Employers and other GINA Title II covered entities would remain liable for any of their actions that violate Title II, even where those actions involve access to health benefits, because such benefits are within the definition of compensation, terms, conditions, or privileges of employment. For example, an employer that fires an employee because of anticipated high health claims based on genetic information remains subject to liability under Title II. On the other hand, health plan or issuer provisions or actions related to the imposition of a preexisting condition exclusion; a health plan's or issuer's discrimination in health plan eligibility, benefits, or premiums based on genetic information; a health plan's or issuer's request that an individual

undergo a genetic test; and/or a health plan's or issuer's collection of genetic information remain subject to enforcement under Title I exclusively. For example:

(i) If an employer contracts with a health insurance issuer to request genetic information, the employer has committed a Title II violation. In addition, the issuer may have violated Title I of GINA.

(ii) If an employer directs his employees to undergo mandatory genetic testing in order to be eligible for health benefits, the employer has committed a Title II violation.

(iii) If an employer or union amends a health plan to require an individual to undergo a genetic test, then the employer or union is liable for a violation of Title II. In addition, the health plan's implementation of the requirement may subject the health plan to liability under Title I.

(c) Relationship to authorities under GINA Title I. GINA Title II does not prohibit any group health plan or health insurance issuer offering group health insurance coverage in connection with a group health plan from engaging in any action that is authorized under any provision of law noted in §1635.11(b) of this part, including any implementing regulations noted in §1635.11(b).

(d) Relationship to HIPAA Privacy Regulations. This part does not apply to genetic information that is protected health information subject to the regulations issued by the Secretary of Health and Human Services pursuant to section 264(c) of the Health Insurance Portability and Accountability Act of 1996.

§1635.12 Medical information that is not genetic information

(a) Medical information about a manifested disease, disorder, or pathological condition.

(1) A covered entity shall not be considered to be in violation of this part based on the use, acquisition, or disclosure of medical information that is not genetic information about a manifested disease, disorder, or pathological condition of an employee or member, even if the disease, disorder, or pathological condition has or may have a genetic basis or component.

(2) Notwithstanding paragraph (a)(1) of this section, the acquisition, use, and disclosure of medical information that is not genetic information about a manifested disease, disorder, or pathological condition is subject to applicable limitations under sections 103(d)(1)-(4) of the Americans with Disabilities Act (42 U.S.C. 12112(d)(1)-(4)), and regulations at 29 CFR 1630.13, 1630.14, and 1630.16.

(b) Genetic information related to a manifested disease, disorder, or pathological condition. Notwithstanding paragraph (a) of this section, genetic information about a manifested disease, disorder, or pathological condition is subject to the requirements and prohibitions in sections 202 through 206 of GINA and §§1635.4 through 1635.9 of this part.

TABLE OF CASES

Bold indicates principal cases.

473

TABLE OF SELECTED SECONDARY AUTHORITIES